C++

IN A NUTSHELL

C++

IN A NUTSHELL

Ray Lischner

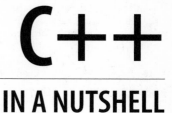

O'REILLY®

Beijing • Cambridge • Farnham • Köln • Sebastopol • Taipei • Tokyo

C++ in a Nutshell

by Ray Lischner

Copyright © 2003 O'Reilly Media, Inc. All rights reserved.
Printed in the United States of America.

Published by O'Reilly Media, Inc., 1005 Gravenstein Highway North, Sebastopol, CA 95472.

O'Reilly Media, Inc. books may be purchased for educational, business, or sales promotional use. Online editions are also available for most titles (*safari.oreilly.com*). For more information, contact our corporate/institutional sales department: 800-998-9938 or *corporate@oreilly.com*.

Editor:	Jonathan Gennick
Production Editor:	Matt Hutchinson
Cover Designer:	Ellie Volckhausen
Interior Designer:	David Futato

Printing History:

May 2003:	First Edition.

 This book uses RepKover™, a durable and flexible lay-flat binding.

ISBN: 978-0-596-00298-5

[M] 42.5# [11/08]

Table of Contents

Preface

C++ in a Nutshell is a reference to the C++ language and library. Being a Nutshell guide, it is not a comprehensive manual, but it is complete enough to cover everything a working professional needs to know. Nonetheless, C++ is such a large and complex language that even this Nutshell guide is a large book.

This book covers the C++ standard, the international standard published as ISO/IEC 14882:1998(E), *Programming Languages—C++*, plus Technical Corrigendum 1. Many implementations of C++ extend the language and standard library. Except for brief mentions of language and library extensions in the appendixes, this book covers only the standard. The standard library is large—it includes strings, containers, common algorithms, and much more—but it omits much that is commonplace in computing today: concurrency, network protocols, database access, graphics, windows, and so on. See Appendix B for information about nonstandard libraries that provide additional functionality.

This book is a reference. It is not a tutorial. Newcomers to C++ might find portions of this book difficult to understand. Although each section contains some advice on idioms and the proper use of certain language constructs, the main focus is on the reference material. Visit *http://www.tempest-sw.com/cpp/* for links to sites and lists of books that are better suited for beginners.

Structure of This Book

This book is divided into two interleaved sections that cover the language and the library, and a section of appendixes. Roughly speaking, the language is the part of C++ that does not require any additional #include headers or files. The library is the part of C++ that is declared in the standard headers.

Chapters 1–7, 11, and 12 cover the language. The first seven chapters form the main language reference, organized by topic. It is customary for a programming reference to contain a formal grammar, and this book does so in Chapter 12, which is organized alphabetically by keyword (with some additional entries for major syntactic categories, such as expressions). Chapter 11 is a reference for the preprocessor.

Chapter 13 is the library reference, organized alphabetically by header. Chapters 8–10 present an overview of the library and introduce the topics that span individual headers.

Sometimes, information is duplicated, especially in Chapter 12. My goal has been to present information when you need it, where you need it. I tried to balance the need for a single, clear, complete description of each language feature with the desire to reduce the number of cross references you must chase before you can understand that language feature.

Here are more detailed descriptions of each chapter.

Chapter 1, *Language Basics*, describes the basic rules for the C++ language: character sets, tokens, literals, and so on.

Chapter 2, *Declarations*, describes how objects, types, and namespaces are declared and how names are looked up.

Chapter 3, *Expressions*, describes operators, precedence, and type casts.

Chapter 4, *Statements*, describes all the C++ statements.

Chapter 5, *Functions*, describes function declarations and definitions, overload resolution, argument passing, and related topics.

Chapter 6, *Classes*, describes classes (and unions and structures), members, virtual functions, inheritance, accessibility, and multiple inheritance.

Chapter 7, *Templates*, describes class and function template declarations, definitions, instantiations, specializations, and how templates are used.

Chapter 8, *Standard Library*, introduces the standard library and discusses some overarching topics, such as traits and allocators.

Chapter 9, *Input and Output*, introduces the I/O portion of the standard library. Topics include formatted and unformatted I/O, stream buffers, and manipulators.

Chapter 10, *Containers, Iterators, and Algorithms*, introduces the suite of container class templates, their iterators, and generic algorithms. This is the portion of the library that has traditionally been called the Standard Template Library (STL).

Chapter 11, *Preprocessor Reference*, is an alphabetical reference for the preprocessor, which is part of the language, but with a distinct set of syntactic and semantic rules.

Chapter 12, *Language Reference*, is an alphabetical reference for the language and grammar. Backus-Naur Form (BNF) syntax descriptions are given for each keyword and other language elements, with pointers to the first seven chapters for the main reference material.

Chapter 13, *Library Reference*, is a reference for the entire standard library, organized alphabetically by header, and alphabetically by name within each header section.

Appendix A, *Compiler Extensions*, describes ways that some compilers extend the language: to satisfy customer need, to meet platform-specific requirements, and so on.

Appendix B, *Projects*, describes a few interesting, open source C++ projects. You can find information about additional projects on this book's web site (*http://www.tempest-sw.com/cpp/*).

The Glossary defines some words and phrases used throughout this book and in the C++ community.

About the Examples

Whenever possible, the examples in this book are complete, compilable programs. You can tell which examples fall into this category because they start with #include directives and contain a main( ) function. You can download these examples as text files from the book's web site at *http://www.tempest-sw.com/cpp/* or from O'Reilly's catalog page for this book: *http://www.oreilly.com/catalog/cplsian/*.

Most examples are shortened to eliminate excess code that might interfere with the clarity of the example. In particular, these examples are fragments that lack a main function. Sometimes, an ellipsis indicates missing code, such as a function body. In other cases, the omissions are clear from the context. Most abbreviated examples have complete and compilable versions available for download.

All of the examples have been checked with several different compilers, including Comeau Computing's compiler with the Dinkumware standard library (widely acknowledged as the most complete and correct implementations of the C++ standard). Not all compilers can compile all the examples due to limitations and bugs in the compilers and libraries. For best results, try to work with the latest version of your compiler. Recent releases of several major compilers have made dramatic progress toward conformance with the standard. When possible, I have tried to alter the example files to work around the bugs without interfering with the intent of the example.

I have checked all the examples with the following compilers:

Linux
- Borland Kylix 3.0
- Comeau 4.3.0.1
- GNU 3.2
- Intel 7.0

Microsoft Windows
- Borland C++ Builder 6.4
- Metrowerks CodeWarrior 8.3
- Microsoft Visual Studio.NET 7.0

Conventions Used in This Book

This book uses the following conventions:

Constant Width

> Used for identifiers and symbols, including all keywords. In the language reference, constant width shows syntax elements that must be used exactly as shown. For example, the if keyword, parentheses, and else keyword must be used exactly as follows:
>
>> if (*condition*) *statement* else *statement*
>
> A function name that is followed by parentheses refers to a function call, typically to obtain the function result. The function name without the parentheses refers to the function in more general terms. For example:
>
>> The empty function returns true if the container is empty, e.g., size( ) == 0.

Constant Width Italic

> Used in the language reference chapters for syntax elements that must be replaced by your code. In the previous example, you must supply the *condition* and the two *statement*s.

Constant Width Bold

> Used in examples to highlight key lines, and in complex declarations to highlight the name being declared. In some C++ declarations, especially for templates, the name gets buried in the middle of the declaration and can be hard to spot.

Italic

> Used in the language reference for nonterminal syntax elements. Italic is also used for filenames, URLs, emphasis, and for the first use of a technical term.

...

> Indicates statements and declarations that have been removed for the sake of brevity and clarity. An ellipsis is also a symbol in C++, but context and comments make it clear when an ellipsis is a language element and when it represents omitted code.

[first, last)

> Indicates a range of values from first to last, including first and excluding last.

 This icon indicates a tip, suggestion, or general note.

 This icon indicates a warning or caution.

This icon indicates an issue or feature that might affect the portability of your code. In particular, some aspects of C++ are implementation-defined, such as the size of an integer, which allows the compiler or library author to decide what the best implementation should be.

For More Information

Visit the C++ *in a Nutshell* web site at *http://www.tempest-sw.com/cpp/* to find links to newsgroups, frequently asked questions, tool and library web sites, free compilers, open source projects, other C++ books, and more. The web site also has information about the ongoing activities of the C++ Standardization Committee.

If you are a glutton for punishment, or if you need more details than are provided in this book, you might want to read the actual standard: ISO/IEC 14882:1998(E), *Programming Languages—C++*. The standard is not easy to read, and even its authors sometimes disagree on its interpretation. Nonetheless, it is the one specification for the C++ language, and all other books, including this one, are derivatives, subject to error and misinterpretation. The C++ standard library includes the entire C standard library, which is documented in ISO/IEC 9899:1990, *Programming Languages—C*, plus Amendment 1:1995(E), *C Integrity*.

The C and C++ standards are evolving documents; the committees meet regularly to review defect reports and proposals for language extensions. As I write this, the C++ standard committee has approved a technical corrigendum (TC1), which is an update to the C++ standard that corrects defects and removes ambiguities in the original standard. TC1 is winding its way through the ISO bureaucracy. By the time you read this, TC1 will have probably completed its journey and been added to the official standard for the C++ programming language. The book's web site has up-to-date information about the status of the C++ and C standards.

Comments and Questions

Please address comments and questions concerning this book to the publisher:

O'Reilly & Associates, Inc.
1005 Gravenstein Highway North
Sebastopol, CA 95472
(800) 998-9938 (in the United States or Canada)
(707) 829-0515 (international/local)
(707) 829-0104 (fax)

There is a web page for this book, which lists errata, examples, or any additional information. You can access this page at:

http://www.oreilly.com/catalog/cplsian

To comment or ask technical questions about this book, send email to:

bookquestions@oreilly.com

For more information about books, conferences, Resource Centers, and the O'Reilly Network, see the O'Reilly web site at:

http://www.oreilly.com

Acknowledgments

Special thanks go to my technical reviewers: Ron Natalie, Uwe Schnitker, and Bruce Krell. Their corrections and suggestions have greatly improved this book.

I posted early drafts of this book to my web site, and solicited comments. David Cattarin and Roshan Naik were especially helpful. I thank everyone who also provided comments: David Abrahams, Frank Brown, Cyrille Chepelov, Jerry Coffin, Buster Copley, Gerhard Doeppert, Nicolas Fleury, Jarrod Hollingworth, James Kanze, Michael Kochetkov, Clare Macrae, Thomas Maeder, Brian McAndrews, Jeff Raft, Allan Ramacher, Torsten Robitzki, and John Spicer.

Thanks to Comeau Computing, Dinkumware, Metrowerks, Borland, and Microsoft for giving me free versions of their compilers and libraries to use while preparing this book. Thanks also to Intel for making its compiler freely available to download for evaluation purposes. I thank VMware for licenses to its virtual machine software.

I thank my editor, Jonathan Gennick, for his patience and advice.

Most of all, I thank my wife, Cheryl, and my son, Arthur, for their love and support, without which I could not have written this book.

Language Basics

C++ is a case-sensitive, free-form programming language that supports procedural, object-oriented, and generic programming. This chapter presents the basic rules for the language, such as lexical rules and basic syntax elements.

Compilation Steps

A C++ source file undergoes many transformations on its way to becoming an executable program. The initial steps involve processing all the #include and conditional preprocessing directives to produce what the standard calls a *translation unit*. Translation units are important because they have no dependencies on other files. Nonetheless, programmers still speak in terms of source files, even if they actually mean translation units, so this book uses the phrase *source file* because it is familiar to most readers. The term "translation" encompasses compilation and interpretation, although most C++ translators are compilers. This section discusses how C++ reads and compiles (translates) source files (translation units).

A C++ program can be made from many source files, and each file can be compiled separately. Conceptually, the compilation process has several steps (although a compiler can merge or otherwise modify steps if it can do so without affecting the observable results):

1. Read physical characters from the source file and translate the characters to the source character set (described in "Character Sets" later in this chapter). The source "file" is not necessarily a physical file; an implementation might, for example, retrieve the source from a database. Trigraph sequences are reduced to their equivalent characters (see "Trigraphs" later in this chapter). Each native end-of-line character or character sequence is replaced by a newline character.

2. If a backslash character is followed immediately by a newline character, delete the backslash and the newline. The backslash/newline combination must not fall in the middle of a universal character (e.g., \u1234) and must not be at the end of a file. It can be used in a character or string literal, or to continue a preprocessor directive or one-line comment on multiple lines. A non-empty file must end with a newline.

3. Partition the source into preprocessor tokens separated by whitespace and comments. A preprocessor token is slightly different from a compiler token (see the next section, "Tokens"). A preprocessor token can be a header name, identifier, number, character literal, string literal, symbol, or miscellaneous character. Each preprocessor token is the longest sequence of characters that can make up a legal token, regardless of what comes after the token.

4. Perform preprocessing and expand macros. All #include files are processed in the manner described in steps 1–4. For more information about preprocessing, see Chapter 11.

5. Convert character and string literals to the execution character set.

6. Concatenate adjacent string literals. Narrow string literals are concatenated with narrow string literals. Wide string literals are concatenated with wide string literals. Mixing narrow and wide string literals results in an error.

7. Perform the main compilation.

8. Combine compiled files. For each file, all required template instantiations (see Chapter 7) are identified, and the necessary template definitions are located and compiled.

9. Resolve external references. The compiled files are linked to produce an executable image.

Tokens

All source code is divided into a stream of *tokens*. The compiler tries to collect as many contiguous characters as it can to build a valid token. (This is sometimes called the "max munch" rule.) It stops when the next character it would read cannot possibly be part of the token it is reading.

A token can be an identifier, a reserved keyword, a literal, or an operator or punctuation symbol. Each kind of token is described later in this section.

Step 3 of the compilation process reads *preprocessor tokens*. These tokens are converted automatically to ordinary compiler tokens as part of the main compilation in Step 7. The differences between a preprocessor token and a compiler token are small:

- The preprocessor and the compiler might use different encodings for character and string literals.

- The compiler treats integer and floating-point literals differently; the preprocessor does not.

- The preprocessor recognizes ⟨*header*⟩ as a single token (for #include directives); the compiler does not.

Identifiers

An identifier is a name that you define or that is defined in a library. An identifier begins with a nondigit character and is followed by any number of digits and nondigits. A nondigit character is a letter, an underscore, or one of a set of universal characters. The exact set of nondigit universal characters is defined in the C++ standard and in ISO/IEC PDTR 10176. Basically, this set contains the universal characters that represent letters. Most programmers restrict themselves to the characters a...z, A...Z, and underscore, but the standard permits letters in other languages.

 Not all compilers support universal characters in identifiers.

Certain identifiers are reserved for use by the standard library:

- Any identifier that contains two consecutive underscores (like__this) is reserved, that is, you cannot use such an identifier for macros, class members, global objects, or anything else.

- Any identifier that starts with an underscore, followed by a capital letter (A–Z) is reserved.

- Any identifier that starts with an underscore is reserved in the global namespace. You can use such names in other contexts (i.e., class members and local names).

- The C standard reserves some identifiers for future use. These identifiers fall into two categories: function names and macro names. Function names are reserved and should not be used as global function or object names; you should also avoid using them as "C" linkage names in any namespace. Note that the C standard reserves these names regardless of which headers you #include. The reserved function names are:
  - is followed by a lowercase letter, such as isblank
  - mem followed by a lowercase letter, such as memxyz
  - str followed by a lowercase letter, such as strtof
  - to followed by a lowercase letter, such as toxyz
  - wcs followed by a lowercase letter, such as wcstof
  - In <cmath> with f or l appended, such as cosf and sinl

- Macro names are reserved in all contexts. Do not use any of the following reserved macro names:
  - Identifiers that start with E followed by a digit or an uppercase letter
  - Identifiers that start with LC_ followed by an uppercase letter
  - Identifiers that start with SIG or SIG_ followed by an uppercase letter

Keywords

 A *keyword* is an identifier that is reserved in all contexts for special use by the language. The following is a list of all the reserved keywords. (Note that some compilers do not implement all of the reserved keywords; these compilers allow you to use certain keywords as identifiers. See the section "Alternative Tokens" later in this chapter for more information.)

and	continue	goto	public	try
and_eq	default	if	register	typedef
asm	delete	inline	reintepret_cast	typeid
auto	do	int	return	typename
bitand	double	long	short	union
bitor	dynamic_cast	mutable	signed	unsigned
bool	else	namespace	sizeof	using
break	enum	new	static	virtual
case	explicit	not	static_cast	void
catch	export	not_eq	struct	volatile
char	extern	operator	switch	wchar_t
class	false	or	template	while
compl	float	or_eq	this	xor
const	for	private	throw	xor_eq
const_cast	friend	protected	true	

Literals

A *literal* is an integer, floating-point, Boolean, character, or string constant.

Integer literals

An integer literal can be a decimal, octal, or hexadecimal constant. A prefix specifies the base or radix: 0x or 0X for hexadecimal, 0 for octal, and nothing for decimal. An integer literal can also have a suffix that is a combination of U and L, for unsigned and long, respectively. The suffix can be uppercase or lowercase and can be in any order. The suffix and prefix are interpreted as follows:

- If the suffix is UL (or ul, LU, etc.), the literal's type is unsigned long.
- If the suffix is L, the literal's type is long or unsigned long, whichever fits first. (That is, if the value fits in a long, the type is long; otherwise, the type is unsigned long. An error results if the value does not fit in an unsigned long.)
- If the suffix is U, the type is unsigned or unsigned long, whichever fits first.
- Without a suffix, a decimal integer has type int or long, whichever fits first.
- An octal or hexadecimal literal has type int, unsigned, long, or unsigned long, whichever fits first.

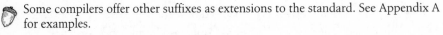 Some compilers offer other suffixes as extensions to the standard. See Appendix A for examples.

Here are some examples of integer literals:

```
314       // Legal
314u      // Legal
314LU     // Legal
0xFeeL    // Legal
0ul       // Legal
078       // Illegal: 8 is not an octal digit
032UU     // Illegal: cannot repeat a suffix
```

Floating-point literals

A floating-point literal has an integer part, a decimal point, a fractional part, and an exponent part. You must include the decimal point, the exponent, or both. You must include the integer part, the fractional part, or both. The signed exponent is introduced by e or E. The literal's type is double unless there is a suffix: F for type float and L for long double. The suffix can be uppercase or lowercase.

Here are some examples of floating-point literals:

```
3.14159        // Legal
.314159F       // Legal
314159E-5L     // Legal
314.           // Legal
314E           // Illegal: incomplete exponent
314f           // Illegal: no decimal or exponent
.e24           // Illegal: missing integer or fraction
```

Boolean literals

There are two Boolean literals, both keywords: true and false.

Character literals

Character literals are enclosed in single quotes. If the literal begins with L (uppercase only), it is a wide character literal (e.g., L'x'). Otherwise, it is a narrow character literal (e.g., 'x'). Narrow characters are used more frequently than wide characters, so the "narrow" adjective is usually dropped.

The value of a narrow or wide character literal is the value of the character's encoding in the execution character set. If the literal contains more than one character, the literal value is implementation-defined. Note that a character might have different encodings in different locales. Consult your compiler's documentation to learn which encoding it uses for character literals.

A narrow character literal with a single character has type char. With more than one character, the type is int (e.g., 'abc'). The type of a wide character literal is always wchar_t.

> In C, a character literal always has type int. C++ changed the type of character literals to support overloading, especially for I/O (e.g., cout << '\n' starts a new line and does not print the integer value of the newline character).

A character literal can be a plain character (e.g., 'x'), an escape sequence (e.g., '\b'), or a universal character (e.g., '\u03C0'). Table 1-1 lists the possible escape sequences. Note that you must use an escape sequence for a backslash or single-quote character literal. Using an escape for a double quote or question mark is optional. Only the characters shown in Table 1-1 are allowed in an escape sequence. (Some compilers extend the standard and recognize other escape sequences.)

Table 1-1. Character escape sequences

Escape sequence	Meaning
\\	\ character
\'	' character
\"	" character
\?	? character (used to avoid creating a trigraph, e.g., \?\?-)
\a	Alert or bell
\b	Backspace
\f	Form feed
\n	Newline
\r	Carriage return
\t	Horizontal tab
\v	Vertical tab
\ooo	Octal number of one to three digits
\xhh...	Hexadecimal number of one or more digits

String literals

String literals are enclosed in double quotes. A string contains characters that are similar to character literals: plain characters, escape sequences, and universal characters. A string cannot cross a line boundary in the source file, but it can contain escaped line endings (backslash followed by newline).

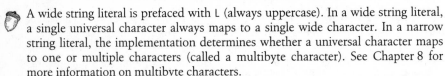 A wide string literal is prefaced with L (always uppercase). In a wide string literal, a single universal character always maps to a single wide character. In a narrow string literal, the implementation determines whether a universal character maps to one or multiple characters (called a multibyte character). See Chapter 8 for more information on multibyte characters.

Two adjacent string literals (possibly separated by whitespace, including new lines) are concatenated at compile time into a single string. This is often a convenient way to break a long string across multiple lines. Do not try to combine a narrow string with a wide string in this way.

After concatenating adjacent strings, the null character ('\0' or L'\0') is automatically appended after the last character in the string literal.

Here are some examples of string literals. Note that the first three form identical strings.

```
"hello, reader"
"hello, \
reader"
"hello, " "rea" "der"

"Alert: \a; ASCII tab: \010; portable tab: \t"
"illegal: unterminated string
L"string with \"quotes\""
```

A string literal's type is an array of const char. For example, "string"'s type is const char[7]. Wide string literals are arrays of const wchar_t. All string literals have static lifetimes (see Chapter 2 for more information about lifetimes).

As with an array of const anything, the compiler can automatically convert the array to a pointer to the array's first element. You can, for example, assign a string literal to a suitable pointer object:

```
const char* ptr;
ptr = "string";
```

As a special case, you can also convert a string literal to a non-const pointer. Attempting to modify the string results in undefined behavior. This conversion is deprecated, and well-written code does not rely on it.

Symbols

Nonalphabetic symbols are used as operators and as punctuation (e.g., statement terminators). Some symbols are made of multiple adjacent characters. The following are all the symbols used for operators and punctuation:

{	(	%:	.	^	.	=	!=	-=	&=
}	)	%:%:	+	&	.*	==	<<	+=	|=
[	<:	;	-	|	->	<	>>	*=	^=
]	:>	:	*	?	->*	>	<<=	/=	++
#	<%	...	/	:	~	<=	>>=	%=	--
##	%>	,	%	::	!	>=			

You cannot insert whitespace between characters that make up a symbol, and C++ always collects as many characters as it can to form a symbol before trying to interpret the symbol. Thus, an expression such as x+++y is read as x ++ + y. A common error when first using templates is to omit a space between closing angle brackets in a nested template instantiation. The following is an example with that space:

```
std::list<std::vector<int> > list;
                         ↑
             Note the space here.
```

The example is incorrect without the space character because the adjacent greater than signs would be interpreted as a single right-shift operator, not as two separate closing angle brackets. Another, slightly less common, error is instantiating a template with a template argument that uses the global scope operators:

```
::std::list< ::std::list<int> > list;
           ↑               ↑
      Space here       and here
```

Again, a space is needed, this time between the angle-bracket (<) and the scope operator (::), to prevent the compiler from seeing the first token as <: rather than <. The <: token is an alternative token, as described in "Alternative Tokens" later in this chapter.

Comments

Comments start with /* and end with */. These comments do not nest. For example:

```
/* this is a comment /* still a comment */
int not_in_a_comment;
```

A comment can also start with //, extending to the end of the line. For example:

```
const int max_widget = 42; // Largest size of a widget
```

Within a /* and */ comment, // characters have no special meaning. Within a // comment, /* and */ have no special meaning. Thus, you can "nest" one kind of comment within the other kind. For example:

```
/* Comment out a block of code:
const int max_widget = 42; // Largest size of a widget
*/

///* Inhibit the start of a block comment
const int max_widget = 10; // Testing smaller widget limit
//*/
```

A comment is treated as whitespace. For example, str/*comment*/ing describes two separate tokens, str and ing.

Character Sets

The character sets that C++ uses at compile time and runtime are implementation-defined. A source file is read as a sequence of characters in the *physical character set*. When a source file is read, the physical characters are mapped to the compile-time character set, which is called the *source character set*. The mapping is implementation-defined, but many implementations use the same character set.

At the very least, the source character set always includes the characters listed below. The numeric values of these characters are implementation-defined.

```
Space
Horizontal tab
Vertical tab
Form feed
Newline
a ... z
A ... Z
0 ... 9
_ { } [ ] # ( ) < > % : ; . ? * + - / ^ & | ~ ! = , \ " '
```

The runtime character set, called the *execution character set*, might be different from the source character set (though it is often the same). If the character sets are different, the compiler automatically converts all character and string literals from the source character set to the execution character set. The *basic execution character set* includes all the characters in the source character set, plus the characters listed below. The execution character set is a superset of the basic execution character set; additional characters are implemented-defined and might vary depending on locale.

Alert
Backspace
Carriage return
Null

Conceptually, source characters are mapped to Unicode (ISO/IEC 10646) and from Unicode to the execution character set. You can specify any Unicode character in the source file as a *universal character* in the form \u*XXXX* (lowercase u) or \U*XXXXXXXX* (uppercase U), in which 0000*XXXX* or *XXXXXXXX* is the hexadecimal value for the character. Note that you must use exactly four or eight hexadecimal digits. You cannot use a universal character to specify any character that is in the source character set or in the range 0–0x20 or 0x7F–0x9F (inclusive).

 How universal characters map to the execution character set is implementation-defined. Some compilers don't recognize universal characters at all, or support them only in limited contexts.

Typically, you would not write a universal character manually. Instead, you might use a source editor that lets you edit source code in any language, and the editor would store source files in a manner that is appropriate for a particular compiler. When necessary, the editor would write universal character names for characters that fall outside the compiler's source character set. That way, you might write the following in the editor:

```
const long double π = 3.1415926535897932385L;
```

and the editor might write the following in the source file:

```
const long double \u03c0 = 3.1415926535897932385L;
```

The numerical values for characters in all character sets are implementation-defined, with the following restrictions:

• The null character always has a value that contains all zero bits.
• The digit characters have sequential values, starting with 0.

The space, horizontal tab, vertical tab, form feed, and newline characters are called *whitespace characters*. In most cases, whitespace characters only separate tokens and are otherwise ignored. (Comments are like whitespace; see the "Comments" section earlier in this chapter.)

Alternative Tokens

Some symbols have multiple representations, as shown in Table 1-2. These *alternative tokens* have no special meaning in a character or string literal. They are merely alternative representations of common symbols. Most programmers do not use alternative tokens, especially the nonalphabetic ones. Some programmers find and, or, and not to be easier to read and understand than &&, ||, and !.

Table 1-2. Alternative tokens

Alternative token	Primary token
<%	{
%>	}
<:	[
:>	]
%:	#
%:%:	##
and	&&
and_eq	&=
bitand	&
bitor	|
compl	~
not	!
not_eq	!=
or	||
or_eq	|=
xor	^
xor_eq	^=

 Many compilers do not support some or even all of the alternative tokens. In particular, some compilers do not treat alternative keywords (and, or, etc.) as reserved keywords, but allow you to use them as identifiers. Fortunately, this problem is becoming less common as more vendors hew closer to the standard. Compilers that do not support the alternative keywords might provide them as macros in the <ciso646> header. See Chapter 13 for more information.

Trigraphs

A few characters have an alternative representation, called a trigraph sequence. A *trigraph* is a three-character sequence that represents a single character. The sequence always starts with two question marks. The third character determines which character the sequence represents. All the trigraph sequences are shown in Table 1-3. If the third character is not one of those in the table, the sequence is not a trigraph and is left alone. For example, the characters ???- represent the two characters ?~. Note that trigraphs are expanded anywhere they appear, including within string literals and character literals, in comments, and in preprocessor directives.

Table 1-3. Trigraph sequences

Trigraph	Replacement
??=	#
??/	\
??'	^

Table 1-3. Trigraph sequences (continued)

Trigraph	Replacement
??(	[
??)	]
??!	|
??<	{
??>	}
??-	~

Not all compilers support trigraphs. Some compilers require an extra switch or option. Others use a separate program to convert all trigraphs to their equivalent characters.

Do not use trigraphs. They are confusing to read and use. If you ever write multiple, adjacent question marks, make sure you are not accidentally writing a trigraph. For example:

```
std::cout << "What do you mean??!!\n";
```

To avoid the trigraph interpretation, separate the string literal:

```
std::cout << "What do you mean?" "?!!\n";
```

or escape the question marks:

```
std::cout << "What do you mean\?\?!!\n";
```

2

Declarations

A C++ source file contains a series of zero or more *declarations*. A declaration can be a function, type, object (constant or variable), namespace, template, or a related entity. The first part of this chapter covers general topics that pertain to all declarations. The second part discusses types, objects, and namespaces specifically. Function, class, and template declarations each get their own chapters: Chapter 5 covers functions; Chapter 6 covers classes and friends; and Chapter 7 covers template declarations, specializations, and instantiations.

The syntax descriptions in this chapter are informal. See Chapter 12 for a precise BNF grammar.

Declarations and Definitions

A declaration is the all-encompassing term for anything that tells the compiler about an identifier. In order to use an identifier, the compiler must know what it means: is it a type name, a variable name, a function name, or something else? Therefore, a source file must contain a declaration (directly or in an #include file) for every name it uses.

Definitions

A *definition* defines the storage, value, body, or contents of a declaration. The difference between a declaration and a definition is that a declaration tells you an entity's name and the external view of the entity, such as an object's type or a function's parameters, and a definition provides the internal workings of the entity: the storage and initial value of an object, a function body, and so on.

In a single source file, there can be at most one definition of an entity. In an entire program, there must be exactly one definition of each function or object used in the program, except for inline functions; an inline function must be defined in every source file that uses the function, and the definitions must all be identical.

A program can have more than one definition of a given class, enumeration, inline function, or template, provided the definitions are in separate source files, and each source file has the same definition.

These rules are known as the One Definition Rules, or ODR.

Before you can use an entity (e.g., calling a function or referring to an object), the compiler needs the entity's declaration, but not necessarily its definition. You can use a class that has an incomplete declaration in some contexts, but usually you need a complete definition. (See Chapter 6 for details about incomplete classes.) The complete program needs definitions for all the declared entities, but those definitions can often reside in separate source files. The convention is to place the declarations for classes, functions, and global objects in a header file (whose name typically ends with *.h* or *.hpp*), and their definitions in a source file (whose name typically ends with *.cpp*, *.c*, or *.C*). Any source file that needs to use those entities must #include the header file. Templates have additional complications concerning declarations and definitions. (See Chapter 7 for details.)

In this and subsequent chapters, the description of each entity states whether the entity (type, variable, class, function, etc.) has separate definitions and declarations, states when definitions are required, and outlines any other rules pertaining to declarations and definitions.

Ambiguity

Some language constructs can look like a declaration or an expression. Such ambiguities are always resolved in favor of declarations. A related rule is that a declaration that is a type specifier followed by a name and empty parentheses is a declaration of a function that takes no arguments, not a declaration of an object with an empty initializer. (See "Initializers" later in this chapter for more information about empty initializers.) Example 2-1 shows some examples of how declarations are interpreted.

Example 2-1. Disambiguating declarations

```
#include <iostream>
#include <ostream>

class T
{
public:
  T()    { std::cout << "T( )\n"; }
  T(int) { std::cout << "T(int)\n"; }
};

int a, x;

int main( )
{
  T(a);       // Variable named a of type T, not an invocation of the T(int)
              // constructor
  T b( );     // Function named b of no arguments, not a variable named b of
              // type T
```

Example 2-1. Disambiguating declarations (continued)

```
    T c(T(x));    // Declaration of a function named c, with one argument of
                  // type T
}
```

The last item in Example 2-1 deserves further explanation. The function parameter T(x) could be interpreted as an expression: constructing an instance of T with the argument x. Or it could be interpreted as a declaration of a function parameter of type T named x, with a redundant set of parentheses around the parameter name. According to the disambiguation rule, it must be a declaration, not an expression. This means that the entire declaration cannot be the declaration of an object named c, whose initializer is the expression T(x). Instead, it must be the declaration of a function named c, whose parameter is of type T, named x.

If your intention is to declare an object, not a function, the simplest way to do this is not to use the function-call style of type cast. Instead, use a keyword cast expression, such as static_cast<>. (See Chapter 3 for more information about type casts.) For example:

```
    T c(static_cast<T>(x)); // Declares an object named c whose initial value is
                            // x, cast to type T
```

This problem can crop up when you least expect it. For example, suppose you want to construct a vector of integers by reading a series of numbers from the standard input. Your first attempt might be to use an istream_iterator:

```
    using namespace std;
    vector<int> data(istream_iterator<int>(cin), istream_iterator<int>());
```

This declaration actually declares a function named data, which takes two parameters. The first is named cin and has type istream_iterator<int>. The second is an unnamed pointer to a function that returns istream_iterator<int>. You can force the compiler to interpret the declaration as an object definition by enclosing one or more arguments in parentheses:

```
    using namespace std;
    vector<int> data((istream_iterator<int>(cin)), (istream_iterator<int>()));
```

or by using additional objects for the iterators:

```
    std::istream_iterator<int> start(std::cin), end;
    std::vector<int> data(start, end);
```

Scope

A *scope* is a region of source code that contains declarations. Every declaration adds a name to a scope, and every use of a name requires the compiler to identify which scope contains that name's declaration. Sometimes you tell the compiler exactly which scope contains the name, and at other times the compiler determines the scope. Once the compiler knows the scope, it can look up the name to learn what the name is (object, function, class, etc.) and how the name can be used. Thus, you can think of a scope as a dictionary of names mapped to declarations.

A scope can be named or unnamed. Classes and namespaces (see "Namespaces" later in this chapter) define named scopes. Statement blocks, function bodies, and unnamed namespaces define unnamed scopes. You can *qualify* a name with a scope name to tell the compiler where to look up the qualified name, but you cannot qualify names from unnamed scopes. In a typical program, most names are unqualified, so the compiler must determine which scope declares the name. (See "Name Lookup" later in this chapter.)

Scopes can be nested, and names in inner scopes can hide names that are declared in outer scopes. Example 2-2 illustrates abuses of the simple scope rules: the body of the for loop is a scope, in which the variable x is declared as an int; the if statement creates a nested scope, in which another declaration of x hides the outer x. The reference to x at the end of main is invalid: no x is in scope at that point.

Example 2-2. Names in inner scopes can hide names in outer scopes

```
#include <iostream>
#include <ostream>

int main( )
{
  for (int i = 0; i < 100; ++i)
  {
    int x = 42;
    if (x < i)
    {
      double x = 3.14;
      std::cout << x; // Prints 3.14
    }
    std::cout << x;   // Prints 42
  }
  std::cout << x;     // Error: no x declared in this scope
}
```

At the same scope level, you cannot have multiple declarations for the same name, unless every declaration of that name is for an overloaded function or function template, or if the declarations are identical typedef declarations.

Example 2-2 shows that a name can be hidden by a different declaration in an inner scope level. Also, a class name or enumeration type name can be hidden by an object, function, or enumerator at the same scope level. For example:

```
enum x { a, b, c };
const int x = 42;   // OK: hides enum x
const int a = 10;   // Error: int cannot hide enumerator a
{
  const int a = 10; // OK: inner scope can hide outer a
}
```

Different entities (functions, statements, classes, namespaces, etc.) establish scope in different ways. The description of each entity (in this and subsequent chapters) includes scoping rules. The general rule of thumb is that curly braces delimit a scope region. The outermost scope region is outside of all the curly braces and is called the *global scope*. (See "Namespaces" later in this chapter.)

Name Lookup

When the compiler reads an identifier, it must look up the identifier to determine which declaration it comes from. In most cases, you can readily tell which identifier is which, but it is not always so simple. A small mistake can sometimes lead to code that compiles successfully but runs incorrectly because an identifier refers to a different object from the one you intended. To understand name lookup fully, you must first understand namespaces (covered later in this chapter), functions (Chapter 5), classes (Chapter 6), and templates (Chapter 7).

Name lookup takes place before overloaded functions are resolved and before the access level of class members is checked. If a name is found in an inner scope, the compiler uses that declaration, even if a better declaration would be found in an outer scope. Example 2-3 shows how problems can arise when an overloaded function is declared in more than one namespace. The function func(int) is global, and func(double) is defined in namespace N. Inside call_func, the compiler looks up the name func by searching first in the local scope (that is, the function body), then in namespace N, where it finds func(double). Name lookup stops at that point because the compiler found a match. Therefore, func(3) converts 3 to type double and calls func(double). The main function brings all the overloaded func functions into its scope (with using declarations, which are described at the end of this chapter), so name lookup can find the best match, which is func(int).

Example 2-3. Name lookup trumps overload resolution

```
void func(int i)
{
  std::cout << "int: " << i << '\n';
}

namespace N {
  void func(double d)
  {
    std::cout << "double: " << std::showpoint << d << '\n';
  }

  void call_func()
  {
    // Even though func(int) is a better match, the compiler finds
    // N::func(double) first.
    func(3);
  }
}

int main()
{
  N::call_func();       // Prints "double: 3.000000"
  using N::func;
  using ::func;
  // Now all overloaded func()s are at the same scope level.
  func(4);              // Prints "int: 4"
}
```

Refer to Chapter 5 for more information about overloaded functions and to Chapter 6 for information about access levels in a class declaration.

Qualified Name Lookup

To specify a particular namespace for looking up a name, qualify the name using the scope operator (::). A name that follows the global scope operator (the unary ::) is looked up in the global scope (outside of all namespaces). The name must be declared in the global scope, not in a nested scope, or the name must have been introduced into the global scope by a using directive or using declaration (see "Namespaces" later in this chapter).

Use the global scope operator to access names that have been hidden by an inner scope. Example 2-4 shows this use of the :: operator to access the global x from within main after an inner x has been declared.

Example 2-4. The global scope operator

```
#include <iostream>
#include <ostream>

int x = 42;

int main( )
{
  double x = 3.1415;        // Hides the global x
  std::cout << x << '\n';    // Prints 3.1415
  std::cout << ::x << '\n';  // Prints 42
}
```

The binary scope resolution operator (also ::) requires a namespace or class name as its lefthand operand, and an identifier as its righthand operand. The identifier is looked up in the scope of the lefthand namespace or class. Example 2-5 shows the scope resolution operator untangling a mess made by using the same names for different kinds of entities. Notice how the inner counter hides the outer counter, so the simple name counter refers to the int variable. The lefthand operand to ::, however, must be a class or namespace, so in the expression counter::c, the inner counter does not hide the outer counter.

Example 2-5. The scope resolution operator

```
#include <iostream>
#include <ostream>

namespace n {
  struct counter {
    static int n;
  };
  double n = 2.71828;
}

int n::counter::n = 42; // Defines static data member
```

Example 2-5. The scope resolution operator (continued)

```
int main( )
{
  int counter = 0;      // Unrelated to n::counter
  int n = 10;           // Hides namespace n
  ::n::counter x;       // Refers to namespace n

  std::cout << n::counter::n; // Prints 42
  std::cout << n::n;          // Prints 2.71828
  std::cout << x.n;           // Prints 42
  std::cout << n;             // Prints 10
  std::cout << counter;       // Prints 0
}
```

Unqualified Name Lookup

The compiler looks up an unqualified name, that is, a bare identifier or operator symbol, in a series of scopes in order to find its declaration. The simple rule is that the innermost scope is searched first, and succeeding outer scopes are searched until a matching declaration is found. Additional named scopes are searched, depending on the context of the usage, as explained in this section and the next ("Argument-Dependent Name Lookup"). An associated simple rule is that a name must be declared before it is used, reading the source file from top to bottom.

In a class definition, the class is searched first; the declaration must appear before it is used, reading the class definition from top to bottom. The immediate base classes are searched next (in declaration order), and their base classes are searched. If the class is nested in another class, the containing class is searched, and its base classes are searched. If the class is local to a function, the block that contains the class is searched, then enclosing blocks are searched. Finally, the namespaces that contain the class declaration are searched. That is, the namespace that immediately contains the class is searched first; if that namespace is nested within another namespace, the outer namespace is searched next, and so on. If the class is nested, the namespaces that contain the outer class or classes are searched.

In the body of a member function, names are looked up first in the local scope and nested scopes of the function body. Then the class is searched; the name can be declared anywhere in the class definition, even if that declaration appears after the member function definition. (This is an exception to the "declare-before-use" rule.) Such names can be used in a parameter type, a default argument value, or the function body, but not in the function's return type. The name is then looked up in the manner described earlier for other names used in a class definition.

The name lookup rules permit a member function to use a name that is declared later in the class definition, but the name lookup rules do not trump the syntax and parsing rules. In particular, the parser must be able to distinguish between names used as types from other names. In the following example, the name big is used as a type, and is declared as a type in the class definition, but when the compiler first sees the name big in the member function declaration, the only big in scope is the global object, so the compiler parses the function declaration incorrectly:

```
int big;
// typedef big float;
struct demo {
  void func(big); // Error
  typedef big long;
};
```

If the declaration int big were a typedef instead, the declaration of func would be parsed as intended, and name lookup would find the nested type demo::big for the parameter type of func. A simpler solution is to move the typedef big long; to the start of the class definition, which is the style used throughout this book.

If a class or namespace contains a using directive (described later in this chapter), the used class or namespace is also searched.

A friend declaration does not add its name to the class scope. Thus, the rules for name lookup are slightly different than they are for a member function. If a friend function is defined within the body of the class granting friendship, the name is looked up in the class scope, just as it would be for a member function. If the function is defined outside the class, the class is not searched, so the rules are the same as for an ordinary function. Example 2-6 shows how the two different lookup rules can cause confusion.

Example 2-6. Looking up names in a friend function

```
class foo {
public:
  friend void bar1(foo& f) {
    ++y;           // OK: refers to foo::y
  }
  friend void bar2(foo& f);
private:
  static int y;
  int x;
};

void bar2(foo& f) {
  ++y;             // Error: y not in scope
}
```

If the friend is a member function, the function and other names in its declaration are looked up first in the class granting friendship, and, if not found, in the class that contains the friend declaration. (See Example 2-7.)

Example 2-7. Declaring friend member functions

```
class test {
public:
  typedef int T1;
  typedef float T2;
  void f(T1);
  void f(T2);
};
class other {
  typedef char T2;
  friend void test::f(T1); // Look up f and T1 in test.
  friend void test::f(T2); // Look up f and T2 in test before looking it up in
                           // other.
};
```

In the definition of a class member (function or static data) outside of the class declaration, the lookup searches the class and ancestor classes, but only after the class name appears in the declarator. Thus, the type specifier (a function's return type or the type of a static data member) is not looked up in the class declaration unless the type name is explicitly qualified. (Declarators and type specifiers are covered later in this chapter.) Example 2-8 shows the consequences of this rule.

Example 2-8. Defining members outside of a class declaration

```
class node {
public:
  enum color { red, black };
  node(color x);
  color toggle(color c);
private:
  color c;
  static color root_color;
};

// Must qualify node::color and node::root_color, but initializer is in the scope
// of node, so it doesn't need to be qualified

node::color node::root_color = red;

// Similarly, return type must be qualified, but parameter type does not need to
// be.
node::color node::toggle(color c)
{
  return static_cast<color>(1 - c);
}
```

In a template declaration, the lookup rules for unqualified names have an additional wrinkle that depends on the template parameters and arguments. See Chapter 7 for details.

Argument-Dependent Name Lookup

Argument-dependent name lookup is an additional rule for looking up unqualified function names. The rule specifies additional classes and namespaces to search based on the types of the function arguments. Argument-dependent name lookup is also known as *Koenig lookup*, named after Andrew Koenig, the creator of this lookup rule. The short version of the rule is that the compiler looks up a function name in the usual places, and in the namespaces that contain the user-defined types (classes and enumerations) of the function arguments.

The slightly longer version of the Koenig lookup rule is that the compiler first searches all the usual places, as described earlier in this chapter. If it does not find a declaration, it then searches an additional list of classes and namespaces. The additional list depends on the types used for all of the function's argument types:

- For a class type, the compiler searches the class and its namespaces, plus all ancestor classes and their namespaces.
- For a pointer to a data member, the compiler searches its class and its namespaces, plus all ancestor classes and their namespaces.
- For a function pointer or reference, the compiler searches the classes and namespaces associated with the return type and all parameter types. For a pointer or reference to a member function, the compiler also searches its class and all ancestor classes, and their namespaces.
- For a union or enumerated type, the namespace that contains the declaration is searched. If the type is a class member, its class is searched.

Example 2-9 shows a typical case in which argument-dependent name lookup is needed. The operator<< function is declared in the std namespace in the <string> header. It is not a member function of ostream, and the only way the compiler can find the operator is to search the std namespace. The fact that its arguments are in the std namespace tells the compiler to look there.

Example 2-9. Argument-dependent name lookup

```
#include <string>
#include <iostream>
#include <ostream>
int main( )
{
  std::string message("Howdy!\n");
  std::cout << message;
}
```

Another way to look at argument-dependent lookup is to consider a simple class declaration. For example, with rational numbers, to support the customary and usual arithmetic operators, you might choose to declare them as member functions:

```
namespace numeric {
  class rational {
    ...
    rational operator+(const rational& other);
```

```
      rational operator+(int i);
   };
}
```

Expressions such as r1 + 42 compile successfully because they are equivalent to
member function calls such as r1.operator+(42), so the + operator is found as a
member of rational (assuming r1 is an instance of rational). But 42 + r1 does not
work because an integer cannot have a member function—e.g., 42.operator+(r1).
Instead, you must declare an operator at the namespace level:

```
namespace numeric {
   class rational { ... };
   rational operator+(int i, const rational& r);
   ...
}
```

In order to compile the expression 42 + r1, the compiler needs to find operator+ in
the numeric namespace. Without a using directive, the compiler has no way of
knowing it needs to search the numeric namespace, but the compiler knows that the
type of the second argument is declared in numeric. Thus, argument-dependent
lookup allows for the everyday, expected use of overloaded operators.

Linkage

Every name has *linkage*, which determines how the compiler and linker can use
the name. Linkage has two aspects: scope and language. *Scope linkage* dictates
which scopes have access to an entity. *Language linkage* dictates an entity's properties that depend on programming language.

Scope Linkage

Scope linkage can be one of the following:

Internal linkage
> A name with internal linkage can be referred to from a different scope within
> the same source file. At namespace scope (that is, outside of functions and
> classes), static declarations have internal linkage, as do const declarations
> that are not also extern. Data members of anonymous unions have internal
> linkage. Names in an unnamed namespace have internal linkage.

External linkage
> A name with external linkage can be referred to from a different scope,
> possibly in a different source file. Functions and objects declared with the
> extern specifier have external linkage, as do entities declared at namespace
> scope that do not have internal linkage.

No linkage
> A name with no linkage can be referred to only from within the scope where
> it is declared. Local declarations that are not extern have no linkage.

Language Linkage

Every function, function type, and object has a language linkage, which is specified as a simple character string. By default, the linkage is "C++". The only other standard language linkage is "C". All other language linkages and the properties associated with different language linkages are implementation-defined.

You can specify the language linkage for a single declaration (not a definition) or for a series of declarations and definitions. When you specify linkage for a series of declarations and definitions, you must enclose the series in curly braces. A language linkage declaration does not define a scope within the curly braces. For example:

```
extern "C" void cfunction(int);
extern "C++" {
  void cppfunc(int);
  void cppfunc(double);
}
```

Language linkage is part of a function's type, so typedef declarations keep track of the language linkage. When assigning a function to a function pointer, the function and pointer must have the same linkage. In the following example, funcptr is a function pointer with "C" linkage (note the need for curly braces because it is a definition, not a declaration). You can assign a "C" function to funcptr, but not a "C++" function, even though the rest of the function type matches.

```
extern "C" { void (*funcptr)(int); }
funcptr = cfunction; // OK
funcptr = cppfunc;   // Error
```

C does not support function overloading, so there can be at most one function with "C" linkage of a given name. Even if you declare a C function in two different namespaces, both declarations refer to the same function, for which there must be a single definition.

Typically, "C" linkage is used for external functions that are written in C (such as those in the C standard library), but that you want to call from a C++ program. "C++" linkage is used for native C++ code. Sometimes, though, you want to write a function in C++ that can be called from C; in that case, you should declare the C++ function with "C" linkage.

An implementation might support other language linkages. It is up to the implementation to define the properties of each language: how parameters are passed to functions, how values are returned from functions, whether and how function names are altered, and so on. In many C++ implementations, a function with "C++" linkage has a "mangled" name, that is, the external name encodes the function name and the types of all its arguments. So the function strlen(const char*) might have an external name of strlen__FCcP, making it hard to call the function from a C program, which does not know about C++ name-mangling rules. Using "C" linkage, the compiler might not mangle the name, exporting the function under the plain name of strlen, which can be called easily from C.

Type Declarations

One of the hallmarks of C++ is that you can define a type that resembles any built-in type. Thus, if you need to define a type that supports arbitrary-sized integers—call it bigint—you can do so, and programmers will be able to use bigint objects the same way they use int objects.

You can define a brand new type by defining a class (see Chapter 6) or an enumeration (see "Enumerated Types" later in this chapter). In addition to declaring and defining new types, you can declare a typedef, which is a synonym for an existing type. Note that while the name typedef seems to be a shorthand for "type definition," it is actually a type declaration. (See "typedef Declarations" later in this chapter.)

Fundamental Types

This section lists the fundamental type specifiers that are built into the C++ language. For types that require multiple keywords (e.g., unsigned long int), you can mix the keywords in any order, but the order shown in the following list is the conventional order. If a type specifier requires multiple words, one of which is int, the int can be omitted. If a type is signed, the signed keyword can be omitted (except in the case of signed char).

bool
> Represents a Boolean or logical value. It has two possible values: true and false.

char
> Represents a narrow character. Narrow character literals usually have type char. (If a narrow character literal contains multiple characters, the type is int.) Unlike the other integral types, a plain char is not necessarily equivalent to signed char. Instead, char can be equivalent to signed char or unsigned char, depending on the implementation. Regardless of the equivalence, the plain char type is distinct and separate from signed char and unsigned char.
>
> All the narrow character types (char, signed char, and unsigned char) share a common size and representation. By definition, char is the smallest fundamental type—that is, sizeof(char) is 1.

double
> Represents a double-precision, floating-point number. The range and precision are at least as much as those of float. A floating-point literal has type double unless you use the F or L suffix.

float
> Represents a single-precision, floating-point number.

long double
> Represents an extended-precision, floating-point number. The range and precision are at least as much as those of double.

signed char
> Represents a signed byte.

`signed int`
> Represents an integer in a size and format that is natural for the host environment.

`signed long int`
> Represents an integer whose range is at least as large as that of `int`.

`signed short int`
> Represents an integer such that the range of an `int` is at least as large as the range of a `short`.

`unsigned char`
> Represents an unsigned byte. Some functions, especially in the C library, require characters and character strings to be cast to `unsigned char` instead of plain `char`. (See Chapter 13 for details.)

`unsigned int`
> Represents an unsigned integer.

`unsigned long int`
> Represents an unsigned long integer.

`unsigned short int`
> Represents an unsigned short integer.

`void`
> Represents the absence of any values. You cannot declare an object of type `void`, but you can declare a function that "returns" `void` (that is, does not return a value), or declare a pointer to `void`, which can be used as a generic pointer. (See `static_cast<>` under "Postfix Expressions" in Chapter 3 for information about casting to and from a pointer to `void`.)

`wchar_t`
> Represents a wide character. Its representation must match one of the fundamental integer types. Wide character literals have type `wchar_t`.

The representations of the fundamental types are implementation-defined. The integral types (`bool`, `char`, `wchar_t`, `int`, etc.) each require a binary representation: signed-magnitude, ones' complement, or two's complement. Some types have alignment restrictions, which are also implementation-defined. (Note that `new` expressions always return pointers that are aligned for any type.)

The `unsigned` types always use arithmetic modulo 2^n, in which n is the number of bits in the type. Unsigned types take up the same amount of space and have the same alignment requirements as their signed companion types. Nonnegative signed values are always a subset of the values supported by the equivalent unsigned type and must have the same bit representations as their corresponding unsigned values.

> Although the size and range of the fundamental types is implementation-defined, the C++ standard mandates minimum requirements for these types. These requirements are specified in `<climits>` (for the integral types) and `<cfloat>` (for the floating-point types). See also `<limits>`, which declares templates for obtaining the numerical properties of each fundamental type.

Enumerated Types

An *enumerated type* declares an optional type name (the *enumeration*) and a set of zero or more identifiers (*enumerators*) that can be used as values of the type. Each enumerator is a constant whose type is the enumeration. For example:

```
enum logical { no, maybe, yes };
logical is_permitted = maybe;

enum color { red=1, green, blue=4 };
const color yellow = static_cast<color>(red | green);

enum zeroes { a, b = 0, c = 0 };
```

You can optionally specify the integral value of an enumerator after an equal sign (=). The value must be a constant of integral or enumerated type. The default value of the first enumerator is 0. The default value for any other enumerator is one more than the value of its predecessor (regardless of whether that value was explicitly specified). In a single enumeration declaration, you can have more than one enumerator with the same value.

The name of an enumeration is optional, but without a name you cannot declare use the enumeration in other declarations. Such a declaration is sometimes used to declare integer constants such as the following:

```
enum { init_size = 100 };
std::vector<int> data(init_size);
```

An enumerated type is a unique type. Each enumerated value has a corresponding integer value, and the enumerated value can be promoted automatically to its integer equivalent, but integers cannot be implicitly converted to an enumerated type. Instead, you can use static_cast<> to cast an integer to an enumeration or cast a value from one enumeration to a different enumeration. (See Chapter 3 for details.)

The range of values for an enumeration is defined by the smallest and largest bitfields that can hold all of its enumerators. In more precise terms, let the largest and smallest values of the enumerated type be v_{min} and v_{max}. The largest enumerator is e_{max} and the smallest is e_{min}. Using two's complement representation (the most common integer format), v_{max} is the smallest $2^n - 1$, such that $v_{max} \geq$ max(abs(e_{min}) - 1, abs(e_{max})). If e_{min} is not negative, $v_{min} = 0$; otherwise, $v_{min} = -(v_{max} + 1)$.

In other words, the range of values for an enumerated type can be larger than the range of enumerator values, but the exact range depends on the representation of integers on the host platform, so it is implementation-defined. All values between the largest and smallest enumerators are always valid, even if they do not have corresponding enumerators.

In the following example, the enumeration sign has the range (in two's complement) -2 to 1. Your program might not assign any meaning to static_cast<sign> (-2), but it is semantically valid in a program:

```
enum sign { neg=-1, zero=0, pos=1 };
```

Each enumeration has an underlying integral type that can store all of the enumerator values. The actual underlying type is implementation-defined, so the size of an enumerated type is likewise implementation-defined.

The standard library has a type called `iostate`, which might be implemented as an enumeration. (Other implementations are also possible; see `<ios>` in Chapter 13 for details.) The enumeration has four enumerators, which can be used as bits in a bitmask and combined using bitwise operators:

```
enum iostate { goodbit=0, failbit=1, eofbit=2, badbit=4 };
```

The `iostate` enumeration can clearly fit in a char because the range of values is 0 to 7, but the compiler is free to use `int`, `short`, `char`, or the `unsigned` flavors of these types as the underlying type.

Because enumerations can be promoted to integers, any arithmetic operation can be performed on enumerated values, but the result is always an integer. If you want to permit certain operations that produce enumeration results, you must overload the operators for your enumerated type. For example, you might want to overload the bitwise operators, but not the arithmetic operators, for the `iostate` type in the preceding example. The `sign` type does not need any additional operators; the comparison operators work just fine by implicitly converting `sign` values to integers. Other enumerations might call for overloading `++` and `--` operators (similar to the *succ* and *pred* functions in Pascal). Example 2-10 shows how operators can be overloaded for enumerations.

Example 2-10. Overloading operators for enumerations

```
// Explicitly cast to int, to avoid infinite recursion.
inline iostate operator|(iostate a, iostate b) {
  return iostate(int(a) | int(b));
}
inline iostate& operator|=(iostate& a, iostate b) {
  a = a | b;
  return a;
}
// Repeat for &, ^, and ~.

int main( )
{
  iostate err = goodbit;
  if (error( ))
    err |= badbit;
}
```

POD Types

POD is short for Plain Old Data. The fundamental types and enumerated types are POD types, as are pointers and arrays of POD types. You can declare a POD class, which is a `class` or `struct` that uses only POD types for its nonstatic data members. A POD union is a `union` of POD types.

POD types are special in several ways:

- A POD object can be copied byte for byte and retain its value. In particular, a POD object can be safely copied to an array of char or unsigned char, and when copied back, it retains its original value. A POD object can also be copied by calling memcpy; the copy has the same value as the original.

- A local POD object without an initializer is uninitialized, that is, its value is undefined. Similarly, a POD type in a new expression without an initializer is uninitialized. (A non-POD class is initialized in these situations by calling its default constructor.) When initialized with an empty initializer, a POD object is initialized to 0, false, or a null pointer.

- A goto statement can safely branch across declarations of uninitialized POD objects. (See Chapter 4 for more information.)

- A POD object can be initialized using an aggregate initializer. (See "Initializers" later in this chapter for details.)

See Chapter 6 for more information about POD types, especially POD classes.

typedef Declarations

A typedef declares a synonym for an existing type. Syntactically, a typedef is like declaring a variable, with the type name taking the place of the variable name, and with a typedef keyword out in front. More precisely, typedef is a specifier in a declaration, and it must be combined with type specifiers and optional const and volatile qualifiers (called *cv-qualifiers*), but no storage class specifiers. A list of declarators follow the specifiers. (See the next section, "Object Declarations," for more information about *cv* qualifiers, storage class specifiers, and declarators.)

The declarator of a typedef declaration is similar to that for an object declaration, except you cannot have an initializer. The following are some examples of typedef declarations:

```
typedef unsigned int uint;
typedef long int *long_ptr;
typedef double matrix[3][3];
typedef void (*thunk)( );
typedef signed char schar;
```

By convention, the typedef keyword appears before the type specifiers. Syntactically, typedef behaves as a storage class specifier (see "Specifiers" later in this chapter for more information about storage class specifiers) and can be mixed in any order with other type specifiers. For example, the following typedefs are identical and valid:

```
typedef unsigned long ulong;    // Conventional
long typedef int unsigned ulong; // Valid, but strange
```

A typedef is especially helpful with complicated declarations, such as function pointer declarations and template instantiations. They help the author who must concoct the declarations, and they help the reader who must later tease apart the morass of parentheses, asterisks, and angle brackets. The standard library uses them frequently. (See also Example 2-11.)

```
typedef std::basic_string<char, std::char_traits<char> > string;
```

A typedef does not create a new type the way class and enum do. It simply declares a new name for an existing type. Therefore, function declarations for which the parameters differ only as typedefs are not actually different declarations. The two function declarations in the following example are really two declarations of the same function:

```
typedef unsigned int uint;
uint func(uint);         // Two declarations of the
unsigned func(unsigned); // same function
```

Similarly, because you cannot overload an operator on fundamental types, you cannot overload an operator on typedef synonyms for fundamental types. For example, both the following attempts to overload + result in an error:

```
int operator+(int, int);            // Error
typedef int integer;
integer operator+(integer, integer); // Error
```

C programmers are accustomed to declaring typedefs for struct, union, and enum declarations, but such typedefs are not necessary in C++. In C, the struct, union, and enum names are separate from the type names, but in C++, the declaration of a struct, union, class, or enum adds the type to the type names. Nonetheless, such a typedef is harmless. The following example shows typedef being used to create the synonym point for the struct point:

```
struct point { int x, y; }
typedef struct point point; // Not needed in C++, but harmless
point pt;
```

Elaborated Type Specifier

An *elaborated type specifier* begins with an introductory keyword: class, enum, struct, typename, or union. The keyword is followed by a (possibly) qualified name of a suitable type. That is, enum is followed by the name of an enumeration, class is followed by a class name, struct by a struct name, and union by a union name. The typename keyword is used only in templates (see Chapter 7) and is followed by a name that must be a type name in a template instantiation.

A typename-elaborated type specifier is often needed in template definitions. The other elaborated type specifiers tend to be used in headers that must be compatible with C or in type names that have been hidden by other names. For example:

```
enum color { black, red };
color x;                   // No need for elaborated name
enum color color();        // Function hides color
enum color c = color();    // Elaborated name is needed here
```

Object Declarations

An *object* in C++ is a region of storage with a type, a value, and possibly a name. In traditional object-oriented programming, "object" means an instance of a class, but in C++ the definition is slightly broader to include instances of any data type.

An object (variable or constant) declaration has two parts: a series of *specifiers* and a list of comma-separated *declarators*. Each declarator has a name and an optional *initializer*.

Specifiers

Each declaration begins with a series of specifiers. The series can contain a storage class, const and volatile qualifiers, and the object's type, in any order.

Storage class specifiers

A storage class specifier can specify scope linkage and lifetime. The storage class is optional. For function parameters and local variables in a function, the default storage class specifier is auto. For declarations at namespace scope, the default is usually an object with static lifetime and external linkage. C++ has no explicit storage class for such a declaration. (See "Object Lifetime" later in this chapter and "Linkage" earlier in this chapter for more information.) If you use a storage class specifier, you must choose only one of the following:

auto
> Denotes an automatic variable—that is, a variable with a lifetime limited to the block in which the variable is declared. The auto specifier is the default for function parameters and local variables, which are the only kinds of declarations for which it can be used, so it is rarely used explicitly.

extern
> Denotes an object with external linkage, which might be defined in a different source file. Function parameters cannot be extern.

mutable
> Denotes a data member that can be modified even if the containing object is const. See Chapter 6 for more information.

register
> Denotes an automatic variable with a hint to the compiler that the variable should be stored in a fast register. Many modern compilers ignore the register storage class because the compilers are better than people at determining which variables belong in registers.

static
> Denotes a variable with a static lifetime and internal linkage. Function parameters cannot be static.

const and volatile qualifiers

The const and volatile specifiers are optional. You can use either one, neither, or both in any order. The const and volatile keywords can be used in other parts of a declaration, so they are often referred to by the more general term *qualifiers*; for brevity, they are often referred to as *cv*-qualifiers.

const
> Denotes an object that cannot be modified. A const object cannot ordinarily be the target of an assignment. You cannot call a non-const member function of a const object.

volatile

Denotes an object whose value might change unexpectedly. The compiler is prevented from performing optimizations that depend on the value not changing. For example, a variable that is tied to a hardware register should be volatile.

Type specifiers

Every object must have a type in the form of one or more type specifiers. The type specifiers can be any of the following:

- The name of a class, enumeration, or typedef
- An elaborated name
- A series of fundamental type specifiers
- A class definition
- An enumerated type definition

Enumerated and fundamental types are described earlier in this chapter in "Type Declarations." Class types are covered in Chapter 6. The typename keyword is covered in Chapter 7.

Using specifiers

Specifiers can appear in any order, but the convention is to list the storage class first, followed by the type specifiers, followed by *cv*-qualifiers.

```
extern long int const mask; // Conventional
int extern const long mask; // Valid, but strange
```

Many programmers prefer a different order: storage class, *cv*-qualifiers, type specifiers. More and more are learning to put the *cv*-qualifiers last, though. See the examples under "Pointers" later in this chapter to find out why.

The convention for types that require multiple keywords is to place the base type last and the modifiers first:

```
unsigned long int x; // Conventional
int unsigned long y; // Valid, but strange
long double a;       // Conventional
double long b;       // Valid, but strange
```

You can define a class or enumerated type in the same declaration as an object declaration:

```
enum color { red, black } node_color;
```

However, the custom is to define the type separately, then use the type name in a separate object declaration:

```
enum color { red, black };
color node_color;
```

Declarators

A declarator declares a single name within a declaration. In a declaration, the initial specifiers apply to all the declarators in the declaration, but each declarator's modifiers apply only to that declarator. (See "Pointers" in this section for examples of where this distinction is crucial.) A declarator contains the name being declared, additional type information (for pointers, references, and arrays), and an optional initializer. Use commas to separate multiple declarators in a declaration. For example:

```
int plain_int, array_of_int[42], *pointer_to_int;
```

Arrays

An array is declared with a constant size specified in square brackets. The array size is fixed for the lifetime of the object and cannot change. (For an array-like container whose size can change at runtime, see <vector> in Chapter 13.) To declare a multidimensional array, use a separate set of square brackets for each dimension:

```
int point[2];
double matrix[3][4]; // A 3 × 4 matrix
```

You can omit the array size if there is an initializer; the number of initial values determines the size. In a multidimensional array, you can omit only the first (leftmost) size:

```
int data[] = { 42, 10, 3, 4 }; // data[4]
int identity[][3] = { { 1,0,0 }, {0,1,0}, {0,0,1} }; // identity[3][3]
char str[] = "hello";          // str[6], with trailing \0
```

In a multidimensional array, all elements are stored contiguously, with the rightmost index varying the fastest (usually called *row major order*).

When a function parameter is an array, the array's size is ignored, and the type is actually a pointer type, which is the subject of the next section. For a multidimensional array used as a function parameter, the first dimension is ignored, so the type is a pointer to an array. Because the first dimension is ignored in a function parameter, it is usually omitted, leaving empty square brackets:

```
long sum(long data[], size_t n);
double chi_sq(double stat[][2]);
```

Pointers

A pointer object stores the address of another object. A pointer is declared with a leading asterisk (*), optionally followed by *cv*-qualifiers, then the object name, and finally an optional initializer.

When reading and writing pointer declarations, be sure to keep track of the *cv*-qualifiers. The *cv*-qualifiers in the declarator apply to the pointer object, and the *cv*-qualifiers in the declaration's specifiers apply to the type of the pointer's target. For example, in the following declaration, the const is in the specifier, so the pointer p is a pointer to a const int. The pointer object is modifiable, but you cannot change the int that it points to. This kind of pointer is usually called a pointer to const.

```
int i, j;
int const *p = &i;
p = &j;  // OK
*p = 42; // Error
```

When the cv-qualifier is part of the declarator, it modifies the pointer object. Thus, in the following example, the pointer p is const and hence not modifiable, but it points to a plain int, which can be modified. This kind of pointer is usually called a const pointer.

```
int i, j;
int * const p = &i;
p = &j;  // Error
*p = 42; // OK
```

You can have pointers to pointers, as deep as you want, in which each level of pointer has its own cv-qualifiers. The easiest way to read a complicated pointer declaration is to find the declarator, work your way from the inside to the outside, and then from right to left. In this situation, it is best to put cv-qualifiers after the type specifiers. For example:

```
int x;
int *p;                        // Pointer to int
int * const cp = &x;           // const pointer to int
int const * pc;                // Pointer to const int
int const * const cpc = &x;    // const pointer to const int
int *pa[10];                   // Array of 10 pointers to int
int **pp;                      // Pointer to pointer to int
```

When a function parameter is declared with an array type, the actual type is a pointer, and at runtime the address of the first element of the array is passed to the function. You can use array syntax, but the size is ignored. For example, the following two declarations mean the same thing:

```
int sum(int data[], size_t n);
int sum(int *data,  size_t n);
```

When using array notation for a function parameter, you can omit only the first dimension. For example, the following is valid:

```
void transpose(double matrix[][3]);
```

but the following is not valid. If the compiler does not know the number of columns, it does not know how to lay out the memory for matrix or compute array indices.

```
void transpose(double matrix[][]);
```

A useful convention is to use array syntax when declaring parameters that are used in an array-like fashion—that is, the parameter itself does not change, or it is dereferenced with the [ ] operator. Use pointer syntax for parameters that are used in pointer-like fashion—that is, the parameter value changes, or it is dereferenced with the unary * operator.

Declarations

Function pointers

A function pointer is declared with an asterisk (*) and the function signature (parameter types and optional names). The declaration's specifiers form the function's return type. The name and asterisk must be enclosed in parentheses, so the asterisk is not interpreted as part of the return type. An optional exception specification can follow the signature. See Chapter 5 for more information about function signatures and exception specifications.

```
void (*fp)(int); // fp is pointer to function that takes an int parameter
                 // and returns void.
void print(int);
fp = print;
```

A declaration of an object with a function pointer type can be hard to read, so typically you declare the type separately with a typedef declaration, and then declare the object using the typedef name:

```
typedef void (*Function)(int);
Function fp;
fp = print;
```

Example 2-11 shows a declaration of an array of 10 function pointers, in which the functions return int* and take two parameters: a function pointer (taking an int* and returning an int*) and an integer. The declaration is almost unreadable without using typedef declarations for each part of the puzzle.

Example 2-11. Simplifying function pointer declarations with typedef

```
// Array of 10 function pointers
int* (*fp[10])(int*(*)(int*), int);

// Declare a type for pointer to int.
typedef int* int_ptr;
// Declare a function pointer type for a function that takes an int_ptr parameter
// and returns an int_ptr.
typedef int_ptr (*int_ptr_func)(int_ptr);
// Declare a function pointer type for a function that returns int_ptr and takes
// two parameters: the first of type int_ptr and the second of type int.
typedef int_ptr (*func_ptr)(int_ptr_func, int);
// Declare an array of 10 func_ptrs.
func_ptr fp[10];
```

Member pointers

Pointers to members (data and functions) work differently from other pointers. The syntax for declaring a pointer to a nonstatic data member or a nonstatic member function requires a class name and scope operator before the asterisk. Pointers to members can never be cast to ordinary pointers, and vice versa. You cannot declare a reference to a member. (See Chapter 3 for information about expressions that dereference pointers to members.) A pointer to a static member is an ordinary pointer, not a member pointer. The following are some simple examples of member pointers:

```
struct simple {
  int data;
```

```
    int func(int);
};
int simple::* p = &simple::data;
int (simple::*fp)(int) = &simple::func;
simple s;
s.*p = (s.*fp)(42);
```

References

A reference is a synonym for an object or function. A reference is declared just like
a pointer, but with an ampersand (&) instead of an asterisk (*). A local or global
reference declaration must have an initializer that specifies the target of the reference. Data members and function parameters, however, do not have initializers.
You cannot declare a reference of a reference, a reference to a class member, a
pointer to a reference, an array of references, or a cv-qualified reference. For
example:

```
int x;
int &r = x;          // Reference to int
int& const rc = x;   // Error: no cv qualified references
int & &rr;           // Error: no reference of reference
int& ra[10];         // Error: no arrays of reference
int &* rp = &r;      // Error: no pointer to reference
int* p = &x;         // Pointer to int
int *& pr = p;       // OK: reference to pointer
```

A reference, unlike a pointer, cannot be made to refer to a different object at
runtime. Assignments to a reference are just like assignments to the referenced
object.

Because a reference cannot have cv-qualifiers, there is no such thing as a const
reference. Instead, a reference to const is often called a const reference for the sake
of brevity.

References are often used to bind names to temporary objects, implement call-by-
reference for function parameters, and optimize call-by-value for large function
parameters. The divide function in Example 2-12 demonstrates the first two uses.
The standard library has the div function, which divides two integers and returns
the quotient and remainder in a struct. Instead of copying the structure to a local
object, divide binds the return value to a reference to const, thereby avoiding an
unnecessary copy of the return value. Furthermore, suppose that you would
rather have divide return the results as arguments. The function parameters quo
and rem are references; when the divide function is called, they are bound to the
function arguments, q and r, in main. When divide assigns to quo, it actually stores
the value in q, so when divide returns, main has the quotient and remainder.

Example 2-12. Returning results in function arguments

```
#include <cstdlib>
#include <iostream>
#include <ostream>
```

Example 2-12. Returning results in function arguments (continued)

```
void divide(long num, long den, long& quo, long& rem)
{
  const std::ldiv_t& result = std::div(num, den);
  quo = result.quot;
  rem = result.rem;
}

int main()
{
  long q, r;
  divide(42, 5, q, r);
  std::cout << q << " remainder " << r << '\n';
}
```

The other common use of references is to use a const reference for function parameters, especially for large objects. Function arguments are passed by value in C++, which requires copying the arguments. The copy operation can be costly for a large object, so passing a reference to a large object yields better performance than passing the large object itself. The reference parameter is bound to the actual argument, avoiding the unnecessary copy. If the function modifies the object, it would violate the call-by-value convention, so you should declare the reference const, which prevents the function from modifying the object. In this way, call-by-value semantics are preserved, and the performance of call-by-reference is improved. The standard library often uses this idiom. For example, operator<< for std::string uses a const reference to the string to avoid making unnecessary copies of the string. (See <string> in Chapter 13 for details.)

If a function parameter is a non-const reference, the argument must be an lvalue. A const reference, however, can bind to an rvalue, which permits temporary objects to be passed to the function, which is another characteristic of call-by-value. (See Chapter 3 for the definitions of "lvalue" and "rvalue.")

A reference must be initialized so it refers to an object. If a data member is a reference, it must be initialized in the constructor's initializer list (see Chapter 6). Function parameters that are references are initialized in the function call, binding each reference parameter to its corresponding actual argument. All other reference definitions must have an initializer. (An extern declaration is not a definition, so it doesn't take an initializer.)

A const reference can be initialized to refer to a temporary object. For example, if a function takes a const reference to a float as a parameter, you can pass an integer as an argument. The compiler converts the integer to float, saves the float value as an unnamed temporary object, and passes that temporary object as the function argument. The const reference is initialized to refer to the temporary object. After the function returns, the temporary object is destroyed:

```
void do_stuff(const float& f);
do_stuff(42);
// Equivalent to:
{
```

```
    const float unnamed = 42;
    do_stuff(unnamed);
  }
```

The restrictions on a reference, especially to a reference of a reference, pose an additional challenge for template authors. For example, you cannot store references in a container because a number of container functions explicitly declare their parameters as references to the container's value type. (Try using std::vector<int&> with your compiler, and see what happens. You should see a lot of error messages.)

Instead, you can write a wrapper template, call it rvector<typename T>, and specialize the template (rvector<T&>) so references are stored as pointers, but all the access functions hide the differences. This approach requires you to duplicate the entire template, which is tedious. Instead, you can encapsulate the specialization in a traits template called Ref<> (refer to Chapter 7 for more information about templates and specializations, and to Chapter 8 for more information about traits), as shown in Example 2-13.

Example 2-13. Encapsulating reference traits

```
// Ref type trait encapsulates reference type, and mapping to and from the type
// for use in a container.
template<typename T>
struct Ref {
  typedef T value_type;
  typedef T& reference;
  typedef const T& const_reference;
  typedef T* pointer;
  typedef const T* const_pointer;
  typedef T container_type;
  static reference from_container(reference x) { return x; }
  static const_reference from_container(const_reference x)
                                              { return x; }
  static reference to_container(reference x)   { return x; }
};

template<typename T>
struct Ref<T&> {
  typedef T value_type;
  typedef T& reference;
  typedef const T& const_reference;
  typedef T* pointer;
  typedef const T* const_pointer;
  typedef T* container_type;
  static reference from_container(pointer x) { return *x; }
  static const_reference from_container(const_pointer x)
                                            { return *x; }
  static pointer to_container(reference x)   { return &x; }
};

// rvector<> is similar to vector<>, but allows references by storing references
// as pointers.
template<typename T, typename A=std::allocator<T> >
```

Example 2-13. Encapsulating reference traits (continued)

```
class rvector {
  typedef typename Ref<T>::container_type container_type;
  typedef typename std::vector<container_type> vector_type;
public:
  typedef typename Ref<T>::value_type value_type;
  typedef typename Ref<T>::reference reference;
  typedef typename Ref<T>::const_reference const_reference;
  typedef typename vector_type::size_type size_type;
  ...  // Other typedefs are similar.
  class iterator { ... }; // Wraps a vector<>::iterator
  class const_iterator { ... };
  ...  // Constructors pass arguments to v.
  iterator begin()          { return iterator(v.begin()); }
  iterator end()            { return iterator(v.end()); }
  void push_back(typename Ref<T>::reference x) {
    v.push_back(Ref<T>::to_container(x));
  }
  reference at(size_type n)   {
    return Ref<T>::from_container(v.at(n));
  }
  reference front()            {
    return Ref<T>::from_container(v.front());
  }
  const_reference front() const {
    return Ref<T>::from_container(v.front());
  }
  ...  // Other members are similar.
private:
  vector_type v;
};
```

Initializers

An initializer supplies an initial value for an object being declared. You must supply an initializer for the definition of a reference or const object. An initializer is optional for other object definitions. An initializer is not allowed for most data members within a class definition, but an exception is made for static const data members of integral or enumerated type. Initializers are also not allowed for extern declarations and function parameters. (Default arguments for function parameters can look like initializers. See Chapter 5 for details.)

The two forms of initializers are *assignment-like* and *function-like*. (In the C++ standard, assignment-like is called copy initialization, and function-like is called direct initialization.) An assignment-like initializer starts with an equal sign, which is followed by an expression or a list of comma-separated expressions in curly braces. A function-like initializer is a list of one or more comma-separated expressions in parentheses. Note that these initializers look like assignment statements or function calls, respectively, but they are not. They are initializers. The difference is particularly important for classes (see Chapter 6). The following are some examples of initializers:

```
int x = 42;              // Initializes x with the value 42
int y(42);               // Initializes y with the value 42
int z = { 42 };          // Initializes z with the value 42
int w[4] = { 1, 2, 3, 4 }; // Initializes an array
std::complex<double> c(2.0, 3.0); // Calls complex constructor
```

When initializing a scalar value, the form is irrelevant. The initial value is converted to the desired type using the usual conversion rules (as described in Chapter 3).

Without an initializer, all non-POD class-type objects are initialized by calling their default constructors. (See Chapter 6 for more information about POD and non-POD classes.) All other objects with static lifetimes are initialized to 0; objects with automatic lifetimes are left uninitialized. (See "Object Lifetime" later in this chapter.) An uninitialized reference or const object is an error.

Function-like initializers

You must use a function-like initializer when constructing an object whose constructor takes two or more arguments, or when calling an explicit constructor. The usual rules for resolving overloaded functions apply to the choice of overloaded constructors. (See Chapter 5 for more information about overloading and Chapter 6 for more information about constructors.) For example:

```
struct point {
  point(int x, int y);
  explicit point(int x);
  point( );
  ...
};

point p1(42, 10);  // Invokes point::point(int x, int y);
point p2(24);      // Invokes point::point(int x);
point p3;          // Invokes point::point( );
```

Empty parentheses cannot be used as an initializer in an object's declaration, but can be used in other initialization contexts (namely, a constructor initializer list or as a value in an expression). If the type is a class type, the default constructor is called; otherwise, the object is initialized to 0. Example 2-14 shows an empty initializer. No matter what type T is, the wrapper<> template can rely on T( ) to be a meaningful default value.

Example 2-14. An empty initializer

```
template<typename T>
struct wrapper {
  wrapper( ) : value_(T( )) {}
  explicit wrapper(const T& v) : value_(v) {}
private:
  T value_;
};
```

Example 2-14. An empty initializer (continued)

```
wrapper<int> i;     // Initializes i with int( ), or zero
enum color { black, red, green, blue };
wrapper<color> c;  // Initializes c with color( ), or black
wrapper<bool> b;    // Initializes b with bool( ), or false
wrapper<point> p;   // Initializes p with point( )
```

Assignment-like initializers

In an assignment-like initializer, if the object is of class type, the value to the right of the equal sign is converted to a temporary object of the desired type, and the first object is constructed by calling its copy constructor.

The generic term for an array or simple class is *aggregate* because it aggregates multiple values into a single object. "Simple" in this case means the class does not have any of the following:

- User-declared constructors
- Private or protected nonstatic data members
- Base classes
- Virtual functions

To initialize an aggregate, you can supply multiple values in curly braces, as described in the following sections. A POD object is a special kind of an aggregate. (See "POD Types" earlier in this chapter for more information about POD types; see also Chapter 6 for information about POD classes.)

To initialize an aggregate of class type, supply an initial value for each nonstatic data member separated by commas and enclosed in curly braces. For nested objects, use nested curly braces. Values are associated with members in the order of the members' declarations. More values than members results in an error. If there are fewer values than members, the members without values are initialized by calling each member's default constructor or initializing the members to 0.

An initializer list can be empty, which means all members are initialized to their defaults, which is different from omitting the initializer entirely. The latter causes all members to be left uninitialized. The following example shows several different initializers for class-type aggregates:

```
struct point { double x, y, z; };
point origin = { };     // All members initialized to 0.0
point unknown;          // Uninitialized, value is not known
point pt = { 1, 2, 3 }; // pt.x==1.0, pt.y==2.0, pt.z==3.0
struct line { point p1, p2; };
line vec = { { }, { 1 } }; // vec.p1 is all zero.
           // vec.p2.x==1.0, vec.p2.y==0.0, vec.p2.z==0.0
```

Only the first member of a union can be initialized:

```
union u { int value; unsigned char bytes[sizeof(int)]; };
u x = 42; // Initializes x.value
```

Initializing arrays

Initialize elements of an array with values separated by commas and enclosed in curly braces. Multidimensional arrays can be initialized by nesting sets of curly braces. An error results if there are more values than elements in the array; if an initializer has fewer values than elements in the array, the remaining elements in the array are initialized to zero values (default constructors or 0). If the declarator omits the array size, the size is determined by counting the number of values in the initializer.

An array initializer can be empty, which forces all elements to be initialized to 0. If the initializer is empty, the array size must be specified. Omitting the initializer entirely causes all elements of the array to be uninitialized (except non-POD types, which are initialized with their default constructors).

In the following example the size of vec is set to 3 because its initializer contains three elements, and the elements of zero are initialized to 0s because an empty initializer is used:

```
int vec[] = { 1, 2, 3 }; // Array of three elements
                         // vec[0]==1 ... vec[2]==3
int zero[4] = { }; // Initialize to all zeros.
```

When initializing a multidimensional array, you can flatten the curly braces and initialize elements of the array in row major order (last index varies the fastest). For example, both id1 and id2 end up having the same values in their corresponding elements:

```
// Initialize id1 and id2 to the identity matrix.
int id1[3][3] = { { 1 }, { 0, 1 }, { 0, 0, 1 } };
int id2[3][3] = { 1, 0, 0, 0, 1, 0, 0, 0, 1 };
```

An array of char or wchar_t is special because you can initialize such arrays with a string literal. Remember that every string literal has an implicit null character at the end. For example, the following two char declarations are equivalent, as are the two wchar_t declarations:

```
// The following two declarations are equivalent.
char str1[] = "Hello";
char str2[] = { 'H', 'e', 'l', 'l', 'o', '\0' };

wchar_t ws1[] = L"Hello";
wchar_t ws2[] = { L'H', L'e', L'l', L'l', L'o', L'\0' };
```

The last expression in an initializer list can be followed by a comma. This is convenient when you are maintaining software and find that you often need to change the order of items in an initializer list. You don't need to treat the last element differently from the other elements.

```
const std::string keywords[] = {
  "and",
  "asm",
  ...
  "while",
  "xor",
};
```

Because the last item has a trailing comma, you can easily select the entire line containing "xor" and move it to a different location in the list, and you don't need to worry about fixing up the commas afterward.

Initializing scalars

You can initialize any scalar object with a single value in curly braces, but you cannot omit the value the way you can with a single-element array:

```
int x = { 42 };
```

Object Lifetime

Every object has a *lifetime*, that is, the duration from when the memory for the object is allocated and the object is initialized to when the object is destroyed and the memory is released. Object lifetimes fall into three categories:

Automatic
> Objects are local to a function body or a nested block within a function body. The object is created when execution reaches the object's declaration, and the object is destroyed when execution leaves the block.

Static
> Objects can be local (with the static storage class specifier) or global (at namespace scope). Static objects are constructed at most once and destroyed only if they are successfully constructed. Local static objects are constructed when execution reaches the object's declaration. Global objects are constructed when the program starts but before main is entered. Static objects are destroyed in the opposite order of their construction. For more information, see "The main Function" in Chapter 5.

Dynamic
> Objects created with new expressions are dynamic. Their lifetimes extend until the delete expression is invoked on the objects' addresses. See Chapter 3 for more information about the new and delete expressions.

Namespaces

A *namespace* is a named scope. By grouping related declarations in a namespace, you can avoid name collisions with declarations in other namespaces. For example, suppose you are writing a word processor, and you use packages that others have written, including a screen layout package, an equation typesetting package, and an exact-arithmetic package for computing printed positions to high accuracy with fixed-point numbers.

The equation package has a class called fraction, which represents built-up fractions in an equation; the arithmetic package has a class called fraction, for computing with exact rational numbers; and the layout package has a class called fraction for laying out fractional regions of a page. Without namespaces, all three names would collide, and you would not be able to use more than one of the three packages in a single program.

With namespaces, each class can reside in a separate namespace—for example, layout::fraction, eqn::fraction, and math::fraction.

 C++ namespaces are similar to Java packages, with a key difference: in Java, classes in the same package have additional access rights to each other; in C++, namespaces confer no special access privileges.

Namespace Definitions

Define a namespace with the namespace keyword followed by an optional identifier (the namespace name) and zero or more declarations in curly braces. Namespace declarations can be discontiguous, even in separate source files or headers. The namespace scope is the accumulation of all definitions of the same namespace that the compiler has seen at the time it looks up a given name in the namespace. Namespaces can be nested. Example 2-15 shows a sample namespace definition.

Example 2-15. Defining a namespace

```
// The initial declaration
namespace numeric {
  class rational { ... }
  template<typename charT, typename traits>
  basic_ostream<charT,traits>& operator<<(
    basic_ostream<charT,traits>& out, const rational& r);
}

...

// This is a second definition. It adds an operator  to the namespace.
namespace numeric {
  rational operator+(const rational&, const rational&);
}

// The definition of operator+ can appear inside or outside the namespace
// definition. If it is outside, the name must be qualified with the scope
// operator.
numeric::rational numeric::operator+(const rational& r1,
                                     const rational& r2)
{
  ...
}

int main( )
{
  using numeric::rational;
  rational a, b;
  std::cout << a + b << '\n';
}
```

You can define a namespace without a name, in which case the compiler uses a unique, internal name. Thus, each source file's unnamed namespace is separate from the unnamed namespace in every other source file.

You can define an unnamed namespace nested within a named namespace (and vice versa). The compiler generates a unique, private name for the unnamed namespace in each unique scope. As with a named namespace, you can use multiple namespace definitions to compose the unnamed namespace, as shown in Example 2-16.

Example 2-16. Unnamed namespaces

```
#include <iostream>
#include <ostream>

namespace {
  int i = 10;
}

namespace {
  int j;          // Same unnamed namespace
  namespace X {
    int i = 20;   // Hides i in outer, unnamed namespace
  }
  namespace Y = X;
  int f() { return i; }
}

namespace X {
  int i = 30;
  // X::unnamed is different namespace than ::unnamed.
  namespace {
    int i = 40;   // Hides ::X::i, but is inaccessible outside the unnamed
                  // namespace
    int f() { return i; }
  }
}

int main()
{
  int i = X::i;   // ambiguous: unnamed::X or ::X?
  std::cout << ::X::f() << '\n'; // Prints 40
  std::cout << Y::i << '\n';      // Prints 20
  std::cout << f() << '\n';       // Prints 10
}
```

The advantage of using an unnamed namespace is that you are guaranteed that all names declared in it can never clash with names in other source files. The disadvantage is that you cannot use the scope operator (::) to qualify identifiers in an unnamed namespace, so you must avoid name collisions within the same source file.

C programmers are accustomed to using global static declarations for names that are private to a source file. You can do the same in C++, but it is better to use an unnamed namespace because a namespace can contain any kind of declaration (including classes, enumerations, and templates), whereas static declarations are limited to functions and objects.

Declarations of static objects and functions at namespace scope are deprecated in C++.

Declarations outside of all namespaces, functions, and classes are implicitly declared in the global namespace. A program has a single global namespace, which is shared by all source files that are compiled and linked into the program. Declarations in the global namespace are typically referred to as *global declarations*. Global names can be accessed directly using the global scope operator (the unary ::), as described earlier in "Qualified Name Lookup."

Namespace Aliases

A namespace alias is a synonym for an existing namespace. You can use an alias name to qualify names (with the :: operator) in using declarations and directives, but not in namespace definitions. Example 2-17 shows some alias examples.

Example 2-17. Namespace aliases

```
namespace original {
  int f( );
}

namespace ns = original;     // Alias

int ns::f( ) { return 42; }   // OK
using ns::f;                  // OK

int g( ) { return f( ); }

namespace ns { // Error: cannot use alias here
  int h( );
}
```

A namespace alias can provide an abbreviation for an otherwise unwieldy namespace name. The long name might incorporate a full organization name, deeply nested namespaces, or version numbers:

```
namespace tempest_software_inc {
  namespace version_1 { ... }
  namespace version_2 { ... }
}
namespace tempest_1 = tempest_software_inc::version_1;
namespace tempest_2 = tempest_software_inc::version_2;
```

using Declarations

A using declaration imports a name from one namespace and adds it to the namespace that contains the using declaration. The imported name is a synonym for the original name. Only the declared name is added to the target namespace, which means using an enumerated type does not bring with it all the enumerated literals. If you want to use all the literals, each one requires its own using declaration.

Because a name that you reference in a using declaration is added to the current namespace, it might hide names in outer scopes. A using declaration can also interfere with local declarations of the same name.

Example 2-18 shows some examples of using declarations.

Example 2-18. using declarations

```
namespace numeric {
  class fraction { ... };
  fraction operator+(int, const fraction&);
  fraction operator+(const fraction&, int);
  fraction operator+(const fraction&, const fraction&);
}

namespace eqn {
  class fraction { ... };
  fraction operator+(int, const fraction&);
  fraction operator+(const fraction&, int);
  fraction operator+(const fraction&, const fraction&);
}

int main()
{
  numeric::fraction nf;
  eqn::fraction qf;

  nf = nf + 1;         // OK: calls numeric::operator+
  qf = 1 + qf;         // OK: calls eqn::operator+
  nf = nf + qf;        // Error: no operator+

  using numeric::fraction;
  fraction f;          // f is numeric::fraction
  f = nf + 2;          // OK
  f = qf;              // Error: type mismatch
  using eqn::fraction; // Error: like trying to declare
                       // fraction twice in the same scope
  if (f > 0) {
    using eqn::fraction; // OK: hides outer fraction
    fraction f;          // OK: hides outer f
    f = qf;              // OK: same types
    f = nf;              // Error: type mismatch
  }
  int fraction;        // Error: name fraction in use
}
```

You can copy names from one namespace to another with a using declaration. Suppose you refactor a program and realize that the numeric::fraction class has all the functionality you need in the equation package. You decide to use numeric::fraction instead of eqn::fraction, but you want to keep the eqn interface the same. So you insert using numeric::fraction; in the eqn namespace.

Incorporating a name into a namespace with a using declaration is not quite the same as declaring the name normally. The new name is just a synonym for the original name in its original namespace. When the compiler searches namespaces under argument-dependent name lookup, it searches the original namespace. Example 2-19 shows how the results can be surprising if you are not aware of the using declaration. The eqn namespace declares operator<< to print a fraction, but fraction is declared in the numeric namespace. Although eqn uses numeric::fraction, when the compiler sees the use of operator<<, it looks in only the numeric namespace, and never finds operator<<.

Example 2-19. Creating synonym declarations with using declarations

```
namespace eqn {
  using numeric::fraction;
  // Big, ugly declaration for ostream << fraction
  template<typename charT, typename traits>
  basic_ostream<charT,traits>& operator<<(
    basic_ostream<charT,traits>& out, const fraction& f)
  {
    out << f.numerator() << '/' << f.denominator();
    return out;
  }
}

int main()
{
  eqn::fraction qf;
  numeric::fraction nf;
  nf + qf;        // OK because the types are the same
  std::cout << qf; // Error: numeric namespace is searched for operator<<, but
                  // not eqn namespace
}
```

The using declaration can also be used within a class. You can add names to a derived class from a base class, possibly changing their accessibility. For example, a derived class can promote a protected member to public visibility. Another use of using declarations is for private inheritance, promoting specific members to protected or public visibility. For example, the standard container classes are not designed for public inheritance. Nonetheless, in a few cases, it is possible to derive from them successfully. Example 2-20 shows a crude way to implement a container type to represent a fixed-size array. The array class template derives from std::vector using private inheritance. A series of using declarations make selected members of std::vector public and keep those members that are meaningless for a fixed-size container, such as insert, private.

Example 2-20. Importing members with using declarations

```cpp
template<typename T>
class array: private std::vector<T>
{
public:
  typedef T value_type;
  using std::vector<T>::size_type;
  using std::vector<T>::difference_type;
  using std::vector<T>::iterator;
  using std::vector<T>::const_iterator;
  using std::vector<T>::reverse_iterator;
  using std::vector<T>::const_reverse_iterator;

  array(std::size_t n, const T& x = T()) : std::vector<T>(n, x) {}
  using std::vector<T>::at;
  using std::vector<T>::back;
  using std::vector<T>::begin;
  using std::vector<T>::empty;
  using std::vector<T>::end;
  using std::vector<T>::front;
  using std::vector<T>::operator[];
  using std::vector<T>::rbegin;
  using std::vector<T>::rend;
  using std::vector<T>::size;
};
```

See Chapter 6 for more information about using declarations in class definitions.

using Directives

A using directive adds a namespace to the list of scopes that is used when the compiler searches for a name's declaration. Unlike a using declaration, no names are added to the current namespace. Instead, the used namespace is added to the list of namespaces to search right after the innermost namespace that contains both the current and used namespaces. (Usually, the containing namespace is the global namespace.) The using directive is transitive, so if namespace A uses namespace B, and namespace B uses namespace C, a name search in A also searches C. Example 2-21 illustrates the using directive.

Example 2-21. The using directive

```cpp
#include <iostream>
#include <ostream>

namespace A {
  int x = 10;
}
namespace B {
  int y = 20;
}
namespace C {
  int z = 30;
```

Example 2-21. The using directive (continued)

```
  using namespace B;
}
namespace D {
  int z = 40;
  using namespace B;        // Harmless but pointless because D::y hides B::y
  int y = 50;
}

int main( )
{
  int x = 60;
  using namespace A;        // Does not introduce names, so there is no conflict
                            // with x

  using namespace C;

  using namespace std;      // To save typing std::cout repeatedly

  cout << x << '\n';        // Prints 60 (local x)
  cout << y << '\n';        // Prints 20
  cout << C::y << '\n';     // Prints 20
  cout << D::y << '\n';     // Prints 50

  using namespace D;
  cout << y << '\n'; // Error: y is ambiguous. It can be found in D::y and C's
                     // use of B::y.
}
```

How to Use Namespaces

Namespaces have no runtime cost. Don't be afraid to use them, especially in large projects in which many people contribute code and might accidentally devise conflicting names. The following are some additional tips and suggestions for using namespaces:

- When you define a class in a namespace, be sure to declare all associated operators and functions in the same namespace.

- To make namespaces easier to use, keep namespace names short, or use aliases to craft short synonyms for longer names.

- Never place a using directive in a header. It can create name collisions for any user of the header.

- Keep using directives local to functions to save typing and enhance clarity.

- Use using namespace std outside functions only for tiny programs or for backward compatibility in legacy projects.

3

Expressions

An expression combines literals, names, operators, and symbols to express or compute a value, or to achieve a side effect. This chapter describes the rules for writing and understanding expressions, including information on lvalues and rvalues, type conversion, constant expressions, and how C++ evaluates expressions. It contains detailed descriptions of all the operators and other forms of expressions.

The syntax descriptions in this chapter are informal. See Chapter 12 for a precise BNF grammar.

Lvalues and Rvalues

Lvalues and rvalues are fundamental to C++ expressions. Put simply, an *lvalue* is an object reference and an *rvalue* is a value. The difference between lvalues and rvalues plays a role in the writing and understanding of expressions.

An lvalue is an expression that yields an object reference, such as a variable name, an array subscript reference, a dereferenced pointer, or a function call that returns a reference. An lvalue always has a defined region of storage, so you can take its address.

An rvalue is an expression that is not an lvalue. Examples of rvalues include literals, the results of most operators, and function calls that return nonreferences. An rvalue does not necessarily have any storage associated with it.

Strictly speaking, a function is an lvalue, but the only uses for it are to use it in calling the function, or determining the function's address. Most of the time, the term lvalue means object lvalue, and this book follows that convention.

C++ borrows the term lvalue from C, where only an lvalue can be used on the left side of an assignment statement. The term rvalue is a logical counterpart for an expression that can be used only on the righthand side of an assignment. For example:

```
#define rvalue 42
int lvalue;
lvalue = rvalue;
```

In C++, these simple rules are no longer true, but the names remain because they are close to the truth. The most significant departure from traditional C is that an lvalue in C++ might be const, in which case it cannot be the target of an assignment. (C has since evolved and now has const lvalues.)

The built-in assignment operators require an lvalue as their lefthand operand. The built-in address (&) operator also requires an lvalue operand, as do the increment (++) and decrement (--) operators. Other operators require rvalues. The rules are not as strict for user-defined operators. Any object, including an rvalue, can be used to call member functions, including overloaded =, &, ++, and -- operators.

Some other rules for lvalues and rvalues are:

- An array is an lvalue, but an address is an rvalue.
- The built-in array subscript ([ ]), dereference (unary *), assignment (=, +=, etc.), increment (++), and decrement (--) operators produce lvalues. Other built-in operators produce rvalues.
- A type cast to a reference type produces an lvalue; other casts produce rvalues.
- A function call (including overloaded operators) that returns a reference returns an lvalue; otherwise, it returns an rvalue.
- An lvalue is converted implicitly to an rvalue when necessary, but an rvalue cannot be implicitly converted to an lvalue.

Example 3-1 shows several different kinds of lvalues and rvalues.

Example 3-1. Lvalues and rvalues

```
class number {
public:
  number(int i = 0) : value(i) {}
  operator int( ) const { return value; }
  number& operator=(const number& n);
private:
  int value;
};

number operator+(const number& x, const number& y);

int main( )
{
  number a[10], b(42);
  number* p;
  a;            // lvalue
  a[0];         // lvalue
  &a[0];        // rvalue
  *a;           // lvalue
```

Example 3-1. Lvalues and rvalues (continued)

```
p;          // lvalue
*p;         // lvalue
10;         // rvalue
number(10); // rvalue
a[0] + b;   // rvalue
b = a[0];   // lvalue
}
```

Type Conversions

In an arithmetic expression, binary operators require operands of the same type. If this is not the case, the type of one operand must be converted to match that of the other operand. When calling a function, the argument type must match the parameter type; if it doesn't, the argument is converted so its type matches. C++ has cast operators, which let you define a type conversion explicitly, or you can let the compiler automatically convert the type for you. This section presents the rules for automatic type conversion.

Arithmetic Types

An *arithmetic type* is a fundamental integral or floating-point type: bool, char, signed char, unsigned char, int, short, long, unsigned int, unsigned short, unsigned long, float, double, or long double. Some operations are permitted only on arithmetic types, pointer types, enumerations, class types, or some combination of types. The description of each operator tells you which types the operator supports.

Type Promotion

Type promotion is an automatic type conversion that applies only to arithmetic types, converting a "smaller" type to a "larger" type while preserving the original value. Contrast promotions with other automatic type conversions (described in later subsections), which can lose information. Promotions involve either integral or floating-point values. The rules for integral promotion are:

- A "small" integral rvalue is converted to an int if the type int can represent all of the values of the source type; otherwise, it is converted to unsigned int. A "small" value is an integral bit-field (see Chapter 6) whose size is smaller than an int, or a value with one of the following types: char, signed char, unsigned char, short int, unsigned short int.

- An rvalue whose type is wchar_t or an enumeration (including bit-fields with enumeration type) is converted to the first type that can hold all the values of the source type. The type is one of: int, unsigned int, long, or unsigned long.

- An rvalue of type bool can be converted to an int; the value true becomes 1, and the value false becomes 0.

One floating-point promotion rule is defined:

- An rvalue of type float can be converted to type double.

Arithmetic Type Conversions

An arithmetic type conversion is an automatic type conversion that the compiler applies to the operands of the built-in arithmetic and comparison operators. For the arithmetic operators, the result type is the same as the operand type.

 The arithmetic type conversions try to preserve the original values as much as possible. However, they do not always succeed. For example, -1 / 1u does not produce -1 as a result because -1 has type int, which is converted to type unsigned int, yielding an implementation-defined arithmetic value. On a 32-bit, two's-complement system, the result is 4294967295u.

The rules for arithmetic type conversion are applied in the following order:

1. If one operand has type long double, the other is converted to long double.
2. Otherwise, if one operand is double, the other is converted to double.
3. Otherwise, if one operand is float, the other is converted to float.
4. Otherwise, integral promotions are performed (see the section "Type Promotion").
5. After integral promotion, if one operand is unsigned long, the other is converted to unsigned long.
6. Otherwise, if one operand is long, and the other is unsigned int, type conversion occurs as follows:
   a. If all values of type unsigned int fit in a long int, the unsigned int is converted to long int.
   b. Otherwise, both operands are converted to unsigned long.
7. Otherwise, if one operand is long, the other is converted to long.
8. Otherwise, if one operand is unsigned, the other is converted to unsigned.
9. Otherwise, both operands are int.

Implicit Numeric Conversions

An arithmetic value can be converted implicitly to a different arithmetic value, even if that conversion loses information. These implicit conversions can take place in assignments, initializers, arguments to function calls, returning values from a function, and template arguments. Do not confuse these conversions with the arithmetic type conversions described earlier, which can take place in any arithmetic operation.

The basic rule is that any arithmetic type can be converted to any other. If the destination type cannot hold the converted value, the behavior is undefined. When assigning a floating-point number to an integer, the floating-point value is truncated toward zero by discarding the fractional part. When converting an integer or enumerated value to a floating-point number, if the integer value falls between two floating-point values (that is, the integer is not representable in the floating-point format), the implementation chooses one of the two neighboring values.

A value can be converted to a class type if the class has a suitable constructor that does not use the explicit specifier. A value of class type can be converted to a non-class type if the source class has a type conversion operator of the target type. When converting a class type to another class type, the compiler considers the constructors for the target class and the type conversion operators for the source class.

Lvalue Conversions

Lvalue conversions automatically convert an lvalue to an rvalue for contexts in which an rvalue is required. The need to convert an lvalue to an rvalue is usually transparent, and these conversions are listed only for the sake of completeness:

- An array lvalue can be converted to a pointer rvalue, pointing to the first element of the array.
- A function lvalue can be converted to an rvalue pointer to the function.
- Any other lvalue can be converted to an rvalue with the same value. If the type is not a class type, cv-qualifiers are removed from the type. Thus, a const int lvalue is converted to an int rvalue.

Conversion to bool

Arithmetic, enumeration, and pointer values can be converted to bool, in which null pointers and zero arithmetic values are false, and everything else is true. A common idiom is to test whether a pointer is a null pointer:

```
if (ptr)
    ... // Do something with *ptr.
else
    ... // Pointer is null

if (! ptr)
    // Another way to test if ptr is null
```

This idiom is so common that some classes have operators to convert an object to void*, so void* can be converted to bool. (Any pointer type would do, but void* is used because the pointer is not meant to be dereferenced, only converted to bool.) The void* operator is used instead of a direct conversion to bool to avoid automatic promotion to an integer. For example, basic_ios defines operator void*( ) to return a null pointer if the iostream's failbit is set. (See <ios> in Chapter 13 for details.)

Type Casts

A *type cast* is an explicit type conversion. C++ offers several different ways to cast an expression to a different type. The different ways expose the evolution of the language. The six forms of type cast expressions are:

- (*type*) *expr*
- *type* (*expr*)
- const_cast< *type* >(*expr*)

- dynamic_cast< *type* >(*expr*)
- reinterpret_cast< *type* >(*expr*)
- static_cast< *type* >(*expr*)

The first form was inherited from C; the second form was added in the early days of C++ and has the same meaning as the first, but with a slightly different syntax. The final four forms supplant the two older forms and are preferred because they are more specific, thus reducing the risk of error. All type cast expressions are described in detail later in this chapter; the first form is covered in the section "Cast Expressions," and the other five forms are covered in "Postfix Expressions." The remainder of this section briefly discusses when to use each form.

If you simply want to force an expression to be const, or to remove a const (e.g., prior to passing a pointer to a legacy library that is not written in C++ and does not know about const declarations), use const_cast<>. (You can also change the volatile qualifier, but that is less common.)

If you have a pointer or reference to an object whose declared type is a base class, but you need to obtain a derived class pointer or reference, you should use dynamic_cast<>. The dynamic cast performs a runtime check to make sure the cast is valid. A dynamic cast works only with polymorphic classes, which have at least one virtual function.

The common uses of static_cast<> are to force one enumeration to a different enumerated type, force an arithmetic type to a different type, or force a particular conversion from a class-type object that has multiple type conversion operators. The simpler type casts are sometimes used in these cases, for the sake of brevity. For example, sqrt(float(i)) can be easier to read than sqrt(static_cast<float>(i)). Use static_cast to reverse any implicit type conversion. For example, C++ automatically converts an enum to an integer; use static_cast if you want to convert an integer to an enum. You can use static_cast to cast a pointer to and from void*.

A reinterpret_cast<> is reserved for potentially unsafe type casts, such as converting one type of pointer to another. You can also convert a pointer to an integer or vice versa. For example, an internal debugging package might record debug log files. The logger might convert pointers to integers using reinterpret_cast<> and print the integers using a specific format.

If you try to perform the wrong kind of cast with one of the template-like cast operators, the compiler informs you of your mistake. For example, if you use static_cast<> and accidentally cast away const-ness, the compiler complains. Or if you use static_cast<> where you should have used reinterpret_cast<>, the compiler complains. The short forms of casting do not provide this extra level of error-checking because one form must suffice for the several different kinds of type casts.

When you see a type cast, you should read it as a warning that something unusual is happening. The longer forms of type casts provide additional clues about the programmer's intent, and help the compiler enforce that intent.

Constant Expressions

A constant expression is an expression that can be evaluated at compile time. Constants of integral or enumerated type are required in several different situations, such as array bounds, enumerator values, and case labels. Null pointer constants are a special case of integral constants.

Integral Constant Expressions

An integral constant expression is an expression that can be evaluated at compile time, and whose type is integral or an enumeration. The situations that require integral constant expressions include array bounds, enumerator values, case labels, bit-field sizes, static member initializers, and value template arguments. The compiler must be able to evaluate the expression at compile time, so you can use only literals, enumerators, const objects that have constant initializers, integral or enumerated template parameters, sizeof expressions, and constant addresses. The address of a static lvalue object is a constant address, as is the address of a function. A string literal, being a static array of characters, is also a constant address.

An integral static const data member can be initialized in the class definition if the initializer is a constant integral or enumerated expression. The member can then be used as a constant expression elsewhere in the class definition. For example:

```
template<typename T, size_t size>
class array {
public:
  static const size_t SIZE = size;
  ...
private:
  T data[SIZE];
};
```

See Chapter 6 for more information about static data members.

Null Pointers

A constant expression with a value of 0 can be a *null pointer constant*. A null pointer constant can be converted to a *null pointer value*. The colloquial term null pointer almost always means null pointer value.

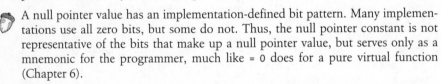 A null pointer value has an implementation-defined bit pattern. Many implementations use all zero bits, but some do not. Thus, the null pointer constant is not representative of the bits that make up a null pointer value, but serves only as a mnemonic for the programmer, much like = 0 does for a pure virtual function (Chapter 6).

When you assign a null pointer constant to a pointer-type variable, the compiler converts the null pointer constant to a null pointer value of the appropriate type. Similarly, when comparing pointers, the compiler ensures that the comparison is meaningful. In particular, a null pointer value is never equal to any valid pointer value, is always equal to another null pointer value, and is always equal to a null pointer constant. A null pointer value, when converted to bool, is false. A pointer that is initialized with an empty initializer is initialized to a null pointer value.

The NULL macro, defined in <cstdlib> and other headers (see Chapter 13), expands to a null pointer constant. Using NULL instead of 0 can be a helpful reminder to the reader or maintainer of a program, especially when typedefs obscure the nature of a type:

```
Token tok1 = 0;      // Is Token a pointer or an integer?
Token tok2 = NULL;   // Token is probably a pointer.
```

Dereferencing a null pointer results in undefined behavior.

Expression Evaluation

At its most fundamental level, the execution of a C++ program is the successive evaluation of expressions, under the control of statements (Chapter 4), in which some expressions can produce side effects. Any expression might have one or more of the following side effects:

- Accessing a volatile object
- Modifying an object
- Calling a function in the standard library
- Calling any other function that has side effects

Sequence Points

During the execution of a program, there are well-defined points in time called *sequence points*, at which the side effects have all been completed for expressions that have been evaluated, and no side effects have been started for any unevaluated expression. Between sequence points, the compiler is free to reorder expressions in any way that preserves the original semantics. The same term also refers to the positions in the source code that produce sequence points when the code executes. You can usually ignore the details of sequence points, but when you are using global or volatile objects, it is important that you know exactly when it is safe to access those objects. That time is after a sequence point. Also, any expression that modifies a scalar object more than once between sequence points, or that examines a scalar object's value after modifying it, yields undefined behavior. This rule often bites the unwary programmer who uses the increment and decrement operators. For example:

```
int i = 0;
i = ++i - ++i;            // Error: undefined behavior
printf("%d,%d", ++i, ++i); // Error: undefined behavior
i = 3, ++i, i++;          // OK: i == 5
```

There are sequence points in the following positions:

- At the end of every expression that is not a subexpression. Such an expression might be used in an expression statement, in an initializer, as a condition in an if statement, etc.
- After evaluating all function arguments but before calling the function.
- When a function returns: after copying the return value from the function call (if any), but before evaluating any other expressions outside the function.
- After evaluating the first expression (expr1) in each of the following expressions, provided they use the built-in operators and not overloaded operators:
  - expr1 && expr2
  - expr1 || expr2
  - expr1 ? expr2 : expr3
  - expr1 , expr2

Order of Evaluation

In general, the order in which operands are evaluated is unspecified, so you should never write code that depends on a particular order. For example, in the expression f( ) / g( ), f( ) might be called first, or g( ) might be called first. The difference can be significant when the functions have side effects. Example 3-2 shows a contrived situation in which a program prints 2 if g( ) is called first, or 1 if f( ) is called first.

Example 3-2. Demonstrating order of evaluation

```
#include <iostream>
#include <ostream>

int x = 1;

int f( )
{
  x = 2;
  return x;
}

int g( )
{
  return x;
}

int main( )
{
  std::cout << f( ) / g( ) << '\n';
}
```

A simpler example follows. The increment of i can happen before or after the assignment, so i might be 2 or 3.

```
int i = 1;
i = i++ + 1; // Value of i is unspecified
```

In a function call, all arguments are evaluated before the function is called. As you might expect, the order in which the arguments are evaluated is unspecified.

Short-Circuit Evaluation

The logical operators (&& and ||) perform *short-circuit evaluation*. The left operand is evaluated, and if the expression result can be known at that point, the right operand is *not* evaluated:

```
if (false && f()) ... // f() is never called.
if (true || f()) ... // f() is never called.
```

If the logical operator is overloaded, however, it cannot perform short-circuit evaluation. Like any other function, all the arguments are evaluated before the function is called. For this reason, you should avoid overloading the && and || operators.

Expression Rules

C++ has the usual unary operators such as logical negation (!a), binary operators such as addition (a+b), and even a ternary operator (a?b:c). Unlike many other languages, an array subscript is also an operator (a[b]), and a function call is an *n*-ary operator (e.g., a(b, c, d)).

Every operator has a *precedence*. Operators with higher precedence are grouped so that they are logically evaluated before operators with lower precedence. (Note that precedence determines how the compiler parses the expression, not necessarily the actual order of computation. For example, in the expression a( ) + b( ) * c( ), the multiplication has higher precedence, but a( ) might be called first.)

Some operators group from left to right. For example, the expression x / y / z is equivalent to (x / y) / z. Other operators group right to left, as in x = y = z, which is equivalent to x = (y = z). The order of grouping is called the operator's *associativity*.

When reading C++ expressions, you must be aware of the precedence and associativity of the operators involved. For example, *ptr++ is read as *(ptr++) because the postfix ++ operator has higher precedence than the unary * operator.

Table 3-1 summarizes the syntax, precedence, and associativity of each kind of expression. The subsections that follow describe the kinds of expressions in depth; each subsection covers a single precedence group.

Table 3-1. *Expression syntax and associativity, grouped by precedence*

Group	Associativity	Expression
Primary (highest precedence)	Left-to-right	*literal* this (*expr*) *name* :: *name* *class-or-namespace* :: *name*
Postfix	Left-to-right	*pointer* [*expr*] *expr* (*expr* , ...) *type* (*expr* , ...) *object.* member *pointer* -> member *cast_keyword* < *type* >(*expr*) typeid(*expr*) typeid(*type*) *lvalue* ++ *lvalue* --
Unary	Right-to-left	++ *lvalue* -- *lvalue* ~ *expr* compl *expr* ! *expr* not *expr* + *expr* - *expr* * *pointer* & *lvalue* sizeof *expr* sizeof(*type*) *new-expr* *delete-expr*
Cast	Right-to-left	(*type*) *expr*
Pointer to Member	Left-to-right	*object* .* *expr* *pointer* ->* *expr*
Multiplicative	Left-to-right	*expr* * *expr* *expr* / *expr* *expr* % *expr*
Additive	Left-to-right	*expr* + *expr* *expr* - *expr*
Shift	Left-to-right	*expr* << *expr* *expr* >> *expr*
Relational	Left-to-right	*expr* < *expr* *expr* > *expr* *expr* <= *expr* *expr* >= *expr*
Equality	Left-to-right	*expr* == *expr* *expr* != *expr* *expr* not_eq *expr*
Bitwise And	Left-to-right	*expr* & *expr* *expr* bitand *expr*
Bitwise Exclusive Or	Left-to-right	*expr* ^ *expr* *expr* xor *expr*
Bitwise Inclusive Or	Left-to-right	*expr* | *expr* *expr* bitor *expr*

Group	Associativity	Expression
Logical And	Left-to-right	`expr && expr` `expr and expr`
Logical Or	Left-to-right	`expr || expr` `expr or expr`
Conditional	Right-to-left	`expr ? expr : expr`

Assignment	Right-to-left	`lvalue = expr`
		`lvalue op= expr`
		`throw expr`
		`throw`

Comma (lowest precedence)	Left-to-right	`expr , expr`

Primary Expressions

A primary expression is the basic building block for more complex expressions. It is an expression in parentheses, a literal, or a name (possibly qualified). The various forms of primary expressions are:

literal
A constant value. String literals (being arrays of const char or const wchar_t) are lvalues. All other literals are rvalues. (See Chapter 1.)

this
Refers to the target object in a nonstatic member function. Its type is a pointer to the class type; its value is an rvalue.

`( expression )`
Has the type and value of *expression*.

unqualified-name
Names an entity according to the name lookup rules in Chapter 2. The expression result is the entity itself, and the expression type is the entity's type. The result is an lvalue if the entity is an object, data member, or function. The following are the various kinds of unqualified identifiers:

identifier
Names an object, function, member, type, or namespace. The name is looked up according to the rules in Chapter 2. The type is the declared type of the entity. If the entity is an object, data member, or function, the value is an lvalue.

operator *symbol*
Names an operator. See Chapter 5 for more information.

template-name < optional-template-args >
Names a template instance. See Chapter 7 for more information.

operator *type*
Names a type conversion operator. The *type* is a type specifier, possibly with one or more pointer symbols in the declarator. (See Chapter 2 for details about type specifiers and declarators.)

`~ class-name`
Names the destructor for *class-name*.

qualified-name
> Uses the scope operator to qualify an identifier, operator, or destructor. The qualified name can be in the global scope or in the scope of a class or namespace:
>
> :: *identifier*
>> Names a global identifier. The type is the declared type of the entity. If the entity is an object, data member, or function, the value is an lvalue; otherwise, it is an rvalue.
>
> :: operator *symbol*
>> Names a global operator. Note that type conversion operators must be member functions, so there cannot be a global type conversion operator. See Chapter 5 for more information.
>
> *nested-name* :: *unqualified-name*
> *nested-name* :: template *unqualified-name*
>> Names an entity in a class or namespace scope. The *nested-name* can be a class or namespace name, or it can have the form *class-or-namespace-name* :: *nested-name* or *class-name* :: template *nested-name*. Use the template keyword when instantiating a template. See Chapter 7 for information about template members.
>
> :: *nested-name* :: *unqualified-name*
> :: *nested-name* :: template *unqualified-name*
>> Names an entity in a class or namespace scope. The first (left-most) class or namespace name is looked up in the global scope.

In the rest of this chapter, the syntax element *name-expr* refers to a qualified or unqualified name, as described in this section. In particular, a *name-expr* can be used to the right of the . or -> in a postfix expression.

Example 3-3 shows some primary expressions.

Example 3-3. Primary expressions

```
namespace ns {
  int x;
  class cls {
  public:
    cls(int);
    ~cls();
  };
}
int x;

3.14159          // Literal
(2 + 3 * 4)      // Parenthesized expression
x                // Unqualified identifier
ns::x            // Qualified identifier
ns::cls::cls     // Qualified constructor
operator*        // Unqualified operator name
```

Postfix Expressions

A postfix expression is an expression that uses postfix syntax (operator follows the operand) with some exceptions that just happen to have the same precedence. The postfix expressions are:

pointer [*expr*]

Returns an element of an array. The subscript operator requires a pointer as the left operand. An array is implicitly converted to a pointer. The right operand is converted to an integer, and the expression is evaluated as *((*pointer*) + (*expr*)). If the array index is out of bounds, the behavior is undefined. The result is an lvalue whose type is the base type of *pointer*.

expr (*optional-expr-list*)

Calls a function. The function call operator requires one of the following as a left operand: a function name, an expression that returns a function pointer, or an expression that returns an object that has a function call operator. (An operator name is the same as a function name in this case.) The *optional-expr-list* is a comma-separated list of zero or more assignment expressions. (See "Assignment Expressions" later in this chapter.) All the expressions in the expression list are evaluated, and then the function is called. The result type is the return type of the function. If the return type is a reference type, the result is an lvalue; otherwise, the result is an rvalue. If the return type is void, no value is returned. See Chapter 5 for more information about functions.

simple-type-specifier (*optional-expr-list*)

Performs type conversion or construction. A *simple-type-specifier* is a single name: a fundamental type or a qualified name of a class, an enumeration, or a typedef. The result is an instance of the specified type, initialized as follows:

- If the expression list is empty, the result is an rvalue that is initialized with a default constructor, or that is initialized to 0. (See Chapter 2 for details about initialization.)

- If the expression list contains one expression, that value is cast to the desired type in the same manner as a cast expression—that is, (*type*) *expr*. If the type is a reference, the result is an lvalue; otherwise, it is an rvalue.

- If the expression list contains more than one expression, the type must be a class, and the expression list is passed as arguments to a suitable constructor to create an instance of the class, which is returned as an rvalue.

object . *name-expr*

Returns a member of an object. The name can be qualified to refer to a name in a base class (see Chapter 2). The return type is the type of *name-expr*. The return value depends on whether *name-expr* is a data member, member function, or enumerator:

- If *name-expr* names a static data member, the member is returned as an lvalue.

- If *name-expr* names a nonstatic data member, the result is an lvalue only if *object* is an lvalue. If *name-expr* is declared mutable, the result is not const even if *object* is const; otherwise, the result is const if either *object* or *name-expr* is const. Similarly, the result is volatile if either *object* or *name-expr* is volatile.

- If *name-expr* names a member function, the usual rules for overload resolution apply (see Chapter 5). If the function is a static member function, the result is an lvalue. You can take the function's address (with &) or call the function.

- If the function is a nonstatic member function, it must be used in a function call—for example, obj.memfun(arg).

- If *name-expr* is an enumerator, the result is an rvalue.

pointer -> name-expr

  Returns (*(pointer)).name-expr.

lvalue ++

  Increments *lvalue* and returns its value prior to incrementing (as an rvalue). The type of *lvalue* must be arithmetic or a pointer. The new value is *lvalue* + 1.

  If *lvalue* has type bool, the new value is always true. This bool-specific behavior is deprecated.

lvalue --

  Decrements *lvalue* and returns its value prior to decrementing (as an rvalue). The type must be arithmetic or a pointer and cannot be bool. The new value is *lvalue* − 1.

const_cast< *type* >(*expr*)

  Casts *expr* to *type*. If *type* is a reference, the result is an lvalue; otherwise, it is an rvalue. The new type must match the type of *expr*, but the const and volatile qualifiers can be changed.

  A const_cast that removes a const qualifier is generally a bad idea. Nonetheless, it is sometimes necessary to cast away const-ness, especially when passing pointers to legacy libraries.

  See Chapter 6 for a discussion of the mutable modifier, which lets you modify a data member of a const object.

dynamic_cast< *type* >(*expr*)

  Casts a base class pointer or reference *expr* to a derived class *type*. A runtime check is performed to make sure the true class of *expr* is *type* or a class derived from *type*. The class must be polymorphic, that is, have at least one virtual function. The base class can be virtual. A dynamic_cast<> cannot cast away *cv*-qualifiers. The cast works as follows:

- If *type* is void*, the return value is a pointer to the most-derived object that *expr* points to. The type does not have to be polymorphic in this case.

- If *expr* is a pointer, *type* must be a pointer type. If the type of *expr* does not match *type* (is not the same as *type* or derived from *type*), a null pointer value is returned. Otherwise, the value of *expr* cast to *type* is returned. If *expr* is a null pointer, a null pointer is returned.

- If *expr* is an object and *type* is a reference, *expr* is cast to *type*. If the type of *expr* does not match, a bad_cast exception is thrown.

- You can also cast from a derived class to a base class, which is the same as an ordinary implicit conversion. The type does not have to be polymorphic in this case.

Example 3-4 shows some uses of dynamic_cast<>.

Example 3-4. Using dynamic_cast<>

```
#include <iostream>
#include <ostream>

class base {
public:
  virtual ~base( ) {}
};

class derived : public base {};
class most_derived : public derived {};
class other : public base {};

int main( )
{
  base* b = new derived;
  dynamic_cast<most_derived*>(b); // Null pointer
  dynamic_cast<derived&>(*b);     // OK
  dynamic_cast<other*>(b);        // Null pointer

  derived* d = new most_derived;
  b = d;
  b = dynamic_cast<base*>(d);     // OK, but dynamic_cast<>
                                  // is unnecessary.
}
```

reinterpret_cast< *type* >(*expr*)

Casts *expr* to *type*. When using reinterpret_cast<>, no conversion functions or constructors are called. Casting to a reference yields an lvalue; otherwise, it yields an rvalue. Only the following conversions are allowed:

- A pointer can be converted to an integer. The integer must be large enough to hold the pointer's value. Which integer type you should use is implementation-defined, as is the mapping from pointer to integer.

- An integer or enumerated value can be converted to a pointer. The mapping is implementation-defined. Casting from a pointer to an integer back to the original pointer type yields the original pointer value, provided the integer type is large enough.

- Casting an integer constant of value 0 to a pointer always produces a null pointer value. Casting any other integer expression of value 0 to a pointer produces an implementation-defined pointer, which may or may not be a null pointer.

- A function pointer can be converted to a function pointer of a different type. Calling such a function results in undefined behavior. Converting back to the original pointer type produces the original pointer value.

- An object pointer can be converted to an object pointer of a different type. Using such an object results in undefined behavior. Converting back to the original pointer type produces the original pointer value.

- A pointer to a member can be converted to a pointer to a different member. Using the pointer to a member has undefined behavior, except that casting a pointer to a data member to a different pointer to a data member and back to the original type produces the original value, and casting a pointer to a member function to a different member function and back produces the original value.

- A null pointer constant or value can be converted to a null pointer of the target type.

- A reference can be cast in the same manner as a pointer (except that the pointer is dereferenced). That is, casting reinterpret_cast<T&>(x) is just like casting *reinterpret_cast<T*>(&x).

A reinterpret_cast has the following restrictions:

- A function pointer cannot be converted to an object pointer, or an object pointer to a function pointer.

- A member function pointer cannot be converted to a data member pointer, or a data member pointer to a member function pointer.

- A member pointer cannot be converted to a nonmember pointer, or a nonmember pointer to a member pointer.

- The target type must not cast away *cv*-qualifiers.

The need for reinterpret_cast<> is rare in an ordinary application.

Example 3-5 shows some uses of reinterpret_cast<>. The first use reinterprets the representation of a float as an int to show the underlying representation of a float. This use is implementation-dependent and requires sizeof(int) to be greater than or equal to sizeof(float). The second use is a simple conversion from a function pointer to an integer to print the address in a specific format. It requires that an int be large enough to hold a function pointer.

Example 3-5. Using reinterpret_cast<>

```
#include <cassert>
#include <iomanip>
#include <iostream>
#include <ostream>

int foo()
{
  return 0;
}
```

Example 3-5. Using reinterpret_cast<> (continued)

```
int main( )
{
  using namespace std;
  float pi = 3.1415926535897;
  int   ipi;

  // Print numbers in pretty hexadecimal.
  cout << setfill('0') << showbase << hex << internal;

  // Show the representation of a floating-point number.
  assert(sizeof(int) == sizeof(float));
  ipi = reinterpret_cast<int&>(pi);
  cout << "pi bits=" << setw(10) << ipi << '\n';

  // Show the address of foo( ).
  cout << "&foo=" << setw(10) <<
    reinterpret_cast<int>(&foo) << '\n';
}
```

static_cast< *type* >(*expr*)

> Casts *expr* to *type* using a standard or user-defined conversion, as though you declared a temporary *type tmp*(*expr*) and used the value of *tmp* in place of the cast expression. The result is an lvalue if *type* is a reference; otherwise the result is an rvalue. A static_cast<> cannot cast away *cv*-qualifiers. The rules of permitted conversions are:
>
> - The *type* can be void, in which case the result of *expr* is discarded.
> - A base-class lvalue can be cast to a reference to a derived class, provided a standard conversion exists from a derived-class pointer to the base class. The base class must not be virtual. If *expr* is not actually a subobject of *type*, the behavior is undefined. (See dynamic_cast<> to learn how to make error-checking safe.)
> - A base-class pointer can be converted to a derived-class pointer in the manner described for class references.
> - A pointer to a member of a derived class can be converted to a pointer to a member of a base class if there is a standard conversion in the other direction. The target class (or an ancestor class) must contain the original member.
> - Standard arithmetic conversions can work in reverse—for example, long can be cast to short. Integers can be cast to enumerations.
> - Enumerations can be cast to other enumerations.
> - A void pointer can be converted to any object pointer. Converting a pointer to void* (with the same *cv*-qualifiers as the original pointer) and back produces the original pointer value.
>
> Example 3-6 shows some uses of static_cast<>.

Example 3-6. Using static_cast<>

```
#include <iostream>
#include <ostream>

class base {};
class derived : public base {};
class other : public base {};

enum color  { red, black };
enum logical { no, yes, maybe };

int main()
{
  base* b = new derived;
  static_cast<derived&>(*b); // OK
  static_cast<other*>(b);    // Undefined behavior

  derived* d = new derived;
  b = d;
  b = static_cast<base*>(d); // OK, but unnecessary

  color c = static_cast<color>(yes);

  int i = 65;
  std::cout << static_cast<char>(i);
}
```

typeid(*expr*)

Returns type information for the type of *expr* without evaluating *expr*. The type information is an lvalue of type const std::type_info (or an implementation-defined type that derives from type_info). See <typeinfo> in Chapter 13 for information about this class.

If *expr* is an lvalue of a polymorphic type (a class with at least one virtual function), the type information is for the most-derived class of *expr*. If *expr* is a dereference of a null pointer, bad_typeid is thrown.

If *expr* is not an lvalue, or the type is not polymorphic, the type information is for the static type of *expr*.

typeid(*type*)

Returns the type information for *type* as described for typeid(*expr*). Example 3-7 shows some uses of typeid.

Example 3-7. Using typeid

```
#include <iostream>
#include <ostream>
#include <typeinfo>

class base {
public:
  virtual ~base() {}
};
```

Example 3-7. Using typeid (continued)

```
class derived : public base {};
enum color   { red, black };

// The actual output is implementation-defined, but should reflect the types
// shown in the comments.
int main( )
{
  base* b = new derived;
  std::cout << typeid(*b).name( ) << '\n';       // Derived
  std::cout << typeid(base).name( ) << '\n';      // Base
  derived* d = new derived;
  std::cout << typeid(*d).name( ) << '\n';       // Derived
  std::cout << typeid(derived).name( ) << '\n';  // Derived
  std::cout << typeid(red).name( ) << '\n';       // Color
  std::cout << typeid(color).name( ) << '\n';     // Color
}
```

Expressions

Unary Expressions

A unary expression uses a unary prefix operator:

++ *lvalue*
> Increments *lvalue*, which must be of arithmetic or pointer type, and returns the new value as an lvalue. The expression ++x is equivalent to x += 1, unless x is of type bool, in which case the expression ++x is equivalent to x=true. The special-case behavior for bool is deprecated.

-- *lvalue*
> Decrements *lvalue*, which must be of arithmetic or pointer type (not bool), and returns the new value as an lvalue. The expression --x is equivalent to x -= 1.

* *pointer*
> Dereferences *pointer* and returns an lvalue for the object that *pointer* points to. If *pointer* has type *T**, the expression has type *T* (preserving any *cv*-qualifiers).

& *lvalue*
& *qualified-name*
> Returns the address of *lvalue* or *qualified-name*. If *lvalue* has type *T* or if *qualified-name* is a static member of type *T*, the result is the object's address, which is an rvalue of type pointer to *T*. If *qualified-name* is a nonstatic member of class *C*, the result type is a pointer to a member of class *C*.

> Note that a pointer to a member is formed only by applying the & operand to a qualified name. Even in the scope of a class, &*unqualified-name* is not a pointer to a member, but an ordinary pointer to an object.

> You cannot take the address of a bit-field. To take the address of an over-loaded function, the context must make it clear which function you mean. Example 3-8 shows uses of the & operator.

Example 3-8. Using the & operator

```
class demo
{
public:
  int x;
  static int y;
  int get_x() { return x; }
};

int demo::y = 10;

int add(int a, int b) { return a + b; }
double add(double a, double b) { return a + b; }

int main()
{
  demo d;
  int demo::*p;
  int (demo::*func)();
  int *i;
  int local = 42;
  int *ptr = &local;

  p = &demo::x;
  i = &demo::y;
  func = &demo::get_x;
  d.*p = *ptr;
  *i = (d.*func)();

  int (*adder)(int, int);
  adder = &add;
  d.*p = adder(42, *i);

  return d.y;
}
```

+ *expr*

   Returns *expr*, which must have arithmetic, enumeration, or pointer type. The usual type promotions take place, and the result type is the promoted type. The result is an rvalue.

- *expr*

   Negates *expr*, which must have arithmetic or enumerated type. The usual type promotions take place, and the result type is the promoted type. The result is an rvalue. If the type is unsigned, the result is $2^n - expr$, in which n is the number of bits in the result type.

~ *expr*

compl *expr*

   Returns the bitwise complement of *expr*, which must have integral or enumeration type. The type is promoted according to the usual rules, and the result type is the promoted type. The result is an rvalue. Every zero bit in *expr* is converted to a one bit, and every one bit is converted to a zero bit.

In the ambiguous case of ~C( ), in which C is a class name, ~C( ) is interpreted as the complement operator, not the destructor of C. If C does not have an over-loaded operator~ or an implicit conversion to an integral or enumerated type, the expression ~C( ) results in an error. To force a reference to C's destructor, use a member reference (e.g., this->~C( )) or a qualified name (e.g., C::~C( )).

! *expr*
not *expr*

Returns the logical negation of *expr* after converting it to bool. The result is an rvalue of type bool. If *expr* is true, the result is false; if *expr* is false, the result is true.

sizeof *expr*
sizeof (*type*)

Returns the size in bytes of *type* or the type of *expr* (without evaluating *expr*). By definition, sizeof(char) == 1. You cannot take the size of a bit-field, a function, or an incomplete type. The size of a reference is the size of the refer-enced type.

The sizeof operator always returns a value greater than zero for a class or object of class type. The size of a base-class subobject within a derived-class object can be zero, so the compiler is not necessarily wasting space. You can see this in Example 3-9, which shows that the size of the derived class is the same as the size of the base class. The expression result is an rvalue of type size_t. (See <cstdlib> in Chapter 13.)

Example 3-9. Using the sizeof operator

```
#include <iostream>
#include <ostream>

class base {};
class derived : public base {};

int main( )
{
  // The values actually printed depend on the implementation, but many
  // common implementations print the values shown.
  using namespace std;
  cout << sizeof(base)    << '\n';      // Prints 1
  cout << sizeof(derived) << '\n';      // Prints 1
  base b[3];
  cout << sizeof(b) << '\n';            // Prints 3
  derived d[5];
  cout << sizeof(d) << '\n';            // Prints 5
}
```

new *type*
new *type* (*optional-expr-list*)
new (*expr-list*) *type*
new (*expr-list*) *type* (*optional-expr-list*)

Allocates and initializes a dynamic object or array of objects. The new expres-sion first calls an allocation function (operator new) to allocate memory. It then constructs the object in the allocated memory. A class can provide its own allocation function by overriding operator new as a member function. Otherwise, a global operator new is called. (See <new> in Chapter 13 for the standard allocation functions.)

The parts of a new expression are:

new
::new
> The new keyword can be prefixed with the global scope operator to call the global operator new as the allocation function.

(*expr-list*)
> An expression list in parentheses is called the *placement*. The placement is optional, but if it is used, it must contain at least one expression. If present, the expressions are passed directly to the allocation function without further interpretation.
>
> The standard library defines two placement new functions, which are discussed in Chapter 13. You can also write your own overloaded operator new functions for other forms of placement new. The first operand to operator new is always the amount of memory to allocate followed by the placement parameters.

type
> The type to allocate. It has the following form (optionally in parentheses):
>
> > *type-specifiers ptr-operators dimensions*
>
> (See Chapter 2 for information about type specifiers.) The *ptr-operators* are optional and can be * or & for pointers or references. The array *dimensions* are optional. All dimensions of an array except the first must be constant integral expressions (enclosed in square brackets). The first dimension can be any integral expression.
>
> The compiler reads the longest sequence of declarators as the *type*, even if it results in a syntax error. If *type* contains parentheses (e.g., a function pointer) or if you want to force a particular type declaration, surround *type* with parentheses. For example, (new int[*n*])[2] allocates an array of *n* integers and extracts the element at index 2. Without the parentheses, new int[*n*][2] allocates a two-dimensional array of int.

(*optional-expr-list*)
> An optional initializer that follows the usual rules for initializers. (See Chapter 2 for more information about initializers.)
>
> If the expression list has a single expression, and a single object is allocated, the expression is the object's initial value.
>
> If multiple expressions are in the initializer, the type must be a class type, and the expression list is passed to a suitable constructor, which is found by the usual rules for resolving overloaded functions (Chapter 5).
>
> An array cannot have an initializer. If the base type is a POD type, the array elements are uninitialized; otherwise, they are initialized by calling the default constructor for each array element.
>
> See Chapter 6 for a comparison of POD and non-POD types.

The allocation function (operator new) is called with at least one argument: the number of bytes to allocate (of type size_t). If a placement is used, the placement arguments are passed as additional arguments to the allocation function to the right of the size. If the allocation function cannot fulfill the request, it typically throws std::bad_alloc. However, if you pass std::nothrow as the placement argument, the standard allocation function returns a null pointer as an error indicator instead of throwing bad_alloc.

Allocating an array is different from allocating a scalar. The allocation function is operator new[]. The requested size is the number of elements in the array times the size of each element. An implementation is free to request additional memory for its own use, perhaps to store the number of elements in the array. The amount of additional memory is implementation-defined. Even if the array size is zero, the returned pointer is not null. The allocated memory is aligned to the most restrictive boundary for any type. (More precisely, the allocation function must return a pointer that is aligned for any type, and the new expression simply uses that pointer.) Thus, you can, for example, allocate an array of char and use the memory to store any object. The standard containers often do this. See <memory> in Chapter 13 for algorithms that work with uninitialized memory.

If an exception is thrown during initialization, the memory is freed by calling a corresponding deallocation function (corresponding to the equivalent delete expression). If placement new is used, a placement delete operator with the same additional parameters is the deallocation function, if such a function exists; otherwise, no deallocation function is called.

The following are some examples of new expressions:

```
int n = 10;                     // Note that n is not const
new int                         // Pointer to uninitialized int
new int( )                      // Pointer to int, initialized to 0
new int[n]                      // n uninitialized ints
new (int*)                      // Pointer to uninitialized pointer to int
new (int (*[n])( ))             // n function pointers
   typedef int (*int_func)( );
new int_func[n];                // n function pointers
new (int*[n][4])                // n 4 array of pointers to int
new complex<int>(42)            // Pointer to a complex object
new complex<int>[5]             // Five default-initialized complex objects
```

delete *pointer*
delete[] *pointer*

Destroys and frees a dynamic object or array of objects and returns void. The actual memory deallocation is performed by a deallocation function. A class can provide its own deallocation function by overriding operator delete. A plain delete expression looks up the deallocation function first in the class (if the *pointer* type is a pointer to a class type) and, if it is not found, in the global scope. Use the global scope operator to look only in the global scope. (See <new> in Chapter 13 for the default deallocation functions.)

To free an array, you must use delete[]. To free a scalar, you must use delete. If you make a mistake, the results are undefined. Note that the compiler cannot generally help you avoid mistakes because a pointer to a scalar cannot be distinguished from a pointer to an array. (Some libraries are more forgiving of this error than others.)

The *pointer* expression is evaluated once. If *pointer* is a pointer to a class type, the scalar form calls the object's destructor first, and the array form calls the destructor for each element of the array. The value of *pointer* is then passed to the deallocation function as a void*. If the expression's static type does not match the object's dynamic type, the static class must have a virtual destructor, or else the behavior is undefined. See Chapter 6 for more information.

You can delete a pointer to a const object. It is also safe to delete a null pointer value, in which case the deallocation function does nothing.

Cast Expressions

A cast expression performs an explicit type conversion. The cast expression is a holdover from C. In C++, the preferred cast syntax uses one of the explicit cast operators (described in "Postfix Expressions" earlier in this chapter). The C-style casts are still used for their brevity, however.

(*type*) *expr*
> The C-style cast converts *expr* to *type* using one or more template-like type conversions. If *type* is a reference, the result is an lvalue; otherwise the result is an rvalue. The following type conversions are tried in order. The first one that is syntactically allowed is the one used, even if the expression is not permitted semantically.
>
> 1. const_cast< *type* >(*expr*)
> 2. static_cast< *type* >(*expr*)
> 3. const_cast< *type* >(static_cast< *type1* >(*expr*))
> 4. reinterpret_cast< *type* >(*expr*)
> 5. const_cast< *type* >(reinterpret_cast< *type1* >(*expr*))
>
> The type *type1* is the same as *type*, but its *cv*-qualifiers are changed to match the type of *expr*. Thus, the C-style type cast can mix a const cast with a static or reinterpret cast. A C-style cast can also cast to an otherwise inaccessible base class (see Chapter 6 for information about accessibility). That is, you can cast a derived class to an inaccessible base class, cast a pointer to a member of a derived class to a pointer to a member of an inaccessible base class, or cast from an inaccessible base class to an accessible derived class.

Pointer-to-Member Expressions

A pointer-to-member expression takes an object or a pointer to an object as the lefthand operand and a pointer-to-member as the righthand operand, and it binds the pointer-to-member to the object. The result can be a data member or a member function. A member function can be used only to call the function.

Example 3-8 shows some uses of pointers to members. The pointer-to-member operator has the following syntax:

object **.*** *expr*

> Binds *expr* to *object*, in which *expr* is a pointer-to-member of class *C*, and the type of *object* is *C* or a class derived from *C*. The result is an lvalue if *object* is an lvalue and *expr* points to a data member; otherwise, the result is an rvalue. The type of the result is determined by the type of *expr*. The behavior is undefined if *expr* is a null pointer-to-member.

pointer **->*** *expr*

> Binds *expr* to the object that *pointer* points to, in which *expr* is a pointer-to-member of class *C*, and the type of *object* is *C* or a class derived from *C*. The result is an lvalue if *expr* points to a data member. The type of the result is determined by the type of *expr*. The behavior is undefined if *pointer* is null or if *expr* is a null pointer-to-member.

If *expr* points to a virtual function, the usual rules apply. That is, the actual function called is that of the most-derived type of *pointer or object. See Chapter 6 for more information about virtual functions.

Multiplicative Expressions

A multiplicative expression is used for multiplication, division, and remainders. The multiplicative operators require arithmetic or enumeration types; the usual conversions are performed, and an rvalue is returned. If the result is too large, the behavior is undefined (except for unsigned types, for which arithmetic is performed modulo the integer size; see Chapter 1 for details). Many C++ implementations ignore integer overflow. The multiplicative operators have the following syntax:

expr1 ***** *expr2*

> Performs multiplication.

expr1 **/** *expr2*

> Performs division. If the divisor is zero, the behavior is undefined.

expr1 **%** *expr2*

> Returns the remainder of dividing *expr1* by *expr2*. The operands must have integral or enumerated types. If *expr2* is 0, the behavior is undefined; otherwise, the value is such that `(a/b)*b + a%b == a`. If both operands are nonnegative, the result is nonnegative; otherwise, the sign of the result is implementation-defined.

Additive Expressions

An additive expression is used for addition and subtraction. The additive operators require arithmetic, enumerated, or pointer types. The usual conversions are performed, and an rvalue is returned. If the result of an additive expression is too large, the behavior is undefined (except for unsigned types, for which arithmetic is performed modulo the integer size; see Chapter 1 for details). Many C++

implementations ignore integer overflow. The additive operators have the following syntax:

expr + *expr*
> Performs addition. If one operand has a pointer type, the other must have an integral or enumeration type. The result is a pointer to the same array, but with the index offset by *N* positions (*N* can be positive, negative, or 0), in which *N* is the integral operand. The resulting pointer must be within the bounds of the array or point to one past the end of the array; otherwise, the behavior is undefined. Note that a pointer to any object can be treated as a one-element array.

expr - *expr*
> Performs subtraction. If both operands have arithmetic or enumeration types, the usual promotions apply and the result is the difference of the operands.
>
> If both operands are pointers, they must point to elements of the same array, or to one element past the end of the array. The result has type ptrdiff_t (declared in <cstdlib>) and is equal to the difference of the indices of the two objects.
>
> If the left operand is a pointer and the right operand has integral or enumeration type, the result is the same as *expr1* - *expr2*.

Shift Expressions

A shift expression shifts the bits of the left operand by an amount specified by the right operand. The operands must be have integral or enumerated types; both types are promoted to integral types. The result type is the promoted type of the left operand.

The result of a shift operation is undefined if the right operand is negative or is larger than the number of bits in the left operand.

The shift operators have the following syntax:

expr1 << *expr2*
> Performs a left shift of *expr1* by *expr2* bits. Vacated bits are filled with zeros. If *expr1* is unsigned, the result is equal to multiplying *expr1* by 2 raised to *expr2* (modulo the integer size; see Chapter 1 for more information about unsigned integer arithmetic).

expr1 >> *expr2*
> Performs a right shift of *expr1* by *expr2* bits. If the *expr1* is unsigned, or if it is signed and has a positive value, vacated bits are filled with zeros. The result is equal to dividing *expr1* by 2 raised to *expr2* (truncated to an integer). If *expr1* has a signed type and negative value, the result is implementation-defined.

The standard library overloads the shift operators for the I/O stream class templates. As with any overloaded function, the syntax (precedence and associativity) remains the same. Only the runtime behavior is different. See Chapter 9 for more information.

Relational Expressions

A relational expression compares two values for relative order. Relational operators have higher precedence than equality operators, so the following two expressions are equivalent:

```
a < b == c > d
(a < b) == (c > d)
```

The result of a relational expression is an rvalue of type bool. The operands must have arithmetic, enumeration, or pointer types. For arithmetic and enumeration types, the usual conversions are performed, and the resulting values are compared.

When comparing pointers, the pointers must have the same types (after the usual conversions and ignoring *cv*-qualification), one must be a pointer to void, or one operand must be a null pointer constant. If the pointer types are compatible, they are compared as follows (L is the left operand and R is the right operand):

- If L and R point to the same function, the same object, or one element past the end of the same array, or if both are null pointers, they are considered to be equal to each other. That is, L <= R and L >= R are true, and L < R and L > R are false.

- If L and R point to different objects (that are not members of a common object and not elements of the same array), different functions, or if only one is a null pointer, the result of the relational operators depends on the implementation.

- If L and R point to data members (as ordinary pointers, not pointers-to-members) within the same object (members of the same object, elements of arrays that are data members, and so on, recursively applied), and if the members are not separated by an access specifier label, and if the object is not a union, then L > R if the member to which L points is declared later than the member to which R points. Similarly, L < R if the member to which L points is declared earlier than the member to which R points. If the members are separated by an access specifier label, the results are implementation-dependent.

- If L and R point to data members (as ordinary pointers, not pointers-to-members) of the same union, they are considered to be equal to each other.

- If L and R point to elements of the same array, including one element past the end of the same array, the pointer with the higher subscript is larger.

Example 3-10 shows some pointer comparisons.

Example 3-10. Comparing pointers

```cpp
#include <iostream>
#include <ostream>

struct Demo {
  int x;
  int y;
};
```

Example 3-10. Comparing pointers (continued)

```cpp
union U {
  int a;
  double b;
  char c[5];
  Demo d;
};

int main( )
{
  Demo demo[10];
  std::cout << std::boolalpha;
  // Everything prints "true".
  std::cout << (&demo[0]   <  &demo[2])  << '\n';
  std::cout << (&demo[0]   == demo)      << '\n';
  std::cout << (&demo[10]  >  &demo[9])  << '\n';
  std::cout << (&demo[0].x <  &demo[0].y) << '\n';

  U u;
  std::cout << (&u.d == static_cast<void*>(u.c)) << '\n';
  std::cout << (&u.a == static_cast<void*>(&u.b)) << '\n';
}
```

The relational operators have the following syntax:

expr1 < *expr2*
> Returns true if *expr1* is less than *expr2*

expr1 > *expr2*
> Returns true if *expr1* is greater than *expr2*

expr1 <= *expr2*
> Returns true if *expr1* is less than or equal to *expr2*

expr1 >= *expr2*
> Returns true if *expr1* is greater than or equal to *expr2*

Equality Expressions

An equality expression compares two values to see if they are equal or different. Equality operators have lower precedence than relational operators, so the following two expressions are equivalent:

```cpp
a < b == c > d
(a < b) == (c > d)
```

The result of an equality expression is an rvalue of type bool. The operands must have arithmetic, enumeration, or pointer types. For arithmetic and enumeration types, the usual conversions are performed, and the resulting values are compared.

 Note that comparing the results of floating-point values for equality rarely gives the result you want. Instead, you probably want a fuzzy comparison that allows for floating-point imprecision.

When comparing pointers, the pointers must have the same type (after the usual conversions). The pointers are equal if any of the following conditions hold, and are not equal if none of the conditions hold:

- Both pointers are null pointers.
- Both object pointers point to the same object.
- Both object pointers point to one element past the end of the same array.
- Both function pointers point to the same function.
- Both member pointers point to the same member of the same most-derived object.
- Both member pointers point to any data members of the same union.

The equality operators have the following syntax:

expr == *expr*
> Returns true if the operands are equal.

expr != *expr*
expr not_eq *expr*
> Returns false if the operands are equal.

Bitwise And Expressions

A bitwise *and* expression performs *and* on its operands' bits. The bitwise *and* expression is permitted only on integral types after the usual arithmetic conversions. The bitwise *and* operator has the following syntax:

expr & *expr*
expr bitand *expr*
> Performs bitwise *and* of the operands. Each bit of the result is 1 if the corresponding bits of the operands are both 1; otherwise, the result bit is 0.

Bitwise Exclusive Or Expressions

A bitwise *exclusive or* expression performs *exclusive or* on its operands' bits. The bitwise *exclusive or* expression is permitted only on integral types after the usual arithmetic conversions. The *exclusive or* operator has the following syntax:

expr ^ *expr*
expr xor *expr*
> Performs bitwise *exclusive or* of the operands. Each bit of the result is 1 if the corresponding bits of the operands are not equal; otherwise, the result bit is 0.

Bitwise Inclusive Or Expressions

A bitwise *inclusive or* expression performs *inclusive or* on its operands' bits. The bitwise *inclusive or* expression is permitted only on integral types after the usual arithmetic conversions. The bitwise *inclusive or* operator has the following syntax:

expr | *expr*
expr bitor *expr*
> Performs bitwise *inclusive or* of the operands. Each bit of the result is 0 if the corresponding bits of the operands are both 0; otherwise, the result bit is 1.

Logical And Expressions

A logical *and* expression implicitly converts its operands to type bool. The result has type bool: true if both operands are true; otherwise, it is false. The logical *and* operator is a short-circuit operator, so the second operand is evaluated only if the first evaluates to true. The logical *and* operator has the following syntax:

expr && *expr*
expr and *expr*
> Performs the logical *and* of the operands.

Logical Or Expressions

A logical *or* expression implicitly converts its operands to type bool. The result has type bool: false if both operands are false; otherwise, it is true. The logical *or* operator is a short-circuit operator, so the second operand is evaluated only if the first evaluates to false. The logical *or* operator has the following syntax:

expr || *expr*
expr or *expr*
> Performs the logical *or* of the operands.

Conditional Expressions

A conditional expression is like an if statement in an expression:

condition ? *true-expr* : *false-expr*
> The first operand is converted to bool. If the value is true, only the second operand is evaluated; if it is false, only the third operand is evaluated. The result of the conditional expression is the result of the second or third operand, whichever is evaluated.
>
> The type of the expression depends on the types of the second and third operands: if both operands are lvalues of the same type, the result is an lvalue of that type. If one operand is an lvalue of type *T*, and the other operand is an lvalue that can be implicitly converted to a reference to *T*, the result is an lvalue of type *T*. An error results if the conversion is ambiguous—that is, the second operand can be converted to the type of the third just as readily as the third can be converted to the type of the second. Otherwise, the result is an rvalue, and the type is determined as follows:
> * If both operands have the same type, that is the type of the result.
> * If one operand is a throw expression, the result type is that of the other operand.
> * If one type *S* can be implicitly converted to the other type *T*, *T* is the result type. An error results if each operand can be implicitly converted to the other type.

Assignment Expressions

An assignment expression assigns its right operand to its left operand. In addition to plain assignment (x = y), there are several other assignment operators, each of which is a shorthand for an arithmetic operation and an assignment. The left operand of an assignment expression must be a modifiable lvalue. The result is an lvalue: the left operand after the assignment is complete.

Assignment operators have the following syntax:

lvalue = *expr*
> Assigns *expr* to *lvalue*. If the left operand has class type, a suitable assignment operator is called. (See Chapter 6 for more information.) If the left operand is not of class type, and the operands have different types, the right operand is converted to the type of the left operand.

lvalue += *expr*
lvalue -= *expr*
> The assignment operator x *op*= y is shorthand for x = x *op* y, except that x is evaluated only once. The type of x must be an arithmetic type or a pointer type. The usual conversions are performed for *op*, and the result is converted to the type of x.

lvalue *= *expr*
lvalue /= *expr*
lvalue %= *expr*
lvalue <<= *expr*
lvalue >>= *expr*
lvalue &= *expr*
lvalue and_eq *expr*
lvalue ^= *expr*
lvalue xor_eq *expr*
lvalue |= *expr*
lvalue or_eq *expr*
> The assignment operator x *op*= y is shorthand for x = x *op* y, except that x is evaluated only once. The type of x must be arithmetic (unlike the additive assignment operators, which allow pointers because the additive operators allow pointer operands). The usual conversions are performed for *op*, and the result is converted to the type of x.

throw *expr*
throw
> Throws an exception. The first form throws *expr* as the exception object. The second form rethrows the current exception object. If a program uses the second form, and no exception is being handled, throw calls terminate( ). (See <exception> in Chapter 13 for more information about terminate.)

> You can throw any expression, but the convention is to throw an object of type exception or of a derived class, especially a class derived from one of the standard exception classes (see <stdexcept> in Chapter 13).

> The throw expression initializes a temporary exception object, and that object is thrown to the exception handler, which can copy the exception object in its catch clause. When the handler finishes, the object is destroyed. An implementation can optimize away the extra copy and initialize the catch object directly with the exception *expr*. Even if the object is never copied, the class must have a copy constructor.

See the try statement in Chapter 4 for a description of how exceptions are handled and for examples of throw expressions. See also Chapter 5 for information about throw specifications in function declarations.

Comma Expressions

A comma expression serializes expression evaluation. The comma operator evaluates its left operand, discards the result, and then evaluates the right operand. The result is the value of the right operand, and the type is the type of the right operand. If the right operand is an lvalue, the result is an lvalue; otherwise, the result is an rvalue. Typically, the left operand is evaluated for a side effect, such as an assignment or a function call.

The comma operator can be overloaded, in which case the serial nature is lost. Both operands are evaluated, and the operator function is called. Overloading the comma operator is seldom done.

The syntax of the comma operator is:

expr1 , *expr2*

> Evaluates *expr1*, then *expr2*, and returns *expr2*. To use a comma expression as a function argument or in other contexts in which a comma is significant, enclose the comma expression in parentheses:
>
> ```
> sin((angle = 0.0, angle + 1.0));
> ```

4

Statements

Statements define and control what a program does. This chapter describes the syntax and rules for C++ statements: expressions, loops, selection, and control. The statement syntax rules apply recursively, and wherever a statement is called for, you can use (almost) any of the statements in this chapter.

The syntax descriptions in this chapter are informal. See Chapter 12 for a precise BNF grammar.

Expression Statements

An expression statement computes an expression, such as a function call or assignment. The expression result is discarded, so the expression is typically evaluated for its side effects. (See Chapter 3 for details about expressions.) The statement syntax is simply an optional expression followed by a semicolon:

> *expr* ;

or:

> ;

A statement with no expression is called a *null statement*. Null statements are most often used for loops when no code is needed in the loop body.

Here are several examples of expression statements:

```
42;           // Valid but pointless
cout << 42;   // More typical
x = y * z;    // Remember that assignment is an expression
;             // Null statement
```

Declarations

A declaration can appear anywhere a statement appears, and certain statements permit additional declarations within those statements.

Declarations made in a substatement (of a selection or loop statement) are limited in scope to the substatement, even if the substatement is not a compound statement. For example, the following statement:

```
while ( test( ) )
    int x = init( );
```

is equivalent to:

```
while ( test( ) ) {
    int x = init( );
}
```

The first example uses a declaration as the entire loop body, and the second uses a compound statement (enclosing the loop body in curly braces). In both cases, though, the scope of x is limited to the body of the while loop.

Declaration Statements

A simple declaration can appear wherever a statement can be used. You can declare an object, a type, or a namespace alias. You can also write a using declaration or using directive. You can declare a function, but not define a function, although there is rarely any reason to declare a function locally. You cannot define a namespace or declare a template.

In traditional C programming, declarations appear at the start of each block or compound statement. In C++ (and in the C99 standard), declarations can appear anywhere a statement can, which means you can declare variables close to where they are used. Example 4-1 shows examples of how declarations can be mixed with statements.

Example 4-1. Mixing declarations and statements

```
#include <cctype>
#include <cstddef>
#include <iomanip>
#include <iostream>
#include <ostream>
#include <string>

// Count lines, words, and characters in the standard input.
int main( )
{
    unsigned long num_lines, num_words, num_chars;

    num_lines = num_words = num_chars = 0;

    using namespace std;
    string line;
    while (getline(cin, line)) {
```

Example 4-1. Mixing declarations and statements (continued)

```
    ++num_lines;
    num_chars += line.length( ) + 1;

    bool in_word = false;
    for (size_t i = 0; char c = line[i]; ++i)
      if (isspace(static_cast<unsigned char>(c))) {
        if (in_word)
          ++num_words;
        in_word = false;
      } else if (! in_word)
        in_word = true;
    if (in_word)
      ++num_words;
  }
  cout << right <<
    setw(10) << num_lines <<
    setw(10) << num_words <<
    setw(10) << num_chars << '\n';
}
```

Sometimes a construct can look like an expression statement or a declaration. These ambiguities are resolved in favor of declarations. Example 4-2 shows some declarations that look like they might be expressions.

Example 4-2. Declarations that seem like expressions

```
class cls {
public:
  cls( );
  cls(int x);
};

int x;
int* y = &x;

int main( )
{
  // The following are unambiguously expressions, constructing instances of cls.
  cls(int(x));
  cls(*static_cast<int*>(y));

  // Without the redundant casts, though, they would look like declarations, not
  // expressions.
  cls(x);    // Declares a variable x
  cls(*y);   // Declares a pointer y
}
```

Condition Declarations

The for, if, switch, and while statements permit a declaration within each statement's condition:

```
    if (int x = test_this(a, b)) { cout << x; }
```

If the condition contains a declaration, the scope of the declared name extends to the end of the entire statement. In particular, a name declared in the condition of an if statement is visible in the else part of the statement. In a loop, the condition object is created and destroyed for each iteration of the loop. The name cannot be redeclared in the immediate substatement (but can be redeclared in a nested statement). The name is not visible in subsequent statements. For example:

```
if (derived* d = dynamic_cast<derived*>(b)) {
  d->derived_only_func( );
} else {
  assert(d == NULL); // Same d as above
  double d;          // Error: can't redeclare d
  if (d == 0)
    int d;           // Valid: inner block
}
cout << d;           // Invalid: d no longer in scope
```

Like the if, switch, and while statements, a for loop permits a declaration in its condition. Unlike those other statements, it also allows a declaration to initialize the loop. Both declarations are in the same scope. See "for Statements" for details.

The syntax for a condition declaration is:

```
type-specifiers declarator = expression
```

This syntax is similar to the syntax of a simple object declaration. In this case, the initializer is required (without it, the condition would not have a value), and only one declarator is permitted. See Chapter 2 for more information about type specifiers and declarators.

Compound Statements

A compound statement is a sequence of zero or more statements enclosed within curly braces. Compound statements are frequently used in selection and loop statements. They enable you to write loop bodies that are more than one statement long, among other things. A compound statement is sometimes called a *block*.

Here is the syntax of a compound statement:

```
{ statement ... }
```

or:

```
{ }
```

A compound statement can be used as a single statement wherever a statement is called for. A compound statement delimits a declarative scope, that is, any name declared in the compound statement is not visible outside the statement, and names in the statement can hide names from outside the statement. The lifetime of any automatic object declared in a compound statement is confined to that statement. All such objects are destroyed when execution leaves the compound statement for any reason (e.g., branching outside the statement, execution reaches the end of the statement, or an exception is thrown).

Compound statements are most often used as the bodies of selection and loop statements, but you can also stick a compound statement in the middle of a compound statement to restrict the scope of variables that are local to the compound statement. See the examples in this chapter for uses of compound statements.

Selections

A selection statement chooses one branch from multiple possibilities and executes the statements in that branch. The two selection statements supported by C++ are if and switch.

if Statements

An if statement has one of the following forms:

    if (condition) statement

or:

    if (condition) statement else statement

In the first form, the *condition* is converted to a bool, and if it is true, the *statement* is executed. Otherwise, the statement is skipped, and execution continues with the subsequent statement.

The second form chooses one of two alternative code paths. The *condition* is converted to a bool, and if it is true, the first *statement* is executed. Otherwise, the second *statement* is executed. Declarations in the first statement are not visible in the second. If if statements are nested, the else part binds with the closest, preceding if statement. Example 4-3 shows nested if statements.

Example 4-3. Nested if statements

```
if (c1)
  if (c2)
    cout << "c1 and c2 are true\n";
  else
    cout << "c1 is true, but c2 is false\n";
else if (c2)
  cout << "c1 is false, but c2 is true\n";
else
  cout << "c1 and c2 are false\n";
```

switch Statements

A switch statement chooses one execution path from among many alternatives. The syntax is:

    switch (condition) statement

The *condition* must have an integral or enumerated type, or be of a class type in which the class has a single conversion function to an integral or enumerated type. The *condition* is evaluated once. Its value is compared against the case labels in the *statement*. If a case label matches the *condition*, execution continues with the statement immediately after the case label. If no case matches the *condition*, execution continues after the default label, if one is present. If there is no default label, the switch's *statement* is skipped and execution continues with the subsequent statement.

The *statement* part of a switch statement is typically a compound statement, in which every substatement has one or more case labels or a default label. The syntax for case and default labels is:

```
case constant-expression : statement
default : statement
```

The *constant-expression* must have an integral or enumerated type. The value is implicitly converted to the type of the *condition*. In a single switch statement, all case *constant-expression*s must have different values. A single statement in the switch's substatement can have multiple case labels, and a single switch statement can have any number of cases.

 In C++, like C and Java, but unlike most other languages, a case or default label does not affect control flow. Execution continues from one case to the next, which is known as "falling through" to the next case. Use the break statement (described later in this chapter) to exit from a switch statement.

There can be at most one default case in a switch statement; it can appear anywhere in the statement. (The default case does not have to be last, as in some languages.)

By convention, case and default labels appear at the top level of the switch's substatement. They can appear in nested statements, but that makes the statements hard to read. In nested switch statements, case and default labels apply only to the innermost switch statement.

You should not define any objects in the switch's substatement unless they are enclosed in a nested compound statement. When the switch dispatches control to a particular case, it might jump over the declaration. Jumping over a declaration results in undefined behavior unless the declared object has POD type and is not initialized.

Example 4-4 shows sample switch statements.

Example 4-4. Switch statements

```
enum color { black, red, green, yellow, blue,
             magenta, cyan, white };
color get_pixel(unsigned r, unsigned c) { ... }

void demo( )
{
  using std::cout;
  int r = ...
  int c = ...
```

Example 4-4. Switch statements (continued)

```
switch (get_pixel(r, c))
{
  cout << "this is never executed, but it is valid\n";
  case black:
    cout << "no color\n";
    break; // Don't forget the break statements!
  case red: case green: case blue:
    cout << "primary\n";
    break; // Omitting break is a common mistake.
  default:
    cout << "mixed\n";
    switch (get_pixel(r+1, c+1))
    case white: {
      const int x = 0;
      cout << "  white\n"; // This case is private to the inner switch
                           // statement.
      c = x;
    }
    if (r > 0)
      // If the color is yellow, the switch branches directly to here. For
      // colors other than red, green, blue, and black, execution jumps to the
      // default label and arrives here if r > 0.
      case yellow:
        cout << " yellow or r > 0\n";

    break; // A break after the last case is not necessary, but is a good idea
           // if you add a case later.
}
}
```

The outer switch statement has one case for black; another case for red, green, or blue; a default case; and a final case for yellow. The first two branches are conventional, and each ends with a break statement to exit the switch.

The case for yellow is unusual and hard to read because it is buried in an if statement. The same statement can be reached from the default case when the if condition is true (that is, r > 0).

The default case has a nested switch, which has a single case, white. The inner switch statement is atypical because it does not have a compound statement as its body.

Loops

A loop statement allows you to execute a statement multiple times. Two loop statements, for and while, test at the top of the loop. The do statement tests at the bottom, thereby ensuring that the loop body executes at least once. This section describes the loop statements. See "Control Statements" for additional statements that affect or control loop execution.

A loop statement can declare variables in the scope of the loop's substatement. Every time the loop iterates, it reenters the substatement scope. This means objects that are declared in the substatement (and in the loop's condition) are created and destroyed with every loop iteration.

while Statements

A while statement repeats a statement while a condition is true. The syntax is:

```
while ( condition ) statement
```

The *condition* is evaluated and converted to bool. If the value is true, *statement* is executed, and the loop repeats. If the value is false, the loop finishes and execution continues with the subsequent statement. Thus, if *condition* is false the first time it is evaluated, the *statement* is never executed.

A continue statement in a while loop branches to the top of the loop, and execution continues with the evaluation of *condition*. A break statement exits immediately.

A while loop is typically used for unbounded iteration, that is, when you don't know beforehand how many times a loop will iterate. Example 4-5 shows how the while loop can be used to control I/O.

Example 4-5. Controlling I/O with the while loop

```
#include <algorithm>
#include <iostream>
#include <iterator>
#include <ostream>
#include <string>
#include <vector>

// Sort lines of text.
int main( )
{
  using namespace std;
  string line;
  vector<string> data;
  while (getline(cin, line))
    data.push_back(line);
  sort(data.begin( ), data.end( ));
  copy(data.begin( ), data.end( ),
    ostream_iterator<string>(cout, "\n"));
}
```

for Statements

A for loop is a generalization of the traditional counted loop that appears in most programming languages. The syntax for a for loop is:

```
for ( init ; condition ; iterate-expr ) statement
```

The *init*, *condition*, and *iterate-expr* parts are optional. The *init* part of the for statement can be an expression or a simple declaration. The *init* part offers more flexibility than a condition. While a condition can declare only one name, the *init* part can declare multiple names. The syntax for the *init* part is:

    specifier-list declarator-list

or:

    expression

As with the *condition*, the scope of the *init* part extends to the end of *statement*. The *init*, *condition*, and *iterate-expr* parts are in the same scope as the loop body. See Chapter 2 for more information about specifiers and declarators.

The for loop starts by executing the *init* part, if present. It then evaluates the *condition* (just like a while loop). If the *condition* is true, the loop executes *statement*. It then evaluates *iterate-expr* and reevaluates *condition*. This process continues while *condition* is true. If *condition* is false, the loop finishes and execution continues with the subsequent statement. Thus, the *init* part is evaluated exactly once. The *condition* is evaluated at least once. The *statement* might be executed zero times.

The most common use of a for loop is to count a bounded loop, although its flexibility makes it useful for unbounded loops, too, as you can see in Example 4-6.

Example 4-6. Multiple uses of for loops

```
// One way to implement the for_each standard algorithm
template<typename InIter, typename Function>
Function for_each(InIter first, InIter last, Function f)
{
  for ( ; first != last; ++first)
    f(*first);
  return f;
}

// One way to implement the generate_n standard algorithm
template<typename OutIter, typename Size, typename Generator>
void generate_n(OutIter first, Size n, Generator gen)
{
  for (Size i = 0; i < n; ++i, ++first)
    *first = gen;
}
```

A continue statement in a for loop branches to the top of the loop, and execution continues by evaluating the *iterate-expr* and then the *condition*. A break statement exits the loop without evaluating the *iterate-expr*. See "Control Statements" later in this chapter for examples of break and continue.

The *init*, *condition*, and *interate-expr* parts are all optional. If the *init* or *iterate-expr* parts are omitted, nothing happens to initialize the loop or after the statement executes. If the *condition* is omitted, it defaults to true.

do Statements

The do statement is like a while statement, except that it tests at the end of the loop body. The syntax is:

    do statement while (expression) ;

The *statement* is executed, then the *expression* is evaluated and converted to bool. If the value is true, the *statement* is repeated and the *expression* is checked again. If the *expression* is false, the loop finishes and execution continues with the subsequent statement. Thus, *statement* is always executed at least once.

A continue statement in a do loop jumps to the end of *statement*, and execution continues with the evaluation and test of *expression*. A break statement exits immediately.

Control Statements

Control statements change execution from its normal sequence. When execution leaves a scope, all automatic objects that were created in that scope are destroyed. (see Chapter 2 for a discussion of automatic and other object lifetimes)

C++ supports the following control statements:

break;

A break statement can be used only in the body of a loop or switch statement. It terminates the loop or switch statement and transfers execution to the statement immediately following the loop or switch.

In a nested loop or switch, the break applies only to the innermost statement. To break out of multiple loops and switches, you must use a goto statement or redesign the block to avoid nested loops and switches (by factoring the inner statement into a separate function, for example). Example 4-7 shows a simple use of break.

Example 4-7. Using break to exit a loop

```
// One way to implement the find_if standard algorithm.
template<typename InIter, typename Predicate>
InIter find_if(InIter first, InIter last, Predicate pred)
{
  for ( ; first != last; ++first)
    if (pred(*first))
      break;

  return first;
}
```

continue;

A continue statement can be used only in the body of a loop. It causes the loop to skip the remainder of its body and immediately retest its condition prior to reiterating (if the condition is true). In a for loop, the *iterate-expr* is evaluated before testing the condition. Example 4-8 shows how continue is used in a loop.

Example 4-8. Using continue in a loop

```cpp
#include <cmath>
#include <iostream>
#include <istream>
#include <limits>
#include <ostream>

int main()
{
  using std::cin;
  using std::cout;
  while(true) {
    cout << "Enter a number: ";
    double x;
    cin >> x;
    if (cin.eof() || cin.bad())
      // Input error: exit
      break;
    else if (cin.fail()) {
      // Invalid input: skip the rest of the line
      cin.clear();
      cin.ignore(std::numeric_limits<int>::max(), '\n');
      continue;
    }
    cout << "sqrt(" << x << ")=" << std::sqrt(x) << std::endl;
  }
}
```

goto *identifier* ;

The goto statement transfers control to the statement that has *identifier* as a label. The goto statement and the labeled statement must be in the same function. Jumping into a block is usually a bad idea. In particular, if the jump bypasses the declaration of an object, the results are undefined unless the object has POD type and no initializer. (See Chapter 2 for information about POD types and initializers.) Example 4-9 shows some uses of goto statements.

Example 4-9. goto statements

```cpp
#include <iostream>
#include <ostream>

int main(int argc, char* argv[])
{
  int matrix[4][5];
  for (int i = 0; i < 4; ++i)
    for (int j = 0; j < 5; ++j)
      if (! (std::cin >> matrix[i][j]))
        goto error;
  goto end;

error:
  std::cerr << "Need 20 values for the matrix\n";
```

Example 4-9. goto statements (continued)

```
end:
  return 0;
}
```

`return` ;
`return` *expr* ;

> The `return` statement transfers execution out of a function to the caller. The first form does not return a value, so it should be used only in functions of type void, in constructors, and in destructors. The latter form cannot be used in constructors and destructors. In a function of type void, you can use the second form, but only if *expr* has type void. See Chapter 5 for more information about returning from functions.
>
> The value of *expr* is converted to the function's return type and returned to the caller. The compiler is free to construct a temporary object and copy *expr* when returning. Some compilers optimize away the extra copy.
>
> If execution reaches the last statement of a function without executing a return statement, an implicit `return`; is assumed. If the function has a non-void return type, the behavior is undefined.
>
> The main function is special. If it ends without a return statement, return 0; is assumed.

identifier : *statement*

> Any statement can have a label. A label is used only as a target of a goto statement. Label identifiers must be unique within a function; the scope of a label is the function in which it is declared. Label identifiers do not conflict with any other identifiers.
>
> A statement can have multiple labels, including case and default labels.

Handling Exceptions

An *exception* interrupts the normal flow of control in a program. An exception *throws* an object from the point where the exception is raised to the point where the exception is handled. In between those points, function calls are aborted, and local scopes are abruptly exited. Local and temporary objects in those scopes are destroyed.

This section discusses exception handling in general and the try statement in particular. For information about other aspects of exception handling, see Chapter 3, which describes the throw expression, and Chapter 5, which describes function try blocks and throw specifications. See also <exception> and <stdexcept> in Chapter 13 for information about the standard exception classes and related functions.

> As the name implies, an exception is used for exceptional circumstances, such as indexing a vector with an index that is out of bounds. The intention in C++ is that try statements should have near zero cost, but throwing and handling an exception can be expensive in terms of performance.

A try statement establishes a local scope plus exception handlers. A try statement begins with the try keyword followed by a compound statement and one or more catch handlers. Each catch handler has an exception type in parentheses followed by a compound statement. The exception type can be a sequence of type specifiers followed by an optional declarator, or it can be an ellipsis:

```
try compound-statement
catch(type declarator) compound-statement
catch(type) compound-statement
catch(...) compound-statement
```

Each compound statement (after try and for each exception handler) forms a separate local scope, following the rules for any other compound statement.

Every time a local scope is entered—for example, by calling a function or by entering a compound statement or other statement that establishes a scope—you can think of the scope as pushing an entry on an execution stack. When execution leaves the scope, the scope is popped from the stack. Each try statement is also pushed on the stack.

When an exception is thrown, the execution stack is *unwound*. Local scopes are popped from the stack (destroying any automatic objects that were declared in each scope) until a try statement is found. The try statement is popped from the exception stack. Then the type of the exception object is compared with each exception handler. If a match is found, the exception object is copied to the locally-declared exception object, and execution transfers to the compound statement for that handler. After the handler finishes, the exception object is destroyed, and execution continues with the statement that follows the try statement (and its handlers).

If no matching handler is found, the stack continues to be popped until the next try statement is reached. Its handlers are compared with the exception type, and the process repeats until a matching handler is found. If no try statement has a matching handler, and the entire execution stack is popped, the terminate function is called. (See <exception> in Chapter 13.)

An exception handler can throw an exception, in which case, the usual rules apply for unwinding the stack. Note that the try statement has already been popped from the stack, so the same try statement cannot catch the exception. The handler can throw a new exception or rethrow the existing exception (in which case, the exception object is not freed yet).

A catch handler can use an ellipsis to mean it catches any type of exception. When an ellipsis is used, the handler must be last in the list of exception handlers.

Handlers are checked in order. The *type* in each catch clause is compared with the type T of the exception object according to the following rules:

- If *type* is the same as T or T& (not considering *cv*-qualifiers), the handler matches.
- If *type* is a base class of T, the handler matches.

- If *type* is a pointer that can be converted to *T* using a standard conversion (Chapter 3)—e.g., *type* is void*—the handler matches.
- An ellipsis (...) always matches.

Thus, it is important to put the most specific exceptions first, and put base classes later. If you use an ellipsis, it must be last.

A common idiom is to throw an exception object and catch a reference. This avoids unnecessary copies of the exception object.

Example 4-10 shows a typical use of a try statement. It also shows a try function block, which is covered in Chapter 5.

Example 4-10. Throwing and catching exceptions

```cpp
#include <cstdlib>
#include <fstream>
#include <iostream>
#include <numeric>
#include <ostream>
#include <sstream>
#include <stdexcept>
#include <string>
#include <vector>

class bad_data : public std::out_of_range {
public:
  bad_data(int value, int min, int max)
  : std::out_of_range(make_what(value, min, max))
  {}
private:
  std::string make_what(int value, int min, int max);
};

std::string bad_data::make_what(int value, int min, int max)
{
  std::ostringstream out;
  out << "Invalid datum, " << value << ", must be in [" <<
         min << ", " << max << "]";
  return out.str();
}

// Read a set of numbers from an input stream. Verify that all data is within the
// defined boundaries. Throw bad_data if any data is invalid. If an exception is
// thrown, tmp's destructor is automatically called (if it has a destructor).
template<typename T, typename charT, typename traits>
void getdata(std::basic_istream<charT,traits>& in,
             std::vector<T>& data, T min, T max)
{
  T tmp;
  while (in >> tmp)
  {
    if (tmp < min)
      throw bad_data(tmp, min, max);
```

Example 4-10. Throwing and catching exceptions (continued)

```
    else if (tmp > max)
      throw bad_data(tmp, min, max);
    else
      data.push_back(tmp);
  }
}

// Arbitrary precision integer
class bigint {
public:
  bigint( );
  ~bigint( );
  ...
};

int main(int argc, char** argv)
{
  using namespace std;
  if (argc < 2) {
    cerr << "usage: " << argv[0] << " FILE\n";
    return EXIT_FAILURE;
  }

  vector<bigint> data;
  ifstream in(argv[1]);
  if (! in) {
    perror(argv[1]);
    return EXIT_FAILURE;
  }
  try {
    getdata(in, data, bigint(0), bigint(10));
  } catch (const bad_data& ex) {
    cerr << argv[1] << ": " << ex.what( ) << '\n';
    return EXIT_FAILURE;
  } catch(...) {
    std::cerr << "fatal error: unknown exception\n";
    return EXIT_FAILURE;
  }

  if (data.size( ) == 0)
    cout << "no data\n";
  else {
    bigint sum(accumulate(data.begin(),data.end( ),bigint( )));
    std::cout << "avg=" << sum / data.size( ) << '\n';
  }
}
```

5

Functions

Every C++ program has at least one function (main), and all but the most trivial programs define additional functions. The C++ standard library provides numerous functions that your program can call. This chapter discusses how to declare, define, and call functions. A function *declaration* tells the compiler about a function's name, return type, and parameters. A function *definition* also provides the body of the function.

See Chapter 3 for more information about function call expressions and Chapter 4 for information about statements, which make up function bodies. This chapter presents information that is common to all kinds of functions. For characteristics that are unique to member functions, see Chapter 6, and for information that pertains specifically to function templates, see Chapter 7.

The syntax descriptions in this chapter are informal. See Chapter 12 for a precise BNF grammar.

Function Declarations

A function declaration tells the compiler about a function name and how to call the function. The actual body of the function can be defined separately (described later in this chapter). A function declaration has the following parts:

> *type name* (*parameters*) *cv-qualifiers except-spec* ;

The *parameters*, *cv-qualifiers*, and *except-spec* are optional. The *type* is required, except for constructors, destructors, and type conversion operators. The *name* is the function name. (Each of these parts is described later in this chapter.) Example 5-1 shows a variety of function declarations.

Example 5-1. Declaring functions

```
// Function named "add", which returns type int, and takes two parameters, each
// of type int. The names a and b are optional.
int add(int a, int b);

// Function named "print", which takes a const string reference, and does not
// return anything. The function is expanded inline.
inline void print(const std::string& str)
{
  std::cout << str;
}

// Function named "test", which takes two floating-point arguments and returns an
// enumeration. This function does not throw any exceptions.
enum fptest { less=-1, equal, greater };
fptest test(double, double) throw( );

class demo {
public:
  // Member function named "value", which returns type int, takes no arguments,
  // and is const, which means it can be called for a const object.
  int value( ) const;
  // Function named "~demo", that is, a destructor, that is virtual. Constructors
  // and destructors do not have return types. Destructors do not take arguments.
  virtual ~demo( );
  // Inline, overloaded, const type conversion operator
  operator bool( ) const { return value( ) != 0; }
};
```

Return Type

The *type* in a function declaration is the function's return type. It is a series of type specifiers (see Chapter 2) with pointer and reference operators. You can mix any of the following function specifiers freely with the type specifiers, but the convention is to list function specifiers before other type specifiers:

explicit
> Applies only to constructors. An explicit constructor cannot be used in an implicit type conversion. See Chapter 6 for details.

inline
> Tells the compiler to expand the function body at the point of the function call. An inline function must be defined in every file in which it is used, and the definition must be identical in every file. If the function body contains a local static object, including string literals, every expansion of the function in every file refers to a common object.
>
> A function definition in a class definition is an inline function definition, even without the use of the inline specifier.

The inline specifier is a hint to the compiler, and the compiler is free to ignore the hint. Most compilers impose a variety of restrictions on which functions can be expanded inline. The restrictions vary from one compiler to another. For example, most compilers cannot expand a recursive function.

Inline functions are most often used for extremely simple functions. For example, all standard containers have a member function empty, which returns true if the container is empty. Some containers might implement the function as the following inline function:

```
inline bool empty( ) const { return size( ) != 0; }
```

virtual
> Applies only to nonstatic member functions. A virtual function's definition is bound to the function call at runtime instead of at compile time. See Chapter 6 for details.

If a function's return type is void, no value is returned to the caller. The function does not need a return statement. The form return; is permitted, or the return expression must have type void.

If the return type is anything other than void, every return statement must have an expression, the type of which can be implicitly converted to the function's return type. See Chapter 4 for more information about the return statement.

A function's return type cannot be an array or function type, but it can be a pointer or reference to an array or function.

In a function declaration (but not a definition), you can use the extern storage class specifier. Declarations and definitions can have linkage specifications, e.g., extern "C". See Chapter 2 for more information about storage class and linkage.

A friend specifier can be used to declare a friend function. See Chapter 6 for more information.

Note that the return type is not considered in overload resolution. See "Overloading" later in this chapter for details.

Parameters

Function parameters are optional. If a function takes no parameters, you can leave the parentheses empty or use the keyword void. If a function requires parameters, the parameter list is comma-separated, in which each parameter is a simple declaration of the following form:

```
type-specifiers declarator = expr
```

expr is optional; if it is omitted, the = symbol is also omitted. The type-specifiers allow for the optional register and auto storage class specifiers and pointer and reference operators. See Chapter 2 for more information about declarators and specifiers.

In C, a function that takes no arguments requires the void keyword, but in C++, void is optional. Thus, void appears most often in headers that must be used in both C and C++ programs. For example:

```
#ifdef __cplusplus
  #define EXTERN extern "C"
#else
  #define EXTERN extern
#endif
EXTERN int get_version(void);
```

In other situations, you can use whichever style you prefer.

You can omit the parameter name from the *declarator*. In a function declaration, the name is important only to the human reader. In a function definition, a nameless parameter cannot be used in the function body. For example, suppose a graphics package defines a variety of shape classes, all deriving from a common base class, shape. Among the operations permitted on a shape is scale, which takes two arguments: the scaling amounts in the x and y directions. Also, suppose that the square shape (unlike rectangle) heeds only the x scale factor. The square::scale function might be written as:

```
void square::scale(double xscale, double)
{
  this->size *= xscale;
}
```

A parameter can have *cv*-qualifiers (const and volatile, as discussed in Chapter 2). The qualifiers have their usual meaning in the function body. The qualifiers and storage class specifier are not part of the function type and do not participate in overload resolution.

Default Arguments

A parameter can have a default argument (separated from the declarator by an equal sign). Only the right-most parameters can have default arguments. If any given parameter does not have a default argument, all parameters to its left cannot have default arguments. The default argument can be any expression. (If you want to use a comma operator, enclose the expression in parentheses.)

In a function call, arguments that have default values can be omitted, starting from the right. For each omitted argument, the default argument is substituted in the function call. Each default argument is implicitly converted to the parameter type, applying the same rules that govern initializers in declarations. The default argument expressions are evaluated every time the argument is needed in a function call. Names used in the default arguments are looked up at the point of declaration, not the point of use, as shown in Example 5-2.

Example 5-2. Declaring and using default arguments

```
#include <iostream>
#include <ostream>

namespace demo {
  int f( )
  {
    return 20;
  }
}

int f( )
{
  return 10;
}

// The default argument for y is always the global f( ), even if a different f( )
// is visible where func( ) is called.
int func(int x, int y = f( ))
{
  return x + y;
}

int main( )
{
  using demo::f;
  std::cout << f( ) << '\n';        // Prints 20
  std::cout << func(32) << '\n';    // Prints 42
}
```

Default arguments are cumulative in multiple declarations of the same function in the same scope. Later declarations can provide default arguments for additional parameters, in which case the declaration must omit the default arguments for parameters that already have default arguments, as shown in Example 5-3.

Example 5-3. Accumulating default arguments

```
void func(int x, int y);
void func(int x, int y = 10);
void func(int x = 20, int y);
void other( )
{
  func( ); // Same as func(20, 10)
}
```

Different scopes can have different default arguments. For example, the source file in which a function is defined might have different default arguments from those used in function declarations where the function is used. However, most of the time, different default arguments suggests programmer errors.

In a derived class, an overridden virtual function can have different default arguments than its counterpart in the base class. The default argument is chosen at compile time, based on the object's static type. Thus, the default arguments are typically those of the base class, even if the function actually called is from the derived class. To avoid confusion, it is best to avoid default arguments with virtual functions, or make sure they are the same for all overridden functions. (See Chapter 6 for more information about virtual functions.)

In a member function declaration, you cannot use a nonstatic data member as a default argument unless it is the member of a specific object. If you want to use the value of a data member as the default value for a parameter, use an overloaded function, as shown in Example 5-4. (See "Function Overloading" for more on overloaded functions.)

Example 5-4. Default arguments in member functions

```
class example {
public:
  void func(int x, int y = data_); // Error

  // Achieve the desired effect with overloaded functions.
  void func(int x, int y);
  void func(int x)          { func(x, data_); }
private:
  int data_;
};
```

Variable Number of Arguments

The last parameter in a function declaration can be an ellipsis (...), which permits a variable number of arguments to be passed to the function. The comma that separates the next-to-last parameter from the ellipsis is optional. However, if portability with C is important, be sure to include the comma. (See <cstdarg> in Chapter 13 to learn how to access the additional arguments.) You can use an ellipsis as the sole parameter in a function, but there is no mechanism in standard C++ to access the arguments from the function body. Such a declaration might be used for an external function, however.

cv-qualifiers

Only nonstatic member functions (but not constructors or destructors) can have *cv*-qualifiers (const and volatile). They are optional, and if used in a member function declaration, apply to the implicit object parameter of the member function (this). You can use const, volatile, neither, or both in any order. Place *cv*-qualifiers after the closing parenthesis of the function parameters and before the exception specification. The qualifiers are part of the function type and participate in overload resolution, so you can have multiple functions with the same name and parameters, but with different qualifiers (but only if you do not also have a static member function of the same name and parameters; see "Function Overloading" later in this chapter for details).

A pointer-to-member function and a function typedef can also have *cv*-qualifiers. Only a top-level typedef can have *cv*-qualifiers; you cannot declare a typedef that combines a function typedef and a qualifier.

cv-qualifiers are most often used to declare const member functions. These functions can be called for a const object. In general, member functions that do not change *this should be declared const. (See Chapter 6 for more information on how *cv*-qualifiers affect member functions.) Example 5-5 shows some simple uses of qualifiers.

Example 5-5. Using qualifiers with member functions

```
class point
{
public:
  point(int x, int y) : x_(x), y_(y) {}
  int x()       const   { return x_; }
  int y()       const   { return y_; }
  double abs() const    { return sqrt(double(x())*x() + y()*y()); }
  void offset(const point& p) {
    // Cannot be const because offset() modifies x_ and y_
    x_ += p.x();
    y_ += p.y();
  }
private:
  int x_, y_;
};
```

Exception Specifications

An exception specification tells the compiler which exceptions a function can throw. Exception specifications are optional in a function declaration and are rarely used. The syntax is:

```
throw ( type-list )
```

The *type-list* is optional. The exception specification follows the function header and *cv*-qualifiers. If present, it is a comma-separated list of type names. (See Chapter 2 for details about type names.) Each type name is an exception type that the function can throw. If the function throws an exception that is not listed in the exception specification, the unexpected function is called. If the function declaration does not have an exception specification, the function can throw any exception.

The default implementation of unexpected calls terminate to terminate the program. You can set your own unexpected handler, which must call terminate or throw an exception. If your handler throws an exception that is not listed in the function's exception specification, bad_exception is thrown. If bad_exception is not listed in the function's exception specification, terminate is called. In other words, if there is an exception specification, only exceptions of the listed types (or derived from one of the listed types) can be thrown from the function, or else the program terminates. See <exception> in Chapter 13 for details.

An overridden virtual function must have an exception specification that lists only types that are also listed in the base-class exception specifications. In particular, if the base-class function does not throw any exceptions, the derived class function must not throw any exceptions.

An exception specification most often marks functions that do not throw exceptions at all (throw( )). Example 5-6 shows various uses of exception specifications.

Example 5-6. Declaring exception specifications

```
class base {
public:
  virtual void f( ) throw( );
  virtual void g( ); // Can throw anything
  virtual void h( ) throw(std::string);
};

class derived : public base {
public:
  virtual void f( ) throw( );     // OK: same as base
  virtual void g( ) throw(int); // OK: subset of base
  virtual void h( ) throw(int); // Error: int not in base
};

class more : public derived {
public:
  virtual void f( );              // Error: can throw anything
  virtual void g( ) throw( );     // OK
};

// Function does not throw any exceptions
int noproblem(int x, int y) throw( )
try
{
  dostuff(x);
  dostuff(y);
  return 1;
}
catch(...)
{
  return 0;
}

derived* downcast(base* b) throw(std::bad_cast)
{
  return dynamic_cast<derived*>(b);
}
```

 Java programmers should note two significant differences between C++ and Java with respect to exception specifications:

- The exception specification is introduced by throw, not throws.
- The correctness of the exception specification is checked at runtime, not at compile time.

Function Definitions

Every function that a program uses must be defined exactly once in the program, except for inline functions. (Function templates are a little different; see Chapter 7 for details.) An inline function must be defined in every source file that uses the function. This section discusses function definitions and their relationship to their declarations.

Declarations and Definitions

In a source file, every function must be declared or defined before it is used. For functions defined in libraries or other source files, the convention is to declare the function in a header (*.h* or *.hpp*) file, and the source file where the function is called must #include the header file. Every function that is used in the program must have a definition.

Inline functions must be defined in every source file in which they are used. This is typically accomplished by defining them in a header file, which you must #include in each source file that calls the inline function. Every definition of an inline function must be identical.

Function Types and Signatures

A *function type* includes the language linkage, return type, parameter types, and *cv*-qualifiers. Note that for each parameter, only its type is significant; its name, storage class, and *cv*-qualifiers are not part of the function type. Exception specifications are not part of a function's type.

A single source file can have multiple declarations of the same function (that is, functions with the same type), even if those declarations differ in other ways. For example, one declaration can declare a parameter const and another might declare it volatile. Because *cv*-qualifiers on parameters do not affect a function's type, both declarations are equivalent. (Parameter qualifiers matter only in the function definition, not the declaration.) Example 5-7 shows several declarations and one definition, all for a single function.

Example 5-7. Declaring and defining functions

```
// Three declarations of the same function type
int add(const int a, const int b);
int add(int x, volatile int);
int add(signed int, int signed);

// Definition of the function. The parameter qualifiers in the declarations are
// irrelevant. Only those in the definition matter.
int add(int x, int y)
{
  return x + y;
}
```

Array and pointer parameter types are also equivalent. In a function body, a parameter with an array type is actually a pointer, not an array. The first (leftmost) size in a multidimensional array is ignored and can be omitted. Similarly, a parameter of function type is the same as a parameter of function pointer type. The rules for function types apply recursively to function and function pointer parameters. Thus, a parameter with a type that is a pointer to a function that takes an int is equivalent to one with a type that is a pointer to a function that takes a const int parameter. Example 5-8 illustrates equivalent pointer types.

Example 5-8. Equivalent pointer types

```
int first(int const array[10]); // Size is ignored
int first(int const array[]);    // Equivalent declaration
int first(int const *array);     // Equivalent declaration
int first(int const *array)      // Definition
{
  return array[0];
}

int apply(int func(int), int arg);
int apply(int func(int const), int);        // Equivalent
int apply(int (*func)(int), int arg);       // Equivalent
int apply(int (*func)(int const), int arg)  // Definition
{
  return func(arg);
}
```

Because typedef declarations do not create new types, but only synonyms for existing types, parameters that differ only in their use of typedef types are equivalent, as shown in Example 5-9.

Example 5-9. Using typedef in equivalent parameter types

```
typedef int INT;
typedef int const CINT;
void func(int);
void func(INT);           // Equivalent
void func(INT const);     // Equivalent
void func(CINT);          // Equivalent
void func(signed int i)   // Definition
{
  std::cout << i;
}
```

You can declare a function type from a typedef, but you cannot use the typedef in a function definition. This usage is uncommon. For example:

```
    typedef int func(int, int);
    func add;                 // Declares int add(int, int);
    int add(int a, int b)     // Cannot use "func add" here
    {
      return a + b;
    }
```

Be careful to distinguish between a function type and a function pointer type. A function can be implicitly converted to a function pointer and can be called using a function pointer. A function pointer, however, cannot be used to declare a function. The following is an example of the implicit conversion of a function, add, to a function pointer, and the use of a function pointer, a, to call the function:

```
typedef func* funcptr;  // Pointer-to-function type
funcptr a = add;        // Pointer-to-function object
int i = a(1, 2);        // Call the function that a points to.
```

A *function signature* is similar to a function type, but it ignores the return type. Overload resolution relies on function signatures to determine which overloaded function to call. See "Function Overloading" later in this chapter.

Function Bodies and try Blocks

A function definition consists of a function declaration followed by a function body. The function body has one of two forms:

compound-statement
> Executed when the function is called. When execution reaches a return statement or the end of the compound statement, the function returns.

try *ctor-initializers compound-statement handlers*
> Sets up a try block that surrounds the constructor initializers and function body. If an exception is thrown from any of the *ctor-initializers*, it is handled by the handlers in the same manner as any exception thrown from the compound statement. Thus, this form is typically used only with constructors that have initializers. See Chapter 6 for more information about constructor initializers.

The constructor initializers in the second form are optional. Without them, the form can be used for any function. It is equivalent to having a try statement around the entire function body. Example 5-10 shows a try function body used in this way.

Example 5-10. A try function body

```
void func1()
try {
  // Statements
} catch (...) {
  // Handler
}

void func2()
{
  try {
    // Statements
  } catch(...) {
    // Handler
  }
}
```

Function Overloading

A single function name can have multiple declarations. If those declarations specify different function signatures, the function name is *overloaded*. A function call to an overloaded function requires the compiler to resolve the overloaded name and decide which function to call. The compiler uses the argument types (but not the return type) to resolve calls to overloaded functions. Example 5-11 shows simple examples of two overloaded functions named sqrt: one for int arguments and the other for double arguments. The rest of this section explains the rules for overloading and resolution.

Example 5-11. Overloaded functions

```
int sqrt(int);
double sqrt(double);

int main( )
{
  std::cout << sqrt(3) << '\n';    // sqrt(int)
  std::cout << sqrt(3.14) << '\n'; // sqrt(double)
}
```

Declaring Overloaded Functions

Whenever you declare more than one function with the same name in the same scope, you are overloading the function name. The function can be an ordinary function, member function, constructor, or overloaded operator.

Overloaded functions must differ in their parameter lists: they must have a different number of parameters, or the parameter types must be different. Refer to "Function Types and Signatures" earlier in this chapter for information on equivalent parameter types.

Default arguments are not considered when declaring overloaded functions (but are important when resolving a call to an overloaded function, as described in "Calling Overloaded Functions"). Example 5-12 shows overloaded constructors and member functions for the point class, and overloaded declarations for the add function.

Example 5-12. Overloaded constructors, member functions, and function declarations

```
class point {
public:
  point(int x = 0);        // Overloaded constructors
  point(int x, int y);
  point(const point& pt);
  // x and y are overloaded.
  int x()     const { return x_; }
  void x(int newx) { x_ = newx; }
  int y()     const { return y_; }
  void y(int newy) { y_ = newy; }
```

Example 5-12. Overloaded constructors, member functions, and function declarations (continued)

```
private:
  int x_, y_;
};

// add is overloaded.
int    add(int, int);
int    add(int);
double add(double, double);
double add(double);
long   add(long, long);
long   add(long);

// The following declarations are not overloaded, but are redeclarations of the
// add functions.
int  add(int a = 0, int b = 0);
long add(signed long, long signed);

long add(int, int); // Error: cannot overload on return type
```

Calling Overloaded Functions

A function call expression (Chapter 3) must identify the function being called, based on its name and arguments. For example, the simple expression f(x) might be a call to a function named f, a function call through a function pointer named f, a function template named f, the construction of an object of class f, a conversion of x to a type named f, or the invocation of the function call operator of an object named f. In each situation, the compiler might use different rules for interpreting f and x.

The compiler first uses the function name and context to create a list of *candidate functions*. The number and types of the arguments are used to select the best match from the candidates, and that function is the one that is called. If no match is found, the compiler reports an error. If more than one match ties for "best," the compiler reports an ambiguity error.

For example, the C++ standard library declares three different sqrt functions (see <cmath> in Chapter 13):

```
float sqrt(float);
double sqrt(double);
long double sqrt(long double);
```

Suppose you add another function named sqrt, such as the following, to apply it to each element of an array :

```
void sqrt(const double data[], size_t count);
```

In a function call to sqrt (e.g., sqrt(x)), the compiler first uses the ordinary rules of name lookup (Chapter 2) to find the first suitable object or function named sqrt. Suppose you used using namespace std; to import the standard sqrt functions into the same namespace as your sqrt function. The compiler would collect all the overloaded sqrt functions as the candidate list, which has four elements in this case (the three original functions plus the array version). The list is then pruned to eliminate functions with the wrong number of arguments. In this case, the array version of the function is eliminated because the expression has only one argument. Finally, the type of x is used to determine which function to call. If there is an exact match, the corresponding function is called. If x is, for example, an integer, the compiler reports an error because the three floating-point sqrt functions look equally good. If x has class type, and the class has a conversion function to one of the floating-point types, the compiler implicitly calls that conversion and then calls the corresponding function:

```
struct FixedPoint {
  ...
  operator long double( );
};
void demo( )
{
  FixedPoint x;
  std::cout << sqrt(x) << '\n'; // Prints a long double
}
```

If a candidate is a function template, the compiler deduces the argument types (see Chapter 7), and from that point on, the template instance is treated as a normal function.

The rules for creating the candidate list and argument list depend on the context of the function call. The argument list can also depend on context: when choosing an overloaded function to call, a member function's class is treated as an argument type. More precisely, member functions have an *implicit object parameter* whose type is a reference to *T*, in which *T* is the class that defines the member function. Any qualifiers on the member function also qualify the type (that is, the object type for a const function is const *T&*). In the function body, the type of this is a pointer to qualified *T*. (See Chapter 6 for more information about this.)

A call to a member function applies to a specific object, which is the *implicit object argument*. When calling a member function with the -> or . operator, the implicit object argument is the left operand. For an overloaded binary operator (such as operator<<), the implicit object argument is the left operand. For a unary operator, the implicit object argument is the operand. When calling an unqualified function inside a nonstatic member function, the implicit object argument is *this. The implicit object argument is considered the first argument in the argument list. Unlike normal arguments, implicit type conversions do not take place for the implicit object argument.

Candidate Functions

This section describes how the compiler creates its list of candidate functions. Table 5-1 summarizes the various categories of function calls, and the subsequent subsections provide the details.

Table 5-1. Function calls and candidate lists

Category	Function call syntax	Candidate functions
Qualified member function call	`expr . name ( args )` `expr -> name ( args )`	Member functions
Unqualified function call	`name ( args )` `expr ( args )`	Member functions Nonmember functions
Operator	`expr op expr`	Member functions Nonmember functions
Function-like initialization	`type name ( args )`	Constructors
Assignment-like initialization	`type name = expr`	Constructors Type conversion operators
Conversion initialization	`type name = expr`	Type conversion operators
Reference bound to initialization	`type& name = expr`	Type conversion operators

Qualified member function call

An expression that uses the . or -> operator to call a function must call a member function. The function name is looked up in the class of the left operand and in its base classes (using the name lookup rules listed in Chapter 2). The search starts in the most-derived class. If that class declares a member function with the desired name, the search stops, and the candidate functions are all the member functions with the same name in that class. If no matching member function is found, the search continues with the immediate base classes. The search stops when a matching name is found.

In other words, a derived class cannot overload a function that is declared in a base class. Instead, if the derived class has a function with the same name, the derived class hides the name that would be inherited from the base class (or the derived class might override a virtual function; see Chapter 6). Insert a using declaration in the derived class if you want the compiler to consider the base class functions as candidates, as shown in Example 5-13.

Example 5-13. Overloading inherited functions

```
#include <iostream>
#include <ostream>

class base {
public:
  void f(int) { std::cout << "f(int)\n"; }
  void g(int) { std::cout << "g(int)\n"; }

};

class derived : public base {
public:
  void f(double) { std::cout << "f(double)\n"; }
  void g(double) { std::cout << "g(double)\n"; }
  using base::g; // g(int) and g(double) are visible.
};
```

Example 5-13. Overloading inherited functions (continued)

```
int main( )
{
  derived d;

  d.f(3);   // Calls derived::f(double)
  d.g(42);  // Calls base::g(int)
}
```

If a class has multiple immediate base classes, overload resolution must find a
name in only one of the base classes. If functions with the desired name are found
in multiple immediate base classes, the compiler reports an ambiguity error. To
resolve this ambiguity, use the scope operator (::) to qualify the function name in
the derived class, as shown in Example 5-14.

Example 5-14. Avoiding ambiguous base-class overloads

```
struct base1 {
  void func(int);
};
struct base2 {
  void func(double);
};
struct derived : base1, base2 {
  // Call to overloaded func is ambiguous.
  void demo1(long x) { func(x); }
  // Qualify the name to resolve ambiguity.
  void demo2(long x) { base2::func(x); }
};
```

Unqualified function call

An ordinary-looking function call can be a nonmember function, a member function, an object of class type, a type name, or a variable of type pointer-to-function.
For a variable of type pointer-to-function, overload resolution takes place when a
value is assigned to the variable (discussed later in this chapter). In the other
cases, the usual name lookup rules apply when finding the candidate functions.

A function call in a member function searches first for matching member functions in the same class or an ancestor class. The search for a match begins in the
class that is declaring the member function. If a match is found, candidate functions are taken from that class. If no matches are found, the search continues with
ancestor classes, following the same rules as for qualified member function calls.
If no matches are found in any ancestor classes, the namespace of the class is
searched for nonmember functions. Example 5-15 shows how a matching
member function in a base class precludes finding a better match in the global
namespace.

Example 5-15. Finding candidate member functions

```
#include <iostream>
#include <ostream>
```

Example 5-15. Finding candidate member functions (continued)

```cpp
void proc(int x)
{
  std::cout << "proc(int:" << x << ")\n";
}

class base {
public:
  void f(int) { std::cout << "f(int)\n"; }
  void g(int) { std::cout << "g(int)\n"; }
  void proc(double) { std::cout << "base::proc(double)\n"; }
};

class derived : public base {
public:
  void f(double) { std::cout << "f(double)\n"; }
  void g(double x) {
    std::cout << "g(double)\n";
    proc(42); // Calls base::proc(double), not ::proc(int)
  }
  using base::g;
};

// Declared after derived, so call to proc() inside g() never sees this proc().
void proc(double x)
{
  std::cout << "proc(double:" << x << ")\n";
}

int main()
{
  derived d;
  d.g(3.14159); // Calls g(double)
}
```

If a function call expression resolves to an object of class type, the class must have a function call operator or a conversion operator, in which the conversion is to a function type: pointer-to-function, reference-to-function, or reference-to-pointer-to function.

A conversion operator is rarely used. The compiler constructs a wrapper function so that the conversion function is the first argument. The conversion type followed by the types of the actual arguments is the new list of argument types to use in overload resolution. In other words, all of a class's function-type conversion operators participate in overload resolution.

Example 5-16 shows how a class-type object is used as the left operand of a function call.

Example 5-16. Calling a class-type object as a function

```cpp
#include <iostream>
#include <ostream>
```

Example 5-16. Calling a class-type object as a function (continued)

```
typedef void (*strproc)(const char*);

void print(const char* str)
{
  std::cout << "const char*:" << str << '\n';
}

void print(int x)
{
  std::cout << "int:" << x << '\n';
}

void print(double x)
{
  std::cout << "double:" << x << '\n';
}

struct simple
{
  void operator()(int x)    { print(x); } // print(int)
  void operator()(double x) { print(x); } // print(double)
};

typedef void (*intfunc)(int);
typedef void (*dblfunc)(double);

struct indirect
{
  operator intfunc() { return print; } // print(int)
  operator dblfunc() { return print; } // print(double)
  operator strproc() { return print; } // print(const char*)
};

int main()
{
  simple sim;
  indirect ind;

  sim(42);                    // Prints "int:42"
  sim.operator()(42);         // Prints "int:42"
  sim(42.0);                  // Prints "double:42"
  ind(42);                    // Prints "int:42"
  ind.operator intfunc()(42); // Prints "int:42"
  ind(42.0);                  // Prints "double:42"
  ind("forty-two");           // Prints "const char*:forty-two"
}
```

Operator

The function for an overloaded operator is chosen according to the usual rules for resolving overloaded functions, in which the operator's operands are the function's arguments. You can overload operators only if at least one operand has a user-defined type. If all operands have built-in types, an operator has its built-in meaning.

If the left operand of an operator has class type, the operator can be a nonstatic member function or a nonmember function. Otherwise, the function must be a nonmember function. The operator function name is formed from the keyword operator followed by the operator symbol, e.g., operator[], operator++, or operator-. Unary operators can be member functions with no arguments or nonmember functions of one argument. Binary operators are member functions of one argument or nonmember functions of two arguments. Postfix increment and decrement operators are different. They are implemented as binary operators for which the right operand is an int. (See Chapter 3 for more information.)

The -> operator is also different. Although it is a binary operator, it is treated as a unary operator. It must be implemented as a member function, so the function takes no arguments. It returns a pointer or another object that overloads the -> operator. Ultimately, the overloaded operators must resolve to a pointer of class type, to which the built-in -> operator can be applied.

The candidate functions for the overloaded operator include all member, nonmember, and built-in candidate functions. Member functions do not take precedence over nonmember functions.

Example 5-17 shows how operator functions are different from named functions. In particular, it shows how operators are resolved by considering member functions and global functions, whereas named member functions take precedence over named global functions.

Example 5-17. Calling overloaded operators

```
class demo
{
public:
  demo(int v) : value_(v) {}

  demo add(const demo& d) const;
  demo sub(const demo& d) const;
  demo mul(const demo& d) const;
  demo operator+(const demo& d) const;
  demo operator-(const demo& d) const;
  demo operator*(const demo& d) const;
  operator int( ) const { return value_; }
private:
  int value_;
};

// Silly examples, but illustrative
demo add(const demo& a) { return a; }
demo mul(const demo& a) { return a; }
demo div(const demo& a) { return a; }

demo operator+(const demo& a, const demo& b)
{
```

Example 5-17. Calling overloaded operators (continued)

```
  return a.operator+(b); // Force use of member function.
}

demo demo::add(const demo& d)
const
{
  return *this + d; // Error: calls ::operator+( ) or demo::operator+( )?
}

demo demo::sub(const demo& d) const
{
  return this->operator-(d); // Member operator
}

demo demo::mul(const demo& d) const
{
    return ::operator*(*this, d); // Global operator
}

demo demo::operator+(const demo& d) const
{
  return demo(int(*this) + int(d));
}

demo demo::operator-(const demo& d) const
{
  return sub(d); // Calls demo::sub (recurses infinitely)
}

demo demo::operator*(const demo& d) const
{
  return ::mul(d); // Scopes operator to call global mul( )
}
```

Function-like initialization

An object can be initialized using function-like syntax (see Chapter 2). When an object of class type is so initialized, the candidate functions are constructors of the named class. The same syntax applies to conversion initialization covered later in this chapter. Example 5-18 shows function-like initializers that call an overloaded constructor.

Example 5-18. Calling an overloaded constructor

```
class point {
public:
  point( ) : x_(0), y_(0) {}
  point(int x) : x_(x), y_(0) {}
  point(int x, int y): x_(x), y_(y) {}
private:
  int x_, y_;
};
```

Example 5-18. Calling an overloaded constructor (continued)

```
point p1(42);
point p2(4, 2);
point p3(p1);
```

Assignment-like initialization

An object can be initialized using assignment-like syntax (see Chapter 2). The candidate functions for "T x = i" are single-argument, non-explicit constructors of T. If i has class type, the candidates are conversion functions that convert i to type T, as shown in Example 5-19. The compiler is free to call T's copy constructor to copy a temporary T object to x. Even if the compiler optimizes away this extra copy, T must have an accessible copy constructor.

Example 5-19. Resolving assignment-like initialization

```
class point {
public:
  point( ) : x_(0), y_(0) {}
  point(int x) : x_(x), y_(0) {}
  point(int x, int y) : x_(x), y_(y) {}
  int x( ) const { return x_; }
  int y( ) const { return y_; }
private:
  int x_, y_;
};

class dot {
public:
  dot(int x, int y) : center_(point(x, y)) {}
  dot(const point& center) : center_(center) {}
  operator point( ) const { return center_; }
private:
  point center_;
};

point p1 = 3;      // Invokes point(int) constructor
point p2 = 4.2;    // Converts 4.2 to 4, and invokes point(int)
dot   d1 = p1;     // Invokes dot(const point&) constructor
point p3 = d1;     // Invokes dot::operator point( ) and implicit
                   // point(const point&) copy constructor
```

Conversion initialization

An object that does not have class type can be initialized with an object of class type. The candidate functions are the conversion functions of that class type. Example 5-20 shows two cases of conversion initialization. In the first, the object c is initialized with an rbnode<int> object, n, and the compiler calls operator color( ). The second invokes operator T( ), in which T is int, to initialize i to the value 42.

Example 5-20. Initializing non-class-type objects by calling conversion functions

```
enum color { red, black };

template<typename T>
class rbnode {
public:
  rbnode(const T& value, color c);
  operator color() const { return color_; }
  operator T() const { return value_; }
private:
  T value_;
  color color_;
};

rbnode<int> n(42, black);

color c = n;
int i = n;
```

Reference bound to conversion

Similar to initializing an object of non-class type with an expression of class type, you can initialize a reference to an lvalue that results from a conversion function and initialize a const reference to an rvalue. Most conversion operators do not return lvalues, so the const reference version of this rule is used more often. Example 5-21 shows some examples of binding references to conversions. The object c1 is bound to a temporary copy of n.color_, and i1 is bound directly to n.value_.

Example 5-21. Binding references to conversion lvalues

```
enum color { red, black };

template<typename T>
class rbnode {
public:
  rbnode(const T& value, color c);
  operator color()  { return color_; }
  operator T&()     { return value_; }
private:
  T value_;
  color color_;
};

rbnode<int> n(42, black);
const color& c1 = n;
int& i1 = n;
```

Addresses of Overloaded Functions

When taking the address of a function, the compiler does not have the benefit of an argument list to help resolve overloading. Instead, it collects a list of candidate functions and picks one based on the type required by the context. The context can be an initializer, an assignment, a function argument, the return value of a function, or an explicit type cast.

Of the potentially matching functions, nontemplate functions are better than template functions, and more-specific template functions are better than less-specific template functions. There must be exactly one best function, or else the compiler reports an error. Example 5-22 shows simple examples of resolving the addresses of overloaded functions.

Example 5-22. Taking the address of an overloaded function

```
int abs(int);
long abs(long);
double abs(double);

template<typename T>
T abs(T x);

template<typename T, typename U>
T abs(T x, U = U( ));

int main( )
{
  int (*intfunc)(int) = &abs;          // abs(int)
  double (*dblfunc)(double) = &abs;    // abs(double)
  float (*fltfunc)(float) = &abs;      // abs<float>
  short (*shrtfunc1)(short, int) = &abs; // abs<short,int>
  short (*shrtfunc2)(short) = &abs;    // abs<short>
}
```

Best Overloaded Function

Once the compiler has found the list of candidate functions, it must choose the "best" match from the list. The candidate list is first pruned by removing functions with the wrong number of arguments. Then the remaining functions are checked to determine how to convert the actual arguments to the desired parameter types. The function with the simplest conversions wins. This section discusses these two steps.

Pruning the candidate list

Once the compiler has assembled its list of candidate functions, it prunes the list by removing functions that have the wrong number of arguments. If the function call has *n* argument expressions, a function is kept in the list if any of the following apply:

- It has exactly *n* parameters.
- It has fewer than *n* parameters followed by an ellipsis parameter.
- It has more than *n* parameters, and the extra parameters have default arguments.

Also, each actual argument must be convertible (applying the rules described in the next section) to the parameter type.

Overloading Versus Default Arguments

Overloading functions can have the same effect as using default arguments. The question is when to use overloading and when to use default arguments. As usual, the answer is, "It depends."

If a default argument is complicated, you are probably better off using overloading. With default arguments, the complicated code would be duplicated at every function call. With overloading, you can concentrate it at a single point.

Ask yourself whether it makes sense to omit arguments, starting from the right. If so, you might be able to use default arguments. If some arguments cannot be omitted singly, you might need to use overloading. In the following example, omitting y without also omitting x is unusual:

```
void circle(float radius, float x, float y);
void circle(float radius); // x=0, y=0
```

If a function is complicated, you might want to use default arguments so you can write the function only once. Even if you use overloading, write a single base function and let the overloaded functions call the base function:

```
class shape {
public:
  // Using default arguments keeps the code simple because there is
  // only one constructor.
  explicit shape(color c = black, size s = 1);
  ...
};
```

Choosing the best function

Of the remaining candidate functions, the "best" function is the one that is called. If multiple functions are tied for best, the compiler reports an error. The best function is found by comparing the implicit type conversion sequences needed for each argument type (and possibly an implicit object argument). As described in the next section, some sequences are better than others. When comparing two functions, the better function is the one with the better conversion sequences:

- If two functions A and B have argument conversion sequences that are equally good, but A has at least one argument with a better sequence, A is the better function.

- If all the argument conversion sequences are equally good, a nontemplate function is better than a template function.

- If the conversion sequences for two template functions are equally good, a more-specific template function is better than a less-specific template function.

Argument conversion sequences

An actual argument is implicitly converted to the desired parameter type by undergoing a series of transformations. Basically, a better conversion is one in which the argument type is closer to the parameter type and, therefore, the type undergoes fewer transformations.

A *standard conversion sequence* is a sequence of built-in transformations that are based on automatic type conversions (Chapter 3). A sequence is built from at most one of each of three kinds of transformations. The quality of a standard conversion sequence is dictated by its worst transformation, in which the value-preserving transformations are better than those that might discard information. The transformations are as follows, ordered from best to worst:

Lvalue transformation and qualification adjustment
> An lvalue transformation is the conversion of an array to a pointer, an lvalue to an rvalue, or a function to a function pointer. A qualification adjustment is adding const or volatile qualifiers to match the parameter. These transformations are just as good as no transformation at all:
> ```
> void func1(const int& x);
> void func2(const char* str);
> func1(42);
> func2("Hello");
> ```

Promotion
> The built-in type promotions are listed in Chapter 3. In general, type promotions are from smaller types to larger types, so information cannot be lost:
> ```
> void func3(long l);
> func3(42);
> ```

Conversion
> A built-in type conversion is one that might lose information, such as converting a number to a smaller type, or a floating point to an integer. Certain conversions are better than others:
> - A conversion of a pointer to bool is worse than other conversions.
> - Converting a derived-class pointer to a base-class pointer is better than converting the pointer to void*.
> - Converting a derived-class pointer to void* is better than converting a base-class pointer to void*.
> - When converting classes, class pointers, and pointers to members, shorter distances in a class hierarchy are better than longer distances; for example, if A inherits from B and B inherits from C, A* to B* is better than A* to C*.

The following are some examples of conversion transformations:
```
void func4(bool b);
func4(3.14);
void func5(void* ptr);
func5(&x);
```

A *user-defined conversion sequence* has up to three parts: a standard conversion sequence followed by a single, user-defined conversion (constructor or type conversion operator) followed by another standard conversion sequence.

A standard conversion sequence is better than a user-defined conversion sequence. A user-defined conversion sequence is better than matching an ellipsis parameter.

If one sequence of transformations is a subsequence of another, the shorter sequence is better than the longer one.

Among sequences that differ only by qualification, the one with fewer qualification adjustments is better than one with more adjustments.

Example 5-23 shows how overloaded functions are chosen. Notice that type promotions are preferred to the conversion to Num, even though Num has an exact type conversion to long. Also note how an unsigned long cannot be promoted, so it must undergo a built-in conversion. The compiler has no preference of int, long or double, so the conversion is ambiguous and, therefore, results in an error. The same applies to long double; even though you might consider the conversion to double to be "better" than conversion to int, the rules of overloading say otherwise. The final example results in an error because there is no matching function. An array of wchar_t cannot be converted to any of the types used as func parameters.

Example 5-23. Resolving overloaded functions

```
#include <string>

void func(double);
void func(long);
void func(int);
void func(const std::string&);

class Num {
public:
  Num(int i) : num_(i) {}
  operator long() const { return num_; }
private:
  int num_;
};

int main()
{
  short n = 42;
  func(n);                // func(int)
  func(Num(n));           // func(long)
  func(true);             // func(int)
  func(3.1415f);          // func(double)
  func("string");         // func(string);
  std::string s("string");
  func(s);                // func(string);
  func(3.14159L);         // Error: ambiguous
```

Example 5-23. Resolving overloaded functions (continued)

```
  func(42UL);        // Error: ambiguous
  func(L"widestr");  // Error: no match
}
```

Operator Overloading

For user-defined types (classes and enumerations), you can define alternate behavior for the C++ operators. This is called overloading the operators. You cannot define new operators, and not all operators can be overloaded. Table 5-2 lists all the operators and indicates which can be overloaded. For these, it shows whether the overload must be a member function. Overloaded operators that are implemented as member functions must be nonstatic member functions.

Table 5-2. Operators and overloading

Operator	Meaning	Overloading permitted?	Must be member function?
+	Addition, unary plus	yes	no
&	Address of	yes	no
[ ]	Array subscript	yes	yes
&=	Assign bitwise and	yes	no
^=	Assign bitwise exclusive or	yes	no
|=	Assign bitwise or	yes	no
-=	Assign difference	yes	no
<<=	Assign left shift	yes	no
=	Assignment	yes	yes
*=	Assign product	yes	no
/=	Assign quotient	yes	no
%=	Assign remainder	yes	no
>>=	Assign right shift	yes	no
+=	Assign sum	yes	no
&	Bitwise and	yes	no
~	Bitwise complement	yes	no
^	Bitwise exclusive or	yes	no
|	Bitwise or	yes	no
? :	Conditional	no	N/A
new	Create dynamic object	yes	no
new[ ]	Create dynamic array	yes	no
--	Decrement	yes	no
delete	Destroy dynamic object	yes	no
delete[ ]	Destroy dynamic array	yes	no
/	Division	yes	no
==	Equal	yes	no
( )	Function call	yes	yes

Table 5-2. Operators and overloading (continued)

Operator	Meaning	Overloading permitted?	Must be member function?
>	Greater than	yes	no
>=	Greater than or equal	yes	no
++	Increment	yes	no
<<	Left shift	yes	no
<	Less than	yes	no
<=	Less than or equal	yes	no
&&	Logical and	yes	no
!	Logical complement	yes	no
||	Logical or	yes	no
.*	Member reference	no	N/A
->*	Member reference	yes	yes
.	Member reference	no	N/A
->	Member reference	yes	yes
*	Multiplication, dereference	yes	no
!=	Not equal	yes	no
%	Remainder	yes	no
>>	Right shift	yes	no
::	Scope	no	N/A
,	Serial evaluation	yes	no
-	Subtraction, negation	yes	no
type	Type conversion	yes	yes

An overloaded operator is a function in which the function name has the form operator followed by the operator symbol, or in the case of a type conversion member function, a list of type specifiers (with pointer, reference, and array operators). For example, the following code declares functions to overload the ! and && operators:

```
enum logical { no, maybe, yes };
logical operator !(logical x);
logical operator &&(logical a, logical b);
```

Some overloaded operators must be member functions, and others can be member or nonmember functions (as shown in Table 5-2). When you define a member function, the object is always the lefthand operand. A unary operator, therefore, takes no arguments because the one operand is the object itself. Likewise, a binary operator takes one argument: the righthand operand; the lefthand operand is the object. For a nonmember function, a unary operator takes one argument and a binary operator takes two arguments: the first argument is the lefthand operand, and the second is the righthand operand.

Use overloaded operators as you would built-in operators. You can also use function notation, in which the function name is operator followed by the operator

Functions

symbol, but this usage is uncommon. You can use the function notation with built-in operators, too, but such usage is extremely uncommon. For example:

```
operator-(42, 10) // Same as 42 - 10
operator-(33)     // Same as -33
```

The usual rules for resolving overloaded functions applies to overloaded operators. The only difference is that the built-in operators are added to the list of candidates along with the user-defined operators. Remember that you cannot overload operators when all the operands have fundamental types. At least one operand must have a user-defined type (class or enumeration).

Defining Commutative Operators

When overloading a binary operator, consider whether the operator should be commutative ($a + b$ is the same as $b + a$). If that is the case, you might need to define two overloaded operators:

```
enum priority { idle, low, normal, high };
// Adding an integer to a priority commutes. For example:
//    setpriority(priority( ) + 2);
//    setpriority(2 + priority( ));
priority operator+(priority p, int i);
priority operator+(int i, priority p);
// Subtracting an integer from a priority does not commute. For
// example:
//    setpriority(priority( ) - 1);
priority operator-(priority p, int i);
```

Short-Circuit Operators

A key difference between the overloaded operators and the built-in operators is that the logical && and || operators are *short-circuit operators*. If the expression result is known by evaluating only the left operand, the right operand is never evaluated. For overloaded operators, all operands are evaluated before a function is called, so short-circuit evaluation is impossible.

In other words, you cannot tell whether the && and || operators perform short-circuit evaluation by merely glancing at them. You must study the types of the operands. It is safest, therefore, never to overload these operators. If the operators are never overloaded, you know that they are always short-circuit operators.

Comma Operator

You can overload the comma operator (,), but you will rarely have any reason to do so. If you do, however, you change its semantics in a subtle way. The built-in comma operator has a sequence point (see Chapter 3) between its operands, so you know that the lefthand expression is completely evaluated before the righthand

---

expression. If you overload the operator, you lose that guarantee. The ordinary rules apply, so the operands might be evaluated in any order.

Increment and Decrement

When overloading the increment and decrement operators, remember that they have two forms: prefix and postfix. To distinguish between the two forms, the postfix form takes an additional int parameter. The compiler always passes 0 as the additional argument. Example 5-24 shows one way to overload the increment operator. (Decrement is analogous.)

Example 5-24. Overloading the increment operator

```
enum status { stopped, running, waiting };
status& operator++(status& s) { // Prefix
  if (s != waiting)
    s = status(s + 1);
  return s;
}
status operator++(status& s, int) {    // Postfix
  status rtn = s;
  ++s;
  return rtn;
}
int main( )
{
  status s(stopped);
  ++s;                  // Calls operator++(s);
  s++;                  // Calls operator++(s, 0);
}
```

Member Reference

The -> operator is different from the other operators. Although you use it as a binary operator, you overload it as a unary operator. It must be implemented as a member function, so the function takes no arguments. It must return one of the following:

- An object of class type, for which the type overloads the -> operator
- A pointer to a class type

A chain of -> operators is followed until it ends with a pointer to a class type. The actual right operand must name a member of that class. The -> operator is most often overloaded to implement a smart pointer. See the auto_ptr<> template in the <memory> section of Chapter 13 for an example.

Function Call

The function call operator (operator( )) takes any number of arguments. It must be implemented as a member function. To invoke the operator, use an object of class type as the "name" of the function. Pass the arguments as you would any other function arguments. With a simple variable of class type, the syntax looks like an ordinary function call.

An object that overloads the function call operator is often called a *functor*. Functors are typically used with the standard algorithms to better encapsulate functionality. Some algorithms, such as for_each, also permit the functor to store state information, which cannot be done with a plain function. Comparison functions for the associative containers are easier to implement as functors. See <algorithm> and <functional> in Chapter 13 for examples.

operator new and operator delete

A new expression (Chapter 3) calls operator new to allocate memory, and a delete expression calls operator delete. (A new[] expression calls operator new[], and a delete[] expression calls operator delete[]. For the sake of simplicity, whenever I refer to a new expression, I mean a new expression or new[] expression. Similarly, operator new refers to operator new and operator new[]. Ditto for delete.)

You can overload operator new and operator delete in the global scope or as members of a class. In the global scope, the functions must not be static, nor can you declare them in a namespace. When you define these operators as member functions, the functions are always static, even if you omit the static specifier. If you do not overload the global operators, the C++ library provides an implementation for you. (See <new> in Chapter 13.) If you do not overload the operators for a class, the global operators are used.

If a class overloads the operator new and operator delete functions, the corresponding operator functions are called for new and delete expressions involving that class. When overloading operator new or operator delete as member functions or with placement arguments, you can call the global operator, as shown in Example 5-25.

Example 5-25. Overloading operator new and operator delete

```
#include <cstddef>
#include <iostream>
#include <memory>
#include <new>
#include <ostream>

class demo
{
public:
  static void* operator new(std::size_t size)
  throw (std::bad_alloc)
  {
    std::cout << "demo::new\n";
    if (instance == 0)
      instance = ::new demo;
    ++count;
    return instance;
  }
  static void operator delete(void* p) {
```

Example 5-25. Overloading operator new and operator delete (continued)

```
    std::cout << "demo::delete\n";
    if (--count == 0) {
        ::delete instance;
        instance = 0;
    }
}

static demo* make( ) { return new demo( ); }

private:
    demo( ) {}
    demo(const demo&);
    static demo* instance;
    static std::size_t count;
};

demo* demo::instance;
std::size_t demo::count;

int main( )
{
    std::auto_ptr<demo> s1(demo::make( ));
    std::auto_ptr<demo> s2(demo::make( ));
    return s1.get( ) == s2.get( );
}
```

The first parameter to operator new has type size_t and is the amount of memory to allocate. The function returns a pointer to the allocated memory as a void*. Additional parameters are allowed for placement new functions (see Chapter 3). The first parameter to operator delete is a void* pointer to the memory; the function returns void. Additional parameters are allowed for placement delete. See <new> in Chapter 13 for more information about overloaded operator new and operator delete.

When you overload the operator new and operator delete functions, you will probably want to overload the scalar (operator new) and array versions (operator new[]) of the operator. The scalar and array versions often behave identically, but you have the option of making them behave differently. Note that the compiler initializes the objects, so your allocation or deallocation function does not need to know the number of objects being allocated or freed.

If you overload operator new, you should probably also overload operator delete. In the case of placement new, the corresponding placement delete function is called if an exception is thrown while constructing the newly allocated object or array. Without a corresponding placement delete function, no operator delete function is called. This is the only time a placement delete function is called. A delete expression always calls the plain, single-argument form of operator delete.

Type Conversion

A class can declare type conversion operators to convert class-type objects to other types. The operator functions must be nonstatic member functions. The name of each operator is the desired type, which can be a series of type specifiers with pointer, reference, and array operators, but cannot be a function or array type:

```
class bigint {
public:
  operator long( ); // Convert object to type long.
  operator unsigned long( );
  operator const char*( ); // Return a string representation
  ...
};
```

The main Function

Every program must have a function in the global namespace called main, which is the main program. This function must return type int. The C++ environment calls main; your program must never call main. The main function cannot be declared inline or static. It can be called with no arguments or with two arguments:

```
int main( )
```

or:

```
int main(int argc, char* argv[])
```

The argc parameter is the number of command-line arguments, and argv is an array of pointers to the command-line arguments, which are null-terminated character strings. By definition, argv[argc] is a null pointer. The first element of the array (argv[0]) is the program name or an empty string.

An implementation is required to support at least two forms of main: one that takes no parameters, and one that takes the two parameters for command-line arguments. An implementation can support other forms of main. The standard recommends that the first two parameters should be the same as they are in the standard, and that additional parameters follow them.

Static objects at namespace scope can have constant or dynamic initial values, those of POD type with constant values are initialized by constant data before the program starts, and those with dynamic values are initialized by code when the program begins. When, exactly, the objects are initialized is implementation-defined. It might happen before main is called, or it might be after.

You should avoid writing code that depends on the order in which static objects are initialized. If you cannot avoid it, you can work around the problem by defining a class that performs the required initialization and defining a static instance of your class. For example, you can guarantee that the standard I/O

---

stream objects are created early so they can be used in the constructor of a static object. See <ios> in Chapter 13 for more information and an example.

A local static object is initialized when execution first reaches its declaration. If the function is never called, or if execution never reaches the declaration, the object is never initialized.

When main returns or when exit is called (see <cstdlib> in Chapter 13), static objects are destroyed in the reverse order of their construction, and the program terminates. All local, static objects are also destroyed. If a function that contains a local, static object is called during the destruction of static objects, the behavior is undefined.

The value returned from main is passed to the host environment. You can return 0 or EXIT_SUCCESS (declared in <cstdlib>) to indicate success, or EXIT_FAILURE to tell the environment that the program failed. Other values are implementation-defined. Some environments ignore the value returned from main; others rely on the value.

6

Classes

C++ supports object-oriented programming with a traditional, statically-typed, class-based object model. That is, a class defines the behavior and the state of objects that are instances of the class. Classes can inherit behavior from ancestor classes. Virtual functions implement type polymorphism, that is, a variable can be declared as a pointer or reference to a base class, and at runtime it can take on the value of any class derived from that base class. C++ also supports C-style structures and unions using the same mechanism as classes. This chapter describes classes in all their glory. For information about class templates, see Chapter 7. Member functions are a special kind of function; see Chapter 5 for general information about functions.

The syntax descriptions in this chapter are informal. See Chapter 12 for a precise BNF grammar.

Class Definitions

A class definition starts with the class, struct, or union keyword. The difference between a class and a struct is the default access level. (See "Access Specifiers" later in this chapter for details.) A union is like a struct for which the storage of all the data members overlap, so you can use only one data member at a time. (See "Unions" later in this section for details.)

A class definition can list any number of base classes, some or all of which might be virtual. (See "Inheritance" later in this chapter for information about base classes and virtual base classes.)

In the class definition are declarations for data members (called instance variables or fields in some other languages), member functions (sometimes called methods), and nested types.

A class definition defines a scope, and the class members are declared in the class scope. The class name itself is added to the class scope, so a class cannot have any members, nested types, or enumerators that have the same name as the class. As with any other declaration, the class name is also added to the scope in which the class is declared.

You can declare a name as a class, struct, or union without providing its full definition. This incomplete class declaration lets you use the class name in pointers and references but not in any context in which the full definition is needed. You need a complete class definition when declaring a nonpointer or nonreference object, when using members of the class, and so on. An incomplete class declaration has a number of uses:

Forward class declarations
> If two classes refer to each other, you can declare one as an incomplete class, then provide the full definitions of both:
> ```
> class graphics_context;
> class bitmap {
>   ...
>   void draw(graphics_context*);
>   ...
> };
> class graphics_context {
>   ...
>   bitblt(const bitmap&);
>   ...
> };
> ```

Opaque types
> Sometimes a class uses hidden helper classes. The primary class can hold a pointer to an incomplete helper class, and you do not need to publish the definition of the helper class. Instead, the definition might be hidden in a library. This is sometimes called a *pimpl* (for a number of reasons, one of which is "pointer to implementation"). For example:
> ```
> class bigint {
> public:
>   bigint();
>   ~bigint();
>   bigint(const bigint&);
>   bigint& operator=(const bigint&);
>   ...
> private:
>   class bigint_impl;
>   std::auto_ptr<bigint_impl> pImpl_;
> };
> ```

For a complete discussion of the pimpl idiom, see *More Exceptional C++*, by Herb Sutter (Addison-Wesley).

Example 6-1 shows several different class definitions.

Example 6-1. Class definitions

```cpp
#include <string>

struct point {
  double x, y;
};

class shape {
public:
  shape();
  virtual ~shape();
  virtual void draw();
};

class circle : public shape {
public:
  circle(const point& center, double radius);
  point center() const;
  double radius() const;
  void move_to(const point& new_center);
  void resize(double new_radius);
  virtual void draw();
private:
  point center_;
  double radius_;
};

class integer {
public:
  typedef int value_type;
  int value() const;
  void set_value(int value);
  std::string to_string() const;
private:
  int value_;
};

class real {
public:
  typedef double value_type;
  double value() const;
  void set_value(double value);
  std::string to_string() const;
private:
  double value_;
};

union number {
  number(int value);
  number(double value);
  integer i;
  real    r;
};
```

In C, a struct or union name is not automatically a type name, as it is in C++. A variable declaration in C, for example, would need to be elaborated as struct demo x instead of simply demo x. There is no harm in using the fully elaborated form in C++, and this is often done in headers that are meant to be portable between C and C++.

There are times, even in C++, when the fully elaborated form is needed, such as when a function or object declaration hides a class name. In this case, use the elaborated form to refer to the class name. For example, the POSIX API has a structure named stat, which is hidden by a function stat:

```
extern "C" int stat(const char* filename, struct stat* st);
int main(int argc, char* argv[])
{
  struct stat st;
  if (argc > 1 && stat(argv[1], &st) == 0) show_stats(st);
}
```

See Chapter 2 for more information about elaborated type specifiers.

Plain Old Data

Some programming languages differentiate between records and classes. Typically, a record is a simple storage container that lacks the more complex features of a class (inheritance, virtual functions, etc.). In C++, classes serve both purposes, but you can do things with simple classes (called POD, for *plain old data*) that you cannot do with complicated classes.

Basically, a POD class is a structure that is compatible with C. More precisely, a POD class or union does not have any of the following:

- User-defined constructors
- User-defined destructor
- User-defined copy assignment operator
- Virtual functions
- Base classes
- Private or protected nonstatic members
- Nonstatic data members that are references

Also, all nonstatic data members must have POD type. A POD type is a fundamental type, an enumerated type, a POD class or union, or a pointer to or array of POD types

Unlike C structures, a POD class can have static data members, nonvirtual functions, and nested types (members that do not affect the data layout in an object).

POD classes are often used when compatibility with C is required. In that case, you should avoid using any access specifier labels because they can alter the layout of data members within an object. (A POD class cannot have private or protected members, but you can have multiple public: access specifier labels and still have a class that meets the standard definition of a POD class.)

Example 6-2 shows POD types (point1 and info) and non-POD types (point2 and employee).

Example 6-2. Declaring POD and non-POD types

```
struct point1 {                     // POD
  int x, y;
};

class point2 {                      // Not POD
public:
  point2(int x, int y);
private:
  int x, y;
};

struct info {                       // POD
  static const int max_size = 50;
  char name[max_size];
  bool is_name_valid() const;
  bool operator<(const info& i); // Compare names.
};

struct employee : info {            // Not POD
  int salary;
};
```

The virtue of a POD object is that it is just a contiguous area of storage that stores some value or values. Thus, it can be copied byte for byte and retain its value. In particular, a POD object can be safely copied to an array of char or unsigned char, and when copied back, it retains its original value. A POD object can also be copied by calling memcpy; the copy has the same value as the original.

A local POD object without an initializer is left uninitialized, but a non-POD object is initialized by calling its default constructor. Similarly, a POD type in a new expression is uninitialized, but a new non-POD object is initialized by calling its default constructor. If you supply an empty initializer to a new expression or other expression that constructs a POD object, the POD object is initialized to 0.

A POD class can contain padding between data members, but no padding appears before the first member. Therefore, a pointer to the POD object can be converted (with reinterpret_cast<>) into a pointer to the first element.

A goto statement can safely branch into a block, skipping over declarations of uninitialized POD objects. A goto that skips any other declaration in the block results in undefined behavior. (See Chapter 2 for more information about initializing POD objects, and Chapter 4 for more information about the goto statement.)

Trivial Classes

A *trivial class* is another form of restricted class (or union). It cannot have any of the following:

- User-defined constructors
- User-defined destructor
- User-defined copy assignment operator
- Virtual functions
- Virtual base classes

Also, all base classes must be trivial, and all nonstatic data members must be trivial or have non-class type. Unlike POD classes, a trivial class can have base classes, private and protected members, and members with reference type.

Trivial classes are important only because members of a union must be trivial. Fundamental types are trivial, as are pointers to and arrays of trivial types.

Unions

A union is like a struct, but with the following restrictions:

- It cannot have base classes.
- It cannot be a base class.
- It cannot have virtual functions.
- It cannot have static data members.
- Its data members cannot be references.
- All of its data members must be trivial.

An object of union type has enough memory to store the largest member, and all data members share that memory. In other words, a union can have a value in only one data member at a time. It is your responsibility to keep track of which data member is "active."

A union can be declared without a name (an *anonymous* union), in which case it must have only nonstatic data members (no member functions, no nested types). The members of an anonymous union are effectively added to the scope in which the union is declared. That scope must not declare any identifiers with the same names as the union's members. In this way, an anonymous union reduces the nesting that is needed to get to the union members, as shown in Example 6-3.

Example 6-3. An anonymous union

```
struct node {
  enum kind { integer, real, string } kind;
  union {
    int intval;
    double realval;
    char strval[8];
  };
};

node* makeint(int i)
{
  node* rtn = new node;
  rtn->kind = node::integer;
```

Example 6-3. An anonymous union (continued)

```
  rtn->intval = i;
  return rtn;
}
```

 Unions are used less often in C++ than in C. Two common uses for unions in C have been supplanted with other alternatives in C++:

- Unions can be used to peek inside the data representation for certain types, but a reinterpret_cast<> can do the same thing.

- Unions were sometimes used to save memory when storing different kinds of data in a structure, but inheritance is safer and offers more flexibility.

Local Classes

You can declare a local class, that is, a class definition that is local to a block in a function body. A local class has several restrictions when compared to nonlocal classes:

- A local class cannot have static data members.

- Member functions must be defined inline in the class definition.

- You cannot refer to nonstatic objects from within a local class, but you can refer to local static objects, local enumerators, and functions that are declared locally.

- A local class cannot be used as a template argument, so you cannot use a local functor with the standard algorithms.

Local classes are not used often. Example 6-4 shows one use of a local class.

Example 6-4. A local class

```
// Take a string and break it up into tokens, storing the tokens in a vector.
void get_tokens(std::vector<std::string>& tokens, const std::string& str)
{
  class tokenizer {
  public:
    tokenizer(const std::string& str) : in_(str) {}
    bool next()
    {
      return in_ >> token_;
    }
    std::string token() const { return token_; }
  private:
    std::istringstream in_;
    std::string token_;
  };

  tokens.clear();
  tokenizer t(str);
  while (t.next())
    tokens.push_back(t.token());
}
```

Data Members

A class can have static and nonstatic data members. The static storage class specifies a static data member; with no storage class, a data member is nonstatic. No other storage class specifier is allowed. Every object has its own copy of the class's nonstatic data members, and they share a single copy of each static data member. A data member can also be declared with *cv*-qualifiers. See Chapter 2 for more information about storage class specifiers and *cv*-qualifiers.

You declare data members as you would local variables in a function, except you cannot usually supply initializers. Instead, nonstatic data members are initialized in the class's constructors. See "Member Functions" later in this chapter for details.

Data members are typically declared at the private access level. See "Access Specifiers" later in this chapter for details.

Data Layout

Nonstatic data members are organized so that members declared later have higher addresses than those declared earlier. Access specifier labels, however, can interrupt the order, and the relative order of members separated by an access specifier label is implementation-defined. Writing code that depends on the layout of a class is usually a bad idea, but when interfacing with external code, it is sometimes unavoidable. See "POD Types" earlier in this chapter for more information.

The layout of base-class subobjects within a derived-class object is also unspecified. If a base class appears more than once in the inheritance graph, it will have multiple copies of its data members in the derived-class object, unless the inheritance is virtual. See "Inheritance" later in this chapter for more information.

Individual data members might have specific alignment requirements, so the compiler can insert padding between members. Thus, adjacent member declarations might not have adjacent addresses.

Even if a class has no nonstatic data members, the size of the object is guaranteed to be greater than zero. If the class is used as a base class, however, the compiler can optimize the base-class subobject so it has a size of 0 within the derived class.

Mutable Data Members

A nonstatic data member can be declared with the mutable type specifier. A mutable member can be changed even when the object is const.

Mutable members are often used to implement a class that can have objects that are logically constant, even if they are not physical constants. For example, a class can implement a private cache with a mutable data member. Suppose you are writing a class, bigint, that implements very large integers. The to_double member function computes an approximation of the value as a floating-point number. Instead of computing this value each time to_double is called, the bigint class saves the value after the first call and returns the cached value for the second and subsequent calls. When calling to_double for a const bigint, you still want to

Classes

be able to modify the `bigint` object to cache the floating-point value, so the cache is declared `mutable`, as shown in Example 6-5.

Example 6-5. Caching a value in a mutable data member

```cpp
class bigint {
public:
  bigint() : has_approx_(false) { ... }
  double to_double()
  const
  {
    if (! has_approx_) {
      approx_ = as_double();
      has_approx_ = true;
    }
    return approx_;

  }
  ...
private:
  double as_double() const;
  mutable double approx_;
  mutable bool has_approx_;
  ...
};
```

Bit-Fields

A nonstatic data member can be a *bit-field*, which is a sequence of bits packed into an object. The declarator for a bit-field uses a colon followed by an integral constant expression, which specifies the number of bits in the field. Example 6-6 shows the layout of the control word for an Intel x87 floating-point processor. (Whether this struct definition accurately maps to the actual control word layout is implementation-defined, but using the x87 control word is inherently nonportable, anyway.)

Example 6-6. Using bit-fields for a control word

```cpp
// Intel x87 FPU control word.
struct fpu_control {
  enum precision_control { single, double_prec=2, extended };
  enum rounding_control  { nearest, down, up, truncate };
  int                               : 4; // Reserved
  rounding_control  round_ctl       : 2;
  precision_control prec_ctl        : 2;
  int                               : 2; // Reserved
  bool              precision        : 1;
  bool              underflow        : 1;
  bool              overflow         : 1;
  bool              zero_divide      : 1;
  bool              denormal         : 1;
  bool              invalid_op       : 1;
};
```

Use a bit-field as you would any other data member, but with the following caveats:

- You cannot take the address of a bit-field.
- You cannot bind a bit-field to a non-const reference.
- When you bind a bit-field to a const reference, the compiler creates a temporary object and binds that to the reference.
- Whether a bit field is signed or unsigned is implementation defined unless you explicitly declare it with the signed or unsigned specifier. Thus, the bit-field int bf : 1; might take the values 0 and 1 or -1 and 0 (two's complement), or even -0 and +0 (signed magnitude).
- A bit-field size can be larger than the declared type of the member, in which case the excess bits are used as padding and are not part of the member's value.
- Order and alignment of bit-fields are implementation-defined.

A bit-field without a name cannot be used or referred to, and is typically used for padding. A nameless bit-field can have size 0, which pads the object so the next bit-field is aligned on a natural memory boundary.

If you need to work with large bit-fields or treat a set of bits as an object, consider using the bitset template. (See <bitset> in Chapter 13.)

Static Data Members

A static data member is similar to an object declared at namespace scope; the class name assumes the role of the namespace name. In other words, there is a single copy of each static data member regardless of the number of instances of the class. Derived classes also share the single static data member. In some languages, static data members are called class variables.

The lifetime of a static data member is similar to the lifetime of a global static object. See Chapter 2 for details.

Local classes and anonymous unions cannot have static data members. A static data member cannot be mutable.

The member declaration in the class definition is just a declaration. You must supply a definition elsewhere in the program. The definition can have an initializer.

Only an integral or enumerated static data member can have an initializer in the class definition. The initializer must be a constant integral expression. The value of the member can be used as a constant elsewhere in the class definition. The definition of the member must then omit the initializer. This feature is often used to define the maximum size of data member arrays, as shown in Example 6-7.

Example 6-7. Declaring static data members

```
// filename.h
class filename
{
```

Example 6-7. Declaring static data members (continued)

```
public:
  static const int max_length = 1024;
  static const char path_separator = '/';
  static filename current_directory;
  filename(const char* str);
  ...
private:
  char name_[max_length];
};

// filename.cpp
// Definitions for the static data members and member functions
const int filename::max_length;
const char filename::path_separator;
filename filename::current_directory(".");

filename::filename(const char* str)
{
  strncpy(name_, str, max_length-1);
}
...
```

Member Functions

Member functions implement the behavior of a class. Member functions can be defined within the class definition or separately. You can use the inline function specifier and either the static or virtual (but not both) specifier. (See Chapter 2 for more about function specifiers.) Defining a member function within the class definition declares the function inline, even if you do not use the inline specifier.

A nonstatic member function can have const, volatile, or both function qualifiers. Qualifiers appear after the function parameters and before the exception specification. Function qualifiers are discussed in the next section, "this Pointer."

Example 6-8 shows various member function declarations and definitions.

Example 6-8. Declaring and defining member functions

```
#include <cmath>
#include <iostream>
#include <istream>
#include <ostream>

class point {
public:
  typedef double value_type;
  // Constructors are special member functions.
  explicit point(value_type x = 0.0, value_type y = 0.0);
  value_type x()      const { return x_; }
  value_type y()      const { return y_; }
  void x(value_type x)      { x_ = x; }
  void y(value_type y)      { y_ = y; }
```

Example 6-8. Declaring and defining member functions (continued)

```
  value_type distance( ) const;
  bool operator==(const point& pt) const;

  inline static point origin( );
private:
  value_type x_, y_;
};

point::point(value_type x, value_type y)
: x_(x), y_(y)
{}

point::value_type point::distance( )
const
{
  return std::sqrt(x() * x() + y() * y());
}

bool point::operator==(const point& pt)
const
{
  return x() == pt.x() && y() == pt.y();
}

inline point point::origin( )
{
  return point();
}

int main( )
{
  point p1;
  point::value_type n;
  std::cin >> n;
  p1.x(n);
  std::cin >> n;
  p1.y(n);
  if (p1 == point::origin())
    std::cout << "Origin\n";
  else
    std::cout << p1.distance() << '\n';
}
```

When defining a function inside a class definition, the entire function definition is in the scope of the class. Thus, name lookup for the return type and all parameter types looks first in the class, then in all base classes, and then in the surrounding namespaces. (See Chapter 2 for more information about name lookup.)

If the function definition is outside the class definition, the function return type is at namespace scope. Thus, if the type is a nested type in the class, you must fully qualify the type name. The function name must also be qualified so the compiler knows which class contains the function. After the compiler has seen the class name that qualifies the function name, it enters the class scope. Parameter types are then looked up in the class scope.

Pointers-to-Members

The address of a static member is no different than the address of an ordinary function or object at namespace scope. The address of a nonstatic member that is taken in a member function with an unqualified name is also an ordinary address. The address of a nonstatic member taken with a qualified member name (e.g., &cls::mem), however, is quite different from any other kind of address. The address even has a special name: *pointer-to-member*. You cannot use reinterpret_cast<> to cast a pointer-to-member to or from an ordinary data pointer or function pointer.

A pointer-to-member does not necessarily point to a particular function or object. Instead, think of it as a handle that keeps track of which function or data member you have selected but does not refer to a specific object. To use a pointer-to-member, you must use the .* or ->* operator, which requires an object or pointer as the lefthand operand and the pointer-to-member as the righthand operand. The operator looks up the member in the object and then obtains the actual data member or member function. (See Chapter 3 for more information about pointer-to-member expressions.) Example 6-9 shows one use of a pointer-to-member.

Example 6-9. A pointer-to-member

```
#include <iostream>
#include <ostream>

class base {
public:
  base(int i) : x_(i) {}
  virtual ~base() {}
  virtual void func() { std::cout << "base::func()\n"; }
private:
  int x_;
};

class derived : public base {
public:
  derived(int i) : base(i) {}
  virtual void func() { std::cout << "derived::func()\n"; }
};

int main()
{
  base *b = new derived(42);
  void (base::*fp)() = &base::func;
  (b->*fp)();                         // Prints derived::func()
}
```

this Pointer

A nonstatic member function can be called only for an object of its class or for a derived class. The object is implicitly passed as a hidden parameter to the function, and the function can refer to the object by using the this keyword, which represents an rvalue pointer to the object. That is, if the object has type T, this is an rvalue of static type T*. In a call to a virtual function, the object's dynamic type might not match the static type of this.

Static member functions do not have this pointers. (See the next section, "Static Member Functions.")

If the function is qualified with const or volatile, the same qualifiers apply to this within the member function. In other words, within a const member function of class T, this has type const T*. A const function, therefore, cannot modify its nonstatic data members (except those declared with the mutable specifier).

Within a member function, you can refer to data members and member functions using just their names, and the compiler looks up the unqualified names in the class, in its ancestor classes, and in namespace scopes. (See Chapter 2 for details.) You can force the compiler to look only in the class and ancestor classes by explicitly using this to refer to the members—for example, this->*data* and this->*func*( ). (When using templates, an explicit member reference can reduce name lookup problems; see Chapter 7 for details.)

Example 6-10 shows some typical uses of this.

Example 6-10. The this keyword

```
class point {
public:
  point(int x=0, int y=0) : x_(x), y_(y) {}
  int x() const { return this->x_; }
  int y() const { return y_; }
  void x(int x) { this->x_ = x; }
  void y(int y) { y_ = y; }
  bool operator==(const point& that) {
    return this->x() == that.x() &&
           this->y() == that.y();
  }
  void move_to(context*) const { context->move_to(*this); }
  void draw_to(context*) const { context->draw_to(*this); }
  void get_position(context*)  { context->getpos(this); }
private:
  int x_, y_;
};
```

Static Member Functions

A static member function is like a function declared at namespace scope; the class name assumes the role of the namespace name. Within the scope of the class, you can call the function using an unqualified name. Outside the class scope, you must qualify the function name with the class name (e.g., cls::*member*) or by calling the function as a named member of an object (e.g., *obj*.*member*). In the latter case, the object is not passed as an implicit parameter (as it would be to a nonstatic member function), but serves only to identify the class scope in which the function name is looked up.

Classes

Static member functions have the following restrictions:

- They do not have this pointers.
- They cannot be virtual.
- They cannot have const or volatile qualifiers.
- They cannot refer to nonstatic members, except as members of a specific object (using the . or -> operator).
- A class cannot have a static and nonstatic member function with the same name and parameters.

Example 6-11 shows some uses of static member functions.

Example 6-11. Static member functions

```
class point {
public:
  point(int x, int y);

  static point origin() { return point(0, 0); }

  // Error: calls non-static function, x()
  static bool is_zero() { return x() == 0; }

  int x() const;
  int y() const;
private:
  int x_, y_;
};
```

Constructors

Constructors and destructors are special forms of member functions. A constructor is used to initialize an object, and a destructor is used to finalize an object.

Declaring constructors

A constructor's name is the same as the class name. If you use typedef to create a synonym for the class name, you cannot use the typedef name as the constructor name:

```
    struct point {
      point(int x, int y);
    ...
    typedef point p;

    p::point(int x, int y)     { ... } // OK
    point::point(int x, int y) { ... } // OK
    p::p(int x, int y)         { ... } // Error
    point::p(int x, int y)     { ... } // Error
```

A constructor cannot have a return type, and you cannot return a value. That is, you must use a plain return; or return an expression of type void. A constructor cannot have const or volatile qualifiers, and it cannot be virtual or static.

Constructors can initialize data members with a list of member initializers, which appear after the function header but before the function body. A colon separates the header from the comma-separated initializers. Each initializer names a data member, an immediate base class, or a virtual base class. The value of the initializer follows in parentheses:

```
class-name(parameters)
: member(expr), base-class(expr-list), ...
compound-statement
```

You can also use a function try block, which wraps the constructor initializers as part of the try block. (See Chapter 4 for more information about try blocks and exception handlers.) The syntax is:

```
class-name(parameters)
try
   : member(expr), base-class(expr-list), ...
   compound-statement
exception-handlers
```

You can initialize a base class by invoking any of its constructors, passing zero or more expressions as arguments. See "Inheritance" later in this chapter for more information.

The order in which initializers appear in the initializer list is irrelevant. The order of initialization is determined by their declarations according to the following rules:

- Virtual base classes are initialized first, in order of declaration in a depth-first traversal of the inheritance graph. Each virtual base class is initialized exactly once for the most-derived object.
- Nonvirtual, direct base classes are initialized next, in order of declaration.
- Nonstatic data members are initialized next, in order of declaration.
- Finally, the body of the constructor is executed.

Note that each base class is constructed according to the same rules. This causes the root of the inheritance tree to be initialized first, and the most-derived class to be initialized last.

A constructor can be declared with the explicit specifier. An explicit constructor is never called for an implicit type conversion, but only for function-like initialization in a declaration and for explicit type casts. See the next section for more information.

Special constructors

Two kinds of constructors are special, so special they have their own names: *default constructors* and *copy constructors*.

A default constructor can be called with no arguments. It might be declared with no parameters, default arguments for every parameter, or an ellipsis as the sole parameter. (The last case is uncommon.) Default constructors are called when you construct an array of objects, when you omit the initializer for a scalar object, or when you use an empty initializer in an expression:

```
point corners[2];
point p;
point *ptr = new point( );
```

(Remember not to use an empty initializer in a declaration. For example, point p( ); declares a function named p, not a default-initialized point object. See Chapter 2 for details.)

A copy constructor can take a single argument whose type is a reference to the class type. (Additional parameters, if any, must have default arguments.) The reference is usually const, but it does not have to be. The copy constructor is called to copy objects of the class type when passing objects to functions and when returning objects from functions.

The following example shows a default and a copy constructor:

```
struct point {
    point( );                  // Default constructor
    point(const point& pt);    // Copy constructor
    ...
```

Default and copy constructors are so important, the compiler might generate them for you. See "Implicit Member Functions" later in this chapter for details.

Calling constructors

Constructors are special because you never call them directly. Instead, the compiler calls the constructor as part of the code it generates to create and initialize an object of class type. Objects can be created in several different ways:

- With automatic variables and constants in a function body:
  ```
  void demo( )
  {
    point p1(1, 2);
    const point origin;
    ...
  ```
- With static objects that are local or global:
  ```
  point p2(3, 4);
  void demo( )
  {
      static point p3(5, 6);
      ...
  ```
- Dynamically, with new expressions:
  ```
  point *p = new point(7, 8);
  ```

- With temporary objects in expressions:

```
set_bounds(point(left, top), point(right, bottom));
```

- With function parameters and return values:

```
point offset(point p) { p.x(p.x() + 2); return p; }
point x(1,2);
x = offset(x); // Calls point(const point&) twice
```

- With implicit type conversions:

```
point p = 2; // Invokes point(int=0, int=0), then point(const point&)
```

- With constructor initializers:

```
derived::derived(int x, int y) : base(x, y) {}
```

In each case, memory is set aside for the object, then the constructor is called. The constructor is responsible for initializing the object's members. Members that are listed in the initializer list are initialized as requested: scalar and pointer types are initialized with their given values; class-type objects are initialized by invoking the appropriate constructors. Class-type objects that are not listed are initialized by calling their default constructors; other types are left uninitialized. Every const member and reference-type member must have an initializer (or you must be willing to accept the default constructor for a class-type const member). Within the body of the constructor, you are free to change any non-const member. Many simple constructors are written with empty bodies:

```
struct point {
  point(int x, int y) : x_(x), y_(y) {}
  point()            : x_(0), y_(0) {}
  point(double radius, double angle) {
    x = radius * cos(angle);
    y = radius * sin(angle);
  }
  ...
```

If a constructor is declared with the explicit specifier, it can never be called for an implicit type conversion. An implicit type conversion is commonly used during assignment-like construction. In the following example, two constructors are called: complex(1.0, 0.0) is implicitly called to construct a nameless temporary object, then the copy constructor is called to copy the temporary object into z. (The compiler is allowed to optimize away the copy and initialize z directly. Most modern compilers perform this optimization, but point must have a copy constructor even if it is never called.)

```
struct complex {
  complex(double re, double im = 0.0);
  ...
};
complex z = 1;
```

Implicit type conversions can produce some surprising results by calling conversion constructors when you least expect it. In the following example, a nameless temporary complex object is created as complex(42.0, 0.0), and this temporary object is bound to the z parameter in the call to add2.

```
complex add2(const complex) {
  z.real(z.real() + 2);
  return z;
}
z = add2(42.0);
```

To avoid unexpected constructor calls, declare a constructor with the explicit
specifier if that constructor can be called with a single argument. Calls to an
explicit constructor require function-like construction or an explicit type cast:

```
struct complex {
  explicit complex(double re, double im = 0.0);
  ...
};
complex z = 1;                        // Error
complex z(1);                         // OK
add2(42);                             // Error
add2(static_cast<complex>(42));       // OK
add2(p);                              // OK
```

Throwing exceptions during construction

A constructor can also use a function try block as its function body. The try
keyword comes before the initializers. If an exception is thrown during the initialization of any member, the corresponding catch blocks are examined for
matching handlers in the usual manner. (See Chapter 4 for information about try
blocks and exception handlers.) Example 6-12 shows a constructor with a function try block.

Example 6-12. Catching exceptions in constructors

```
struct array {
  // Initialize the array with all the items in the range (first, last). If an
  // exception is thrown while copying the items, be sure to clean up by
  // destroying the items that have been added so far.
  template<typename InIter>
  array(InIter first, InIter last)
  try
    : data_(0), size_(0)
  {
    for (InIter iter(first); iter != last; ++iter)
      push_back(*iter);
  } catch (...) {
    clear();
  }
  ...
private:
  int* data_;
  std::size_t size_;
};
```

Regardless of whether the function body is a plain compound statement or a function try block, the compiler keeps track of which base-class subobjects and which

members have been initialized. If an exception is thrown during initialization, the destructors of only those objects that have been fully constructed are called.

If the object is being created as part of a new expression, and an exception is thrown, the object's memory is deallocated by calling the appropriate deallocation function. If the object is being created with a placement new operator, the corresponding placement delete operator is called—that is, the delete function that takes the same additional parameters as the placement new operator. If no matching placement delete is found, no deallocation takes place. (See Chapter 3 for more information on new and delete expressions.)

Example 6-13 shows a silly class that allocates two dynamic arrays in its constructor. Suppose the first allocation fails (member str_). In that case, the compiler knows that str_ has not been initialized and so does not call the auto_ptr<> destructor, nor does the compiler call the destructor for the wstr_ member. If, however, the allocation for str_ succeeds and fails for wstr_, the compiler calls the auto_ptr<> destructor for str_ to free the memory that had been allocated successfully. Note that if auto_ptr<> were not used, the class would have a memory leak because the compiler would not be able to free the memory for str_. (Pointers don't have destructors.)

Example 6-13. Exception-safe constructor

```
struct silly {
  silly(std::size_t n)
  : size_(n), str_(new char[n+1]), wstr_(new wchar_t[n+1])
  {}
  silly(const silly& that);
  silly& operator=(silly that);
private:
  std::size_t size_;
  std::auto_ptr<char> str_;
  std::auto_ptr<wchar_t> wstr_;
};
```

Destructors

A destructor finalizes an object when the object is destroyed. Typically, finalization frees memory, releases resources (such as open files), and so on. A destructor is a special member function. It has no return type, no arguments, and cannot return a value. A destructor can be virtual, it can be inline, but it cannot be static, const, or volatile. The name of a destructor is a tilde (~) followed by the class name. A class has only one destructor (although it may have several constructors).

Just as constructors automatically construct base-class objects, a destructor automatically calls destructors for nonstatic data members, direct base classes, and virtual base classes after the derived-class destructor body returns. Member and base-class destructors are called in reverse order of their constructors. If you do not write a destructor, the compiler does so for you. (See the next section, "Implicit Member Functions.") Any class that has virtual functions should have a virtual destructor, as explained in "Inheritance" later in this chapter.

You can call a destructor explicitly, but there is rarely any reason to do so. The compiler calls destructors automatically when objects are destroyed. Dynamically allocated objects are destroyed by delete expressions. Static objects are destroyed when a program terminates. Other named objects are destroyed automatically when they go out of scope. Temporary, unnamed objects are destroyed automatically at the end of the expression that created them.

When you write a destructor, make sure that it never throws an exception. When an exception causes the stack to be unwound (see Chapter 5), objects are automatically destroyed. If a destructor throws an exception during stack unwinding, the program terminates immediately. (See <exception> in Chapter 13.)

Example 6-14 shows how a simple destructor is declared.

Example 6-14. Declaring a destructor

```
class string {
public:
  string(std::size_t n, char c = '\0')
  : str_(new char[n+1]), size_(n) {
    std::fill(str_, str_+size_+1, c);
  }
  string( ) : str_(new char[1]), size_(0) {
    str_[0] = '\0';
  }
  ~string( ) { delete[] str_; }
  const char* c_str( ) const { return str_; }
  std::size_t size( )        const { return size_; }
private:
  std::size_t size_;
  char*  str_;
};
```

Implicit Member Functions

The compiler implicitly declares and defines default and copy constructors, the copy assignment operator, and the destructor in certain circumstances. All these implicit functions are inline public members. This section describes what each function does and the circumstances under which the function is implicitly declared and defined. Example 6-15 explicitly shows how each implicit member function is defined.

Example 6-15. Implicit member functions

```
// These classes show explicitly what the implicit member functions would be.
class base {
public:
  base( ) {}
  base(const base& that) : m1_(that.m1_), m2_(that.m2_) {}
  base& operator=(const base& that) {
    this->m1_ = that.m1_;
    this->m2_ = that.m2_;
    return *this;
```

Example 6-15. Implicit member functions (continued)

```
  }
  ~base( ) {}
private:
  int m1_;
  char* m2_;
};

class demo {
public:
  demo( ) {}          // Default constructs three base objects
  demo(demo& d) {}    // Copies three base objects in ary_[]
  demo& operator=(const demo& that) {
    this->ary_[0] = that.ary_[0];
    this->ary_[1] = that.ary_[1];
    this->ary_[2] = that.ary_[2];
    return *this;
  }
  ~demo( ) {}          // Default destructs three base objects
private:
  base ary_[3];
};

class derived : public base {
public:
  derived( ) : base( ) {}                   // Constructs m3_[]
  derived(derived& that) : base(that) {} // Copies m3_[]
  derived& operator=(const derived& that) {
    static_cast<base&>(*this) =
      static_cast<const base&>(that);
    this->m3_[0] = that.m3_[0];
    this->m3_[1] = that.m3_[1];
    this->m3_[2] = that.m3_[2];
    return *this;
  }
  ~derived( ) {} // Calls ~base( ), destructs 3 demo objects
private:
  demo m3_[3];
};
```

For classes whose data members have fundamental, class, or enumeration types, the implicit functions are often adequate. The most common case in which you must implement these functions explicitly is when an object manages pointers to memory that the object controls. In this case, a copy constructor or copy assignment operator must not blindly copy a member that is a pointer, which results in two pointers to the same memory. Instead, you should allocate a new pointer and copy the contents. In such cases, you will often find yourself providing the copy constructor, copy assignment operator, and destructor.

Classes

A useful guideline is that if you write one of the three special functions (copy constructor, copy assignment operator, or destructor), you will probably need to write all three.

If you want to store objects in a standard container, you must make sure it has a copy constructor and a copy assignment operator (implicit or explicit). See Chapter 10 for information about the standard containers.

Implicit default constructor

The compiler implicitly declares a default constructor if a class has no user-defined constructors. The implicit default constructor calls the default constructor for all base classes and for all nonstatic data members of class type. Other nonstatic data members are left uninitialized. In other words, the behavior is the same as if you wrote the default constructor with no initializers and an empty function body.

Implicit copy constructor

The compiler implicitly declares a copy constructor if a class has no copy constructor. If every direct base class and virtual base class has a copy constructor that takes a const reference parameter, and every nonstatic data member has a copy constructor with a const reference parameter, the implicit copy constructor also takes a const reference parameter. Otherwise, the implicit copy constructor takes a plain reference parameter.

In other words, the compiler tries to declare the implicit copy constructor so it takes a const reference parameter. If it cannot because the implicit function would end up calling an inherited or member copy constructor that does not take a const parameter, the compiler gives up and declares a copy constructor that takes a non-const parameter.

An implicit copy constructor calls the copy constructor for each direct base class and each virtual base class and then performs a member-by-member copy of all nonstatic data members. It calls the copy constructor for each member of class type and copies the values for members of nonclass type.

Implicit copy assignment operator

The compiler implicitly declares a copy assignment operator (operator=) if a class does not have one. If every direct base class and virtual base class has a copy assignment operator that takes a const reference parameter, and if every nonstatic data member has a copy assignment operator with a const reference parameter, the implicit copy assignment operator also takes a const reference parameter. Otherwise, the implicit copy assignment operator takes a plain reference parameter.

In other words, the compiler tries to declare the implicit copy assignment operator, so it takes a const reference parameter. If it cannot because the implicit function would end up calling an inherited or member copy assignment operator that does not take a const parameter, the compiler gives up and declares a copy assignment operator that takes a non-const parameter.

An implicit copy assignment operator calls the copy assignment operator for each direct base class and each virtual base class and then performs a member-by-member assignment of all nonstatic data members. It calls the copy assignment operator for each member of class type and assigns the values for members of nonclass type.

Implicit destructor

The compiler declares an implicit destructor if the programmer does not provide one. If a base class has a virtual destructor, the implicit destructor is also virtual. The implicit destructor is like a programmer-supplied destructor with an empty function body.

Inheritance

A class can inherit from zero or more *base classes*. A class with at least one base class is said to be a *derived class*. A derived class inherits all the data members and member functions of all of its base classes and all of their base classes, and so on. A class's immediate base classes are called *direct base classes*. Their base classes are *indirect base classes*. The complete set of direct and indirect base classes is sometimes called the *ancestor classes*.

A class can derive directly from any number of base classes. The base-class names follow a colon and are separated by commas. Each class name can be prefaced by an access specifier (described later in this chapter). The same class cannot be listed more than once as a direct base class, but it can appear more than once in the inheritance graph. For example, derived3 in the following code has base2 twice in its inheritance tree, once as a direct base class, and once as an indirect base class (through derived2):

```
class base1 { ... };
class derived1 : public base1 { ... };
class base2 { ... }
class derived2 : public derived1, public base2 { ... }
class derived3 : protected derived2, private base2 { ... }
```

A derived class can access the members that it inherits from an ancestor class, provided the members are not private. (See "Access Specifiers" later in this chapter for details.) To look up a name in class scope, the compiler looks first in the class itself, then in direct base classes, then in their direct base classes, and so on. See Chapter 2 for more information about name lookup.

To resolve overloaded functions, the compiler finds the first class with a matching name and then searches for overloads in that class. Chapter 5 lists the complete rules for overload resolution.

An object with a derived-class type can usually be converted to a base class, in which case the object is *sliced*. The members of the derived class are removed, and only the base class members remain:

```
struct file {
  std::string name;
};
struct directory : file {
  std::vector<file*> entries;
};
directory d;
file f;
f = d; // Only d.name is copied to f; entries are lost.
```

Slicing usually arises from a programming error. Instead, you should probably use a pointer or reference to cast from a derived class to a base class. In that case, the derived-class identity and members are preserved. This distinction is crucial when using virtual functions, as described in the next section. For example:

```
directory* dp = new directory;
file* fp;
fp = dp; // Keeps entries and identity as a directory object
```

As you can see in the previous examples, the compiler implicitly converts a derived class to a base class. You can also use an explicit cast operator, but if the base class is virtual, you must use `dynamic_cast<>`, not `static_cast<>`. See Chapter 3 for more information about cast expressions.

If a base class is ambiguous (see "Multiple Inheritance" later in this chapter) or inaccessible (see "Access Specifiers" later in this chapter), you cannot slice a derived class to the base class, nor can you cast a pointer or reference to the inaccessible base class (an old-style cast allows it but such use is not recommended).

Virtual Functions

A nonstatic member function can be declared with the `virtual` function specifier, and is then known as a *virtual function*. A virtual function can be *overridden* in a derived class. To override a virtual function, declare it in a derived class with the same name and parameter types. The return type is usually the same but does not have to be identical (as described in the next section, "Covariant Return Types"). The `virtual` specifier is optional in the derived class but is recommended as a hint to the human reader. A constructor cannot be virtual, but a destructor can be. A virtual function cannot be `static`.

A class that has at least one virtual function is *polymorphic*. This form of polymorphism is more precisely known as *type polymorphism*. (C++ also supports *parametric polymorphism* with templates; see Chapter 7.) Most programmers mean type polymorphism when they talk about object-oriented programming.

When calling virtual functions, you must distinguish between the declared type of the object, pointer, or reference and the actual type at runtime. The declared type is often called the static type, and the actual type is the dynamic type. For example:

```
struct base {
  virtual void func( );
};
struct derived : base {
  virtual void func( ); // Overload
};
base* b = new derived; // Static type of b is base*.
                       // Dynamic type is derived*.
b->func( );            // Calls dynamic::func( )
```

When any function is called, the compiler uses the static type to pick a function signature. If the function is virtual, the compiler generates a virtual function call. Then, at runtime, the object's dynamic type determines which function is actually called—namely, the function in the most-derived class that overrides the virtual function. This is known as a *polymorphic function call*.

Dispatching Virtual Functions

Virtual functions are most commonly implemented using *virtual function tables*, or *vtables*. Each class that declares at least one virtual function has a hidden data member (e.g., __vtbl). The __vtbl member points to an array of function pointers. Every derived class has a copy of the table. Every instance of a class shares a common table. Each entry in the table points to a function in a base class, or if the function is overridden, the entry points to the derived class function. Any new virtual functions that the derived class declares are added at the end of the table.

When an object is created, the compiler sets its __vtbl pointer to the vtable for its dynamic class. A call to a virtual function is compiled into an index into the table and into a call to the function at that index. Note that the dynamic_cast<> operator can use the same mechanism to identify the dynamic type of the object.

Multiple inheritance complicates matters slightly, yet the basic concept remains the same: indirection through a table of pointers.

Compilers do not have to use vtables, but they are used so widely, the term "vtable" has entered the common parlance of many C++ programmers.

An object's dynamic type can differ from its static type only if the object is accessed via a pointer or reference. Thus, to call a virtual function, you typically access the target object via a pointer (e.g., ptr->func( )). Inside a member function, if you call a virtual member function using its unqualified name, that is the same as calling the function via this->, so the function is called virtually. If a nonpointer, nonreference object calls a virtual function, the compiler knows that the static type and dynamic type always match, so it can save itself the lookup time and call the function in a nonvirtual manner.

Example 6-16 shows a variety of virtual functions for implementing a simple calculator. A parser constructs a parse tree of expr nodes, in which each node can be a literal value or an operator. The operator nodes point to operand nodes, and an operand node, in turn, can be any kind of expr node. The virtual evaluate function evaluates the expression in the parse tree, returning a double result. Each kind of node knows how to evaluate itself. For example, a node can return a literal value or add the values that result from evaluating two operands.

Example 6-16. Declaring and using virtual functions

```
class expr {
public:
  virtual ~expr() {}
  virtual double evaluate() const = 0;
  std::string as_string() const {
    std::ostringstream out;
    print(out);
    return out.str();
  }
  virtual void print(std::ostream& out) const {}
  virtual int precedence() const = 0;
  template<typename charT, typename traits>
  static std::auto_ptr<expr> parse(
    std::basic_istream<charT,traits>& in);
};

// cout << *expr prints any kind of expression because expr->print() is virtual.
template<typename charT, typename traits>
std::basic_ostream<charT,traits>&
  operator<<(std::basic_ostream<charT,traits>& out, const expr& e)
{
  e.print(out);
  return out;
}

class literal : public expr {
public:
  literal(double value) : value_(value) {}
  virtual double evaluate() const { return value_; }
  virtual void print(std::ostream& out) const {
    out << value_;
  }
  virtual int precedence() const { return 1; }
private:
  double value_;
};

// Abstract base class for all binary operators
class binop : public expr {
public:
  binop(std::auto_ptr<expr> left, std::auto_ptr<expr> right)
  : left_(left), right_(right) {}
  virtual double evaluate() const {
    return eval(left_->evaluate(), right_->evaluate());
  }
```

Example 6-16. Declaring and using virtual functions (continued)

```cpp
  virtual void print(std::ostream& out) const {
    if (left_->precedence() > precedence())
      out << '(' << *left_ << ')';
    else
      out << *left_;

    out << op();

    if (right_->precedence() > precedence())
      out << '(' << *right_ << ')';
    else
      out << *right_;
  }
  // Reminder that derived classes must override precedence
  virtual int precedence() const = 0;
protected:
  virtual double eval(double left, double right) const = 0;
  virtual const char* op() const = 0;
private:
  // No copying allowed (to avoid messing up auto_ptr<>s)
  binop(const binop&);
  void operator=(const binop&);
  std::auto_ptr<expr> left_;
  std::auto_ptr<expr> right_;
};

// Example binary operator.
class plus : public binop {
public:
  plus(std::auto_ptr<expr> left, std::auto_ptr<expr> right)
  : binop(left, right) {}
  virtual int precedence() const { return 3; }
protected:
  virtual double eval(double left, double right) const {
    return left + right;
  }
  virtual const char* op() const { return "+"; }
};

int main()
{
  while(std::cin) {
    std::auto_ptr<expr> e(expr::parse(std::cin));
    std::cout << *e << '\n';
    std::cout << e->evaluate() << '\n';
  }
}
```

Sometimes you do not want to take advantage of the virtualness of a function. Instead, you may want to call the function as it is defined in a specific base class.

In such a case, qualify the function name with the base-class name, which tells the compiler to call that class's definition of the function:

```
literal* e(new literal(2.0));
e->print(std::cout);       // Calls literal::print
e->expr::print(std::cout); // Calls expr::print
```

A class that has at least one virtual function should also have a virtual destructor. If a delete expression (see Chapter 3) deletes a polymorphic pointer (for which the dynamic type does not match the static type), the static class must have a virtual destructor. Otherwise, the behavior is undefined.

Covariant Return Types

The return type of an overriding virtual function must be the same as that of the base function, or it must be *covariant*. In a derived class, a covariant return type is a pointer or reference to a class type that derives from the return type used in the base class. Note that the return type classes do not necessarily have to match the classes that contain the functions, but they often do. The return type in the derived class can have additional const or volatile qualifiers that are not present in the base-class return type.

In a function call, the actual return value is implicitly cast to the static type used in the function call. Example 6-17 shows one typical use of covariant types.

Example 6-17. Covariant return types

```
struct shape {
  virtual shape* clone( ) = 0;
};
struct circle : shape {
  virtual circle* clone( ) {
    return new circle(*this);
  }
  double radius( ) const { return radius_; }
  void radius(double r) { radius_ = r; }
private:
  double radius_;
  point center_;
};
struct square : shape {
  virtual square* clone( ) {
    return new square(*this);
  }
private:
  double size_;
  point corners_[4];
};

circle unit_circle;

circle* big_circle(double r)
{
  circle* result = unit_circle.clone( );
```

Example 6-17. Covariant return types (continued)

```
  result->radius(r);
  return result;
}

int main()
{
  shape* s = big_circle(42.0);
  shape* t = s->clone();
  delete t;
  delete s;
}
```

Pure Virtual Functions

A virtual function can be declared with the pure specifier (=0) after the function header. Such a function is a *pure virtual function* (sometimes called an *abstract function*). The syntax for a pure specifier requires the symbols = 0. You cannot use an expression that evaluates to 0.

Even though a function is declared pure, you can still provide a function definition (but not in the class definition). A definition for a pure virtual function allows a derived class to call the inherited function without forcing the programmer to know which functions are pure. A pure destructor must have a definition because a derived-class destructor always calls the base-class destructor.

A derived class can override a pure virtual function and provide a body for it, override it and declare it pure again, or simply inherit the pure function. See the next section, "Abstract Classes."

Example 6-18 shows some typical uses of pure virtual functions. A base class, shape, defines several pure virtual functions (clone, debug, draw, and num_sides). The shape class has no behavior of its own, so its functions are pure virtual.

Example 6-18. Pure virtual functions

```
class shape {
public:
  virtual ~shape();
  virtual void draw(graphics* context)      = 0;
  virtual size_t num_sides()         const = 0;
  virtual shape* clone()             const = 0;
  virtual void debug(ostream& out)   const = 0;
};

class circle : public shape {
public:
  circle(double r) : radius_(r) {}
  virtual void draw(graphics* context);
  virtual size_t num_sides()    const { return 0; }
  virtual circle* clone()       const { return new circle(radius()); }
  virtual void debug(ostream& out) const {
    shape::debug(out);
```

Example 6-18. Pure virtual functions (continued)

```
    out << "radius=" << radius_ << '\n';
  }
  double radius() const { return radius_; }
private:
  double radius_;
};

class filled_circle : public circle {
public:
  filled_circle(double r, ::color c) : circle(r), color_(c) {}
  virtual filled_circle* clone() const {
    return new filled_circle (radius(), color());
  }
  virtual void draw(graphics* context);
  virtual void debug(ostream& out) const {
    circle::debug(out);
    out << "color=" << color_ << '\n';
  }
  ::color color() const { return color_;}
private:
  color color_;
};

void shape::debug(ostream& out)
const
{}
```

Even though shape::debug is pure, it has a function body. Derived classes must override shape::debug, but they can also call it, which permits uniform implementation of the various debug functions. In other words, every implementation of debug starts by calling the base class debug. Classes that inherit directly from shape do not need to implement debug differently from classes that inherit indirectly.

Abstract Classes

An *abstract class* declares at least one pure virtual function or inherits a pure virtual function without overriding it. A *concrete class* has no pure virtual functions (or all inherited pure functions are overridden). You cannot create an object whose type is an abstract class. Instead, you must create objects of concrete type. In other words, a concrete class that inherits from an abstract class must override every pure virtual function.

Abstract classes can be used to define a pure interface class, that is, a class with all pure virtual functions and no nonstatic data members. Java and Delphi programmers recognize this style of programming because it is the only way these languages support multiple inheritance. Example 6-19 shows how interface classes might be used in C++.

Example 6-19. Using abstract classes as an interface specification

```
struct Runnable {
  virtual void run( ) = 0;
};

struct Hashable {
  virtual size_t hash( ) = 0;
};

class Thread : public Runnable, public Hashable {
public:
  Thread( )                           { start_thread(*this); }
  Thread(const Runnable& thread) { start_thread(thread); }
  virtual void run( );
  virtual size_t hash( ) const { return thread_id( ); }
  size_t thread_id( )     const;
  ...
private:
  static void start_thread(const Runnable&);
};

// Derived classes can override run to do something useful.
void Thread::run( )
{}
```

Multiple Inheritance

A class can derive from more than one base class. You cannot name the same class more than once as a direct base class, but a class can be used more than once as an indirect base class, or once as a direct base class and one or more times as an indirect base class. Some programmers speak of inheritance trees or hierarchies, but with multiple base classes, the organization of inheritance is a directed acyclic graph, not a tree. Thus, C++ programmers sometimes speak of *inheritance graphs*.

If multiple base classes declare the same name, the derived class must qualify references to the name or else the compiler reports an ambiguity error:

```
struct base1 { int n; };
struct base2 { int n; };
struct derived : base1, base2 {
  int get_n( ) { return base1::n; } // Plain n is an error.
};
```

Objects of a derived-class type contain separate subobjects for each instance of every base class to store the base class's nonstatic data members. To refer to a member of a particular subobject, qualify its name with the name of its base class. Static members, nested types, and enumerators are shared among all instances of a repeated base class, so they can be used without qualification (unless the derived class hides a name with its own declaration), as shown in Example 6-20.

Example 6-20. Multiple inheritance

```
struct base1 {
  int n;
};
struct base2 {
  enum color { black, red };
  int n;
};
struct base3 : base2 {
  int n; // Hides base2::n
};
struct derived : base1, base2, base3 {
  color get_color(); // OK: unambiguous use of base2::color
  int get_n() { return n; } // Error: ambiguous
  int get_n1() { return base2::n; } // Error: which base2?
  int get_n2() { return base3::n; } // OK
  int get_n3() {          // OK: another way to get to a specific member n
    base3& b3 = *this;
    base2& b2 = b3;
    return b2.n;
  }
};
```

A well-designed inheritance graph avoids problems with ambiguities by ensuring that names are unique throughout the graph, and that a derived class inherits from each base class no more than once. Sometimes, however, a base class must be repeated in an inheritance graph. Figure 6-1 illustrates the organization of multiple base classes, modeled after the standard I/O stream classes. Because basic_iostream derives from basic_istream and from basic_ostream, it inherits two sets of flags, two sets of buffers, and so on, even though it should have only one set of each. This problem is solved by virtual base classes, as explained in the next section.

Virtual Inheritance

A base class can be declared with the virtual specifier, which is important when a class has multiple base classes. Ordinarily, each time a class is named in an inheritance graph, the most-derived class is organized so that an object has a distinct subobject for each occurrence of each base class. Virtual base classes, however, are combined into a single subobject. That is, each nonvirtual base class results in a distinct subobject, and each virtual base class gets a single subobject, no matter how many times that base class appears in the inheritance graph.

Figure 6-2 illustrates virtual base classes as they are used in the standard I/O streams. Because basic_istream and basic_ostream derive virtually from basic_ios, the basic_iostream class inherits a single copy of basic_ios, with its single copy of flags, buffer, and so on.

If a base class is used as a virtual and nonvirtual base class in an inheritance graph, all the virtual instances are shared, and all the nonvirtual instances are

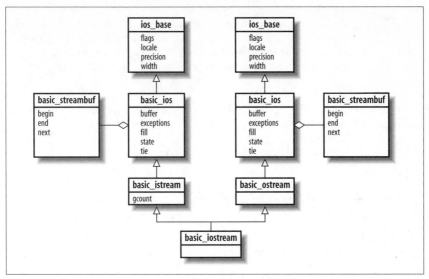

Figure 6-1. Deriving from multiple base classes

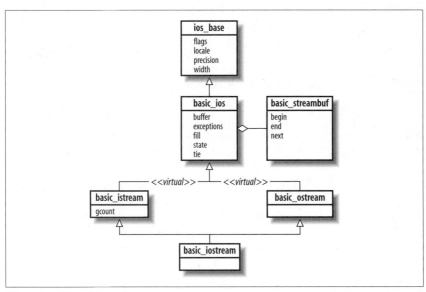

Figure 6-2. Virtual base classes

separate from the virtual instances. This situation is rare, and usually indicates a programming error.

When constructing a class that has virtual base classes, the most-derived class's constructors must initialize all the virtual base classes. If a constructor does not explicitly initialize a virtual base class, the virtual base class's default constructor is used. Initializers for the virtual base classes are ignored when all base class constructors run.

You should design your virtual base classes so they require only the default constructor. Otherwise, you impose a burden on every derived class to initialize the virtual base class properly. Any change to the parameters of the virtual base class constructor necessitates a corresponding change to every constructor for every class that derives, directly or indirectly, from the virtual base class.

Example 6-21 shows the skeletons of the declarations for the standard I/O streams, as illustrated in Figure 6-2.

Example 6-21. Virtual inheritance in the standard I/O classes

```
class ios_base;

template<typename charT, typename traits>
class basic_ios : public ios_base;

template<typename charT, typename traits>
class basic_istream : public virtual basic_ios<charT,traits>;

template<typename charT, typename traits>
class basic_ostream : public virtual basic_ios<charT,traits>;

template<typename charT, typename traits>
class basic_iostream : public basic_istream<charT,traits>,
                       public basic_ostream<charT,traits>;
```

Polymorphic Constructors and Destructors

When an object is constructed, the class of the object being created is called the *most-derived class*. When a constructor body runs, the class identity and virtual functions are those of the class whose constructor is running, which is not necessarily the most-derived class. If you call a pure virtual function, the behavior is undefined.

Destructors run in the opposite order of constructors. In the body of a destructor, the class identity and virtual functions are those of the destructor's class, not the most-derived class. As mentioned earlier, any class that has a virtual function should also have a virtual destructor. Example 6-22 illustrates how an object's identity changes as it is being constructed.

Example 6-22. Constructing and destroying an object

```
#include <iostream>
#include <ostream>

struct base {
  base() { whoami(); }
  ~base() { whoami(); }
  virtual void whoami() { std::cout << "I am base\n"; }
};
```

Example 6-22. Constructing and destroying an object (continued)

```
struct derived : base {
  derived( )  { whoami( ); }
  ~derived( ) { whoami( ); }
  virtual void whoami( ) { std::cout << "I am derived\n"; }
};

struct most_derived : virtual derived {
  most_derived( )  { whoami( ); }
  ~most_derived( ) { whoami( ); }
  virtual void whoami( )
  {
    std::cout << "I am most_derived\n";
  }
};

int main( )
{
  most_derived md;
  // Prints:
  // I am base
  // I am derived
  // I am most_derived
  // I am most_derived
  // I am derived
  // I am base
}
```

Access Specifiers

Access specifiers restrict who can access a member. You can use an access speci-fier before a base-class name in a class definition and have access specifier labels within a class definition. The access specifiers are:

`public`
> Anyone can access a public member.

`protected`
> Only the class, derived classes, and friends can access protected members.

`private`
> Only the class and friends can access private members.

In a `class` definition, the default access for members and base classes is `private`. In a `struct` definition, the default is `public`. That is the only difference between a `class` and a `struct`, although by convention, some programmers use `struct` only for POD classes and use `class` for all other classes.

The access level of a base class affects which members of the base class are acces-sible to users of a derived class (not the derived class's access to the base class). The access level caps the accessibility of inherited members. In other words, private inheritance makes all inherited members private in the derived class. Protected inheritance reduces the accessibility of public members in the base class to protected in the derived class. Public inheritance leaves all accessibility as it is in the base class.

The access level of a base class also limits type casts and conversions. With public inheritance, you can cast from a derived class to a base class in any function. Only derived classes and friends can cast to a protected base class. For private inheritance, only the class that inherits directly and friends can cast to the base class.

Access level labels in a class definition apply to all data members, member functions, and nested types. A label remains in effect until a new access label is seen or the class definition ends.

Access specifier labels affect the layout of nonstatic data members. In the absence of access specifier labels, nonstatic data members are at increasing addresses within an object in the order of declaration. When separated by access specifier labels, however, the order is implementation-defined.

When looking up names and resolving overloaded functions, the access level is not considered. The access level is checked only after a name has been found and overloaded functions have been resolved, and if the level does not permit access, the compiler issues an error message. Example 6-23 shows how the compiler ignores the access level when resolving names and overloading.

Example 6-23. The access level and overloading

```
class base {
public:
  void func(double);
protected:
  void func(long);
private:
  void func(int);
};

class demo : public base {
public:
  demo()   { func(42L); } // Calls base::func(long)
  void f() { func(42); }  // Error: func(int) is private
};

class closed : private demo {
public:
  closed() { f(); } // OK: f() is accessible from closed
};

int main()
{
  demo d;
  d.func(42L); // Error: func(long) accessibly only from base and demo
  d.func(42);  // Error: func(int) is private

  closed c;
  c.f();       // Error: private inheritance makes demo::f() private in closed.
}
```

A derived class can change the accessibility of inherited members with using declarations. A derived class can restore the accessibility of a member whose access was reduced by protected or private inheritance, or it can increase the accessibility of an inherited protected member. Example 6-24 shows how using declarations work. (You can omit the using keyword, leaving only the qualified name, but such usage is deprecated.)

Example 6-24. Adjusting accessibility with using declarations

```
struct base { // struct is public by default.
  int x;
protected:
  int y;
};
// Private inheritance makes x and y private in derived1.
class derived1 : private base {
public:
  using base::x; // x is now public.
};
// public inheritance menas x is public and y is protected in derived2.
class derived2 : public base {
public:
  using base::y; // y is now public.
private:
  using base::x; // Pointless: x is still public
};

int main( )
{
  base b;
  derived1 d1;
  derived2 d2;
  b.x = 0;        // OK: x is public in base
  b.y = 42;       // Error: y is protected in base
  d1.x = b.x;     // OK: x is public in derived1
  d2.x = d1.x;    // OK: x is public in derived2
  d1.y = 42;      // Error: y is private in derived1
  d2.y = b.x;     // OK: y is public in derived2
  return d2.y;
}
```

A member's accessibility depends on how it is accessed. In particular, a protected, nonstatic member can be accessed only through its own class or a derived class, but not through a base class. Example 6-25 demonstrates this principle.

Example 6-25. Accessing a protected member

```
class base {
protected:
  int m;
};
```

Example 6-25. Accessing a protected member (continued)

```
struct derived : base {
  void reset( ) {
    this->m = 0;  // OK
  }
  void set(base* b) {
    b->m = 0;      // Error: cannot refer to m through base
  }
  bool operator==(const derived& d) {
    return this->m == d.m; // OK
  }
};
```

Friends

A *friend* is permitted full access to private and protected members. A friend can be a function, function template, or member function, or a class or class template, in which case the entire class and all of its members are friends.

Use the friend specifier to declare a friend in the class granting friendship. Note that friendship is given, not taken. In other words, if class A contains the declaration friend class B;, class B can access the private members of A, but A has no special privileges to access B (unless B declares A as a friend).

By convention, the friend specifier is usually first, although it can appear in any order with other function and type specifiers. The friend declaration can appear anywhere in the class; the access level is not relevant.

You cannot use a storage class specifier in a friend declaration. Instead, you should declare the function before the class definition (with the storage class, but without the friend specifier), then redeclare the function in the class definition (with the friend specifier and without the storage class). The function retains its original linkage. If the friend declaration is the first declaration of a function, the function gets external linkage. (See Chapter 2 for more information about storage classes and linkage.) For example:

```
class demo;
static void func(demo& d);
class demo {
  friend void func(demo&);
  ...
```

Friendship is not transitive—that is, the friend of my friend is not my friend (unless I declare so in a separate friend declaration)—nor is a nested class a friend just because the outer class is a friend. (See the next section, "Nested Types," for more information.)

Friendship is not inherited. If a base class is a friend, derived classes do not get any special privileges.

You cannot define a class in a friend declaration, but you can define a function, provided the class granting friendship is not local to a block. The function body is in the class scope, which affects name lookup (see Chapter 2). The friend function is automatically inline. Usually, friend functions are declared, not defined, in the class.

A declaration or definition of a friend function does not make that function a member of the class and does not introduce the name into the class scope. Example 6-26 shows several different kinds of friends.

Example 6-26. Friend functions and classes

```cpp
#include <iterator>

// Simple container for singly-linked lists
template<typename T>
class slist {
  // Private type for a link (node) in the list
  template<typename U>
  struct link {
    link* next;
    U value;
  };
  typedef link<T> link_type;

  // Base class for iterator and const_iterator. Keeps track of current node, and
  // previous node to support erase( ).
  class iter_base :
  public std::iterator<std::forward_iterator_tag, T> {
  protected:
    friend class slist; // So slist can construct iterators
    iter_base(slist::link_type* prv, slist::link_type* node);
    slist::link_type* node_;
    slist::link_type* prev_;
  };

public:
  typedef T value_type;
  typedef std::size_t size_type;

  class iterator : public iter_base {
    // Members omitted for bevity...
  private:
    friend class slist; // So slist can call constructor
    iterator(slist::link_type* prev, slist::link_type* node)
    : iter_base(prev, node) {}
  };

  friend class iter_base; // So iter_base can use link_type
  friend class iterator;  // So iterator can use link_type
  template<typename U>
  friend void swap(slist<U>& a, slist<U>& b);

  iterator begin( )    { return iterator(0, head_); }
  iterator end( )      { return iterator(0, 0); }
private:
  link_type* head_;
```

Classes

Example 6-26. Friend functions and classes (continued)

```
  size_type  count_;
};

template<typename T>
slist<T>::iter_base::iter_base(slist::link_type* prev,
                              slist::link_type* node)
: prev_(prev), node_(node)
{}

// Swap two lists in constant time by swapping members.
template<typename T>
void swap(slist<T>& a, slist<T>& b)
{
  typename slist<T>::link_type* tmp_head = a.head_;
  typename slist<T>::size_type  tmp_count = a.count_;
  a.head_  = b.head_;
  a.count_ = b.count_;
  b.head_  = tmp_head;
  b.count_ = tmp_count;
}
```

Nested Types

You can declare and define types within a class definition. Accessing these nested types is similar to using types declared within a namespace; the class name serves as the namespace name.

 Java programmers have several different kinds of nested classes to choose from, but C++ has only one. A C++ nested class is like a static member class in Java. You can construct the other forms of nested classes by adding the appropriate declarations and support code. For example:

```
class outer {
public:
  friend inner;    // Implicit in Java
  class inner {
  friend outer; // Implicit in Java
  public:
    // Inner member class keeps track of outer instance.
    inner(outer& out) : out_(out) {}
    int get() const { return out_.x(); }
  private:
    outer& out_;
  }
  int x();
  int y() { inner i(*this); return i.get(); }
};
```

Nested types obey access specifiers, so private types are usable only by the class and its friends; protected types are usable by the class, derived classes, and friends. Public types are usable anywhere. To use a nested type outside the containing class and derived classes, it must be qualified with the class name.

Nested enumerations add every enumerator to the class scope:

```
class Graphics {
public:
   enum color { black, red, green, yellow, blue, magenta, cyan, white };
   color pixel(int row, int col) const;
   ...
};
Graphics::color background = Graphics::white;
```

A typedef declaration can also be nested in a class. This technique is often used for traits (see Chapter 8):

```
template<typename T, std::size_t N>
class array {
public:
   typedef T value_type;
   typedef T* pointer_type;
   typedef T& reference_type;
   typedef std::size_t size_type;
   ...
};
```

A nested-class definition is like an ordinary class definition, except the name is local to the outer class. The inner class has no special access privileges to the outer class, and vice versa. A nested class can be declared within its outer class definition and later defined at namespace scope. In that case, the nested name must be qualified with the outer class name. Often, nested classes are fully defined within their outer classes:

```
struct outer {
   struct inner1 {
      int foo( ) { return 10; }
   };
   class inner2;
};
struct outer::inner2 {
   int foo( );
};
int outer::inner2::foo( ) {
   outer::inner2 x;
   return x.foo( );
}
```

Classes

7

Templates

C++ is more than a mere object-oriented programming language. The full power of C++ is seen when programming with templates. Templates lie at the heart of the standard library: strings, I/O streams, containers, iterators, algorithms, and more.

A *template* is a pattern for creating classes or functions as instances of the template at compile time, similar to the manner in which a class is a pattern for creating objects as instances of the class at runtime. A template takes one or more parameters, and when you instantiate a class or function template, you must supply arguments for the parameters. The classes and functions can have different behaviors or implementations, depending on the arguments. This style of programming is often called *generic programming*. Templates can also be used to select code at compile time, affect the behavior of generated code, and set policies. This style of programming is often known as *template metaprogramming*.

Programming with templates is unlike traditional object-oriented programming. Object-oriented programming centers around type polymorphism (requiring classes, objects, and virtual functions). Template-based programming centers around *parametric polymorphism*, in which a function or class is defined independently of its parameters (which can be values, types, or even other templates).

This chapter describes the syntax and semantics of declaring, specializing, instantiating, and using templates. See Chapter 8 for information about some typical uses of templates in the standard library. See Appendix B for information about template-oriented projects.

The syntax descriptions in this chapter are informal. See Chapter 12 for a precise BNF grammar.

Overview of Templates

A template declaration can be a function declaration, function definition, class declaration, or class definition. The template declaration takes one or more parameters, which can be values, types, or class templates.

In most cases, you can use a template simply by naming the template and providing arguments for the template parameters: constant expressions, types, or template references. This is known as *instantiating* the template. You can instantiate a template at its point of use, or declare a separate instantiation as a class or function declaration. An instance of a function template creates a function; an instance of a class template creates a class and all of its members.

A template lets you define a class or function once for a wide range of template arguments, but sometimes you need to customize a template for particular arguments. This is known as *specializing* the template. A template specialization, as its name implies, is a special case of the template pattern. When you instantiate a template, the compiler uses the template arguments to pick a specialization, or if no specialization matches the arguments, the original template declaration. A specialization can be total or partial. A *total specialization* specifies values for all of the template arguments, and a *partial specialization* specifies only some of the template arguments.

The terminology used in this book reflects the terminology that many C++ programmers have adopted, even though that terminology differs slightly from that used in the C++ standard. In the standard, "specialization" means an instance of a template. "Instantiation" also refers to an instance of a template. When you declare a special case of a template, that is known as *explicit specialization*.

Many C++ programmers prefer to keep specialization and instantiation as separate concepts and separate terms, and I have adopted the simpler terminology for this book.

Note that a template declaration defines only the pattern. A specialization defines a pattern that applies to a specific set of template arguments. Only by instantiating a template do you declare or define a function or class. When you instantiate a template, the compiler uses the template arguments to pick which pattern to instantiate: a specialization or the main template.

Writing a template is more difficult than writing a non-template class or function. The template can be instantiated in almost any context, and the context can affect how the template definition is interpreted. Name lookup rules are more complicated for templates than for non-templates.

Example 7-1 shows several different kinds of templates and their uses.

Example 7-1. Declaring and using templates

```
#include <cmath>
#include <complex>
#include <iostream>
#include <ostream>
```

Example 7-1. Declaring and using templates (continued)

```cpp
// Template declaration of point
template<typename T>
class point {
public:
  typedef T value_type;
  point(const T& x, const T& y) : x_(x), y_(y) {}
  point() : x_(T()), y_(T()) {}
  T x()             const { return x_; }
  T& x()                  { return x_; }
  void x(const T& new_x) { x_ = new_x; }
  T y()             const { return y_; }
  T& y()                  { return y_; }
  void y(const T& new_y) { y_ = new_y; }
private:
  T x_, y_;
};


// Instantiate point<>.
typedef point<std::complex<double> > strange;
strange s(std::complex<double>(1, 2),
          std::complex<double>(3, 4));

// Specialize point<int> to use call-by-value instead of const references.
template<>
class point<int> {
public:
  typedef int value_type;
  point(int x, int y) : x_(x), y_(y) {}
  point() : x_(0), y_(0) {}
  int x()     const { return x_; }
  int& x()          { return x_; }
  void x(int new_x) { x_ = new_x; }
  int y()     const { return y_; }
  int& y()          { return y_; }
  void y(int new_y) { y_ = new_y; }
private:
  int x_, y_;
};


// Instance of the specialized point<int>
point<int> p(42, 0);
// Instance of the general point<>, using long as the template argument
point<long> p(42, 0);

// Function template
template<typename T>
T abs(T x)
{
  return x < 0 ? -x : x;
}
```

Example 7-1. Declaring and using templates (continued)

```
namespace {
  // Explicit instantiation
  const int abs_char_min1 = abs<int>(CHAR_MIN);
  // Implicit instantiation
  const int abs_char_min2 = abs(CHAR_MIN);
}

// Overload abs() with another function template.
template<typename floatT, typename T>
floatT abs(const point<T>& p)
{
  return std::sqrt(static_cast<floatT>(p.x()*p.x() +
                                       p.y()*p.y()));
}

int main()
{
  point<double> p;
  // Call instance of function template. Compiler deduces second template
  // argument (double) from the type of p.
  double x = abs<long double>(p);
  std::cout << x << '\n'; // prints 0
  std::cout << abs_char_min1 << '\n';
}
```

Template Declarations

A template declaration begins with a template header followed by a function declaration or definition, or a class declaration or definition. Template declarations can appear only at namespace or class scope. The template name must be unique in its scope (except for overloaded functions).

The template header starts with the template keyword followed by the template parameters enclosed in angle brackets (<>). Multiple parameters are separated by commas. The syntax is:

```
template < parameter-list > declaration
```

There are three kinds of template parameters: values, types, and class templates. Similar to a function parameter, a template parameter has an optional name and an optional default argument.

Function templates cannot have default template arguments. If a class template has member definitions that are outside the class definition, only the class template takes default arguments; the individual member definitions do not. If a default argument is present, it is preceded by an equal sign. Only the rightmost parameters can have default arguments. If any parameter has a default argument, all parameters to its right must also have default arguments. Example 7-2 shows valid and invalid member definitions.

Example 7-2. Defining members of a class template

```
// OK: default argument for template parameter A
template<typename T, typename A = std::allocator<T> >
class hashset {
  bool empty() const;
  size_t size() const;
  ...
};
// Error: do not use default argument here
template<typename T, typename A = std::allocator<T> >
bool hashset<T,A>::empty() { return size() == 0; }

// OK
template<typename T, typename A>
size_t hashset<T,A>::size() { ... }
```

Each template header defines the template name and template parameters. The scope of a parameter name extends from its declaration to the end of the declaration or definition of the class or function. A parameter name can be used in subsequent template parameters in the same template header (such as std::allocator<T> in Example 7-2). The template parameter name must be unique in the template declaration and cannot be redeclared in its scope. If a class template has separate definitions for its members, each member definition is free to use different names for the template parameters. (See "Member Templates" later in this chapter for more information.)

There are three kinds of template parameters:

Value template parameter
    Declared in the same manner as a function parameter:

```
type-specifiers declarator
type-specifiers declarator = expr
```

The type must be an integral, enumeration, pointer, reference, or pointer-to-member type. When the template is instantiated, the argument must be a constant integral or enumeration expression, the address of a named object or function with external linkage, or the address of a member:

```
template<unsigned Size>
struct name {
  // ...
  unsigned size() const { return Size; }
private:
  char name_[Size+1];
};
name<100> n;
```

Note that a string literal is an unnamed object with internal linkage, so you cannot use it as a template argument:

```
template<const char* Str> void print(const char* s = Str);
print<"default">(); // Error
const char def[] = "default";
print<def>();        // OK
```

The *type-specifiers* can be elaborated type specifiers that start with typename, that is, typename followed by a qualified type name. (If typename is followed by a plain identifier, the template parameter is a type parameter, as described later.) For more information about this use of typename, see "Name Lookup" later in this chapter.

```
template<typename list<int>::value_type value>
int silly( ) { return value; }
```

Type template parameter

Introduced with the keyword typename followed by the optional parameter name:

```
typename identifier
typename identifier = type
```

The class keyword can be used in place of typename and has the same meaning in this context. (A useful convention is to use class when the argument must be a class and typename when the argument can be any type.) When the template is instantiated, the argument must be a type (that is, a list of type specifiers with optional pointer, reference, array, and function operators). In the following example, the point template is instantiated with unsigned long int as the template argument:

```
template<typename T> struct point {
  T x, y;
};
point<unsigned long int> pt;
```

If typename is followed by a qualified type name instead of a plain identifier, it declares a value parameter of that type, as described earlier.

Template template parameter

Must be a class template. It has the form of a template declaration:

```
template < parameter-list > class identifier
template < parameter-list > class identifier = template-id
```

When the template is instantiated, the argument must be a class template:

```
// Erase all occurrences of item from a sequence container.
template<template<typename T, typename A> class C, typename T,
         typename A>
void erase(C<T,A>& c, const T& item)
{
  c.erase(std::remove(c.begin(), c.end( ), item), c.end( ));
}
...
list<int> l;
...
erase(l, 42);
```

To use a template declaration, you must create an instance of the template, either explicitly (by naming the template and enclosing a list of template arguments in angle brackets) or implicitly (by letting the compiler deduce the template arguments from context) for a function template. In either case, the compiler must know about a template declaration before the template is used. Typically, a template is declared in an #include file or header. The header declares the function or class template and possibly provides the definition of the function template or the definitions of all the members of the class template. See "Compiling Templates" later in this chapter for details about the files that declare and define templates.

A template instance must provide an argument for each template parameter. If a class template has fewer arguments than parameters, the remaining parameters must have default arguments, which are used for the template instance.

If a function template has fewer arguments than parameters, the remaining arguments are deduced from the context of the function call (as explained in the next section). If the arguments cannot be deduced, the compiler reports an error. See "Instantiation" later in this chapter for more information.

Function Templates

A function template defines a pattern for any number of functions whose definitions depend on the template parameters. You can overload a function template with a non-template function or with other function templates. You can even have a function template and a non-template function with the same name and parameters.

Function templates are used throughout the standard library. The best-known function templates are the standard algorithms (such as copy, sort, and for_each).

Declare a function template using a template declaration header followed by a function declaration or definition. Default template arguments are not allowed in a function template declaration or definition. In the following example, round is a template declaration for a function that rounds a number of type T to N decimal places (see example 7-14 for the definition of round), and min is a template definition for a function that returns the minimum of two objects:

```
// Round off a floating-point value of type T to N digits.
template<unsigned N, typename T>  T round(T x);
// Return the minimum of a and b.
template<typename T> T min(T a, T b)
{ return a < b ? a : b; }
```

To use a function template, you must specify a template instance by providing arguments for each template parameter. You can do this explicitly, by listing arguments inside angle brackets:

```
long x = min<long>(10, 20);
```

However, it is more common to let the compiler deduce the template argument types from the types of the function arguments:

```
int x = min(10, 20); // Calls min<int>( )
```

See the section "Deducing Argument Types" later in this chapter for details.

Function Signatures

The signature of a function template includes the template parameters even if those parameters are never used in the function's return type or parameter types.

Thus, instances of different template specializations produce distinct functions. The following example has two function templates, both named func. Because their template parameters differ, the two lines declare two separate function templates:

```
template<typename T> void func(T x = T( ));
template<typename T, typename U> void func(T x = U( ));
```

Typically, such function templates are instantiated in separate files; otherwise, you must specify the template arguments explicitly to avoid overload conflicts.

The function signature also includes expressions that use any of the template parameters. In the following example, two function templates overload func. The function parameter type is an instance of the demo class template. The template parameter for demo is an expression that depends on func's template parameter (T or i):

```
template<int x> struct demo {};
template<typename T> void func(demo<sizeof(T)>);
template<int i> void func(demo<i+42>);
```

Just as you can have multiple declarations (but not definitions) of a single function, you can declare the same function template multiple times using expressions that differ only by the template parameter names. Even if the declarations are in separate files, the compiler and linker ensure that the program ends up with a single copy of each template instance.

If the expressions differ by more than just the parameter names, they result in distinct functions, so you can have distinct function template definitions. If the argument expressions result in the same value, the program is invalid, although the compiler is not required to issue an error message:

```
template<int i> void func(demo<i+42>);
template<int x> void func(demo<x+42>) {}    // OK
template<int i> void func(demo<i+41>) {}    // OK
template<int i> void func(demo<i+40+2>) {} // Error
```

Follow the standard procedure of declaring templates in header files and using those headers in the source files where they are needed, thereby ensuring that every source file sees the same template declarations. Then you will not have to be concerned about different source files seeing declarations that differ only by the form of the template argument expressions. The compiler tries to ensure that the program ends up with a single copy of functions that are meant to be the same, but distinct copies of those that are meant to be distinct.

Deducing Argument Types

Most uses of function templates do not explicitly specify all of the template arguments, letting the compiler deduce the template arguments from the function call. You can provide explicit arguments for the leftmost template parameters, leaving the rightmost parameters for the compiler to deduce. If you omit all the template arguments, you can also choose to omit the angle brackets.

In the following discussion, make sure you distinguish between the parameters and arguments of a template and those of a function. Argument type deduction is the process of determining the template arguments, given a function call or other use of a function (such as taking the address of a function).

The basic principle is that a function call has a list of function arguments, in which each function argument has a type. The function argument types must be matched to function parameter types; in the case of a function template, the function parameter types can depend on the template parameters. The ultimate goal, therefore, is to determine the appropriate template arguments that let the compiler match the function parameter types with the given function argument types.

Usually, the template parameters are type or template template parameters, but in a few cases, value parameters can also be used (as the argument for another template or as the size of an array).

The function parameter type can depend on the template parameter in the following ways, in which the template parameter is *v* for a value parameter, *T* for a type parameter, or *TT* for a template template parameter:

- `T, T*, T&, const T, volatile T, const volatile T`
- Array of *T*
- Array of size *v*
- Template *TT*, or any class template whose template argument is *T* or *v*
- Function pointer in which *T* is the return type or the type of any function parameter
- Pointer to a data member of *T*, or to a data member whose type is *T*
- Pointer to a member function that returns *T*, to a member function of *T*, or to a member function in which *T* is the type of any function parameter

Types can be composed from any of these forms. Thus, type deduction can occur for a struct in which the types of its members are also deduced, or a function's return type and parameter types can be deduced.

A single function argument can result in the deduction of multiple template parameters, or multiple function arguments might depend on a single template parameter.

If the compiler cannot deduce all the template arguments of a function template, you must provide explicit arguments. Example 7-3 shows several different ways the compiler can deduce template arguments.

Example 7-3. Deducing template arguments

```
#include <algorithm>
#include <cstddef>
#include <iostream>
#include <list>
#include <ostream>
#include <set>

// Simple function template. Easy to deduce T.
template<typename T>
```

Example 7-3. Deducing template arguments (continued)

```
T min(T a, T b)
{
  return a < b ? a : b;
}

template<typename T, std::size_t Size>
struct array
{
  T value[Size];
};

// Deduce the row size of a 2D array.
template<typename T, std::size_t Size>
std::size_t dim2(T [][Size])
{
  return Size;
}

// Overload the function size( ) to return the number of elements in an array<>
// or in a standard container.
template<typename T, std::size_t Size>
std::size_t size(const array<T,Size>&)
{
  return Size;
}

template<template<typename T, typename A> class container,
         typename T, typename A>
typename container<T,A>::size_type size(container<T,A>& c)
{
  return c.size( );
}

template<template<typename T, typename C, typename A>
           class container,
         typename T, typename C, typename A>
typename container<T,C,A>::size_type
size(container<T,C,A>& c)
{
  return c.size( );
}

// More complicated function template. Easy to deduce Src, but impossible to
// deduce Dst.
template<typename Dst, typename Src>
Dst cast(Src s)
{
  return s;
}

int main( )
{
```

Example 7-3. Deducing template arguments (continued)

```
  min(10, 100);       // min<int>
  min(10, 1000L);     // Error: T cannot be int and long

  array<int,100> data1;
  // Deduce T=int and SIZE=100 from type of data1.
  std::cout << size(data1) << '\n';

  int y[10][20];
  std::cout << dim2(y) << '\n';  // Prints 20

  std::list<int> lst;
  lst.push_back(10);
  lst.push_back(20);
  lst.push_back(10);
  std::cout << size(lst) << '\n';  // Prints 3

  std::set<char> s;
  const char text[] = "hello";
  std::copy(text, text+5, std::inserter(s, s.begin()));
  std::cout << size(s) << '\n';  // Prints 4

  // Can deduce Src=int, but not return type, so explicitly set Dst=char
  char c = cast<char>(42);
}
```

Overloading

Function templates can be overloaded with other function templates and with non-template functions. Templates introduce some complexities, however, beyond those of ordinary overloading (as covered in Chapter 5).

As with any function call, the compiler collects a list of functions that are candidates for overload resolution. If the function name matches that of a function template, the compiler tries to determine a set of template arguments, deduced or explicit. If the compiler cannot find any suitable template arguments, the template is not considered for overload resolution. If the compiler can find a set of template arguments, they are used to instantiate the function template, and the template instance is added to the list of candidate functions. Thus, each template contributes at most one function to the list of overload candidates. The best match is then chosen from the list of template and non-template functions according to the normal rules of overload resolution: non-template functions are preferred over template functions, and more specialized template functions are preferred over less specialized template functions. See Chapter 5 for more details on overload resolution.

Example 7-4 shows how templates affect overload resolution. Sometimes, template instantiation issues can be subtle. The last call to print results in an error, not because the compiler cannot instantiate print, but because the instantiation contains an error, namely, that operator << is not defined for std::vector<int>.

Example 7-4. Overloading functions and function templates

```cpp
#include <cctype>
#include <iomanip>
#include <iostream>
#include <ostream>
#include <string>
#include <vector>

template<typename T>
void print(const T& x)
{
  std::cout << x;
}

void print(char c)
{
  if (std::isprint(c))
    std::cout << c;
  else
    std::cout << std::hex << std::setfill('0')
              << "'\\x" << std::setw(2) << int(c) << '\''
              << std::dec;
}

template<>
void print(const long& x)
{
  std::cout << x << 'L';
}

int main()
{
  print(42L);     // Calls print<long> specialization
  print('x');     // Calls print(char) overload
  print('\0');    // Calls print(char) overload
  print(42);      // Calls print<int>
  print(std::string("y"));   // Calls print<string>
  print();                    // Error: argument required
  print(std::vector<int>()); // Error
}
```

Operators

You can create operator templates in the same manner as function templates. The usual rules for deducing argument types apply as described earlier in this section. If you want to specify the arguments explicitly, you can use the operator keyword:

```cpp
template<typename T>
bigint operator+(const bigint& x, const T& y);
bigint a;
a = a + 42;                  // Argument type deduction
a = operator+<long>(a, 42);  // Explicit argument type
```

When using operator<, be sure to leave a space between the operator symbol and the angle brackets that surround the template argument, or else the compiler will think you are using the left-shift operator:

```
operator<<long>(a, 42);  // Error: looks like left-shift
operator< <long>(a, 42); // OK
```

Type conversion operators can use ordinary type cast syntax, but if you insist on using an explicit operator keyword, you cannot use the usual syntax for specifying the template argument. Instead, the target type specifies the template argument type:

```
struct demo {
  template<typename T>
  operator T*() const { return 0; }
};
demo d;
char* p = d.operator int*();            // Error: illegal cast
char* c = d; // d.operator char*();     // OK
```

Class Templates

A class template defines a pattern for any number of classes whose definitions depend on the template parameters. The compiler treats every member function of the class as a function template with the same parameters as the class template.

Class templates are used throughout the standard library for containers (list<>, map<>, etc.), complex numbers (complex<>), and even strings (basic_string<>) and I/O (basic_istream<>, etc.).

The basic form of a class template is a template declaration header followed by a class declaration or definition:

```
template<typename T>
struct point {
  T x, y;
};
```

To use the class template, supply an argument for each template parameter (or let the compiler substitute a default argument). Use the template name and arguments the way you would a class name.

```
point<int> pt = { 42, 10 };
typedef point<double> dpoint;
dpoint dp = { 3.14159, 2.71828 };
```

In member definitions that are separate from the class definition, you must declare the template using the same template parameter types in the same order, but without any default arguments. (You can change the names of the template parameters, but be sure to avoid name collisions with base classes and their members. See "Name Lookup" later in this chapter for more information.) Declare the member definitions the way you would any other definition, except that the class name is a template name (with arguments), and the definition is preceded by a template declaration header.

In the class scope (in the class definition, or in the definition of a class member), the bare class name is shorthand for the full template name with arguments. Thus, you can use the bare identifier as the constructor name, after the tilde in a destructor name, in parameter lists, and so on. Outside the class scope, you must supply template arguments when using the template name. You can also use the template name with different arguments to specify a different template instance when declaring a member template. The following example shows how the template name can be used in different ways:

```
template<typename T> struct point {
  point(T x, T y); // Or point<T>(T x, T y);
  ~point<T>( );     // Or ~point( );
  template<typename U>
  point(const point<U>& that);
  ...
};
```

Example 7-5 shows a class template with several different ways to define its member function templates.

Example 7-5. Defining class templates

```
template<typename T, typename U = int>
class demo {
public:
  demo(T t, U u);
  ~demo( );
  static T data;
  class inner; // inner is a plain class, not a template.
};

template<typename T, typename U>
demo<T,U>::demo(T, U)    // Or demo<T,U>::demo<T,U>(T, U)
{}

template<typename T, typename U>
demo<T,U>::~demo<T,U>( ) // Or demo<T,U>::~demo( )
{}

template<typename U, typename T> // Allowed, but confusing
U demo<U,T>::data;

template<typename T, typename U>
class demo<T,U>::inner {
public:
  inner(T, demo<T,U>& outer);
private:
  demo<T,U>& outer;
};

// The class name is "demo<T,U>::inner", and the constructor name is "inner".
template<typename T, typename U>
demo<T,U>::inner::inner(T, demo<T,U>& outer)
: outer(outer)
{}
```

The template defines only the pattern; the template must be instantiated to declare or define a class. See the sections "Specialization" and "Instantiation" later in this chapter for more information.

Member Templates

A *member template* is a template inside a class template or non-template class that has its own template declaration header, with its own template parameters. It can be a member function or a nested type. Member templates have the following restrictions:

- Local classes cannot have member templates.
- A member function template cannot be a destructor.
- A member function template cannot be virtual.
- If a base class has a virtual function, a member function template of the same name and parameters in a derived class does not override that function.

Type conversion functions have additional rules because they cannot be instantiated using the normal template instantiation or specialization syntax:

- A using declaration cannot refer to a type conversion template in a base class.
- Use ordinary type conversion syntax to instantiate a type conversion template:

```
template<typename T>
struct silly {
  template<typename U> operator U*() { return 0; }
};
...
silly<int> s, t(42);
if (static_cast<void*>(s))
  std::cout << "not null\n";
```

A class can have a non-template member function with the same name as a member function template. The usual overloading rules apply (Chapter 5), which means the compiler usually prefers the non-template function to the function template. If you want to make sure the function template is called, you can explicitly instantiate the template:

```
template<typename T>
struct demo {
  template<typename U> void func(U);
  void func(int);
};

demo<int> d;
d.func(42);       // Calls func(int)
d.func<int>(42); // Calls func<int>
```

Friends

A friend (of a class template or an ordinary class) can be a template, a specialization of a template, or a non-template function or class. A friend declaration cannot be a partial specialization. If the friend is a template, all instances of the template are friends. If the class granting friendship is a template, all instances of the template grant friendship. A specialization of a template can be a friend, in which case instances of only that specialization are granted friendship:

```
template<typename T> class buddy {};
template<typename T> class special {};
class demo {
  // All instances of buddy<> are friends.
  template<typename T> friend class buddy;
  // special<int> is a friend, but not special<char>, etc.
  friend class special<int>;
};
```

When you use the containing class template as a function parameter, you probably want friend functions to be templates also:

```
template<typename T>
class outer {
  friend void func1(outer& o);      // Wrong

  template<typename U>
  friend void func2(outer<U>& o); // Right
};
```

A friend function can be defined in a class template, in which case every instance of the class template defines the function. The function definition is compiled even if it is not used.

You cannot declare a friend template in a local class.

If a friend declaration is a specialization of a function template, you cannot specify any default function arguments, and you cannot use the `inline` specifier. These items can be used in the original function template declaration, however.

All the rules for function templates apply to friend function templates. (See "Function Templates" earlier in this chapter for details.) Example 7-6 shows examples of friend declarations and templates.

Example 7-6. Declaring friend templates and friends of templates

```
#include <algorithm>
#include <cstddef>
#include <iostream>
#include <iterator>
#include <ostream>

template<typename T, std::size_t Size>
class array {
public:
  typedef T value_type;

  class iterator_base :
    std::iterator<std::random_access_iterator_tag, T> {
  public:
    typedef T value_type;
```

```
  typedef std::size_t size_type;
  typedef std::ptrdiff_t distance_type;

  friend inline bool operator==(const iterator_base& x,
                                const iterator_base& y)
  {
    return x.ptr_ == y.ptr_;
  }
  friend inline bool operator!=(const iterator_base& x,
                                const iterator_base& y)
  {
    return ! (x == y);
  }
  friend inline ptrdiff_t operator-(const iterator_base& x,
                                    const iterator_base& y)
  {
    return x.ptr_ - y.ptr_;
  }

protected:
  iterator_base(const iterator_base& that)
    : ptr_(that.ptr_) {}
  iterator_base(T* ptr) : ptr_(ptr) {}
  iterator_base(const array& a, std::size_t i)
    : ptr_(a.data_ + i) {}

  T* ptr_;
};

friend class iterator_base;

class iterator : public iterator_base {
public:
  iterator(const iterator& that) : iterator_base(that) {}
  T& operator*()         const { return *this->ptr_; }
  iterator& operator++() { ++this->ptr_; return *this; }
  T* operator->()        const { return this->ptr_; }

private:
  friend class array;
  iterator(const array& a, std::size_t i = 0)
    : iterator_base(a, i) {}
  iterator(T* ptr) : iterator_base(ptr) {}

  friend inline iterator operator+(iterator iter, int off)
  {
    return iterator(iter.ptr_ + off);
  }
};

array() : data_(new T[Size]) {}
array(const array& that);
```

Example 7-6. Declaring friend templates and friends of templates (continued)

```
~array( )                   { delete[] data_; }
iterator begin( )           { return iterator(*this); }
const_iterator begin( ) const { return iterator(*this); }
iterator end( );
const_iterator end( )   const;
T& operator[](std::size_t i);
T operator[](std::size_t i);

  template<typename U, std::size_t USize>
  friend void swap(array<U,USize>& a, array<U,USize>& b);

private:
  T* data_;
};

template<typename T, std::size_t Size>
void swap(array<T,Size>& a, array<T,Size>& b)
{
  T* tmp = a.data_;
  a.data_ = b.data_;
  b.data_ = tmp;
}
```

Specialization

A template declares a set of functions or classes from a single declaration, which is a powerful tool for writing code once and having it work in a multitude of situations. A single, one-size-fits-all approach is not always appropriate, however. You can therefore specialize a template for specific values of one or more template arguments and provide a completely different definition for that special case.

You can specialize a class template, a function template, or a member of a class template. Declare a specialization with an empty set of template parameters in the template header followed by a declaration that provides arguments for all the template parameters:

```
template<> declaration
```

Specializations must appear after the declaration of the primary template, and they must be declared in the same namespace as the primary template. You can also have a *partial specialization*, which provides some of the template arguments. (See the next section.)

When a template is instantiated, if the template arguments of the instantiation match the arguments used in a specialization, the compiler instantiates the matching specialization. Otherwise, it instantiates the primary template. See the section "Instantiation" later in this chapter for details.

To specialize a function template, the function return type and parameter types must match the primary template declaration. The function name can be followed by the specialized template arguments (enclosed in angle brackets and separated by commas), or you can omit them and let the compiler deduce the specialized arguments. See "Deducing Argument Types" earlier in this chapter for details.

If you need to change the function parameters, you can overload the function, but that requires an entirely new function or function template declaration, not a specialization. Example 7-7 shows two specializations of a function template.

Example 7-7. Specializing a function template

```
// Primary template declaration
template<typename T> T root(T x, T y)
{
  return pow(x, 1.0/y);
}

// Specialization in which T is deduced to be long
template<> long root(long x, long y)
{
  if (y == 2)
    return sqrt((long double)x);
  else
    return pow((long double)x, 1.0l/y);
}

// Specialization for explicit T=int
template<> int root<int>(int x, int y)
{
  if (y == 2)
    return sqrt(double(x));
  else
    return pow(double(x), 1.0/y);
}

// Overload with a different function template, such as valarray<T>.
template<template<typename T> class C, typename T>
C<T> root(const C<T>& x, const C<T>& y)
{
  return pow(x, C<T>(1.0)/y);
}
```

A specialization of a class template requires an entirely new class declaration or definition. The members of the specialized class template can be entirely different from the members of the primary class template. If you want to specialize only some members, you can specialize just those members instead of specializing the entire class.

In a specialization of a static data member, you must supply an explicit initializer to define the data member. Without an initializer, the member template declaration is just a declaration of the data member, not a definition. If you want to use the static data member, you must make sure it is defined:

```
    template<typename T>
    struct demo {
      static T data;
```

```
  };
  template<> int demo<int>::data;        // Declaration
  template<> int demo<int>::data = 42; // Definition
```

Declare specializations before the template is used. (See ""Instantiation" later in this chapter for information on how templates are "used.") A program must have a single specialization for a given set of template arguments.

Example 7-8 shows some specializations of a class template, type_traits, which exposes a few attributes, or traits, of a type. The primary template describes the default traits, and the template is specialized for specific types, such as int. See Chapter 8 for more information about traits.

Example 7-8. Specializing a class template

```cpp
#include <iostream>
#include <ostream>
#include <sstream>
#include <string>
#include <typeinfo>

template<typename T>
struct type_traits
{
  typedef T base_type;
  enum { is_fundamental = 0 };
  enum { is_integer = 0 };
  enum { is_float = 0 };
  enum { is_pointer = 0 };
  enum { is_reference = 0 };
  static std::string to_string(const T&);
};

template<typename T>
std::string type_traits<T>::to_string(const T& x)
{
  return typeid(x).name( );
}

// Specialize entire class for each fundamental type.
template<>
struct type_traits<int>
{
  typedef int base_type;
  enum { is_fundamental = 1 };
  enum { is_integer = 1 };
  enum { is_float = 0 };
  enum { is_pointer = 0 };
  enum { is_reference = 0 };
  static std::string to_string(const int& x) {
    std::ostringstream out;
    out << x;
    return out.str( );
  }
};
```

Example 7-8. Specializing a class template (continued)

```
struct point
{
  int x, y;
};

// Specialize only the to_string() member function for type point.
template<>
std::string type_traits<point>::to_string(const point& p)
{
  std::ostringstream out;
  out << '(' << p.x << ',' << p.y << ')';
  return out.str();
}

int main()
{
  using std::cout;
  cout << type_traits<point>::is_fundamental << '\n';
  cout << type_traits<point>::is_pointer << '\n';
  cout << type_traits<point>::to_string(point()) << '\n';
  cout << type_traits<int>::is_fundamental << '\n';
  cout << type_traits<int>::is_pointer << '\n';
  cout << type_traits<int>::is_integer << '\n';
  cout << type_traits<int>::to_string(42) << '\n';
}
```

Partial Specialization

You can choose to specialize only some of the parameters of a class template. This is known as partial specialization. Note that function templates cannot be partially specialized; use overloading to achieve the same effect.

A partial specialization is declared with a template header that contains one or more template parameters. (With no template parameters, it is a total specialization, not a partial specialization; see the previous section for details.) The class declaration that follows the template header must supply an argument for each parameter of the primary template (or rely on default arguments), and the arguments can depend on the template parameters of the partial specialization. For example, suppose you have a simple pair class, similar to the one in the standard library, but you want to allow one member of the pair to be void. In this case, an object can be made smaller and store only one item:

```
template<typename T, typename U>
struct pair {
  T first;
  U second;
};
template<typename X> struct pair<X, void> {
  X first;
};
```

The partial specialization of a class is a distinct template and must provide a complete class definition. You cannot partially specialize a member of a class template, only the entire class template.

Example 7-9 shows partial specializations of the `type_traits` template from Example 7-8. The first partial specialization applies to all pointer types. It sets the `is_pointer` member to 1, for example. The second partial specialization applies to all const types. It sets most members to their values obtained from the non-const template instance. Thus, `type_traits<const int*>::base_type` is plain int.

Example 7-9. Partially specializing a class template

```
// Specialize for all pointer types.
template<typename T>
struct type_traits<T*>
{
  typedef T base_type;
  enum { is_fundamental = type_traits<T>::is_fundamental };
  enum { is_integer = 0 };
  enum { is_float = 0 };
  enum { is_pointer = 1 };
  enum { is_reference = 0 };
  static std::string to_string(const T& x) {
    std::ostringstream out;
    out << x;
    return out.str();
  }
};

// Specialize for const types, so base_type refers to the non-const type.
template<typename T>
struct type_traits<const T>
{
  typedef T base_type;
  typedef type_traits<base_type> base_type_traits;
  enum { is_fundamental = base_type_traits::is_fundamental };
  enum { is_integer = base_type_traits::is_integer };
  enum { is_float =  base_type_traits::is_float };
  enum { is_pointer =  base_type_traits::is_pointer };
  enum { is_reference =  base_type_traits::is_reference };
  static std::string to_string(const base_type& x) {
    return type_traits<base_type>::to_string(x);
  }
};
```

Instantiation

Template declarations and specializations describe the form that a class or function can take but do not create any actual classes or functions. To do these things, you must instantiate a template.

Most often, you implicitly instantiate a template by using it in a function call, object declaration, or similar context. The template instance requires a template argument for each template parameter. The arguments can be explicit (enclosed in angle brackets and separated by commas) or implicit (default arguments for class templates or deduced arguments for function templates):

```
template<typename T> T plus(T a, T b) { return a + b; }
template<typename T = int> struct wrapper {
  T value;
};
int x = plus(10, 20); // Instantiate plus<int>.
wrapper<double> x;     // Instantiate wrapper<double>.
wrapper<> w;           // Instantiate wrapper<int>.
```

A class member expression (. or -> operator) that names an instance of a member function template with template arguments must use the `template` keyword before the member name. Similarly, a qualified name of a member template must use `template` before the member name. Otherwise, the < symbol that introduces the template argument list is interpreted as the less-than operator:

```
class bigfloat {
  template<unsigned N> double round();
  template<unsigned N> static double round(double);
};

bigfloat f;
std::cout << f.template round<2>() << '\n';
std::cout << bigfloat::template round<8>(PI) << '\n';
```

Instantiating a class template does not necessarily instantiate all the members. Members of a class template are instantiated only when they are needed. A static data member is "needed" if the program refers to the member. A member function is "needed" if the function is called, has its address taken, or participates in overload resolution. An implementation is permitted to define every virtual function in a class template, and most implementations do. Each instance of a class template has its own, separate copy of the class's static data members.

If a class template has any specializations, the compiler must choose which specialization to instantiate. It starts by choosing which partial specializations match the template arguments. A partial specialization matches if the specialized template arguments can be deduced from the actual template arguments. See "Deducing Argument Types" earlier in this chapter.

If no specializations match, the compiler instantiates the primary template. If one specialization matches, that one is instantiated. Otherwise, the best match is chosen, in which "best" means most specific. An error results if two or more specializations are tied for best. Template specialization A is at least as specific as template specialization B if the parameters of A can be deduced from B's template parameter list. No implicit conversion takes place when comparing specializations. The following example shows several instances of the demo class template. The template instantiations are instances of the primary template or one of the three partial specializations:

```
template<typename T, typename U, int N> class demo {};
template<typename T, int N> class demo<T, int, N> {};
template<typename T> class demo<T, T, 0> {};
```

```
template<typename T> class demo<T*, T, 1> {};
demo<int,  char,  1> w;      // Primary template
demo<char, int,  10> x;      // First specialization
demo<char, char,  0> y;      // Second specialization
demo<char, char,  1> z;      // Primary template
demo<char*,char,  1> p;      // Third template
demo<char*,char,  0> q;      // Primary template
demo<char*,char*, 0> r;      // Second template
demo<int*, int,   1> s;      // Error: ambiguous
```

In addition to the obvious points at which a function or class is needed (e.g., calling the function, taking the address of the function, declaring an object whose type is the class, or casting an object to the class), there are more subtle points of instantiation. For example, a template can be instantiated if it is used in the value of a default function argument, and the default argument is needed in a function call.

A function template is needed if an instance of the template is needed for overload resolution. If a class template participates in function overloading (that is, as part of a function parameter type), but the template does not need to be instantiated to resolve the overload (e.g., because the function parameter is a pointer or reference to the class template), the class template may or may not be instantiated. The standard leaves this up to the implementation.

If a template declaration contains an error, the compiler might diagnose the error when it compiles the template or when it instantiates the template. If a program does not instantiate the template, you might find that you can compile a program successfully using one compiler (which reports errors only when a template is instantiated), but not a different compiler (which reports errors when a template is declared).

You can explicitly instantiate a template. Use a bare `template` keyword followed by a declaration that supplies the template arguments for the template:

```
template long int plus<long int>(long int a, long int b);
template short plus(short a, short b); // Deduce plus<short>.
template struct wrapper<unsigned const char*>;
```

The class, function, or member template must be defined before it can be instantiated. If you are instantiating a specialization, the template specialization must appear before the instantiation in the source. The behavior is undefined if a template is specialized after it has been instantiated for the same template arguments. Example 7-10 illustrates template instantiation.

Example 7-10. Instantiating templates

```
#include <iomanip>
#include <iostream>
#include <ostream>
const double pi = 3.1415926535897932;
// Function template
template<typename T> T sqr(T x)
{
  return x * x;
}
```

Example 7-10. Instantiating templates (continued)

```
// Class template
template<typename T>
class circle
{
public:
  circle(T r) : radius_(r) {}
  // sqr<> is instantiated when circle<> is instantiated.
  T area() const { return pi * sqr(radius_); }
  T radius() const { return radius_; }
private:
  T radius_;
};

// Function template
template<typename T>
void print(T obj)
{
  std::cout << obj << '\n';
}

// Overload the function template with another template.
template<typename T>
void print(const circle<T>& c)
{
  std::cout << "circle(" << c.radius() << ")\n";
}

template int sqr<int>(int); // Explicit instantiation

// Explicit instantiation of circle<double> and implicit instantiation of
// sqr<double>
template class circle<double>;

// Error: after instantiation of sqr<double>, illegal to specialize it
template<> double sqr(double x)
{
  return x * x;
}

int main()
{
  using namespace std;
  // No circle<> instance is needed yet, even to resolve overloaded print
  // function.
  print(42);
  for (int i = 0; i < 10; ++i)
    // Implicit instantiation of sqr<int>
    cout << setw(2) << i << setw(4) << sqr(i) << '\n';
  // Instantiation of circle<float> and therefore sqr<float>
  circle<float> unit(1.0f);
```

Example 7-10. Instantiating templates (continued)

```
  // Implicit instantiation of print<circle<float> >
  print(unit);
}
```

Name Lookup

Templates introduce a new wrinkle to name lookup. (See Chapter 2 for the non-template rules of name lookup.) When compiling a template, the compiler distinguishes between names that depend on the template parameters (called *dependent names*) and those that do not (*nondependent names*). Nondependent names are looked up normally when the template is declared. Dependent names, on the other hand, must wait until the template is instantiated, when the template arguments are bound to the parameters. Only then can the compiler know what those names truly mean. This is sometimes known as *two-phase lookup*.

Dependent Names

This section describes dependent names, and the following section describes what the compiler does with them.

A dependent name can have different meanings in different template instantiations. In particular, a function is dependent if any of its arguments are type-dependent. An operator has a dependent name if any of its operands are type-dependent.

A *dependent type* is a type that that can change meaning if a template parameter changes. The following are dependent types:

- The name of a type template parameter or template template parameter:
  ```
  template<typename T> struct demo { T dependent; }
  ```
- A template instance with template arguments that are dependent:
  ```
  template<typename T> class templ {};
  template<typename U> class demo { templ<U> dependent; }
  ```
- A nested class in a dependent class template (such as the class template that contains the nested class):
  ```
  template<typename T> class demo { class dependent {}; }
  ```
- An array that has a base type that is a dependent type:
  ```
  template<typename T> class demo { T dep[1]; }
  ```
- An array with a size that is value-dependent (defined later in this section):
  ```
  template<typename T> class demo { int dep[sizeof(T)]; }
  ```
- Pointers and references to dependent types or functions (that is, functions whose return types or parameter types are dependent or whose default arguments are dependent):
  ```
  template<typename T> class demo { T& x; T (*func)(); }
  ```

- A class, struct, or union that depends on a template parameter for a base class or member (note that a non-template class nested in a class template is always dependent):

  ```
  template<typename T> class demo { class nested { T x; }; };
  ```

- A const- or volatile-qualified version of a dependent type:

  ```
  template<typename T> class demo { const T x; };
  ```

- A qualified name, in which any qualifier is the name of a dependent type:

  ```
  template<typename T> struct outer { struct inner {}; };
  template<typename T> class demo { outer<T>::inner dep; };
  ```

A *type-dependent expression* has a dependent type. It can be any of the following:

- `this`, if the class type is dependent
- A qualified or unqualified name if its type is dependent
- A cast to a dependent type
- A `new` expression, creating an object of dependent type
- Any expression that is built from at least one dependent subexpression, except when the result type is not dependent, as in the following:
  - A `sizeof` or `typeid` expression
  - A member reference (with the `.` or `->` operators)
  - A `throw` expression
  - A `delete` expression

A constant expression can also be *value-dependent* if its type is dependent or if any subexpression is value-dependent. An identifier is value-dependent in the following cases:

- When it is the name of an object with a dependent type
- When it is the name of a value template parameter
- When it is a constant of integral or enumerated type, and its initial value is a value-dependent expression

A `sizeof` expression is value-dependent only if its operand is type-dependent. A cast expression is dependent if its operand is a dependent expression. Example 7-11 shows a variety of dependent types and expressions.

Example 7-11. Dependent names

```
template<typename T> struct base {
  typedef T value_type; // value_type is dependent.
  void func(T*);        // func is dependent.
  void proc(int);       // proc is nondependent.

  class inner {         // inner is dependent.
    int x;              // x is nondependent.
  };
  template<unsigned N>
  class data {          // data is dependent.
    int array[N];       // array is dependent.
  };
```

Example 7-11. Dependent names (continued)

```
class demo : inner {  // demo is dependent.
    char y[sizeof(T)];  // y is dependent.
  };
};

int main( )
{
  base<int> b;
}
```

Resolving Names

When writing a template declaration or definition, you should use qualified names as much as possible. Use member expressions to refer to data members and member functions (e.g., this->data). If a name is a bare identifier, the name lookup rules are different from the rules for non-templates.

The compiler looks up unqualified, nondependent names at the point where the template is declared or defined. Dependent base classes are not searched (because, at the point of declaration, the compiler does not know anything about the instantiation base class). This can give rise to surprising results. In the following example, the get_x member function does not see base<T>::x, so it returns the global x instead:

```
template<typename T> struct base {
  double x;
};
int x;
template<typename T>
struct derived : base<T> {
  int get_x() const { return x; } // Returns ::x
};
```

Dependent names are looked up twice: first in the context of the declaration and later in the context of the instantiation. In particular, when performing argument-dependent name lookup (Chapter 2), the compiler searches the declaration and instantiation namespaces for the function argument types.

Essentially, the instantiation context is the innermost namespace scope that encloses the template instantiation. For example, a template instance at global scope has the global scope as its instantiation context. The context for an instance that is local to a function is the namespace where the function is defined. Thus, the instantiation context never includes local declarations, so dependent names are never looked up in the local scope.

A function template can have multiple instantiation points for the same template arguments in a single source file. A class template can have multiple instantiations for the same template arguments in multiple source files. If the different contexts for the different instantiations result in different definitions of the templates for the same template arguments, the behavior is undefined. The best way to avoid this undefined behavior is to avoid using unqualified dependent names.

Example 7-12 shows several ways dependent name lookup affects a template. In particular, note that iterator_base can refer to its members without qualification or member expressions. However, the derived classes, such as iterator, must use this-> or qualify the member name with the base class because the base class is not searched for unqualified names. The print member function is also interesting. It prints the array by using an ostream_iterator, which calls operator<< to print each element. The name operator<< is dependent, so it is not looked up when the template is declared, but when the template is instantiated. At that time, the compiler knows the template argument, big::integer, so it also knows to search the big namespace for the right overloaded operator<<.

Example 7-12. Resolving dependent names

```cpp
#include <algorithm>
#include <iostream>
#include <iterator>
#include <ostream>
#include <stdexcept>

template<unsigned Size, typename T>
class array {
  template<unsigned Sz, typename U>
    friend class array<Sz,U>::iterator;
  template<unsigned Sz, typename U>
    friend class array<Sz,U>::const_iterator;
  class iterator_base {
  public:
    iterator_base& operator++() {
      ++ptr;
      return *this;
    }
    T operator*() const { check(); return *ptr; }
  protected:
    iterator_base(T* s, T* p) : start(s), ptr(p) {}
    void check() const {
      if (ptr >= start + Size)
        throw std::out_of_range("iterator out of range");
    }
    T* ptr;
    T* start;
  };
public:
  array(): data(new T[Size]) {}
  class iterator : public iterator_base,
    public std::iterator<std::random_access_iterator_tag,T>
  {
  public:
    iterator(T* s, T* p) : iterator_base(s, p) {}
    operator const_iterator() const {
      return const_iterator(this->start, this->ptr);
    }
    T& operator*() {
      iterator_base::check();
```

Example 7-12. Resolving dependent names (continued)

```
      return *this->ptr;
    }
  };
  iterator begin( ) { return iterator(data, data); }
  iterator end( )   { return iterator(data, data + Size); }
  template<typename charT, typename traits>
  void print(std::basic_ostream<charT,traits>& out)
  const
  {
    std::copy(begin( ), end( ), std::ostream_iterator<T>(out));
  }
private:
  T* data;
};

namespace big {
  class integer {
  public:
    integer(int x = 0) : x_(x) {}
    operator int( ) const { return x_; }
  private:
    int x_; // Actual big integer implementation is left as an exercise.
  };

  template<typename charT, typename traits>
  std::basic_ostream<charT,traits>&
    operator<<(std::basic_ostream<charT,traits>& out,
               const integer& i)
  {
    out << int(i);
    return out;
  }
}

int main( )
{
  const array<10, big::integer> a;
  a.print(std::cout);
}
```

Hiding Names

When using templates, several situations can arise in which template parameters hide names that would be visible in a non-template class or function. Other situations arise in which template parameter names are hidden by other names.

If a member of a class template is defined outside of the namespace declaration that contains the class template, a template parameter name hides members of the namespace:

```
    namespace ns {
      template<typename T>
      struct demo {
```

```
    demo( );
    T x;
  };
  int z;
}
template<typename z>
ns::demo::demo( )
{
  x = z( ); // Template parameter z, not ns::z
}
```

Template parameter names are hidden in the following cases:

- If a member is defined outside of its class template, members of the class or class template hide template parameter names:

  ```
  template<typename T>
  struct demo {
    T x;
    demo( );
  };
  template<typename x>
  demo::demo( ) { x = 10; } // Member x, not parameter x
  ```

- In the definition of a member of a class template that lies outside the class definition, or in the definition of a class template, a base class name or the name of a member of a base class hides a template parameter if the base class is nondependent:

  ```
  struct base {
    typedef std::size_t SZ;
  };
  template<int SZ>
  struct derived : base {
    SZ size; // base::SZ hides template parameter.
  };
  ```

If a base class of a class template is a dependent type, it and its members do not hide template parameters, and the base class is not searched when unqualified names are looked up in the derived-class template.

Using Type Names

When parsing a template definition, the compiler must know which names are types and which are objects or functions. Unqualified names are resolved using the normal name lookup rules (described earlier in this section). Qualified dependent names are resolved according to a simple rule: if the name is prefaced with typename, it is a type; otherwise, it is not a type.

Use typename only in template declarations and definitions, and only with qualified names. Although typename is meant to be used with dependent names, you can use it with nondependent names. Example 7-13 shows a typical use of typename.

Example 7-13. Using typename in a template definition

```
// Erase all items from an associative container for which a predicate returns
// true.
template<typename C, typename Pred>
void erase_if(C& c, Pred pred)
{
  // Need typename because iterator is qualified
  for (typename C::iterator it = c.begin(); it != c.end();)
    if (pred(*it))
      c.erase(*it++);
    else
      ++it;
}
```

Tricks with Templates

Template syntax permits recursion, selection, and computation. In other words, it is a full-fledged programming language, albeit a language that is hard to write and even harder to read. The full scope and power of programming with templates is beyond the scope of this book. This section presents some tips for starting your own exploration of this exciting field. Appendix B tells you about some interesting projects in this area.

Suppose you want to write a function to round off floating-point values to a fixed number of decimal places. You decide to write the function by multiplying by a power of 10, rounding off to an integer, and dividing by the same power of 10. You can hardcode the amount, (e.g., 100) in the routine, but you prefer to use a template, in which a template parameter specifies the number of decimal digits to retain. To avoid computing the same power of 10 every time the function is called, you decide to use template programming to compute the constant at compile time.

The ipower<> template in Example 7-14 uses recursion to compute the power of any integer raised to any nonnegative integer value. Three base cases for the recursion are defined as specializations: raising any value to the 0th power is always 1, raising 0 to any power is always 0, and raising 0 to the 0th power is undefined. (As an exercise, try to define ipower more efficiently.) Finally, the ipower<> class template is used to define the round<> function template.

Example 7-14. Computing at compile time

```
template<int x, unsigned y>
struct ipower {
  enum { value = x * ipower<x, y-1>::value };
};
template<int x>
struct ipower<x, 0> {
  enum { value = 1 };
};
template<unsigned y>
struct ipower<0, y> {
  enum { value = 0 };
```

Example 7-14. Computing at compile time (continued)

```
};
template<> struct ipower<0, 0> {};

// Round off a floating-point value to a fixed number of digits.
template<unsigned N, typename T>
T round(T x)
{
  if (x < 0.0)
    return std::floor(x * ipower<10,N>::value - 0.5) /
           ipower<10,N>::value;
  else
    return std::floor(x * ipower<10,N>::value + 0.5) /
           ipower<10,N>::value;
}
```

In addition to compile-time computation, you can write more complicated programs that are evaluated at compile time. For example, the Boost project (described in Appendix B) uses templates to create type lists, that is, lists of types that are manipulated at compile time. Such lists can greatly simplify certain programming tasks, such as implementing type traits. Example 7-15 shows a simplified version of type lists. A list is defined recursively as an empty list or a node that contains a type (head) and a list (tail). (This definition should be familiar to anyone with experience using functional programming languages.)

Example 7-15. Defining type lists

```
struct empty {};
template<typename H, typename T>
struct node {
  typedef H head;
  typedef T tail;
};

template<typename T1  = empty, typename T2  = empty,
         typename T3  = empty, typename T4  = empty,
         typename T5  = empty, typename T6  = empty,
         typename T7  = empty, typename T8 = empty,
         typename T9  = empty, typename T10 = empty,
         typename T11 = empty, typename T12 = empty
>
struct list {
  typedef node<T1, node<T2, node<T3, node<T4,
          node<T5, node<T6, node<T7, node<T8,
          node<T9, node<T10, node<T11, node<T12,
          empty
          > > > > > > > > > > > > type;
};

template<typename L>
struct length {
  enum { value = 1 + length<typename L::tail>::value };
};
```

Example 7-15. Defining type lists (continued)

```
template<>
struct length<empty> {
  enum { value = 0 };
};

template<typename L>
struct is_empty {
  enum { value = false };
};
template<>
struct is_empty<empty> {
  enum { value = true };
};
```

Actions on type lists are inherently recursive. Thus, to count the number of items in a type list, count the head as one, and add the length of the tail. The recursion stops at the end of the list, which is implemented as a specialization of the length<> template for the empty type.

An important action when using type lists is to test membership. To do this, you must be able to compare two types to see if they are the same. The is_same_type class template uses partial specialization to determine when two types are the same. If the two types specified as template arguments are the same, the specialization sets value to true. If the arguments are different, the primary template is instantiated, and value is false. Example 7-16 shows is_same_type and how it is used in the is_member template.

Example 7-16. Testing membership in a type list

```
template<typename T, typename U>
struct is_same_type {
  enum  { value = false };
};
template<typename T>
struct is_same_type<T, T> {
  enum { value = true };
};

template<typename T, typename L>
struct is_member {
  enum { value = is_same_type<T, typename L::head>::value
              || is_member<T, typename L::tail>::value };
};

template<typename T>
struct is_member<T, empty> {
  enum { value = false };
};
```

Once you can define type lists and test whether a type is in a type list, you can use these templates to implement simple type traits. For example, you can create a list of the integral types and test whether a type is one of the fundamental integral types. (Testing for integral types is important when implementing standard containers, as discussed in Chapter 10.) Example 7-17 shows some simple uses of type lists.

Example 7-17. Using type lists

```
#include <iostream>
#include <ostream>

typedef list<bool, char, unsigned char, signed char,
             int, short, long, unsigned,
             unsigned long, unsigned short>::type int_types;
typedef list<float, double, long double>::type real_types;

int main()
{
  using namespace std;
  cout << is_same_type<int,int>::value << '\n';
  cout << is_same_type<int, signed int>::value << '\n';
  cout << is_same_type<int, unsigned int>::value << '\n';
  cout << is_member<int, int_types>::value << '\n';
  cout << is_member<float, int_types>::value << '\n';
  cout << is_member<ostream, int_types>::value << '\n';
}
```

Compiling Templates

Like an ordinary function, a function template requires a definition before the function can be called. Like an ordinary class, a class template requires a definition for each member function and static data member before they can be used. Unlike ordinary functions or members, however, templates are typically defined in every source file.

Templates are often used by placing a template declaration and all supporting definitions in a header file, (e.g., *template.h*). Then #include that file anywhere the template is needed. For every implicit or explicit instantiation, the compiler generates the necessary code for the template's instantiation. If multiple source files instantiate the same template with the same arguments, the compiler and linker ensure that the program contains a single copy of the instantiated functions and members.

Different compilers use different techniques to ensure that the program contains a single copy of each template instance. The following are four different approaches:

- The most common approach is to have the compiler keep track of which source files require which instantiations. When the program is linked, the compiler combines all the lists of required instantiations and compiles the template instantiations at that time. As an optimization, the compiler saves the compiled instantiations, so an instantiation that does not change does not need to be recompiled.

- Another approach is to have the compiler generate the code for all needed instantiations when it compiles each source file. The linker identifies duplicate instantiations and ensures that the linked program gets a single copy of each instantiation.

- A third approach is to separate the template declaration from its associated definitions. If the declaration is in *template.h*, the definitions are in *template.cc*. The compiler automatically locates the definition file from the name of the declaration file. In this scenario, the compiler keeps track of which instantiations it needs and compiles each of them only once.

- Another approach uses the export keyword to declare and define templates. An exported template lets you define a function template or all the members of a class template in a separate source file. The template's header contains only the declarations.

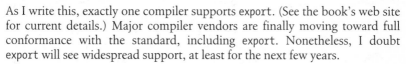 As I write this, exactly one compiler supports export. (See the book's web site for current details.) Major compiler vendors are finally moving toward full conformance with the standard, including export. Nonetheless, I doubt export will see widespread support, at least for the next few years.

If portability is important to you, do not use export.

Consult your compiler's documentation to learn how it handles templates. When writing a template that can be used by multiple compilers, a common technique is to put the declaration in a header file (e.g., *template.h*), and the definitions in another file (e.g., *template.cc*), and at the end of *template.h*, use conditional directives to #include "template.cc" for those compilers where it is needed. Use conditional compilation to define a macro only for compilers that support export. Example 7-18 shows this common pattern.

Example 7-18. Declaring and defining a template

```
// point.h
#ifndef POINT_H
#define POINT_H

#ifdef HAS_EXPORT
 #define EXPORT export
#else
 #define EXPORT
#endif

EXPORT template<typename T>
class point {
public:
  point(T a, T b);
  point();
  T x() const { return x_; }
  T y() const { return y_; }
private:
  T x_, y_;
};
```

Example 7-18. Declaring and defining a template (continued)

```
#ifdef NEED_TEMPLATE_DEFINITIONS
 #include "point.cc"
 #endif
#endif // POINT_H

// point.cc
#include "point.h"
EXPORT template<typename T>
point<T>::point(T a, T b)
: x_(a), y_(b)
{}

EXPORT template<typename T>
point<T>::point( )
: x_(T( )), y_(T( ))
{}

// program.cc
#include "point.h"
int main( )
{
  point<float> ptf;
  point<int> pti;
  ...
}
```

If your compiler supports export, define HAS_EXPORT. If the compiler requires
template definitions in every source file, define NEED_TEMPLATE_DEFINITIONS. Most
compilers offer a way to define macros globally (e.g., in a project definition file, in
a makefile, etc.). Another alternative is to use conditional compilation to test the
predefined macros that most compilers define, and use those to set the template
macros accordingly. Put these definitions in a configuration file that is included
first by every other file, as shown in Example 7-19.

Example 7-19. Configuring template compilation macros

```
// config.h
#ifndef CONFIG_H
#define CONFIG_H

#ifdef __COMO__
  #define HAS_EXPORT
  #undef NEED_TEMPLATE_DEFINITIONS
#endif
#if defined(__BORLANDC__) || defined(__GNUC__)
  #undef HAS_EXPORT
  #define NEED_TEMPLATE_DEFINITIONS
#endif
...

#endif // CONFIG_H
```

8

Standard Library

The previous seven chapters describe the C++ language. This and the next two chapters describe the library. The library consists of a number of headers, in which each header declares types, macros, and functions for use in C++ programs. Much of the standard library is implemented using templates, so the implementation is typically embodied entirely in header files. Nonetheless, parts of the library are separately compiled and must be linked into a C++ program, the details of which are dictated by the implementation.

This chapter presents an overview of the standard library and some of its more important components: wide and multibyte characters, traits, policies, allocators, and numerics. Other important parts of the library get their own chapters: Chapter 9 introduces the input and output classes, and Chapter 10 describes the containers, iterators, and algorithms that make up what is most often known as the "standard template library," or STL.

Overview of the Standard Library

The standard library has 51 headers, each containing a set of macro, function, type, and object declarations. A header is sometimes called a header file, but that phrase is misleading. An implementation does not need to implement headers as external files, although it is often simplest to think of a header as a file that contains macro, type, and function declarations.

Almost all the names declared in the standard library are in the std namespace. Macros, of course, are not in any namespace, so it is important that you know which names are macros and which are not. The detailed descriptions in Chapter 13 tell you this information. The only other names that are outside the std namespace are the global operator new and operator delete functions, declared in the <new> header.

To use the standard library, you must #include the desired header or headers. Some implementations #include headers within other headers (e.g., <set> might #include <iterator>). The headers that a vendor includes within a header vary from one implementation to another, so code that compiles successfully with one vendor's environment might not compile in a different environment. The solution is to get in the habit of including all the headers you need.

If you see headers of the form <iostream.h>, the program was probably written in the days before the C++ standard. It might also mean that your compiler and library were written before C++ was standardized. Although some popular, old compilers are still in wide use, they have newer versions that provide much better support for the C++ standard. Following the C++ standard is the best way to achieve portability across recent compilers and libraries.

You must not add any declarations to the std namespace, although you can specialize templates that are declared in std. When you add your own specialization, you must obey all the constraints specified for the template, and the specialization must depend on at least one user-defined name that has external linkage. Otherwise, the behavior is undefined.

The following are brief descriptions of the contents of each header. The headers inherited from the C standard are marked as "C header." Some of these headers have improved C++ equivalents, which are also shown. For complete descriptions of these headers, see Chapter 13.

<algorithm>
  Standard algorithms for copying, searching, sorting, and otherwise operating on iterators and containers. See Chapter 10 for more information about the standard algorithms.

<bitset>
  Class template to hold a fixed-sized sequence of bits.

<cassert>
  Runtime assertion-checking; C header.

<cctype>
  Character classification and case conversion; C header (see also <locale>).

<cerrno>
  Error codes; C header.

<cfloat>
  Limits of floating-point types; C header (see also <limits>).

<ciso646>
  Empty header because C declarations are incorporated in the C++ language; C header.

<climits>
  Limits of integer types; C header (see also <limits>).

<clocale>
  Locale-specific information; C header (see also <locale>).

`<cmath>`
    Mathematical functions; C header.

`<complex>`
    Complex numbers.

`<csetjmp>`
    Nonlocal goto; C header.

`<csignal>`
    Asynchronous signals; C header.

`<cstdarg>`
    Macros to help implement functions that take a variable number of arguments; C header.

`<cstddef>`
    Miscellaneous standard definitions; C header.

`<cstdio>`
    Standard input and output; C header (see also `<iostream>` and related headers).

`<cstdlib>`
    Miscellaneous functions and related declarations; C header.

`<cstring>`
    String-handling functions; C header (see also `<string>`).

`<ctime>`
    Date and time functions and types; C header.

`<cwchar>`
    Wide character functions, including I/O; C header (see also `<locale>`, `<iostream>`, `<string>`, and other I/O-related headers).

`<cwctype>`
    Wide character classification and case conversion; C header (see also `<locale>`).

`<deque>`
    Deque (double-ended queue) standard container.

`<exception>`
    Base exception class and functions related to exception-handling.

`<fstream>`
    File-based stream I/O.

`<functional>`
    Function objects; typically used with standard algorithms.

`<iomanip>`
    I/O manipulators; used with standard I/O streams.

`<ios>`
    Base class declarations for all I/O streams.

`<iosfwd>`
    Forward declarations for I/O objects.

`<iostream>`
    Declarations of standard I/O objects.

`<istream>`
 Input streams and input/output streams.

`<iterator>`
 Additional iterators for working with standard containers and algorithms. See Chapter 10 for more information.

`<limits>`
 Limits of numerical types.

`<list>`
 Standard linked list container.

`<locale>`
 Locale-specific information for formatting and parsing numbers, dates, times, and currency values, plus character-related functions for classifying, converting, and comparing characters and strings.

`<map>`
 Associative map (sometimes called a dictionary) standard container.

`<memory>`
 Allocators, algorithms for uninitialized memory, and smart pointers (`auto_ptr`).

`<new>`
 Global `operator new` and `operator delete` and other functions related to managing dynamic memory.

`<numeric>`
 Numerical algorithms.

`<ostream>`
 Output streams.

`<queue>`
 Queue and priority queue container adapters.

`<set>`
 Associative set container.

`<sstream>`
 String-based I/O streams.

`<stack>`
 Stack container adapter.

`<stdexcept>`
 Standard exception classes.

`<streambuf>`
 Low-level stream buffers; used by high-level I/O streams.

`<string>`
 Strings and wide-character strings.

`<strstream>`
 String streams that work with character arrays (see also `<sstream>`).

`<typeinfo>`
 Runtime type information.

`<utility>`
> Miscellaneous templates, such as `pair`, most often used with standard containers and algorithms.

`<valarray>`
> Numerical arrays.

`<vector>`
> Vector (array-like) standard container.

C Library Wrappers

The C++ library includes the entire C standard library (from the 1990 C standard, plus Amendment 1), in which each C header, such as `<stdio.h>`, is wrapped as a C++ header (e.g., `<cstdio>`). Being part of the C++ standard, all types, functions, and objects are declared in the `std` namespace.

The external names are also reserved in the global namespace. Thus, proper practice is to use the names in the `std` namespace (e.g., `std::strlen`), but realize that these names are also reserved in the global namespace, so you cannot write your own `::strlen` function.

The C standard permits macros to be defined to mask function names. In the C++ wrappers for these headers, the names must be declared as functions, not macros. Thus, the C `<stdio.h>` header might contain the following:

```
extern int printf(const char* fmt, ...);
#define printf printf
```

In C++, the `printf` macro is not permitted, so the `<cstdio>` header must declare the `printf` function in the `std` namespace, so you can use it as `std::printf`.

A deprecated feature of C++ is that the C standard headers are also available as their original C names (e.g., `<stdio.h>`). When used in this fashion, their names are in the global namespace, as though a `using` declaration were applied to each name (e.g., `using std::printf`). Otherwise, the old style headers are equivalent to the new headers. The old C header names are deprecated; new code should use the `<cstdio>`, etc., style C headers.

Wide and Multibyte Characters

The familiar `char` type is sometimes called a *narrow character*, as opposed to `wchar_t`, which is a *wide character*. The key difference between a narrow and wide character is that a wide character can represent any single character in any character set that an implementation supports. A narrow character, on the other hand, might be too small to represent all characters, so multiple narrow `char` objects can make up a single, logical character called a *multibyte character*.

Beyond some minimal requirements for the character sets (see Chapter 1), the C++ standard is purposely open-ended and imposes few restrictions on an implementation. Some basic behavioral requirements are that conversion from a narrow character to a wide character must produce an equivalent character. Converting back to a narrow character must restore the original character. The open nature of the standard gives the compiler and library vendor wide latitude. For example, a compiler for Japanese customers might support a variety of Japanese Industrial Standard (JIS) character sets, but not any European character sets. Another vendor might support multiple ISO 8859 character sets for Western and Eastern Europe, but not any Asian multibyte character sets. Although the standard defines universal characters in terms of the Unicode (ISO/IEC 10646) standard, it does not require any support for Unicode character sets.

This section discusses some of the broad issues in dealing with wide and multi-byte characters, but the details of specific characters and character sets are implementation-defined.

Wide Characters

A program that must deal with international character sets might work entirely with wide characters. Although wide characters usually require more memory than narrow characters, they are usually easier to use. Searching for substrings in a wide string is easy because you never have the problem of matching partial characters (which can happen with multibyte characters).

A common implementation of wchar_t is to use Unicode UTF-32 encoding, which means each wide character is 32 bits and represents a single Unicode character. Suppose you want to declare a wide string that contains the Greek letter pi (π). You can specify the string with a universal name (see Chapter 1):

```
wchar_t wpi[] = "\u03c0";
```

Using UTF-32, the string would contain L"\x03c0". With a different wchar_t implementation, the wpi string would contain different values.

The standard wstring class supports wide strings, and all the I/O streams support wide characters (e.g., wistream, wostream).

Multibyte Characters

A multibyte character represents a single character as a series of one or more bytes, or narrow characters. Because a single character might occupy multiple bytes, working with multibyte strings is more difficult than working with wide strings. For example, if you search a multibyte string for the character '\x20', when you find a match, you must test whether the matching character is actually part of a multibyte character and is therefore not actually a match for the single character you want to find.

Consider the problem of comparing multibyte strings. Suppose you need to sort the strings in ascending order. If one string starts with the character '\xA1' and other starts with '\xB2', it seems that the first is smaller than the second and therefore should come before the second. On the other hand, these characters might be the first of multibyte character sequences, so the strings cannot be compared until you have analyzed the strings for multibyte character sequences.

Multibyte character sets abound, and a particular C++ compiler and library might support only one or just a few. Some multibyte character sets specifically support a particular language, such as the Chinese Big5 character set. The UTF-8 character set supports all Unicode characters using one to six narrow characters.

For example, consider how an implementation might encode the Greek letter pi (π), which has a Unicode value of 0x03C0:

```
char    pi[] = "\u03c0";
```

If the implementation's narrow character set is ISO 8859-7 (8-bit Greek), the encoding is 0xF0, so pi[] contains "\xf0". If the narrow character set is UTF-8 (8-bit Unicode), the representation is a multibyte character, and pi[] would contain "\xe0\x8f\x80". Many character sets do not have any encoding for π, in which case the contents of pi[] might be "?", or some other implementation-defined marker for unknown characters.

Shift State

You can convert a multibyte character sequence to a wide character and back using the functions in <cwchar>. When performing such conversions, the library might need to keep track of state information during the conversion. This is known as the *shift state* and is stored in an mbstate_t object (also defined in <cwchar>).

For example, the Japanese Industrial Standard (JIS) encodes single-byte characters and double-byte characters. A 3-byte character sequence shifts from single- to double-byte mode, and another sequence shifts back. The shift state keeps track of the current mode. The initial shift state is single-byte. Thus, the multibyte string "\x1B$B&P\x1B(B" represents one wide character, namely, the Greek letter pi (π). The first three characters switch to double-byte mode. The next two characters encode the character, and the final three characters restore single-byte mode.

Shift states are especially important when performing I/O. By definition, file I/O uses multibyte characters. That is, a file is treated as a sequence of narrow characters. When reading a wide-character stream, the narrow characters are converted to wide characters, and when writing a wide stream, wide characters are converted back to multibyte characters. Seeking to a new position in a file might seek to a position that falls in the middle of a multibyte sequence. Therefore, a file position is required to keep track of a shift state in addition to a byte position in the file. See <ios> in Chapter 13.

Traits and Policies

Traits are used throughout the C++ library. A *trait* is a class or class template that characterizes a type, possibly a template parameter. At first glance, it seems that traits obscure information, hiding types and other declarations in a morass of templates. This is true, but traits are also powerful tools used in writing templates. Traits are often used to obtain information from built-in types in the same manner as user-defined types.

A *policy* is a class or class template that defines an interface as a service to other classes. Traits define type interfaces, and policies define function interfaces, so they are closely related. Sometimes, a single class template implements traits and policies.

The typical application programmer might never use traits and policies directly. Indirectly, however, they are used in the string class, I/O streams, the standard containers, and iterators—just about everywhere in the standard library.

Character Traits

One of the most commonly used trait and policy templates is char_traits<> in the <string> header. The standard declares two specializations: char_traits<char> and char_traits<wchar_t>.

The rest of the C++ library uses character traits to obtain types and functions for working with characters. For example, the basic_istream class template takes a character type, charT, and a character traits type as template parameters. The default value for the traits parameter is char_traits<charT>, which is a set of character traits defined in <string>. The basic_istream template declares the get( ) function, which reads a character and returns its integer equivalent. The return type is obtained from the character traits template, specifically int_type.

As a policy template, char_traits<> provides member functions that compare characters and character arrays, copy character arrays, and so on. For example, compare compares two character arrays for equality. The char_traits<char> specialization might implement compare by calling memcmp.

At a basic level, the typical C++ programmer does not need to be concerned with the implementation of traits. Instead, you can use the istream and string classes, and everything just works. If you are curious, you can trace the declaration of, for example, istream::int_type:

```
istream::int_type → basic_istream<char>::int_type → traits::int_type →
char_traits<char>::int_type → int
```

As you can see, traits can be difficult to follow when you need to know the exact type of one of the types declared in a standard container.

Once you get used to them, however, you can see how valuable traits can be. Consider what happens when you change from istream::int_type to wistream::int_type:

```
wistream::int_type → basic_istream<wchar_t>::int_type →
traits::int_type → char_traits<wchar_t>::int_type → wint_t
```

Note that the declarations of basic_istream and the other templates do not differ when the template parameter changes from char to wchar_t. Instead, you end up with a different template specialization for char_traits<>, which directs you to a different integer type.

You can implement your own character traits and policy template. For example, suppose you want to use strings that compare themselves without regard to case differences. Comparison is a policy issue, typically implemented by the char_traits<> template. You can define your own template that has the same trait and policy implementation, but one that implements compare to

ignore case differences. Using your template, you can specialize basic_string<>
to create a case-insensitive string class and then store those strings in sets and
maps. The keys will be compared using your policy function that ignores case
differences, as shown in Example 8-1.

Example 8-1. Case-insensitive character policy

```
template<typename T> struct ci_char_traits {};
template<> struct ci_char_traits<char> {
  typedef char char_type;
  typedef int int_type;
  typedef std::streamoff off_type;
  typedef std::streampos pos_type;
  typedef std::mbstate_t state_type;

  static void assign(char_type& dst, const char_type src) {
    dst = src;
  }
  static char_type* assign(char* dst, std::size_t n, char c) {
    return static_cast<char_type*>(std::memset(dst, n, c));
  }
  static bool eq(const char_type& c1, const char_type& c2) {
    return lower(c1) == lower(c2);
  }
  static bool lt(const char_type& c1, const char_type& c2) {
    return lower(c1) < lower(c2);
  }
  static int compare(const char_type* s1,
  const char_type* s2, std::size_t n) {
    for (size_t i = 0; i < n; ++i)
    {
      char_type lc1 = lower(s1[i]);
      char_type lc2 = lower(s2[i]);
      if (lc1 < lc2)
        return -1;
      else if (lc1 > lc2)
        return 1;
    }
    return 0;
  }
  ...
private:
  static int_type lower(char_type c) {
    return std::tolower(to_int_type(c));
  }
};

typedef std::basic_string<char, ci_char_traits<char> >
  ci_string;

void print(const std::pair<const ci_string, std::size_t>& item)
{
  std::cout << item.first << '\t' << item.second << '\n';
}
```

Example 8-1. Case-insensitive character policy (continued)

```
int main( )
{
  std::map<ci_string, std::size_t> count;
  ci_string word;
  while (std::cin >> word)
    ++count[word];
  std::for_each(count.begin( ), count.end( ), print);
}
```

Iterator Traits

Traits are also useful for iterators (Chapter 10). An algorithm often needs to know the iterator category to provide specializations that optimize performance for random access iterators, for example. Traits provide a standard way to convey this information to the algorithm—namely, by using the iterator_category typedef. They also permit algorithms to use plain pointers as iterators.

For example, the distance function returns the distance between two iterators. For random access iterators, the distance can be computed by subtraction. For other iterators, the distance must be computed by incrementing an iterator and counting the number of increments needed. Example 8-2 shows a simple implementation of distance that uses the iterator traits to choose the optimized random access implementation or the slower implementation for all other input iterators.

Example 8-2. Implementing the distance function template

```
// Helper function, overloaded for random access iterators
template<typename InputIter>
typename std::iterator_traits<InputIter>::difference_type
compute_dist(InputIter first, InputIter last,
             std::random_access_iterator_tag)
{
  return last - first;
}

// Helper function, overloaded for all other input iterators
template<typename InputIter>
typename std::iterator_traits<InputIter>::difference_type
compute_dist(InputIter first, InputIter last,
             std::input_iterator_tag)
{
  typename std::iterator_traits<InputIter>::difference_type
    count = 0;
  while (first != last) {
    ++first;
    ++count;
  }
  return count;
}
```

Example 8-2. Implementing the distance function template (continued)

```
// Main distance function, which calls the helper function, using the iterator
// tag to differentiate the overloaded functions.
template<typename InputIter>
typename std::iterator_traits<InputIter>::difference_type
distance(InputIter first, InputIter last)
{
  return compute_dist(first, last,
    std::iterator_traits<InputIter>::iterator_category( ));
}
```

Being able to optimize algorithms for certain kinds of iterators is one benefit of using traits, but the real power comes from the iterator_traits<T*> specialization. This class permits the use of any pointer type as an iterator. (See <iterator> in Chapter 13 for details.) Consider how the distance function is called in the following example:

```
int data[] = { 10, 42, 69, 13, 100, -1 };
distance(&data[1], &data[4]);
```

The compiler infers the InputIter template parameter as type int*. The iterator_traits<T*> template is expanded to obtain the iterator_category type (random_access_iterator_tag) and difference_type (ptrdiff_t).

Custom Traits

Traits can be useful whenever you are using templates. You never know what the template parameters might be. Sometimes, you want to specialize your own code according to a template parameter.

For example, all the standard sequence containers have a constructor that takes two iterators as arguments:

```
template<typename InputIterator>
list(InputIterator first, InputIterator last);
```

But take a closer look at the declaration. The author's intent is clear: that the template parameter must be an input iterator, but nothing in the declaration enforces this restriction. The compiler allows any type to be used (at least any type that can be copied).

If the InputIterator type actually is an input iterator, the list is constructed by copying all the elements in the range [first, last). But if the InputIterator type is an integral type, the first argument is interpreted as a count, and the last argument is interpreted as an integer value, which is converted to the value type of the container; the container is then initialized with first copies of the last value, which is ordinarily the work of a different constructor. See Chapter 10 for more information about these constructors.

If you need to implement your own container template, you must find a way to implement this kind of constructor. The simplest way is to define a traits template that can tell you whether a type is an integral type. Example 8-3 shows one possible implementation and how it can be used by a container.

Example 8-3. Differentiating between integral types using traits

```
// Type trait to test whether a type is an integer.
struct is_integer_tag {};
struct is_not_integer_tag {};

// The default is that a type is not an integral type.
template<typename T>
struct is_integer {
  typedef is_not_integer_tag tag;
};

// Override the default explicitly for all integral types.
template<>
struct is_integer<int> {
  typedef is_integer_tag tag;
};
template<>
struct is_integer<short> {
  typedef is_integer_tag tag;
};
template<>
struct is_integer<unsigned> {
  typedef is_integer_tag tag;
};
// And so on for char, signed char, short, etc.

// Constructor uses the is_integer trait to distinguish integral from nonintegral
// types and dispatches to the correct overloaded construct function.
template<typename T, typename A>
template<typename InputIter>
list<T,A>::list(InputIter first, InputIter last)
{
   construct(first, last, is_integer<InputIter>::tag( ));
}

// The construct member functions finish the initialization of the list. The
// integral version casts the arguments to the size and value types.
template<typename T, typename A>
template<typename InputIter>
void list<T,A>::construct(InputIter first, InputIter last,
                          is_integer_tag)
{
  insert(begin( ), static_cast<size_type>(first),
            static_cast<T>(last));
}

// The non-integral version copies elements from the iterator range.
template<typename T, typename A>
template<typename InputIter>
void list<T,A>::construct(InputIter first, InputIter last,
                          is_not_integer_tag)
{
  insert(begin( ), first, last);
}
```

Traits can be used to characterize any type and specialize templates for a wide variety of situations. See the Boost project (described in Appendix B) for other definitions and uses of traits.

Allocators

An *allocator* is a policy class that defines an interface for managing dynamic memory. You already know about the new and delete expressions for allocating and freeing dynamic memory. They are simple, expressive, and useful, but the standard library does not necessarily use them internally. Instead, the standard library uses allocators, which let you provide alternative mechanisms for allocating and freeing memory.

The standard library provides a standard allocator (see <memory> in Chapter 13). If you don't want to use the standard allocator, you can use your own, provided it satisfies the same interface that is defined by the standard allocator.

Using Allocators

An allocator is a simple object that manages dynamic memory, abstracting new and delete expressions. All the container class templates take an allocator template parameter and use the allocator to manage their internal memory. You can use allocators in your own container classes or wherever you want to offer flexibility to the user of your class or template.

If you do not want to bother with allocators, you don't need to. All the standard containers have a default argument for their allocator template parameters: std::allocator, which uses standard new and delete expressions to manage dynamic memory.

If you write a new container class template, make sure it takes an allocator parameter, as the standard containers do. Use the allocator to manage internal memory for your container. See Chapter 10 for more information about containers.

If you simply want to use an allocator to manage memory, you can do so. Your class would use the allocator to allocate and free memory, initialize and finalize objects, and take the address of an allocated object. (See <memory> in Chapter 13 for a complete description of the allocator policy interface.) Example 8-4 shows a simple class that wraps a dynamic instance of any object. It is not particularly useful, but it illustrates how a class can use an allocator. Note how the allocation of memory is separated from the construction of the object. If allocate fails to allocate the desired memory, it throws bad_alloc, so the wrapper constructor fails before it tries to construct the object. If the allocation succeeds, but the call to construct fails, the memory must be freed, hence the try statement. The destructor assumes that wrapped class is well-written and never throws an exception.

Example 8-4. Wrapping a dynamic object

```
template<typename T, typename Alloc=std::allocator<T> >
class wrapper {
public:
```

Example 8-4. Wrapping a dynamic object (continued)

```
typedef T value_type;
typedef typename Alloc::pointer pointer;
typedef typename Alloc::reference reference;

// Allocate and save a copy of obj.
wrapper(const T& obj = T( ), const Alloc& a = Alloc( ))
: alloc_(a), ptr_(0)
{
  T* p = a.allocate(sizeof(T));
  try {
    alloc_.construct(p, obj);
  } catch(...) {
    // If the construction fails, free the memory without trying to finalize
    // the (uninitialized) object.
    alloc_.deallocate(p);
    throw;
  }
  // Everything succeeded, so save the pointer.
  ptr_ = p;
}
~wrapper( )
{
  alloc_.destroy(ptr_);
  alloc_.deallocate(ptr_);
}
  typename Alloc::reference operator*( )     { return *ptr_; }
  value_type operator*( ) const             { return *ptr_; }
private:
  Alloc alloc_;
  typename Alloc::pointer ptr_;
};
```

Custom Allocators

Writing a custom allocator requires care and patience. One particularly difficult point is that an implementation of the standard library is free to assume that all instances of an allocator class are equivalent, that is, allocators cannot maintain state. The standard permits this behavior without mandating it.

Thus, you need to be aware of the standard library's requirements for your implementation. Once you know the requirements, you can write a custom allocator. As a starting point, see Example 13-30 (under <memory>), which implements the allocator as trivial wrappers around new and delete expressions. Other allocators might manage memory that is shared between processes or differentiate between different kinds of pointers (such as near and far pointers found on old PC operating systems). More sophisticated allocators can implement debugging or validity checks to detect programmer errors, such as memory leaks or double frees.

Numerics

The C++ library has several headers that support numerical programming. The most basic header is <cmath>, which declares transcendental and other mathematical functions. This C header is expanded in C++ to declare overloaded versions of every function. For example, whereas C declares only exp(double), C++ also declares exp(float) and exp(long double).

The <complex> header declares a class template for complex numbers, with the specializations you would probably expect for float, double, and long double. Transcendental and I/O functions are also declared for complex numbers.

The <numeric> header declares a few algorithms (that use standard iterators) for numerical sequences.

The most interesting numerical functions are in <valarray>. A valarray is like an ordinary numerical array, but the compiler is free to make some simplifying assumptions to improve optimization. A valarray is not a container, so it cannot be used with standard algorithms or the standard numeric algorithms.

You can use the complex template as an example of how to define custom numeric types. For example, suppose you want to define a type to represent rational numbers (fractions). To use rational objects in a valarray, you must define the class so it behaves the same as ordinary values, such as ints. In other words, a custom numeric type should have the following:

- A public default constructor (e.g., rational( ))
- A public copy constructor (e.g., rational(const rational&))
- A public destructor
- A public assignment operator (e.g., rational& operator=(const rational&))
- Reasonable arithmetic and comparison operators

When you implement a class, make sure that the copy constructor and assignment operator have similar, reasonable results.

When overloading arithmetic and comparison operators, think about which operators are meaningful (e.g., most arithmetic types should have addition, subtraction, multiplication, and division, but only integral types will probably have remainder, bitwise, and shift operators). You should provide overloaded operators that accept the built-in types as operands. For example, the complex template defines the following functions for operator+:

```
template<typename T> complex<T> operator+(const complex<T>& z);
template<typename T> complex<T> operator+(const complex<T>& x, const
                                          complex<T>& y);
template<typename T> complex<T> operator+(const complex<T>& x, const T& y);
template<typename T> complex<T> operator+(const T& x, const complex<T>& y);
```

Example 8-5 shows excerpts from a simple rational class template.

Example 8-5. The rational class template for rational numbers

```
template<typename T>
class rational
```

Example 8-5. The rational class template for rational numbers (continued)

```
{
public:
  typedef T value_type;

  rational()                      : num_(0),     den_(1) {}
  rational(value_type num)    : num_(num), den_(1) {}
  rational(value_type num, value_type den)
    : num_(num), den_(den) { reduce(); }
  rational(const rational& r): num_(r.num_), den_(r.den_) {}
  template<typename U>
  rational(const rational<U>& r)
    : num_(r.num_), den_(r.den_) { reduce(); }

  rational& operator=(const rational& r)
    { num_ = r.num_; den_ = r.den_; return *this; }
  template<typename U>
  rational& operator=(const rational<U>& r)
    { assign(r.numerator(), r.denominator()); return *this; }

  void assign(value_type n, value_type d)
    { num_ = n; den_ = d; reduce(); }

  value_type numerator()   const { return num_; }
  value_type denominator() const { return den_; }

private:
  void reduce();
  value_type num_;
  value_type den_;
};

// Reduce the numerator and denominator by the gcd. Make sure that the
// denominator is nonnegative.
template<typename T>
void rational<T>::reduce()
{
  if (den_ < 0) {
    den_ = -den_;
    num_ = -num_;
  }
  T d = gcd(num_, den_);
  num_ /= d;
  den_ /= d;
}

// Greatest common divisor using Euclid's algorithm
template<typename T>
T gcd(T n, T d)
{
  n = abs(n);
  while (d != 0) {
    T t = n % d;
```

```
      n = d;
      d = t;
    }
    return n;
}


// Multiplication assignment operator. Often implemented as a member function,
// but there is no need to do so.
template<typename T, typename U>
rational<T>& operator*=(rational<T>& dst,
                        const rational<U>& src)
{
  dst.assign(dst.numerator( ) * src.numerator( ),
             dst.denominator( ) * src.denominator( ));
  return dst;
}


// Multiply two rational numbers.
template<typename T>
rational<T> operator*(const rational<T>& a,
                      const rational<T>& b)
{
  rational<T> result(a);
  result *= b;
  return result;
}


// Multiply rational by an integral value.
template<typename T>
rational<T> operator*(const T& a, const rational<T>& b)
{
  return rational<T>(a * b.numerator( ), b.denominator( ));
}


template<typename T>
rational<T> operator*(const rational<T>& a, const T& b)
{
  return rational<T>(b * a.numerator( ), a.denominator( ));
}
// Other arithmetic operators are similar.
// Comparison. All other comparisons can be implemented in terms of operator==
// and operator<.
template<typename T>
bool operator==(const rational<T>& a, const rational<T>& b)
{
  // Precondition. Both operands are reduced.
  return a.numerator( ) == b.numerator( ) &&
         a.denominator( ) == b.denominator( );
}


template<typename T>
bool operator<(const rational<T>& a, const rational<T>& b)
```

Standard
Library

Example 8-5. The rational class template for rational numbers (continued)

```
{
  return a.numerator( ) * b.denominator( ) <
         b.numerator( ) * a.denominator( );
}
```

Many numerical programmers find the C++ standard library to be lacking. However, the Blitz++ project is a popular, high-performance numerical library. Boost also has some numerical headers, such as a full-featured rational class template. See Appendix B for information about these and other C++ libraries.

9

Input and Output

C++ has a rich I/O library, which is often called *I/O streams*. This chapter presents an overview of the C++ I/O library. For details of individual classes and functions, see Chapter 13. The I/O streams often use templates; refer to Chapter 7 for information about templates. See also Chapter 8 for information about character traits.

The standard I/O streams can also be used with standard iterator adapters. See Chapter 10 for details.

Introduction to I/O Streams

As with C and many modern languages, input and output in C++ is implemented entirely in the library. No language features specifically support I/O.

The C++ I/O library is based on a set of templates parameterized on the character type. Thus, you can read and write plain char-type characters, wide wchar_t characters, or some other, exotic character type that you might need to invent. (Read about character traits in Chapter 8 first.) Figure 9-1 depicts the class hierarchy. Notice that the names are of the form basic_*name*. These are the template names; the specializations have the more familiar names (e.g., istream specializes basic_istream<char>).

One advantage of using inheritance in the I/O library is that the basic I/O functions are defined once in the base classes, and that interface is inherited by the derived classes and overridden when necessary. Using inheritance, you perform I/O with files as you would with strings. With only a little effort, you can derive your own I/O classes for specialized situations. (See Example 9-6.) Thus, to understand I/O in C++, you must start with the base classes.

Another advantage of the I/O stream classes is that you can implement your own overloaded functions that look and behave like the standard functions. Thus, you

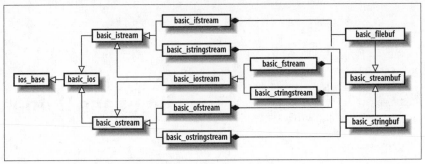

Figure 9-1. The I/O stream class hierarchy

can read and write objects of your custom classes just as easily as the fundamental types.

The ios_base class declares types and constants that are used throughout the I/O library. Formatting flags, I/O state flags, open modes, and seek directions are all declared in ios_base.

The basic_istream template declares input functions, and basic_ostream declares output functions. The basic_iostream template inherits input and output functions through multiple inheritance from basic_istream and basic_ostream.

The stream class templates handle high-level I/O of numbers, strings, and characters. For low-level I/O, the streams rely on *stream buffers*, which control reading and writing buffers of characters. The basic_streambuf template defines the stream buffer interface, and the actual behavior is implemented by derived-class templates.

I/O to and from external files is handled by basic_fstream, basic_ifstream, and basic_ofstream, using basic_filebuf as the stream buffer. These class templates are declared in <fstream>.

You can also treat a string as a stream using basic_istringstream, basic_ostringstream, and basic_stringstream. The stream buffer template is basic_stringbuffer. These class templates are declared in <sstream>.

The I/O library supports formatted and unformatted I/O. Unformatted I/O simply reads or writes characters or character strings without interpretation. The I/O streams have a number of functions for performing unformatted I/O.

Formatted input can skip over leading whitespace, parse text as numbers, and interpret numbers in different bases (decimal, octal, hexadecimal). Formatted output can pad fields to a desired width and write numbers as text in different bases. Formatted I/O uses a stream's *locale* to parse numeric input or format numeric output.

A locale is an object of type locale. It stores character attributes, formatting preferences, and related information about a particular culture or environment. This information is organized into a set of *facets*. For example, the num_get facet defines how numbers are read and parsed from an input stream; the num_put facet defines how numbers are formatted and written to an output stream; and the numpunct facet specifies the punctuation characters used for decimal points, minus signs, and so on. Locales are used primarily by I/O streams, but they have other uses, as well. See <locale> in Chapter 13 for details.

To perform formatted I/O, the I/O streams overload the shift operators: left shift (<<) writes and right shift (>>) reads. Think of the shift operators as arrows pointing in the direction of data flow: output flows from an expression to the stream (cout << expr). Input flows from the stream to a variable (cin >> var). The string, complex, and other types in the standard library overload the shift operators, so you can perform I/O with these objects just as easily as you can with fundamental types.

Custom I/O Operators

When you define your own classes for which I/O is meaningful, you should also override the shift operators to perform I/O in the same manner as the standard I/O operators. A common simplification is to overload the shift operators for istream and ostream, but that prevents your operators from being used with wide-character streams or streams with custom character traits. You should consider writing function templates instead, using basic_istream and basic_ostream, to take advantage of the generality that the I/O stream templates offer.

Other guidelines to follow when writing custom I/O functions are:

- Pay attention to the stream's flags, locale, and state.
- Set failbit for malformed input.
- Be careful with internal whitespace.
- When writing an object that has multiple parts, be careful of how you treat the stream's field width. Remember that the width is reset to 0 after each formatted output function.

Example 9-1 shows an example of I/O for the rational class, which represents a rational number. For input, two numbers are read, separated by a slash (/). If the slash is missing, the input is malformed, so failbit is set. (See the <ios> header in Chapter 13 for more information about failbit and the other state bits.) For output, the two parts of the rational number are formatted as a string, and the entire string is written to the output stream. Using a temporary string lets the caller set the field width and apply the width to the entire rational number as a single entity. If the numerator and denominator were written directly to the output stream, the width would apply only to the numerator. (See Example 9-3 for more information about rational.)

Example 9-1. Performing I/O with the rational class template

```
// Read a rational number. The numerator and denominator must be written as two
// numbers (the first can be signed) separated by a slash (/). For example:
// "2/3", "-14/19".
template<typename T, typename charT, typename traits>
std::basic_istream<charT, traits>&
operator>>(std::basic_istream<charT, traits>& in, rational<T>& r)
{
    typename rational<T>::numerator_type n;
```

Example 9-1. Performing I/O with the rational class template (continued)

```
   typename rational<T>::denominator_type d;
   char c;

   if (! (in >> n)) return in;
   // Allow whitespace before and after the dividing '/'.
   if (! (in >> c)) return in;
   if (c != '/') {
      // Malformed input
      in.setstate(std::ios_base::failbit);
      return in;
   }
   if (! (in >> d)) return in;
   r.set(n, d);
   return in;
}

// Write a rational number as two integers separated by a slash. Use a string
// stream so the two numbers are written without padding, and the overall
// formatted string is then padded to the desired width.
template<typename T, typename charT, typename traits>
std::basic_ostream<charT, traits>&
operator<<(std::basic_ostream<charT, traits>& out, const rational<T>& r)
{
   // Use the same flags, locale, etc. to write the
   // numerator and denominator to a string stream.
   std::basic_ostringstream<charT, traits> s;
   s.flags(out.flags());
   s.imbue(out.getloc());
   s.precision(out.precision());
   s << r.numerator() << '/' << r.denominator();
   // Write the string to out. The field width, padding, and alignment are already
   // set in out, so they apply to the entire rational number.
   out << s.str();
   return out;
}
```

The C Standard I/O Library

Because the C++ library includes the C library, you can use any of the C standard I/O functions, such as fopen and printf. The C standard I/O library is contained in <cstdio> for narrow I/O and <cwchar> for wide-character I/O. The C++ library inherits many attributes from the C library. For example, the C++ end-of-file marker, char_traits<char>::eof( ), has the same value as the C end-of-file marker, EOF. In most cases, however, a C++ program should use C++ I/O functions rather than C functions.

The printf and scanf functions are noteworthy for their lack of safety. Although some compilers now check the format strings and compare them with the actual arguments, many compilers do not. It is too easy to make a simple mistake. If you are lucky, your program will fail immediately. If you are unlucky, your program will appear to work on your system and fail only when it is run on your customers' systems. The following is an example of a common mistake made when using printf:

```
size_t s;
printf("size=%u\n", s);
```

The problem here is that the size_t type might be unsigned long, which means the argument s and the format %u do not match. On some systems, the mismatch is harmless, but on others, wrong information will be printed, or worse.

Other functions, such as gets and sprintf, are unsafe because they write to character arrays with no way to limit the number of characters written. Without a way to prevent buffer overruns, these functions are practically useless.

Another limitation of the C I/O library is that it has little support for alternate locales. In C++, every stream can have a different locale. For example, this lets you write a program that reads a datafile in a fixed format (using the "C" locale), but prints the human-readable results in the native locale. Writing such a program using the C I/O library requires that locales be changed between each read and write call, which is much less convenient.

In spite of all these problems, some C++ programmers still use the C library. In some implementations, the C library performs better than the C++ library. Another reason is that some C++ functions, such as printf, have a brevity that appeals to C and C++ programmers. Compare the following examples, one using printf and the other using the << operator, which both print the same count and mask values in the same formats:

```
unsigned long count, mask;
...
printf("count=%-9.9ld\n"
       "mask=%#-8.8lx\n", count, mask);

cout.fill('0');
cout << "count=" << right << dec << setw(9) << count <<
        "\nmask=0x" << hex << setw(8) << mask << '\n';
```

Even though the printf approach seems more concise and easier to understand, I recommend using the C++ I/O streams. You might think printf is saving you time now, but the lack of safety can present major problems in the future. (Reread the example and imagine what would happen if count exceeded the maximum value for type long.)

Sometimes, using the C I/O library is necessary (e.g., perhaps legacy C code is being called from C++ code). To help in such situations, the standard C++ I/O objects are associated with their corresponding C FILEs. The C++ cin object is associated with the C stdin object, cout is associated with stdout, and cerr and clog are associated with stderr. You can mix C and C++ I/O functions with the standard I/O objects.

C++ I/O Headers

This section lists the I/O-related headers in the C++ standard library, with a brief description of each. See the corresponding sections in Chapter 13 for more detailed descriptions.

`<fstream>`

File streams—that is, input and output using external files. Declares `basic_filebuf`, `basic_fstream`, `basic_ifstream`, `basic_ofstream`, `fstream`, `ifstream`, `ofstream`, `wfstream`, `wistream`, `wostream`, and other types.

`<iomanip>`

Declares several manipulators—that is, function objects that affect an I/O stream object. A manipulator offers an alternate, often more convenient, syntax for calling member functions of an I/O stream object.

`<ios>`

Base template definitions of `ios_base`, `basic_ios` and some common manipulators. All I/O streams derive from `basic_ios`, which derives from `ios_base`.

`<iosfwd>`

Forward declarations of the standard I/O classes and templates. Judicious use of `<iosfwd>` can reduce the compile-time burden in certain situations.

`<iostream>`

Declarations of the standard I/O objects: `cin`, `cout`, etc.

`<istream>`

Declares types and functions for input-only streams (`basic_istream`, `istream`, and `wistream`), and for input and output streams (`basic_iostream`, `iostream`, and `wiostream`).

`<ostream>`

Declares types and functions for output-only streams (`basic_ostream`, `ostream`, and `wostream`).

`<sstream>`

Declares string streams (`basic_istringstream`, `basic_ostringstream`, `basic_stringbuf`, `basic_stringstream`, `istringstream`, `ostringstream`, and `stringstream`), which read from and write to strings using the stream protocol.

`<streambuf>`

Declares low-level stream buffers (`basic_streambuf`) for the I/O stream classes. Most programs do not need to deal with the stream buffers, but stick to the high-level interfaces presented by the stream classes.

`<strstream>`

Declares string streams (`istrstream`, `ostrstream`, `strstream`, `strstreambuf`), which read and write to character arrays using a stream protocol. These classes are not template-based so they do not work for wide characters or alternative character traits. This header is deprecated.

Text I/O

By default, an I/O stream performs text I/O, also known as formatted I/O, in which text is converted to and from numeric and other values. For output, values are converted to text, and padding, alignment, and other formatting is applied to the text. For input, formatting controls how text is converted to values and whether whitespace is skipped prior to reading an input field.

Different systems have different ways of representing the end of a line. A text I/O stream hides these details and maps all line endings in a file to the newline character ('\n'). Thus, the number of characters read from or written to a file might not match the actual file size. An implementation might require a newline at the end of the last line of a file.

To control formatting, a stream keeps track of a set of flags, a field width, and a precision. Table 13-12 (in the <ios> section) lists all the formatting flags.

Formatted Input

The formatted input functions are the overloaded operator>> functions. If the skipws flag is set (which is the default), whitespace characters (according to the locale imbued in the stream) are skipped, and input begins with the first non-whitespace character.

If reading into a string or character array, all non-whitespace characters are read into the string, ending with the first whitespace character or when width characters have been read (if width > 0), whichever comes first. The width is then reset to 0.

For all other types, the width is not used. To read a number from a fixed-width field, read the field into a string, then use a string stream to read the number, as shown in Example 9-2.

Example 9-2. Reading a number from a fixed-width field

```
template<typename T, typename charT, typename traits>
std::basic_istream<charT, traits>&
  fixedread(std::basic_istream<charT, traits>& in, T& x)
{
  if (in.width( ) == 0)
    // Not fixed size, so read normally.
    in >> x;
  else {
    std::string field;
    in >> field;
    std::basic_istringstream<charT, traits> stream(field);
    if (! (stream >> x))
      in.setstate(std::ios_base::failbit);
  }
  return in;
}
```

Input and Output

The only other flags that affect input are basefield and boolalpha:

- The basefield flag determines how integers are interpreted. If basefield is nonzero, it specifies a fixed radix (oct, hex, or dec), or if basefield is 0 (the default), the input determines the radix: leading 0x or 0X for hexadecimal, leading 0 for octal, decimal otherwise.

- If the boolalpha flag is set, a formatted read of bool reads a string, which must match the names true or false (in the stream's locale, according to the numpunct facet). If the boolalpha flag is not set, a bool is read as a long integer, and the number is converted to bool using the standard rules: nonzero is true and 0 is false. By default, the flag is clear (false).

Floating-point numbers are accepted in fixed or scientific format.

The decimal point character is determined by the stream's locale, as is the thousands separator. Thousands separators are optional in the input stream, but if present, they must match the locale's thousands separator character and grouping rules. For example, assuming that the thousands separator is , and the grouping is for every 3 characters (grouping( ) returns "\3"), the following are three valid input examples and one invalid example:

```
1,234,567      // Valid
1,234,56       // Invalid
1234567        // Valid
1234,567       // Valid
```

When reading data that the user types, you should imbue the input stream with the user's native locale (e.g., cin.imbue(locale(""))). For input that is being read from files or other sources that require portable data formats, be sure to use the "C", or classic, locale (e.g., cin.imbue(locale::classic( ))).

See the num_get facet in the <locale> section of Chapter 13 for details on how numeric input is parsed and interpreted.

Formatted Output

The formatted output functions are the overloaded operator<< functions. They all work similarly, using the flags and other information to format a value as a string. The string is then padded with zero or more copies of a fill character to achieve the desired width. The adjustfield flags are used to determine where the fill characters are added (to the left, right, or internal, with internal meaning after a sign or a leading 0x or 0X).

The padded string is written to the output stream, and the stream's width is reset to 0. The width is the only formatting parameter that is reset. The flags, precision, and the fill character are "sticky" and persist until they are changed explicitly.

Formatting an integer depends on the basefield (hex, oct, or dec), uppercase (0X for hexadecimal), showpos (insert a + for positive numbers), and showbase (to insert a prefix of 0x or 0X for hexadecimal or 0 for octal) flags. The defaults are decimal, lowercase, no positive sign, and no base. If the locale's numpunct facet specifies thousands grouping, thousands separators are inserted at the specified positions.

Formatting a floating-point number depends on the floatfield (fixed, scientific, or 0 for general), uppercase (E for exponent), showpoint (insert decimal point even if not needed), and showpos (insert a + for positive numbers) flags. The defaults are general, lowercase, no point unless needed, and no positive sign.

If the boolalpha flag is set, bool values are written as names (e.g., true or false, or other strings, depending on the locale). If boolalpha is not set, bool values are written as integers (described earlier). The default flag is clear (false).

When writing output for a user's immediate consumption, you should imbue the output stream with the user's native locale (e.g., cout.imbue(locale(""))). For output that is being written to files or other sources that require portable data formats, be sure to use the "C", or classic, locale (e.g., cout.imbue(locale::classic())).

See the num_put facet in the <locale> section of Chapter 13 for details on how numeric output is formatted.

Binary I/O

Binary, or unformatted, I/O involves characters, character arrays, or strings, which are read or written without interpretation, padding, or other adjustments. End-of-lines are not treated specially.

The unformatted read functions (such as get and read) can read into a string or character array. The gcount function returns the number of characters read.

The unformatted output functions (such as put and write) can write a string or character array. You can specify the exact number of characters to write from a character array or write all characters up to a null character (to write a C-style null-terminated string).

You can also dip down the stream buffer level to perform unformatted I/O, although this is seldom done except for bulk I/O of entire streams. See the next section for more information.

Stream Buffers

The I/O stream classes rely on stream buffers for the low-level input and output. Most programmers ignore the stream buffer and deal only with high-level streams. You might find yourself dealing with stream buffers from the client side—for example, using stream buffers to perform low-level I/O on entire streams at once—or you might find yourself on the other side, implementing a custom stream buffer. This section discusses both of these aspects.

You can copy a file in several ways. Example 9-3 shows how a C programmer might copy a stream once he has learned about templates.

Example 9-3. Copying streams one character at a time

```
template<typename charT, typename traits>
void copy(std::basic_ostream<charT, traits>& out,
          std::basic_istream<charT, traits>& in)
{
```

Example 9-3. Copying streams one character at a time (continued)

```
  charT c;
  while (in.get(c))
    out.put(c);
}
```

After measuring the performance of this solution, the intrepid programmer might decide that copying larger buffers is the right way to go. Example 9-4 shows the new approach. On my system, the new version runs roughly twice as fast as the original version. (Of course, performance measures depend highly on compiler, library, environment, and so on.)

Example 9-4. Copying streams with explicit buffers

```
template<typename charT, typename traits>
void copy(std::basic_ostream<charT, traits>& out,
          std::basic_istream<charT, traits>& in)
{
  const unsigned BUFFER_SIZE = 8192;
  std::auto_ptr<charT> buffer(new charT[BUFFER_SIZE]);
  while (in) {
    in.read(buffer.get( ), BUFFER_SIZE);
    out.write(buffer.get( ), in.gcount( ));
  }
}
```

After reading more about the C++ standard library, the programmer might try to improve performance by delegating all the work to the stream buffer, as shown in Example 9-5.

Example 9-5. Copying streams via stream buffers

```
template<typename charT, typename traits>
void copy(std::basic_ostream<charT, traits>& out,
          std::basic_istream<charT, traits>& in)
{
  out << in.rdbuf( );
}
```

The version in Example 9-5 runs about as fast as the version in Example 9-4 but is much simpler to read and write.

Another reason to mess around with stream buffers is that you might need to write your own. Perhaps you are implementing a network I/O package. The user opens a network stream that connects to a particular port on a particular host and then performs I/O using the normal I/O streams. To implement your package, you must derive your own stream buffer class template (basic_networkbuf) from the basic_streambuf class template in <streambuf>.

A stream buffer is characterized by three pointers that point to the actual buffer, which is a character array. The pointers point to the beginning of the buffer, the current I/O position (that is, the next character to read or the next position for writing), and the end of the buffer. The stream buffer class manages the array and the pointers. When the array empties upon input, the stream buffer must obtain additional input from the network (the underflow function). When the array fills upon output, the stream buffer must write the data to the network (the overflow function). Other functions include putting back a character after reading it, seeking, and so on. (See <streambuf> in Chapter 13 for details about each member function.) Example 9-6 shows an extremely oversimplified sketch of how the basic_networkbuf class template might work.

Example 9-6. The basic_networkbuf class template

```
template<typename charT,
         typename traits = std::char_traits<char> >
class basic_networkbuf :
  public std::basic_streambuf<charT, traits> {
public:
  typedef charT                      char_type;
  typedef traits                     traits_type;
  typedef typename traits::int_type int_type;
  typedef typename traits::pos_type pos_type;
  typedef typename traits::off_type off_type;

  basic_networkbuf();
  virtual ~basic_networkbuf();

  bool is_connected();
  basic_networkbuf* connect(const char* hostname, int port,
    std::ios_base::openmode mode);
  basic_networkbuf* disconnect();

protected:
  virtual std::streamsize showmanyc();
  virtual int_type underflow();
  virtual int_type overflow(int_type c = traits::eof());
  virtual pos_type seekoff(off_type offset,
    std::ios_base::seekdir dir,
    std::ios_base::openmode);
  virtual pos_type seekpos(pos_type sp,
    std::ios_base::openmode);
  virtual basic_networkbuf* setbuf(char_type* buf,
    std::streamsize size);
  virtual int sync();

private:
  char_type* buffer_;
  std::streamsize size_;
  bool ownbuf_; // true means destructor must delete buffer_
  // network connectivity stuff...
};

// Construct initializes the buffer pointers.
template<typename charT, typename traits>
basic_networkbuf<charT,traits>::basic_networkbuf()
: buffer_(new char_type[DEFAULT_BUFSIZ]),
```

Example 9-6. The basic_networkbuf class template (continued)

```
  size_(DEFAULT_BUFSIZ), ownbuf_(true)
{
  this->setg(buffer_, buffer_ + size_, buffer_ + size_);
  // Leave room in the output buffer for one last character.
  this->setp(buffer_, buffer_ + size_ - 1);
}


// Return the number of characters available in the input buffer.
template<typename charT, typename traits>
std::streamsize basic_networkbuf<charT,traits>::showmanyc()
{
  return this->egptr() - this->gptr();
}


// Fill the input buffer and set up the pointers.
template<typename charT, typename traits>
typename basic_networkbuf<charT,traits>::int_type
basic_networkbuf<charT,traits>::underflow()
{
  // Get up to size_ characters from the network, storing them in buffer_. Store
  // the actual number of characters read in the local variable, count.

  std::streamsize count;
  count = netread(buffer_, size_);
  this->setg(buffer_, buffer_, buffer_ + count));
  if (this->egptr() == this->gptr())
    return traits::eof();
  else
    return traits::to_int_type(*this->gptr());
}


// The output buffer always has room for one more character, so if c is not
// eof(), add it to the output buffer. Then write the buffer to the network
// connection.
template<typename charT, typename traits>
typename basic_networkbuf<charT,traits>::int_type
basic_networkbuf<charT,traits>::overflow(int_type c)
{
  if (c != traits::eof()) {
    *(this->pptr()) = c;
    this->pbump(1);
  }
  netwrite(this->pbase(), this->pptr() - this->pbase());
  // The output buffer is now empty. Make sure it has room for one last
  // character.
  this->setp(buffer_, buffer_ + size_ - 1);
  return traits::not_eof(c);
}


// Force a buffer write.
template<typename charT, typename traits>
int basic_networkbuf<charT,traits>::sync()
```

Example 9-6. The basic_networkbuf class template (continued)

```
{
  overflow(traits::eof());
  return 0;
}
```

Manipulators

A *manipulator* is a function object that can be used as an operand to an input or output operator to manipulate the stream. Manipulators can send additional output to a stream, read input from a stream, set flags, and more. For example, to output a zero-padded, hexadecimal integer, you can use an ostream's member functions or manipulators, whichever you prefer. Example 9-7 shows both ways.

Example 9-7. Manipulating an output stream to format a number

```
using namespace std;

// Output a value using ostream's member functions.
cout.fill('0');
cout.width(8);
cout.setf(ios_base::internal, ios_base::adjustfield);
cout.setf(ios_base::hex, ios_base::basefield);
cout << value;

// Output the same value using manipulators.
cout << setfill('0') << setw(8) << hex << internal << value;
```

Standard Manipulators

The standard library defines several manipulators for setting formatting flags, setting other formatting parameters, skipping whitespace, flushing output, and more. The following is a list of all the standard manipulators, grouped by header:

<ios>
>   Declares the manipulators that set the formatting flags: boolalpha, dec, fixed, hex, internal, left, noboolalpha, noshowbase, noshowpoint, noshowpos, noskipws, nouppercase, nounitbuf, oct, right, scientific, showbase, showpoint, showpos, skipws, uppercase, and unitbuf

<istream>
>   Declares the input manipulator: ws

<ostream>
>   Declares the output manipulators: endl, ends, and flush

<iomanip>
>   Declares several additional manipulators: resetioflags, setioflags, setbase, setfill, setprecision, and setw

Most manipulators are declared in the same header as the stream type they manipulate. The only time you need to #include an additional header is when you

Input and Output

use a manipulator that takes an argument. These manipulators are in the <iomanip> header.

Custom Manipulators

To write your own manipulator, use the standard manipulators as patterns. The easiest to use are manipulators that take no arguments. A manipulator is simply a function that takes a stream as an argument and returns the same stream. The standard streams overload operator<< and operator>> to take a pointer to such a function as an operand.

Suppose you want to write an input manipulator that skips all characters up to and including a newline. (Perhaps this manipulator is used by a command processor after reading a // comment sequence.) Example 9-8 shows one way to write the skipline manipulator.

Example 9-8. Skipping a line in an input stream

```
template<typename charT, typename traits>
std::basic_istream<charT,traits>&
skipline(std::basic_istream<charT,traits>& in)
{
  charT c;
  while (in.get(c) && c != '\n')
    ;
  return in;
}
...
int x;
std::string next;
std::cin >> x >> skipline >> next;
```

Manipulators that take arguments are harder to write, but only slightly. You need to write some supporting infrastructure, such as additional overloaded operator>> or operator<< functions.

For example, suppose you want to parameterize your input skipline manipulator so it skips everything up to a caller-supplied character. This manipulator is defined as a class template, in which the constructor takes the manipulator's argument, that is, the delimiter character. You must overload operator>> so it recognizes your manipulator as an operand and invokes the manipulator's operator( ). You don't need to use operator( ), but this is a good choice when building a reusable infrastructure for manipulators. Example 9-9 shows the new skip manipulator.

Example 9-9. Writing a manipulator that takes an argument

```
template<typename charT>
class skipper
{
public:
  typedef charT char_type;
  skipper(char_type delim) : delim_(delim) {}
```

Example 9-9. Writing a manipulator that takes an argument (continued)

```
  template<typename traits>
  void operator()(std::basic_istream<charT,traits>&) const;
private:
  char_type delim_;
};

// Skip the rest of the line. The compiler deduces the traits type from the
// stream argument.
template<typename charT>
template<typename traits>
void skipper<charT>::operator()(std::basic_istream<charT,traits>& stream)
const
{
  char_type c;
  while (stream.get(c) && c != delim_)
    ;
}

// Invoke the skipper manipulator.
template<typename charT, typename traits>
std::basic_istream<charT,traits>&
operator>>(std::basic_istream<charT,traits>& stream,
           const skipper<charT>& f)
{
  f(stream);
  return stream;
}

// Let the compiler deduce the character type.
template<typename charT>
skipper<charT> skip(charT c)
{
  return skipper<charT>(c);
}
...
int x;
std::string next;
std::cin >> x >> skip('\n') >> next;
```

Errors and Exceptions

By default, I/O streams do not raise exceptions for errors. Instead, each stream keeps a mask of error bits called the *I/O state*. The state mask keeps track of formatting failures, end-of-file conditions, and miscellaneous error conditions. The ios_base class template defines several member functions for testing and modifying the state flags (rdstate, setstate, fail, etc.).

A common idiom is to read from an input stream until an input operation fails. Because this idiom is so common, the standard library makes it easy. Instead of calling rdstate and testing the state explicitly, you can simply treat the stream object as a Boolean value: true means the state is good, and false means the state has an error condition. Most I/O functions return the stream object, which makes the test even easier:

```
while (cin.get(c))
  cout.put(c);
```

The basic_ios class overloads operator void* to return a non-null pointer if the state is good or a null pointer for any error condition. Similarly, it overloads operator! to return true for any error condition. (As explained later in this section, an end-of-file is not an error condition.) This latter test is often used in conditional statements:

```
if (! cout)
  throw("write error");
```

The state mask has three different error bits:

badbit
> An unrecoverable error occurred. For example, an exception was thrown from a formatting facet, an I/O system call failed unexpectedly, and so on.

eofbit
> An end-of-file upon input.

failbit
> An I/O operation failed to produce any input or output. For example, when reading an integer, if the next input character is a letter, no characters can be read from the stream, which results in an input failure.

The basic_ios conditional operators define "failure" as when badbit or failbit is set, but not when eofbit is set. To understand why, consider the following canonical input pattern. During a normal program run, the input stream's state is initially zero. After reading the last item from the input stream, eofbit is set in the state. At this time, the state does not indicate "failure," so the program continues by processing the last input item. The next time it tries to read from the input stream, no characters are read (because eofbit is set), which causes the input to fail, so the stream sets failbit. Now a test of the input stream returns false, indicating failure, which exits the input loop.

Sometimes, instead of testing for failure after each I/O operation, you may want to simplify your code. You can assume that every operation succeeds and arrange for the stream to throw an exception for any failure. In addition to the state mask, every stream has an exception mask, in which the bits in the exception mask correspond to the bits in the state mask. When the state mask changes, if any bit is set in both masks, the stream throws an ios_base::failure exception.

For example, suppose you set the exception mask to failbit | badbit. Using the canonical input pattern, after reading the last item from the input stream, eofbit is set in the state. At this time, rdstate( ) & exceptions( ) is still 0, so the program continues. The next time the program tries to read from the input stream, no characters are read, which causes the input to fail, and the stream sets failbit. Now rdstate( ) & exceptions( ) returns a nonzero value, so the stream throws ios_base::failure.

A stream often relies on other objects (especially locale facets) to parse input or format output. If one of these other objects throws an exception, the stream catches the exception and sets badbit. If badbit is set in the exceptions( ) mask, the original exception is rethrown.

When testing for I/O success, be sure to test for badbit as a special indicator of a serious failure. A simple test for ! cin does not distinguish between different reasons for failure: eofbit | failbit might signal a normal end-of-file, but failbit | badbit might tell you that there is something seriously wrong with the input stream (e.g., a disk error). One possibility, therefore, is to set badbit in the exceptions( ) mask so normal control flow deals with the normal situation of reading an end-of-file. However, more serious errors result in exceptions, as shown in Example 9-10.

Example 9-10. Handling serious I/O errors

```
#include <algorithm>
#include <cstddef>
#include <exception>
#include <iostream>
#include <map>
#include <string>

void print(const std::pair<std::string, std::size_t>& count)
{
  std::cout << count.first << '\t' << count.second << '\n';
}

int main( )
{
  using namespace std;

  try {
    string word;
    map<string, size_t> counts;
    cin.exceptions(ios_base::badbit);
    cout.exceptions(ios_base::badbit);
    while (cin >> word)
      ++counts[word];
    for_each(counts.begin( ), counts.end( ), print);
  } catch(ios_base::failure& ex) {
    std::cerr << "I/O error: " << ex.what( ) << '\n';
    return 1;
  } catch(exception& ex) {
    std::cerr << "Fatal error: " << ex.what( ) << '\n';
    return 2;
  } catch(...) {
    std::cerr << "Total disaster.\n";
    return 3;
  }
}
```

10

Containers, Iterators, and Algorithms

Containers (sometimes called collections) are a staple of computer programming. Every major programming language has fundamental containers, such as arrays or lists. Modern programming languages usually have an assortment of more powerful containers, such as trees, for more specialized needs.

The C++ library has a basic suite of containers (deques, lists, maps, sets, and vectors), but more important, it has *generic algorithms*, which are function templates that implement common algorithms, such as searching and sorting. The algorithms operate on *iterators*, which are an abstraction of pointers that apply to any container or other sequence.

This chapter presents an overview of the standard C++ containers, the iterators used to examine the containers, and the algorithms that can be used with the iterators. It covers how to use the standard containers, iterators, and algorithms, as well as how to write your own.

In this chapter, the mathematical notation of [first, last) is often used to denote a range. The square bracket marks an inclusive endpoint of a range, and the parenthesis marks an exclusive endpoint of a range. Thus, [first, last) means a range that extends from first to last, including first, but excluding last. Read more about ranges in "Iterators" later in this chapter.

For complete details about the various containers, iterators, and algorithms, see Chapter 13.

Containers

The fundamental purpose of a container is to store multiple objects in a single container object. Different kinds of containers have different characteristics, such as speed, size, and ease of use. The choice of container depends on the characteristics and behavior you require.

In C++, the containers are implemented as class templates, so you can store anything in a container. (Well, almost anything. The type must have *value semantics*, which means it must behave as an ordinary value, such as an int. Values can be copied and assigned freely. An original and its copy must compare as equal. Some containers impose additional restrictions.)

Standard Containers

The standard containers fall into two categories: sequence and associative containers. A sequence container preserves the original order in which items were added to the container. An associative container keeps items in ascending order (you can define the order relation) to speed up searching. The standard containers are:

deque
> A deque (double-ended queue) is a sequence container that supports fast insertions and deletions at the beginning and end of the container. Inserting or deleting at any other position is slow, but indexing to any item is fast. Items are not stored contiguously. The header is <deque>.

list
> A list is a sequence container that supports rapid insertion or deletion at any position but does not support random access. Items are not stored contiguously. The header is <list>.

map
multimap
> A map (or dictionary) is an associative container that stores pairs of keys and associated values. The keys determine the order of items in the container. map requires unique keys. multimap permits duplicate keys. The header for map and multimap is <map>.

set
multiset
> A set is an associative container that stores keys in ascending order. set requires unique keys. multiset permits duplicate keys. The header for set and multiset is <set>.

vector
> A vector is a sequence container that is like an array, except that it can grow as needed. Items can be rapidly added or removed only at the end. At other positions, inserting and deleting items is slower. Items are stored contiguously. The header is <vector>.

The set and map containers perform insertions, deletions, and searches in logarithmic time, which implies a tree or tree-like implementation. Items must be kept in sorted order, so a hash table implementation is not allowed. Many programmers consider the lack of a standard hash table to be a serious omission. When the C++ standard is revised, a hash table is likely to be added. The STLport project includes hash table–based containers. See Appendix B for information about STLport.

Container Adapters

In addition to the standard containers, the standard library has several container adapters. An adapter is a class template that uses a container for storage and provides a restricted interface when compared with the standard containers. The standard adapters are:

priority_queue
> A priority queue is organized so that the largest element is always the first. You can push an item onto the queue, examine the first element, or remove the first element. The header is <queue>.

queue
> A queue is a sequence of elements that lets you add elements at one end and remove them at the other end. This organization is commonly known as FIFO (first-in, first-out). The header is <queue>.

stack
> A stack is a sequence that lets you add and remove elements only at one end. This organization is commonly known as LIFO (last-in, first-out). The header is <stack>.

Pseudo-Containers

The standard library has a few class templates that are similar to the standard containers but fail one or more of the requirements for a standard container:

bitset
> Represents a bitmask of arbitrary size. The size is fixed when the bitset is declared. There are no bitset iterators, so you cannot use a bitset with the standard algorithms. See <bitset> in Chapter 13 for details.

basic_string
string
wstring
> Represent character strings. The string class templates meet almost all of the requirements of a sequence container, and you can use their iterators with the standard algorithms. Nonetheless, they fall short of meeting all the requirements of a container, such as lacking front and back member functions. The header is <string>.

valarray
> Represents an array of numeric values optimized for computational efficiency. A valarray lacks iterators, and as part of the optimization, the compiler is free to make assumptions that prevent valarray from being used with the standard algorithms. See <valarray> in Chapter 13 for details.

vector<bool>
> A specialization of the vector template. Although vector<> usually meets the requirements of a standard container, the vector<bool> specialization does not because you cannot obtain a pointer to an element of a vector<bool> object. See <vector> in Chapter 13 for details.

Container Requirements

This section presents the rules that govern containers. Some rules apply to all the standard containers, and you can rely on the standard behavior for all C++ implementations. Other rules apply only to sequence containers, and some apply only to associative containers. If you write your own container class template, be sure to follow the same conventions and rules that apply to the standard containers.

Member types

const_iterator
> The iterator type for const values.

const_reference
> A const lvalue type for the items stored in the container. This is typically the same as the allocator's const_reference type.

difference_type
> A signed integral type denoting the difference between two iterators.

iterator
> The iterator type.

reference
> An lvalue type for the items stored in the container. This is typically the same as the allocator's reference type.

size_type
> An unsigned integral type that can hold any nonnegative difference_type value.

value_type
> The type of item stored in the container. This is typically the same as the first template parameter.

A container that supports bidirectional iterators should also define the reverse_iterator and const_reverse_iterator types.

An associative container should define key_type as the key type, compare_type as the key compare function or functor, and value_compare as a function or functor that compares two value_type objects.

Optionally, a container can declare pointer and const_pointer as synonyms of the allocator's types of the same name, and allocator_type for the allocator, which is typically the last template parameter.

Member functions

Most of the standard member functions have a complexity that is constant or linear in the number of elements in the container. Some of the member functions for associative members are logarithmic in the number of elements in the container. Each of the descriptions in this section notes the complexity of the function.

A container template should have the following constructors. You do not need to write separate constructors in all cases; sometimes you can use default arguments instead of overloading. If an allocator object is supplied, it is copied to the container; otherwise, a default allocator is constructed. In each of the following descriptions, **container** is the name of the container class template.

container( )
container(allocator_type)
> Initializes the container to be empty. Complexity is constant.

container(const container& that)
> Initializes the container with a copy of all the items and the allocator from that. Complexity is linear.

A sequence container should have the following additional constructors:

container(size_type n, const value_type& x)
container(size_type n, const value_type& x, allocator_type)
> Initializes the container with n copies of x. Complexity is linear with respect to n.

template<InIter> **container**(InIter first, InIter last)
template<InIter>
container(InIter first, InIter last, allocator_type)
> Initializes the container with copies of the items in the range [first, last). Complexity is linear with respect to last − first.
>
> If InIter is an integral type, the container is initialized with first copies of last (converted to value_type). Complexity is linear with respect to first.

An associative container should have the following additional constructors:

container(key_compare compare)
container(key_compare compare, allocator_type)
> Initializes an empty container that uses compare to compare keys. Complexity is constant.

template<InIter> **container**(InIter first, InIter last, key_compare compare)
template<InIter> **container**(InIter first, InIter last, key_compare compare,
  allocator_type)
> Initializes the container with copies of the items in the range [first, last), comparing keys with compare. Complexity is linear.

All containers must have a destructor:

~container( )
> Calls the destructor for every object in the container, perhaps by calling clear. Complexity is linear.

Many member functions are the same for all the container templates, and when you write your own container template, you should implement the same member functions with the same behaviors. Some are specific to sequence containers, and some to associative containers. Each container template can define additional members.

```
iterator begin( )
const_iterator begin( ) const
```
> Returns an iterator that points to the first item of the container. Complexity is constant.

```
void clear( )
```
> Erases all the items in the container. Complexity is linear.

```
bool empty( ) const
```
> Returns true if the container is empty (size( ) == 0). Complexity is constant.

```
iterator end( )
const_iterator end( ) const
```
> Returns an iterator that points to one past the last item of the container. Complexity is constant. (See "Iterators" later in this chapter for a discussion of what "one past the last item" means.)

```
erase(iterator p)
```
> Erases the item that p points to. For a sequence container, erase returns an iterator that points to the item that comes immediately after the deleted item or end( ). Complexity depends on the container.

> For an associative container, erase does not return a value. Complexity is constant (amortized over many calls).

```
erase(iterator first, iterator last)
```
> Erases all the items in the range [first, last). For a sequence container, erase returns an iterator that points to the item that comes immediately after the last deleted item or end( ). Complexity depends on the container.

> For an associative container, erase does not return a value. Complexity is logarithmic, plus last – first.

```
size_type max_size( ) const
```
> Returns the largest number of items the container can possibly hold. Although many containers are not constrained, except by available memory and the limits of size_type, other container types, such as an array type, might have a fixed maximum size. Complexity is usually constant.

```
container& operator=(const container& that)
```
> Erases all items in this container and copies all the items from that. Complexity is linear in size( ) + that.size( ).

```
size_type size( ) const
```
> Returns the number of items in the container. Complexity is usually constant.

```
void swap(const container& that)
```
> Swaps the elements of this container with that. An associative container also swaps the comparison function or functions. Complexity is usually constant.

Each container should have all of its equality and relational operators defined, either as member functions or, preferably, as functions at the namespace level. Namespace-level functions offer more flexibility than member functions. For example, the compiler can use implicit type conversions on the lefthand operand but only if the function is not a member function.

A container that supports bidirectional iterators should define rbegin and rend member functions to return reverse iterators.

The following functions are optional. The standard containers provide only those functions that have constant complexity.

reference **at**(size_type n)
const_reference **at**(size_type n) const
 Returns the item at index n, or throws out_of_range if n >= size( ).

reference **back**( )
const_reference **back**( ) const
 Returns the last item in the container. Behavior is undefined if the container is empty.

reference **front**( )
const_reference **front**( ) const
 Returns the first item in the container. Behavior is undefined if the container is empty.

reference **operator[]**(size_type n)
const_reference **operator[]**(size_type n)
 Returns the item at index n. Behavior is undefined if n >= size( ).

void **pop_back**( )
 Erases the last item in the container. Behavior is undefined if the container is empty.

void **pop_front**( )
 Erases the first item in the container. Behavior is undefined if the container is empty.

void **push_back**(const value_type& x)
 Inserts x as the new last item in the container.

void **push_front**(const value_type& x)
 Inserts x as the new first item in the container.

A sequence container should define the following member functions. The complexity of each depends on the container type.

iterator **insert**(iterator p, const value_type& x)
 Inserts x immediately before p and returns an iterator that points to x.

void **insert**(iterator p, size_type n,
const value_type& x)
 Inserts n copies of x before p.

template<InIter>
void **insert**(iterator p, InIter first, InIter last)
 Copies the values from [first, last) and inserts them before p.

An associative container should define the following member functions. In the descriptions of the complexity, N refers to the number of elements in the container, M refers to the number of elements in the argument range (e.g., last − first), and *count* is the value that the function returns. Some of these member functions seem to duplicate standard algorithms (as discussed in "Algorithms" later in this chapter), but the associative containers can implement them with better performance than the generic algorithms.

size_type **count**(const key_type& k) const
> Returns the number of items equivalent to k. Complexity is log N + *count*.

pair<const_iterator,const_iterator>
equal_range(const key_type& k) const
pair<iterator,iterator> **equal_range**(const key_type& k)
> Returns the equivalent of make_pair(lower_bound(k), upper_bound(k)). Complexity is log N.

size_type **erase**(const key_type& k)
> Erases all the items equivalent to k. Returns the number of items erased. Complexity is log N + *count*.

const_iterator **find**(const key_type& k) const
iterator **find**(const key_type& k)
> Finds an item equivalent to k and returns an iterator that points to one such item, or end( ) if not found. Complexity is log N.

insert(const value_type& x)
> Inserts x. If the container permits duplicate keys, insert returns an iterator that points to the newly inserted item. If the container requires unique keys, insert returns pair<iterator,bool>, in which the first element of the pair is an iterator that points to an item equivalent to x, and the second element is true if x was inserted or false if x was already present in the container. Complexity is log N.

iterator **insert**(iterator p, const value_type& x)
> Inserts x and returns an iterator that points to x. The iterator p hints to where x might belong. Complexity is log N in general, but is constant (amortized over many calls) if the hint is correct, that is, if x is inserted immediately after p.

template<InIter>
void **insert**(InIter first, InIter last)
> Copies the items from [first, last) and inserts each item in the container. Complexity is $M \log(N + M)$, but is linear if the range is already sorted.

key_compare **key_comp**( ) const
> Returns the key compare function or functor. Complexity is constant.

const_iterator **lower_bound**(const key_type& k) const
iterator **lower_bound**(const key_type& k)
> Returns an iterator that points to the first item in the container that does not come before k. That is, if k is in the container, the iterator points to the position of its first occurrence; otherwise, the iterator points to the first position where k should be inserted. Complexity is log N.

value_compare **value_comp**( ) const
> Returns the value compare function or functor. Complexity is constant.

const_iterator **upper_bound**(const key_type& k) const
iterator **upper_bound**(const key_type& k)
> Returns an iterator that points to the first item in the container that comes after all occurrences of k. Complexity is log N.

Exceptions

The standard containers are designed to be robust in the face of exceptions. The exceptions that the containers themselves can throw are well-defined (for example, at might throw out_of_range), and most member functions do not throw any exceptions of their own.

If a single value is being added to a container (by calling insert, push_front, or push_back), and an exception is thrown, the container remains in a valid state without adding the value to the container.

When inserting more than one value, different containers have different behaviors. A list, for example, ensures that all items are inserted or none, that is, if an exception is thrown, the list is unchanged. A map or set, however, ensures only that each individual item is inserted successfully. If an exception is thrown after inserting some of the items from a range, the destination container retains the elements that had been inserted successfully.

The erase, pop_back, and pop_front functions never throw exceptions.

The swap function throws an exception only if an associative container's Compare object's copy constructor or assignment operator throws an exception.

Example 10-1 shows an slist container, which implements a singly-linked list. A singly-linked list requires slightly less memory than a doubly-linked list but offers, at best, a forward iterator, not a bidirectional iterator.

Example 10-1. Implementing a custom container: a singly-linked list

```
// Simple container for singly-linked lists.
template<typename T, typename Alloc = std::allocator<T> >
class slist {
  // Private type for a link (node) in the list.
  template<typename U>
  struct link {
    link* next;
    U value;
  };
  typedef link<T> link_type;

public:
  typedef typename Alloc::reference reference;
  typedef typename Alloc::const_reference const_reference;
  typedef typename Alloc::pointer pointer;
  typedef typename Alloc::const_pointer const_pointer;
  typedef Alloc allocator_type;
  typedef T value_type;
  typedef size_t size_type;
  typedef ptrdiff_t difference_type;

  class iterator;        // See the section "Iterators" later in this chapter for
  class const_iterator;  // the iterators.

  slist(const slist& that);
  slist(const Alloc& alloc = Alloc());
```

Example 10-1. Implementing a custom container: a singly-linked list (continued)

```
  slist(size_type n, const T& x, const Alloc& alloc=Alloc());
  template<typename InputIter>
  slist(InputIter first, InputIter last,
        const Alloc& alloc = Alloc());
  ~slist()                             { clear(); }

  slist& operator=(const slist& that);
  allocator_type get_allocator() const { return alloc_; }

  iterator begin()          { return iterator(0, head_); }
  const_iterator begin() const
    { return const_iterator(0, head_); }
  iterator end()            { return iterator(0, 0); }
  const_iterator end() const { return const_iterator(0, 0); }

  void pop_front()                   { erase(begin()); }
  void push_front(const T& x)        { insert(begin(), x); }
  T front()                    const { return head_->value; }
  T& front()                         { return head_->value; }

  iterator insert(iterator p, const T& x);
  void insert(iterator p, size_type n, const T& x);
  template<typename InputIter>
  void insert(iterator p, InputIter first, InputIter last);

  iterator erase(iterator p);
  iterator erase(iterator first, iterator last);

  void clear()             { erase(begin(), end()); }
  bool empty()       const { return size() == 0; }
  size_type max_size() const
    { return std::numeric_limits<difference_type>::max(); }
  void resize(size_type sz, const T& x = T());
  size_type size()     const { return count_; }
  void swap(slist& that);

private:
  typedef typename
    allocator_type::template rebind<link_type>::other
    link_allocator_type;

  link_type* newitem(const T& x, link_type* next = 0);
  void delitem(link_type* item);

  template<typename InputIter>
  void construct(InputIter first, InputIter last,
                 is_integer_tag);

  template<typename InputIter>
  void construct(InputIter first, InputIter last,
                 is_not_integer_tag);
```

Example 10-1. Implementing a custom container: a singly-linked list (continued)

```
  link_type* head_;
  link_type* tail_;
  size_t count_;
  allocator_type alloc_;
  link_allocator_type linkalloc_;
};

// Constructor. If InputIter is an integral type, the standard requires the
// constructor to interpret first and last as a count and value, and perform the
// slist(size_type, T) constructor. Use the is_integer trait to dispatch to the
// appropriate construct function, which does the real work.
template<typename T, typename A>
template<typename InputIter>
slist<T,A>::slist(InputIter first, InputIter last,
                  const A& alloc)
: alloc_(alloc), linkalloc_(link_allocator_type()),
  head_(0), tail_(0), count_(0)
{
  construct(first, last, is_integer<InputIter>::tag());
}


template<typename T, typename A>
template<typename InputIter>
void slist<T,A>::construct(InputIter first, InputIter last,
                           is_integer_tag)
{
  insert(begin(), static_cast<size_type>(first),
         static_cast<T>(last));
}


template<typename T, typename A>
template<typename InputIter>
void slist<T,A>::construct(InputIter first, InputIter last,
                           is_not_integer_tag)
{
  insert(begin(), first, last);
}


// Private function to allocate a new link node.
template<typename T, typename A>
typename slist<T,A>::link_type*
   slist<T,A>::newitem(const T& x, link_type* next)
{
  link_type* item = linkalloc_.allocate(1);
  item->next = next;
  alloc_.construct(&item->value, x);
  return item;
}


// Private function to release a link node.
template<typename T, typename A>
void slist<T,A>::delitem(link_type* item)
```

```
{
  alloc_.destroy(&item->value);
  linkalloc_.deallocate(item, 1);
}


// Basic insertion function. All insertions eventually find their way here.
// Inserting at the head of the list (p == begin()) must set the head_ member.
// Inserting at the end of the list (p == end()) means appending to the list,
// which updates the tail_'s next member, and then sets tail_. Anywhere else in
// the list requires updating p.prev_->next. Note that inserting into an empty
// list looks like inserting at end(). Return an iterator that points to the
// newly inserted node.
template<typename T, typename A>
typename slist<T,A>::iterator
  slist<T,A>::insert(iterator p, const T& x)
{
  // Allocate the new link before changing any pointers. If newitem throws an
  // exception, the list is not affected.
  link_type* item = newitem(x, p.node_);
  if (p.node_ == 0) {
    p.prev_ = tail_;
    // At end
    if (tail_ == 0)
      head_ = tail_ = item; // Empty list
    else {
      tail_->next = item;
      tail_ = item;
    }
  }
  else if (p.prev_ == 0)
    head_ = item;              // New head of list
  else
    p.prev_->next = item;
  p.node_ = item;
  ++count_;
  return p;
}


// Erase the item at p. All erasures come here eventually. If erasing begin(),
// update head_. If erasing the last item in the list, update tail_. Update the
// iterator to point to the node after the one being deleted.
template<typename T, typename A>
typename slist<T,A>::iterator slist<T,A>::erase(iterator p)
{
  link_type* item = p.node_;
  p.node_ = item->next;
  if (p.prev_ == 0)
    head_ = item->next;
  else
    p.prev_->next = item->next;
  if (item->next == 0)
    tail_ = p.prev_;
```

Example 10-1. Implementing a custom container: a singly-linked list (continued)

```
    --count_;
  delitem(item);
  return p;
}

// Comparison functions are straightforward.
template<typename T>
bool operator==(const slist<T>& a, const slist<T>& b)
{
  return a.size() == b.size() &&
         std::equal(a.begin(), a.end(), b.begin());
}
```

Using Containers

A container holds stuff. Naturally, you need to know how to add stuff to a container, remove stuff from a container, find stuff in a container, and so on.

Value type requirements

Every container stores values and imposes certain restrictions on the values' types. Most important, the value must be copyable and assignable. The result of the copy constructor or assignment operator must be an exact copy of the original. (Note that you cannot store auto_ptr<> objects in a container because copies are not exact duplicates.)

In a sequence container, operator== is used to compare objects when searching. If you compare entire containers with any relational operators, the value types must also support operator<. All the relational operators are defined in terms of operator== and operator<.

In an associative container, values are stored in ascending order according to a comparison function or functor that you supply. The default is std::less<>, which uses operator<. Two objects A and B are considered to be equal (more precisely, *equivalent*) when A < B is false and B < A is false, so there is no need for operator==.

Inserting values

To add an item to a container, call an insert member function. Sequence containers might also have push_front or push_back to insert an item at the beginning or end of the sequence. The push_front and push_back members exist only if they can be implemented in constant time. (Thus, for example, vector does not have push_front.)

Every container has an insert(*iter, item*) function, in which *iter* is an iterator and *item* is the item to insert. A sequence container inserts the item before the indicated position. Associative containers treat the iterator as a hint: if the item belongs immediately after the iterator's position, performance is constant instead of logarithmic.

Sequence containers have additional `insert` functions: for inserting many copies of an item at a position and for copying a range to a given position. Associative containers have additional `insert` functions for inserting an item (with no positional hint) and for copying a range into the container.

Erasing values

To remove an item from a container, call an `erase` member function. All containers have at least two `erase` functions: one that takes a single iterator to delete the item that the iterator points to, and another two iterators to delete every item in the range. Associative containers also have an `erase` function that takes a value as an argument to erase all matching items.

The standard containers are designed to be used with the standard iterators (see "Iterators" later in this chapter) and standard algorithms (see "Algorithms" later in this chapter). The standard algorithms offer much more functionality than the containers' member functions, but they also have limitations. In particular, the standard algorithms cannot insert or erase items. For example, among the standard algorithms are `remove` and `remove_if`. Their names are suggestive but misleading. They do not remove anything from the container. Instead, they rearrange the elements of the container so that the items to retain are at the beginning. They return an iterator that points to the first item to be erased. Call `erase` with this iterator as the first argument and `end()` as the second to erase the items from the container. This two-step process is needed because an iterator cannot erase anything. The only way to erase an item from a container is to call a member function of the container, and the standard algorithms do not have access to the containers, only to iterators. Example 10-2 shows how to implement a generic erase function that calls `remove` and then the `erase` member function.

Example 10-2. Removing matching items from a sequence container

```
// Erase all items from container c that are equal to item.
template<typename C>
void erase(C& c, const typename C::value_type& item)
{
  c.erase(std::remove(c.begin(), c.end(), item), c.end());
}

template<typename C, typename Pred>
void erase_if(C& c, Pred pred)
{
  c.erase(std::remove_if(c.begin(), c.end(), pred), c.end());
}

int main()
{
  std::list<int> lst;
  ...
  // Erase all items == 20.
  erase(lst, 20);
  ...
```

Example 10-2. Removing matching items from a sequence container (continued)

```
  // Erase all items < 20.
  erase_if(lst, std::bind2nd(std::less<int>( ), 20));
  ...
}
```

Searching

The standard algorithms provide several ways to search for items in a container: adjacent_find, find, find_end, find_first_of, find_if, search, and search_n. These algorithms essentially perform a linear search of a range. If you know exactly which item you want, you can search an associative container much faster by calling the find member function. For example, suppose you want to write a generic function, contains, that tells you whether a container contains at least one instance of an item. Example 10-3 shows one way, which relies on find, to implement this function.

Example 10-3. Determining whether a container contains an item

```
// Need a type trait to tell us which containers are associative and which are
// not (see Chapter 8).
struct associative_container_tag {};
struct sequence_container_tag {};

template<typename C>
struct is_associative
{};

template<typename T, typename A>
struct is_associative<std::list<T,A> >
{
  typedef sequence_container_tag tag;
};
// Ditto for vector and deque

template<typename T, typename C, typename A>
struct is_associative<std::set<T,C,A> >
{
  typedef associative_container_tag tag;
};
// Ditto for multiset, map, and multimap

template<typename C, typename T>
inline bool do_contains(const C& c, const T& item,
                        associative_container_tag)
{
  return c.end( ) != c.find(item);
}

template<typename C, typename T>
inline bool do_contains(const C& c, const T& item,
                        sequence_container_tag)
{
```

Example 10-3. Determining whether a container contains an item (continued)

```
  return c.end() != std::find(c.begin( ), c.end( ), item);
}

// Here is the actual contains function. It dispatches to do_contains, picking
// the appropriate overloaded function depending on the type of the container c.
template<typename C, typename T>
bool contains(const C& c, const T& item)
{
  return do_contains(c, item, is_associative<C>::tag( ));
}
```

As you can see, iterators are important for using containers. You need them to insert at a specific position, identify an item for erasure, or specify ranges for algorithms. The next section discusses iterators in more depth.

Iterators

An iterator is an abstraction of a pointer used for pointing into containers and other sequences. An ordinary pointer can point to different elements in an array. The ++ operator advances the pointer to the next element, and the * operator dereferences the pointer to return a value from the array. Iterators generalize the concept so that the same operators have the same behavior for any container, even trees and lists. See the <iterator> section of Chapter 13 for more details.

Iterator Categories

There are five categories of iterators:

Input
> Permits you to read a sequence in one pass. The increment (++) operator advances to the next element, but there is no decrement operator. The dereference (*) operator returns an rvalue, not an lvalue, so you can read elements but not modify them.

Output
> Permits you to write a sequence in one pass. The increment (++) operator advances to the next element, but there is no decrement operator. You can dereference an element only to assign a value to it. You cannot compare output iterators.

Forward
> Permits unidirectional access to a sequence. You can refer to and assign to an item as many times as you want. You can use a forward iterator wherever an input iterator is required or wherever an output iterator is required.

Bidirectional
> Similar to a forward iterator but also supports the -- (decrement) operator to move the iterator back one position.

Random access
> Similar to a bidirectional iterator but also supports the [ ] (subscript) operator to access any index in the sequence. Also, you can add or subtract an

integer to move a random access iterator by more than one position at a time. Subtracting two random access iterators yields an integer distance between them. Thus, a random access iterator is most like a conventional pointer, and a pointer can be used as a random access iterator.

An input, forward, bidirectional, or random access iterator can be a const_iterator. Dereferencing a const_iterator yields a constant value, but otherwise behaves as described previously. See "const_iterator" later in this chapter for details.

Iterator Safety

The most important point to remember about iterators is that they are inherently unsafe. Like pointers, an iterator can point to a container that has been destroyed or to an element that has been erased. You can advance an iterator past the end of the container the same way a pointer can point past the end of an array. With a little care and caution, however, iterators are safe to use.

The first key to safe use of iterators is to make sure a program never dereferences an iterator that marks the end of a range. Two iterators can denote a range of values, typically in a container. One iterator points to the start of the range and another marks the end of the range by pointing to a position one past the last element in the range. The mathematical notation of [first, last) tells you that the item that first points to is included in the range, but the item that last points to is excluded from the range.

A program must never dereference an iterator that points to one past the end of a range (e.g., last) because that iterator might not be valid. It might be pointing to one past the end of the elements of a container, for example.

Even a valid iterator can become invalid and therefore unsafe to use, for example if the item to which the iterator points is erased. The detailed descriptions in Chapter 13 tell you this information for each container type. In general, iterators for the node-based containers (list, set, multiset, map, multimap) become invalid only when they point to an erased node. Iterators for the array-based containers (deque, vector) become invalid when the underlying array is reallocated, which might happen for any insertion and for some erasures.

Special Iterators

Iterators are often used with containers, but they have many more uses. You can define iterators for almost any sequence of objects. The standard library includes several examples of non-container iterators, most notably I/O iterators and inserters.

At the lowest level, a stream is nothing more than a sequence of characters. At a slightly higher level, you can think of a stream as a sequence of objects, which would be read with operator>> or written with operator<<. Thus, the standard library includes the following I/O iterators: istreambuf_iterator, ostreambuf_iterator, istream_iterator, and ostream_iterator. Example 10-4 shows how to use streambuf iterators to copy one stream to another.

Example 10-4. Copying streams with streambuf iterators

```
template<typename charT, typename traits>
void copy(std::basic_ostream<charT,traits>& out,
          std::basic_istream<charT,traits>& in)
{
  std::copy(std::istreambuf_iterator<charT>(in),
            std::istreambuf_iterator<charT>(),
            std::ostreambuf_iterator<charT>(out));
}
```

Another kind of output iterator is an *insert iterator*, which inserts items into a sequence collection. The insert iterator requires a container and an optional iterator to specify the position where the new items should be inserted. You can insert at the back of a sequence with back_insert_iterator, at the front of a sequence with front_insert_iterator, or at a specific position in any kind of container with insert_iterator. Each of these iterator class templates has an associated function template that creates the iterator for you and lets the compiler deduce the container type. Example 10-5 shows how to read a series of numbers from a stream, store them in reverse order in a list, and print the list, one number per line.

Example 10-5. Inserting numbers in a vector

```
#include <algorithm>
#include <iostream>
#include <iterator>
#include <list>

int main()
{
  using namespace std;

  list<double> data;
  copy(istream_iterator<double>(cin),
      istream_iterator<double>(),
      front_inserter(data));
  // Use the data...
  // Write the data, one number per line.
  copy(data.begin(), data.end(),
      ostream_iterator<double>(cout, "\n"));
}
```

Custom Iterators

The simplest way to write your own iterator is to derive from the iterator class template. Specify the iterator category as the first template parameter and the item type as the second parameter. In most cases, you can use the default template arguments for the remaining parameters. (See <iterator> in Chapter 13 for details.) The slist container from Example 10-1 needs an iterator and a const_iterator. The only difference is that a const_iterator returns rvalues instead of lvalues. Most of the iteration logic can be factored into a base class. Example 10-6 shows iterator and base_iterator; const_iterator is almost identical to iterator, so it is not shown.

Example 10-6. Writing a custom iterator

```
// The declaration for iterator_base is nested in slist.
class iterator_base :
  public std::iterator<std::forward_iterator_tag, T> {
    friend class slist;
public:
  bool operator==(const iterator_base& iter) const
  { return node_ == iter.node_; }
  bool operator!=(const iterator_base& iter) const
  { return ! (*this == iter); }

protected:
  iterator_base(const iterator_base& iter)
  : prev_(iter.prev_), node_(iter.node_) {}
  iterator_base(slist::link_type* prev,
                slist::link_type* node)
  : prev_(prev), node_(node) {}
  // If node_ == 0, the iterator == end().
  slist::link_type* node_;
  // A pointer to the node before node_ is needed to support erase(). If
  // prev_ == 0, the iterator points to the head of the list.
  slist::link_type* prev_;
private:
  iterator_base();
};

// The declaration for iterator is nested in slist.
class iterator : public iterator_base {
  friend class slist;
public:
  iterator(const iterator& iter) : iterator_base(iter) {}
  iterator& operator++() {                  // Pre-increment
    this->prev_ = this->node_;
    this->node_ = this->node_->next;
    return *this;
  }
  iterator  operator++(int) {               // Post-increment
    iterator tmp = *this;
    operator++();
    return tmp;
  }
  T& operator*()         { return  this->node_->value; }
  T* operator->()        { return &this->node_->value; }
private:
  iterator(slist::link_type* prev, slist::link_type* node)
  : iterator_base(prev, node) {}
};
```

---

const_iterators

Every container must provide an iterator type and a const_iterator type. Functions such as begin and end return iterator when called on a non-const container and return const_iterator when called on a const container.

Note that a const_iterator (with underscore) is quite different from a const iterator (without underscore). A const iterator is a constant object of type iterator. Being constant, it cannot change, so it cannot advance to point to a different position. A const_iterator, on the other hand, is a non-const object of type const_iterator. It is not constant, so its value can change. The key difference between iterator and const_iterator is that iterator returns lvalues of type T, and const_iterator returns unmodifiable objects, either rvalues or const lvalues of type T. The standard requires that a plain iterator be convertible to const_iterator, but not vice versa.

One problem is that some members of the standard containers (most notably erase and insert) take iterator as a parameter, not const_iterator. If you have a const_iterator, you cannot use it as an insertion or erasure position.

Another problem is that it might be difficult to compare an iterator with a const_iterator. If the compiler reports an error when you try to compare iterators for equality or inequality, try swapping the order of the iterators, that is, if a == b fails to compile, try b == a. Most likely, the problem is that b is a const_iterator and a is a plain iterator. By swapping the order, you let the compiler convert a to a const_iterator and allow the comparison.

For a full explanation of how best to work with const_iterators, see Scott Meyers's *Effective STL* (Addison-Wesley).

Reverse Iterators

Every container that supports bidirectional or random access iterators also provides reverse iterators, that is, iterators that start with the last element and "advance" toward the first element of the container. These iterators are named reverse_iterator and const_reverse_iterator.

The standard library includes the reverse_iterator class template as a convenient way to implement the reverse_iterator type. The reverse_iterator class template is an iterator adapter that runs in the reverse direction of the adapted iterator. The adapted iterator must be a bidirectional or random access iterator. You can obtain the adapted iterator, given a reverse iterator, by calling the base function.

On paper, the reverse iterator seems like a good idea. After all, a bidirectional iterator can run in two directions. There is no reason why an iterator adapter could not implement operator++ by calling the adapted iterator's operator-- function.

Reverse iterators share a problem with const_iterators, namely that several members, such as insert and erase, do not take an iterator template parameter but require the exact iterator type, as declared in the container class. The reverse_iterator type is not accepted, so you must pass the adapted iterator instead, which is returned from the base function.

As an insertion point, the base iterator works fine, but for erasing, it is one off from the desired position. The solution is to increment the reverse iterator, then call base, as shown in Example 10-7.

Example 10-7. A reverse iterator

```
int main( )
{
  std::list<int> l;
  l.push_back(10); l.push_back(42); l.push_back(99);
  print(l);
  std::list<int>::reverse_iterator ri;
  ri = std::find(l.rbegin( ), l.rend( ), 42);
  l.insert(ri.base( ), 33);
  // OK: 33 inserted before 42, from the point of view of a reverse iterator,
  // that is, 33 inserted after 42

  ri = std::find(l.rbegin( ), l.rend( ), 42);
  l.erase(ri.base( ));
  // Oops! Item 33 is deleted, not item 42.

  ri = std::find(l.rbegin( ), l.rend( ), 42);
  l.erase((++ri).base( ));
  // That's right! In order to delete the item ri points to, you must advance ri
  // first, then delete the item.
}
```

For a full explanation of how best to work with reverse iterators, see Scott Meyer's *Effective STL* (Addison-Wesley).

Algorithms

The so-called algorithms in the standard library distinguish C++ from other programming languages. Every major programming language has a set of containers, but in the traditional object-oriented approach, each container defines the operations that it permits, e.g., sorting, searching, and modifying. C++ turns object-oriented programming on its head and provides a set of function templates, called *algorithms*, that work with iterators, and therefore with almost any container.

The advantage of the C++ approach is that the library can contain a rich set of algorithms, and each algorithm can be written once and work with (almost) any kind of container. And when you define a custom container, it automatically works with the standard algorithms (assuming you implemented the container's iterators correctly). The set of algorithms is easily extensible without touching the container classes. Another benefit is that the algorithms work with iterators, not containers, so even non-container iterators (such as the stream iterators) can participate.

C++ algorithms have one disadvantage, however. Remember that iterators, like pointers, can be unsafe. Algorithms use iterators, and therefore are equally unsafe. Pass the wrong iterator to an algorithm, and the algorithm cannot detect the error and produces undefined behavior. Fortunately, most uses of algorithms make it easy to avoid programming errors.

Most of the standard algorithms are declared in the <algorithm> header, with some numerical algorithms in <numeric>. Refer to the respective sections of Chapter 13 for details.

How Algorithms Work

The generic algorithms all work in a similar fashion. They are all function templates, and most have one or more iterators as template parameters. Because the algorithms are templates, you can instantiate the function with any template arguments that meet the basic requirements. For example, for_each is declared as follows:

```
template<typename InIter, typename Function>
Function for_each(InIter first, InIter last, Function func);
```

The names of the template parameters tell you what is expected as template arguments: InIter must be an input iterator, and Function must be a function pointer or functor. The documentation for for_each further tells you that Function must take one argument whose type is the value_type of InIter. That's all. The InIter argument can be anything that meets the requirements of an input iterator. Notice that no container is mentioned in the declaration or documentation of for_each. For example, you can use an istream_iterator.

For a programmer trained in traditional object-oriented programming, the flexibility of the standard algorithms might seem strange or backwards. Thinking in terms of algorithms takes some adjustment.

For example, some object-oriented container classes define sort as a member function or as a function that applies only to certain kinds of objects. (For example, Java defines sort only on arrays and List objects). If you have a new kind of container, you must duplicate the implementation of sort or make sure the implementation of your container maps to one of the standard implementations of sort. In C++, you can invent any kind of crazy container, and as long as it supports a random access iterator, you can use the standard sort function.

Whenever you need to process the contents of a container, you should think about how the standard algorithms can help you. For example, suppose you need to read a stream of numbers into a data array. Typically, you would set up a while loop to read the input stream and, for each number read, append the number to the array. Now rethink the problem in terms of an algorithmic solution. What you are actually doing is copying data from an input stream to an array, so you could use the copy algorithm:

```
std::copy(std::istream_iterator<double>(stream),
          std::istream_iterator<double>(),
          std::back_inserter(data));
```

The copy algorithm copies all the items from one range to another. The input comes from an `istream_iterator`, which is an iterator interface for reading from an `istream`. The output range is a `back_insert_iterator` (created by the `back_inserter` function), which is an output iterator that pushes items onto a container.

At first glance, the algorithmic solution doesn't seem any simpler or clearer than a straightforward loop:

```
double x;
while (stream >> x)
  data.push_back(x);
```

More complex examples demonstrate the value of the C++ algorithms. For example, all major programming languages have a type for character strings. They typically also have a function for finding substrings. What about the more general problem of finding a subrange in any larger range? Suppose a researcher is looking for patterns in a data set and wants to see if a small data pattern occurs in a larger data set. In C++, you can use the `search` algorithm:

```
std::vector<double> data;
...
if (std::search(data.begin( ), data.end( ), pattern.begin( ),
    pattern.end( )) != data.end( ))
{
  // found the pattern...
}
```

A number of algorithms take a function pointer or functor (that is, an object that overloads `operator( )`) as one of the arguments. The algorithms call the function and possibly use the return value. For example, `count_if` counts the number of times the function returns a true (nonzero) result when applied to each element in a range:

```
bool negative(double x)
{
  return x < 0;
}

std::vector<double>::iterator::difference_type neg_cnt;
std::vector<double> data;
...
neg_cnt = std::count_if(data.begin( ), data.end( ), negative);
```

In spite of the unwieldy declaration for neg_cnt, the application of `count_if` to count the number of negative items in the data vector is easy to write and read.

If you don't want to write a function to be used only with an algorithm, you might be able to use the standard functors or function objects (which are declared in the `<functional>` header). For example, the same count of negative values can be obtained with the following:

```
std::vector<double>::iterator::difference_type neg_cnt;
std::vector<double> data;
...
neg_cnt = std::count_if(data.begin( ), data.end( ),
            std::bind2nd(std::less<double>, 0.0));
```

The std::less class template defines operator( ), so it takes two arguments and applies operator< to those arguments. The bind2nd function template takes a two-argument functor and binds a constant value (in this case 0.0) as the second argument, returning a one-argument function (which is what count_if requires). The use of standard function objects can make the code harder to read, but also helps avoid writing one-off custom functions. (The Boost project expands and enhances the standard library's binders. See Appendix B for information about Boost.)

When using function objects, be very careful if those objects maintain state or have global side effects. Some algorithms copy the function objects, and you must be sure that the state is also properly copied. The numerical algorithms do not permit function objects that have side effects.

Example 10-8 shows one use of a function object. It accumulates statistical data for computing the mean and variance of a data set. Pass an instance of Statistics to the for_each algorithm to accumulate the statistics. The copy that is returned from for_each contains the desired results.

Example 10-8. Computing statistics with a functor

```
#include <algorithm>
#include <cstddef>
#include <cmath>
#include <iostream>
#include <ostream>

template<typename T>
class Statistics {
public:
  typedef T value_type;
  Statistics( ) : n_(0), sum_(0), sumsq_(0) {}
  void operator( )(double x) {
    ++n_;
    sum_ += x;
    sumsq_ += x * x;
  }
  std::size_t count( ) const { return n_; }
  T sum( )        const { return sum_; }
  T sumsq( )      const { return sumsq_; }
  T mean( )       const { return sum_ / n_; }
  T variance( )   const
      { return (sumsq_ - sum_*sum_ / n_) / (n_ - 1); }
private:
  std::size_t n_;
  T sum_;
  T sumsq_; // Sum of squares
};

int main( )
{
  using namespace std;
```

Example 10-8. Computing statistics with a functor (continued)

```
Statistics<double> stat = for_each(
  istream_iterator<double>(cin),
  istream_iterator<double>( ),
  Statistics<double>( ));

cout << "count=" << stat.count( ) << '\n';
cout << "mean =" << stat.mean( ) << '\n';
cout << "var  =" << stat.variance( ) << '\n';
cout << "stdev=" << sqrt(stat.variance( )) << '\n';
cout << "sum  =" << stat.sum( ) << '\n';
cout << "sumsq=" << stat.sumsq( ) << '\n';
}
```

Standard Algorithms

Chapter 13 describes all the algorithms in detail. This section presents a categorized summary of the algorithms.

It is always your responsibility to ensure that the output range is large enough to accommodate the input.

If the algorithm name ends with _if, the final argument must be a *predicate*, that is, a function pointer or function object that returns a Boolean result (a result that is convertible to type bool).

Nonmodifying operations

The following algorithms examine every element of a sequence without modifying the order:

count
    Returns the number of items that match a given value

count_if
    Returns the number of items for which a predicate returns true

for_each
    Applies a function or functor to each item

Comparison

The following algorithms compare objects or sequences (without modifying the elements):

equal
    Determines whether two ranges have equivalent contents

lexicographical_compare
    Determines whether one range is considered less than another range

max
    Returns the maximum of two values

```
max_element
```
Finds the maximum value in a range

```
min
```
Returns the minimum of two values

```
min_element
```
Finds the minimum value in a range

```
mismatch
```
Finds the first position where two ranges differ

Searching

The following algorithms search for a value or a subsequence in a sequence (without modifying the elements):

```
adjacent_find
```
Finds the first position where an item is equal to its neighbor

```
find
```
Finds the first occurrence of a value in a range

```
find_end
```
Finds the last occurrence of a subsequence in a range

```
find_first_of
```
Finds the first position where a value matches any one item from a range of values

```
find_if
```
Finds the first position where a predicate returns true

```
search
search_n
```
Finds a subsequence in a range

Binary search

The following algorithms apply a binary search to a sorted sequence. The sequence typically comes from a sequence container in which you have already sorted the elements. You can use an associative containers, but they provide the last three functions as member functions, which might result in better performance.

```
binary_search
```
Finds an item in a sorted range using a binary search

```
equal_range
```
Finds the upper and lower bounds

```
lower_bound
```
Finds the lower bound of where an item belongs in a sorted range

```
upper_bound
```
Finds the upper bound of where an item belongs in a sorted range

Modifying sequence operations

The following algorithms modify a sequence:

copy
> Copies an input range to an output range

copy_backward
> Copies an input range to an output range, starting at the end of the output range

fill
fill_n
> Fills a range with a value

generate
generate_n
> Fills a range with values returned from a function

iter_swap
> Swaps the values that two iterators point to

random_shuffle
> Shuffles a range into random order

remove
> Reorders a range to prepare to erase all elements equal to a given value

remove_copy
> Copies a range, removing all items equal to a given value

remove_copy_if
> Copies a range, removing all items for which a predicate returns true

remove_if
> Reorders a range to prepare to erase all items for which a predicate returns true

replace
> Replaces items of a given value with a new value

replace_copy
> Copies a range, replacing items of a given value with a new value

replace_copy_if
> Copies a range, replacing items for which a predicate returns true with a new value

replace_if
> Replaces items for which a predicate returns true with a new value

reverse
> Reverses a range in place

reverse_copy
> Copies a range in reverse order

rotate
> Rotates items from one end of a range to the other end

rotate_copy
> Copies a range, rotating items from one end to the other

`swap_ranges`
>   Swaps values in two ranges

`transform`
>   Modifies every value in a range by applying a transformation function

`unique`
>   Reorders a range to prepare to erase all adjacent, duplicate items

`unique_copy`
>   Copies a range, removing adjacent, duplicate items

Sorting

The following algorithms are related to sorting and partitioning. You can supply a comparison function or functor or rely on the default, which uses the < operator.

`nth_element`
>   Finds the item that belongs at the nth position (if the range were sorted) and reorders the range to partition it into items less than the nth item and items greater than or equal to the nth item.

`partial_sort`
>   Reorders a range so the first part is sorted.

`partial_sort_copy`
>   Copies a range so the first part is sorted.

`partition`
>   Reorders a range so that all items for which a predicate is true come before all items for which the predicate is false.

`sort`
>   Sorts items in ascending order.

`stable_partition`
>   Reorders a range so that all items for which a predicate is true come before all items for which the predicate is false. The relative order of items within a partition is maintained.

`stable_sort`
>   Sorts items in ascending order. The relative order of equal items is maintained.

Merging

The following algorithms merge two sorted sequences:

`inplace_merge`
>   Merges two sorted, consecutive subranges in place, so the results replace the original ranges

`merge`
>   Merges two sorted ranges, copying the results to a separate range

Set operations

The following algorithms apply standard set operations to sorted sequences:

includes
> Determines whether one sorted range is a subset of another

set_difference
> Copies the set difference of two sorted ranges to an output range

set_intersection
> Copies the intersection of two sorted ranges to an output range

set_symmetric_difference
> Copies the symmetric difference of two sorted ranges to an output range

set_union
> Copies the union of two sorted ranges to an output range

Heap operations

The following algorithms treat a sequence as a heap data structure:

make_heap
> Reorders a range into heap order

pop_heap
> Reorders a range to remove the first item in the heap

push_heap
> Reorders a range to add the last item to the heap

sort_heap
> Reorders a range that starts in heap order into fully sorted order

Permutations

The following reorder the elements of a sequence to generate permutations:

next_permutation
> Reorders a range to form the next permutation

prev_permutation
> Reorders a range to form the previous permutation

Custom Algorithms

Writing your own algorithm is easy. Some care is always needed when writing function templates (as discussed in Chapter 7), but generic algorithms do not present any special or unusual challenges. Be sure you understand the requirements of the different categories of iterators and write your algorithm to use the most general category possible. You might even want to specialize your algorithm to improve its performance with some categories.

The first generic algorithm that most programmers will probably write is copy_if, which was inexplicably omitted from the standard. The copy_if function copies an input range to an output range, copying only the values for which a predicate returns true (nonzero). Example 10-9 shows a simple implementation of copy_if.

Example 10-9. One way to implement the copy_if function

```
template<typename InIter, typename OutIter, typename Pred>
OutIter copy_if(InIter first, InIter last, OutIter result, Pred pred)
{
  for (; first != last; ++first)
    if (pred(*first)) {
      *result = *first;
      ++result;
    }
  return result;
}
```

You can also specialize an algorithm. For example, you might be able to implement the algorithm more efficiently for a random access iterator. In this case, you can write helper functions and use the iterator_category trait to choose a specialized implementation. (Chapter 8 has more information about traits, including an example of how to use iterator traits to optimize a function template.)

The real trick in designing and writing algorithms is being able to generalize the problem and then find an efficient solution. Before running off to write your own solution, check the standard library. Your problem might already have a solution.

For example, I recently wanted to write an algorithm to find the median value in a range. There is no median algorithm, but there is nth_element, which solves the more general problem of finding the element at any sorted index. Writing median became a trivial matter of making a temporary copy of the data, calling nth_element, and then returning an iterator that points to the median value in the original range. Because median makes two passes over the input range, a forward iterator is required, as shown in Example 10-10.

Example 10-10. Finding the median of a range

```
template<typename FwdIter, typename Compare>
FwdIter median(FwdIter first, FwdIter last, Compare compare)
{
  typedef typename std::iterator_traits<FwdIter>::value_type value_type;
  std::vector<value_type> tmp(first, last);
  typename std::vector<value_type>::size_type median_pos = tmp.size() / 2;
  std::nth_element(tmp.begin(), tmp.begin() + median_pos,
             tmp.end(), compare);
  return std::find(first, last, tmp[median_pos]);
}
```

11

Preprocessor Reference

The preprocessing step occurs before the main compilation step. Historically, the preprocessor has been a separate program, but compilers are not required to implement the preprocessor in that way. Because of its history, though, the preprocessor has syntax and semantics that are quite different from the rest of C++. See Chapter 1 for information about all the steps in compiling a source file.

The preprocessor handles preprocessing *directives*, which can define and undefine macros, establish regions of conditional compilation, include other source files, and control the compilation process somewhat. A *macro* is a name that represents other text, called the *macro replacement text*. When the macro name is seen in the source file, the preprocessor replaces the name with the replacement text. A macro can have formal parameters, and actual arguments are substituted in the expansion.

Preprocessor directives obey different syntax rules from the rest of the language. Directives are line-oriented. Each directive starts with whitespace characters followed by # as the first non-space character on a line. After the # is more optional whitespace (no newlines are permitted) followed by the directive name. Each directive extends to the end of the line. A backslash (\) at the end of the line continues the directive onto the subsequent line.

The directive name must be one of the names listed in this chapter. Any other preprocessing token after the initial # character is an error.

 # operator and directive   Stringify operator and null directive

```
# // Null directive
# identifier
```

A preprocessor directive with no directive name is called a *null directive*. It has no effect.

The # operator can also be used as a unary operator, sometimes called the *stringify operator* because it turns its operand into a string. It can be used only in the macro replacement text of a #define directive. It must be followed by a parameter name for the macro being defined. The # operator and the parameter name are replaced by a string literal whose contents are the text of the macro argument that corresponds to the macro parameter. The macro argument is not expanded before being converted to a string. Whitespace in the argument is condensed to a single space character between tokens; leading and trailing whitespace is removed.

The evaluation order of # and ## operators is undefined. If the order is important, you can control the order by using multiple macros.

Example

The following example prints the text [now is the time]:

```
#define now then
#define is was
#define print(stuff)  std::cout << "[" #stuff "]\n"
print( now   is the   time   );
```

See Also

operator, #define directive

---

operator   Concatenation operator

identifier ## identifier

The ## operator is a binary operator, sometimes called the *concatenation operator* because it concatenates preprocessor tokens. It can be used only in the macro replacement text of a #define directive. It must not appear at the start or end of the macro replacement text. The operands of the ## operator must be parameter names for the macro being defined. They are replaced by the corresponding macro arguments, which are not expanded. The tokens immediately adjacent to the ## operator are concatenated to form a single token. If the result is not a valid token, the behavior is undefined; otherwise, the token is expanded normally.

The evaluation order of # and ## operators is undefined. If the order is important, you can control the order by using multiple macros.

Example

The following example prints std to cout because the concat macro assembles the token std from s, t, and d:

```
#define s this is not expanded by the concatenation operator
#define t nor is this, so the result is the token std
#define concat(part1, part2, part3) part1 ## part2 ## part3
concat(s, t, d)::cout << "std";
```

See Also

operator, #define directive

#define directive Defines a macro

```
#define identifier definition
#define identifier() definition
#define identifier(identifier-list) definition
```

The #define directive defines a macro named *identifier*. The macro's replacement text is the list of tokens shown as *definition*. The macro can be simple, with no arguments, or can have an argument list. The argument list is introduced by a left parenthesis that immediately follows the macro name. If there is a space between *identifier* and (, the (is interpreted as the start of the definition of a simple macro. The *identifier-list* can be empty, or it can be a list of identifiers separated by commas. Whitespace is permitted in the *identifier-list* and before the closing parenthesis.

C programmers are accustomed to using macros to declare constants and simple inline functions, but C++ offers const declarations, true inline functions, and templates. Macros are therefore used much less often in C++ than in C. The main drawback to macros is that they do not obey scope or namespace rules. When you must use macros, a common convention is to use all uppercase letters for the macro names, and never use all uppercase letters for non-macro names.

A macro's scope is from the point of definition to the end of the source file, or until you undefine the macro with the #undef directive. If you try to repeat a macro definition, the new definition must be identical to the original definition. The only way to give a macro a different definition is to undefine it first.

If you #include any standard header, a macro name cannot be the same as a reserved keyword or any of the names declared in the header. Many compilers accept keywords as macro names, but your program would still be wrong and would not be portable to a compiler that is more strict about detecting this particular error. Even if you do not #include a standard header, using macros to redefine keywords is usually a bad idea.

Wherever a macro name appears as a distinct token after its definition, it is replaced with the replacement text. Macro names are not replaced inside string and character literals, however. The replacement text is rescanned for macro names, which are recursively expanded until no more replacements take place. During replacement, the original macro name is not expanded if it appears in any replacement text. Here is a simple example of a macro definition and use:

```
#define NAME "NAME = Tempest Software, Inc."
char companyName[] = NAME;
```

During the macro expansion phase of compilation, the token NAME will be replaced by its expansion, with the following result:

```
char companyName[] = "NAME = Tempest Software, Inc.";
```

The replacement text is never interpreted as a preprocessing directive. This means, for example, you cannot #define a macro within a macro's replacement text. Also, directive names are not subject to macro replacement (although directive arguments are).

You can also declare a macro with a parameter list, which is sometimes called a *function-like macro*:

```
#define DECLARE(x,y, z)   x y = z
#define PRINT(a)  (::std::cout << (a) << '\n')
```

To use a function-like macro, the macro name must be followed by a comma-separated argument list in parentheses. A single argument can contain balanced parentheses, and within those parentheses, you can have commas, which are not interpreted as argument separators. The macro invocation must have the same number of arguments as the macro definition has parameters. Newlines are permitted as ordinary whitespace characters in a macro invocation.

The following example uses the DECLARE and PRINT macros defined in the previous example:

```
int main( )
{
  DECLARE(int, x, 42);
  PRINT((x = 10, x+2));
}
```

In the macro replacement text, each occurrence of a parameter name is replaced by the corresponding argument. For example, the macro expansion for the previous example results in the following:

```
int main( )
{
  int x = 42;
  (::std::cout << (x = 10, x + 2) << '\n');
}
```

You must be extra cautious when using a template instantiation as a macro argument. The angle brackets that surround the template arguments are not treated specially for macro arguments, so commas that separate the template arguments are interpreted as separators for the macro arguments. In the following example, the DECL macro attempts to declare an object named n with type t. This works fine for a simple type, such as int, but fails with a template instantiation. When used with map<int,int>, the comma separates macro arguments, so the preprocessor sees three macro arguments—std::map<int, int>, and m—and reports an error:

```
#define DECL(t, n) t n = t( )
DECL(int, zero);            // Expands to int zero = int( )
DECL(std::map<int,int>, m); // Error
```

When a macro is expanded, the macro arguments are expanded, and each parameter is replaced by its corresponding expanded argument unless the parameter is an operand to the # or ## operator. After the arguments have been expanded, the # and ## operators are evaluated, and the resulting text is rescanned for macros. The macro name is expanded only once, so rescanning does not expand the name of the macro being expanded.

Predefined Macros

The following macros are predefined. Do not undefine or redefine any of the predefined macros.

__cplusplus
> Has the value 199711L. Future versions of the C++ standard will use a larger value. Nonconforming compilers should use a different value.

__DATE__
> Expands to the date of compilation, as a string literal, in the form "Mmm dd yyyy", in which dd begins with a space for numbers less than 10. An implementation is free to substitute a different date, but the form is always the same, and the date is always valid.

__FILE__
> Expands to the name, as a string literal, of the source file being compiled.

__LINE__
> Expands to the line number, as a decimal constant, of the source file being compiled.

__STDC__
> Is implementation-defined. C++ compilers might define this macro; if it is defined, the value is implementation-defined. Note that C compilers are required to define __STDC__ as 1, and in some implementations, the same preprocessor might be used for C and C++.

__TIME__
> Expands to the compilation time, as a string literal, in the form "hh:mm:ss". An implementation is free to substitute a different time, but the form is always the same, and the time is always valid.

An implementation is free to predefine other macros that use any of the reserved names, such as names that contain two adjacent underscores or a leading underscore followed by an uppercase letter. For example, compilers often define macros to indicate the host or target platform—e.g., __linux__. Consult your compiler's documentation for details.

Examples

When writing a container class template (see Chapter 10), it is important to detect when a template parameter is an integral type. There are several ways to do this. One way is to use type traits (Chapter 8). A template declares a special tag for all integral types and a different tag for all other types. The traits template is then specialized for the integral types, which is repetitive, tedious, and error-prone. Using a macro, however, reduces the opportunity for errors because the macro body is written once. Example 11-1 shows how the DECL_IS_INTEGER macro specializes the is_integer class template for each built-in integral type.

Example 11-1. Defining type traits with a macro

```
// Type trait to test whether a type is an integer.
struct is_integer_tag {};
struct is_not_integer_tag {};

// The default is that a type is not an integral type.
template<typename T>
struct is_integer {
  enum { value = 0 };
  typedef is_not_integer_tag tag;
};
```

Example 11-1. Defining type traits with a macro (continued)

```
// Explicitly override the default for all integral types.
#define DECL_IS_INTEGER(T)       \
template<>                       \
struct is_integer<T> {           \
  enum { value = 1 };            \
  typedef is_integer_tag tag;    \
}
DECL_IS_INTEGER(bool);
DECL_IS_INTEGER(char);
DECL_IS_INTEGER(signed char);
DECL_IS_INTEGER(unsigned char);
DECL_IS_INTEGER(int);
DECL_IS_INTEGER(unsigned int);
DECL_IS_INTEGER(short);
DECL_IS_INTEGER(unsigned short);
DECL_IS_INTEGER(long);
DECL_IS_INTEGER(unsigned long);

#undef  DECL_IS_INTEGER
```

Example 11-2 shows another way that macros are used when testing the string class. The TEST macro calls a function and prints the result. The TEST macro cannot be implemented as a function because it uses the # operator.

Example 11-2. Testing functions

```
#include <iostream>
#include <string>

int main( )
{
  using namespace std;

  string s("hello, world");

#define TEST(func) cout << #func "=" << s.func << '\n'

  TEST(erase(9, 1));
  TEST(erase(5));
  TEST(find_first_not_of("aeiou"));
  ...
}
```

 Most compilers have an option in which the compiler runs only the preprocessor, and you can examine the results after all macros have been expanded and all preprocessor directives have been evaluated. This mode can be helpful when debugging an incorrect macro expansion.

Example 11-3 is a contrived example that illustrates how macros are expanded. Try running the example through your compiler to see if the results are correct. (Other than whitespace, the results should be the same as what is shown in the rest of this section.)

Example 11-3. Expanding macros

```
#define x            x.y
#define STR(x)       #x
#define XSTR(s)      STR(s)
#define CONCAT(x, y) x ## y
#define PARENS(x)    (x)
#define APPLY(x,y)   x(y)
#define hello        HI


x                             // x.y
CONCAT(ST, R)(hello)          // "hello"
CONCAT(X,STR)(hello)          // "HI"
CONCAT(S, TR)PARENS(hello)    // STR(HI)
CONCAT(S, TR)(PARENS(hello))  // "PARENS(hello)"
APPLY(CONCAT(S, TR), hello)   // "HI"
```

The first macro expansion shows how the macro name x is not expanded in the replacement text. The result is simply:

> x.y

The second macro expansion shows how the CONCAT macro forms a new token STR from its arguments. After the CONCAT macro is evaluated, the text is rescanned. The STR macro is then invoked with the hello argument. Because the x parameter is an operand of #, the argument is not expanded. Instead, # is applied to hello to produce the result:

> "hello"

The third macro expansion is like the second, except it invokes XSTR instead of STR. The difference is that XSTR expands its argument, s, because the replacement text, STR(s), does not use the # or ## operators. Thus, XSTR(hello) expands to STR(HI), which has the following result:

> "HI"

The fourth expansion also invokes CONCAT to produce STR, but STR is not followed by a left parenthesis, so it is not expanded as a macro. Instead, it is followed by the PARENS macro. The parameter of PARENS is not an operand of # or ##, so it is expanded, which means the argument hello expands to HI, and the final result is:

> STR(HI)

The fifth expansion is just like the second, but emphasizes how the argument to STR is not expanded. The result is:

> "PARENS(hello)"

The final macro expansion shows how to expand hello as an argument to STR, even when STR is the result of the CONCAT macro. The parameters of APPLY are expanded, resulting in the text STR(HI), which expands to:

> "HI"

See Also

#undef directive

defined operator
Tests whether a macro is defined

defined(*identifier*)

defined *identifier*

The unary operator defined(*identifier*) (also written as defined *identifier*, without the parentheses) evaluates to 1 if *identifier* is a known macro name at the point of the defined operator, or 0 if it is not known. The operator is evaluated only in the argument to an #if or #elif directive.

The behavior is undefined if the defined operator is used in any other way, or if the token defined results from macro expansion.

See Also
#define directive, #elif directive, #if directive, #ifdef directive, #ifndef directive, #undef directive

#elif directive
Else-if for conditional compilation

#elif *constant-expression*

The #elif directive marks a region of conditional compilation. Every #elif must be paired with an introductory directive: #if, #ifdef, or #ifndef. If the initial condition was false (0), and every subsequent #elif condition is false, and *constant-expression* is true (nonzero), subsequent statements are compiled until the next #elif, #else, or #endif directive is reached for this level of nesting.

See Also
#else directive, #if directive

#else directive
Else for conditional compilation

#else

The #else directive marks a region of conditional compilation. Every #else must be paired with an introductory directive: #if, #ifdef, or #ifndef. There can be any number of intervening #elif directives. If the initial condition was false (0), and every subsequent #elif condition is false, statements that follow the #else directive are compiled until the corresponding #endif directive is reached.

See Also
#if directive

#endif directive
Ends conditional compilation

#endif

The #endif directive ends a region of conditional compilation.

See Also
#if directive

#error directive

#error *message*

The #error directive tells the preprocessor to issue an error message and mark the source file as ill-formed, just as if the programmer made a programming error that the compiler detected. You can supply any sequence of preprocessor tokens as the *message*, and those tokens are echoed in the error message.

Example

```
#if !defined(__cplusplus) || (__cplusplus < 199711L)
  #error Not a conforming C++ compiler.
#endif
```

See Also

#line directive

#if directive

#if *constant-expression*

The #if directive begins a region of conditional compilation, that is, a region within a source file where preprocessor directives determine whether the code in the region is compiled. A conditional region starts with #ifdef, #ifndef, or #if and ends with #endif. Each region can have any number of #elif directives and an optional #else directive after all the #elif directives. The basic form to use is:

```
#if defined(__win32__)
  const char os[] = "Microsoft Windows";
#elif defined(__linux__) or defined(__unix__)
  const char os[] = "UNIX (or variant)";
#elif defined(__vms__)
  const char os[] = "VMS";
#else
  const char os[] = "(unknown)";
#endif
```

Macros in the directive argument are expanded, except for the operands of the defined operator. The constant expression is evaluated, and if the result is nonzero, the #if condition is true, and the code in the region that immediately follows is compiled. The region ends with #else, #elif, or #endif. If the #if expression is false, the condition for the next #elif is evaluated, and if that expression is true, its region is compiled, and so on. If all #elif expressions are false, and #else is present, its region is compiled. Conditional processing ends with the corresponding #endif directive.

Conditionals can be nested. Within an inner region, the preprocessor keeps track of conditional directives even if the region is not being compiled, so conditional directives can be properly matched.

The #if and #elif directives take a single parameter, a constant expression. The expression differs slightly from non-preprocessor constant expressions:

- You can use the defined operator.

- Integers are long, that is, int values (and values that are promoted to int) have the same representation as long int, and unsigned int values have the same repre-

---

sentation as unsigned long. All bool values are promoted to integers, including the keywords true and false.

- Character literals are converted to the execution character set. The numeric value of a character in a preprocessor expression is not necessarily the same as the value of the same character in a non-preprocessor expression. A character may have a negative value.

- Keywords that are alternative operators for symbolic operators (i.e., and, and_eq, bitand, bitor, compl, not, not_eq, or, or_eq, xor, and xor_eq) have their usual meaning, although it is ineffective to try using assignment operators (and_eq, or_eq, and xor_eq) in an #if or #elif condition.

- Other identifiers and keywords that remain after macro expansion are replaced by 0. (It might seem strange to convert keywords, such as sizeof, to the integer 0, but that is the rule. Some compilers fail to follow this particular rule.) One consequence of this rule is that you cannot use type casts or new, delete, sizeof, throw, or typeid expressions in an #if or #elif condition.

Conditional directives are most often used to guard header files from multiple inclusion. All the standard headers are guarded, so including them more than once has no harmful effects. This is important because an implementation might include one header in another header. For example, <map> might include <utility> to get the declaration for the pair<> template. If you explicitly #include <map> and #include <utility>, you might end up including <utility> more than once.

Another common use is for system- or compiler-specific code. Every compiler predefines one or more macros to identify the compiler and possibly the host operating system (such as __linux__ or __GNUC__). Consult your compiler's documentation to learn which macro names are predefined.

Examples

Example 11-4 shows one way to nest conditional directives.

Example 11-4. Nesting conditional directives

```
#define zero zero  // Identifiers are converted to 0.
#define one  true  // Bool expressions are promoted to int.

#if one
// This region is compiled.
  #if zero
  This region can contain erroneous C++ code. The code is not
  compiled, so the errors do not matter.
  #else // This #else matches the inner #if.
    // This region is compiled.
    const int zero = 0;
  #endif // This #endif matches the inner #if.
  int x = zero;
#else
  This #else matches the outer #if. Because the #if
  condition was true, the #else region is not compiled.
#endif
```

You can guard your own headers by using conditional directives to define a guard macro and using the guard macro to ensure the file's contents are compiled only when the macro is not defined, as shown in Example 11-5.

Example 11-5. Guarding a header against multiple inclusion

```
// In the header file employee.h
#ifndef EMPLOYEE_H
#define EMPLOYEE_H
// Thus, the entire contents of the file are compiled only when EMPLOYEE_H is not
// defined. The first time the file is #included, the macro is not defined, in
// which case it is immediately defined. The second and subsequent times the same
// header is included in the same source file; the macro and conditional
// directives ensure that the entire file is skipped.

class employee { ... };

#endif   // End of employee.h
```

See Also

#elif directive, #else directive, #endif directive, #ifdef directive, #ifndef directive

---

#ifdef directive
Tests whether a macro is defined

#ifdef *identifier*

The #ifdef directive begins a region of conditional compilation. It takes a single *identifier* as an argument and is equivalent to #if defined *identifier*.

See Also

defined operator, #if directive, #ifndef directive

#ifndef directive
Tests whether a macro is undefined

#ifndef *identifier*

The #ifndef directive begins a region of conditional compilation. It takes a single *identifier* as an argument and is equivalent to #if not defined *identifier*.

See Also

defined operator, #if directive, #ifdef directive

#include directive
Includes another source file

#include <*header*>

#include "*sourcefile*"

The #include directive includes the contents of a standard header or source file. The first form searches for *header* and replaces the directive with the entire contents of the header. The second form searches for *sourcefile* and replaces the directive with the entire contents of the named source file.

The basic action of #include is to read the named file or header as though its entire contents appeared in the source file at the position of the #include directive. Typically, common declarations are placed in a separate file, such as *decl.h*, and #include "decl.h" is used in every source file that depends on those declarations.

If a source file contains the directive #include "*filename*", and the compiler cannot find the external file named *filename*, the compiler also tries the form #include <*filename*>. Most compilers implement these two forms of #include by searching in different folders or directories. For example, the quote form searches in the current directory or in the directory that contains the source file, and the angle-bracket form searches only in "system" directories. Such details are implementation-defined, and some compilers might introduce further distinctions between the two forms.

It is possible, for example, for a compiler to recognize only the standard headers in the <*header*> form and use built-in knowledge of the standard headers without referencing any external files. This hypothetical compiler might report an error for all other uses of the angle-bracket form and require all external file inclusions to use the quote form. Such a compiler would not be very popular, however, because common practice is to treat <*header*> and "*header*" as equivalent forms, except when applying the rules for locating the external file named *header*.

It is common practice to install third-party libraries in common directories and to configure compilers to look in these directories for <*header*> inclusions. For example, if you use Boost (described in Appendix B), you might use #include <any.hpp> to obtain the boost::any class template. Another common practice is to install such libraries in subdirectories. On a Unix system, for example, you might install Boost in the *boost* subdirectory of one of the standard system directories and use #include <boost/any.hpp>. You should be careful, however, because using system-specific filenames is not portable.

The only guarantee that the standard offers is that if *filename* consists of a sequence of letters and underscore characters followed by a period and a single letter or underscore, then the implementation must provide a unique mapping of *filename* to a source file (optionally ignoring case distinctions). The standard permits universal characters in *filename*, but you should avoid them when you need maximum portability because some compilers do not support universal characters.

The implementation defines how and where the preprocessor searches for *header* or *filename*, how *filename* maps to an external filename, whether filenames heed or ignore case distinctions, and whether different character sequences for *filename* represent distinct external files. For example, under Windows, "foo.h" and "FOO.H" are usually the same file, but under Unix, they are usually different files. If the filesystem supports links, such as Unix, two names such as "foo.h" and "bar.h" might name the same file; in other environments, you might be guaranteed that different filenames refer to distinct files.

The most common convention is that <*header*> refers only to standard headers and to vendor-supplied extensions to the standard. Compilers typically have a way for you to supply your own additional libraries and use the associated headers as <*header*> includes. The quoted form is used for all header files that are part of the application, and those are typically located in the same directory or folder as the application's source files. The most common filename convention is to end header names with *.h* (for header), although *.hpp* is also common. For example, suppose you wrote a class to represent an employee. Put the class definition in *employee.h* and the definitions of the members in *employee.cpp*. Any other file that needs to use the employee class can #include "employee.h" and use the class definition:

```
#include <set>
#include "employee.h"
```

```
class business_group {
private:
  std::set<employee> employees_;
  ...
};
```

You can use other preprocessor tokens in an #include directive, provided they expand to one of the two standard forms. Each header name or filename must be a single preprocessor token; you cannot combine tokens to form a name. To preserve portability, use macros only for the entire sequence of the #include argument:

```
#define HEADER "this.h"
#include HEADER
```

See Also

#if directive

#line directive

Changes the line number in error messages

#line *digits*

#line *digits string*

The #line directive changes the compiler's notion of the current filename and line number. The first form changes the line number (as expressed by the __LINE__ directive and used in error messages) to *digits*. The second form changes the line number to *digits* and the filename to the contents of *string*. The new file name is used as the value of the __FILE__ macro.

The #line directive is typically used by programs that generate C++ as output from some other input. The directive records the original filename and line number that produced the C++ code. Error messages and debuggers can point to the original file instead of to the intermediate C++ source file.

See Also

#error directive

#pragma directive

Controls the compiler

#pragma *tokens*

The #pragma directive is implementation-defined. An implementation can define certain pragma parameters to control the compiler. The preprocessor ignores any pragma that it does not recognize.

Because pragmas are highly compiler-dependent, you should avoid using them as much as possible. Most compilers let you control the compiler by providing command-line options, configuration files, or project files. Do your best to keep compiler-specific information out of your source files. When you must use pragmas, protect them with conditional directives for specific compilers.

Example

```
#ifdef __BORLANDC__
  #pragma pack
#endif
```

```
#ifdef __COMO__
  #pragma instantiate
#endif
```

#undef directive

#undef *identifier*

The #undef directive deletes the definition of the macro named *identifier*. If *identifier* is not a macro name, the directive has no effect. If you attempt to undefine the identifier defined or any predefined macro, the behavior is undefined.

See Also

#define directive

12

Language Reference

Here begins the alphabetic reference. This chapter presents each language keyword with a syntax summary, description, and, in some cases, an example. The syntax summaries use a modified BNF (Backus Normal Form or Backus-Naur Form):

- Terminal symbols (keywords and operator symbols) are in a `constant-width` typeface.

- To avoid ambiguity, a terminal symbol that might be mistaken for a BNF metacharacter (e.g., a vertical bar or a square bracket) is enclosed in quotes (e.g., `"|"`).

- Nonterminal symbols (syntax elements) are in an *italic* typeface.

- Optional elements are in square brackets ([*like this*]).

- Choices are separated by vertical bars (|).

- A *production* (syntax description) is introduced with := or ::=. The traditional symbol (::=) is used for a complete definition. The abbreviated symbol (:=) is used when the righthand side is incomplete. For example, here is the complete definition of *function-specifier* as it is given under *declaration*:

  function-specifier ::= explicit | inline | virtual

  The following is a partial production of *function-specifier*:

  function-specifier := inline

  The abbreviated symbol (:=) lets you see that the syntax summary is incomplete. Whenever an incomplete rule is used, a cross reference (under "See Also") leads you to the complete rule.

The starting point for parsing a C++ source file (the start symbol) is *translation-unit*, which you can find under *declaration*.

C++ syntax is complicated, and even simple statements require an understanding of many different syntax elements. To help you, this chapter duplicates some syntax rules and has plenty of cross references to help you find the parts you need.

Almost every language element is discussed at greater length in Chapters 1–7; each description in this chapter includes a reference to the relevant chapter or chapters. References to specific headers (e.g., <new>) are for the corresponding sections in Chapter 13.

and operator Logical and operator

logical-and-expr := *logical-and-expr* && *inclusive-or-expr* |
   logical-and-expr and *inclusive-or-expr*

The *logical and* operator converts its operands to type bool and returns a bool result. This built-in operator is a short-circuit operator, so if the left operand is false, the expression yields false without evaluating the right operand. Note that an overloaded operator and cannot be short-circuited and must evaluate both operands. The keyword and is interchangeable with the && token.

Example
```
int* p;
if (p != NULL and *p != 0)
  do_stuff(*p);
```

See Also
bitand, bool, *expression*, not, or, Chapter 3, <ciso646>

and_eq operator Bitwise and assignment operator

assignment-expr := *logical-or-expr* &= *assignment-expr* |
   logical-or-expr and_eq *assignment-expr*

The and_eq operator is an assignment operator that performs bitwise *and*. It is equivalent to *logical-or-expr* = *logical-or-expr* & *assignment-expr* except that *logical-or-expr* is evaluated only once. The keyword and_eq is interchangeable with the &= token.

Example
```
unsigned bitmask = 0xFFFF;
bitmask &= ~0x7E; // bitmask becomes 0xFF81.
```

See Also
bitand, *expression*, or_eq, xor_eq, Chapter 3, <ciso646>

asm definition Inline assembler definition

block-decl := *asm-defn*

asm-defn ::= asm (*string-literal*) ;

The asm definition is implementation-defined. Typically, the *string-literal* contains assembler instructions. Some compilers extend the asm syntax to make it easier to write larger blocks of assembler code.

Example

```
asm("mov 4, %eax"); // GNU on Intel IA32
asm("mov eax, 4");  // Borland on Intel IA32
```

See Also

declaration

---

auto storage class
Automatic variable specifier

storage-class-specifier := auto

The auto storage class specifier declares a local variable to be automatic. The object is constructed when execution reaches the variable's declaration, and the object is destroyed when execution leaves the scope where it is declared.

All local variables and function parameters are auto by default, so the explicit auto specifier is rarely used.

Example

```
int foo(auto int parm)
{
  auto int sqr = parm * parm;
  return sqr;
}
```

See Also

declaration, register, Chapter 2

---

bitand operator
Bitwise and operator

and-expr := *and-expr* & *equality-expr* | *and-expr* bitand *equality-expr*

The *bitwise and* operator requires integer or enumeration operands. It performs the usual arithmetic conversions, then does an *and* operation on pairs of bits in the operands, resulting in an integer.

The bitand keyword is interchangeable with the & token.

Example

```
unsigned bitmask = 0xFFFF;
bitmask = bitmask & ~0x7E; // bitmask becomes 0xFF81
```

See Also

and, and_eq, bitor, compl, *expression*, xor, Chapter 3, <ciso646>

---

bitor operator
Bitwise inclusive or operator

inclusive-or-expr := *inclusive-or-expr* "|" *exclusive-or-expr* |
  inclusive-or-expr bitor *exclusive-or-expr*

The *bitwise or* operator requires integer or enumeration operands. It performs the usual arithmetic conversions, then does an *inclusive or* operation on pairs of bits in the operands, resulting in an integer. The bitor operator is interchangeable with the | token.

Example

```
unsigned bitmask = 0xF0F0;
bitmask = bitmask | 0x0102; // bitmask becomes 0xF1F2.
```

See Also

bitand, compl, *expression*, or, or_eq, xor, Chapter 3, <ciso646>

bool type
Boolean (logical) type specifier

simple-type-specifier := bool

The bool type represents Boolean or logical values. The only valid values of the bool type are the literals true and false. A bool expression can be promoted to an integer: false becomes 0 and true becomes 1. Arithmetic, enumerated, and pointer values can be converted to bool: 0 is false, a null pointer is false, and anything else is true.

See Also

and, false, not, or, true, *type*, Chapter 2, Chapter 3

break statement
Exits from a loop or switch statement

statement := break ;

The break statement exits from the nearest enclosing loop (do, for, or while) or switch statement. Execution continues with the statement immediately following the end of the loop or switch. An error results if break is used outside of a loop or switch statement.

Example

```
while(std::cin >> x) {
  if (x < 0)
    break;
  data.push_back(x);
}
```

See Also

continue, do, for, *statement*, switch, while, Chapter 4

case keyword
Case label for switch statement

statement := case *constant-expression* : *statement*

The case keyword labels a statement in a switch statement. A single statement can have multiple labels. You cannot use case outside of a switch statement.

Note that case labels have no effect on the order in which substatements are executed within a switch statement. Use the break statement to exit from a switch statement.

Example

```
switch(c) {
case '+':
  z = add(x, y);
  break;
```

```
      case '-':
        z = subtract(x, y);
        break;
    }
```

See Also

break, default, *statement*, switch, Chapter 4

---

catch keyword   Exception handler in try statement

handler ::= catch (*exception-declaration*) *compound-statement*

exception-declaration ::= *type-specifier-seq declarator* |
  type-specifier-seq abstract-declarator | *type-specifier-seq* | . . .

The catch keyword introduces an exception handler in a try statement. A single try statement must have one or more catch blocks. The *exception*-declaration declares an exception handler object. If an exception is thrown in the try's *compound-statement*, the type of the exception object is compared with the type of each catch declaration. The *compound-statement* of the first catch block whose type matches that of the exception object is executed. A catch block (typically the last one in a try statement) can have an ellipsis (. . .) as the *exception-declaration* to match all exceptions.

Example

```
    int main( )
    try {
      run_program( );
    } catch(const std::exception& ex) {
      std::cerr << ex.what( ) << '\n';
      std::abort( );
    } catch(...) {
      std::cerr << "Unknown exception. Program terminated.\n";
      std::abort( );
    }
```

See Also

declarator, *statement*, throw, try, *type*, Chapter 4

---

char type   Character type specifier

simple-type-specifier := char

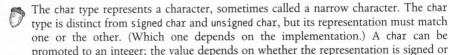 The char type represents a character, sometimes called a narrow character. The char type is distinct from signed char and unsigned char, but its representation must match one or the other. (Which one depends on the implementation.) A char can be promoted to an integer; the value depends on whether the representation is signed or unsigned.

By definition, sizeof(char) is 1, so a char is often used as the basic unit of memory allocation. Raw memory is often allocated as arrays of char or unsigned char.

See Also

type, wchar_t, Chapter 1, Chapter 2, <cstring>, <memory>

---

class keyword

Declares a class or template parameter, or elaborates a type name

class-specifier ::= *class-head* { [*member-specification*] }

class-head ::= *class-key* [*identifier*] [*base-clause*] |
  class-key nested-name :: *identifier* [*base-clause*] |
  class-key [*nested-name* ::] *template-id* [*base-clause*] *class-key* ::= class |
  struct | union

member-specification ::= *member-decl* [*member-specification*] |
  access-specifier : [*member-specification*]

member-decl ::= [*decl-specifier-seq*] [*member-declarator-list*] ; |
  function-definition [;] | *qualified-id* ; | *using-decl* | *template-decl*

member-declarator-list ::= *member-declarator* |
  member-declarator-list , *member-declarator*

member-declarator ::= *declarator* [= 0] | *declarator* [= *constant-expression*] |
  [*identifier*] : *constant-expression*

base-clause ::= : *base-specifier-list*

base-specifier-list ::= *base-specifier* | *base-specifier-list* , *base-specifier*

base-specifier ::= [*base-modifiers*] [::] [*nested-name* ::] *class-name*

base-modifiers ::= virtual [*access-specifier*] | *access-specifier* [virtual]

access-specifier ::= private | protected | public

class-name ::= *identifier* | *template-id*

type-parm := class [*identifier*] [= *type-id*] |
  template < *template-parm-list* > class [*identifier*] [= *id-expression*]

elaborated-type-specifier := *class-key* [::] [*nested-name* ::] *identifier* |
  class-key [::] [*nested-name* ::] [template] *template-id*

The class keyword introduces a class declaration or definition, names a type template parameter (*type-parm*), or names a class type in an *elaborated-type-specifier*. In a class definition, the only difference between class and struct is that the default access level is private for class and public for struct.

When declaring a type template parameter, typename and class are interchangeable.

Example

```
template<class T> // Can use typename instead of class
class point {
public:
  point(T x = 0, T y = 0);
private:
  T x_, y_;
};
point<int> pt1;
class point<int> pt2; // redundant use of class
```

See Also

declaration, *declarator*, *expression*, *function*, *identifier*, private, protected, public, struct, template, *type*, typename, union, virtual, Chapter 6, Chapter 7

compl operator

Bitwise complement operator

unary-expr := ~ *cast-expr* | compl *cast-expr*

The *bitwise complement* operator requires an integer or enumeration operand. It performs the usual arithmetic promotion and toggles each bit of its operand, resulting in an integer.

The compl keyword is interchangeable with the ~ token.

Example

```
unsigned bitmask;
bitmask = ~0xF107; // bitmask becomes 0xFFFF0EF8 (32 bits).
```

See Also

bitand, bitor, *expression*, not, xor, Chapter 3, <ciso646>

---

const qualifier

Marks objects and functions as constant

cv-qualifier ::= const | volatile

cv-qualifier-seq ::= const | volatile | const volatile | volatile const

The const keyword can be used as a qualifier when declaring objects, types, or member functions. When qualifying an object, using const means that the object cannot be the target of an assignment, and you cannot call any of its non-const member functions. When qualifying the target of a pointer, it means the destination cannot be modified. When member functions of a const object are called, this is a const pointer. When qualifying a member function, using the const qualifier means that within the member function, this is a const pointer to const, and the member function can be called for const objects. (Member functions without the const modifier cannot be called for a const object.)

When declaring pointers and references, be sure to distinguish between a const pointer (for which the pointer cannot be assigned, but what it points to can be modified) and a pointer to const (for which the pointer can be assigned, but what it points to cannot be modified).

Example

```
struct rect {
  rect(int x, int y) : x_(x), y_(y) {}
  void x(int x) { x_ = x; }
  void y(int y) { y_ = y; }
  int x() const { return x_; }
  int y() const { return y_; }
  int area() const;
private:
  int x_, y_;
};
int rect::area() const { return x() * y(); }
const rect zero(0, 0);
const rect unit(1, 1);
rect p(4, 2), q(2, 4);
const rect* ptr1 = &zero;    // OK: pointer to const
ptr1->x(42);                 // Error: *ptr is const
ptr1 = &p;                   // Error: p is not const
```

```
ptr1 = &unit;            // OK: unit is const
rect* const ptr2 = &p;   // OK: const pointer
ptr2 = &q;               // Error: cannot set ptr2
ptr2->x(42);             // OK: *ptr2 is not const
```

See Also

const_cast, *declaration*, mutable, *type*, volatile, Chapter 2

---

const_cast operator
Cast to modify qualifiers

postfix-expr := const_cast < *type-id* > (*expression*)

The const_cast operator performs a type cast that can add or remove const and volatile qualifiers. No other modifications to the type are permitted.

If you cast away a const or volatile qualifier from an object, and then modify the object, the behavior is undefined.

Example

```
template<typename T>
T& unsafe(const T& x)
{
  return const_cast<T&>(x);
}
```

See Also

const, dynamic_cast, *expression*, reinterpret_cast, static_cast, *type*, volatile, Chapter 3

---

continue statement
Reiterates a loop statement

statement := continue ;

The continue statement iterates a loop statement without executing the rest of the loop body. Control passes directly to the loop condition in a do or while loop or to the iterate expression in a for loop. You cannot use continue outside of a loop statement.

Example

```
while (getline(cin, line)) {
  if (line.empty())
    continue;
  parse(line);
  do_more_stuff();
};
```

See Also

break, do, for, *statement*, while, Chapter 4

---

declaration
Function, namespace, object, type, template declaration

translation-unit ::= [*declaration-seq*]

declaration-seq ::= *declaration* | *declaration-seq declaration*

declaration ::= *block-decl* | *function-decl* | *template-decl* | *explicit-instantiation* |
  explicit-specialization | *linkage-specification* | *namespace-defn*

block-decl ::= *simple-decl* | *asm-defn* | *namespace-alias-defn* | *using-decl* |
  using-directive

simple-decl ::= [*decl-specifier-seq*] [*init-declarator-list*] ;

decl-specifier ::= *storage-class-specifier* | *type-specifier* | *function-specifier* |
  friend | typedef

decl-specifier-seq ::= *decl-specifier* | *decl-specifier-seq* *decl-specifier*

storage-class-specifier ::= auto | register | static | extern | mutable

function-specifier ::= inline | virtual | explicit

A source file is a sequence of zero or more declarations. See Chapter 2 for a full discussion of declarations.

See Also

asm, *declarator*, *function*, namespace, template, *type*, typedef, using, Chapter 2

---

declarator   Provides information about a single identifier in a declaration

declarator ::= *direct-declarator* | *ptr-operator* *declarator*

init-declarator-list ::= *init-declarator* | *init-declarator-list* , *init-declarator*

init-declarator ::= *declarator* [*initializer*]

initializer ::= = *initializer-clause* | (*expr-list*)

initializer-clause ::= *assignment-expr* | { *initializer-list* [,] } | { }

initializer-list ::= *initializer-clause* | *initializer-list* , *initializer-clause*

direct-declarator ::= *declarator-id* |
  direct-declarator (*parm-decl-clause*) [*cv-qualifier-seq*] [*exception-specification*] |
  direct-declarator "[" [*constant-expr*] "]" | (*declarator*)

ptr-operator ::= * [*cv-qualifier-seq*] | & | [::] *nested-name* :: * [*cv-qualifier-seq*]

declarator-id ::= *id-expression* | [::] [*nested-name* ::] *type-name*

abstract-declarator ::= *ptr-operator* [*abstract-declarator*] | *direct-abstract-declarator*

direct-abstract-declarator ::= [*direct-abstract-declarator*] (*parm-decl-clause*)
  [*cv-qualifier-seq*] [*exception-specification*] |
  [*direct-abstract-declarator*] "[" [*constant-expr*] "]" | (*abstract-declarator*)

parm-decl-clause ::= [*parm-decl-list*] [...] | *parm-decl-list* , ...

parm-decl-list ::= *parm-decl* | *parm-decl-list* , *parm-decl*

parm-decl ::= *decl-specifier-seq* *declarator* [= *assignment-expr*] |
  decl-specifier-seq [*abstract-declarator*] [= *assignment-expr*]

exception-specification ::= throw ([*type-id-list*])

type-id-list ::= *type-id* | *type-id-list* , *type-id*

A declarator provides additional information about a single identifier in a declaration. The declarator can be part of an object declaration, a class member declaration, a typedef declaration, a parameter in a function declaration, and so on.

See Also

declaration, *expression*, *function*, *identifier*, *type*, Chapter 2

---

default keyword

statement := default : *statement*

A switch statement jumps to the default label if no case matches the switch expression. A switch statement can have at most one default label. If there is no default and the expression does not match any cases, control jumps directly to the statement that follows the switch statement.

Example

```
switch(c) {
case '+': ... break;
case '-': ... break;
default:
  cerr << "unknown operator: " << c << '\n';
  break;
};
```

See Also

break, case, *statement*, switch, Chapter 4

delete operator

delete-expr ::= [::] delete *cast-expr* | [::] delete "[" "]" *cast-expr*

The delete expression destroys dynamically-allocated objects and frees their memory. A scalar allocated with new must be freed with delete. An array allocated with new[] must be freed with delete[]. Do not mix scalar allocation or deallocation with array allocation or deallocation.

It is safe to delete a null pointer; nothing will happen.

You can overload operator delete and operator delete[] (as described in Chapter 5). Two global placement operator delete functions are provided by the standard library (see the <new> header); you can define additional functions if you wish.

The first argument to operator delete is the pointer to the memory that must be freed. Additional arguments can be used for placement delete operations, which cannot be used directly but are matched with placement new operations if the new expression throws an exception.

Example

```
void operator delete(void* p)
{
  debug(p);
  std::free(p);
}
int* p = new int;
int* array = new int[10];
...
delete p;
delete[] array;
```

See Also

expression, new, Chapter 3, Chapter 5, <new>

do statement   Test-at-bottom loop statement

statement := do *statement* while (*expression*) ;

The do statement is a loop that executes *statement*, then tests *expression*. The loop iterates while *expression* is true and ends if *expression* is false. The loop body always executes at least once.

Example
```
do {
  cout << "Number: ";
  if (cin >> num)
    data.push_back(num);
} while(cin);
```

See Also
break, continue, *expression*, for, *statement*, while, Chapter 4

double type   Double-precision, floating-point type specifier

simple-type-specifier := double

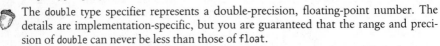

The double type specifier represents a double-precision, floating-point number. The details are implementation-specific, but you are guaranteed that the range and precision of double can never be less than those of float.

The type long double has at least the range and precision of a plain double.

See Also
float, long, *type*, Chapter 2

dynamic_cast operator   Polymorphic cast of class type objects

postfix-expr := dynamic_cast < *type-id* > (*expression*)

The dynamic_cast operator performs a polymorphic cast on a pointer or reference to an object of class type. If *expression* is a pointer or reference to a base class, *type-id* can be a pointer or reference to a derived class. If the dynamic type of the object is not that of *type-id* or a class derived from *type-id*, the cast fails. If *expression* is a pointer, failure returns a null pointer; if *expression* is a reference, failure throws std::bad_cast. Casts from a derived to an unambiguous, accessible base class always succeed.

If *expression* is a null pointer, the result is a null pointer. If *type-id* is a pointer to void, the cast succeeds and returns a pointer to the most-derived object that *expression* represents.

Example
```
struct base {};
struct derived : base {};
base* b = new derived;
derived* d = dynamic_cast<derived*>(b);
```

See Also
const_cast, *expression*, reinterpret_cast, static_cast, *type*, Chapter 3, <typeinfo>

else keyword

Else part of if statement

statement := if (*condition*) *statement* else *statement*

The else keyword introduces the else part of an if statement. If the *condition* is false, the else *statement* is executed.

Example

```
template<typename T>
T abs(T x)
{
  if (x < T())
    return -x;
  else
    return x;
}
```

See Also

if, *statement*, Chapter 4

---

enum keyword

Declares enumerated type or elaborates an enumerated type name

enum-specifier ::= enum [*identifier*] { [*enumerator-list*] }

enumerator-list ::= *enumerator-defn* | *enumerator-list* , *enumerator-defn*

enumerator-defn ::= *enumerator* | *enumerator* = *constant-expr*

enumerator ::= *identifier*

elaborated-type-specifier := enum [::] [*nested-name* ::] *identifier*

The enum keyword declares a new enumerated type (as an *enum-specifier*) or names an existing enumerated type (in an *elaborated-type-specifier*). An enumerated type is an integral type that defines a set of named constants (the *enumerator-list*). Each *enumerator* is an identifier optionally followed by a value (an equal sign and a constant expression of integral or enumerated type). Without an explicit value, the value of an enumerator is one more than the value of the preceding enumerator. The implicit value of the first enumerator is 0.

 Every enumerated type is stored as an integral type. The size of the integer is implementation-defined but is large enough to hold all the enumerated values. The valid values of an enumeration include the declared enumerators and every value that can be stored in the same number of bits, even if those values are not named as enumerators.

Example

```
enum logical { no, maybe, yes };
bool logical_to_bool(enum logical x) // Redundant enum
{
  return x != no;
}
```

See Also

expression, *identifier*, *type*, Chapter 2

explicit specifier

function-specifier := explicit

The explicit specifier can be used with a constructor to prevent implicit type conversions. It is permitted for any constructor but makes sense only for constructors that can be called with a single argument. An explicit constructor can be invoked from a declaration that uses function-like initialization or from an explicit type cast but not from a declaration that uses assignment-like initialization, nor from an implicit type cast.

Example

```
struct point {
  explicit point(int x, int y = 0);
};
point p1(10);   // OK
point p2 = 10; // Error: would be OK without explicit
point p3;
p3 = 20;        // Error: would be OK without explicit
p3 = static_cast<point>(40); // OK
```

See Also

class, *declaration*, *function*, static_cast, *type*, Chapter 2, Chapter 6

---

export specifier

template-decl ::= [export] template < *template-parm-list* > *declaration*

The export specifier declares a template to be exported. An exported template lets you compile the definitions of a function template, or the member definitions of a class template, separately from the template's declaration.

 Most compilers do not support export.

Example

```
export template<typename T>
class point {
public:
  point(T x, T y);
};
export template<typename T>
point::point(T x, T y) {
  ...
}
```

See Also

template, Chapter 7

---

expression

expression ::= *assignment-expr* | *expression* , *assignment-expr*

constant-expr ::= *conditional-expr*

expr-list ::= *assignment-expr* | *expr-list* , *assignment-expr*

---

assignment-expr ::= *conditional-expr* |
  logical-or-expr *assignment-op* *assignment-expr* | *throw-expr*

assignment-op ::= = | *= | /= | %= | += | -= | >>= | <<= | &= | and_eq | "|=" |
  or_eq | ^= | xor_eq

throw-expr ::= throw [*assignment-expr*]

conditional-expr ::= *logical-or-expr* | *logical-or-expr* ? *expression* : *assignment-expr*

logical-or-expr ::= *logical-and-expr* | *logical-or-expr* "||" *logical-and-expr* |
  logical-or-expr or *logical-and-expr*

logical-and-expr ::= *inclusive-or-expr* | *logical-and-expr* && *inclusive-or-expr* |
  logical-and-expr and *inclusive-or-expr*

inclusive-or-expr ::= *exclusive-or-expr* | *inclusive-or-expr* "|" *exclusive-or-expr* |
  inclusive-or-expr bitor *exclusive-or-expr*

exclusive-or-expr ::= *and-expr* | *exclusive-or-expr* ^ *and-expr* |
  exclusive-or-expr xor *and-expr*

inclusive-or-expr ::= *equality-expr* | *and-expr* & *equality-expr* |
  and-expr bitand *exclusive-or-expr*

equality-expr ::= *relational-expr* | *equality-expr* == *relational-expr* |
  equality-expr != *relational-expr* | *equality-expr* not_eq *relational-expr*

relational-expr ::= *shift-expr* | *relational-expr* < *shift-expr* |
  relational-expr > *shift-expr* | *relational-expr* <= *shift-expr* |
  relational-expr >= *shift-expr*

shift-expr ::= *add-expr* | *shift-expr* << *add-expr* | *shift-expr* >> *add-expr*

add-expr ::= *mul-expr* | *add-expr* + *mul-expr* | *add-expr* - *mul-expr*

mul-expr ::= *pm-expr* | *mul-expr* * *pm-expr* | *mul-expr* / *pm-expr* |
  mul-expr % *pm-expr*

pm-expr ::= *cast-expr* | *pm-expr* .* *cast-expr* | *pm-expr* ->* *cast-expr*

cast-expr ::= *unary-expr* | (*type-id*) *cast-expr*

unary-expr ::= *postfix-expr* | ++ *cast-expr* | -- *cast-expr* | *unary-op* *cast-expr* |
  sizeof *unary-expr* | sizeof (*type-id*) | *new-expr* | *delete-expr*

postfix-expr ::= *primary-expr* | *postfix-expr* "[" *expression* "]" |
  postfix-expr ([*expr-list*]) | *simple-type-specifier* ([*expr-list*]) |
  typename [::] *nested-name* :: *identifier* ([*expr-list*]) |
  typename [::] *nested-name* :: [template] *template-id* ([*expr-list*]) |
  postfix-expr . [template] *id-expr* | *postfix-expr* -> [template] *id-expr* |
  postfix-expr . *pseudo-dtor-name* | *postfix-expr* -> *pseudo-dtor-name* |
  postfix-expr ++ | *postfix-expr* -- | const_cast < *type-id* > (*expression*) |
  dynamic_cast < *type-id* > (*expression*) |
  reinterpret_cast < *type-id* > (*expression*) |
  static_cast < *type-id* > (*expression*) | typeid (*expression*) |
  typeid (*type-id*)

pseudo-dtor-name ::= [::] [*nested-name* ::] *type-name* :: ~ *type-name* |
  [::] *nested-name* :: template *template-id* :: ~ *type-name*

primary-expr ::= *literal* | this | (*expression*) | *id-expr*

An expression represents a value and a type. See Chapter 3 for details about expressions, precedence, associativity, lvalues and rvalues, and more. Some syntax rules are presented here and in the various keyword sections. The *new-expr* and *delete-expr* rules are not duplicated here; see new and delete for details. The *id-expr* rules are under *identifier*. See Chapter 1 for information about literals.

See Also

and, and_eq, bitand, bitor, compl, const_cast, delete, dynamic_cast, *identifier*, new, not, not_eq, or, or_eq, reinterpret_cast, sizeof, static_cast, template, *type*, typeid, xor, xor_eq, Chapter 3

---

extern storage class External storage class specifier

storage-class-specifier := extern

linkage-specification ::= extern *string-literal* { [*declaration-seq*] } |
   extern *string-literal declaration*

The extern storage class specifier marks a declaration as having external linkage. An external object or function can be defined in one file and used in other files.

 The extern keyword can also be used to specify language linkage: you provide the language name as a string literal. The "C++" language is the default. "C" linkage is also supported. Other languages are implementation-defined.

Example

```
extern "C" int callable_from_C(int x, int y);
extern void func(int);
extern const double pi;
```

See Also

declaration, static, *type*, Chapter 2

---

false literal Boolean false literal

literal := false

The false literal has type bool and integer value 0.

See Also

bool, *expression*, true, Chapter 2

---

float type Single-precision, floating-point type specifier

simple-type-specifier := float

 The float type is a single-precision, floating-point number. The range and precision are implementation-defined. They can never be more than those of double or long double.

See Also

double, long, *type*, Chapter 2

---

for statement

statement := for (*for-init-stmt* [*condition*] ; [*expression*]) *statement*
  for-init-stmt ::= *expression-stmt* | *simple-decl*
  condition ::= *expression* | *type-specifier-seq declarator* = *assignment-expr*

The for loop is used for bounded loops and for unbounded loops that have well-defined iterations. Execution starts with *for-init-stmt*, which can be an expression statement or a declaration. (Note that the syntax for *expression-stmt* and *simple-decl* both include a terminating semicolon.)

condition is then evaluated. If *condition* evaluates to true, *statement* is executed. The iteration *expression* is then evaluated, and the *condition* is tested again. When *condition* is false, the loop ends and control passes to the statement following the end of the for statement.

Declarations in *for-int-stmt* and *condition* are in the same scope as *expression* and *statement*. A continue statement inside *statement* transfers control to the evaluation of the iteration *expression*.

Example

```
for (int i = 0; i < 10; ++i)
  cout << i << '\n';
for (node* n = head; n != 0 ; n = n->next)
  link_node(n);
```

See Also

break, continue, do, *expression*, *statement*, while, Chapter 4

---

friend specifier

decl-specifier := friend

The friend specifier declares a friend function, class, or template. A friend declaration can appear only in a class or class template definition. A friend has full access to the private members of the class that contains the friend declaration. A friend function declaration can be a function definition.

If a class template contains a friend declaration, all instantiations of the template grant friendship. If the friend is a template declaration, all instantiations of the template are friends. If the friend is a template specialization or instantiation, only that specialization or instantiation is a friend.

Friendship is not transitive, nor is it inherited.

Example

```
class list {
  friend bool operator==(const list& a, const list& b);
  friend class node;
  ...
};
```

See Also

class, *declaration*, template, Chapter 6, Chapter 7

function

Function definition

declaration := *function-defn*

function-defn ::= [*decl-specifier-seq*] *declarator* [*ctor-initializer*] *function-body* |
  [*decl-specifier-seq*] *declarator* *function-try-block*

function-body ::= *compound-statement*

function-try-block ::= try [*ctor-initializer*] *function-body* *handler-seq*

ctor-initializer ::= : *member-initializer-list*

member-initializer-list ::= *member-initializer* |
  member-initializer-list , *member-initializer*

member-initializer ::= *member-initializer-id* ([*expr-list*])

member-initializer-id ::= *identifier* | [::] [*nested-name* ::] *class-name*

See Chapter 5 for information about functions and Chapter 6 for information about the special member functions, such as constructors. (A *ctor-initializer* applies only to the definition of a class constructor.)

See Also

class, *declaration*, *declarator*, *statement*, try, Chapter 5

goto statement

Transfers execution to a labeled statement

statement := goto *identifier* ;

The goto statement transfers control to another statement in the same function. The *identifier* must match a statement label elsewhere in the function. Statement labels have the form *identifier* : *statement*.

Control cannot transfer into a try block. Transferring control into the middle of a block and across a declaration results in undefined behavior unless the declaration is for an uninitialized POD object.

Example

```
while (getline(cin, line))
  for (size_t i = 0; i < line.size(); ++i)
    if (line[i] == '.')
      goto exit; // Break out of nested loops.
  exit:
  ...
```

See Also

break, continue, *statement*, Chapter 4

identifier

Name of an entity

id-expression ::= *unqualified-id* | *qualified-id*

unqualified-id ::= *identifier* | *operator-function-id* | *conversion-function-id* |
  ~ *class-name* | *template-id*

qualified-id ::= [::] *nested-name* :: [template] *unqualified-id* | :: *identifier* |
  :: *operator-function-id* | :: *template-id*

nested-name ::= *class-or-namespace-name* |
  nested-name [:: *class-or-namespace-name*] |
  nested-name [:: template *class-name*]

class-or-namespace-name ::= *class-name* | *namespace-name*

class-name ::= *identifier* | *template-id*

namespace-name ::= *identifier*

An entity name can be a simple identifier, an operator name, or a qualified name. See Chapter 1 for the rules that apply to valid identifiers. See Chapter 5 for more information on overloaded operators. See operator for the rules that apply to *operator-function-id* and *conversion-function-id*.

See Also

class, *declarator*, namespace, operator, Chapter 1, Chapter 2

if statement

Selection statement

statement := if (*condition*) *statement* |
  if (*condition*) *statement* else *statement*

condition ::= *expression* | *type-specifier-seq declarator* = *assignment-expr*

The if statement tests *condition*, and if it is true, executes the first *statement*. If *condition* is false, and an else part is present, the else *statement* is executed; if there is no else part, execution continues with the statement immediately after the end of the if statement. If *condition* contains a declaration, the declared name is in the scope of both the if and else statements.

Example

```
template<typename T>
T abs(T x)
{
  if (x < T())
    return -x;
  else
    return x;
}
```

See Also

expression, else, *statement*, Chapter 4

inline specifier

Inline function specifier

function-specifier := inline

The inline function specifier can be used with any function or member function to hint to the compiler that the function should be expanded inline at the point of call. The compiler is free to ignore the hint. The compiler is also free to expand functions inline that are declared without the inline specifier, so long as this does not affect the semantics of the program.

An inline function must be defined in the same source file where it is used, before it is used. An inline function can be defined in more than one file (unlike other functions); the definition in every file must be the same.

A member function that is defined within a class definition is implicitly declared inline.

Example

```
struct point {
  inline point(int x, int y) : x_(x), y_(y) {} // Redundant
  inline point();
private:
  int x_, y_;
};
inline point::point() : x_(0), y_(0) {}
```

See Also

class, *declaration*, *function*, *type*, Chapter 5

---

int type   Integer type specifier

simple-type-specifier := int

The int type specifier denotes an integral type. Alone, it represents a signed integer whose size is the natural size of an integer on the host platform. With the short or long specifier, it represents an integer type whose range is possibly smaller or larger than that of plain int. With the unsigned specifier, it represents an unsigned type. The signed specifier is allowed, but it is the default, so it is rarely used with int.

See Also

char, *declaration*, *declarator*, long, short, signed, *type*, unsigned, Chapter 2

---

long type   Long type specifier

simple-type-specifier := long

When used alone or with int, the long type specifier represents a long integer whose range is at least as large as a plain int. It can be combined with unsigned to denote an unsigned integer whose range is at least as large as a plain unsigned. A plain long is signed by default, but you can use the signed specifier to be explicit.

When combined with double, long represents an extended-precision, floating-point number, whose range and precision are at least as great as those of a plain double.

See Also

declaration, *declarator*, double, float, int, short, signed, *type*, unsigned, Chapter 2

---

mutable specifier   Mutable data member specifier

storage-class-specifier := mutable

The mutable specifier can be used with the declaration of a data member. Using it means that the member can be modified even if the containing object is const.

Example

```
// Represent a point in Cartesian coordinates. If the user requests polar
// coordinates, compute and cache the polar coordinates. If the Cartesian
// coordinates change, the polar coordinates must be recomputed. The polar
// coordinates are computed only if they are needed.
```

```
struct point {
  double angle() const {
    if (! has_angle_) {
      angle_ = tan2(y, x);
      has_angle_ = true;
    }
    return angle_;
  }
  void x(double x) { x_ = x; has_angle_ = has_arg_ = false; }
  ...
private:
  double x_, y_;
  mutable double angle_, arg_;
  mutable bool has_angle_, has_arg_;
};

int main()
{
  const point pt(1, 2);
  std::cout << pt.angle();
}
```

See Also

class, const, *declaration*, *type*, Chapter 6

---

namespace keyword   Declares namespace

declaration := *namespace-defn*

block-decl := *namespace-alias-defn* | *using-directive*

namespace-defn ::= *named-namespace-defn* | *unnamed-namespace-defn*

named-namespace-defn ::= namespace *identifier* { *namespace-body* }

unnamed-namespace-defn ::= namespace { *namespace-body* }

namespace-body ::= [*declaration-seq*]

namespace-alias-defn ::= namespace *identifier* = *namespace-specifier* ;

namespace-specifier ::= [::] [*nested-name* ::] *namespace-name*

namespace-name ::= *identifier*

using-directive ::= using namespace *namespace-specifier* ;

The namespace keyword can be used in a namespace definition, a namespace alias definition, or a using directive. A namespace is a scope for declarations of classes, templates, functions, objects, and other namespaces. Outside a namespace, you can refer to a name that is declared in the namespace by qualifying the name with the scope operator (::), such as ns::name, or with a using directive or declaration.

Multiple namespace declarations can name the same namespace, each one adding more declarations to the namespace. The standard namespace, std, is built this way, with many different headers all placing their declarations in the std namespace. A namespace can be anonymous, which prevents the enclosed declarations from being visible in other source files.

A namespace alias defines an identifier as a synonym for an existing namespace. See using for information on the using directive.

Example

```
namespace math_version_2 {
  const long double pi = 3.1415926535897932385L;
};
namespace math = math_version_2;
using namespace math;
```

See Also

class, *declaration*, *identifier*, using, Chapter 2

---

new operator   Allocates a dynamic object or array of objects

new-expr ::= [::] new [*placement*] *new-type-id* [*new-initializer*] |
  [::] new [*placement*] (*type-id*) [*new-initializer*]

placement ::= (*expr-list*)

new-type-id ::= *type-specifier-seq* [*new-declarator*]

new-declarator ::= *ptr-operator* [*new-declarator*] | *direct-new-declarator*

direct-new-declarator ::= "[" *expression* "]" |
  direct-new-declarator "[" *constant-expr* "]"

new-initializer ::= ([*expr-list*])

ptr-operator ::= * [*cv-qualifier-seq*] | & | [::] *nested-name* :: * [*cv-qualifier-seq*]

The new expression allocates memory and constructs an object. It has many forms, the simplest being a simple type name (e.g., new int). The *new-type-id* can be a sequence of type specifiers and qualifiers, with pointer operators, a reference operator, and an array size (e.g., new int*[n][42], which allocates a two-dimensional array of pointers to int with n rows and 42 columns). The first dimension can be an integral expression; the second and subsequent dimensions must be constant expressions. If the type contains parentheses, such as function pointers, you should enclose it in parentheses to avoid ambiguity.

The new expression calls an allocator function to allocate the necessary memory, then initializes the memory. The *new-initializer* is an optional list of expressions in parentheses. If no *new-initializer* is present, the new object is initialized to its default value: POD objects are uninitialized, and other objects are initialized with their default constructors. If the *new-initializer* consists of just empty parentheses, POD objects are initialized to 0, and other objects are initialized with their default constructors. The *new-initializer* can be the value of a scalar or a list of expressions to pass to a suitable constructor.

The allocator function is operator new or operator new[], which can be overloaded (as described in Chapter 5). Two global placement operator new functions are provided by the standard library (see the <new> header); you can define additional functions if you wish.

The allocator function takes a size_t as its first parameter, which is the number of bytes of memory to allocate. It returns a pointer to the memory. The *placement* syntax is a list of expressions in parentheses. The expression list is passed to the allocator functions after the size argument. The compiler chooses which overloaded operator new according to the usual rules of overload resolution (Chapter 5).

Example

```
void* operator new(std::size_t nbytes)
{
  void* result = std::malloc(nbytes);
  debug(result);
  if (result == 0)
    throw std::bad_alloc("no more memory");
  return result;
}

int* p = new int;
int* array = new int[10];
int* placement = new(p) int;
...
delete p;
delete[] array;
```

See Also

declarator, delete, *expression*, *type*, Chapter 3, Chapter 5, <new>

not operator   Logical negation operator

unary-expr := ! *cast-expr* | not *cast-expr*

The not operator converts its operand to type bool, inverts its value, and returns a bool result. The not keyword is interchangeable with the ! token.

Example

```
template<typename C>
typename C::value_type checked_first(const C& c)
{
  if (not c.empty())
    return c[0];
  throw std::out_of_range("container is empty");
}
```

See Also

and, bool, *expression*, or, Chapter 3, <ciso646>

not_eq operator   Inequality operator

equality-expr := *equality-expr* != *relational-expr* |
  equality-expr not_eq *relational-expr*

The not_eq operator compares two expressions for inequality. It returns true if the operands are different or false if they are the same. The not_eq keyword is interchangeable with the != token. Note that there is no keyword equivalent for the == operator.

See Also

expression, Chapter 3, <ciso646>

operator keyword   Function call syntax for operators

operator-function-id ::= operator *op-symbol* |
  operator *op-symbol* < [*template-arg-list*] >

conversion-function-id ::= operator *conversion-type-id*

conversion-type-id ::= *type-specifier-seq* [*conversion-declarator*]

conversion-declarator ::= *ptr-operator* [*conversion-declarator*]

ptr-operator ::= * [*cv-qualifier-seq*] | & | [::] *nested-name* :: * [*cv-qualifier-seq*]

The operator keyword converts an operator symbol into function notation. You can use the operator keyword when invoking an operator or when overloading an operator.

Example

```
int x = operator+(10, 32);
complex<double> c, d;
c.operator+=(d);
operator+=(c, d); // Same as above
bigint operator*(const bigint& a, const bigint* b);
```

Table 12-1 lists the operator symbols (*op-symbol*) that can be overloaded. Alternative tokens (shown in parentheses) are interchangeable with their symbolic equivalents.

Table 12-1. Operator symbols that can be overloaded

delete	/	=	%=	<<=	++
delete [ ]	%	<	^=(xor_eq)	==	--
new	^ (xor)	>	&=(and_eq)	!=(not_eq)	,
new [ ]	&(bitand)	+=	|=(or_eq)	<=	->*
+	|(bitor)	-=	<<	>=	->
-	~(compl)	*=	>>	&&(and)	( )
*	!(not)	/=	>>=	||(or)	[ ]

See Also

expression, *identifier*, template, *type*, Chapter 5

---

or operator   Logical or operator

logical-or-expr := *logical-or-expr* "||" *logical-and-expr* |
  logical-or-expr or *logical-and-expr*

The *logical or* operator converts its operands to type bool and returns a bool result. This built-in operator is a short-circuit operator, so if the left operand is true, the expression yields true without evaluating the right operand. Note that if operator or is overloaded, it cannot be short-circuited and must evaluate both operands.

The keyword or is interchangeable with the || token.

Example

```
int* p;
if (p == NULL or *p == 0)
  skip( );
```

See Also

and, bitor, bool, *expression*, not, Chapter 3, <ciso646>

---

or_eq operator
Bitwise or assignment operator

assignment-expr := *logical-or-expr* "|=" *assignment-expr* |
  logical-or-expr or_eq *assignment-expr*

The or_eq operator is an assignment operator that performs *bitwise inclusive or*. It is equivalent to *logical-or-expr* = *logical-or-expr* | *assignment-expr* except that *logical-or-expr* is evaluated only once.

The keyword or_eq is interchangeable with the |= token.

Example

```
unsigned bitmask = 0xF0F0;
bitmask |= 0x0102; // bitmask becomes 0xF1F2.
```

See Also

and_eq, bitor, *expression*, xor_eq, Chapter 3, <ciso646>

---

private access specifier
Restricts member access to the class

access-specifier := private

The private keyword can be used within a class definition (followed by a colon) to mark subsequent member declarations as private or before a base-class name in the class header to mark the inheritance as private. The default access level of a class is private, both for members and base classes.

Private members can be used by the class itself or by friends.

Private inheritance means all public and protected members in the base class are private to the derived class.

Example

```
class rational {
public:
  rational(int n, int d) : num_(n), den_(d) { reduce(); }
  rational() : num_(0), den_(1) {}
  int num() const { return num_; }
  int den() const { return den_; }
protected:
  void reduce(); // Reduce num_ and den_ by gcd.
private:
  int num_, den_;
};
class derived : public rational {};
class myrational : private rational {
public:
  using rational::num;
  using rational::den;
};
```

See Also

class, protected, public, struct, Chapter 6

protected access specifier

Restricts member access to the class and derived classes

access-specifier := protected

The protected keyword can be used within a class definition (followed by a colon) to mark subsequent member declarations as protected or before a base-class name in the class header to mark the inheritance as protected.

Protected members can be used by the class itself, derived classes, or by friends. When accessing a protected member, the access must be through this or an instance of the same class or a derived class. It cannot be through a base class.

Protected inheritance means all public members of the base class become protected in the derived class.

See private for an example.

See Also

class, private, public, struct, Chapter 6

public access specifier

No restrictions on member access

access-specifier := public

The public keyword can be used within a class definition (followed by a colon) to mark subsequent member declarations as public or before a base-class name in the class header to mark the inheritance as public. The default access level of a struct is public, both for members and base classes.

Public members can be used freely by any other class or function.

Public inheritance means all members of the base class retain their accessibility levels.

See private for an example.

See Also

class, private, protected, struct, Chapter 6

register storage class

Register storage class specifier

storage-class-specifier := register

The register storage class is like auto: it can be used for local objects and function parameters, and using it means that the declared object has automatic lifetime. It also provides a hint to the compiler that the object will be used frequently, so the compiler can optimize access, perhaps by storing the object in a machine register.

Many modern compilers routinely ignore register because the compilers are better than humans at allocating registers.

Example

```
int foo(register int parm)
{
    register int sqr = parm * parm;
    return sqr;
}
```

See Also

auto, *type*, Chapter 2

---

reinterpret_cast operator   Cast for unsafe pointer conversions

postfix-expr := reinterpret_cast < *type-id* > (*expression*)

The reinterpret_cast operator performs potentially unsafe type casts. It is most often used to cast a pointer to a different pointer type. Casting a pointer to a different pointer and back is usually safe and yields the original value. The limitations are that object pointers can be cast only to object pointers with similar or stricter alignment requirements, and function pointers can be cast only to function pointers. Pointers-to-members can be cast only to pointers-to-members. You can cast an integer to a pointer and vice versa. In all cases, the destination pointer must be large enough to hold the result. Casting a null pointer results in a null pointer of the destination type. Any other cast results in undefined behavior.

Example

```
template<typename T>
unsigned long addressof(const T& obj)
{
   return reinterpret_cast<unsigned long>(&obj);
}
```

See Also

const_cast, dynamic_cast, *expression*, static_cast, Chapter 3

---

return statement   Returns from a function

statement := return [*expression*] ;

The return statement returns control from a function to its caller. If the function returns void, the *expression* is typically omitted, or else *expression* must be of type void. If the function returns a non-void type, the *expression* must be convertible to the return type.

A function that returns non-void must have a return statement (except for main, which has an implicit return 0; if control reaches the end of the function).

See Also

expression, *statement*, Chapter 5

---

short type   Short integer type specifier

simple-type-specifier := short

When used alone or with int, the short type specifier represents a short integer, whose range is no bigger than a plain int. It can be combined with unsigned to denote an unsigned integer whose range is no bigger than a plain unsigned. A plain short is signed by default, but you can use the signed specifier to be explicit.

See Also

int, long, signed, *type*, unsigned, Chapter 2

signed specifier
Signed integer type specifier

simple-type-specifier := `signed`

The `signed` keyword can be used alone to mean `signed int` or combined with other type specifiers to force the type to be signed. The `int`, `short`, and `long` types are implicitly signed, so it is most often used with `signed char` to implement a signed integral value whose range is the smallest that the compiler allows.

 A signed integer can be represented using two's complement, ones' complement, or signed magnitude.

See Also

char, int, long, short, *type*, unsigned, Chapter 2

sizeof operator
Size of type operator

unary-expr := `sizeof` (*type-id*) | `sizeof` *unary-expr*

At compile time, the `sizeof` operator returns the amount of memory required to hold an object whose type is *type-id* or the type of *unary-expr*. In the latter case, *unary-expr* is not evaluated. The size of a type includes any padding that the compiler adds to it, so the size of an array of *N* elements is always equal to *N* times the size of a single element.

By definition, sizeof(char) is 1, so you can think of the size of other types as multiples of the size of a character. The expression type is std::size_t.

Example

```
class point { ... };
point* p = malloc(sizeof(point));
point corners[] = { { 2, 4 }, {4, 2}, ..., { 42, 10 } };
const unsigned count = sizeof(corners) / sizeof(corners[0]);
```

See Also

expression, *type*, Chapter 3, <cstdlib>

statement
Statement syntax

statement ::= *labeled-stmt* | *expr-stmt* | *compound-stmt* | *decl-stmt* | *try-block* |
  `if` (*condition*) *statement* | `if` (*condition*) *statement* `else` *statement* |
  `switch` (*condition*) *statement* | `while` (*condition*) *statement* |
  `do` *statement* `while` (*expression*) |
  `for` (*for-init-stmt* [*condition*] ; [*expression*]) *statement* | `break` ; |
  `continue` ; | `goto` *identifier* ; | `return` [*expression*] ;

expr-stmt ::= [*expression*] ;

compound-stmt ::= { [*statement-seq*] }

statement-seq ::= *statement* | *statement-seq*

labeled-stmt ::= *identifier* : *statement* | `case` *constant-expr* : *statement* |
  `default` : *statement*

decl-stmt ::= *block-decl*

for-init-stmt ::= *expr-stmt* | *simple-decl*

condition ::= *expression* | *type-specifier-seq declarator* = *assignment-expr*

See Chapter 4 for a complete discussion of statements.

See Also

break, case, continue, *declaration*, *declarator*, default, do, else, *expression*, for, goto, if, return, switch, try, *type*, while, Chapter 4

---

static storage class
Static storage class specifier

storage-class-specifier := static

The static storage class specifier can be used with objects, functions, and class members. Its purpose varies slightly depending on how you use it:

- For local objects, static affects the object's lifetime: instead of being constructed anew every time the function is called, a static local object is constructed at most once, and the object retains its value across function calls.

- A static class member is not tied to a specific object. Instead, it is similar to a global object or function, but in the scope of the class that declares it.

- For global declarations, using static means the object or function has internal linkage instead of the default external linkage, that is, the object or function is not visible in other source files. This use is deprecated; use anonymous namespaces instead.

Example

```
struct demo {
  static const int size = 10;
  static void func() {
    return size;
  }
private:
  int data_[size];
};
static int local_data = 10;
static int local_func() { return demo::func(); }
```

See Also

auto, class, extern, namespace, register, *type*, Chapter 2

---

static_cast operator
Explicit cast operator

postfix-expr := static_cast < *type-id* > (*expression*)

The static_cast operator performs type conversions from one static type to another. It cannot cast away const or volatile qualifiers. A static cast can invoke built-in type promotions or conversions or user-defined type conversions with type conversion operators or constructors (including explicit constructors).

Example

```
char c;
if (isalpha(static_cast<unsigned char>(c))
  handle_alpha(c);
```

See Also

const_cast, dynamic_cast, explicit, *expression*, reinterpret_cast, Chapter 3

---

struct keyword   Declares class with public members

class-key := struct

The struct keyword declares a class that has public access by default. Inheritance is also public by default. See class for syntax rules.

Example

```
struct point {
   int x, y;
};
struct point p1; // "struct" is redundant here.
point p2;
```

See Also

class, union, Chapter 6

---

switch statement   Multibranch selection statement

statement := switch (*condition*) *statement*

condition ::= *expression* | *type-specifier-seq declarator* = *assignment-expr*

The switch statement evaluates *condition* and saves the value. It compares the value to each case label in *statement* (which is typically a compound statement). The statements that follow the matching case label are executed. If no case label matches, the statements following the default label are executed. If there is no default, execution continues with the statement following the end of the switch statement.

All case labels in *statement* must be unique. Use the break statement to exit the switch statement at the end of each case.

Example

```
switch(c) {
case '+':
   z = add(x, y);
   break;
default:
   z = noop( );
   break;
};
```

See Also

break, case, *declarator*, default, *expression*, if, *statement*, *type*, Chapter 4

---

template keyword   Declares a template, specialization, or instantiation

declaration := *template-decl* | *explicit-instantiation* | *explicit-specialization*

template-decl ::= [export] template < *template-parm-list* > *declaration*

template-parm-list ::= *template-parm* | *template-parm-list* , *template-parm*

template-parm ::= *type-parm* | *parm-decl*

---

type-parm ::= class [*identifier*] [= *type-id*] | typename [*identifier*] [= *type-id*] |
  template < *template-parm-list* > class [*identifier*] [= *id-expr*]

template-id ::= *template-name* < [*template-arg-list*] >

typename-name ::= *identifier*

template-arg-list ::= *template-arg* | *template-arg-list* , *template-arg*

template-arg ::= *assignment-expr* | *type-id* | *id-expr*

explicit-instantiation ::= template *declaration*

explicit-specialization ::= template < > *declaration*

elaborated-type-specifier := *class-key* [::] [*nested-name* ::] [template]
  template-id | typename [::] *nested-name* :: [template] *template-id*

simple-type-specifier := [::] *nested-name* :: template *template-id*

postfix-expr := *postfix-expr* . [template] *id-expr* |
  postfix-expr -> [template] *id-expr*

pseudo-dtor-name := [::] *nested-name* :: template *template-id* :: ~ *class-name*

nested-name := *nested-name* [:: template *class-name*]

qualified-id := [::] *nested-name* :: [template] *unqualified-id*

The template keyword declares a template, a specialization of a template, or an instance of a template. The *declaration* can be a function declaration, function definition, class declaration, or class definition.

A template instance provides arguments for the template parameters, enclosing the arguments in angle brackets (<>). If the template is a member of a class, and the . or -> operator is used to access the member template, you must use the template keyword to tell the compiler to interpret the < symbol as the start of the template arguments. Similarly, use the template keyword in a qualified name when the name is used to instantiate the template in a context in which the compiler would interpret the < symbol as the less-than operator.

Example

```
template<typename T>
T min(const T& a, const T& b) { return a < b ? a : b; }

typedef complex<float> cfloat;
template<> min<cfloat>(const cfloat& a, const cfloat& b)
{
  return cfloat(min(a.real(), b.real()), min(a.imag(), b.imag()));
}

template int min<int>(const int&, const int&);
```

See Also

class, *expression*, *identifier*, *type*, Chapter 7

this keyword

Object pointer in member function

primary-expr := this

The this keyword can be used only in nonstatic member functions. Its value is a pointer to the target object of a member function call. If the member function is qualified (with const or volatile), the same qualifiers apply to the type of this.

Example

```
struct point {
  bool operator==(const point& that) {
    return this->x() == that.x() && this->y() == that.y();
  }
  bool operator!=(const point& that) {
    return !(*this == that);
  }
  bool write(FILE* fp) {
    fwrite(static_cast<void*>(this), sizeof(*this), 1, fp);
  }
};
```

See Also

class, *expression*, Chapter 6

---

throw operator   Throws an exception

throw-expr ::= throw [*assignment-expr*]

The throw operator throws *assignment-expr* as an exception. The throw expression has type void. With no operand, throw rethrows the current pending exception. If no exception is pending, terminate( ) is called.

Example

```
template<typename C>
typename C::value_type checked_first(const C& c)
{
  if (not c.empty())
    return c[0];
  throw std::out_of_range("container is empty");
}
```

See Also

expression, try, Chapter 3, <exception>, <stdexcept>

---

true literal   Logical true literal

literal := true

The true literal has type bool and an integer value of 1.

See Also

bool, *expression*, false, Chapter 2

---

try statement   Handles exceptions in statements

statement := *try-block*

try-block ::= try *compound-statement* *handler-seq*

function-try-block ::= try [*ctor-initializer*] *function-body* *handler-seq*

handler-seq ::= *handler* | *handler-seq* *handler*

---

handler ::= catch (*exception-declaration*) *compound-statement*

exception-declaration ::= *type-specifier-seq declarator* |
  type-specifier-seq abstract-declarator | *type-specifier-seq* | ...

The try statement executes *compound-statement*, and if an exception is thrown in any of the statements within that compound statement (and not caught and handled by another try statement), the catch handlers are tested to see if any of them can handle the exception. Each catch handler is tested in turn. The first one to match the exception type handles the exception. If no handler matches, the exception propagates up the call stack to the next try statement. If there is no further try statement, terminate( ) is called.

Example

```
int main( )
try {
  run_program( );
} catch(const exception& ex) {
  std::cerr << ex.what( ) << '\n';
  abort( );
} catch(...) {
  std::cerr << "Unknown exception. Program terminated.\n";
  abort( );
}
```

See Also

catch, *declarator*, *function*, throw, *type*, Chapter 4, <exception> in Chapter 13

---

type

type-specifier ::= *simple-type-specifier* | *class-specifier* | *enum-specifier* |
  elaborated-type-specifier | *cv-qualifier*

simple-type-specifier ::= [::] [*nested-name* ::] *type-name* |
  [::] *nested-name* :: template *template-id* | bool | char | double | float | int |
  long | short | signed | unsigned | void | wchar_t

type-name ::= *class-name* | *enum-name* | *typedef-name*

typedef-name ::= *identifier*

elaborated-type-specifier ::= *class-key* [::] [*nested-name* ::] *identifier* |
  class-key [::] [*nested-name* ::] [template] *template-id* |
  enum [::] [*nested-name* ::] *identifier* | typename [::] *nested-name* :: *identifier* |
  typename [::] *nested-name* :: [template] *template-id*

Type specifiers are used throughout C++: in declarations, type casts, new expressions, and so on. Although the syntax rules shown here are quite flexible, the semantic rules impose many limits. For example, the simple syntax rules permit short long as a type (specifically, as a *decl-specifier-seq*; see *declaration*), but that combination of type specifiers is not permitted. See Chapter 2 for details about semantics for valid type specifiers.

See Also

class, const, *declaration*, *declarator*, enum, *identifier*, struct, template, typedef, typename, union, volatile, Chapter 2

typedef keyword

Declares a type synonym

decl-specifier := typedef

A typedef declaration creates a synonym for an existing type. It does not create a new type (as class and enum do).

Example

```
typedef unsigned int UINT;
typedef map<string,string> dictionary;
```

See Also

class, *declaration*, enum, struct, typeid, union, Chapter 2

---

typeid operator

Runtime type identification operator

postfix-expr := typeid (*expression*) | typeid (*type-id*)

The typeid operator returns a const reference to a type_info object that describes *type-id* or the type of *expression*. If *expression* is an lvalue (not a pointer) of a polymorphic class, the type_info of the most-derived class is returned. Otherwise, *expression* is not evaluated, and the type_info of its static type is returned.

Each distinct type has its own associated type_info object, but type synonyms (such as those created with typedef) have the same type_info object.

Example

```
template<typename T>
void debug(const T& obj)
{
   std::clog << typeid(obj).name() << ':' << &obj << '\n';
}
```

See Also

expression, typedef, Chapter 3, <typeinfo>

---

typename keyword

Introduces a type name

elaborated-type-specifier := typename [::] *nested-name* :: *identifier* |
  typename [::] *nested-name* :: [template] *template-id*

using-decl := using [typename] [::] *nested-name* :: *unqualified-id* ;

type-parm := typename [*identifier*] [= *id-expr*]

The typename keyword is used in two different situations:

- When referring to a qualified member of a class template, the compiler cannot tell whether the name refers to a type, object, or function. Use typename before the qualified name to tell the compiler that it names a type.

- In a template declaration, use typename to name a type parameter. In this context, class means the same thing as typename.

Example

```
template<typename C>
typename C::value_type checked_first(const C& c)
```

```
{
  if (not c.empty())
    return c[0];
  throw std::out_of_range("container is empty");
}
```

See Also

class, *expression*, template, *type*, using, Chapter 7

---

unsigned specifier

simple-type-specifier := unsigned

The unsigned type specifier can be used with any integral type to make the type unsigned. Unsigned integer arithmetic is always performed modulo 2^n, in which n is the number of bits in the value representation of the integer. When used alone, unsigned means unsigned int.

Example

```
char c;
if (isalpha(static_cast<unsigned char>(c))
  handle_alpha(c);
```

See Also

char, int, long, short, signed, *type*, Chapter 2

---

union keyword

class-key := union

The union keyword declares an aggregate type, similar to a struct, but the union object can store only one member at a time. The storage for all members overlaps. A union can have member functions (including constructors and destructors) but not virtual member functions. A union cannot be or have a base class. Union members cannot be static or references. Data members cannot have constructors, a destructor, copy-assignment operators, virtual functions, or virtual base classes. An initializer for a union can initialize only its first member.

See class for the syntax rules.

Example

```
enum kind { integer, real, text };
struct data {
  kind data_kind;
  data(int i) : data_kind(integer), integerval(i) {}
  data(double d) : data_kind(real), realval(d) {}
  union {
    int integerval;
    double realval;
  };
};
```

See Also

class, struct, Chapter 2, Chapter 6

Language Reference

using keyword

Looks up names in alternate classes or namespaces

block-decl := *using-decl* | *using-directive*

using-decl ::= using [typename] [::] *nested-name* :: *unqualified-id* ; |
  using [::] *unqualified-id* ;

using-directive ::= using namespace [::] [*nested-name* ::] *namespace-name* ;

The using keyword starts a using declaration or using directive.

A using declaration imports a name from another namespace into the current namespace. It can also be used to introduce a name into a class scope; this is most often used to promote the access level of an inherited member or bring an inherited member into the derived class for overload resolution.

A using directive tells the compiler to search an additional namespace when looking up unqualified names.

Example

```
namespace math {
   const long double pi = 3.1415926535897932385L;
};

using math::pi;
long double tan(long double x = pi);

int main()
{
   using namespace std;
   cout << "pi=" << math::pi << '\n';
}
```

See Also

class, *declaration*, *identifier*, namespace, Chapter 2, Chapter 6

---

virtual specifier

Polymorphic function specifier or shared base class

function-specifier := virtual

base-modifiers ::= virtual [*access-specifier*] | *access-specifier* [virtual]

The virtual keyword has two unrelated uses; it is used in virtual functions and virtual base classes:

- As a function specifier, virtual can be used only with a nonstatic member function. It makes the function and class polymorphic. A virtual function can be declared with = 0 after the function header, which means the function is abstract. You cannot create an instance of a class with an abstract function; instead, a derived class must override the function. You can create an instance of the derived class.

- Using virtual as a base-class modifier means the base class subobject is shared when it is used more than once in an inheritance graph.

Example

```
struct shape {
   virtual void draw(canvas&) = 0;
```

```
    virtual void debug( );
};
struct square : virtual shape {
    virtual void draw(canvas&);
    virtual void debug( );
};
```

See Also

class, *declaration*, Chapter 6

---

void keyword
Absence of type or function arguments

simple-type-specifier := void

The void keyword can be used as a type specifier to indicate the absence of a type or as a function's parameter list to indicate that the function takes no parameters.

When used as a type specifier, it is most often used as a function return type to indicate that the function does not return a value. It is also used as a generic pointer (e.g., void*), although this usage is needed less often in C++ than in C.

C++ does not require that void be used to indicate that there are no function parameters, but it is often used in this way for compatibility with C.

Example

```
void func(void)
{
    std::cout << "hello, world\n";
}
```

See Also

declaration, *type*, Chapter 2, Chapter 5

---

volatile qualifier
Volatile qualifier

cv-qualifier ::= const | volatile

cv-qualifier-seq ::= const | volatile | const volatile | volatile const

The volatile qualifier can be used with objects and member functions. The volatile qualifier tells the compiler to avoid certain optimizations because the object's value can change in unexpected ways. As a function qualifier, volatile tells the compiler to treat this as a volatile pointer in the member function body.

Example

```
volatile sig_atomic_t interrupted = false;
```

See Also

const, const_cast, *type*, Chapter 2, Chapter 5

---

wchar_t type
Wide-character type specifier

simple-type-specifier := wchar_t

 The wchar_t type specifier denotes a wide character. The representation and interpretation of wide characters is implementation-defined.

Example
```
wchar_t Hellas[] = L"\u0397\u03b5\u03bb\u03bb\u03b1\u03c2";
```

See Also
char, *type*, Chapter 1, Chapter 2

---

while statement   Test-at-top unbounded loop statement

statement := while (*condition*) *statement*

condition ::= *expression* | *type-specifier-seq declarator* = *assignment-expr*

The while loop tests *condition*, and if *condition* is true, while executes *statement*. This repeats until *condition* is false. If *condition* contains a declaration, the declaration is in the same scope as *statement*.

Example
```
while (cin >> num)
    data.push_back(num);
```

See Also
break, continue, do, *expression*, for, *statement*, Chapter 4

---

xor operator   Bitwise exclusive or operator

exclusive-or-expr := *exclusive-or-expr* ^ *and-expr* | *exclusive-or-expr* xor *and-expr*

The *bitwise exclusive or* operator requires integer or enumeration operands. It performs the usual arithmetic conversions, then does an *exclusive or* operation on pairs of bits in the operands, resulting in an integer.

The xor operator is interchangeable with the ^ token.

Example
```
unsigned bitmask = 0xFFF0;
bitmask = bitmask ^ 0x0F12;  // bitmask becomes 0xF0E2.
```

See Also
bitand, bitor, *expression*, xor_eq, Chapter 3, <ciso646>

---

xor_eq operator   Bitwise exclusive or assignment operator

assignment-expr := *logical-or-expr* ^= *assignment-expr* |
  logical-or-expr xor_eq *assignment-expr*

The xor_eq operator is an assignment operator that performs *bitwise exclusive or*. It is equivalent to *logical-or-expr* = *logical-or-expr* ^ *assignment-expr*, except that *logical-or-expr* is evaluated only once.

The keyword xor_eq is interchangeable with the ^= token.

Example
```
unsigned bitmask = 0xFFF0;
bitmask ^= 0x0F12;  // bitmask becomes 0xF0E2.
```

See Also
and_eq, *expression*, or_eq, xor, Chapter 3, <ciso646>

13

Library Reference

This chapter is a reference for the entire runtime library. As you can see, it is a big one. To help you find what you need, each header in this chapter is organized in alphabetical order. If you are not sure which header declares a particular type, macro, or other identifier, check the index. Once you find the right page, you can quickly see which header you must #include to define the identifier you need.

The subsections in each header's section describe the functions, macros, classes, and other entities declared and defined in the header. The name of the subsection tells you what kind of entity is described in the subsection—e.g., "terminate function," "basic_string class template," and so on. Cross references in each "See Also" heading list intrasection references first, followed by references to other headers (in this chapter) and references to keywords (in Chapter 12).

The subsection for each class or class template contains descriptions of all important members. A few obvious or do-nothing members are omitted (such as most destructors) for the sake of brevity.

The entire standard library resides in the std namespace, except that macros reside outside any namespace. Be sure to check the subsection name closely so you know whether an identifier is a macro or something else. To avoid cluttering the reference material, the std:: prefix is omitted from the descriptions. Examples, however, are complete and show how each namespace prefix is properly used.

Some C++ headers are taken from the C standard. For example, the C standard <stdio.h> has its C++ equivalent in <cstdio>. The C++ version declares all the C names (other than macros) in the std:: namespace but reserves the same names in the global namespace, so you must not declare your own names that conflict with those of the C headers.

Each C header can be used with its C name, in which case the declarations in the header are explicitly introduced into the global namespace. For example, <cstdio> declares std::printf (and many other names), and <stdio.h> does the same, but adds "using std::printf" to bring the name printf into the global namespace. This use of the C headers is deprecated.

The syntax description for most macros shows the macro name as an object or function declaration. These descriptions tell you the macro's type or expected arguments. They do not reflect the macro's implementation. For macros that expand to values, read the textual description to learn whether the value is a compile-time constant.

For an overview of the standard library, see Chapter 8. Chapter 9 presents the I/O portions of the library, and Chapter 10 discusses containers, iterators, and algorithms.

C++ permits two kinds of library implementations: *freestanding* and *hosted*. The traditional desktop computer is a hosted environment. A hosted implementation must implement the entire standard.

 A freestanding implementation is free to implement a subset of the standard library. The subset must provide at least the following headers, and can optionally provide more:

```
<cstdarg>
<cstddef>
<cstdlib>
<exception>
<limits>
<new>
<typeinfo>
```

<algorithm>

The <algorithm> header declares the generic algorithm function templates for operating on iterators and other objects. Refer to Chapter 10 for more information about using and writing generic algorithms and about the iterators they use. See Chapter 8 for a discussion of iterator traits.

 If you are at all confused by the removal algorithms (such as pop_heap, remove, and unique), be sure to read Chapter 10 first.

This section uses a number of abbreviations and conventions. First, each algorithm is described using plain English. Then, a more mathematical description of the algorithm, which tends to be harder to read, is given in a "Technical Notes" section.

The names of the template parameters tell you which category of iterator is expected. The iterator category is the minimal functionality needed, so you can, for example, use a random access iterator where at least a forward iterator is needed. (See Chapter 10 for more information on iterators and iterator categories.) To keep the syntax summaries short and readable, the iterator categories are abbreviated, as shown in Table 13-1.

Table 13-1. Template parameter names for iterator categories

Parameter name	Iterator category
BidiIter	Bidirectional iterator
FwdIter	Forward iterator
InIter	Input iterator
OutIter	Output iterator
RandIter	Random access iterator

Other template parameter names are chosen to be self-explanatory. For example, any name that ends in Predicate is a function that returns a Boolean result (which can be type bool or any other type that is convertible to bool) or a Boolean functional object (an object that has a function call operator that returns a Boolean result).

A number of algorithms require sorted ranges or otherwise use a comparison function to test the less-than relationship. The library overloads each algorithm: the first function uses operator<, and the second accepts a function pointer or function object to perform the comparison. The comparison function takes two arguments and returns a Boolean result. In the "Technical Notes" sections, the < relationship signifies operator< or the caller-supplied function, depending on the version of the algorithm you are using. If you overload operator< or provide your own comparison function, make sure it correctly implements a less-than relationship. In particular, a < a must be false for any a.

In this section, the following conventions are used:

- Iterators are usually used in ranges that represent all the elements in the range or sequence. A range is written using standard mathematical notation: a square bracket denotes an inclusive endpoint of a range, and a parenthesis denotes an exclusive endpoint of a range. Thus, $[x, y)$ is a range that starts at x, including x, and ends at y, excluding y. Chapter 10 also discusses this aspect of iterators.

- Arithmetic expressions that involve iterators work as though each iterator were a random access iterator, even if the iterator is from a different category. For example, $i - 1$ for an input iterator is not allowed in C++ code, but in this section, it means the input iterator that points to one position before i.

- The names used for input ranges are typically first and last, in which first is an iterator that points to first the element of the range, and last is an iterator that points to one past the end of the range. Thus, the range is written as [first, last).

- An iterator that advances from first to last is typically called iter.

- Output iterators are typically named result. Most algorithms specify only the start of the output range. It is your responsibility to ensure that the output range has room to accommodate the entire output. The behavior is undefined if the output range overflows.

In each "Technical Notes" section, conventional mathematical notation is used with some aspects of C++ notation, such as *, which dereferences an iterator. Also, a single equal sign (=) means assignment, and a double equal sign (==) means comparison for equality. The following conventions are used for names:

i, j, k
> Denote iterators, and **i*, **j*, and **k* denote the values that the iterators point to.

n, m
> Denote integers.

a, b, c
> Denote values, which are usually of types that can be assigned to or from a dereferenced iterator (e.g., **i = a*).

---

adjacent_find function template

Searches for a pair of adjacent, equal items

```
template<typename FwdIter>
  FwdIter adjacent_find(FwdIter first, FwdIter last);

template<typename FwdIter, typename BinaryPredicate>
  FwdIter adjacent_find(FwdIter first, FwdIter last, BinaryPredicate pred);
```

The adjacent_find function template looks for the first set of adjacent items in the range [first, last) that are equal (first version) or in which pred(*iter, *(iter+1)) is true (second version). Items are "adjacent" when their iterators differ by one position.

The return value is an iterator that points to the first of the adjacent items, or last if no matching items are found. See Figure 13-1 for an example.

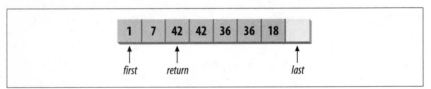

Figure 13-1. Using adjacent_find to find two adjacent, equivalent items

Technical Notes

The adjacent_find function template returns *i*, in which *i = first + n*, and *n* is the smallest value such that **(first + n) == *(first + n + 1)* and *first + n + 1 < last*, or, if there is no such *n*, *i = last*.

Complexity is linear: the standard is muddled, but any reasonable implementation calls the predicate (operator== or pred) exactly *n + 1* times.

See Also

find function template, find_if function template

---

binary_search function template

Searches using a binary search

```
template<typename FwdIter, typename T>
  bool binary_search(FwdIter first, FwdIter last, const T& value);

template<typename FwdIter, typename T, typename Compare>
  bool binary_search(FwdIter first, FwdIter last, const T& value,
                     Compare comp);
```

The binary_search function template uses a binary search to test whether value is in the range [first, last). It returns true upon success and false if the value is not found. The contents of the range must be sorted in ascending order.

The first version compares items using the < operator. The second version uses comp(X, Y) to test whether X < Y.

Technical Notes

Precondition: !(*(*i* + 1) < **i*) for all *i* in [*first*, *last* − 1).

The binary_search function template returns true if there is an *i* in [*first*, *last*) such that !(**i* < *value*) and !(*value* < **i*). It returns false if there is no such *i*.

Complexity is logarithmic. The number of comparisons is at most log(*last* − *first*) + 2. Although the iterator can be a forward iterator, the best performance is obtained with a random access iterator. With a forward or bidirectional iterator, the iterator is advanced a linear number of times, even though the number of comparisons is logarithmic.

See Also

equal_range function template, find function template, find_if function template, lower_bound function template, upper_bound function template

---

copy function template

Copies every item in a range

```
template<typename InIter, typename OutIter>
    OutIter copy(InIter first, InIter last, OutIter result);
```

The copy function template copies items from [first, last) to the output iterator starting at result. You must ensure that the output sequence has enough room for last − first items. The return value is the value of the result iterator after copying all the items, as shown in Figure 13-2.

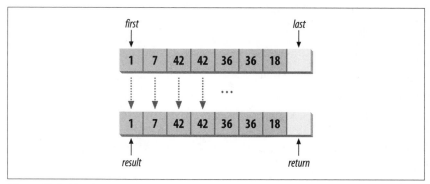

Figure 13-2. Copying a range

The result iterator cannot be in the source range [first, last), but other parts of the destination range can overlap with the source.

See Example 13-2 (under generate).

Technical Notes

The copy function template assigns *(result + n) = *(first + n) for all *n* in the range [0, last − first).

Complexity is linear: exactly *last* − *first* assignments are performed.

See Also

copy_backward function template, partial_sort_copy function template, replace_copy function template, remove_copy function template, reverse_copy function template, rotate_copy function template, unique_copy function template

copy_backward function template
Copies a range, starting at the end

```
template<typename BidiIter1, typename BidiIter2>
  BidiIter2 copy_backward(BidiIter1 first, BidiIter1 last, BidiIter2 result);
```

The copy_backward function template does the same thing as copy, but it works backward, starting at the element before last and copying elements toward first. The result iterator must point to one past the end of the destination and is decremented before copying each element. The return value is an iterator that points to the first element of the destination, as shown in Figure 13-3.

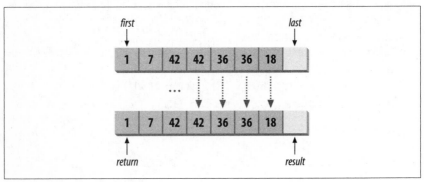

Figure 13-3. Copying a range backward

The result iterator cannot be in the source range [first, last), but other parts of the destination range can overlap with the source.

Technical Notes

The copy_backward function template assigns *(result − n) = *(last − n) for all n in the range [1, last − first].

Complexity is linear: exactly last − first assignments are performed.

See Also

copy function template, reverse_copy function template

count function template
Counts the occurrences of a value

```
template<typename InIter, typename T>
  typename iterator_traits<InIter>::difference_type
    count(InIter first, InIter last, const T& value);
```

The count function template returns the number of elements in the range [first, last) that are equal to value.

Technical Notes

Complexity is linear: exactly last − first comparisons are performed.

See Also

count_if function template, equal_range function template

---

count_if function template Counts the number of times a predicate returns true

```
template<typename InIter, typename Predicate>
  typename iterator_traits<InIter>::difference_type
    count_if(InIter first, InIter last, Predicate pred);
```

The count_if function template returns the number of elements in the range [first, last) for which pred(*iter) returns true.

Technical Notes

Complexity is linear: pred is called exactly *last − first* times.

See Also

count function template, find_if function template

---

equal function template Tests whether ranges have same contents

```
template<typename InIter1, typename InIter2>
  bool equal(InIter1 first1, InIter1 last1, InIter2 first2);
```

```
template<typename InIter1, typename InIter2, typename BinaryPredicate>
  bool equal(InIter1 first1, InIter1 last1, InIter2 first2,
             BinaryPredicate pred);
```

The equal function template returns true if two ranges contain the same elements in the same order. The first range is [first1, last1), and the second range has the same number of elements, starting at first2. The ranges can overlap.

The first form compares items using the == operator. The second form calls pred(*iter1, *iter2).

Technical Notes

The equal function template returns true if $*(first1 + n) == *(first2 + n)$ for all n in the range $[0, last1 - first1)$.

Complexity is linear: at most $last1 - first1$ comparisons are performed.

See Also

lexicographical_compare function template, mismatch function template, search function template

---

equal_range function template Finds all occurrences of a value in a sorted range using binary search

```
template<typename FwdIter, typename T>
  pair<FwdIter, FwdIter>
    equal_range(FwdIter first, FwdIter last, const T& value);
```

```
template<typename FwdIter, typename T, typename Compare>
  pair<FwdIter, FwdIter>
    equal_range(FwdIter first, FwdIter last, const T& value, Compare comp);
```

The equal_range function template determines where value belongs in the sorted range [first, last). It returns a pair of iterators that specify the start and one past the end of the range of items that are equivalent to value, or both iterators in the pair point to where you can insert value and preserve the sorted nature of the range.

The first form compares values using the < operator. The second form calls comp(*iter, value).

Figure 13-4 shows how bounds are found with the value 36. The result of calling equal_range is pair(lb, ub). Note that for values in the range [19, 35], the upper and lower bound are both equal to lb, and for values in the range [37, 41], the upper and lower bound are both equal to ub.

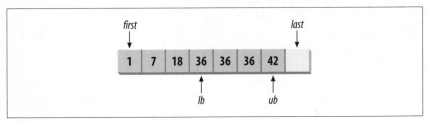

Figure 13-4. Finding the limits of where the value 36 belongs in a sorted range

Technical Notes

Precondition: !(*(*i* + 1) < *i*) for all *i* in [*first*, *last* − 1).

The equal_range function template returns the equivalent of calling the following, although the actual implementation might be different:

```
std::make_pair(std::lower_bound(first, last, value),
               std::upper_bound(first, last, value))
```

or:

```
std::make_pair(std::lower_bound(first, last, value, comp),
               std::upper_bound(first, last, value, comp))
```

Complexity is logarithmic. The number of comparisons is at most 2 × log(*last* − *first*) + 1. Although the iterator can be a forward iterator, the best performance is obtained with a random access iterator. With a forward or bidirectional iterator, the iterator is advanced a linear number of times, even though the number of comparisons is logarithmic.

See Also

binary_search function template, lower_bound function template, upper_bound function template, pair in <utility>

---

fill function template

Fills a range with copies of a value

```
template<typename FwdIter, typename T>
  void fill(FwdIter first, FwdIter last, const T& value);
```

The fill function template fills the destination range [first, last) by assigning value to each item in the range.

Technical Notes

The fill function template assigns *i* = *value* for all *i* in the range [*first*, *last*).

Complexity is linear: exactly *last* − *first* assignments are performed.

See Also

fill_n function template, generate function template

fill_n function template
Fills a counted range with copies of a value

```
template<typename OutIter, typename Size, typename T>
  void fill_n(OutIter first, Size n, const T& value);
```

The fill_n function template assigns value to successive items in the destination range, starting at first and assigning exactly n items.

The Size template parameter must be convertible to an integral type.

Technical Notes

The fill_n function template assigns $*(first + n) = value$ for all n in the range $[0, n)$.

Complexity is linear: exactly n assignments are performed.

See Also

fill function template, generate_n function template

find function template
Searches for a value using linear search

```
template<typename InIter, typename T>
  InIter find(InIter first, InIter last, const T& value);
```

The find function template returns an iterator that points to the first occurrence of value in [first, last). It returns last if value is not found. The == operator is used to compare items.

Technical Notes

The find function template returns $i = first + n$, in which n is the smallest value such that $*(first + n) == value$. If there is no such n, $i = last$.

Complexity is linear: at most $last - first$ comparisons are performed.

See Also

find_end function template, find_first function template, find_if function template, search function template

find_end function template
Searches for the last occurrence of a sequence

```
template<typename FwdIter1, typename FwdIter2>
  FwdIter1 find_end(FwdIter1 first1, FwdIter1 last1, FwdIter2 first2,
                    FwdIter2 last2);

template<typename FwdIter1, typename FwdIter2, typename BinaryPredicate>
  FwdIter1 find_end(FwdIter1 first1, FwdIter1 last1, FwdIter2 first2,
                    FwdIter2 last2, BinaryPredicate pred);
```

The find_end function template finds the last (rightmost) subsequence [first2, last2) within the range [first1, last1), as illustrated in Figure 13-5. It returns an iterator, find_end in Figure 13-5, that points to the start of the matching subsequence or last1 if a match cannot be found.

The first form compares items with the == operator. The second form calls pred(*iter1, *iter2).

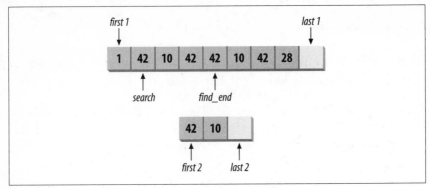

Figure 13-5. Finding a subsequence with find_end and search

Technical Notes

Let $length1 = last1 - first1$ and $length2 = last2 - first2$.

The find_end function template returns $first1 + n$, in which n is the highest value in the range $[0, length1 - length2)$ such that $*(i + n + m) == (first2 + m)$ for all i in the range $[first1, last1)$ and m in the range $[0, length2)$. It returns $last1$ if no such n can be found.

Complexity: at most $length1 \times length2$ comparisons are performed.

See Also

find function template, search function template

---

find_first_of function template   Searches for any one of a sequence of values

```
template<typename FwdIter1, typename FwdIter2>
  FwdIter1 find_first_of(FwdIter1 first1, FwdIter1 last1, FwdIter2 first2,
                         FwdIter2 last2);

template<typename FwdIter1, typename FwdIter2, typename BinaryPredicate>
  FwdIter1 find_first_of(FwdIter1 first1, FwdIter1 last1, FwdIter2 first2,
                         FwdIter2 last2, BinaryPredicate pred);
```

The find_first_of function template searches the range [first1, last1) for any one of the items in [first2, last2). If it finds a matching item, it returns an iterator that points to the matching item, in the range [first1, last1). It returns last1 if no matching item is found. Figure 13-6 shows an example.

The first form compares items with the == operator. The second form calls pred(*iter1, *iter2).

Technical Notes

Let $length1 = last1 - first1$ and $length2 = last2 - first2$.

The find_first_of function template returns $first1 + n$ where n is the smallest value in the range $[0, length1)$ such that $*(first1 + n) == (first2 + m)$ for some m in the range $[0, length2)$. It returns $last1$ if no such n and m can be found.

Complexity: at most $length1 \times length2$ comparisons are performed.

See Also

find function template

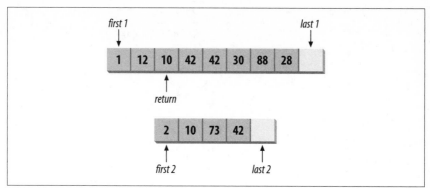

Figure 13-6. Finding any one of a list of items

---

find_if function template
Searches for when a predicate returns true

```
template<typename InIter, typename Predicate>
  InIter find_if(InIter first, InIter last, Predicate pred);
```

The find_if function template (similar to find) searches the range [first, last) for the first item for which pred(*iter) is true. It returns an iterator that points to the matching item. If no matching item is found, last is returned.

Technical Notes
The find_if function template returns $i = first + n$, in which n is the smallest value such that $pred(*(first + n), value)$ is true. If there is no such n, $i = last$.

Complexity is linear: pred is called at most $last - first$ times.

See Also
find function template

---

for_each function template
Calls a function for each item in a range

```
template<typename InIter, typename Func>
  Function for_each(InIter first, InIter last, Func f);
```

The for_each function template calls f for each item in the range [first, last), passing the item as the sole argument to f. It returns f.

Example
Example 13-1 shows how the use for_each to test whether a sequence is sorted. The is_sorted object remembers the previous item in the sequence, which it compares with the current item. The overloaded bool operator returns true if the sequence is sorted so far or false if the sequence is out of order. The example takes advantage of the fact that for_each returns the f parameter as its result.

Example 13-1. Using for_each to test whether a list is sorted

```
#include <iostream>
#include <algorithm>
#include <list>
```

Example 13-1. Using for_each to test whether a list is sorted (continued)

```
template<typename T>
class is_sorted
{
public:
  is_sorted( ) : first_time(true), sorted(true) {}
  void operator( )(const T& item) {
    // for_each calls operator( ) for each item.
    if (first_time)
      first_time = false;
    else if (item < prev_item)
      sorted = false;
    prev_item = item;
  }
  operator bool( ) { return sorted; }
private:
  bool first_time;
  bool sorted;
  T prev_item;
};

int main( )
{
  std::list<int> l;
  l.push_back(10);
  l.push_back(20);
  ...
  if (std::for_each(l.begin( ), l.end( ), is_sorted<int>( )))
    std::cout << "list is sorted" << '\n';
}
```

Technical Notes

Complexity is linear: f is called exactly *last − first* times.

See Also

copy function template, accumulate in <numeric>

---

generate function template Fills a range with values returned from a function

```
template<typename FwdIter, typename Generator>
  void generate(FwdIter first, FwdIter last, Generator gen);
```

The generate function template fills the sequence [first, last) by assigning the result of calling gen( ) repeatedly.

Example

Example 13-2 shows a simple way to fill a sequence with successive integers.

Example 13-2. Using generate to fill a vector with integers

```
#include <algorithm>
#include <iostream>
#include <iterator>
#include <vector>
```

Example 13-2. Using generate to fill a vector with integers (continued)

```
// Generate a series of objects, starting with "start".
template <typename T>
class series {
public:
  series(const T& start) : next(start) {}
  T operator()() { return next++; }
private:
  T next;
};

int main()
{
  std::vector<int> v;
  v.resize(10);
  // Generate integers from 1 to 10.
  std::generate(v.begin(), v.end(), series<int>(1));
  // Print the integers, one per line.
  std::copy(v.begin(), v.end(),
            std::ostream_iterator<int>(std::cout, "\n"));
}
```

Technical Notes

Complexity is linear: gen is called exactly *last – first* times.

See Also

fill function template, generate_n function template

---

generate_n function template   Fills a counted range with values returned from a function

```
template<typename OutIter, typename Size, typename Generator>
  void generate_n(OutIter first, Size n, Generator gen);
```

The generate_n function template calls gen() exactly n times, assigning the results to fill the sequence that starts at first. You must ensure that the sequence has room for at least n items. The Size type must be convertible to an integral type.

Example

Example 13-3 shows a simple way to print a sequence of integers.

Example 13-3. Using generate_n to print a series of integers

```
#include <algorithm>
#include <iostream>
#include <iterator>

// Use the same series template from Example 13-2.

int main()
{
  // Print integers from 1 to 10.
  std::generate_n(std::ostream_iterator<int>(std::cout,"\n"),
                  10, series<int>(1));
}
```

Technical Notes

Complexity is linear: gen is called exactly *n* times.

See Also

fill_n function template , generate function template

---

includes function template   Tests sorted ranges for subset

```
template<typename InIter1, typename InIter2>
  bool includes(InIter1 first1, InIter1 last1, InIter2 first2, InIter2 last2);
template<typename InIter1, typename InIter2, typename Compare>
  bool includes(InIter1 first1, InIter1 last1, InIter2 first2, InIter2 last2,
                Compare comp);
```

The includes function template checks for a subset relationship, that is, it returns true if every element in the sorted sequence [first2, last2) is contained in the sorted sequence [first1, last1). It returns false otherwise.

Both sequences must be sorted. The first form uses the < operator to compare the elements. The second form calls comp(*iter1, *iter2).

Technical Notes

Precondition: !(*(*i* + 1) < **i*) for all *i* in [*first1*, *last1* − 1) and !(*(*j* + 1) < **j*) for all *j* in [*first2*, *last2* − 1).

The includes function template returns true if there is an *i* in [*first1*, *last1*) such that *(*i* + *n*) = *(*first2* + *n*) for all *n* in [0, (*last2* − *first2*)). It returns *last1* if there is no such *i*.

Complexity is linear: at most, $2 \times ((last1 - first1) + (last2 - first2)) - 1$ comparisons are performed.

See Also

set_difference function template, set_intersection function template, set_symmetric_difference function template, set_union function template

---

inplace_merge function template   Merges sorted, adjacent ranges in place

```
template<typename BidiIter>
  void inplace_merge(BidiIter first, BidiIter middle, BidiIter last);
template<typename BidiIter, typename Compare>
  void inplace_merge(BidiIter first, BidiIter middle, BidiIter last,
                     Compare comp);
```

The inplace_merge function template merges two sorted, consecutive ranges in place, creating a single sorted range. The two ranges are [first, middle) and [middle, last). The resulting range is [first, last).

The merge is stable, so elements retain their respective orders, with equivalent elements in the first range coming before elements in the second.

Both sequences must be sorted. The first form uses the < operator to compare elements. The second form calls comp(*iter1, *iter2).

Figure 13-7 shows how inplace_merge operates.

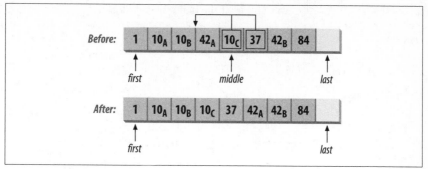

Figure 13-7. Merging two sorted ranges

Technical Notes

Precondition: !(*(*i* + 1) < *i*) for all *i* in [*first, middle* – 1) and !(*(*j* + 1) < *j*) for all *j* in [*middle, last* – 1).

Postcondition: !(*(*i* + 1) < *i*) for all *i* in [*first, last* – 1).

Complexity is usually linear with *n* + 1 comparisons, but if enough temporary memory is not available, the complexity might be *n* log *n*, in which *n* is *last* – *first*.

See Also

merge function template, sort function template

iter_swap function template
Swaps values that iterators point to

```
template<typename FwdIter1, typename FwdIter2>
  void iter_swap(FwdIter1 a, FwdIter2 b);
```

The iter_swap function template swaps the values pointed to by a and b. You can think of its functionality as:

```
FdwIter1::value_type tmp = *b*;
*b = *a;
*a = tmp;
```

Technical Notes

Complexity is constant.

See Also

copy function template, swap function template, swap_ranges function template

lexicographical_compare function template
Compares ranges for less-than

```
template<typename InIter1, typename InIter2>
  bool lexicographical_compare(InIter1 first1, InIter1 last1, InIter2 first2,
                               InIter2 last2);
```

```
template<typename InIter1, typename InIter2, typename Compare>
  bool lexicographical_compare(InIter1 first1, InIter1 last1, InIter2 first2,
                               InIter2 last2, Compare comp);
```

The lexicographical_compare function template returns true if the sequence [first1, last1) is less than the sequence [first2, last2). If the sequences have the same length and contents, the return value is false. If the first sequence is a prefix of the second, true is returned. (The use of "lexicographical" emphasizes that the ranges are compared element-wise, like letters in words.)

The first form uses the < operator to compare elements. The second form calls comp(*iter1, *iter2).

Technical Notes

Let *length1* = *last1* − *first1*, *length2* = *last2* − *first2*, and *minlength* = min(*length1*, *length2*).

The lexicographical_compare function template returns true if either of the following conditions is true:

- There is an *n* in [0, *minlength*) such that *(first1 + m) == *(first2 + m) for all *m* in [0, *n* − 1), and *(first1 + n) < *(first2 + n).
- *(first1 + n) == *(first2 + n) for all *n* in [0, *length1*) and *length1* < *length2*.

Complexity is linear: at most, *minlength* comparisons are performed.

Example

```
#include <algorithm>
#include <iostream>
#include <ostream>

int main( )
{
  using namespace std;

  int a[] = { 1, 10, 3, 42 };
  int b[] = { 1, 10, 42, 3 };
  int c[] = { 1, 10 };

  cout << boolalpha;
  cout << lexicographical_compare(a, a+4, b, b+4); // true
  cout << lexicographical_compare(a, a+4, c, c+2); // false
  cout << lexicographical_compare(a, a+4, a, a+4); // false
  cout << lexicographical_compare(c, c+2, b, b+4); // true
}
```

See Also

equal function template

---

lower_bound function template

Finds lower bound for a value's position in a sorted range using binary search

```
template<typename FwdIter, typename T>
  FwdIter lower_bound(FwdIter first, FwdIter last, const T& value);
```

```
template<typename FwdIter, typename T, typename Compare>
  FwdIter lower_bound(FwdIter first, FwdIter last, const T& value, Compare comp);
```

The lower_bound function template determines where value belongs in the sorted range [first, last). The return value is an iterator that points to the first (leftmost) occurrence of value in the range, if value is present. Otherwise, the iterator points to the first position where you can insert value and preserve the sorted nature of the range.

The first form compares values using the < operator. The second form calls comp(*iter, value).

Figure 13-4 (under equal_range) shows how to find the bounds for the value 36. The lower_bound function returns lb as the lower bound of 36 in the given range. Note that lb is the lower bound for all values in the range [19, 36], and for values in the range [37, 41], the lower bound is equal to ub.

Technical Notes

Precondition: !(*(i + 1) < *i) for all i in [first, last − 1).

The lower_bound function template returns *first* + n, in which n is the highest value in [0, *last* − *first*) such that *(first + m) < value for all m in [0, n).

Complexity is logarithmic. The number of comparisons is at most log(*last* − *first*) + 1. Although the iterator can be a forward iterator, the best performance is obtained with a random access iterator. With a forward or bidirectional iterator, the iterator is advanced a linear number of times, even though the number of comparisons is logarithmic.

See Also

binary_search function template, equal_range function template, upper_bound function template

---

make_heap function template

Reorders a range to convert it into a heap

```
template<typename RandIter>
  void make_heap(RandIter first, RandIter last);
```

```
template<typename RandIter, typename Compare>
  void make_heap(RandIter first, RandIter last, Compare comp);
```

The make_heap function template reorders the elements in the range [first, last) to form a heap in place.

The first form compares values using the < operator. The second form calls comp(*iter, value).

Heap Data Structure

A *heap* is a data structure that is ideally suited for implementing priority queues. C++ defines a range as a heap if two properties are satisfied:

- The first element of the range is the largest, which strictly means that **first* < *(first* + n) is false for all n in [1, *last* − *first*).
- Adding or removing an element can be done in logarithmic time, and the result is still a heap.

The classic example of a heap is a binary tree, in which each node is greater than or equal to its children, but the relative order of the children is not specified. Thus, the root of the tree is the largest element in the entire tree.

Library Reference

Technical Notes

Postcondition: [*first*, *last*) is a heap.

Complexity is linear: at most, $3 \times (last - first)$ comparisons are performed.

See Also

pop_heap function template, push_heap function template, sort_heap function template, <queue>

---

max function template   Returns the maximum of two values

```
template<typename T>
  const T& max(const T& a, const T& b);

template<typename T, typename Compare>
  const T& max(const T& a, const T& b, Compare comp);
```

The max function template returns the larger of a and b. If neither is larger, it returns a. The first form compares values using the < operator. The second form calls comp(a, b).

See Also

max_element function template, min function template

---

max_element function template   Finds the largest element in a range

```
template<typename FwdIter>
  FwdIter max_element(FwdIter first, FwdIter last);

template<typename FwdIter, typename Compare>
  FwdIter max_element(FwdIter first, FwdIter last, Compare comp);
```

The max_element function template returns an iterator that points to the largest element in the range [first, last). If there are multiple instances of the largest element, the iterator points to the first such instance.

The first form compares values using the < operator. The second form calls comp(*iter1, *iter2).

Technical Notes

The max_element function template returns $first + n$, in which n is the smallest value in $[0, last - first)$ such that for all m in $[0, last - first)$, $*(first + n) < *(first + m)$ is false.

Complexity is linear: exactly $\max(last - first - 1, 0)$ comparisons are performed.

See Also

max function template, min_element function template

---

merge function template   Merges sorted ranges

```
template<typename InIter1, typename InIter2, typename OutIter>
  OutIter merge(InIter1 first1, InIter1 last1, InIter2 first2, InIter2 last2,
                OutIter result);

template<typename InIter1, typename InIter2, typename OutIter, typename Compare>
  OutIter merge(InIter1 first1, InIter1 last1, InIter2 first2, InIter2 last2,
                OutIter result, Compare comp);
```

The merge function template merges the sorted ranges [first1, last1) and [first2, last2), copying the results into the sequence that starts with result. You must ensure that the destination has enough room for the entire merged sequence.

The return value is the end value of the destination iterator, that is, result + (last1 − first1) + (last2 − first2).

The destination range must not overlap either of the input ranges.

The merge is stable, so elements preserve their relative order. Equivalent elements are copied, so elements from the first range come before elements from the second range.

The first form compares values using the < operator. The second form calls comp(*iter1, *iter2).

Technical Notes

Let $length1 = last1 − first1$ and $length2 = last2 − first2$.

Precondition: $!(*(i + 1) < *i)$ for all i in [first1, last1 − 1) and $!(*(j + 1) < *j)$ for all j in [first2, last2 − 1).

Postcondition: $!(*(i + 1) < *i)$ for all i in [result, result + length1 + length2 − 1).

Complexity is linear: at most, $length1 + length2 - 1$ comparisons are performed.

See Also

inplace_merge function template, sort function template

___

min function template
Returns the minimum of two values

```
template<typename T>
  const T& min(const T& a, const T& b);
```
```
template<typename T, typename Compare>
  const T& min(const T& a, const T& b, Compare comp);
```

The min function template returns the smaller of a and b. If neither is smaller, it returns a.

The first form compares values using the < operator. The second form calls comp(a, b).

See Also

max function template, min_element function template

___

min_element function template
Finds the smallest value in a range

```
template<typename FwdIter>
  FwdIter min_element(FwdIter first, FwdIter last);
```
```
template<typename FwdIter, typename Compare>
  FwdIter min_element(FwdIter first, FwdIter last, Compare comp);
```

The min_element function template returns an iterator that points to the smallest element in the range [first, last). If there are multiple instances of the smallest element, the iterator points to the first such instance.

The first form compares values using the < operator. The second form calls comp(*iter1, *iter2).

Technical Notes

The min_element function template returns *first* + *n*, in which *n* is the smallest value in [0, *last* − *first*) such that for all m in [0, *last* − *first*), *(*first* + *m*) < *(*first* + *n*) is false.

Complexity is linear: exactly max(*last* − *first* − 1, 0) comparisons are performed.

See Also

max_element function template, min function template

---

mismatch function template   Finds first position where two ranges differ

```
template<typename InIter1, typename InIter2>
  pair<InIter1, InIter2>
    mismatch(InIter1 first1, InIter1 last1, InIter2 first2);

template<typename InIter1, typename InIter2, typename BinaryPredicate>
  pair<InIter1, InIter2>
    mismatch(InIter1 first1, InIter1 last1, InIter2 first2,
             BinaryPredicate pred);
```

The mismatch function template compares two sequences pairwise and returns a pair of iterators that identifies the first elements at which the sequences differ. The first sequence is [first1, last1), and the second sequence starts at first2 and has at least as many elements as the first sequence.

The return value is a pair of iterators; the first member of the pair points to an element of the first sequence, and second member of the pair points to an element of the second sequence. The two iterators have the same offset within their respective ranges. If the two sequences are equivalent, the pair returned is last1 and an iterator that points to the second sequence at the same offset (let's call it last2).

The first form compares items with the == operator. The second form calls pred(*iter1, *iter2).

Figure 13-8 illustrates how the mismatch function template works.

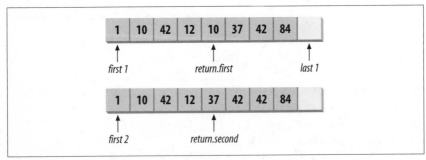

Figure 13-8. Checking two sequences for a mismatch

Technical Notes

The mismatch function template returns the pair (*first1* + *n*, *first2* + *n*), in which *n* is the smallest value in [0, *last1* − *first1*) such that *(*first1* + *n*) == *(*first2* + *n*) is false and *(*first1* + *m*) == *(*first2* + *m*) is true for all *m* in [0, *n*). If there is no such *n*, *n* = *last1* − *first1*.

Complexity is linear: at most *last1* − *first1* comparisons are performed.

See Also

equal function template, search function template, pair in <utility>

---

next_permutation function template

Generates next permutation

```
template<typename BidiIter>
  bool next_permutation(BidiIter first, BidiIter last);

template<typename BidiIter, typename Compare>
  bool next_permutation(BidiIter first, BidiIter last, Compare comp);
```

The next_permutation function template rearranges the contents of the range [first, last) for the next permutation, assuming that there is a set of lexicographically ordered permutations. The return value is true if the next permutation is generated, or false if the range is at the last permutation, in which case the function cycles, and the first permutation is generated (that is, with all elements in ascending order).

Figure 13-9 shows all the permutations, in order, for a sequence. The next_permutation function swaps elements to form the next permutation. For example, if the input is permutation 2, the result is permutation 3. If the input is permutation 6, the result is permutation 1, and next_permutation returns false.

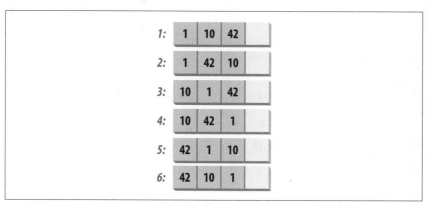

Figure 13-9. Permutations of a sequence

Example

Example 13-4 shows a simple program that prints all the permutations of a sequence of integers. You can use this program to better understand the next_permutation function template.

Example 13-4. Generating permutations

```cpp
#include <algorithm>
#include <iostream>
#include <istream>
#include <iterator>
#include <ostream>
#include <vector>

void print(const std::vector<int>& v)
{
```

Example 13-4. Generating permutations (continued)

```
  std::copy(v.begin( ), v.end( ),
           std::ostream_iterator<int>(std::cout, " "));
  std::cout << '\n';
}

int main( )
{
  std::cout << "Enter a few integers, followed by EOF:";
  std::istream_iterator<int> start(std::cin);
  std::istream_iterator<int> end;
  std::vector<int> v(start, end);

  // Start with the first permutation (ascending order).
  std::sort(v.begin( ), v.end( ));
  print(v);

  // Print all the subsequent permutations.
  while (std::next_permutation(v.begin( ), v.end( )))
    print(v);
}
```

Technical Notes

Complexity is linear: at most, there are *(last – first)* / 2 swaps.

See Also

lexicographical_compare function template, prev_permutation function template, swap function template

---

nth_element function template   Reorders a range to properly place an item at the nth position

```
template<typename RandIter>
  void nth_element(RandIter first, RandIter nth, RandIter last);

template<typename RandIter, typename Compare>
  void nth_element(RandIter first, RandIter nth, RandIter last, Compare comp);
```

The nth_element function template reorders the range [first, last) so that *nth is assigned the value that would be there if the entire range were sorted. It also partitions the range so that all elements in the range [first, nth) are less than or equal to the elements in the range [nth, last).

The order is not stable—that is, if there are multiple elements that could be moved to position nth and preserve the sorted order, you cannot predict which element will be moved to that position.

Figure 13-10 illustrates how the nth_element function template works.

Technical Notes

Precondition: *nth* is in the range [*first, last*).

Postcondition: $*i < *nth$ for all *i* in [*first, nth*), $!(*j < *nth)$ for all *j* in [*nth, last*), and $!(*k < *nth)$ for all *k* in [*nth* + 1, *last*).

Complexity is linear for the average case but is allowed to perform worse in the worst case.

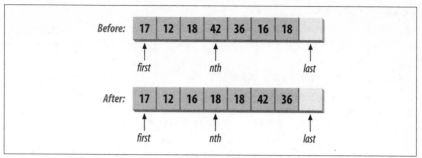

Figure 13-10. Reordering a range with nth_element

See Also

partition function template, partial_sort function template, sort function template

partial_sort function template   Sorts the first part of a range

```
template<typename RandIter>
  void partial_sort(RandIter first, RandIter middle, RandIter last);

template<typename RandIter, typename Compare>
  void partial_sort(RandIter first, RandIter middle, RandIter last,
                    Compare comp);
```

The partial_sort function template sorts the initial middle − first elements of the range [first, last) into the range [first, middle). The remaining elements at [middle, last) are not in any particular order.

The first form compares values using the < operator. The second form calls comp(*iter1, *iter2).

See Figure 13-11 for an illustration of the partial-sort algorithm.

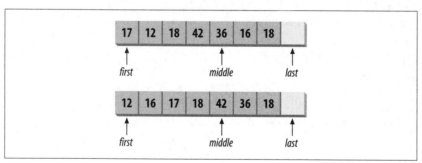

Figure 13-11. The partial-sort algorithm

Technical Notes

Postcondition: for all i in [first, middle − 1), *(i + 1) < *i is false, and for all j in [middle, last) and for all i in [first, middle), *j < *i is false.

Complexity is logarithmic, taking about (last − first) × log(middle − first) comparisons.

See Also

nth_element function template, partial_sort_copy function template, partition function template, sort function template

---

partial_sort_copy function template
Sorts and copies the first part of a range

```
template<typename InIter, typename RandIter>
  RandIter partial_sort_copy(InIter first, InIter last, RandIter result_first,
                             RandIter result_last);

template<typename InIter, typename RandIter, typename Compare>
  RandIter partial_sort_copy(InIter first, InIter last, RandIter result_first,
                             RandIter result_last, Compare comp);
```

The partial_sort_copy function template copies and sorts elements from the range [first, last) into the range [result_first, result_last). The number of items copied (N) is the smaller of last − first and result_last − result_first. If the source range is smaller than the result range, the sorted elements are taken from the entire source range [first, last) and copied into the first N positions of the result range, starting at result_first. If the source range is larger, it is copied and sorted into the first N positions of the result range, leaving the elements in [result_first + N, result_last) unmodified. The return value is result_first + N.

The first form compares values using the < operator. The second form calls comp(*iter1, *iter2).

Technical Notes

Let $n = \min(last - first, result\_last - result\_first)$.

Postcondition: for all i in [$result\_first, result\_first + n - 1$), $^*(i + 1) < {}^*i$ is false.

Complexity is logarithmic, taking about $(last - first) \times \log n$ comparisons.

See Also

nth_element function template, partial_sort_copy function template, partition function template, sort function template

---

partition function template
Partitions a range according to a predicate

```
template<typename BidiIter, typename Predicate>
  BidiIter partition(BidiIter first, BidiIter last, Predicate pred);
```

The partition function template swaps elements in the range [first, last) so that all elements that satisfy pred come before those that do not. The relative order of elements is not preserved.

The return value is an iterator that points to the first element for which pred is false, or last if there is no such element.

Figure 13-12 illustrates the partition function template for a predicate that tests whether a number is even:

```
function iseven(int n)
{
  return n % 2 == 0;
}
```

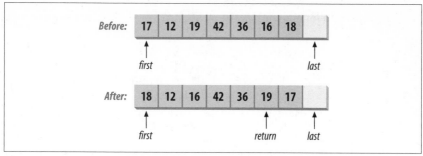

Figure 13-12. *Partitioning a range into even and odd numbers*

Technical Notes

Postcondition: Let *r* be an iterator in the range [*first, last*] such that *pred*(**i*) is true for all *i* in [*first, r*), and *pred*(**j*) is false for all *j* in [*r, last*).

The partition function template returns *r*.

Complexity is linear: pred is called exactly *last − first* times, and at most (*last − first*) / 2 swaps are performed.

See Also

nth_element function template, partial_sort function template, sort function template, stable_partition function template

---

pop_heap function template

Removes largest element from a heap

```
template<typename RandIter>
  void pop_heap(RandIter first, RandIter last);

template<typename RandIter, typename Compare>
  void pop_heap(RandIter first, RandIter last, Compare comp);
```

The pop_heap function template copies the first (largest) element from the heap in [first, last) to the end of the range, that is, *(last − 1). It then ensures that the elements remaining in [first, last − 1) form a heap.

The first form compares values using the < operator. The second form calls comp(*iter1, *iter2).

Technical Notes

Precondition: [*first, last*) is a heap (see make_heap for the definition of a heap).

Postcondition: [*first, last* − 1) is a heap, and !(*(last* − 1) < **i*) for all *i* in [*first, last* − 1).

Complexity is logarithmic: at most 2 × log(*last − first*) comparisons are performed.

See Also

make_heap function template, push_heap function template, sort_heap function template, <queue>

prev_permutation function template

```
template<typename BidiIter>
  bool prev_permutation(BidiIter first, BidiIter last);
template<typename BidiIter, typename Compare>
  bool prev_permutation(BidiIter first, BidiIter last, Compare comp);
```

The prev_permutation function template rearranges the contents of the range [first, last) to the previous permutation, assuming that there is a set of lexicographically ordered permutations. The return value is true if the previous permutation is generated, or false if the range is at the first permutation, in which case the function cycles and generates the last permutation (that is, with all elements in descending order).

Figure 13-9 (under next_permutation) shows all the permutations, in order, for a sequence. The prev_permutation function swaps elements to form the previous permutation. For example, if the input is permutation 3, the result is permutation 2. If the input is permutation 1, the result is permutation 6, and prev_permutation returns false.

Technical Notes

Complexity is linear: at most $(last - first) / 2$ swaps are performed.

See Also

lexicographical_compare function template, next_permutation function template, swap function template

---

push_heap function template

```
template<typename RandIter>
  void push_heap(RandIter first, RandIter last);
template<typename RandIter, typename Compare>
  void push_heap(RandIter first, RandIter last, Compare comp);
```

The push_heap function template adds the item at last − 1 to the heap in [first, last − 1), forming a new heap in the range [first, last).

The first form compares values using the < operator. The second form calls comp(*iter1, *iter2).

Technical Notes

Precondition: [*first*, *last* − 1) is a heap (see make_heap for the definition of a heap).

Postcondition: [*first*, *last*) is a heap.

Complexity is logarithmic: at most log($last - first$) comparisons are performed.

See Also

make_heap function template, pop_heap function template, sort_heap function template, <queue>

---

random_shuffle function template   Reorders a range into a random order

```
template<typename RandIter>
  void random_shuffle(RandIter first, RandIter last);

template<typename RandIter, typename RandomNumberGenerator>
  void random_shuffle(RandIter first, RandIter last,
                      RandomNumberGenerator& rand);
```

 The random_shuffle function template changes the order of elements in the range [first, last) to a random order. The first form uses an implementation-defined random number generator to produce a uniform distribution. The second form calls rand(*n*) to generate random numbers, in which *n* is a positive value of type iterator_traits<RandIter>::difference_type. The return value from rand must be convertible to the same difference_type and be in the range [0, *n*).

Technical Notes

Complexity is linear: exactly (*last* − *first*) + 1 swaps are performed.

See Also

swap function template, rand in <cstdlib>

---

remove function template   Reorders a range to remove all occurrences of a value

```
template<typename FwdIter, typename T>
  FwdIter remove(FwdIter first, FwdIter last, const T& value);
```

The remove function template "removes" items that are equal to value from the range [first, last). Nothing is actually erased from the range; instead, items to the right are copied to new positions so they overwrite the elements that are equal to value. The return value is one past the new end of the range. The relative order of items that are not removed is stable.

> The only way to erase an element from a container is to call one of the container's member functions. Therefore, the remove function template does not and cannot erase items. All it can do is move items within its given range. A typical pattern, therefore, is to call remove to reorder the container's elements, and then call erase to erase the unwanted elements. To help you, the value returned from remove is an iterator that points to the start of the range that will be erased. For example:
>
> ```
> std::vector<int> data
> ...
> // Erase all values that are equal to 42.
> std::erase(std::remove(data.begin( ), data.end( ), 42),
>            data.end( ));
> ```

See Figure 13-13 (under remove_copy) for an example of the removal process.

Technical Notes

The remove function template assigns *(*first* + *n*++) = *(*first* + *m*), in which *n* starts at 0, for all values of *m* in [0, *last* − *first*) in which *(*first* + *m*) == *value* is false. The return value is *first* + *n*.

Complexity is linear: exactly *last* − *first* comparisons are performed.

See Also

remove_copy function template, remove_copy_if function template, remove_if function template, replace function template

---

remove_copy function template
Copies elements that are not equal to a value

```
template<typename InIter, typename OutIter, typename T>
  OutIter remove_copy(InIter first, InIter last, OutIter result, const T& value);
```

The remove_copy function template copies items from the range [first, last) to the range that starts at result. Only items that are not equal to value are copied, that is, cases in which operator== returns false.

The return value is one past the end of the result range. The relative order of items that are not removed is stable.

The source and result ranges must not overlap. Figure 13-13 illustrates the removal process.

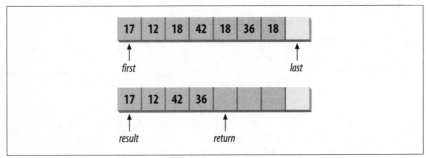

Figure 13-13. Removing 18s from a range by calling remove_copy(first, last, 18)

Technical Notes

The remove_copy function template assigns *(result + n++) = *(first + m), in which n starts at 0, for all values of m in [0, last − first), in which *(first + m) == value is false. The return value is result + n.

Complexity is linear: exactly last − first comparisons are performed.

See Also

remove function template, remove_copy_if function template, replace_copy function template

---

remove_copy_if function template
Copies elements for which a predicate returns false

```
template<typename InIter, typename OutIter, typename Predicate>
  OutIter remove_copy_if(InIter first, InIter last, OutIter result,
                         Predicate pred);
```

The remove_copy_if function template copies items from the range [first, last) to the range that starts at result. Only items for which pred returns false are copied.

The return value is one past the end of the result range. The relative order of items that are not removed is stable.

The source and result ranges must not overlap. See Figure 13-13 (under remove_copy) for an example of the removal process.

Technical Notes

The remove_copy_if function template assigns *(result + n++) = *(first + m), in which n starts at 0, for all values of m in [0, last − first), in which pred(*(first + m)) is false. The return value is result + n.

Complexity is linear: exactly last − first comparisons are performed.

See Also

remove function template, remove_copy function template, replace_copy_if function template

remove_if function template

Reorders a range to remove elements
for which a predicate returns false

```
template<typename FwdIter, typename Predicate>
  FwdIter remove_if(FwdIter first, FwdIter last, Predicate pred);
```

The remove_if function template "removes" items for which pred returns true from the range [first, last). The return value is one past the new end of the range. The relative order of items that are not removed is stable.

Nothing is actually erased from the underlying container; instead, items to the right are assigned to new positions so they overwrite the elements for which pred returns false. See Figure 13-13 (under remove_copy) for an example of the removal process.

Technical Notes

The remove_if function template assigns *(first + n++) = *(first + m), in which n starts at 0, for all values of m in [0, last − first), in which pred(*(first + m)) is false. The return value is first + n.

Complexity is linear: exactly last − first comparisons are performed.

See Also

remove function template, remove_copy_if function template, replace_if function template

replace function template

Replaces all occurrences of one value with another value

```
template<typename FwdIter, typename T>
  void replace(FwdIter first, FwdIter last, const T& old_value,
               const T& new_value);
```

The replace function template replaces all occurrences of old_value in [first, last) with new_value. See Figure 13-14 (under replace_copy) for an example of the replacement process.

Technical Notes

The replace function template assigns *i = (*i == old_value) ? new_value : *i for all i in [first, last).

Complexity is linear: exactly last − first comparisons are performed.

See Also

remove function template, replace_copy function template, replace_copy_if function template, replace_if function template, transform function template

---

replace_copy function template

Copies a range, replacing occurrences of one value with another value

```
template<typename InIter, typename OutIter, typename T>
  OutIter replace_copy(InIter first, InIter last, OutIter result,
                       const T& old_value, const T& new_value);
```

The replace_copy function template copies values from [first, last) to the range that starts at result. Values that are equal to old_value are replaced with new_value; other values are copied without modification.

The return value is an iterator that points to one past the end of the result range. The source and result ranges must not overlap. Figure 13-14 illustrates the replacement process.

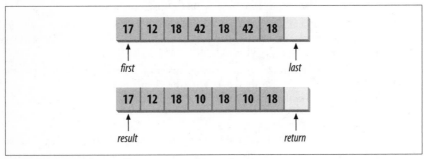

Figure 13-14. Replacing all occurrences of 42 with 10

Technical Notes

The replace_copy function template assigns $*(result + n) = *(first + n) == old\_value\ ?\ new\_value : *(first + n)$ for all n in $[0, last - first)$.

Complexity is linear: exactly $last - first$ comparisons are performed.

See Also

remove_copy function template, replace function template, replace_copy_if function template, transform function template

---

replace_copy_if function template

Copies values, replacing those that satisfy a predicate

```
template<typename InIter, typename OutIter, typename Predicate, typename T>
  OutIter replace_copy_if(InIter first, InIter last, OutIter result, Predicate
                          pred, const T& new_value);
```

The replace_copy_if function template copies values from [first, last) to the range that starts at result. Elements for which pred returns true are replaced with new_value; other elements are copied without modification.

The return value is an iterator that points to one past the end of the result range. The source and result ranges must not overlap. See Figure 13-14 (under replace_copy) for an example of the replacement process.

Technical Notes

The replace_copy_if function template assigns *(result + n) = *(first + n) == pred(*(first + n)) ? new_value : *(first + n) for all n in [0, last − first).

Complexity is linear: exactly *last − first* comparisons are performed.

See Also

remove_copy_if function template, replace function template, replace_copy function template, replace_if function template, transform function template

---

replace_if function template   Replaces values that satisfy a predicate

```
template<typename FwdIter, typename Predicate, typename T>
  void replace_if(FwdIter first, FwdIter last, Predicate pred,
                  const T& new_value);
```

The replace_if function template replaces all values in [first, last) for which pred is true with new_value. See Figure 13-14 (under replace_copy) for an example of the replacement process.

Technical Notes

The replace_if function template assigns *i = pred(*i) ? new_value : *i for all i in [first, last).

Complexity is linear: exactly *last − first* comparisons are performed.

See Also

remove_if function template, replace function template, replace_copy function template, transform function template

---

reverse function template   Reverses the values in a range

```
template<typename BidiIter>
  void reverse(BidiIter first, BidiIter last);
```

The reverse function template reverses the order of the items in the range [first, last). See Figure 13-15 (under reverse_copy) for an example.

Technical Notes

The reverse function template swaps *(first + n) with *(last − n − 1) for all n in [0, (last − first) / 2].

Complexity is linear: exactly (last − first) / 2 swaps are performed.

See Also

reverse_copy function template, rotate function template, swap function template

---

reverse_copy function template

Copies a range in reverse order

```
template<typename BidiIter, typename OutIter>
  OutIter reverse_copy(BidiIter first, BidiIter last, OutIter result);
```

The reverse_copy function template copies items in reverse order from the range [first, last) to the range that starts at result. In other words, *(last − 1) is first copied to *result, then *(last − 2) is copied to *(result + 1), and so on. The return value is an iterator that points to one past the end of the result range. The source and result ranges must not overlap. Figure 13-15 shows an example of reversing a range.

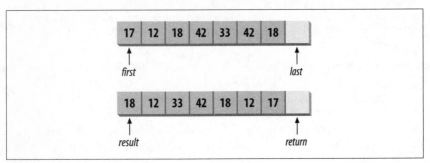

Figure 13-15. Reversing a range

Technical Notes

The reverse_copy function template assigns *(result + n) = *(last − n − 1) for all n in [0, last − first).

Complexity is linear: exactly last − first assignments are performed.

See Also

copy_backward function template, reverse function template, rotate_copy function template

---

rotate function template

Rotates elements in a range

```
template<typename FwdIter>
  void rotate(FwdIter first, FwdIter middle, FwdIter last);
```

The rotate function template rotates elements in the range [first, last) to the left so that the items in the range [middle, last) are moved to the start of the new sequence. Elements in the range [first, middle) are rotated to the end. See Figure 13-16 for an example.

Technical Notes

For all n in [0, last − first), the rotate function template moves *(first + n) into position first + (n + (last − middle)) % (last − first).

Complexity is linear: at most last − first swaps are performed.

See Also

reverse function template, rotate_copy function template

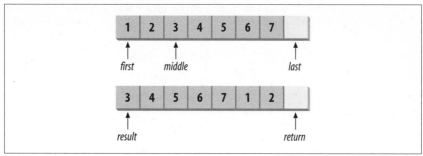

Figure 13-16. Rotating a range by two positions

rotate_copy function template
Rotates and copies items in a range

```
template<typename FwdIter, typename OutIter>
  OutIter rotate_copy(FwdIter first, FwdIter middle, FwdIter last,
                      OutIter result);
```

The rotate_copy function template copies elements from the range [middle, last) to the range that starts at result followed by the elements from [first, middle), thereby effecting a rotation to the left. The return value is one past the end of the result range.

The source and result ranges must not overlap. Figure 13-16 shows an example of rotation.

Technical Notes

The rotate_copy function template assigns *(*result* + (*n* + (*last* − *middle*)) % (*last* − *first*)) = *(*first* + *n*) for all *n* in [0, *last* − *first*). It returns *result* + (*last* − *first*).

Complexity is linear: exactly *last* − *first* assignments are performed.

See Also

reverse_copy function template, rotate function template

search function template
Searches a range for a subsequence

```
template<typename FwdIter1, typename FwdIter2>
  FwdIter1 search(FwdIter1 first1, FwdIter1 last1, FwdIter2 first2,
                  FwdIter2 last2);
```

```
template<typename FwdIter1, typename FwdIter2, typename BinaryPredicate>
  FwdIter1 search(FwdIter1 first1, FwdIter1 last1, FwdIter2 first2,
                  FwdIter2 last2, BinaryPredicate pred);
```

The search function template finds the first (leftmost) subsequence [first2, last2) within the range [first1, last1). It returns an iterator that points to the start of the subsequence or last1 if the subsequence is not found.

The first form compares items with the == operator. The second form calls pred(*iter1, *iter2).

Figure 13-5 (under find_end) illustrates the search function template.

Technical Notes

Let *length1* = *last1* − *first1* and *length2* = *last2* − *first2*.

Library
Reference

The search function template returns *first1* + *n*, in which *n* is the smallest value in the range [0, *length1* − *length2*) such that **(i + n + m)* == (*first2* + *m*) for all *m* in the range [0, *length2*). It returns *last1* if no such *n* can be found.

Complexity: at most *length1* × *length2* comparisons are performed.

See Also

find function template, find_end function template, search_n function template

---

search_n function template   Searches a range for a repeated value

```
template<typename FwdIter, typename Size, typename T>
  FwdIter search_n(FwdIter first, FwdIter last, Size count, const T& value);
```

```
template<typename FwdIter, typename Size, typename T, typename BinaryPredicate>
  FwdIter search_n(FwdIter first, FwdIter last, Size count, const T& value,
                   BinaryPredicate pred);
```

The search_n function template finds the first (leftmost) subsequence of count adjacent occurrences of value in the range [first, last). It returns an iterator that points to the start of the subsequence or last if the subsequence is not found.

The first form compares items with the == operator. The second form calls pred(*iter, value).

Technical Notes

The search_n function template returns *first* + *n*, in which *n* is the smallest value in the range [0, *last* − *first*) such that **(i + n + m)* == *value* for all *m* in the range [0, *count*). It returns *last* if no such *n* can be found.

Complexity: at most *n* × (*last* − *first*) comparisons are performed.

See Also

find function template, search function template

---

set_difference function template   Computes set difference of sorted ranges

```
template<typename InIter1, typename InIter2, typename OutIter>
  OutIter set_difference(InIter1 first1, InIter1 last1, InIter2 first2,
                         InIter2 last2, OutIter result);
```

```
template<typename InIter1, typename InIter2, typename OutIter, typename Compare>
  OutIter set_difference(InIter1 first1, InIter1 last1, InIter2 first2,
                         InIter2 last2, OutIter result, Compare comp);
```

The set_difference function template copies elements from the sorted range [first1, last1) to the range starting at result. Only those elements that are not also present in the sorted range [first2, last2) are copied. An iterator that points to one past the end of the result range is returned.

The result range must not overlap either source range.

The first version compares items using the < operator. The second version uses comp(X, Y) to test whether X < Y.

Figure 13-17 shows an example of a set difference using multisets.

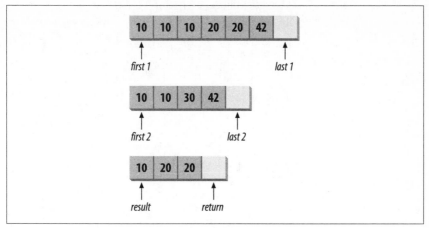

Figure 13-17. Computing the difference between sets

Technical Notes

Precondition: $!(*(i + 1) < *i)$ for all i in $[first1, last1 - 1)$ and $!(*(j + 1) < *j)$ for all j in $[first2, last2 - 1)$.

Postcondition: $!(*(i + 1) < *i)$ for all i in $[result, return - 1)$.

The set_difference function template assigns $*(result + n++) = *(first1 + m)$ for all m in $[first1, last1)$, in which $*(first1 + m)$ is not in $[first2, last2)$. It returns $result + n$.

Complexity is linear: at most $2 \times ((last1 - first1) + (last2 - first2)) - 1$ comparisons are performed.

See Also

includes function template, set_intersection function template, set_symmetric_ difference function template, set_union function template

---

set_intersection function template
Computes intersection of sorted ranges

```
template<typename InIter1, typename InIter2, typename OutIter>
  OutIter set_intersection(InIter1 first1, InIter1 last1, InIter2 first2,
                           InIter2 last2, OutIter result);
```

```
template<typename InIter1, typename InIter2, typename OutIter, typename Compare>
  OutIter set_intersection(InIter1 first1, InIter1 last1, InIter2 first2,
                           InIter2 last2, OutIter result, Compare comp);
```

The set_intersection function template copies elements from the sorted range [first1, last1) to the range starting at result. Only those elements that are also present in the sorted range [first2, last2) are copied. An iterator that points to one past the end of the result range is returned.

The result range must not overlap either source range.

The first version compares items using the < operator. The second version uses comp(X, Y) to test whether X < Y.

Figure 13-18 shows an example of intersection using multisets.

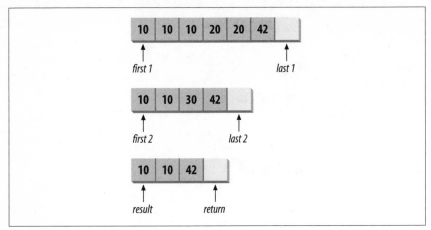

Figure 13-18. Intersecting two sets

Technical Notes

Precondition: !(*(i + 1) < *i) for all i in [first1, last1 − 1) and !(*(j + 1) < *j) for all j in [first2, last2 − 1).

Postcondition: !(*(i + 1) < *i) for all i in [result, return − 1).

The set_intersection function template assigns *(result + n++) = *(first1 + m) for all m in [first1, last1), in which *(first1 + m) is in [first2, last2). It returns result + n.

Complexity is linear: at most 2 × ((last1 − first1) + (last2 − first2)) − 1 comparisons are performed.

See Also

includes function template, set_difference function template, set_symmetric_difference function template, set_union function template

---

set_symmetric_difference function template
Computes symmetric difference
of sorted ranges

```
template<typename InIter1, typename InIter2, typename OutIter>
  OutIter set_symmetric_difference(InIter1 first1, InIter1 last1, InIter2 first2,
                          InIter2 last2, OutIter result);

template<typename InIter1, typename InIter2, typename OutIter, typename Compare>
  OutIter set_symmetric_difference(InIter1 first1, InIter1 last1, InIter2 first2,
                          InIter2 last2, OutIter result, Compare comp);
```

The set_symmetric_difference function template merges elements from the sorted ranges [first1, last1) and [first2, last2), copying the sorted, merged results to the range starting at result. Only those elements that are not also present in the sorted range [first2, last2) are copied from [first1, last1), and only those not present in the range [first1, last1) are copied from [first2, last2). An iterator that points to one past the end of the result range is returned.

The result range must not overlap either source range.

The first version compares items using the < operator. The second version uses comp(X, Y) to test whether X < Y.

Figure 13-19 shows an example of a set symmetric difference using multisets.

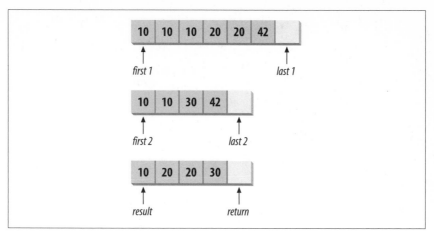

Figure 13-19. Computing the symmetric difference between two sets

Technical Notes

Precondition: $!(*(i + 1) < *i)$ for all i in [*first1*, *last1* − 1] and $!(*(j + 1) < *j)$ for all j in [*first2*, *last2* − 1].

Postcondition: $!(*(i + 1) < *i)$ for all i in [*result*, *return* − 1].

Complexity is linear: at most $2 \times ((last1 - first1) + (last2 - first2)) - 1$ comparisons are performed.

See Also

includes function template, set_difference function template, set_intersection function template, set_union function template

---

set_union function template

Computes union of sorted ranges

```
template<typename InIter1, typename InIter2, typename OutIter>
   OutIter set_union(InIter1 first1, InIter1 last1, InIter2 first2, InIter2 last2,
                   OutIter result);

template<typename InIter1, typename InIter2, typename OutIter, typename Compare>
   OutIter set_union(InIter1 first1, InIter1 last1, InIter2 first2, InIter2 last2,
                   OutIter result, Compare comp);
```

The set_union function template merges elements from the sorted ranges [first1, last1) and [first2, last2), copying the sorted, merged results to the range starting at result. If an element is present in both ranges, only one element is copied to the result range. If the input ranges contain duplicates, each occurrence of an element in an input range results in a copy in the result range. An iterator that points to one past the end of the result range is returned.

The result range must not overlap either source range.

The first version compares items using the < operator. The second version uses comp(X, Y) to test whether X < Y.

Figure 13-20 shows an example of a set union using multisets.

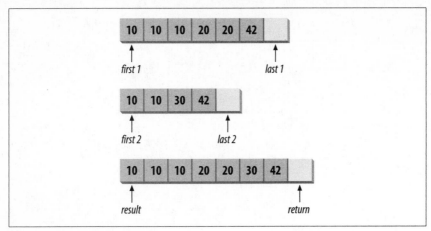

Figure 13-20. Computing the union of two sets

Technical Notes

Precondition: !(*(*i* + 1) < **i*) for all *i* in [*first1*, *last1* − 1) and !(*(*j* + 1) < **j*) for all *j* in [*first2*, *last2* − 1).

Postcondition: !(*(*i* + 1) < **i*) for all *i* in [*result*, *return* − 1).

Complexity is linear: at most 2 × ((*last1* − *first1*) + (*last2* − *first2*)) − 1 comparisons are performed.

See Also

includes function template, merge function template, set_difference function template, set_intersection function template, set_symmetric_difference function template

---

sort function template   Sorts a range in place

```
template<typename RandIter>
  void sort(RandIter first, RandIter last);

template<typename RandIter, typename Compare>
  void sort(RandIter first, RandIter last, Compare comp);
```

The sort function template sorts the range [first, last) in place. The sort is not stable, so equivalent elements do not preserve their original order.

The first version compares items using the < operator. The second version uses comp(X, Y) to test whether X < Y.

Technical Notes

Postcondition: !(*(*i* + 1) < **i*) for all *i* in [*first*, *last* − 1).

Complexity is *n* log *n* comparisons in the average case, in which *n* = *last* − *first*. Worst case performance might be worse. Use stable_sort if the worst-case performance is more important than the average performance.

See Also

merge function template, nth_element function template, partial_sort function template, partition function template, sort_heap function template, stable_sort function template

sort_heap function template

Sorts a heap in place

```
template<typename RandIter>
  void sort_heap(RandIter first, RandIter last);

template<typename RandIter, typename Compare>
  void sort_heap(RandIter first, RandIter last, Compare comp);
```

The sort_heap function template sorts a heap in the range [first, last). The sort is not stable, so equivalent elements do not preserve their original order.

The first version compares items using the < operator. The second version uses comp(X, Y) to test whether X < Y.

Technical Notes

Precondition: [*first, last*) is a heap (see make_heap for the definition of a heap).

Postcondition: !(*(i + 1) < *i) for all i in [*first, last* − 1).

Complexity is at most $n \log n$ comparisons, in which $n = last - first$.

See Also

make_heap function template, pop_heap function template, push_heap function template, sort function template, <queue>

stable_partition function template

Partitions a range in stable order

```
template<typename BidiIter, typename Predicate>
  BidiIter stable_partition(BidiIter first, BidiIter last, Predicate pred);
```

The stable_partition function template swaps elements in the range [first, last) so that all elements that satisfy pred come before those that do not. The relative order of elements in each partition is preserved.

The return value is an iterator that points to the first element for which pred is false, or last if there is no such element.

Figure 13-12 (under partition) illustrates the partition functionality.

Technical Notes

Postcondition: Let r be an iterator in the range [*first, last*] such that *pred*(*i) is true for all i in [*first, r*), and *pred*(*j)is false for all j in [*r, last*).

The stable_partition function template returns r.

Complexity is linear if there is enough memory. Otherwise, at most $n \log n$ swaps are performed, in which $n = last - first$. In all cases, *pred* is called exactly n times.

See Also

nth_element function template, partial_sort function template, partition function template, stable_sort function template

stable_sort function template   Sorts a range in place in stable order

```
template<typename RandIter>
  void stable_sort(RandIter first, RandIter last);
```

```
template<typename RandIter, typename Compare>
  void stable_sort(RandIter first, RandIter last, Compare comp);
```

The stable_sort function template sorts the range [first, last) in place. The sort is stable, so equivalent elements preserve their original order.

The first version compares items using the < operator. The second version uses comp(X, Y) to test whether X < Y.

Technical Notes

Postcondition: !(*(i + 1) < *i) for all *i* in [*first*, *last* − 1).

Complexity is at most $n \log n$ comparisons, in which $n = last - first$, provided that enough memory is available for temporary results. If memory is limited, the complexity is at most $n (\log n)^2$ comparisons.

See Also

merge function template, nth_element function template, partial_sort function template, sort function template, sort_heap function template, stable_partition function template

---

swap function template   Swaps two values

```
template<typename T> void swap(T& a, T& b);
```

The swap function template swaps the values of a and b.

The standard containers all specialize the swap template to call their swap member functions, which usually run in constant time, regardless of the number of elements in the containers.

See Also

iter_swap function template, swap_ranges function template

---

swap_ranges function template   Swaps all values in two ranges

```
template<typename FwdIter1, typename FwdIter2>
  FwdIter2 swap_ranges(FwdIter1 first1, FwdIter1 last1, FwdIter2 first2);
```

The swap_ranges function template swaps all the elements in [first1, last1) with corresponding elements in the range that starts at first2 (and has the same length as the first range). The return value is one past the end of the second range. The two ranges must not overlap.

Technical Notes

The swap_ranges function template performs the equivalent of *swap*(*(first1* + *n*), *(first2* + *n*)) for all *n* in [0, *last1* − *first1*).

Complexity is linear: exactly *last1* − *first1* swaps are performed.

See Also

iter_swap function template, swap function template

---

transform function template   Copies one or two ranges after applying an operator to each element

```
template<typename InIter, typename OutIter, typename UnaryOperation>
  OutIter transform(InIter first, InIter last, OutIter result,
                    UnaryOperation unop);
template<typename InIter1, typename InIter2, typename OutIter,
         typename BinaryOperation>
  OutIter transform(InIter1 first1, InIter1 last1, InIter2 first2,
                    OutIter result, BinaryOperation binop);
```

The transform function template assigns a new value to each element in the range that starts at result. In the first case, the new value is unop(*iter), in which iter is an iterator over [first, last).

In the second case, the new value is binop(*iter1, *iter2), in which iter1 ranges over [first1, last1) and iter2 iterates over the range that starts at first2. The second input range must be at least as long as the first.

The return value is one past the end of the result range. The result range can be the same as any of the input ranges.

Technical Notes

The first form of transform assigns $*(result + n) = unop(*(first + n))$ for all n in [0, $last - first$).

The second form assigns $*(result + n) = binop(*(first1 + n), *(first2 + n))$ for all n in [0, $last1 - first1$).

Complexity is linear: *unop* or *binop* is called exactly n times, in which $n = last - first$ for a unary operator or $last1 - first1$ for a binary operator.

See Also

copy function template, for_each function template

---

unique function template   Removes adjacent, equal values from a range

```
template<typename FwdIter>
  FwdIter unique(FwdIter first, FwdIter last);
template<typename FwdIter, typename BinaryPredicate>
  FwdIter unique(FwdIter first, FwdIter last, BinaryPredicate pred);
```

The unique function template "removes" repetitions of adjacent, identical elements from the range [first, last). The return value is one past the new end of the range. For each sequence of identical elements, only the first is kept. The input range does not have to be sorted, but if it is, all duplicates are "removed," leaving only unique values (hence the function's name).

Nothing is actually erased from the underlying container; instead, items to the right are copied to new positions at lower indices (to the left) so they overwrite the elements that are duplicates. See Figure 13-21 (under unique_copy) for an example of the removal process.

The first form compares items with the == operator. The second form calls pred(a, b).

Technical Notes

The unique function template assigns *(first + n++) = *(first + m) for all m in [0, last − first), in which m == 0 or *(first +m) == *(first + m − 1) is false. It returns first + n.

Complexity is linear: exactly max(0, last − first − 1) comparisons are performed.

See Also

remove function template, unique_copy function template

---

unique_copy function template   Copies unique values

```
template<typename InIter, typename OutIter>
  OutIter unique_copy(InIter first, InIter last, OutIter result);
```

```
template<typename InIter, typename OutIter, typename BinaryPredicate>
  OutIter unique_copy(InIter first, InIter last, OutIter result,
                      BinaryPredicate pred);
```

The unique_copy function template copies items from [first, last) to the range that starts at result, removing duplicates. For each sequence of identical elements, only the first is kept. The return value is one past the end of the result range.

The first form compares items with the == operator. The second form calls pred(a, b).

See Figure 13-21 for an example that calls unique_copy.

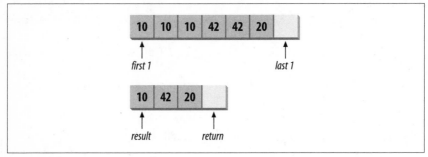

Figure 13-21. Copying unique elements

Technical Notes

The unique_copy function template assigns *(result + n++) = *(first + m) for all m in [0, last − first), in which m == 0 or *(first +m) == *(first + m − 1) is false. It returns result + n.

Complexity is linear: exactly last − first comparisons are performed.

See Also

remove_copy function template, unique function template

upper_bound function template

```
template<typename FwdIter, typename T>
  FwdIter upper_bound(FwdIter first, FwdIter last, const T& value);
template<typename FwdIter, typename T, typename Compare>
  FwdIter upper_bound(FwdIter first, FwdIter last, const T& value, Compare comp);
```

The upper_bound function template determines where value belongs in the sorted range [first, last). The return value is an iterator that points to one past the last (right-most) occurrence of value in the range, if value is present. Otherwise, the iterator points to the last position where you can insert value and preserve the sorted nature of the range.

The first form compares values using the < operator. The second form calls comp(*iter, value).

Figure 13-4 (under equal_range) shows an example of finding the bounds for the value 36. The upper_bound function returns ub as the upper bound of 36 in the given range. Note that it returns ub as the upper bound for all values in the range [36, 41]. For values in the range [19, 35], the upper bound is equal to lb.

Technical Notes

Precondition: !(*(i + 1) < *i) for all i in [first, last − 1).

The upper_bound function template returns first + n, in which n is the highest value in [0, last − first) such that *(first + m) < value is false for all m in [0, n).

Complexity is logarithmic. The number of comparisons is at most log(last − first) + 1. Although the iterator can be a forward iterator, the best performance is obtained with a random access iterator. With a forward or bidirectional iterator, the iterator is advanced a linear number of times, even though the number of comparisons is logarithmic.

See Also

binary_search function template, equal_range function template, lower_bound function template

<bitset>

The <bitset> header declares a single class template, bitset, and some related functions. A bitset is a fixed-size sequence of bits. The bitwise operators (&, |, ^, etc.) are overloaded to work with bitsets in the usual manner, and you can refer to individual bits by index.

The Boost project has a class template for a bit sequence that can change size at runtime. See Appendix B for information about Boost.

bitset class template
Fixed-size sequence of bits

```
template<size_t N>
class bitset {
public:
  // Proxy class to simulate a bit reference
  class reference {
    friend class bitset;
    reference();
  public:
    ~reference();
    reference& operator=(bool x);
    reference& operator=(const reference&);
    bool operator~() const;
    operator bool() const;
    reference& flip();
  };

  // Constructors
  bitset();
  bitset(unsigned long val);

  template<typename charT, typename traits, typename A>
  explicit bitset(const basic_string<charT,traits,A>& s, typename
    basic_string<charT,traits,A>::size_type p=0, typename basic
    string<charT,traits,A>::size_type n = basic_string<charT,traits,A>::npos);

  // bitset operations
  bitset<N>& operator&=(const bitset<N>& rhs);
  bitset<N>& operator|=(const bitset<N>& rhs);
  bitset<N>& operator^=(const bitset<N>& rhs);
  bitset<N>& operator<<=(size_t pos);
  bitset<N>& operator>>=(size_t pos);
  bitset<N>& set();
  bitset<N>& set(size_t pos, int val=true);
  bitset<N>& reset();
  bitset<N>& reset(size_t pos);
  bitset<N>  operator~() const;
  bitset<N>& flip();
  bitset<N>& flip(size_t pos);

  // Element access
  reference operator[](size_t pos);
  bool operator[](size_t pos) const;

  unsigned long  to_ulong() const;
  template <typename charT, typename traits, typename Alloc>
    basic_string<charT, traits, Alloc> to_string() const;

  size_t count() const;
  size_t size()  const;
  bool operator==(const bitset<N>& rhs) const;
  bool operator!=(const bitset<N>& rhs) const;
```

```
    bool test(size_t pos) const;
    bool any( ) const;
    bool none( ) const;
    bitset<N> operator<<(size_t pos) const;
    bitset<N> operator>>(size_t pos) const
};
```

The bitset class template offers a convenient way to manipulate a fixed-sized sequence of bits. The number of bits is specified as a template argument, so each bitset object can have a different size. Each bit in a bitset can be set (1 or true) or reset (0 or false). Bit positions are numbered from right to left, that is, 0 is the least-significant bit, and N − 1 is the most-significant bit.

A bitset is not a standard container and does not provide iterators or support generic algorithms. For a container that holds a sequence of bit values, use vector<int> or deque<bool>. (See <vector> later in this chapter to learn more, including why you should not use vector<bool>.) In the following member function descriptions, N is the template parameter (number of bits):

bitset( )
> Resets all bits.

bitset(unsigned long value)
> Initializes the first m bits to value, in which m == CHAR_BITS * sizeof(unsigned long). If N > m, all other bits are reset to 0. If N < m, excess bits of m are ignored.

```
template<typename charT, typename traits, typename A>
explicit bitset(const basic_string<charT,traits,A>& s,
    typename basic_string<charT,traits,A>::size_type p=0,
    typename basic_string<charT,traits,A>::size_type n=
    basic_string<charT,traits,A>::npos)
```
> Initializes the bitset from the character string s, starting at index p and extending for n characters (or to the end of the string, whichever comes first). The default is to use all characters in the string. A character equal to '0' resets a bit, '1' sets a bit, and any other character causes the constructor to throw invalid_argument.
>
> The rightmost character of the substring (that is, the character s[p+n-1] or the rightmost character of s) initializes the bit at index 0 of the bitset, and subsequent bits are initialized by characters at preceding indices of s. Bits left uninitialized by the string are reset. All of the bitsets in the following example are equal to 000111:
>
> ```
>     bitset<6> a(string("111"));
>     bitset<6> b(string("000111"));
>     bitset<6> c(string("10110011100"), 5, 4);
>     bitset<6> d(string("111111"), 3, 42);
> ```
>
> The unwieldy declaration is due to the basic_string class template. For the common case of a plain string, you can read the declaration as:
>
> ```
>     bitset(const string& s, size_t p=0, size_n n=string::npos)
> ```

bitset<N>& operator&=(const bitset<N>& rhs)
> Performs *this = *this & rhs. Returns *this.

bitset<N>& operator|=(const bitset<N>& rhs)
> Performs *this = *this | rhs. Returns *this.

bitset<N>& operator^=(const bitset<N>& rhs)
> Performs *this = *this ^ rhs. Returns *this.

`bitset<N>& `**`operator<<=`**`(size_t pos)`
    Shifts bits to the left by pos positions. Vacated bits are filled with 0. Returns *this.

`bitset<N>& `**`operator>>=`**`(size_t pos)`
    Shifts bits to the right by pos positions. Vacated bits are filled with 0. Returns *this.

`bool `**`operator==`**`(const bitset<N> rhs)`
    Returns true if every bit in *this has the same value as the corresponding bit in rhs.

`bool `**`operator!=`**`(const bitset<N> rhs)`
    Returns true if any bit in *this has a different value than the corresponding bit in rhs.

`bitset<N> `**`operator<<`**`(size_t pos)`
    Returns a new bitset with its bits shifted to the left by pos positions. Vacated bits are filled with 0.

`bitset<N> `**`operator>>`**`(size_t pos)`
    Returns a new bitset with its bits shifted to the right by pos positions. Vacated bits are filled with 0.

`bitset<N> `**`operator~`**`( ) const`
    Returns a new bitset with all bits flipped.

`reference `**`operator[]`**`(size_t pos)`
    Returns a bitset::reference object for the bit at position pos. The behavior is undefined if pos is out of range.

`bool `**`operator[]`**`(size_t pos) const`
    Returns the value of the bit at position pos. The behavior is undefined if pos is out of range. This member function was added to the standard as part of the technical corrigendum (TC1), so it might not yet be supported by some compilers.

`bool `**`any`**`( ) const`
    Returns true if any bit is set. Returns false if all bits are 0.

`size_t `**`count`**`( ) const`
    Returns the number of bits set.

`bitset<N>& `**`flip`**`( )`
    Toggles all bits, that is, sets 0 bits to 1 and 1 bits to 0. Returns *this.

`bitset<N>& `**`flip`**`(size_t pos)`
    Toggles the bit at position pos. If pos is invalid, throws out_of_range. Returns *this.

`bool `**`none`**`( ) const`
    Returns true if all bits are 0. Returns false if any bit is set.

`bitset<N>& `**`reset`**`( )`
    Resets all bits. Returns *this.

`bitset<N>& `**`reset`**`(size_t pos)`
    Resets the bit at position pos. If pos is invalid, throws out_of_range. Returns *this.

`bitset<N>& `**`set`**`( )`
    Sets all bits. Returns *this.

```
bitset<N>& set(size_t pos, int val = true)
```
Sets the bit at position pos to val != 0. If pos is invalid, throws out_of_range. Returns *this.

```
size_t size( ) const
```
Returns N.

```
bool test(size_t pos) const
```
Returns the value of the bit at position pos. Throws out_of_range if pos is invalid.

```
template <class charT, class traits, class Allocator>
basic_string<charT, traits, Allocator>
to_string( ) const
```
Returns a string representation of the bitset. Each bit is converted to the character '0' if reset or '1' if set. Bit position 0 is the rightmost character (position $N - 1$).

The compiler cannot deduce the template parameters when calling to_string, so you must specify them explicitly:

```
std::bitset<64> bits(std::string("101000111101010101"));
std::string str = bits.template to_string<char, std::char_traits<char>,
                                           std::allocator<char> >( ));
```

```
unsigned long to_ulong( ) const
```
Returns the integral value of the bitset. If N is too large for unsigned long, it throws overflow_error.

See Also

```
<climits>, <vector>
```

---

bitset::reference class   Proxy class for a bit in a bitset

```
class reference {
  friend class bitset;
  reference( )
public:
  ~reference( );
  reference& operator=(bool x);
  reference& operator=(const reference&);
  bool operator~( ) const;
  operator bool( ) const;
  reference& flip( );
};
```

The bitset::reference class is a proxy that refers to a single bit in a bitset. The constructor is private, so instances can be created only by the bitset class, particularly by its operator[ ] function. The member functions are:

```
reference& operator=(bool x)
reference& operator=(const reference& x)
```
Sets the referenced bit to x in the underlying bitset. Returns *this.

```
bool operator~( ) const
```
Returns the logical negation of the referenced bit.

```
operator bool( ) const
```
Returns the value of the referenced bit.

```
reference& flip( )
```
Toggles the referenced bit in the underlying bitset. Returns *this.

See Also

bitset class template

---

operator& function template

Performs bitwise and of two bitsets

```
template <size_t N>
  bitset<N> operator&(const bitset<N>& a, const bitset<N>& b);
```

The & operator takes two bitsets and returns a new bitset that represents the *bitwise and* of the operands. In other words, an output bit is set only when the corresponding bit is set in both operands; otherwise, an output bit is reset.

See Also

bitset class template, operator |, operator ^, <cstddef>, bit_and keyword

---

operator| function template

Performs bitwise inclusive or of two bitsets

```
template <size_t N>
  bitset<N> operator|(const bitset<N>& a, const bitset<N>& b);
```

The | operator takes two bitsets and returns a new bitset that represents the *bitwise inclusive or* of the operands. In other words, an output bit is set when the corresponding bit is set in either operand, and an output bit is reset if the corresponding bits in both operands are 0.

See Also

bitset class template, operator &, operator ^, <cstddef>, bit_or keyword

---

operator^ function template

Performs bitwise exclusive or of two bitsets

```
template <size_t N>
  bitset<N> operator^(const bitset<N>& a, const bitset<N>& b);
```

The ^ operator takes two bitsets and returns a new bitset that represents the *bitwise exclusive or* of the operands. In other words, an output bit is set when the corresponding bits are not equal in either operand, and an output bit is reset if the corresponding bits in both operands are identical.

See Also

bitset class template, operator &, operator |, <cstddef>, xor keyword

---

operator >>function template

Reads a bitset

```
template <typename charT, typename traits, size_t N>
  basic_istream<charT, traits)& operator>>(basic_istream<charT, traits)&
                                 in, const bitset<N>& x);
```

The >> operator reads a bitset from an input stream. It extracts up to N characters and constructs a bitset object using the same format as the string constructor.

Only '0' and '1' characters are extracted. Input stops when it reaches any other character (without extracting that other character).

See Also

bitset class template, operator <<, <istream>, <cstddef>

---

operator<< function template

Writes a bitset

```
template <typename charT, typename traits, size_t N>
  basic_ostream<charT, traits)& operator<<(basic_ostream<charT, traits)& in,
                                           const bitset<N>& x);
```

The << operator writes a bitset on an output stream, using the same format as the to_string member function.

See Also

bitset class template, operator >>, <cstddef>, <ostream>

<cassert>

The <cassert> header (from the C standard <assert.h> header) declares the assert macro. The <cassert> header is unique in that you can #include it multiple times to obtain different effects (depending on whether the NDEBUG macro is defined at the time of #include <cassert>).

Assertions are checked at runtime. You can use templates to craft compile-time assertions. See Appendix B for information about the Boost project, which supports compile-time assertions.

Instead of assertions, consider using exceptions, which offer more flexibility and control.

assert macro

Checks an assertion at runtime

```
void assert(int expression)
```

If enabled, the assert macro ensures the expression is true (nonzero). If so, nothing happens, and execution continues normally. If the expression evaluates to 0, assert prints a message to the standard error file and calls abort. The format of the message is implementation-defined, but it includes a textual representation of expression and the filename and line number where the assert call appears (that is, the values of the __FILE__ and __LINE__ macros).

If disabled, the assert macro does not evaluate expression and has no effect.

See Also

abort function in <cstdlib>, throw keyword

NDEBUG macro

Enables or disables compilation of assertions

```
#define NDEBUG
#include <cassert>
```

The NDEBUG macro is not defined by <cassert> or anywhere else in the standard C++ library. Instead, you can define the macro before including the <cassert> header to disable the assert macro.

In one source file, you can define and undefine NDEBUG multiple times, each time followed by #include <cassert>, to enable or disable the assert macro multiple times in the same source file.

See Also

assert macro

<cctype>

The <cctype> header (from the C standard <ctype.h> header) declares a number of functions for testing and mapping narrow character types. For working with wide characters, see <cwctype>.

All the functions take int parameters, but the value of the parameter must be an unsigned char. Most programs work with ordinary char, so you must cast the parameters and some of the return types:

```
char c;
if (std::isalnum(static_cast<unsigned char>(c)))
...
c = static_cast<char>(std::tolower(static_cast<unsigned char>(c)));
```

The only other value that is permitted is EOF.

These functions get their information from the current locale, as set by calling setlocale. The "C" locale is the only one with behavior that is defined in the standard; all other locales can define these functions to include or exclude different characters. Even in the "C" locale, the behavior of some functions depends on the execution character set (see Chapter 1). One requirement for all locales is that isalpha, iscntrl, isdigit, ispunct, and the space character (' ') are mutually exclusive. See <clocale> for information about the setlocale function.

See the <locale> header for a more flexible (albeit more complicated) mechanism for testing and transforming characters. Each of the functions in this section has a corresponding function in <locale> that takes an explicit locale argument. Also, the ctype facet supports similar functionality.

---

isalnum function   Tests for an alphanumeric character

int **isalnum**(int c)

The isalnum function returns true (nonzero) if c is alphanumeric—that is, it returns isalpha(c) || isnumeric(c).

---

isalpha function   Tests for an alphabetic character

int **isalpha**(int c)

The isalpha function returns true (nonzero) if c is alphabetic. In the "C" locale, this includes only the characters for which islower(c) or isupper(c) is true. For other locales, other characters might be alphabetic.

---

iscntrl function
Tests for a control character

```
int iscntrl(int c)
```

The iscntrl function returns true (nonzero) if c is a control character. The set of control characters depends on the locale and character set. In the 7-bit ASCII character set, the control characters are '\0'–'\x1F' and '\x7F'; other implementations might have different control characters. By definition, a control character is any character that is not a printable character (isprint).

isdigit function
Tests for a digit character

```
int isdigit(int c)
```

The isdigit function returns true (nonzero) if c is a decimal digit character—that is, '0'–'9'—regardless of locale.

isgraph function
Tests for a graphic character

```
int isgraph(int c)
```

The isgraph function returns true (nonzero) if c is any printing character (isprint) except space (' '). The set of printing characters varies with locale and character set.

islower function
Tests for a lowercase letter

```
int islower(int c)
```

The islower function returns true (nonzero) if c is a lowercase letter. In the "C" locale, only the characters 'a'–'z' are lowercase; different locales can define other lowercase characters.

isprint function
Tests for a printable character

```
int isprint(int c)
```

The isprint function returns true (nonzero) if c is a printing character, including space (' '), according to the locale and character set. Informally, a printing character occupies space on a display device.

ispunct function
Tests for a punctuation character

```
int ispunct(int c)
```

The ispunct function returns true (nonzero) for a punctuation character, that is, any printable character (isprint) other than space (' ') and alphanumeric characters (isalnum).

isspace function
Tests for a white space character

```
int isspace(int c)
```

The isspace function returns true (nonzero) if c is a whitespace character. In the "C" locale, the space (' '), form feed ('\f'), newline ('\n'), carriage return ('\r'), horizontal tab ('\t'), and vertical tab ('\v') characters are whitespace, but backspace ('\b') is not. Different locales can define other whitespace characters.

Library Reference

isupper function

int **isupper**(int c)

The isupper function returns true (nonzero) if c is an uppercase letter. In the "C" locale, only the characters 'A'–'Z' are uppercase; different locales can define other uppercase characters

isxdigit function

int **isxdigit**(int c)

The isxdigit function returns true (nonzero) if c is any hexadecimal digit character—that is, '0'–'9', 'a'–'f', or 'A'–'F'—regardless of locale.

tolower function

int **tolower**(int c)

The tolower function converts uppercase characters to lowercase. If c is uppercase (that is, isupper(c) returns true), tolower returns the corresponding lowercase character (for which islower returns true) in the current locale, if there is such a character. Otherwise, it returns c.

toupper function

int **toupper**(int c)

The toupper function converts lowercase characters to uppercase. If c is lowercase (that is, islower(c) returns true), toupper returns the corresponding uppercase character (for which isupper returns true) in the current locale, if there is such a character. Otherwise, it returns c.

<cerrno>

The <cerrno> header (from the C standard <errno.h> header) declares several macros related to error-handling in the standard library, including the errno object.

EDOM macro

int **EDOM**

Standard library functions that report domain errors set errno to EDOM. A domain error occurs when the domain of an argument is out of range, such as when asking for the square root of a negative number.

The EDOM macro expands to a nonzero integer constant. The value of EDOM is implementation-defined.

EILSEQ macro
Code for error in a multibyte character sequence

int **EILSEQ**

Standard library functions that report errors in multibyte character sequences set errno to EILSEQ. For example, passing an invalid wide character to the wcrtomb function results in EILSEQ.

The EILSEQ macro expands to a nonzero integer constant. The value of EILSEQ is implementation-defined.

Note that EILSEQ is not mentioned in the C++ standard, but because C++ includes the C standard library (Amendment 1), and EILSEQ is part of the C standard, it is part of the C++ standard.

ERANGE macro
Code for range error

int **ERANGE**

Standard library functions that report range errors set errno to ERANGE. A range error occurs when the result of a function is out of range, such as when there is overflow from the pow function.

The ERANGE macro expands to a nonzero integer constant. The value of ERANGE is implementation-defined.

errno macro
Global error code object

int& **errno**

The errno macro expands into an int lvalue. Standard library functions can store an error code in errno and return an error status to the caller. You can also store a value in errno (e.g., resetting the error code to 0).

When a program starts, errno is initially 0. No library function resets errno to 0. Any library function might set errno to a nonzero value, even if it is not documented to do so. Therefore, the only time it is safe to check errno is after a library function returns an error status and is documented to set errno in that case.

 The C++ standard is not explicit as to whether errno is truly a macro (versus a variable). The intent of the standard committee is to define errno as a macro, so do not use std::errno, and if your library declares errno as a variable in the std:: namespace, you can define your own macro:

```
#define errno (::std::errno)
```

In a multithreaded environment, a library implementation typically ensures that each thread gets a separate copy of errno. Such considerations fall outside the realm of the C++ standard. Consult your compiler and library documentation for details.

See Also
perror in <cstdio>, strerror in <cstring>

<cfloat>

The <cfloat> header is the C++ version of the C standard <float.h> header. It defines parameters that characterize floating-point types in the same way <climits> does for the integral types. The native C++ header, <limits>, defines the same information (and more) using templates instead of macros.

There are three sets of macros, each describing a different fundamental type. For each type, the corresponding set of macros has a common prefix: float (FLT_), double (DBL_), and long double (LDBL_). Each set characterizes a floating-point value as a sign, a significand (sometimes called the *mantissa*), a base, and an exponent:

$$x = sign \times significand \times base^{\,exponent}$$

In everyday arithmetic, we are used to working with a *base* of 10. (The base is also called the *radix*.) The most common bases for computer arithmetic, however, are 16 and 2. Many modern workstations use the IEC 60559 (IEEE 754) standard for floating-point arithmetic, which uses a base of 2.

The *significand* is a string of digits in the given base. There is an implied radix point at the start of the significand so the value of the significand is always less than 1. (A *radix point* is the generalization of a decimal point for any radix.)

A floating-point value is *normalized* if the first digit of its significand is nonzero, or if the entire value is 0. A value that is not normalized is *denormalized*.

The *precision* of a floating-point type is the maximum number of places in the significand. The *range* of a floating-point type depends primarily on the minimum and maximum values for the exponent.

 The value returned by each macro is implementation-defined because all the fundamental types are implementation-defined. The standard mandates minimum decimal precision and range for each floating-point type. In this section, the descriptions for the decimal characteristics of each type include the minimum value set by the standard.

Only FLT_RADIX expands to a constant expression. All other macros in <cfloat> expand to numeric expressions, but the values might not be compile-time constants.

DBL_DIG macro   Decimal precision

int **DBL_DIG**

Number of significant decimal digits that can be stored in a double. The value is always at least 10.

DBL_EPSILON macro   Limit of accuracy

double **DBL_EPSILON**

The difference between 1 and the smallest value greater than 1 that can be stored in a double. The value is always less than or equal to 10^{-9}.

DBL_MANT_DIG macro   Significand precision

int **DBL_MANT_DIG**

Number of FLT_RADIX digits in the significand of a double.

DBL_MAX macro

Maximum finite value

```
double DBL_MAX
```

Maximum finite double value. The value is always at least 10^{37}.

DBL_MAX_10_EXP macro

Maximum decimal exponent

```
int DBL_MAX_10_EXP
```

Maximum decimal exponent for a finite double. The value is always at least 37.

DBL_MAX_EXP macro

Maximum exponent

```
int DBL_MAX_EXP
```

Maximum exponent of a FLT_RADIX base for a finite double.

DBL_MIN macro

Minimum positive value

```
double DBL_MIN
```

Minimum normalized, positive double value. The value is always less than or equal to 10^{-37}.

DBL_MIN_10_EXP macro

Minimum decimal exponent

```
int DBL_MIN_10_EXP
```

Minimum negative decimal exponent for a normalized double. The value is always less than or equal to −37.

DBL_MIN_EXP macro

Minimum exponent

```
int DBL_MIN_EXP
```

Minimum negative exponent of a FLT_RADIX base for a normalized double.

FLT_DIG macro

Decimal precision

```
int FLT_DIG
```

Number of significant decimal digits that can be stored in a float. The value is always at least 6.

FLT_EPSILON macro

Limit of accuracy

```
float FLT_EPSILON
```

The difference between 1 and the smallest value greater than 1 that can be stored in a float. The value is always less than or equal to 10^{-5}.

FLT_MANT_DIG macro

Significand precision

```
int FLT_MANT_DIG
```

Number of FLT_RADIX digits in the significand of a float.

Library
Reference

FLT_MAX macro
Maximum finite value

float `FLT_MAX`

Maximum finite float value. The value is always at least 10^{37}.

FLT_MAX_10_EXP macro
Maximum decimal exponent

int `FLT_MAX_10_EXP`

Maximum decimal exponent for a finite float. The value is always at least 37.

FLT_MAX_EXP macro
Maximum exponent

int `FLT_MAX_EXP`

Maximum exponent of a FLT_RADIX base for a finite float.

FLT_MIN macro
Minimum positive value

float `FLT_MIN`

Minimum normalized, positive float value. The value is always less than or equal to 10^{-37}.

FLT_MIN_10_EXP macro
Minimum decimal exponent

int `FLT_MIN_10_EXP`

Minimum negative decimal exponent for a normalized float. The value is always less than or equal to -37.

FLT_MIN_EXP macro
Minimum exponent

int `FLT_MIN_EXP`

Minimum negative exponent of a FLT_RADIX base for a normalized float.

FLT_RADIX macro
Implementation base

int `FLT_RADIX`

The FLT_RADIX macro is an integer constant that specifies the radix, or base, for the floating-point implementation. For example, IEC 60559 (IEEE 754) has a FLT_RADIX of 2.

FLT_ROUNDS macro
Rounding mode

int `FLT_ROUNDS`

The FLT_ROUNDS macro specifies how the implementation rounds floating-point numbers. Table 13-2 lists the possible values as defined in the C++ standard. An implementation can define additional values with other meanings.

Table 13-2. Floating-point rounding mode

Value	Description
-1	Indeterminable
0	Rounds toward 0
1	Rounds to nearest
2	Rounds up (toward positive infinity)
3	Rounds down (toward negative infinity)

LDBL_DIG macro   Decimal precision

int **LDBL_DIG**

Number of significant decimal digits that can be stored in a long double. The value is always at least 10.

LDBL_EPSILON macro   Limit of accuracy

long double **LDBL_EPSILON**

The difference between 1 and the smallest value greater than 1 that can be stored in a long double. The value is always less than or equal to 10^{-9}.

LDBL_MANT_DIG macro   Significand precision

int **LDBL_MANT_DIG**

Number of FLT_RADIX digits in the significand of a long double.

LDBL_MAX macro   Maximum finite value

long double **LDBL_MAX**

Maximum finite long double value. The value is always at least 10^{37}.

LDBL_MAX_10_EXP macro   Maximum decimal exponent

int **LDBL_MAX_10_EXP**

Maximum decimal exponent for a finite long double. The value is always at least 37.

LDBL_MAX_EXP macro   Maximum exponent

int **LDBL_MAX_EXP**

Maximum exponent of a FLT_RADIX base for a finite double.

LDBL_MIN macro   Minimum positive value

long double **LDBL_MIN**

Minimum normalized, positive long double value. The value is always less than or equal to 10^{-37}.

Library Reference

LDBL_MIN_10_EXP macro Minimum decimal exponent

int **LDBL_MIN_10_EXP**

Minimum negative decimal exponent for a normalized long double. The value is always less than or equal to −37.

LDBL_MIN_EXP macro Minimum exponent

int **LDBL_MIN_EXP**

Minimum negative exponent of a FLT_RADIX base for a normalized long double.

<ciso646>

The <ciso646> header (from the C standard <iso646.h> header) does nothing in C++. The C header defines a small number of macros, such as and for &&, but these macros are all reserved keywords in C++. The <ciso646> header exists only for the sake of completeness: every header in the C standard has an equivalent in C++.

 Not all C++ compilers correctly implement the alternative tokens such as and. These compilers might use <ciso646> to declare these keywords as macros. For maximum portability to these nonconforming compilers, include the <ciso646> header when you want to use any alternative token keywords. See Chapter 1 for more information about the alternative tokens.

<climits>

The <climits> header (from the C standard <limits.h> header) defines parameters that characterize integral types in the same way <cfloat> does for the floating point types. The native C++ header, <limits>, defines the same information (and more) using templates instead of macros.

 The types used in the descriptions of the _MIN and _MAX macros are meant as reminders and are not descriptive of the actual types of the macro expansions. The actual types are implementation-defined and can be any integral type that would be the result of normal integral promotions for the corresponding type—e.g., if unsigned char is promoted to int, UCHAR_MAX might have type int.

All of the macros in <climits> expand to constant expressions.

CHAR_BIT macro Bits per character

int **CHAR_BIT**

Number of bits per character. The value is always at least 8.

CHAR_MAX macro
Maximum char value

char **CHAR_MAX**

Maximum value for the char type. (Remember that the char type is the same as either signed char or unsigned char, so CHAR_MAX has the same value as SCHAR_MAX or UCHAR_MAX.)

See Also
WCHAR_MAX in <cwchar>

CHAR_MIN macro
Minimum char value

char **CHAR_MIN**

Minimum value for the char type (the same value as SCHAR_MIN or 0).

See Also
WCHAR_MIN in <cwchar>

INT_MAX macro
Maximum int value

int **INT_MAX**

Maximum value for the int type. The value is always at least 32,767.

INT_MIN macro
Minimum int value

int **INT_MIN**

Minimum value for the int type. The value is always less than or equal to −32,767.

LONG_MAX macro
Maximum long value

long int **LONG_MAX**

Maximum value for the long int type. The value is always at least 2,147,483,647.

LONG_MIN macro
Minimum long value

long int **LONG_MIN**

Minimum value for the long int type. The value is always less than or equal to −2,147,483,647.

MB_LEN_MAX macro
Maximum bytes in a multibyte character

int **MB_LEN_MAX**

Maximum number of bytes in any multibyte character, in any locale. The value is always at least 1.

SCHAR_MAX macro
Maximum signed char value

signed char **SCHAR_MAX**

Maximum value for the signed char type. The value is always at least 127.

Library Reference

SCHAR_MIN macro   Minimum signed char value

signed char **SCHAR_MIN**

Minimum value for the signed char type. The value is always less than or equal to −127.

SHRT_MAX macro   Maximum short value

short **SHRT_MAX**

Maximum value for the short type. The value is always at least 32,767.

SHRT_MIN macro   Minimum short value

short **SHRT_MIN**

Minimum value for the short type. The value is always less than or equal to −32,767.

UCHAR_MAX macro   Maximum unsigned char value

unsigned char **UCHAR_MAX**

Maximum value for the unsigned char type. The value is always at least 255.

UINT_MAX macro   Maximum unsigned int value

unsigned int **UINT_MAX**

Maximum value for the unsigned int type. The value is always at least 65,535.

ULONG_MAX macro   Maximum unsigned long value

unsigned long **ULONG_MAX**

Maximum value for the unsigned long type. The value is always at least 4,294,967,295.

USHRT_MAX macro   Maximum unsigned short value

unsigned short **USHRT_MAX**

Maximum value for the unsigned short type. The value is always at least 65,535.

<clocale>

The <clocale> header (from the C standard <locale.h> header) declares types and functions to support internationalization and localization for the C standard library. C++ also offers <locale>, which has more flexibility and functionality, but at a cost of complexity and overhead.

The various locale settings are grouped into categories. Each category has a macro (named LC_*category*) to identify the category in a call to setlocale. Ordinarily, you would use LC_ALL to set all the categories at once, but you can pick a category from one locale and another category from a different locale.

LC_ALL macro

int **LC_ALL**

The LC_ALL macro expands to a constant integer, which sets all categories in a call to setlocale.

LC_COLLATE macro

int **LC_COLLATE**

The LC_COLLATE macro expands to a constant integer, which sets the collation order category in a call to setlocale. The collation order is used by functions such as strcoll (in <cstring>).

LC_CTYPE macro

int **LC_CTYPE**

The LC_CTYPE macro expands to a constant integer, which sets the character type category in a call to setlocale. The <cctype> functions, such as isalpha, use character type information.

LC_MONETARY macro

int **LC_MONETARY**

The LC_MONETARY macro expands to a constant integer, which sets the monetary-formatting category in a call to setlocale. Call localeconv to retrieve this information.

LC_NUMERIC macro

int **LC_NUMERIC**

The LC_NUMERIC macro expands to a constant integer, which sets the numeric-formatting category in a call to setlocale. I/O functions such as printf (in <cstdio>) use this information to format numbers. Call localeconv to retrieve this information.

LC_TIME macro

int **LC_TIME**

The LC_TIME macro expands to a constant integer, which sets the time-formatting category in a call to setlocale. The strftime (in <ctime>) function uses this information.

lconv structure

```
struct lconv {
  char *decimal_point;
  char *thousands_sep;
  char *grouping;
  char *int_curr_symbol;
  char *currency_symbol;
  char *mon_decimal_point;
  char *mon_thousands_sep;
  char *mon_grouping;
```

```
    char *positive_sign;
    char *negative_sign;
    char int_frac_digits;
    char frac_digits;
    char p_cs_precedes;
    char p_sep_by_space;
    char n_cs_precedes;
    char n_sep_by_space;
    char p_sign_posn;
    char n_sign_posn;
};
```

The lconv structure stores information used to format numbers and monetary values. An implementation can add more members to the class and change the order of declaration.

The standard library is responsible for filling an lconv object with values that are appropriate for a locale. Do not modify the lconv object or its data members.

Each locale defines suitable values for the lconv members. The char-type members are all nonnegative integers, in which CHAR_MAX means the information is not available in the current locale. For the char* members, an empty string means the information is not available. The "C" locale uses "." for decimal_point, an empty string ("") for all other char* members, and CHAR_MAX for all char members. All strings are null-terminated.

The localeconv function returns a pointer to the current locale's lconv object.

The following are descriptions of the lconv members:

char* **currency_symbol**
> The currency symbol for the current locale (e.g., "$").

char* **decimal_point**
> The decimal point symbol for the current locale. This member is unique in that it cannot be an empty string. The default is ".".

char **frac_digits**
> The number of digits to appear after the decimal point in monetary formatting.

char* **grouping**
> A string that is interpreted as a series of integers, in which each integer is the number of digits in successive groups of digits for nonmonetary formatting. The value '\0' means to repeat the last grouping for the rest of the value. The value CHAR_MAX means not to group the remaining values. Any other value is the size of a digit group. The first character in the string specifies the size of the rightmost group of digits, the second character in the string specifies the size of the next (moving to the left) group of digits, and so forth. Digit groups are separated by thousands_sep.
>
> A common value is "\3", which means to format digits in groups of three (e.g., "1,234,567").

char* **int_curr_symbol**
> A four-character string, in which the first three characters are the international currency symbol (according to ISO standard 4217:1987), and the fourth character is the separator between the currency symbol and the number. For example, the symbol for United States Dollars is USD. If the locale uses a space as the separator, int_curr_symbol would be "USD ".

char **int_frac_digits**
> The number of digits to appear after the decimal point in an internationally-formatted monetary amount.

char* **mon_decimal_point**
> The monetary decimal point.

char* **mon_grouping**
> The monetary grouping. (This works the same as grouping, except groups are separated by mon_thousands_sep.)

char* **mon_thousands_sep**
> The monetary thousands separator. (This works the same as thousands_sep in monetary groups, as specified by mon_grouping.)

char **n_cs_precedes**
> Equal to 1 if the currency symbol precedes the amount when formatting a negative monetary value. Equal to 0 if the symbol follows the value.

char **n_sep_by_space**
> Equal to 1 if the currency symbol is separated from a negative value by a space. Equal to 0 if there is no space.

char **n_sign_posn**
> The position of the sign for a negative monetary value. Table 13-3 lists all the position values.

Table 13-3. Position values for n_sign_posn and p_sign_posn

Value	Position
0	Parentheses surround the value and the currency symbol.
1	The sign precedes the value and the currency symbol.
2	The sign follows the value and the currency symbol.
3	The sign appears immediately before the currency symbol.
4	The sign appears immediately after the currency symbol.

char* **negative_sign**
> Marker for a negative monetary value (e.g., "-").

char **p_cs_precedes**
> Equal to 1 if the currency symbol precedes the amount when formatting a nonnegative monetary value. Equal to 0 if the symbol follows the value.

char **p_sep_by_space**
> Equal to 1 if the currency symbol is separated from a nonnegative value by a space. Equal to 0 if there is no space.

char **p_sign_posn**
> The position of the sign for a nonnegative monetary value. Table 13-3 lists all the position values.

char* **positive_sign**
> Marker for a nonnegative monetary value.

char* **thousands_sep**
> Thousands separator (e.g., ","), which is used in digit groups, as specified by grouping.

localeconv function
Retrieves numeric-formatting information

lconv* **localeconv**( );

The localeconv function returns a pointer to the current locale's lconv object.

 Do not modify the lconv object. A call to localeconv might over-write the contents of the object returned from an earlier call (or simultaneous call in a multithreaded program). Calls to setlocale for LC_ALL, LC_NUMERIC, or LC_MONETARY categories might also over-write the contents of the lconv object.

NULL macro
Null pointer constant

#define **NULL** ...

The NULL macro expands to a null pointer constant. It is defined in several C headers. See its description in <cstddef> for details.

setlocale function
Sets or queries locale

char* **setlocale**(int category, const char* locale)

The setlocale function sets the locale for a specific category, which you must specify using one of the LC_ macros. Use LC_ALL to set all categories to the same locale.

 The locale parameter is the name of the locale. The default for all categories is the "C" locale. The empty string ("") is an implementation-defined native locale. The implementation can define other possible values for locale.

To query the current locale, pass a null pointer as the locale. Note that each category might have a different locale, so, when querying for LC_ALL, the return value might contain multiple locale names.

The return value is a pointer to a string that contains the new locale (or current locale if you are querying with a null locale parameter) for the specified category. If the locale cannot be set, a null pointer is returned.

 Do not modify the string returned from setlocale. A call to setlocale might overwrite the contents of the string returned from an earlier call (or simultaneous call in a multithreaded program).

<cmath>

The <cmath> header declares a number of mathematical functions (from the C standard <math.h>). In addition to the standard C function, most functions have overloaded versions for different parameter types; each function's syntax shows all the overloaded versions.

 If an argument is out of range, a domain error occurs. The function sets errno to EDOM and returns an error value. The value is defined by the implementation, so the only portable way to test for a domain error is to check errno. If the function's result is an overflow, a range error occurs. The function returns HUGE_VAL and sets errno to ERANGE. If underflow occurs, the function returns 0 and may or may not set errno to ERANGE. (See <cerrno> for more information about errno.)

 HUGE_VAL is defined to be a double, and the C++ standard does not define a suitable value for the float and long double versions of the math functions. If you are using a system that has infinity as an explicit floating-point value (such as IEC 60559/IEEE 754, which is found on PCs, Macintoshes, and modern workstations), the over-loaded versions of a function probably return infinity for overflow, so there is no problem with the float and long double versions of the functions. For maximum portability, however, use only the double versions of the math functions.

All the trigonometric functions use radians. The descriptions of these functions use the common mathematical notation for ranges of values. $[x, y)$ represents all values z such that $x \leq z < y$—that is, the square bracket denotes an inclusive endpoint of a range, and the parenthesis denotes an exclusive endpoint of a range.

Several other headers in the standard library declare additional mathematical functions:

<cfloat>
Declares macros for the limits of floating-point types

<climits>
Declares macros for the limits of integer types

<complex>
Declares types and functions for working with complex numbers

<cstdlib>
Declares integer absolute value functions and functions that compute a quotient and remainder in a single operation

<limits>
Declares the numeric_limits class template for the limits of the numerical types—e.g., the largest float, the precision of double, and so on

<numeric>
Declares generic numerical algorithms

<valarray>
Declares types and functions for computation with arrays of numbers

---

abs function   Computes absolute value

```
float abs(float x)
double abs(double x)
long double abs(long double x)
```

The abs function returns the absolute value of its argument: if $x < 0$, it returns -x; otherwise, it returns x.

The abs function in <cmath> is the same as fabs. The <cstdlib> header declares integer versions of the abs function.

See Also

fabs function, abs function in <cstdlib>

---

acos function
Computes inverse cosine

```
float acos(float x)
double acos(double x)
long double acos(long double x)
```

The acos function returns the inverse cosine of its argument. The parameter x must be in the range [−1, 1], or a domain error occurs. The return value is in the range [0, π].

---

asin function
Computes inverse sine

```
float asin(float x)
double asin(double x)
long double asin(long double x)
```

The asin function returns the inverse sine of its argument. The parameter x must be in the range [−1, 1], or a domain error occurs. The return value is in the range [−π/2, π/2].

---

atan function
Computes inverse tangent

```
float atan(float x)
double atan(double x)
long double atan(long double x)
```

The atan function returns the inverse tangent of its argument. The return value is in the range [−π/2, π/2].

---

atan2 function
Computes inverse tangent

```
float atan2(float y, float x)
double atan2(double y, double x)
long double atan2(long double y, long double x)
```

 The atan2 function returns the inverse tangent of y/x using the sign of both numbers to determine the quadrant for the return value. It correctly handles the case in which x is 0. (That is, it returns π/2 times the sign of y for nonzero y; if y is 0, the result is implementation-defined and might be a range error). The return value is in the range [−π, π].

---

ceil function
Computes ceiling

```
float ceil(float x)
double ceil(double x)
long double ceil(long double x)
```

The ceil function returns the smallest integer that is greater than or equal to x.

See Also

floor function

---

cos function

```
float cos(float x)
double cos(double x)
long double cos(long double x)
```

The cos function returns the cosine of its argument, in radians. The return value is in the range [−1, 1].

cosh function

```
float cosh(float x)
double cosh(double x)
long double cosh(long double x)
```

The cosh function returns the hyperbolic cosine of its argument. Note that <cmath> has no inverse hyperbolic trigonometric functions; the Boost project fills that gap. See Appendix B for information about Boost.

exp function

```
float exp(float x)
double exp(double x)
long double exp(long double x)
```

The exp function returns e^x. If x is too large, a range error occurs.

See Also
log function, pow function

fabs function

```
float fabs(float x)
double fabs(double x)
long double fabs(long double x)
```

The fabs function returns the absolute value of its argument: if x < 0, it returns −x; otherwise, it returns x.

The fabs function is the same as abs for floating-point numbers. It exists only for compatibility with C.

See Also
abs function, abs function in <cstdlib>

floor function

```
float floor(float x)
double floor(double x)
long double floor(long double x)
```

The floor function returns the largest integer that is less than or equal to x.

See Also
ceil function

fmod function

Computes modulus

```
float fmod(float x, float y)
double fmod(double x, double y)
long double fmod(long double x, long double y)
```

 The fmod function returns the floating-point remainder of dividing x by y. If y is 0, the behavior is implementation-defined: the return value might be 0, or a domain error can occur. If y is nonzero, the return value is $x - k \times y$ for some integer k, such that the result has the same sign as x and an absolute value less than the absolute value of y.

frexp function

Computes binary fraction and exponent

```
float frexp(float x, int* exp)
double frexp(double x, int* exp)
long double frexp(long double x, int* exp)
```

The frexp function separates a floating-point number into a fraction and an exponent (with a base of 2) such that $x = frac \times 2^e$, in which $frac$ is in the range [1/2, 1) or is 0 if x is 0. The exponent, e, is stored in *exp. The return value is $frac$. If x is 0, the return value and *exp are 0.

See Also

ldexp function, modf function

HUGE_VAL macro

Range error value

```
double HUGE_VAL
```

 When an overflow occurs, most functions set errno to ERANGE and return HUGE_VAL with the correct sign of the result. The exact value of HUGE_VAL is implementation-defined and is not necessarily a compile-time constant. It might even be a value that can be returned as a valid result from the function. In that case, the only way to discover whether an overflow occurred is to test errno, as shown in Example 13-5.

Example 13-5. Computing a logarithm to any base

```
// Return the logarithm of x to the base n.
template<typename T>
T logn(T x, T n)
{
  errno = 0;
  T logx = log(x);
  if (errno == ERANGE)
    return logx;     // Should be HUGE_VAL
  else if (errno != 0)
    return logx;     // Implementation defined
  T logn = log(n);
  if (errno == ERANGE)
    return logn;     // Should be HUGE_VAL
  else if (errno != 0)
    return logn;     // Implementation defined
  if (logn == 0) {
    errno = EDOM;
    return 0;
```

Example 13-5. Computing a logarithm to any base (continued)

```
  }
  return logx / logn;
}
```

See Also

`<cerrno>`

---

ldexp function   Makes floating point from binary fraction and exponent

```
float ldexp(float frac, int exp)
double ldexp(double frac, int exp)
long double ldexp(long double frac, int exp)
```

The ldexp function returns a floating-point number that it constructs from a fractional part and an exponent (base 2). The return value is $frac \times 2^{exp}$.

See Also

frexp function, modf function

---

log function   Computes natural logarithm

```
float log(float x)
double log(double x)
long double log(long double x)
```

The log function returns the natural (base *e*) logarithm of its argument. A domain error occurs if x is negative. A range error might occur if x is 0.

---

log10 function   Computes common logarithm

```
float log10(float x)
double log10(double x)
long double log10(long double x)
```

The log10 function returns the common (base 10) logarithm of its argument. A domain error occurs if x is negative. A range error might occur if x is 0.

---

modf function   Separates integer and fraction parts

```
float modf(float x, float* iptr)
double modf(double x, double* iptr)
long double modf(long double x, long double* iptr)
```

The modf function splits a floating-point number into integral and fractional parts. Both parts have the same sign as x. The integral part is stored in *iptr; the return value is the fractional part.

See Also

frexp function, ldexp function

pow function

Computes power

```
float pow(float x, float y)
float pow(float x, int y)
double pow(double x, double y)
double pow(double x, int y)
long double pow(long double x, long double y)
long double pow(long double x, int y)
```

The pow function raises x to the y power. If x is negative, and y is not an integral value, a domain error occurs. If x is 0, and y is less than or equal to 0, and the result cannot be represented as a real number, a domain error occurs. A range error can occur if the result is out of range.

See Also

exp function

sin function

Computes sine

```
float sin(float x)
double sin(double x)
long double sin(long double x)
```

The sin function returns the sine of its argument, in radians. The return value is in the range $[-1, 1]$.

sinh function

Computes hyperbolic sine

```
float sinh(float x)
double sinh(double x)
long double sinh(long double x)
```

The sinh function returns the hyperbolic sine of its argument. Note that <cmath> has no inverse hyperbolic trigonometric functions; the Boost project fills that gap. See Appendix B for information about Boost.

sqrt function

Computes square root

```
float sqrt(float x)
double sqrt(double x)
long double sqrt(long double x)
```

The sqrt function returns the square root or its argument. If x is negative, a domain error occurs. The return value is always positive or 0.

tan function

Computes tangent

```
float tan(float x)
double tan(double x)
long double tan(long double x)
```

The tan function returns the tangent of its argument. The standard does not specify the result when the tangent is undefined (that is, when x is $k\pi + \pi/2$ for any integer k), but a reasonable result is a range error. Due to the nature of the tangent function, the sign of the return value (HUGE_VAL) can be positive or negative.

tanh function

```
float tanh(float x)
double tanh(double x)
long double tanh(long double x)
```

The tanh function returns the hyperbolic tangent of its argument. Note that <cmath> has no inverse hyperbolic trigonometric functions; the Boost project fills that gap. See Appendix B for information about Boost.

<complex>

The <complex> header declares the complex class template and specializations for the float, double, and long double types. It also declares mathematical functions that work with complex values.

abs function template
Computes absolute value

```
template<typename T> T abs(const complex<T>& z)
```

The abs function returns the absolute value (or magnitude) of z.

See Also

polar function template, abs function in <cmath>

arg function template
Computes argument (angle)

```
template<typename T> T arg(const complex<T>& z)
```

The arg function returns the argument (angle in polar coordinates) of z.

See Also

polar function template

complex class template
Complex number template

```
template<typename T>
class complex {
public:
  typedef T value_type;
  complex(const T& re = T( ), const T& im = T( ));
  complex(const complex& z);
  template<typename X> complex(const complex<X>& z);
  T real( ) const;
  T imag( ) const;
  complex& operator= (const T& x);
  complex& operator+=(const T& x);
  complex& operator-=(const T& x);
  complex& operator*=(const T& x);
  complex& operator/=(const T& x);
  complex& operator=(const complex& z);
```

```
template<typename X>
  complex& operator= (const complex<X>& z);
template<typename X>
  complex& operator+=(const complex<X>& z);
template<typename X>
  complex& operator-=(const complex<X>& z);
template<typename X>
  complex& operator*=(const complex<X>& z);
template<typename X>
  complex& operator/=(const complex<X>& z);
};
```

The complex class template represents a complex number. The <complex> header specializes the template for the float, double, and long double types. You can instantiate complex<> for any type that behaves in the manner of the fundamental numeric types.

The type definition is a straightforward representation of a complex number. Basic assignment operators are defined as member functions, and arithmetic operators are defined as global functions.

template<typename X> **complex**(const complex<X>& z)
> Constructs a complex<T> object by copying the members from z. Effectively, this converts a complex object instantiated for one type to a complex object of another type.

T **real**( ) const
> Returns the real part of *this.

T **imag**( ) const
> Returns the imaginary part of *this.

complex& **operator=**(const T& x)
> Assigns x to the real part of *this and 0 to the imaginary part. Returns *this.

complex& **operator+=**(const T& x)
> Adds x to the real part of *this, leaving the imaginary part alone. Returns *this.

complex& **operator-=**(const T& x)
> Subtracts x from the real part of *this, leaving the imaginary part alone. Returns *this.

complex& **operator*=**(const T& x)
> Multiplies the real and imaginary parts of *this by x. Returns *this.

complex& **operator/=**(const T& x)
> Divides the real and imaginary parts of *this by x. Returns *this.

complex& **operator=**(const complex& z)
> Assigns the real and imaginary parts of z to *this. Returns *this.

template<typename X> complex& **operator=**(const complex<X>& z)
> Assigns the real and imaginary parts of z to *this. Returns *this. Note that z and *this can have different template parameter types.

template<typename X> complex& **operator+=**(const complex<X>& z)
> Adds z to *this. Returns *this. Note that z and *this can have different template parameter types.

```
template<typename X> complex& operator-=(const complex<X>& z)
```
    Subtracts z from *this. Returns *this. Note that z and *this can have different template parameter types.

```
template<typename X> complex& operator*=(const complex<X>& z)
```
    Multiplies *this by z. Returns *this. Note that z and *this can have different template parameter types.

```
template<typename X> complex& operator/=(const complex<X>& z)
```
    Divides *this by z. Returns *this. Note that z and *this can have different template parameter types.

complex<double> template specialization

Double-precision complex number

```
template<> class complex<double> {
public:
  typedef double value_type;
  complex(double re = 0.0, double im = 0.0);
  complex(const complex<float>&);
  explicit complex(const complex<long double>&);
  double real() const;
  double imag() const;
  complex<double>& operator= (double);
  complex<double>& operator+=(double);
  complex<double>& operator-=(double);
  complex<double>& operator*=(double);
  complex<double>& operator/=(double);
  complex<double>& operator=(const complex<double>&);
  template<typename X>
    complex<double>& operator= (const complex<X>&);
  template<typename X>
    complex<double>& operator+=(const complex<X>&);
  template<typename X>
    complex<double>& operator-=(const complex<X>&);
  template<typename X>
    complex<double>& operator*=(const complex<X>&);
  template<typename X>
    complex<double>& operator/=(const complex<X>&);
};
```

The complex<double> class is a straightforward specialization of the complex class template. It changes the operators to pass double parameters by value instead of by reference, and it adds a new constructor:

```
explicit complex(const complex<long double>& z)
```
    Constructs a complex number by copying from z. Note that you might lose precision or overflow, so the constructor is explicit.

complex<float> template specialization

Single-precision complex number

```
template<> class complex<float> {
public:
  typedef float value_type;
  complex(float re = 0.0f, float im = 0.0f);
  explicit complex(const complex<double>&);
```

```
  explicit complex(const complex<long double>&);
  float real( ) const;
  float imag( ) const;
  complex<float>& operator= (float);
  complex<float>& operator+=(float);
  complex<float>& operator-=(float);
  complex<float>& operator*=(float);
  complex<float>& operator/=(float);
  complex<float>& operator=(const complex<float>&);
  template<typename X>
    complex<float>& operator= (const complex<X>&);
  template<typename X>
    complex<float>& operator+=(const complex<X>&);
  template<typename X>
    complex<float>& operator-=(const complex<X>&);
  template<typename X>
    complex<float>& operator*=(const complex<X>&);
  template<typename X>
    complex<float>& operator/=(const complex<X>&);
};
```

The complex<float> class is a straightforward specialization of the complex class template. It changes the operators to pass float parameters by value instead of by reference, and it adds two new constructors:

```
explicit complex(const complex<double>& z)
explicit complex(const complex<long double>& z)
```

> Constructs a complex number by copying from z. Note that you might lose precision or overflow, so the constructors are explicit.

---

complex<long double> template specialization   Extended-precision complex number

```
template<> class complex<long double> {
public:
  typedef long double value_type;
  complex(long double re = 0.0L, long double im = 0.0L);
  complex(const complex<float>&);
  complex(const complex<double>&);
  long double real( ) const;
  long double imag( ) const;
  complex<long double>&
    operator=(const complex<long double>&);
  complex<long double>& operator= (long double);
  complex<long double>& operator+=(long double);
  complex<long double>& operator-=(long double);
  complex<long double>& operator*=(long double);
  complex<long double>& operator/=(long double);
  template<typename X>
    complex<long double>& operator= (const complex<X>&);
  template<typename X>
    complex<long double>& operator+=(const complex<X>&);
  template<typename X>
    complex<long double>& operator-=(const complex<X>&);
```

```
template<typename X>
  complex<long double>& operator*=(const complex<X>&);
template<typename X>
  complex<long double>& operator/=(const complex<X>&);
};
```

The complex<long double> class is a straightforward specialization of the complex class template. It changes the operators to pass long double parameters by value instead of by reference.

conj function template Computes conjugate

`template<typename T> complex<T> conj(const complex<T>& z)`

The conj function returns the complex conjugate of z.

cos function template Computes cosine

`template<typename T> complex<T> cos(const complex<T>& z)`

The cos function returns the complex cosine of z.

See Also

cos function in <cmath>

cosh function template Computes hyperbolic cosine

`template<typename T> complex<T> cosh(const complex<T>& z)`

The cosh function returns the complex hyperbolic cosine of z.

See Also

cosh function in <cmath>

exp function template Computes exponential

`template<typename T> complex<T> exp(const complex<T>& z)`

The exp function returns the exponential of z, that is, e^z.

See Also

exp function in <cmath>

imag function template Returns imaginary part

`template<typename T> T imag(const complex<T>& z)`

The imag function returns the imaginary part of z, that is, z.imag( ).

See Also

abs function in <cmath>

log function template

Computes natural logarithm

```
template<typename T> complex<T> log(const complex<T>& z)
```

The log function returns the complex natural (base *e*) logarithm of z. The branch cuts are along the negative real axis, which means the imaginary part of the result is in the range $[-\pi i, \pi i]$.

See Also

log function in <cmath>

log10 function template

Computes common logarithm

```
template<typename T> complex<T> log10(const complex<T>& z)
```

The log10 function returns the complex common (base 10) logarithm of z. The branch cuts are along the negative real axis, which means the imaginary part of the result is in the range $[-\pi i, \pi i]$.

See Also

log10 function in <cmath>

norm function template

Computes normalized value

```
template<typename T> T norm(const complex<T>& z)
```

The norm function returns the square of the absolute value of z.

See Also

abs function template

operator+ function template

Persforms unary positive or addition

```
template<typename T>
  complex<T> operator+(const complex<T>& z);

template<typename T> complex<T>
  operator+(const complex<T>& x, const complex<T>& y);
template<typename T> complex<T>
  operator+(const complex<T>& x, const T& y);
template<typename T> complex<T>
  operator+(const T& x, const complex<T>& y);
```

The unary positive operator returns z.

The binary addition operator returns the sum of its operands. If either operand is of type T, the argument is interpreted as the real part, with an imaginary part of T( ) or 0.

operator- function template

Performs negation or subtraction

```
template<typename T>
  complex<T> operator-(const complex<T>&);

template<typename T>
  complex<T> operator-(const complex<T>&, const complex<T>&);
```

```
template<typename T>
    complex<T> operator-(const complex<T>&, const T&);
template<typename T>
    complex<T> operator-(const T&, const complex<T>&);
```

The unary negation operator returns -z.

The binary subtraction operator returns the difference of its operands. If either operand is of type T, the argument is interpreted as the real part, with an imaginary part of T( ) or 0.

operator* function template   Performs multiplication

```
template<typename T>
    complex<T> operator*(const complex<T>&, const complex<T>&);
template<typename T>
    complex<T> operator*(const complex<T>&, const T&);
template<typename T>
    complex<T> operator*(const T&, const complex<T>&);
```

The binary * operator performs complex multiplication. If either operand is of type T, the argument is interpreted as the real part, with an imaginary part of T( ) or 0.

operator/ function template   Performs division

```
template<typename T>
    complex<T> operator/(const complex<T>&, const complex<T>&);
template<typename T>
    complex<T> operator/(const complex<T>&, const T&);
template<typename T>
    complex<T> operator/(const T&, const complex<T>&);
```

The binary / operator performs complex division. If either operand is of type T, the argument is interpreted as the real part, with an imaginary part of T( ) or 0. Division by zero results in undefined behavior.

operator== function template   Checks equality

```
template<typename T>
    bool operator==(const complex<T>&, const complex<T>&);
template<typename T>
    bool operator==(const complex<T>&, const T&);
template<typename T>
    bool operator==(const T&, const complex<T>&);
```

The == operator returns true if the real and imaginary parts of both values are equal. If either operand is of type T, the argument is interpreted as the real part, with an imaginary part of T( ) or 0.

operator!= function template   Checks inequality

```
template<typename T>
    bool operator!=(const complex<T>&, const complex<T>&);
template<typename T>
    bool operator!=(const complex<T>&, const T&);
```

```
template<typename T>
  bool operator!=(const T&, const complex<T>&);
```

The != operator returns true if the real or imaginary parts are not equal. If either operand is of type T, the parameter is interpreted as the real part, with an imaginary part of T( ) or 0.

---

operator<< function template   Writes a complex number

```
template<typename T, typename charT, typename traits>
  basic_ostream<charT, traits>& operator<<(basic_ostream<charT, traits>&,
                                           const complex<T>& z);
```

The << operator prints z to the output stream in the form (x, y), in which x is the real part, and y is the imaginary part. Example 13-6 shows how z is formatted. If you want more control over the formatting, you must print the value yourself.

Example 13-6. Formatting a complex number

```
template<class T, class charT, class traits>
std::basic_ostream<charT, traits>&
operator<<(std::basic_ostream<charT, traits>& o,
           const std::complex<T>& x)
{
  std::basic_ostringstream<charT, traits> s;
  s.flags(o.flags( ));
  s.imbue(o.getloc( ));
  s.precision(o.precision( ));
  s << "(" << x.real( ) << "," << x.imag( ) << ")";
  return o << s.str( );
}
```

---

operator>> function template   Reads a complex number

```
template<typename T, typename charT, typename traits>
  basic_istream<charT, traits>& operator>>(basic_istream<charT, traits>&,
                                           complex<T>& z);
```

The >> operator reads a complex number from an input stream into z. The input format can be any of the following:

x   The value x is the real part, and T( ) or 0 is the imaginary part.

(x)   The value x is the real part, and T( ) or 0 is the imaginary part.

(x, y)
        The value x is the real part, and y is the imaginary part.

---

polar function template   Converts to polar coordinates

```
template<typename T>
complex<T> polar(const T& r, const T& theta)
```

The polar function returns a complex object that represents the value given in polar coordinates, in which r is the magnitude and theta is the angle (in radians). The resulting value has the following real and imaginary parts:

```
real = r * cos(theta)
imag = r * sin(theta)
```

See Also

abs function template, arg function template

---

pow function template
Computes power

```
template<class T>
  complex<T> pow(const complex<T>& x, int y);
template<class T>
  complex<T> pow(const complex<T>& x, const T& y);
template<class T>
  complex<T> pow(const complex<T>& x, const complex<T>& y);
template<class T>
  complex<T> pow(const T& x, const complex<T>& y);
```

The pow function returns the complex power x^y. If x and y are both 0, the result is implementation-defined; otherwise, the result is exp(y * log(x)). The branch cuts are along the negative real axis.

See Also

exp function template, log function template, pow function in <cmath>

---

real function template
Returns real part

```
template<typename T> T real(const complex<T>& z)
```

The real function returns the real part of z, that is, z.real( ).

---

sin function template
Computes sine

```
template<typename T> complex<T> sin(const complex<T>& z)
```

The sin function returns the complex sine of z.

See Also

sin function in <cmath>

---

sinh function template
Computes hyperbolic sine

```
template<typename T> complex<T> sinh(const complex<T>& z)
```

The sinh function returns the complex hyperbolic sine of z.

See Also

sinh function in <cmath>

---

sqrt function template
Computes square root

```
template<typename T> complex<T> sqrt(const complex<T>& z)
```

The sqrt function returns the complex square root of z. The branch cuts are along the negative real axis. The result always has a nonnegative real part.

See Also

sqrt function in <cmath>

tan function template   Computes tangent

```
template<typename T> complex<T> tan(const complex<T>& z)
```

The tan function returns the complex tangent of z.

See Also

tan function in <cmath>

tanh function template   Computes hyperbolic tangent

```
template<typename T> complex<T> tanh(const complex<T>& z)
```

The tanh function returns the complex hyperbolic tangent of z.

See Also

tanh function in <cmath>

<csetjmp>

The <csetjmp> header is the C++ version of the C standard <setjmp.h> header.

 This chapter presents only the most cursory description of this header because its use is limited in a C++ program. Use exceptions instead of the functions in <csetjmp>.

jmp_buf type   Jump buffer

```
typedef ... jmp_buf;
```

The jmp_buf type is an opaque array type that stores information for the setjmp and longjmp functions.

longjmp function   Performs nonlocal goto

```
void longjmp(jmp_buf env, int val);
```

The longjmp function bypasses the normal function return and unwinds the call stack to the point where setjmp was called with the same jmp_buf environment. When setjmp returns to its caller, it returns val; if val is 0, setjmp returns 1.

Calling longjmp is similar to throwing an exception that is caught at the point of the setjmp call. One important difference, however, is that if any objects on the stack would have been destroyed by throwing an exception, the program's behavior is undefined if you call longjmp. This is why you should use exceptions instead of longjmp.

setjmp function   Establishes nonlocal label

```
int setjmp(jmp_buf env);
```

The setjmp function stores the current execution environment in its argument so that the environment can be restored by a call to longjmp. The first time setjmp is called, it returns 0. When longjmp is called, setjmp returns the val argument that was passed to longjmp; that value is guaranteed to be nonzero.

\<csignal\>

The \<csignal\> header is the C++ version of the standard C \<signal.h\> header. It declares functions and macros related to signal handling.

A *signal* is a condition that can arise during program execution. A signal can originate by an explicit call to raise or abort, from external sources (such as the user inter- rupting the program), or from internal events (such as floating-point errors or memory violations). Each signal has a *handler*, which is a function that the C++ library calls when a signal occurs (called *raising* the signal).

Signals are identified by integers. A program can establish different handlers for different signal numbers. You can choose to ignore a signal by using SIG_IGN as the signal handler. If the signal is raised, no handler is called, and the program continues. Each signal also has a default handler (SIG_DFL). When a program starts, every signal number is initialized with SIG_IGN or SIG_DFL. The details are implementation-defined.

You can set your own handler for any signal by calling the signal function. A handler is a function that takes one parameter: the signal number. The signal handler function is limited in what it can do. Unless a signal is raised by an explicit call to raise or abort, the only useful thing the handler can do is to set a global flag. The type of the flag must be sig_atomic_t.

The standard defines a basic set of signals, and an implementation is free to define additional signals. On the other hand, an implementation is not required to raise any signals. Remember that arithmetic overflow, pointer violations, and the like result in undefined behavior. (See Chapter 4.) Thus, an implementation is free to terminate a program immediately, ignore the error, raise a signal, or do anything else. Some signals are meant to reflect external events, such as the user terminating the program. How the user terminates a program is likewise implementation-defined.

Unix and Unix-like operating systems have much more extensive signal-handling facil- ities. The \<csignal\> handler as documented in this section is portable to all hosted C++ environments, regardless of operating system, although the portable behavior is limited. Most uses of \<csignal\> in real programs take advantage of additional, nonstandard capabilities. Consult your compiler's and library's documentation for details.

raise function   Raises a signal

int **raise**(int sig);

The raise function sends a signal to the running program. The sig parameter is the signal number. The return value is 0 for success or nonzero for an error.

SIG_DFL macro   Default handler

void (***SIG_DFL**)(int)

The SIG_DFL macro represents the default handling of a signal. The macro expands to a constant whose value is suitable as the second argument to the signal function.

SIG_ERR macro   Error return

void (***SIG_ERR**)(int)

The SIG_ERR macro represents the value returned from signal in the event of an error. It expands to a constant expression.

SIG_IGN macro   Ignore signal

void (***SIG_IGN**)(int)

The SIG_IGN macro tells signal to ignore a signal. The macro expands to a constant whose value is suitable as the second argument to the signal function.

SIGABRT macro   Abort signal number

int **SIGABRT**

The SIGABRT macro expands to a positive integer constant that represents an abnormal termination. The abort function raises SIGABRT.

SIGFPE macro   Floating-point error signal number

int **SIGFPE**

The SIGFPE macro expands to a positive integer constant that represents a floating-point exception, such as division by zero. An implementation is not required to raise SIGFPE for a floating-point error.

SIGILL macro   Illegal instruction signal number

int **SIGILL**

The SIGILL macro expands to a positive integer constant that represents an illegal instruction.

SIGINT macro   User interrupt signal number

int **SIGINT**

The SIGINT macro expands to a positive integer constant that represents a user interrupt.

SIGSEGV macro   Segmentation violation signal number

int **SIGSEGV**

The SIGSEGV macro expands to a positive integer constant that represents an addressing fault (segmentation violation).

SIGTERM macro   Terminate signal number

int **SIGTERM**

Description

The SIGTERM macro expands to a positive integer constant that represents a request to terminate the program.

sig_atomic_t type Atomic type

typedef ... **sig_atomic_t**;

The sig_atomic_t type is an integral type that can be accessed atomically—that is, even if a signal is delivered, the entire value is read or written. The actual type is implementation-defined.

signal function Sets a signal handler

void (***signal**(int sig, void (*func)(int)))(int);

The signal function controls the program's behavior when a signal is delivered to the program. The first parameter (sig) is the signal number. The second parameter (func) is the function to call when signal sig is delivered.

The func parameter can also be one of the special values SIG_DFL or SIG_IGN. Use SIG_DFL to get the default behavior; use SIG_IGN to ignore a signal.

The default behavior for a signal is implementation-defined, but it usually results in the termination of the program. The signal handler must not use any C++ features (such as throwing an exception), or the results will be implementation-defined. The function must have "C" linkage.

If the func parameter is a function pointer, that function is called when signal sig is delivered. Unless the signal is delivered by calling abort or raise, the function is highly restricted in what it can do:

- The handler must not call any function in the standard library except signal, and the first parameter must be sig.

- The handler must not refer to any variable with static storage except it can assign a value to a variable of type volatile sig_atomic_t.

- If the signal is the result of a computational error such as SIGFPE, the signal handler must not return, but should call abort or exit. (Yes, this item contradicts the first item.)

Real implementations have looser restrictions, such as allowing calls to other library functions from a signal handler. The library functions that are permitted varies, but every practical implementation allows at least abort. If you must use signal handlers in your program, you will probably need to rely on behavior that is dictated by your host environment, extending the limitations of the C++ standard.

If the handler returns normally, and the signal is not the result of a computational error, execution continues from the point where it was interrupted.

The return value of signal is the previous value of the signal handler for sig, or SIG_ERR for an error. If SIG_ERR is returned, errno is set.

Example 13-7 shows a simple signal handler that sets a global flag when the user interrupts the program. Until the user interrupts it, the program reads input and counts the number of lines the user typed.

Example 13-7. Reading input until the program is interrupted

```
#include <csignal>
#include <iostream>
#include <string>

volatile std::sig_atomic_t interrupted;

// Signal handler sets a global flag
extern "C" void sigint(int sig)
{
  interrupted = 1;
}

int main()
{
  //
  if (std::signal(SIGINT, sigint) == SIG_ERR)
    std::cerr << "Cannot set signal handler\n";
  else
  {
    unsigned long count = 0;              // Count lines.
    while(! interrupted)
    {
      std::cout << "> ";                  // User prompt
      std::string s;
      if (! std::getline(std::cin, s))
        // EOF does not terminate the loop; only SIGINT does this.
        std::cin.clear();
      ++count;
    }
    std::cout << "I counted " << count << " line(s).\n";
  }
}
```

<cstdarg>

The <cstdarg> header is the C++ version of the C standard <stdarg.h> header, which declares macros for accessing the arguments to a function that takes a variable number of arguments, that is, a function that is declared with an ellipsis as the last parameter.

A function that takes a variable number of arguments (called a *variadic function*) must have some way of knowing how many arguments have actually been passed to the function and what their types are. For example, the printf function (in <cstdio>) uses its format string to determine the number and type of arguments.

Example 13-8 shows how a function can use the <cstdarg> macros. The max function takes at least two arguments. The first is a count of the number of remaining arguments; the count must be positive. The template parameter specifies the type of each argument that follows the count.

Example 13-8. Finding the maximum value of any number of arguments

```cpp
#include <cassert>
#include <cstdarg>

// Use a trivial wrapper class to ensure that va_end is called.
class varargs {
public:
  ~varargs() { va_end(ap); }
  std::va_list& ap;
};

template <typename T>
T max(unsigned count, ...)
{
  assert(count > 0);
  varargs va;
  va_start(va.ap, count);
  T result = va_arg(va.ap, T);   // Get first argument.
  while (--count > 0) {
    T arg = va_arg(va.ap, T);    // Get successive arguments.
    if (arg > result)
      result = arg;              // Remember the largest.
  }
  return result;
}

int main()
{
  int a, b, c, d;
  ...
  int x = max<int>(4, a, b, c, d);
  int y = max<int>(2, x, 42);
  return y;
}
```

va_arg macro

Gets next argument

T **va_arg**(va_list ap, T)

The va_arg macro fetches the next argument, which must be of type T. The ap parameter must have been initialized by calling va_start. The type T must be a type that results from the standard type promotions (Chapter 3) or else the behavior is undefined. For example, T cannot be char, but must be int because the standard promotion of type char is to type int (or, in rare circumstances, unsigned int). The behavior is undefined if there is no next argument.

va_end macro

Ends getting arguments

void **va_end**(va_list ap)

The va_end macro finishes fetching arguments. You must call va_end once for each call to va_start. You cannot nest calls to va_start and va_end, but you can call them multiple times sequentially in the same function.

va_list type

typedef ... **va_list**;

The va_list type is an opaque type that refers to the function's arguments. Declare a local variable of type va_list and supply the variable to the va_start, va_arg, and va_ end macros.

va_start macro

void **va_start**(va_list& ap, lastNamedParm)

The va_start macro initializes ap and prepares to fetch function arguments with va_ arg. You must call va_end to clean up and finalize ap. The second argument to va_start is the name of the function's last parameter before the ellipsis. The last named parameter must not have a function, array, or reference type.

<cstddef>

The <cstddef> header is the C++ version of the C standard <stddef.h> header, which declares a few types and macros.

The C header declares the wchar_t type, but wchar_t is a reserved keyword in C++, so there is no need to #include <cstddef> to declare this type.

NULL macro

#define **NULL** ...

The NULL macro expands to a null pointer constant, such as 0 or 0L.

Some C libraries declare NULL as ((void*)0) in *stddef.h*. This definition is fine for C, but is wrong for C++. Most C++ compilers correctly declare NULL, but you should be aware of the difference.

offsetof macro

size_t **offsetof**(*type*, *member-name*)

The offsetof macro returns the offset, in bytes, of a member of a struct as a constant integer. The *type* must be a plain, C-style struct (Plain Old Data, or POD), and the expression &(t.*member-name*) must be an address constant, assuming t is an instance of *type*. In particular, this means the *member-name* must not be a bit-field, a static member, or a function member. (See Chapter 6 for more information about POD types.)

ptrdiff_t type

typedef ... **ptrdiff_t**

 The ptrdiff_t type is a signed integral type that represents the difference between two pointers. The exact type is implementation-defined.

size_t type

sizeof result type

typedef ... size_t

The size_t type is the type of the result of the sizeof operator. It is an unsigned integral type. The exact type is implementation-defined.

<cstdio>

The <cstdio> header is a wrapper for the C standard <stdio.h> header, which declares input and output types, macros, and functions. See also <cwchar> for wide character I/O functions.

C++ I/O streams offer more flexibility, type-safety, and clarity. On the other hand, C I/O offers simplicity and compatibility with C libraries. See Chapter 9 for an overview of the C++ I/O stream classes.

_IOFBF macro

Full buffering

int _IOFBF

When passed as the mode parameter to setvbuf, the _IOFBF macro sets an open file to full buffering. A buffer is flushed when it is full. The _IOFBF macro expands to a constant integer.

Support for fully-buffered streams is implementation-dependent.

See Also

setvbuf function

_IOLBF macro

Line buffering

int _IOLBF

When passed as the mode parameter to setvbuf, the _IOLBF macro sets an open file to line buffering. A buffer is flushed when it is full or when a newline character is read or written. The _IOLBF macro expands to a constant integer.

Support for line-buffered streams is implementation-dependent.

See Also

setvbuf function

_IONBF macro

No buffering

const int _IONBF

When passed as the mode parameter to setvbuf, the _IONBF macro disables the buffering of an open file. Characters are read or written as soon as possible, without buffering. The _IONBF macro expands to a constant integer.

Support for unbuffered streams is implementation-dependent. For example, a host operating system might line buffer input from a terminal, even if a program requests unbuffered input.

Library Reference

See Also

setvbuf function

BUFSIZ macro

Buffer size

int **BUFSIZ**

The BUFSIZ macro specifies the minimum buffer size for the setbuf function. The BUFSIZ macro expands to a constant integer.

See Also

setbuf function, setvbuf function

clearerr function

Clears error status

void **clearerr**(FILE* stream)

The clearerr function clears the error and end-of-file indicators for stream.

See Also

feof function, ferror function

EOF macro

End-of-file or error

int **EOF**

The EOF macro represents end-of-file when returned from getchar and other functions. Some functions return EOF to indicate an error.

The value of EOF is a negative integer constant. The precise value is implementation-defined.

fclose function

Closes a file

int **fclose**(FILE* stream)

The fclose function flushes and closes an open file. It returns 0 upon success or EOF when there is an error.

See Also

fopen function

feof function

Tests for end-of-file

int **feof**(FILE* stream)

The feof function returns true (nonzero) if stream is positioned at the end-of-file, or false (0) otherwise.

See Also

clearerr function, ferror function

ferror function

int **ferror**(FILE* stream)

The ferror function returns true (nonzero) if stream has an error condition set, or false (0) otherwise.

See Also

clearerr function, feof function

fgetc function

int **fgetc**(FILE* stream)

The fgetc function reads a single character from stream. It returns the character as an unsigned char converted to int or EOF for an error or end-of-file.

See Also

feof function, ferror function, getc macro, fputc function, fwgetc in <cwchar>

fgetpos function

int **fgetpos**(FILE* stream, fpos_t* pos)

The fgetpos function stores stream's current position in the object that pos points to. The only use for the position is to save it and pass it to fsetpos to set the file's position. You cannot use the position arithmetically, e.g., to advance the position by one character.

The return value is 0 for success or nonzero for failure. If fgetpos fails, it sets errno.

See Also

fpos_t type, fsetpos function, ftell function

fgets function

char* **fgets**(char* s, int n, FILE* stream)

The fgets function reads a line of text from stream into the character array that s points to. It stops reading after a newline character or after n − 1 characters have been read. The newline character, if one is encountered, is copied into s.

The return value is s for success or a null pointer for an error or end-of-file. If fgets fails, the contents of the string s are undefined.

See Also

fgetc function, getc macro, fputs function, fwgets in <cwchar>

FILE type

typedef ... **FILE**

The FILE type represents the contents of an external file. A C++ program works with FILE pointers, in which the actual FILE objects are managed by functions in the standard library. Thus, you never need to allocate or free FILE objects.

See Also

fclose function, fopen function, freopen function, <fstream>

FILENAME_MAX macro
Maximum length of a filename

int **FILENAME_MAX**

FILENAME_MAX is the size you should use when declaring a character array that will store a filename. Some systems do not have a fixed maximum size for a filename, in which case FILENAME_MAX is a recommended size, and the resulting character array might not be large enough to hold all valid filenames. The FILENAME_MAX macro expands to a constant integer.

Use std::string instead of a character array to avoid any problems with character arrays that are too small.

---

fopen function
Opens a file

FILE* **fopen**(const char* filename, const char* mode)

The fopen function opens a file.

 The filename parameter specifies the filename in an implementation-defined manner. The mode parameter specifies how to open the file. The mode must begin with one of the strings listed in Table 13-4. Additional characters can follow, and the interpretation of the extra characters is implementation-defined. Mode strings are case-sensitive.

Table 13-4. File open modes

Mode string	Description
a	Append: opens an existing file for appending, that is, every write is forced to the end of the file. If the file to be opened does not exist, a creates it.
r	Read: opens an existing file for reading.
w	Write: creates a new file for writing. If the file already exists, w truncates it to zero length.
ab	Append in binary mode.
rb	Read in binary mode.
wb	Write in binary mode.
a+	Append update: opens a file in append mode and allows it to be read.
r+	Read update: opens an existing file for reading, and also allows writing.
w+	Write update: creates a new file for writing, and also allows reading. If the file already exists, w+ truncates it to zero length.
ab+ or a+b	Append update in binary mode.
rb+ or r+b	Read update in binary mode.
wb+ or w+b	Write update in binary mode.

See Also

fclose function, freopen function

FOPEN_MAX macro
Minimum limit on the number of open files

int **FOPEN_MAX**

A typical operating system has a maximum number of files that can be open at one time. This number might be variable or fixed; FOPEN_MAX is the guaranteed minimum value of the limit. The FOPEN_MAX macro expands to a constant integer.

See Also

fopen function

---

fpos_t type
File position

typedef ... **fpos_t**

The fpos_t type is an opaque type that represents a position in a file. The only way to set the value of an fpos_t object is to call fgetpos, and the only things you can do with the value are assign an fpos_t value to it and pass it as a function argument, especially to fsetpos.

See Also

fgetpos function, fsetpos function, fpos in <ios>

---

fprintf function
Writes formatted data

int **fprintf**(FILE* stream, const char* format, ...)

The fprintf function writes formatted output to stream. The format parameter contains the formatting information, and the remaining arguments are printed according to the format. The return value is the number of characters printed, or a negative value for an error.

Characters in format are printed verbatim except for conversion specifications, which begin with a percent sign (%). Each conversion specification is made up of the following parts (in order): flags, field width, precision, size, and conversion specifier.

The following are detailed descriptions of the parts of a conversion specification:

Flags
> The flag characters are optional and can appear in any order. Table 13-5 lists the flag characters and their meanings.

Table 13-5. Formatting flag characters

Flag	Description
-	Left-justified (default is right-justified).
+	Signed conversions always begin with a sign (default is to use a sign only if the value is negative).
Space	The output is an initial space character if a signed conversion results in an empty string or a string that does not start with a sign character (+ takes precedence over space).
#	Use an alternate form: insert a 0 for %o; insert 0x for %x or 0X for %X; always output a decimal point for floating-point conversions; do not remove trailing zeros for %g or %G; behavior is undefined for other conversions.
0	Fields are padded with leading zeros (after the sign or base indication). The - flag takes precedence over 0. For integer conversions, a precision takes precedence over the 0 flag.

<cstdio> | 417

Field width

An optional number that specifies the minimum number of characters that the field will occupy. If the field is an asterisk (*), the field width is obtained from the next argument to be processed.

Precision

An optional number of digits for an integer, number of decimal digits for a floating-point number, or maximum size for a string. The precision is specified as a dot (.) followed by a number or an asterisk.

Size

The character h, l, or L. h means an integer is short or unsigned short. l means an integer is long or unsigned long, a character is wint_t, or a string is a pointer to wchar_t. L means a floating-point number is long double.

Conversion character

Specifies the type of the argument containing the data to be printed using a conversion specification. It must be one of the following:

d, i Signed decimal integer.

o   Unsigned octal integer.

u   Unsigned decimal integer.

x, X Unsigned hexadecimal integer. x writes the digits a–f in lowercase, and X writes the digits A–F in uppercase.

f   Fixed-precision floating point.

e, E Exponential floating point. The exponent is introduced with e or E, matching the conversion character.

g, G General floating point. Use style f or e. Use style e if the exponent is less than –4 or greater than the precision; otherwise, use style f. Trailing zeros are dropped, and a trailing decimal point is dropped if it would be the last character.

c   Character. The argument must be an unsigned char promoted to int, or, if the l size modifier is used, the argument must be wchar_t promoted to wint_t, which is then printed as a multibyte character.

s   String. The argument is a pointer to a null-terminated array of characters, or, if the l size modifier is used, the argument must be a pointer to a wchar_t array, which is converted to a series of multibyte characters.

p   Pointer. The argument must be a pointer to void. The output format is implementation-defined.

n   The argument must be a pointer to an integer; fprintf stores in the integer the number of characters written so far. Use the h or l size modifiers if the argument is a pointer to short int or long int.

%   Prints a literal %.

It is your responsibility to ensure that the argument types match the format. Any errors result in undefined behavior. Mismatches between format and the argument is a common and sometimes subtle source of error. You can avoid these problems entirely by using C++ I/O streams instead of fprintf and related functions.

All the printf-related functions interpret the format string identically.

Example

The following are examples of calling printf:

```
long double pi = 3.141592653589792L;
int i = 42;
const char greeting[] = "Hello, how are you?";

printf(">%d %% %Lg<\n", i, pi); // Prints >42 % 3.14159<
printf(">%4d<\n", i);           // Prints >  42<
printf(">%-16.8Le<\n", pi);     // Prints >3.14159265e+00  <
printf(">%#*.*x<\n", 8, 4, i);  // Prints >  0x002a<
printf(">%.5s<\n", greeting);   // Prints >Hello<
```

See Also

fscanf function, printf function, sprintf function, vfprintf function, wcrtomb in <cwchar>, fwprintf in <cwchar>

---

fputc function

Writes a character

```
int fputc(int c, FILE* stream)
```

The fputc function writes a single character to stream. The character must be an unsigned char, which is automatically promoted to int, so the proper way to print a variable of type char is as follows:

```
char ch;
fputc(static_cast<unsigned char>(ch), stream);
```

The return value is EOF for an error or c for success.

See Also

putc macro, fwputc in <cwchar>

---

fputs function

Writes a string

```
int fputs(const char* s, FILE* stream)
```

The fputs function writes the string s to stream. It returns EOF for an error or a nonnegative value for success.

See Also

fputc function, puts function, fwputs in <cwchar>

---

fread function

Reads binary data

```
size_t fread(void* ptr, size_t size, size_t count, FILE* stream)
```

The fread function reads up to count elements from stream into the memory that ptr points to. The memory must have POD type (see Chapter 6). Each element is size bytes long. It returns the number of elements that were read successfully.

See Also

fwrite function

freopen function   Opens a file with an existing stream

`FILE* freopen(const char* filename, const char* mode, FILE* stream)`

The freopen function opens a file using an existing stream. The file previously associated with the stream is closed first, and the named file is opened in the same manner as if fopen were called. See fopen for a description of the mode parameter.

The main purpose of using freopen is to reopen one of the standard files: stdin, stdout, and stderr.

See Also

fclose function, fopen function

fscanf function   Reads formatted data

`int fscanf(FILE* stream, const char* format, ...)`

The fscanf function performs a formatted read from stream. The format parameter contains formatting information, and the remaining arguments are pointers. When fscanf reads items, it stores their values in the objects that successive arguments point to. The return value is the number of items read or a negative value for an error.

Items are read from stream and interpreted according to format, which contains whitespace characters, non-whitespace characters, and conversion specifications, which begin with a percent sign (%). A whitespace character directs fscanf to skip over whitespace in the input stream. Non-whitespace characters must match the input text. Each conversion specification is made up of the following parts (in order): assignment suppression, field width, size, and conversion specifier.

The following are descriptions of the conversion specification elements:

Assignment suppression
> An optional asterisk (*) directs fscanf to read and parse the input according to the conversion specification, but not to assign the value to an argument.

Field width
> An optional number (positive decimal integer) that specifies the maximum number of characters to read.

Size
> The character h, l, or L. h means an integer is short or unsigned short. l means an integer is long or unsigned long; a floating-point number is double, or a string argument is a pointer to wchar_t for the c, s, and [conversion specifiers. L means a floating-point number is long double. The default size for an integer is int or unsigned int, float for a floating-point number, and char for any of the character conversion specifiers.

Conversion character
> Specifies the type of the argument containing the data to be printed using a conversion specification. It must be one of the following:

> d   Signed decimal integer.

> i   Signed integer. Reads and interprets a prefix of 0x or 0X for hexadecimal, 0 for octal, or anything else for decimal.

> o   Unsigned octal integer.

> u   Unsigned decimal integer.

x, X   Unsigned hexadecimal integer.

e, E, f, g, G
       Floating point in fixed or exponential format.

c   Characters. The field width (default 1) specifies the exact number of charac-
       ters to read. The corresponding argument must be a pointer to a character
       array large enough to hold the characters. If the l modifier is used, the input
       is read as multibyte characters, which are converted to wide characters and
       stored in a wchar_t array. In either case, no null character is appended.

s   String. Reads a sequence of non-whitespace characters. The corresponding
       argument must be a pointer to a character array that is large enough to hold
       the sequence plus a terminating null character. If the l modifier is used, the
       input is read as multibyte characters, which are converted to wide characters
       and stored in a wchar_t array, followed by a terminating null wide character.

p   Pointer. The argument must be a pointer to void. The input format is imple-
       mentation-defined and matches the format that fprintf uses.

n   The argument must be a pointer to an integer; fscanf stores in the integer the
       number of characters read so far. The h or l size modifiers can be used if the
       argument is a pointer to short int or long int. Nothing is read from the
       input, and %n does not affect the count returned by fscanf.

[Matches a sequence of characters. The conversion specification lists a set of
       characters (called the *scanset*) in square brackets. The input string is a
       sequence of characters that matches any of the characters in the scanset or, if
       the scanset begins with a circumflex (^), any character not in the scanset. If
       the l modifier is used, the input is read as multibyte characters, which are
       converted to wide characters and stored in a wchar_t array, followed by a
       terminating null wide character.

%   Matches a literal % in the input stream.

It is your responsibility to ensure that the argument types match the
format. Any errors result in undefined behavior. Mismatches
between format and the argument are a common and sometimes
subtle source of error. You can avoid these problems entirely by
using C++ I/O streams instead of fscanf and related functions.

All the scanf-related functions interpret the format string identically.

Example
The following is an example of calling scanf. The input stream is:

    start 3.14 BeefFeed cab42.0e-01, 1234

and the scanf call is:

    char c[10];
    double d;
    float f;
    long int l;
    unsigned short us;
    scanf("start %4lf %4lx%*x %9[abcdefg]%f,%hu", &d, &l, c, &f, &us);

which has the following result:

    c = "cab"

```
d = 3.14
f = 4.2
l = 48879 (0xbeef)
us = 1234
```

See Also

`fprintf` function, `scanf` function, `sscanf` function, `vfscanf` function, `mbrtowc` in `<cwchar>`, `fwscanf` in `<cwchar>`

fseek function   Changes file position

`int fseek(FILE* stream, long int offset, int origin)`

The `fseek` function seeks to a different position in `stream`. The `origin` must be one of `SEEK_CUR`, `SEEK_END`, or `SEEK_SET`. The `offset` is relative to the current position, end-of-file, or start-of-file, respectively. The end-of-file flag is cleared, and any ungetc character is also cleared.

Use `fsetpos` instead of `fseek` when using large files—that is, for which a position does not necessarily fit into a `long int`.

The return value is 0 for success or nonzero for an error.

See Also

`fsetpos` function, `ftell` function, `SEEK_CUR` macro, `SEEK_END` macro, `SEEK_SET` macro

fsetpos function   Changes file position

`int fsetpos(FILE* stream, const fpos_t* pos)`

The `fsetpos` function seeks to a different position in `stream`. The position must have been returned from an earlier successful call to `fgetpos`.

See Also

`fpos_t` type, `fseek` function, `fgetpos` function

ftell function   Returns current file position

`long int ftell(FILE* stream)`

The `ftell` function returns the current file position in `stream`. This position can be used (with an origin of `SEEK_SET`) in a subsequent call to `fseek`. If `ftell` fails, it returns `-1L` (which may be, but is not necessarily, the same value as `EOF`).

See Also

`fgetpos` function, `fseek` function

fwrite function   Writes binary data

`size_t fwrite(const void* ptr, size_t size, size_t count, FILE* stream)`

The `fwrite` function writes up to count elements to `stream`. Each element is size bytes long, and `ptr` points to the first such element. The memory must have POD type (see Chapter 6).

The return value is the number of complete elements successfully written to `stream`.

See Also

fread function

---

getc macro
Reads a character

int **getc**(FILE* stream)

The getc macro reads a character from stream and returns that character as an unsigned char. The return value is EOF for end-of-file or a read error.

See Also

fgetc function, getchar macro, putc macro

---

getchar macro
Reads a character from stdin

int **getchar**( )

The getchar macro is equivalent to getc(stdin).

See Also

fgetc function, getc macro, putchar macro

---

gets function
Reads a string unsafely

char* **gets**(char* s)

The gets function reads a line of text (up to and including a newline) into the string s.

 There is no way to limit the input to the size of s, so you should never call gets. Use fgets instead.

See Also

fgets function, getchar macro

L_tmpnam macro
Length of temporary filename

int **L_tmpnam**

L_tmpnam is the length of a temporary filename for tmpnam. The L_tmpnam macro expands to a constant integer.

See Also

tmpnam function

NULL macro
Null pointer constant

#define **NULL** ...

The NULL macro expands to a null pointer constant. See <cstddef> for more information.

See Also

NULL in <cstddef>

Library Reference

perror function

Writes an error message

void **perror**(const char* s)

The perror function writes an error message to stderr. If s is not null and is not an empty string, it is printed first, followed by a colon and a space. The error message is printed next and is the same text as that returned by strerror, passing errno as its argument.

See Also

errno in <cerrno>, strerror in <cstring>

printf function

Writes formatted data

int **printf**(const char* format, ...)

The printf function is equivalent to calling fprintf to stdout. See fprintf for information about the format string.

See Also

fprintf function, vprintf function, wprintf in <cwchar>

putc macro

Writes a character

int **putc**(int c, FILE* stream)

The putc macro writes the character c, which must be cast to unsigned char, to stream.

See Also

fputc function, putchar macro, wputc in <cwchar>

putchar macro

Writes a character to stdout

int **putchar**(int c)

The putchar macro is equivalent to putc(c, stdout).

See Also

fputc function, putc macro, wputchar in <cwchar>

puts function

Writes a string

int **puts**(const char* s)

The puts function writes a string to stdout.

See Also

fputs function, putc function, wputs in <cwchar>

remove function

Deletes a file

int **remove**(const char* filename)

The remove function deletes the file named by filename. It returns 0 for success or nonzero for an error.

See Also

rename function

rename function
Renames a file

int **rename**(const char* oldname, const char* newname)

The rename function renames the file specified by oldname to newname. The return value is 0 for success or nonzero for failure.

See Also

remove function

rewind function
Resets file position

void **rewind**(FILE* stream)

The rewind function moves a file position to the beginning of a file and is equivalent to fseek(stream, 0, SEEK_SET).

See Also

fseek function, fsetpos function

SEEK_CUR macro
Seek from current file position

int **SEEK_CUR**

Pass SEEK_CUR as the last parameter to fseek to seek from the current file position. Positive offset values seek toward the end of the file, and negative values seek toward the beginning of the file. The SEEK_CUR macro expands to a constant integer.

See Also

fseek function

SEEK_END macro
Seek from end-of-file

int **SEEK_END**

Pass SEEK_END as the last parameter to fseek to seek relative to the end of the file. Positive offset values seek past the end of the file, and negative values seek toward the beginning of the file. The SEEK_END macro expands to a constant integer.

See Also

fseek function

SEEK_SET macro
Seek from beginning of file

int **SEEK_SET**

Pass SEEK_SET as the last parameter to fseek to seek from the start of the file. Positive offset values seek toward the end of the file. The SEEK_SET macro expands to a constant integer.

See Also

fseek function

setbuf function
Sets file buffer

void **setbuf**(FILE* stream, char* buf)

The setbuf function sets the buffer to use when reading from or writing to stream. The size of buf must be at least BUFSIZ characters.

See Also

BUFSIZ macro, setvbuf function

setvbuf function
Sets file buffer

int **setvbuf**(FILE* stream, char* buf, int mode, size_t size)

The setvbuf function sets the buffering for stream. The mode determines the buffering mode: no buffering (_IONBF), line buffering (_IOLBF), or full buffering (_IOFBF). You can supply a buffer in the buf argument, with size as the buffer size, or use a null pointer for the buf argument to let setvbuf allocate the buffer. (The buffer will be freed when the file is closed or setvbuf is called to change the buffering.)

Call setvbuf before performing any I/O on stream.

See Also

_IOFBF macro, _IOLBF macro, _IONBF macro, setbuf function

size_t type
Size type

typedef ... **size_t**;

The size_t type is the type of the result of the sizeof operator. It is an unsigned integral type. The exact type is implementation-defined.

See Also

size_t in <cstddef>

sprintf function
Writes formatted data to a string

int **sprintf**(char* s, const char* format, ...)

The sprintf function is like fprintf, but instead of writing to an open file, it "writes" by copying characters to the string s. See fprintf for a description of the format parameter.

You must ensure that s is large enough for the formatted string. For some formats, this is impossible, which makes sprintf unsafe to use.

See Also

fprintf function, sscanf function, vsprintf function, wsprintf in <cwchar>, <sstream>

sscanf function
Reads formatted data from a string

int **sscanf**(const char* s, const char* format, ...)

The sscanf function is like fscanf, but instead of reading from an open file, it "reads" characters from the string s. See fscanf for a description of the format parameter.

See Also

fscanf function, sprintf function, vsscanf function, swscanf in <cwchar>, <sstream>

---

stderr macro
Standard error file

FILE* **stderr**

The stderr macro is a standard file, suitable for printing error messages. Its buffering is implementation-defined: either unbuffered or line buffered.

See Also

cerr in <iostream>, clog in <iostream>

---

stdin macro
Standard input file

FILE* **stdin**

The stdin macro is a standard file used for reading from the program's standard input device. stdin is fully buffered if the standard input is not an interactive device.

See Also

cin in <iostream>

---

stdout macro
Standard output file

FILE* **stdout**

The stdout macro is a standard file used to print to the program's standard output device. stdout is fully buffered if the standard output is not an interactive device.

See Also

cout in <iostream>

TMP_MAX macro
Size of temporary filename

int **TMP_MAX**

The TMP_MAX macro is the number of unique names the tmpnam function generates.

See Also

tmpnam function

---

tmpfile function
Opens a temporary file

FILE* **tmpfile( )**

The tmpfile function generates a unique filename and opens a file with that name using mode "wb+". When the program terminates normally, the file is automatically deleted. If the temporary file cannot be created, a null pointer is returned.

See Also

tmpnam function

tmpnam function

Returns a temporary filename

char* **tmpnam**(char* s)

The tmpnam function generates a unique filename and returns a pointer to that name. If the s parameter is not null, it must point to an array of at least L_tmpnam characters, the new filename is copied into that array, and s is returned. If s is null, a static character array is returned; the contents of the array are overwritten each time tmpnam is called.

The tmpnam function has a race condition: after it generates a "unique" filename, but before the file is actually created, another program might generate the same "unique" filename. Use tmpfile instead of tmpnam to ensure that the file is created, thereby ensuring that its name is unique.

See Also

L_tmpnam macro, tmpfile function

ungetc function

Pushes a character back for reading later

int **ungetc**(int c, FILE* stream)

The ungetc function pushes back the character c (which must be an unsigned char), so the next read from stream will return c. The standard guarantees that you can push back just one character, though in some situations, you may be able to push back more.

The return value is c for success or EOF for an error.

See Also

fgetc function, getc macro, getchar macro, ungetwc in <cwchar>

vfprintf function

Writes formatted data

```
#include <cstdarg>
int vfprintf(FILE* stream, const char* format, va_list arg)
```

The vfprintf function is like fprintf, but the values to print are taken from successive arguments in arg (obtained by calling va_start(arg, *param*)). Use vfprintf to write your own fprintf-like function.

Example

The following shows how you can implement fprintf in terms of vfprintf:

```
int fprintf(std::FILE* stream, const char* format, ...)
{
  std::va_list ap;
  va_start(ap, format);
  int result = vfprintf(stream, format, ap);
  va_end(ap);
  return result;
}
```

See Also

fprintf function, vfwprintf in <cwchar>, <cstdarg>

---

vprintf function

```
#include <cstdarg>
int vprintf(const char* format, va_list arg)
```

The vprintf function is like printf, but the values to print are taken from successive arguments in arg (obtained by calling va_start(arg, *param*)). Use vprintf to write your own printf-like function.

See Also

printf function, vwprintf in <cwchar>, <cstdarg>

---

vsprintf function

```
#include <cstdarg>
int vsprintf(char* s, const char* format, va_list arg)
```

The vsprintf function is like sprintf, but the values to print are taken from successive arguments in arg (obtained by calling va_start(arg, *param*)). Use vsprintf to write your own sprintf-like function.

See Also

sprintf function, vswprintf in <cwchar>, <cstdarg>

<cstdlib>

The <cstdlib> header is the C++ version of the C standard <stdlib.h> header, which declares macros, types, and functions of general utility. Several functions in <cstdlib> convert character arrays to numbers. You can also use a string stream (see <sstream>) if you want more control over the conversion, or if you need to convert a number to a string.

The multibyte functions (mblen, etc.) have counterparts in <cwchar> that are reentrant, that is, the <cwchar> functions take an explicit mbstate_t* parameter to avoid using an internal, static shift state.

---

abort function

```
void abort()
```

The abort function raises the SIGABRT signal. Unless the program has registered a handler for SIGABRT, the default action is to terminate the program without destroying any automatic or static objects and without calling any atexit functions.

See Also

atexit function, exit function, raise in <csignal>, SIGABRT in <csignal>

abs function Computes an absolute value

```
int abs(int x)
long abs(long x)
```

The abs function returns the absolute value of x. The <cmath> header declares floating-point versions of the abs function.

See Also

labs function, abs function in <cmath>

atexit function Calls a function at program termination

```
extern "C"   int atexit(void (*func)())
extern "C++" int atexit(void (*func)())
```

The atexit function registers a parameterless function, func, which is called when the program exits normally.

Multiple functions can be registered, and registered functions are called in the opposite order of registration. A function can be registered more than once, in which case it will be called as many times as it was registered.

The atexit functions are not called if the program exits due to a signal, such as SIGABRT.

See Also

abort function, exit function

atof function Converts a string to floating point

```
double atof(const char* str)
```

The atof function reads a floating-point number from the character array str and returns the value of the floating-point number. The conversion is similar to calling strtod(str, NULL).

See Also

atoi function, atol function, strtod function

atoi function Converts a string to an integer

```
int atoi(const char* str)
```

The atoi function reads an integer from the character array str and returns the value of the number. The atoi function is equivalent to calling static_cast<int> (strtol(str, NULL, 10)).

See Also

atof function, atol function, strtod function

atol function Converts a string to a long integer

```
long atol(const char* str)
```

The atol function reads an integer from the character array str, and returns the value of the number. The conversion is similar to calling strtol(str, NULL, 10).

See Also

atof function, atoi function, strtol function, strtoul func

---

bsearch function

Performs a binary search

```
extern "C"
  void* bsearch(const void* key, const void* base, size_t count, size_t size, int
          (*compare)(const void*, const void*))
extern "C++"
  void* bsearch(const void* key, const void* base, size_t count, size_t size, int
          (*compare)(const void*, const void*))
```

The bsearch function uses a binary search to search for key in the array base, in which each element takes up size bytes. There are count elements in the array.

The compare function is called with key as the first argument and a pointer into the array as the second. The function should return an integer less than zero if the key is less than the array element, greater than zero if the key is larger, or 0 if the key is the same as the array element.

The bsearch function returns a pointer to the array element that matches key or a null pointer if no element matches.

Two versions of bsearch are declared so the compare function can have "C" linkage or "C++" linkage.

See Also

qsort function, binary_search in <algorithm>

---

calloc function

Allocates memory

```
void* calloc(size_t count, size_t size)
```

The calloc function allocates count elements, each of size bytes, and initializes the allocated memory to all zeros. It returns a pointer to the start of the newly allocated memory or a null pointer if there is insufficient memory to fulfill the request. The pointer is suitably aligned for any type.

C++ programs should use the new operator instead of calling calloc. Call fill or memset to fill the allocated memory with zeros.

See Also

free function, malloc function, realloc function, new keyword, fill in <algorithm>, memset in <cstring>

---

div function

Computes quotient and remainder

```
div_t div(int numerator, int denominator)
ldiv_t div(long numerator, long denominator)
```

The div function divides numerator by denominator and returns the quotient and the remainder in a structure.

See Also

div_t type, ldiv function

div_t type
Quotient and remainder type

struct **div_t** { int quot, rem; }

The div_t type is used only by the div function to return the quotient and remainder of an integer division. The order of the quot and rem members in the structure may vary between implementations.

See Also

div function, ldiv_t type

exit function
Terminates the program normally

void **exit**(int code)

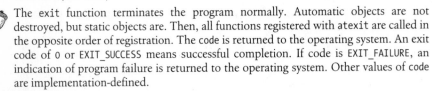 The exit function terminates the program normally. Automatic objects are not destroyed, but static objects are. Then, all functions registered with atexit are called in the opposite order of registration. The code is returned to the operating system. An exit code of 0 or EXIT_SUCCESS means successful completion. If code is EXIT_FAILURE, an indication of program failure is returned to the operating system. Other values of code are implementation-defined.

See Also

abort function, atexit function

EXIT_FAILURE macro
Exit status for unsuccessful termination

int **EXIT_FAILURE**

Pass EXIT_FAILURE to exit to terminate the program normally and informs the operating system that the program was unsuccessful. Returning EXIT_FAILURE from main is the same as calling exit. The EXIT_FAILURE macro expands to an integer constant.

See Also

exit function

EXIT_SUCCESS macro
Exit status for successful termination

int **EXIT_SUCCESS**

Pass EXIT_SUCCESS to exit to terminate the program normally and inform the operating system that the program was successful. Returning EXIT_SUCCESS from main is the same as calling exit.

The value 0 also means success, but EXIT_SUCCESS is not necessarily equal to 0. The EXIT_SUCCESS macro expands to an integer constant.

See Also

exit function

free function

void **free**(void* ptr)

The free function releases the memory that ptr points to. The pointer must have been returned by a call to malloc or calloc. After freeing the pointer, do not refer to the memory again.

See Also

calloc function, malloc function, realloc function, delete keyword

getenv function

char* **getenv**(const char* name)

The getenv function obtains the value of an environment variable. The environment is a system-defined list of name/value pairs. The getenv function searches the environment for name and returns the associated value. The getenv function returns a null pointer if the specified name is not found.

labs function

long **labs**(long x)

The labs function returns the absolute value of x.

See Also

abs function, abs function in <cmath>

ldiv function

ldiv_t **ldiv**(long numerator, long denominator)

The ldiv function divides numerator by denominator and returns the quotient and remainder in a structure.

See Also

div function, ldiv_t type

ldiv_t type

struct **ldiv_t** { long quot, rem; }

The ldiv_t type is used only as the return type for the ldiv function and the overloaded div function. It stores the quotient and remainder of a long integer division.

See Also

div_t type, ldiv function

malloc function

void* **malloc**(size_t size)

The malloc function allocates size bytes of memory. It returns a pointer to the start of the newly allocated memory or a null pointer if there is insufficient memory to fulfill the request. The pointer is suitably aligned for any type.

C++ programs should use the new operator instead of calling `malloc`.

See Also

`calloc` function, `free` function, `realloc` function, `new` keyword

MB_CUR_MAX function   Maximum size of a multibyte character

`int MB_CUR_MAX`

The `MB_CUR_MAX` macro is the maximum number of bytes required to represent a multibyte character in the extended character set, in any locale.

See Also

`mblen` function, `mbtowc` function, `wctomb` function, `MB_LEN_MAX` in `<climits>`, `<clocale>`

---

mblen function   Returns number of bytes in a multibyte character

`int mblen(const char* s, size_t n)`

The `mblen` function returns the length of the multibyte character pointed to by s. The character array s can be null, it can point to an empty string, or it must have at least n bytes, which must form a valid multibyte character.

If s is null, the return value depends on whether multibyte characters have state-dependent encodings. (See Chapter 8 for a discussion of shift state.) The `mblen` function returns a nonzero value if encodings are state-dependent or 0 if encodings are not state-dependent.

If s points to an empty string, 0 is returned.

If s points to a valid multibyte character, the number of bytes that make up that character is returned. If s points to an invalid multibyte character, -1 is returned.

See Also

`MB_CUR_MAX` macro, `mbtowc` function, `mbrlen` in `<cwchar>`

---

mbstowcs function   Converts multibyte string to wide string

`size_t mbstowcs(whcar_t* dst, const char* src, size_t n)`

The `mbstowcs` function converts a multibyte string to a wide character string. The src parameter points to the null-terminated multibyte string. Up to n wide characters are stored in dst. If fewer than n characters are stored, a null wide character is appended to the wide character array.

The return value is the number of wide characters stored in dst. If any multibyte character in src is not valid, the return value is `static_cast<size_t>(-1)`.

See Also

`mbtowc` function, `wcstombc` function, `mbcrtowcs` in `<cwchar>`

---

mbtowc function
Converts multibyte character to wide character

`int `**`mbtowc`**`(wchar_t* pwc, const char* src, size_t n)`

The `mbtowc` function converts a multibyte character sequence to a single wide character. It starts by counting the number of bytes in `src` that make up the first multibyte character. It examines only the first n bytes.

If `src` is null, the return value depends on whether multibyte characters have state-dependent encodings. (See Chapter 8 for a discussion of shift state.) The `mbtowc` function returns a nonzero value if encodings are state-dependent or 0 if encodings are not state-dependent.

If `src` points to an empty string, 0 is returned.

If `src` points to a valid multibyte character, the number of bytes that make up that character is returned. If `dst` is not null, the multibyte character is converted to its equivalent wide character, and the wide character is stored in `*dst`.

If `src` points to an invalid multibyte character, -1 is returned.

See Also

`mblen` function, `mbstowcs` function, `wctomb` function, `mbrtowc` in `<cwchar>`

NULL macro
NULL pointer constant

`#define `**`NULL`**` ...`

The `NULL` macro expands to a null pointer constant. See `<cstddef>` for more information.

See Also

`NULL` in `<cstddef>`

qsort function
Sorts an array

```
extern "C"
  void qsort(void* base, size_t count, size_t size, int
          (*compare)(const void*, const void*))
extern "C++"
  void qsort(void* base, size_t count, size_t size, int
          (*compare)(const void*, const void*))
```

The `qsort` function sorts in ascending order an array of count elements, each of size `size` bytes, in which base is the pointer to the first element. The array must have POD type. The sort is not stable, that is, the relative order of identical elements is not necessarily preserved.

The `compare` function takes two pointers into the array and compares the elements. It returns an integer: negative if the first element is less than the second, positive if the first is greater than the second, or 0 if the two elements are equal.

The name qsort derives from the original implementation, which used the Quick Sort algorithm. The current standard does not specify which sort algorithm is used, nor does it specify any performance characteristics of the sort algorithm.

Two versions of qsort are declared so the `compare` function can have "C" linkage or "C++" linkage.

Library Reference

See Also

bsearch function, sort in <algorithm>

---

rand function

Generates a pseudo-random number

int **rand**( )

The rand function returns a pseudo-random integer in the range 0 to RAND_MAX, inclusive.

See Also

RAND_MAX macro, srand function

RAND_MAX macro

Maximum value returned by rand

int **RAND_MAX**

RAND_MAX is the maximum value that rand can return. The RAND_MAX macro expands to an integer constant.

See Also

rand function

---

realloc function

Reallocates memory

void* **realloc**(void* ptr, size_t size)

The realloc function changes the size of the allocated memory that ptr points to. The new size is size bytes. The return value is a pointer to the newly resized memory block, which might be at a different address than the original block. The pointer is suitably aligned for any type.

The contents of the original memory are preserved, up to the smaller of the new and old sizes. If the new size is larger than the old size, the extra memory above the old size is uninitialized.

The memory might be copied, so you can store only POD values in the memory that you reallocate with realloc.

If ptr is null, realloc behaves just like malloc(size). If size is 0, realloc is like free and frees ptr.

If there is insufficient memory to fulfill the request, the original memory is untouched, and a null pointer is returned.

See Also

calloc function, free function, malloc function, Chapter 6

---

size_t type

Size type

typedef ... **size_t**

 The size_t type is the type of the result of the sizeof operator. It is an unsigned integral type. The exact type is implementation-defined.

See Also

size_t in <cstddef>

---

srand function

void **srand**(unsigned int seed)

The srand function saves seed as the seed for a new sequence of pseudo-random numbers to be returned by successive calls to rand. The default seed is 1.

See Also

rand function

strtod function

double **strtod**(const char* str, char** end)

The strtod function converts a character array to a floating-point number. The string str is divided into three parts: optional whitespace, the text of the floating-point value, and a trailing part, which starts with the first character that cannot be part of a floating-point number. The first part is skipped, and the second part is converted to a floating-point value. If the second part is empty, 0 is returned. If end is not null, *end is assigned a pointer to the start of the third part of str. If the third part is empty, *end points to the terminating null character.

If the result would cause overflow, positive or negative HUGE_VAL is returned, and errno is set to ERANGE. If the result causes underflow, 0 is returned, and errno is set to ERANGE.

See Also

atoi function, strtol function, strtoul function, wcstod in <cwchar>

strtol function

long int **strtol**(const char* str, char** end, int base)

The strtol function converts a character array to a long integer. The string str is divided into three parts: optional whitespace, the text of the integer value, and a trailing part, which starts with the first character that cannot be part of an integer. The first part is skipped, and the second part is converted to a long integer. If the second part is empty, 0 is returned. If end is not null, *end is assigned a pointer to the start of the third part of str. If the third part is empty, *end points to the terminating null character.

If base is 0, the base is determined from the prefix of the integer text: a leading 0x or 0X means hexadecimal, a leading 0 means octal, and anything else is decimal. Otherwise, base must be between 2 and 36, in which the letters a–z (of either case) represent digits with values of 10–35. Only letters that are appropriate for the base are permitted, that is, the corresponding digit value must be less than the base.

If the resulting value is too large or too small to fit in a long int, the value LONG_MAX or LONG_MIN is returned, and errno is set to ERANGE.

See Also

atol function, strtod function, strtoul function, wcstol in <cwchar>

strtoul function
Converts a string to unsigned long

`unsigned long strtoul(const char* str, char** end, int base)`

The strtoul function converts a character array to an unsigned long integer. The string str is divided into three parts: optional whitespace, the text of the integer value, and a trailing part, which starts with the first character that cannot be part of an integer. The first part is skipped, and the second part is converted to an unsigned long integer. If the second part is empty, 0 is returned. If end is not null, *end is assigned a pointer to the start of the third part of str. If the third part is empty, *end points to the terminating null character.

If base is 0, the base is determined from the prefix of the integer text: a leading 0x or 0X means hexadecimal, a leading 0 means octal, and anything else is decimal. Otherwise, base must be between 2 and 36, in which the letters a–z (of either case) represent digits with values of 10–35. Only letters that are appropriate for the base are permitted, that is, the corresponding digit value must be less than the base.

If the resulting value is too large to fit in an unsigned long int, the value ULONG_MAX is returned, and errno is set to ERANGE.

See Also

atol function, strtod function, strtol function, wcstoul in <cwchar>

system function
Runs a program

`int system(const char* command)`

The system function passes command to the host operating system to run as an external command. The use and interpretation of the command string is implementation-defined.

The return value is implementation-defined.

If command is null, the return value is true (nonzero) if a command processor is available; it is false (0) if no command processor is available.

wctomb function
Converts a wide character to a multibyte character

`int wctomb(char* s, wchar_t wc)`

The wctomb function converts a wide character to a multibyte character. It first determines the number of bytes needed to represent wc as a multibyte character. If s is not null, the sequence of multibyte characters is stored there. At most, MB_CUR_MAX bytes are stored, and the return value is the actual number of bytes written to s. If wc does not have a valid multibyte encoding, -1 is returned.

If s is null, the return value is true (nonzero) if multibyte characters have state-dependent encodings, or false (0) if they do not.

See Also

mbtowc function, wcstombs function, wcrtomb in <cwchar>

wcstombs function
Converts a wide string to a multibyte string

size_t **wcstombs**(char* dst, const wchar_t* src, size_t n)

The wcstombs function converts a wide string src to a string dst of multibyte characters. At most, n bytes of dst are written to. If the conversion of src requires fewer than n bytes, a trailing null byte is appended to dst.

If any wide characters cannot be represented as a multibyte character, static_cast<size_t>(-1) is returned. Otherwise, the return value is the number of bytes written to dst (not counting a trailing null byte).

See Also

mbstowcs function, wctomb function, wcsrtombs in <cwchar>

<cstring>

The <cstring> header is for the C++ version of the C standard <string.h> header, which declares string-handling functions.

The functions in this section fall into two categories, identified by the first three letters of the function name:

mem...
> The mem functions operate on arbitrary chunks of memory, treating the memory as arrays of unsigned char. The caller must specify the size of each memory chunk.

str...
> The str functions operate on null-terminated character arrays. Even though the function parameters are declared as type char, they are always interpreted as unsigned char when comparing two characters.

See also <cwchar> for wide character string functions.

> Instead of using C-style, null-terminated character arrays, C++ code should use the string and wstring classes that are declared in the <string> header. C++ strings offer high performance, more flexibility, more safety, and greater ease of use. The char_traits class template in <string> also provides member functions for working with narrow and wide character arrays.

memchr function
Searches for a byte

const void* **memchr**(const void* mem, int c, size_t n)
     void* **memchr**(void* mem, int c, size_t n)

The memchr function searches the memory that mem points to, of size n bytes, for the byte whose value is c (converted to unsigned char). The return value is a pointer into the mem array to the first occurrence of c, or a null pointer if c is not present in the first n bytes of mem.

See Also

strchr function, find in <algorithm>, wmemchr in <cwchar>

---

memcmp function   Compares memory

int **memcmp**(const void* s1, const void* s2, size_t n)

The memcmp function compares the first n bytes of s1 and s2 as arrays of unsigned char. If all n bytes are equal, the return value is 0. Otherwise, the return value is positive if s1 is greater than s2 or negative if s1 is less than s2.

See Also

strcmp function, strncmp function, equal in <algorithm>, lexicographical_compare in <algorithm>, mismatch in <algorithm>, wmemcmp in <cwchar>

---

memcpy function   Copies memory

void* **memcpy**(void* dst, const void* src, size_t n)

The memcpy function copies n bytes from src to dst. If src and dst overlap, the results are undefined. The return value is dst.

If you copy the memory that contains any non-POD objects, the results are undefined. See Chapter 6 for more information about POD objects.

See Also

memmove function, strcpy function, strncpy function, copy in <algorithm>, wmemcpy in <cwchar>, Chapter 6

---

memmove function   Copies possibly overlapping memory

void* **memmove**(void* dst, const void* src, size_t n)

The memmove function copies n bytes from src to dst. The memory regions can overlap. The return value is dst.

If you copy the memory that contains any non-POD objects, the results are undefined. See Chapter 6 for more information about POD objects.

See Also

memcpy function, strcpy function, strncpy function, copy in <algorithm>, copy_backward in <algorithm>, wmemmove in <cwchar>, Chapter 6

---

memset function   Fills memory with a byte

void* **memset**(void* s, int c, size_t n)

The memset function fills the array s with n copies of c (converted to unsigned char). The return value is s.

See Also

memcpy function, fill_n in <algorithm>, wmemset in <cwchar>

NULL macro
NULL pointer constant

`#define NULL ...`

The NULL macro expands to a null pointer constant. See `<cstddef>` for more information.

See Also

NULL in `<cstddef>`

size_t type
Size type

`typedef ... size_t`

 The size_t type is the type of the result of the `sizeof` operator. It is an unsigned integral type. The exact type is implementation-defined.

See Also

size_t in `<cstddef>`

strcat function
Concatenates strings

`char* strcat(char* dst, const char* src)`

The strcat function concatenates src onto the end of dst, overwriting the null byte that ends dst. The src and dst arrays cannot overlap. The caller must ensure that dst points to a region of memory that is large enough to hold the concatenated result, including its null terminator.

See Also

strcpy function, strncat function, wcscat in `<cwchar>`

strchr function
Searches a string for a character

```
const char* strchr(const char* s, int c)
      char* strchr(      char* s, int c)
```

The strchr function returns a pointer to the first occurrence of c (converted to unsigned char) in the null-terminated string s. If c does not appear in s, a null pointer is returned.

See Also

memchr function, strcspn function, strpbrk function, strrchr function, strspn function, wcschr in `<cwchar>`

strcmp function
Compares strings

`int strcmp(const char* s1, const char* s2)`

The strcmp function compares two null-terminated strings as arrays of unsigned char. If the strings are equal, the return value is 0. Otherwise, the return value is positive if s1 is greater than s2 or negative if s1 is less than s2. If one string is a prefix of the other, the longer string is greater than the shorter string.

See Also

memcmp function, strncmp function, wcscmp in <cwchar>

---

strcoll function
Compares strings using locale's collation order

int **strcoll**(const char* s1, const char* s2)

The strcoll function compares two null-terminated strings, interpreting the strings according to the LC_COLLATE (defined in <clocale>) category of the current C locale. The return value is the same as that of strcmp.

See Also

strcmp function, wcscoll in <cwchar>, collate in <locale>, <clocale>

---

strcpy function
Copies a string

char* **strcpy**(char* dst, const char* src)

The strcpy function copies the null-terminated string src to dst. The caller must ensure that dst points to a region of memory that is large enough to hold the entire src string plus its null terminator. The return value is dst.

See Also

memcpy function, strncpy function, wcscpy in <cwchar>

---

strcspn function
Counts initial characters not in a span set

size_t **strcspn**(const char* str, const char* spanset)

The strcspn function returns the number of characters at the start of str that are not in the string spanset. Thus, the c in its name means complement, that is, strcspn counts characters that are in the complement of the span set.

See Also

strchr function, strpbrk function, strspn function, strstr function, wcscspn in <cwchar>

---

strerror function
Retrieves error message text

char* **strerror**(int errnum)

The strerror function returns a pointer to an error message string that corresponds to the error number errnum. The message is the same as that printed by the perror function.

A program must not modify the array returned by strerror, and subsequent calls to strerror can overwrite the array.

See Also

perror in <cstdio>, <cerrno>

---

strlen function

size_t **strlen**(const char* s)

The strlen function returns the length of the null-terminated string s, that is, the number of bytes that come before the null byte at the end of the string.

See Also

wcslen in <cwchar>

strncat function

char* **strncat**(char* dst, const char* src, size_t n)

The strncat function concatenates src onto the end of dst, overwriting the null byte at the end of dst. At most, n characters are copied from src. A terminating null character is always appended to the end of dst. The caller must ensure that dst points to a region of memory that is large enough to hold the concatenated result, including the null terminator. The return value is dst.

See Also

strcat function, wcsncat in <cwchar>

strncmp function

int **strncmp**(const char* s1, const char* s2, size_t n)

The strncmp function compares at most n characters of two null-terminated strings as arrays of unsigned char. If the strings are equal, the return value is 0. Otherwise, the return value is positive if s1 is greater than s2 or negative if s1 is less than s2. If one string is a prefix of the other, the longer string is greater than the shorter string.

See Also

memcmp function, strcmp function, wcsncmp in <cwchar>

strncpy function

char* **strncpy**(char* dst, const char* src, size_t n)

The strncpy function copies at most n characters from the null-terminated string src to dst. If src is shorter than dst, null characters are appended to the end so that exactly n characters are always written to dst.

The return value is dst.

See Also

memcpy function, strcpy function, wcsncpy in <cwchar>

strpbrk function

const char* **strpbrk**(const char* str, const char* spanset)
    char* **strpbrk**(char* str, const char* spanset)

The strpbrk function searches str for any of the characters in spanset and returns a pointer to the first occurrence of such a character. If none of the characters in spanset appear in str, strpbrk returns a null pointer.

See Also

strchr function, strcspn function, strspn function, wcspbrk in <cwchar>

---

strrchr function   Locates rightmost occurrence of a character

```
const char* strrchr(const char* str, int c)
      char* strrchr(      char* str, int c)
```

The strrchr function returns a pointer to the last (rightmost) occurrence of c (converted to unsigned char) in the null-terminated string s. If c does not appear in s, NULL is returned.

See Also

memchr function, strchr function, wcsrchr in <cwchar>

---

strspn function   Counts characters in a span set

```
size_t strspn(const char* str, const char* spanset)
```

The strspn function returns the number of characters at the start of str that are in the string spanset.

See Also

strchr function, strcspn function, strpbrk function, wcsspn in <cwchar>

---

strstr function   Finds a substring

```
const char* strstr(const char* str, const char* substr)
      char* strstr(      char* str, const char* substr)
```

The strstr function returns the address in str of the first occurrence of substr or a null pointer if substr does not appear in str.

See Also

strchr function, wcsstr in <cwchar>

---

strtok function   Tokenizes a string

```
char* strtok(char* str, const char* delimset)
```

The strtok function splits str into separate tokens, separated by one or more characters from delimset. The contents of str are modified when each token is found.

To parse a string str, you must call strtok multiple times. The first time, pass str as the first parameter to strtok; for the second and subsequent calls, pass a null pointer. Because strtok saves str, only one series of strtok calls can be active at a time. Each call to strtok can use a different delimset.

The strtok function skips over initial delimiters, searching str for the first character that is not in delimset. If it reaches the end of the string without finding any token characters, it returns a null pointer. Otherwise, it saves a pointer to the first non-delimiter character as the start of the token. It then searches for the next delimiter character, which ends the token. It changes the delimiter character to a null character and returns a pointer to the start of the token. When strtok is called with a null pointer as the first parameter, it starts searching for the next token at the point where the previous search ended.

See Also

strcspn function, strpbrk function, strspn function, wcstok in <cwchar>

strxfrm function
Transforms a string for collation

size_t **strxfrm**(char* dst, const char* src, size_t n)

The strxfrm function transforms the src string by converting each character to its collation order equivalent. The equivalent is copied into dst. Thus, after transforming two different strings with strxfrm, the transformed strings can be compared by calling strcmp to obtain the same result as calling strcoll on the original strings.

No more than n bytes are stored in dst, including the trailing null character. If n is 0, dst can be null.

The return value is the number of transformed characters written to dst.

See Also

strcmp function, strcoll function, wcsxfrm in <cwchar>, collate in <locale>, <clocale>

<ctime>

The <ctime> header is the C++ version of the C standard <time.h> header, which declares types and functions for working with dates and times.

 The time_t type is the fundamental representation of a date and time. The details of this type and how it encodes a date and time are implementation-defined. Unix programmers recognize this type as the number of seconds since January 1, 1970, but that is only one possible implementation.

A date and time have a secondary representation as a tm object, which breaks down a date and time into constituent parts. The parts facilitate formatting dates and times for output, or you can read a date and time, parse the parts, and build a tm object, which you can then convert to a time_t object.

This section describes the types and functions for working with dates and times. The Boost project has additional date and time classes. See Appendix B for information about Boost.

asctime function
Converts a time to a string

char* **asctime**(const tm* tmptr)

The asctime function formats the date and time pointed to by tmptr as a character string. It returns a pointer to a static buffer that is overwritten with each call. (The static buffer can be shared with ctime.)

The returned value has the format "Ddd Mmm DD HH:MM:SS YYYY\n" followed by a terminating null character. Thus, the result always has a length of 25. The day of the week (Ddd) and month name (Mmm) are English abbreviations and are not localized—that is, Monday is represented by "Mon" regardless of locale. The day of the month (DD) always takes up the same number of characters, using a leading space if necessary. The hours (HH), minutes (MM), and seconds (SS) use a leading zero if necessary.

See Also

ctime function, gmtime function, localtime function, time_put in <locale>

clock function
Gets the processor time

clock_t **clock**( )

 The clock function returns the amount of processor time used since an implementation-defined start time. The time is returned in implementation-defined units. There are CLOCKS_PER_SEC units per second.

The value returned by the clock function is not useful by itself but is intended to be used by comparing it with the value returned from an earlier call to clock. For example, the first statement in the main function might be a call to clock; the difference between subsequent calls and the original call tell you how much time has elapsed since the program started.

If the environment cannot provide the processor time, static_cast<clock_t>(-1) is returned.

See Also

clock_t type, CLOCKS_PER_SEC macro, time function

clock_t type
Represents processor time

typedef ... **clock_t**

The clock_t type is an arithmetic type returned by the clock function.

See Also

clock function

CLOCKS_PER_SEC macro
Processor time resolution

int **CLOCKS_PER_SEC**

The CLOCKS_PER_SEC macro returns the number of clock ticks per second. It is not necessarily a compile-time constant.

See Also

clock function

ctime function
Converts a time to a string

char* **ctime**(const time_t* timeptr)

The ctime function converts the date and time pointed to by timeptr to local time and formats the time as a string. It is equivalent to:

    std::asctime(std::localtime(timeptr));

The text is written to a static buffer, and a pointer to that buffer is returned. Subsequent calls can overwrite the buffer contents. The static buffer can be shared with asctime.

See Also

asctime function, localtime function

difftime function

double **difftime**(time_t t1, time_t t2);

The difftime function computes the difference between two times: t1 − t2. The return value is in seconds.

See Also

time function, time_t type

gmtime function

tm* **gmtime**(const time_t* timeptr)

The gmtime function expands the calendar time pointed to by timeptr into a static tm object using Coordinated Universal Time (UTC). It returns a pointer to the static object. Subsequent calls to gmtime overwrite the object. The static object can be shared with localtime.

If UTC is not available (for example, the host operating system does not provide the time zone offset), a null pointer is returned.

See Also

localtime function, tm struct

localtime function

tm* **localtime**(const time_t* timeptr)

The localtime function expands the calendar time pointed to by timeptr into a static tm object using local time. It returns a pointer to the static object. Subsequent calls to localtime overwrite the object. The static object can be shared with gmtime.

See Also

gmtime function, tm struct

mktime function

time_t **mktime**(tm* tmptr)

The mktime function makes a time_t time by assembling the parts in a tm object, interpreted as local time. The tm_wday and tm_yday members are ignored, and other fields are permitted to be outside their normal ranges.

If the conversion is successful, the corresponding time is returned, the tm_wday and tm_yday members are set, and the other fields are changed if necessary to reflect their normal ranges.

If the time cannot be represented as a time_t value, static_cast<time_t>(-1) is returned.

See Also

localtime function, time_t type, tm struct, time_get in <locale>

NULL macro

NULL pointer constant

`#define NULL ...`

The NULL macro expands to a null pointer constant. See `<cstddef>` for more information.

See Also

NULL in `<cstddef>`

---

size_t type

Size type

`typedef ... size_t`

The size_t type is the type of the result of the `sizeof` operator. It is an unsigned integral type. The exact type is implementation-defined.

See Also

size_t in `<cstddef>`

---

strftime function

Formats a time as a string

`size_t strftime(char* str, size_t n, const char* fmt, const tm* tmptr)`

The strftime function formats a tm object as a string. Up to n bytes are stored in str, including a terminating null character. The return value is the number of characters actually stored, not counting the final null character. If the formatted result requires more than n characters, the return value is 0.

Characters from fmt are copied to str, except conversion specifiers, which start with a percent sign (%) and are followed by one of the letters shown in Table 13-6. The LC_TIME category in the current C locale controls the text that is copied to str for each conversion specifier.

Table 13-6. Conversion specifiers for strftime

Specifier	Description
a	Abbreviated weekday name
A	Full weekday name
b	Abbreviated month name
B	Full month name
c	Complete date and time
D	Day of the month (01–31)
H	Hour (00–23); 24-hour clock
I	Hour (01–12); 12-hour clock
j	Day of the year (001–366)
m	Month (01–12)
M	Minutes (00–59)
P	A.M./P.M. designation for use with a 12-hour clock

Table 13-6. Conversion specifiers for strftime (continued)

Specifier	Description
S	Second (00–61); up to two leap seconds
U	Week number (00–53); week 1 starts with the first Sunday
w	Weekday (0–6); Sunday is day 0
W	Week number (00–53); week 1 starts with first Monday
x	Date
X	Time
y	Year in century (00–99)
Y	Year
Z	Time zone name or abbreviation, or empty string if time zone is unknown
%	Literal %

See Also

asctime function, ctime function, tm struct, time_put in <locale>, <clocale>

---

time function

Gets the current date and time

time_t **time**(time_t *timeptr)

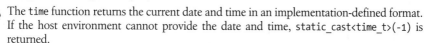

The time function returns the current date and time in an implementation-defined format. If the host environment cannot provide the date and time, static_cast<time_t>(-1) is returned.

If timeptr is not null, the return value is also stored in *timeptr.

See Also

clock function, time_t type

---

time_t type

Represents a date and time

typedef ... **time_t**

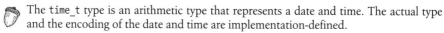

The time_t type is an arithmetic type that represents a date and time. The actual type and the encoding of the date and time are implementation-defined.

See Also

clock_t type, time function, tm struct

---

tm struct

Represents the parts of a date and time

```
struct tm {
  int tm_sec;   /* Seconds: 0-61 */
  int tm_min;   /* Minutes: 0-59 */
  int tm_hour;  /* Hours:   0-23 */
  int tm_mday;  /* Day of month: 1-31 */
  int tm_mon;   /* Month: 0-11 */
  int tm_year;  /* Years since 1900 */
  int tm_wday;  /* Days since Sunday: 0-6 */
```

Library
Reference

```
    int tm_yday;   /* Days since January 1: 0-365 */
    int tm_isdst;  /* Daylight Savings Time */
}
```

The tm structure stores parts of a date and time. The values returned by localtime and gmtime will always be in the ranges shown above. (Note that two extra leap seconds are allowed for tm_sec.)

The tm_isdst member is positive when Daylight Savings Time is in effect, 0 when it is not in effect, or negative if it is unknown.

The order of the members is implementation-defined. An implementation can have additional members.

See Also

gmtime function, localtime function, mktime function, time_t type

---

<cwchar>

The <cwchar> header is the C++ version of the C standard <wchar.h> header, which declares types and functions for working with wide characters. Many of these functions are wide versions of functions found in <cstdio> and <cstring> plus improved versions of the multibyte functions from <cstdlib>.

You can use narrow (byte-oriented) I/O functions, as declared in <cstdio>, or wide I/O functions, as declared in <cwchar>, but you cannot mix wide and narrow functions on a single stream without explicitly changing the stream's orientation (see the fwide function in this section for details).

Wide I/O treats a file as a sequence of multibyte characters. When reading, multibyte characters are converted to wide characters, and when writing, wide characters are converted to multibyte characters. The conversion depends on the C locale (set with setlocale in <clocale>).

See Chapter 1 for information about character sets, Chapter 8 for information about multibyte characters and shift states, and Chapter 9 for information about wide characters and I/O.

When working with wide characters, consider using the C++ I/O streams and wstring class instead of the C functions. (See <string> later in this chapter for the wstring class and the char_traits class template.) The <locale> header provides additional support for converting between narrow and wide characters (the codecvt and related facets).

---

btowc function   Converts a multibyte character to a wide character

wint_t **btowc**(int c)

The btowc function returns a wide character representation of c, which is a multibyte character that can be represented in a single byte (as an unsigned char). If c is not a valid one-byte, multibyte character, or if c is EOF, WEOF is returned.

See Also

mbrtowc function, wctob function, WEOF macro, codecvt in <locale>

---

fgetwc function
Reads a wide character

`wint_t` **`fgetwc`**`(FILE* stream)`

The `fgetwc` function reads the next wide character from `stream`. It returns the character read, or `WEOF` for end-of-file or an error.

See Also

fgetws function, fputwc function, getwc macro, fgetc in <cstdio>

fgetws function
Reads a wide string

`wchar_t*` **`fgetwc`**`(wchar_t* str, int n, FILE* stream)`

The fgetws function reads a line of wide characters from `stream` and stores them in `str`. The newline character is also stored. At most, n wide characters are stored in `str`, including a terminating null wide character.

The return value is `str` for success or a null pointer for end-of-file or an error.

See Also

fgetwc function, fputws function, fgets in <cstdio>

fputwc function
Writes a wide character

`wint_t` **`fputwc`**`(wchar_t wc, FILE* stream)`

The fputwc function writes a wide character, `wc`, to `stream`. It returns `wc`, or `WEOF` for an error.

See Also

fgetwc function, putwc macro, fputc in <cstdio>

fputws function
Writes a wide string

`int` **`fputws`**`(const wchar_t* str, FILE* stream)`

The fputws function writes the wide string `str` to `stream`. It returns `EOF` (not `WEOF`) for an error, or a nonnegative value for success.

See Also

fgetws function, fputwc function, fputs in <cstdio>

fwide function
Gets or sets stream orientation

`int` **`fwide`**`(FILE* stream, int mode);`

The fwide function gets or sets the orientation of stream. The orientation is wide or narrow (byte). When a file is opened, it starts without orientation. Calling any wide I/O function on the stream gives it wide orientation. Calling any narrow I/O function on the stream gives it narrow orientation. Mixing narrow and wide functions on a stream results in an error—that is, calling a narrow function on a stream with wide orientation or calling a wide function on a stream with narrow orientation results in an error.

Before performing any I/O on a newly opened stream, you can force the stream's orientation by calling fwide. Once the orientation is set, it cannot be changed except by closing and reopening the stream (for example, by calling freopen in <cstdio>).

If mode is positive, the orientation is set to wide. If mode is negative, the orientation is set to narrow. If the orientation has already been set, it is not changed, and the stream's true orientation is returned. If mode is 0, the orientation is queried without being changed.

The return value indicates the new orientation: positive for wide, negative for narrow, or 0 if the stream has no orientation.

See Also

fopen in <cstdio>, freopen in <cstdio>

---

fwprintf function   Writes formatted data

int **fwprintf**(FILE* stream, const wchar_t* format, ...)

The fwprintf function writes wide output to stream, formatted according to the conversion specifiers in format. See fprintf in <cstdio> for more information.

See Also

fprintf in <cstdio>

---

fwscanf function   Reads formatted data

int **fwscanf**(FILE* stream, const wchar_t* format, ...)

The fwscanf function reads wide input from stream and interprets it according to the conversion specifiers in format. See fscanf in <cstdio> for more information.

See Also

fscanf in <cstdio>

---

getwc macro   Reads a wide character

wint_t **getwc**(FILE* stream)

The getwc macro reads a wide character from stream. It returns the character converted to wint_t, or WEOF for end-of-file or an error.

See Also

fgetwc function, getwchar macro, getc in <cstdio>

---

getwchar macro   Reads a wide character

wint_t **getwchar**( )

The getwchar macro is equivalent to getwc(stdin).

See Also

getwc macro, getchar in <cstdio>

---

mbrlen function

size_t **mbrlen**(const char* str, size_t n, mbstate_t* ps)

The mbrlen function counts the number of bytes needed to complete the next multibyte character that str points to. At most, n bytes of str are examined.

The ps parameter points to the shift state, which keeps track of the conversion state between calls to mbrlen. If ps is a null pointer, an internal shift state is used (which is similar to calling mblen in <cstdlib>).

The return value is one of the following:

0   If the multibyte character represents the null wide character

static_cast<size_t>(-1)
     If str does not point to a valid multibyte character

static_cast<size_t>(-2)
     If n is too small

Anything else
     If the multibyte character is valid, in which case the value returned is the number of bytes in the multibyte character

See Also

mbrtowc function, mbstate_t type, mblen in <cstdlib>

mbrtowc function

size_t **mbrtowc**(wchar_t* pwc, const char* str, size_t n, mbstate_t* ps)

The mbrtowc function converts a multibyte character to a wide character. First, it counts the number of bytes needed to complete the next multibyte character that str points to. At most, n bytes of str are examined. If str points to a valid multibyte character, that character is converted to a wide character, which is stored in *pwc.

The ps parameter points to the shift state, which keeps track of the conversion state between calls to mbrtowc. If ps is a null pointer, an internal shift state is used (which is similar to calling mbtowc in <cstdlib>).

The return value is one of the following:

0   If the multibyte character represents the null wide character

static_cast<size_t>(-1)
     If str does not point to a valid multibyte character

static_cast<size_t>(-2)
     If n is too small

Anything else
     If the multibyte character is valid, in which case the value returned is the number of bytes in the multibyte character

See Also

mbstate_t type, mbtowc in <cstdlib>, codecvt in <locale>

mbsinit function   Determines whether a state is the initial shift state

int **mbsinit**(const mbstate_t* ps)

The mbsinit function returns true (nonzero) if ps is a null pointer or it points to an mbstate_t object that is in the initial shift state; otherwise, it returns false (0).

See Also

mbstate_t type

---

mbsrtowcs function   Converts a multibyte string to a wide string

size_t **mbsrtowcs**(wchar_t* dst, const char** src, size_t len, mbstate_t* ps)

The mbsrtowcs converts a multibyte string to a wide character string. The src parameter indirectly points to the null-terminated multibyte string, that is, *src points to the start of the multibyte string.

If dst is not null, up to len wide characters are stored in dst. If fewer than len characters are stored, a trailing null character is appended to the wide character array. If conversion stops upon reaching a null character in the src string, a null pointer is assigned to *src; otherwise, *src is assigned a pointer to the byte immediately past the end of the last multibyte character converted.

The dst parameter can be a null pointer, in which case no wide characters are stored and *src is not altered, but ps is updated and the return value is the same as it would be if dst were large enough to hold the entire converted string.

The ps parameter points to the shift state, which keeps track of the conversion state between calls to mbsrtowcs. If ps is a null pointer, an internal shift state is used (which is similar to calling mbstowcs in <cstdlib>). If the conversion ends without a terminating null character in *src, the shift state is reset to an mbstate_t initial state.

The return value is the number of wide characters successfully converted. If any multibyte character is not valid, the return value is static_cast<size_t>(-1).

See Also

mbrtowc function, mbstate_t type, mbstowcs in <cstdlib>, codecvt in <locale>

---

mbstate_t type   Represents a multibyte shift state

typedef ... **mbstate_t**

The mbstate_t type is an opaque, POD type that stores the conversion state used to convert between multibyte and wide characters. The type is implementation-defined, but it is not an array type, so an mbstate_t object can be returned from a function.

A value of 0 for an mbstate_t object corresponds to the initial shift state, although other values might also represent the initial state. Thus, to initialize an mbstate_t object, use a default constructor:

    std::mbstate_t mbs = std::mbstate_t( );

If two mbstate_t objects are identical, they represent the same shift state, but the reverse is not necessarily true.

There is no way to compare two mbstate_t objects to determine whether they represent the same state, but you can call mbsinit to determine whether a state is the initial state.

Typically, you would use an mbstate_t object by initializing it to the initial shift state, then passing it to any of the multibyte functions (such as mbrtowc) repeatedly. Each call to the multibyte function reads the shift state and uses that information for the conversion, updating the shift state depending on which multibyte characters were provided as input. You should not alter the mbstate_t object between calls to the multibyte function.

See Also

mbrlen function, mbrtowc function, mbsinit function, mbsrtowcs function, wcrtomb function, wcsrtombs function

NULL macro

NULL pointer constant

#define **NULL** ...

The NULL macro expands to a null pointer constant. See <cstddef> for more information.

See Also

NULL in <cstddef>

putwc macro

Writes a wide character

wint_t **putwc**(wchar_t wc, FILE* stream)

The putwc macro writes the wide character wc. The return value is the character converted to wint_t, or WEOF for an error.

See Also

fputwc function, putwchar macro, putc in <cstdio>

putwchar macro

Writes a wide character to stdout

wint_t **putwchar**(wchar_t wc)

The putwchar macro is equivalent to puwc(wc, stdout).

See Also

putwc macro, putchar in <cstdio>

size_t type

Size type

typedef ... **size_t**

 The size_t type is the type of the result of the sizeof operator. It is an unsigned integral type. The exact type is implementation-defined.

See Also

size_t in <cstddef>

swprintf function

Writes formatted data to a wide string

```
int swprintf(wchar_t* dst, size_t n, const wchar_t* format, ...)
```

The swprintf function is similar to sprintf, except it stores the formatted output in a wide string, dst, and the format is a wide string. Another difference is that n is the maximum number of wide characters (including a terminating null wide character) that can be written to dst.

The return value is the number of wide characters actually stored in dst (not counting the terminating null wide character) or a negative value if the formatted output requires n or more characters (not including the terminating null character).

See Also

fwprintf function, vswprintf function, sprintf in <cstdio>

swscanf function

Reads formatted data from a wide string

```
int swscanf(const wchar_t* str, const wchar_t* format, ...)
```

The swscanf function is similar to sscanf, except it reads from a wide string, str, and the format string is also wide. Like sscanf, the return value is the number of items converted.

See Also

fwscanf function, sscanf in <cstdio>

tm struct

Represents the parts of a date and time

```
struct tm {
  int tm_sec;   /* Seconds: 0-61 */
  int tm_min;   /* Minutes: 0-60 */
  int tm_hour;  /* Hours:   0-24 */
  int tm_mday;  /* Day of month: 1-31 */
  int tm_mon;   /* Month: 1-12 */
  int tm_year;  /* Years since 1900 */
  int tm_wday;  /* Days since Sunday: 0-6 */
  int tm_yday;  /* Days since January 1: 0-365 */
  int tm_isdst; /* Daylight Savings Time */
}
```

The tm structure stores parts of a date and time. It is the same structure definition as that found in <ctime>. See <ctime> for details.

See Also

tm struct in <ctime>

ungetwc function

Pushes back a wide character

```
wint_t ungetwc(wint_t wc, FILE* stream)
```

The ungetwc function pushes back the wide character wc, so the next read from stream will return wc. The standard guarantees that you can push back just one character, though in some situations you may be able to push back more.

The return value is wc if the pushback was successful, or WEOF if the pushback was not successful.

See Also

fgetwc function, getwc function, ungetc in <cstdio>

vfwprintf function   Writes formatted data

int **vfwprintf**(FILE* stream, const wchar_t* format, va_list arg)

The vfwprintf function is similar to vfprintf in <cstdio>, except it prints wide characters to stream, and the format parameter is a wide string.

See Also

vfprintf in <cstdio>, <cstdarg>

vswprintf function   Writes formatted data to a wide string

int **vswprintf**(wchar_t* dst, size_t n, const wchar_t* format, va_list arg)

The vswprintf function is similar to vsprintf in <cstdio>, except it stores its output in a wide string, dst, and the format parameter is a wide string. Another difference is that no more than n wide characters are written to dst, including a terminating null character.

See Also

swprintf function, vsprintf in <cstdio>, <cstdarg>

vwprintf function   Writes formatted data

int **vwprintf**(const wchar_t* format, va_list arg)

The vwprintf function is similar to vprintf in <cstdio>, except it prints wide characters to stdout, and the format parameter is a wide string.

See Also

wprintf function, vprintf in <cstdio>, <cstdarg>

WCHAR_MAX macro   Largest value of a wide character

wchar_t **WCHAR_MAX**

The WCHAR_MAX macro is the largest value that can be represented by the wchar_t type. It is not necessarily a valid character in the extended character set.

See Also

WCHAR_MIN macro, CHAR_MAX in <climits>, <limits>

WCHAR_MIN macro   Smallest value of a wide character

wchar_t **WCHAR_MIN**

The WCHAR_MIN macro is the smallest value that can be represented by the wchar_t type. It is not necessarily a valid character in the extended character set.

See Also

WCHAR_MAX macro, CHAR_MIN in <climits>, <limits>

---

wcrtomb function
Converts a wide character to a multibyte character

size_t **wcrtomb**(char* dst, wchar_t wc, mbstate_t* ps)

The wcrtomb function converts a wide character to a multibyte character. It first deter-mines the number of bytes needed to represent wc as a multibyte character. If dst is not null, the sequence of multibyte characters is stored there. At most, MB_CUR_MAX (defined in <cstdlib>) bytes are stored, and the return value is the actual number of bytes written to dst. If wc does not have a valid multibyte encoding, static_cast<size_t>(-1) is returned.

If dst is null, wcrtomb ignores wc and converts the null wide character using a private, internal buffer (e.g., wcrtomb(*buffer*, L'\0', ps)).

The ps parameter points to the shift state, which keeps track of the conversion state between calls to wcrtomb. If ps is null, an internal shift state is used (which is similar to calling wctomb in <cstdlib>).

See Also

mbrtowc function, mbstate_t type, MB_CUR_MAX in <cstdlib>, wctomb in <cstdlib>, codecvt in <locale>

---

wcscat function
Concatenates wide strings

wchar_t* **wcscat**(wchar_t* dst, const wchar_t* src)

The wcscat function concatenates src onto the end of dst, overwriting the null char-acter at the end of dst. The caller must ensure that dst points to a region of memory that is large enough to hold the entire string plus its null terminator. The return value is dst.

See Also

wcscpy function, wcsncat function, strcat in <cstring>

---

wcschr function
Searches for a wide character in a wide string

const wchar_t* **wcschr**(const wchar_t* str, wchar_t wc)
    wchar_t* **wcschr**(wchar_t* str, wchar_t wc)

The wcschr function returns a pointer to the first occurrence of wc in the null-termi-nated wide string str. If wc does not appear in str, a null pointer is returned.

See Also

wmemchr function, wcscspn function, wcspbrk function, wcsrchr function, wcsspn func-tion, strchr in <cstring>

---

wcscmp function
Compares wide strings

int **wcscmp**(const wchar_t* s1, const wchar_t* s2)

The wcscmp function compares two null-terminated wide strings. If the strings are equal, the return value is 0. Otherwise, the return value is positive if s1 is greater than

---

s2 or negative if s1 is less than s2. If one string is a prefix of the other, the longer string is greater than the shorter string.

See Also

wmemcmp function, wcsncmp function, strcmp in <cstring>

wcscoll function
Compares wide strings using locale's collation order

int **wcscoll**(const wchar_t* s1, const wchar_t* s2)

The wcscoll function compares two null-terminated wide strings, interpreting the strings according to the LC_COLLATE (defined in <clocale>) category of the current C locale. The return value is the same as that of wcscmp.

See Also

wcscmp function, strcoll in <cstring>, <clocale>, collate in <locale>

wcscpy function
Copies wide strings

wchar_t* **wcscpy**(wchar_t* dst, const wchar_t* src)

The wcscpy function copies the null-terminated wide string src to dst. The caller must ensure that dst points to a region of memory that is large enough to hold the entire src string plus its null terminator. The return value is dst.

See Also

wmemcpy function, wcsncpy function, strcpy in <cstring>

wcscspn function
Counts initial characters that do not match a span set

size_t **wcscspn**(const wchar_t* str, const wchar_t* spanset)

The wcscspn function returns the number of wide characters at the start of str that are not in the wide string spanset. Thus, the c in its name means complement, that is, wcscspn counts characters that are in the complement of the span set.

See Also

wcschr function, wcspbrk function, wcsspn function, wcsstr function, strspn in <cstring>

wcsftime function
Formats a time as a wide string

size_t **wcsftime**(wchar_t* str, size_t n, const wchar_t* format, const tm* tmptr)

The wcsftime function is similar to strftime in <ctime>, except it formats the result as a wide string, str, and the format parameter is a wide string.

See Also

strftime in <ctime>

wcslen function
Gets length of a wide string

size_t **wcslen**(const wchar_t* str)

The wcslen function returns the number of wide characters (not including the terminating null wide character) in str.

See Also

strlen in <cstring>

wcsncat function
Concatenates wide strings

wchar_t* **wcscat**(wchar_t* dst, const wchar_t* src, size_t n)

The wcsncat function concatenates src onto the end of dst. At most, n wide characters are copied from src. A terminating null wide character is always appended to the end of dst. You must ensure that dst points to a region of memory that is large enough to hold the concatenated result plus the null terminator. The return value is dst.

See Also

wcscat function, strncat in <cstring>

wcsncmp function
Compares wide strings

int **wcsncmp**(const wchar_t* s1, const wchar_t* s2, size_t n)

The wcsncmp function compares at most n wide characters of two null-terminated wide strings. If the strings are equal, the return value is 0. Otherwise, the return value is positive if s1 is greater than s2 or negative if s1 is less than s2. If one string is a prefix of the other, the longer string is greater than the shorter string.

See Also

wcscmp function, strncmp in <cstring>

wcsncpy function
Copies wide strings

wchar_t* **wcsncpy**(wchar_t* dst, const wchar_t* src, size_t n)

The wcsncpy function copies at most n wide characters from the null-terminated wide string src to dst. If src is shorter than dst, null wide characters are appended to the end so that exactly n characters are always written to dst.

The return value is dst.

See Also

wcscpy function, strncpy in <cstring>

wcspbrk function
Locates a span set member in a wide string

const wchar_t* **wcspbrk**(const wchar_t* str, const wchar_t* spanset)
    wchar_t* **wcspbrk**(wchar_t* str, const wchar_t* spanset)

The wcspbrk function searches str for any of the wide characters in spanset and returns a pointer to the first occurrence of such a character. If none of the characters in spanset appears in str, strpbrk returns a null pointer.

See Also

wcschr function, wcscspn function, wcsspn function, strpbrk in <cstring>

---

wcsrchr function   Locates rightmost occurrence of a wide character

```
const wchar_t* wcsrchr(const wchar_t* str, wchar_t wc)
      wchar_t* wcsrchr(      wchar_t* str, wchar_t wc)
```

The wcsrchr function returns a pointer to the last (rightmost) occurrence of wc in the null-terminated wide string str. If wc does not appear in str, the function returns a null pointer .

See Also

wmemchr function, wcschr function, strrchr in <cstring>

---

wcsrtombs function   Converts a wide string to a multibyte string

```
size_t wcsrtombs(char* dst, const wchar_t** src, size_t len, mbstate_t* ps)
```

The wcsrtombs function converts a wide string to a string of multibyte characters. The src parameter points indirectly to the source wide string, that is, *src points to the start of the wide string.

If dst is not null, up to len bytes are stored in dst. If fewer than len bytes are stored, a trailing null character is appended to the narrow character array. If conversion stops upon reaching a null wide character in the src string, a null pointer is assigned to *src; otherwise, *src is assigned a pointer to the character immediately past the end of the last wide character converted.

The dst parameter can be null, in which case no narrow characters are stored and *src is not altered, but ps is updated and the return value is the same as it would be if dst were large enough to hold the entire converted string.

The ps parameter points to the shift state, which keeps track of the conversion state between calls to wcsrtombs. If ps is null, an internal shift state is used (which is similar to calling wcstombs in <cstdlib>). If the conversion ends without a terminating null character in *src, the shift state is reset to an mbstate_t initial state.

If any of the wide characters cannot be represented as a multibyte character, static_cast<size_t>(-1) is returned. Otherwise, the return value is the number of bytes successfully converted from wide characters (not counting the trailing null byte).

See Also

mbstate_t type, wmbsrtowcs function, wcrtomb function, wcstombs in <cstdlib>, codecvt in <locale>

---

wcsspn function   Counts characters that match a span set

```
size_t wcsspn(const wchar_t* str, const wchar_t* spanset)
```

The wcsspn function returns the number of wide characters at the start of str that are in the string spanset.

See Also

wcschr function, wcscspn function, wcspbrk function, strspn in <cstring>

wcsstr function
Finds a wide substring

```
const wchar_t* wcsstr(const wchar_t* str, const wchar_t* substr)
    wchar_t* wcsstr(      wchar_t* str, const wchar_t* substr)
```

The wcsstr function returns the index in str of the first occurrence of substr, or a null pointer if substr does not appear in str.

See Also

wcschr function, strstr in <cstring>

wcstod function
Converts a wide string to double

```
double wcstod(const wchar_t* str, wchar_t** end)
```

The wcstod function converts a wide string to double. It is similar to the strtod function.

See Also

wcstol function, wcstoul function, strtod in <cstdlib>

wcstok function
Tokenizes a wide string

```
wchar_t* wcstok(wchar_t* str, const wchar_t* delimset, wchar_t** ptr)
```

The wcstok function is similar to strtok in <cstring>, except it works with wide strings. Another difference is that it is reentrant, taking a third parameter, ptr, which is the address of a wide string. The wcstok function uses ptr for storing working information, which it uses when str is null.

To parse a string str, you must call wcstok multiple times. The first time, pass str as the first parameter to wcstok; for the second and subsequent calls, pass a null pointer. For the final argument, ptr, pass the address of a wchar_t* object. For subsequent calls to wcstok (when str is null), pass the address of the same ptr object. Do not modify ptr between successive calls to wcstok when parsing a single wide string.

Each call to wcstok can use a different delimset.

See Also

wcscspn function, wcspbrk function, wcsspn function, strtok in <cstring>

wcstol function
Converts a wide string to a long integer

```
long int wcstol(const wchar_t* str, wchar_t** end)
```

The wcstol function converts a wide string to long int. It is similar to the strtol function in <cstdlib>.

See Also

wcstod function, wcstoul function, strtol in <cstdlib>

wcstoul function

unsigned long int **wcstoul**(const wchar_t* str, wchar_t** end)

The wcstoul function converts a wide string to unsigned long int. It is similar to the strtoul function in <cstdlib>.

See Also
wcstod function, wcstol function, strtoul in <cstdlib>

wcsxfrm function

size_t **strxfrm**(wchar_t* dst, const wchar_t* src, size_t n)

The wcsxfrm function transforms the src wide string by converting each wide character to its collation order equivalent. The functionality and return value are similar to strxfrm in <cstring>, except wcsxfrm works with wide strings.

See Also
wcscmp function, wcscoll function, strxfrm in <cstring>, collate in <locale>, <clocale>

wctob function

int **wctob**(wint_t wc)

If the wide character wc has a single-byte representation as a multibyte character, wctob returns that byte; otherwise, it returns EOF.

See Also
btowc function, EOF in <cstdio>, codecvt in <locale>

WEOF macro

wint_t **WEOF**

The WEOF macro expands to a constant integer value that does not correspond to any valid wide character value. Unlike EOF, WEOF is not guaranteed to be negative.

See Also
wint_t type, EOF in <cstdio>

wint_t type

typedef ... **wint_t**

The wint_t type is an integral type that represents wide characters. It can hold the value for any character in the extended character set plus the value WEOF.

See Also
WEOF macro

wmemchr function

```
const wchar_t* wmemchr(const wchar_t* mem, wchar_t c, size_t n)
      wchar_t* wmemchr(      wchar_t* mem, wchar_t c, size_t n)
```

The wmemchr function searches the memory that mem points to, of size n wide characters, for the wide character whose value is c. The return value is a pointer in the mem array that points to the first occurrence of c, or a null pointer if c is not present in the first n wide characters of mem.

See Also

wcschr function, find in <algorithm>, memchr in <cstring>

wmemcmp function

```
int wmemcmp(const wchar_t* s1, const wchar_t* s2, size_t n)
```

The wmemcmp function compares the first n wide characters of s1 and s2. If all n wide characters are equal, the return value is 0. Otherwise, the return value is positive if s1 is greater than s2 or negative if s1 is less than s2.

See Also

wcscmp function, wcsncmp function, equal in <algorithm>, lexicographical_compare in <algorithm>, mismatch in <algorithm>, memcmp in <cstring>

wmemcpy function

```
wchar_t* wmemcpy(wchar_t* dst, const wchar_t* src, size_t n)
```

The wmemcpy function copies n wide characters from src to dst. If src and dst overlap, the results are undefined. The return value is dst.

See Also

wcscpy function, wcsncpy function, wmemmove function, copy in <algorithm>, memcpy in <cstring>

wmemmove function

```
wchar_t* memmove(wchar_t* dst, const wchar_t* src, size_t n)
```

The wmemmove function copies n wide characters from src to dst. The memory regions can overlap. The return value is dst.

See Also

wcscpy function, wcsncpy function, wmemcpy function, copy in <algorithm>, copy_backward in <algorithm>, memmove in <cstring>

wmemset function

```
wchar_t* wmemset(wchar_t* str, wchar_t wc, size_t n)
```

The wmemset function fills the array str with n copies of the wide character wc. The return value is str.

See Also

wmemcpy function, fill_n in <algorithm>, memset in <cstring>

wprintf function

int **wprintf**(const wchar_t* format, ...)

The wprintf function is similar to printf in <cstdio>, except it prints wide characters, and the format parameter is a wide string.

See Also

wfprintf function, wsprintf function, wvprintf function, printf in <cstdio>

wscanf function

int **wscanf**(const wchar_t* format, ...)

The wscanf function is similar to scanf in <cstdio>, except it reads wide characters, and the format parameter is a wide string.

See Also

wfscanf function, wsscanf function, scanf in <cstdio>

<cwctype>

The <cwctype> header is the C++ version of the C standard <wctype.h> header, which declares types and functions for classifying and converting wide characters.

Most of the functions in this header are wide equivalents of functions found in <cctype>. For example, iswalnum determines whether a wide character is alphanumeric, just as isalnum determines whether a narrow (byte) character is alphanumeric. The behavior of the wide functions is similar to their narrow equivalents. In particular, for any narrow character c, its wide character equivalent wc, and classification functions isxyz and iswxyx, if isxyz(c) is true, then iswxyz(wc) is true and vice versa. The only exception is that iswgraph and iswpunct behave slightly differently than isgraph and ispunct for whitespace characters other than ' '.

The behavior of the <cwctype> functions depend on the C locale, as set with the setlocale function in <clocale>. For more flexibility in dealing with multiple locales, you can use C++ locales, in particular the ctype facet in <locale>.

iswalnum function

int **iswalnum**(wint_t wc)

The iswalnum function returns true (nonzero) if either iswalpha(wc) or iswdigit(wc) is true.

See Also

iswalpha function, iswdigit function, isalnum in <cctype>

iswalpha function
Determines whether a wide character is alphabetic

int **iswalpha**(wint_t wc)

The iswalpha function returns true (nonzero) if wc is an alphabetic character, that is, a wide character for which iswcntrl, iswdigit, iswpunct, and iswspace all return false (0).

See Also
iswcntrl function, iswdigit function, iswpunct function, iswspace function, isalpha in <cctype>

iswcntrl function
Determines whether a wide character is a control character

int **iswcntrl**(wint_t wc)

The iswcntrl function returns true (nonzero) if wc is a wide control character, that is, a wide character for which iswalnum, iswpunct, and iswspace all return false (0).

See Also
iswalnum function, iswpunct function, iswspace function, iscntrl in <cctype>

iswctype function
Tests any category of a wide character

int **iswctype**(wint_t wc, wctype_t desc)

The iswctype function tests any category of the wide character wc. The category to test is specified by desc, which must be obtained by calling wctype. The setting of the LC_CTYPE category must be the same for the call to iswctype and the call to wctype that returned desc.

Using iswctype, you can implement all the isw… functions. For example, you can implement the iswalnum function as follows:

```
int iswalnum(wint_t wc)
{
  return std::iswctype(wc, std::wctype("alnum"));
}
```

See Also
wctype function, wctype_t type

iswdigit function
Determines whether a wide character is a digit

int **iswdigit**(wint_t wc)

The iswdigit function returns true (nonzero) if wc is a decimal digit character—that is, '0'–'9'—regardless of locale.

See Also
iswxdigit function, isdigit in <cctype>

iswgraph function
Determines whether a wide character is graphic

int **iswgraph**(wint_t wc)

The iswgraph function returns true (nonzero) if iswprint(wc) is true and iswspace(wc) is false. Note that iswgraph is slightly different from isgraph in that it returns true for whitespace characters other than ' '.

See Also
iswprint function, iswspace function

iswlower function
Determines whether a wide character is lowercase

int **iswlower**(wint_t wc)

The iswlower function returns true (nonzero) if wc is a lowercase character.

See Also
iswalpha function, iswupper function, towlower function, islower in <cctype>

iswprint function
Determines whether a wide character is printable

int **iswprint**(wint_t wc)

The iswprint function returns true (nonzero) if wc is a printable wide character.

See Also
iswgraph function, isprint in <cctype>

iswpunct function
Determines whether a wide character is punctuation

int **iswpunct**(wint_t wc)

The iswpunct function returns true (nonzero) if iswalnum(wc), iswcntrl(wc), and iswspace(wc) are false.

See Also
iswalnum function, iswcntrl function, iswspace function, ispunct in <cctype>

iswspace function
Determines whether a wide character is whitespace

int **iswspace**(wint_t wc)

The iswspace function returns true (nonzero) if wc is a whitespace character.

See Also
iswgraph function, iswprint function, isspace in <cctype>

iswupper function
Determines whether a wide character is uppercase

int **iswupper**(wint_t wc)

The iswupper function returns true (nonzero) if wc is an uppercase character.

See Also
iswalpha function, iswlower function, towupper function, isupper in <cctype>

iswxdigit function   Determines whether a wide character is a hexadecimal digit

int **iswxdigit**(wint_t wc)

The iswxdigit function returns true (nonzero) if wc is a hexadecimal digit character—that is, '0'–'9', 'a'–'f', or 'A'–'F'—regardless of locale.

See Also

iswdigit function, isxdigit in <cctype>

---

towctrans function   Translates a wide character's case

wint_t **towctrans**(wint_t wc, wctrans_t desc)

The towctrans function translates the wide character wc according to the description desc, which was returned from the wctrans function. For example, the towlower function can be implemented using towctrans:

```
wint_t towlower(wint_t wc)
{
  return std::towctrans(wc, std::wctrans("tolower"));
}
```

See Also

wctrans function, wctrans_t type

---

towlower function   Converts a wide character to lowercase

wint_t **towlower**(wint_t wc)

The towlower function maps the wide character wc to lowercase. If iswupper(wc) is false, or if wc has no lowercase mapping, wc is returned unchanged.

See Also

towctrans function, towupper function, tolower in <cctype>

---

towupper function   Converts a wide character to uppercase

wint_t **towupper**(wint_t wc)

The towupper function maps the wide character wc to uppercase. If iswlower(wc) is false, or if wc has no uppercase mapping, wc is returned unchanged.

See Also

towctrans function, towlower function, toupper in <cctype>

---

wctrans function   Construct a wctrans_t object

wctrans_t **wctrans**(const char* property)

The wctrans function constructs a wctrans_t object according to the given property. Table 13-7 lists the properties defined in the standard.

Table 13-7. Character translation properties

Property	Description
`"tolower"`	Maps from uppercase to lowercase
`"toupper"`	Maps from lowercase to uppercase

See Also

towctrans function, wctrans_t type

wctrans_t type

Represents a wide character translation

typedef ... **wctrans_t**

The wctrans_t type is a scalar type used to represent character mappings for the towctrans function.

See Also

towctrans function, wctrans function, <clocale>

wctype function

Constructs a wctype_t object

wctype_t **wctype**(const char* property)

The wctype function constructs a wctype_t object that describes wide characters that have the given property. Table 13-8 lists the properties that are supported by this standard.

Table 13-8. Character classification properties

Property	Description
`"alnum"`	Alphanumeric
`"alpha"`	Alphabetic
`"cntrl"`	Control
`"digit"`	Digit
`"graph"`	Non-space printable
`"lower"`	Lowercase
`"print"`	Printable or whitespace
`"punct"`	Punctuation
`"space"`	Whitespace
`"upper"`	Uppercase
`"xdigit"`	Hexadecimal digit

See Also

iswctype function, wctype_t type, <clocale>

wctype_t type   Represents a character classification

typedef ... **wctype_t**

The wctype_t type is a scalar type used to represent character classifications for the iswctype function.

See Also

iswctype function, wctype function, <clocale>

WEOF macro   End-of-file or error

wint_t **WEOF**

The WEOF macro expands to a constant integer value that does not correspond to any valid wide character value. Unlike EOF, WEOF is not guaranteed to be negative.

See Also

WEOF in <cwchar>, EOF in <cstdio>

wint_t type   Integer representation of a wide character

typedef ... **wint_t**

The wint_t type is an integral type that represents wide characters. It can hold the value for any character in the extended character set plus the value WEOF.

See Also

wint_t in <cwchar>

<deque>

The <deque> header is one of the standard container template headers. It declares the deque class template and a few global functions that operate on deque objects.

A *deque*, short for double-ended queue, is similar to a vector, but the performance is constant when adding to or removing from the collection at the beginning and at the end.

If you need a vector of bool that behaves as a normal C++ container, you should use deque<bool> instead of vector<bool>. See <vector> later in this chapter for an explanation.

See Chapter 10 for information about containers in general.

deque class template   Double-ended queue

```
template <class T, class Alloc = allocator<T> >
class deque {
public:
  typedef typename Alloc::reference reference;
  typedef typename Alloc::const_reference const_reference;
  typedef ... iterator;
```

```
typedef ... const_iterator;
typedef ... size_type;
typedef ... difference_type;
typedef T value_type;
typedef Alloc allocator_type;
typedef typename Alloc::pointer pointer;
typedef typename Alloc::const_pointer const_pointer;
typedef std::reverse_iterator<iterator> reverse_iterator;
typedef std::reverse_iterator<const_iterator> const_reverse_iterator;

explicit deque(const Alloc& = Alloc());
explicit deque(size_type n, const T& value = T(), const Alloc& = Alloc());
template <class InputIterator>
deque(InputIterator first, InputIterator last, const Alloc& = Alloc());
deque(const deque<T,Alloc>& x);

~deque();

deque<T,Alloc>& operator=(const deque<T,Alloc>& x);
template <class InputIterator>
void assign(InputIterator first, InputIterator last);
void assign(size_type n, const T& t);
allocator_type get_allocator() const;

iterator begin();
const_iterator begin() const;
iterator end();
const_iterator end() const;
reverse_iterator rbegin();
const_reverse_iterator rbegin() const;
reverse_iterator rend();
const_reverse_iterator rend() const;

size_type size() const;
size_type max_size() const;
void resize(size_type sz, T c = T());
bool empty() const;

reference operator[](size_type n);
const_reference operator[](size_type n) const;
reference at(size_type n);
const_reference at(size_type n) const;
reference front();
const_reference front() const;
reference back();
const_reference back() const;

void push_front(const T& x);
void push_back(const T& x);
iterator insert(iterator position, const T& x);
void insert(iterator position, size_type n, const T& x);
template <class InputIterator>
void insert (iterator position, InputIterator first, InputIterator last);
void pop_front();
```

```
  void pop_back( );
  iterator erase(iterator position);
  iterator erase(iterator first, iterator last);
  void swap(deque<T,Alloc>&);
  void clear( );
};
```

The deque class template represents a double-ended queue. It is one of the standard container types, like list and vector. Like a list, a deque yields amortized, constant performance when adding and removing items from the beginning and end of the container. Like a vector, performance is constant when accessing items at any index in the deque. Performance for inserting or removing items not at the start or end is linear with respect to the size of the container.

After inserting items at the beginning or end of the deque, all iterators become invalid. All references and pointers to items in the deque remain valid. After inserting in the middle of the deque, all iterators, references, and pointers to items in the deque become invalid.

After erasing an element from the beginning or end of the deque, all iterators and references remain valid, except those pointing to the erased element. After erasing an element from the middle of the deque, all iterators, references, and pointers to items in the deque become invalid.

explicit **deque**(const Alloc& = Alloc( ))
> Constructs an empty deque.

explicit **deque**(size_type n, const T& value = T( ), const Alloc& = Alloc( ))
> Constructs a deque with n copies of value.

template <class InputIterator>
deque(InputIterator first, InputIterator last, const Alloc& alloc = Alloc( ))
> Constructs a deque with copies of the elements in [first, last), unless InputIterator is an integral type, in which case the deque is constructed as though the arguments were cast as follows:
> ```
> deque(static_cast<size_type>(first), static_cast<value_type>(last),
>       alloc);
> ```

template <class InputIterator>
void **assign**(InputIterator first, InputIterator last)
> Erases the current contents of the deque and inserts the elements in [first, last), unless InputIterator is an integral type, in which case the arguments are interpreted as though they were cast as follows:
> ```
> assign(static_cast<size_type>(first), static_cast<value_type>(last));
> ```

void **assign**(size_type n, const T& t)
> Erases the current contents of the deque and inserts n copies of t.

allocator_type **get_allocator**( ) const
> Returns the allocator object.

reference **operator[]**(size_type n)
const_reference **operator[]**(size_type n) const
> Returns the element at index n. If n >= size( ), the behavior is undefined.

reference **at**(size_type n)
const_reference **at**(size_type n) const
> Returns the element at index n. If n >= size( ), it throws out_of_range.

```
reference back( )
const_reference back( ) const
```
Returns the last element in the deque. The behavior is undefined if the deque is empty.

```
iterator begin( )
const_iterator begin( ) const
```
Returns an iterator that points to the first element of the deque.

```
void clear( )
```
Erases all elements from the deque.

```
bool empty( ) const
```
Returns size( ) == 0.

```
iterator end( )
const_iterator end( ) const
```
Returns an iterator that points to the last element of the deque.

```
iterator erase(iterator position)
```
Erases the element at position.

```
iterator erase(iterator first, iterator last)
```
Erases all the elements in the range [first, last).

```
reference front( )
const_reference front( ) const
```
Returns the first element of the deque. The behavior is undefined if the deque is empty.

```
iterator insert(iterator position, const T& x)
```
Inserts x at position. If position is begin( ) or end( ), the performance is constant; at any other position, the performance is linear.

```
void insert(iterator pos, size_type n, const T& x)
```
Inserts n copies of x at pos.

```
template <class InputIterator>
void insert (iterator position, InputIterator first, InputIterator last)
```
Inserts the elements in the range [first, last) starting at position, unless InputIterator is an integral type, in which case the arguments are interpreted as though they were cast:

```
        insert(position, static_cast<size_type>(first),
                         static_cast<value_type>(last));
```

If an exception is thrown, such as bad_alloc when there is insufficient memory for a new element, the deque is unchanged, and all iterators and references remain valid. If the exception is thrown from an element's copy constructor or assignment operator, however, the behavior is unspecified.

```
size_type max_size( ) const
```
Returns the size of the largest possible deque.

```
void pop_front( )
```
Erases the first element of the deque. The behavior is undefined if the deque is empty.

```
void pop_back( )
```
Erases the last element of the deque. The behavior is undefined if the deque is empty.

void **push_front**(const T& x)
 Inserts x as the new first element of the deque.

void **push_back**(const T& x)
 Inserts x as the new last element of the deque.

reverse_iterator **rbegin**( )
const_reverse_iterator **rbegin**( ) const
 Returns a reverse iterator that points to the last element of the deque.

reverse_iterator **rend**( )
const_reverse_iterator **rend**( ) const
 Returns a reverse iterator that points to one position before the first element of the deque.

size_type **size**( ) const
 Returns the number of elements in the deque.

void **resize**(size_type n, T c = T( ))
 Changes the size of the deque to n. If n > size( ), one or more copies of c are added to the end of the deque to reach the desired size. If the new size is smaller than the current size, the first n elements are unchanged, and elements are erased from the end to reach the new size.

void **swap**(deque<T,Alloc>& that)
 Exchanges all the elements in the deque with all the elements in that.

See Also

<list>, <vector>

---

operator== function template
Compares two deques for equality

```
template<typename T, typename A>
bool operator==(const deque<T,A>& x, const deque<T,A>& y)
```

The == operator returns true if x and y are the same size and their elements are equal, that is, x.size( ) == y.size( ) && equals(x.begin( ), x.end( ), y.begin( )).

See Also

equals in <algorithm>

---

operator!= function template
Compares two deques for inequality

```
template<typename T, typename A>
bool operator!=(const deque<T,A>& x, const deque<T,A>& y)
```

The != operator is equivalent to ! (x == y).

---

operator< function template
Compares two deques for less-than

```
template<typename T, typename A>
bool operator<(const deque<T,A>& x, const deque<T,A>& y)
```

The < operator determines whether x is less than y using the same algorithm as lexicographical_compare(x.begin( ), x.end( ), y.begin( ), y.end( )).

See Also

lexicographical_compare in <algorithm>

---

operator<= function template

```
template<typename T, typename A>
bool operator<=(const deque<T,A>& x, const deque<T,A>& y)
```

The <= operator is equivalent to ! (y < x).

operator> function template

```
template<typename T, typename A>
bool operator>(const deque<T,A>& x, const deque<T,A>& y)
```

The > operator is equivalent to (y < x).

operator>= function template

```
template<typename T, typename A>
bool operator>=(const deque<T,A>& x, const deque<T,A>& y)
```

The >= operator is equivalent to ! (x < y).

swap function template specialization

```
template<typename T, typename Alloc>
void swap(deque<T, Alloc>& x, deque<T, Alloc>& y)
```

The swap function template specialization is equivalent to calling x.swap(y).

See Also

swap in <algorithm>

<exception>

The <exception> header declares classes, types, and functions related to fundamental exception handling. See <stdexcept> for additional exception classes.

 This section describes a complicated system of exceptions, function calls, and handlers. The end result is simpler than it might seem at first:

> A function can throw only the exception types listed in its exception specification, or else the program terminates immediately.

If a function does not have an exception specification, it can throw any exception. (Virtual functions work a little differently; see Chapter 6 for details.)

bad_exception class

```
class bad_exception : public exception {
public:
  bad_exception() throw();
```

```
  bad_exception(const bad_exception&) throw( );
  bad_exception& operator=(const bad_exception&) throw( );
  virtual const char* what( ) const throw( );
};
```

A bad_exception object is thrown from the unexpected function when unexpected throws an exception that is not listed in the exception specification that caused unexpected to be called. Most programs do not throw or catch bad_exception. You can list bad_exception in an exception specification if you want to handle this unusual situation differently.

See Chapter 5 and unexpected (in this section) for more details.

See Also

terminated function, unexpected function, throw keyword

---

exception class   Base class for all standard exceptions

```
class exception {
public:
  exception( ) throw( );
  exception(const exception&) throw( );
  exception& operator=(const exception&) throw( );
  virtual ~exception( ) throw( );
  virtual const char* what( ) const throw( );
};
```

The exception class is the base class for all exception objects thrown by the standard library or by code generated by the compiler. By convention, user-defined exception classes also derive from exception or from one of its derived classes.

virtual const char* what( ) const throw( );
> Returns a message that describes the nature of the exception. The exact contents of the string are implementation-defined; it might be a multibyte string, which can be converted to a wstring.

See Also

bad_exception class, bad_alloc in <new>, bad_cast in <typeinfo>, bad_typeid in <typeinfo>, ios_base::failure in <ios>, logic_error in <stdexcept>, runtime_error in <stdexcept>

---

set_terminate function   Changes the terminate( ) handler

```
typedef void (*terminate_handler)( );
terminate_handler set_terminate(terminate_handler f) throw( );
```

The set_terminate function saves f to be used by calls to terminate. The previous value of the terminate handler is returned.

See Also

terminate function

---

set_unexpected function

```
typedef void (*unexpected_handler)( );
unexpected_handler set_unexpected(unexpected_handler f)
    throw( );
```

The set_unexpected function saves f to be used by calls to unexpected. The previous value of the unexpected handler is returned.

See Also

unexpected function

terminate function

```
void terminate( )
```

The terminate function is called when normal exception handling cannot handle an exception for any reason—for example, when there is no matching catch block for an exception, or when an exception is thrown and, while the stack is unwinding, another exception is thrown by a destructor.

A program might also call terminate explicitly.

You can change the behavior of the terminate function by calling set_terminate. The default behavior is to call abort.

The terminate function is a last resort because normal exception handling failed. For this reason, you cannot rely on the usual destruction of static objects and objects on the stack.

See Also

set_terminate function, unexpected function, abort function in <cstdlib>, catch keyword

uncaught_exception function

```
bool uncaught_exception( )
```

The uncaught_exception function returns true while an exception is processed: after evaluating the argument of a throw expression but before a matching exception declaration is initialized in a catch block. It also returns true after terminate is called (but not for an explicit call to terminate). It returns false at other times.

Call uncaught_exception to learn whether exception handling is currently underway. If it returns true, throwing a new exception results in a call to terminate.

See Also

terminate function, catch keyword, throw keyword

unexpected function

```
void unexpected( )
```

If a function has an exception specification and throws an exception that is not listed in the exception specification, the unexpected function is called to handle the unexpected exception.

You can implement your own unexpected function. If you do so, you must ensure that unexpected does not return normally. It can terminate the program—for example, by calling terminate—or it can throw an exception.

If your unexpected function throws an exception that is not listed in the function's exception specification, a new exception of type bad_exception is created and thrown. If the function's exception specification does not list bad_exception, terminate is called automatically.

The default implementation of unexpected calls terminate.

In other words, if a function has an exception specification, it is guaranteed that only the specified exceptions can be thrown out of the function, or else the application will be terminated.

See Also

bad_exception class, set_unexpected function, abort in <cstdlib>, throw keyword

<fstream>

The <fstream> header declares classes and other types for performing I/O with external files. A file in C++ is a sequence of bytes. A narrow (byte) stream or buffer simply reads or writes those bytes. A wide stream or buffer reads multibyte characters and converts them to wide characters (according to the stream's locale) or converts wide characters to their multibyte equivalents for writing.

See Chapter 9 for a general discussion of I/O and related topics (stream buffers, locales, and facets), Chapter 1 for more information about character sets, and the <iostream> section in this chapter for information about the base-class templates required by the fstream class templates. Refer to Chapter 8 for information about traits in general and to the <string> section in this chapter for detailed information about the char_traits class template. Refer to the <streambuf> section in this chapter for information about the basic_streambuf class template.

To open a file for reading, use ifstream; for writing, use ofstream; for reading and writing, use fstream; for wide character I/O, use wifstream, wofstream, or wfstream.

basic_filebuf class template   Class template for file buffers

```
template <class charT, class traits = char_traits<charT> >
class basic_filebuf : public basic_streambuf<charT,traits>
{
public:
  typedef charT char_type;
  typedef typename traits::int_type int_type;
  typedef typename traits::pos_type pos_type;
  typedef typename traits::off_type off_type;
  typedef traits traits_type;

  basic_filebuf();
  virtual ~basic_filebuf();
```

```
    bool is_open( ) const;
    basic_filebuf<charT,traits>*
      open(const char* filename, ios_base::openmode mode);
    basic_filebuf<charT,traits>*
      open(const char* filename, ios_base::open_mode mode);
    basic_filebuf<charT,traits>* close( );
protected:
    virtual streamsize showmanyc( );
    virtual int_type underflow( );
    virtual int_type uflow( );
    virtual int_type pbackfail(int_type c = traits::eof( ));
    virtual int_type overflow(int_type c = traits::eof( ));
    virtual basic_streambuf<charT,traits>*
      setbuf(char_type* s, streamsize n);
    virtual pos_type seekoff(off_type off, ios_base::seekdir way,
      ios_base::openmode = ios_base::in | ios_base::out);
    virtual pos_type seekpos(pos_type newpos,
      ios_base::openmode which = ios_base::in | ios_base::out);
    virtual int sync( );
    virtual void imbue(const locale& loc);
};
```

The basic_filebuf class template implements a stream buffer that is associated with an external file. The connection to the external file is equivalent to calling C I/O functions (declared in <cstdio>) but may or may not actually call the C functions. For example, the open function is equivalent to calling fopen and having the filebuf object store the returned FILE pointer.

The external file is treated as a series of bytes, which might form multibyte characters. When converting the multibyte character sequences to characters in the file buffer, which are of type charT, the file buffer uses a code conversion facet from the buffer's locale. This codecvt facet is equivalent to *a_codecvt*, which is declared and initialized as follows:

```
    std::codecvt<charT, char, typename traits::state_type>
      a_codecvt = use_facet<codecvt<charT, char,
                  typename traits::state_type> >(getloc( ));
```

Some of the function descriptions in this section refer to *a_codecvt* and describe functionality, assuming that an actual codecvt facet object exists. An implementation does not have to create a codecvt facet object as long as the file stream acts as though it did create and use an explicit codecvt facet. (See <locale> for more information about codecvt.)

Remember that codecvt<char, char, mbstate_t> is essentially a no-op, mapping a character to itself, so the codecvt facet is most important when charT is wchar_t.

See <streambuf> for a description of the required behavior of a stream buffer, especially for the virtual functions that basic_filebuf overrides.

The following are the member functions of basic_filebuf:

basic_filebuf( )
> Initializes the file buffer in a closed state.

virtual **~basic_filebuf( )**
> Calls close( ) and finalizes the file buffer.

`basic_filebuf<charT, traits>*` **close()**

Closes the file, severing the connection between the external file and the file buffer. If the file is already closed, it returns a null pointer. Otherwise, it calls `overflow(EOF)` to flush the output buffer. If the buffer recently called `overflow`, the external character stream might have an incomplete shift sequence of a multibyte character. The `close` function therefore calls `a_codecvt.unshift()` as often as needed to complete the shift sequence, and then calls `overflow(EOF)` again to flush the buffer. Finally, the external file is closed by calling `fclose` or its equivalent.

The return value is this for success or a null pointer for failure.

`virtual void` **imbue**`(const locale& loc)`

Changes the file buffer's locale, in particular the codecvt facet. It is safe to change the locale when the file is positioned at its beginning, when the character encoding (*a_codecvt*.encoding()) is not state-dependent, or the old and new locales have the same codecvt facet.

`bool` **is_open**`() const`

Returns true if the file is open or false if the file is closed.

`basic_filebuf<charT, traits>*`
open`(const char* filename, ios_base::openmode mode)`
`basic_filebuf<charT, traits>*`
open`(const char* filename, ios_base::open_mode mode)`

Opens the file filename. If the file is already open (is_open() returns true), a null pointer is returned immediately; otherwise, the file buffer is initialized and the named file is opened by calling the equivalent of `fopen(filename, modestr)`. The *modestr* is determined from the mode (without the ios_base::ate bit), as shown in Table 13-9. No other mode combinations are allowed. If the mode includes ios_base::ate, the opened file is positioned at its end by calling the equivalent of `fseek(file, 0, SEEK_END)`.

The second form is deprecated. It has the same functionality as the first form. See ios_base::openmode in <ios> for details.

If the file is opened successfully, this is returned; otherwise, the return value is a null pointer.

Table 13-9. File open modes

ios_base mode bits	fopen equivalent mode string
out	"w"
out | app	"a"
out | trunc	"w"
in	"r"
in | out	"r+"
in | out | trunc	"w+"
binary | out	"wb"
binary | out | app	"ab"
binary | out | trunc	"wb"
binary | in	"rb"
binary | in | out	"r+b"
binary | in | out | trunc	"w+b"

virtual int_type **overflow**(int_type c = traits::eof( ))

> Converts its output using *a_codecvt*.out and writes the converted characters to the external file. The return value is traits::eof( ) for failure, which also occurs if the file is not open. For success, the return value is traits::not_eof(c).

virtual int_type **pbackfail**(int_type c = traits::eof( ))

> Tries to push back the character c so it will be the next character read from the input buffer. If a push-back position is not available (see <streambuf> for a definition of "push-back position"), the file buffer attempts to make one available (e.g., by moving the file position).

> If c is traits::eof( ) or the same character as gptr( )[-1], the file buffer decrements the gptr( ) pointer; otherwise, if the input array is assignable, c is assigned to gptr( )[-1] and gptr( ) is decremented.

> The return value is traits::eof( ) for failure or traits::not_eof(c) for success.

virtual pos_type **seekoff**(off_type off, ios_base::seekdir way,
  ios_base::openmode = ios_base::in | ios_base::out)

> Tries to seek to a new position in the file as an offset from a defined position. If the file is not open, the attempt to seek fails. If the character set encoding uses shift states or otherwise does not have a fixed size per character, off must be 0. Otherwise, if the destination is not the current position (off != 0 or way != basic_ios::cur), the output buffer is flushed and unshift sequences are written as needed (*a_codecvt*.unshift). The new file position is set by calling the equivalent of fseek(file, *width* * off, *origin*), in which *width* is *a_codecvt*.encoding( ) and *origin* is determined as shown in Table 13-10. If *width* < 0, off must be 0, so the call is fseek(file, 0, *origin*). The return value is the new file position or -1 for an error or if the new position is unknown. Note that seekoff does not use its final parameter.

Table 13-10. Seek origins

ios_base::seekdir options	fseek equivalents
basic_ios::beg	SEEK_SET
basic_ios::cur	SEEK_CUR
basic_ios::end	SEEK_END

virtual pos_type **seekpos**(pos_type newpos,
  ios_base::openmode which=ios_base::in|ios_base::out)

> Attempts to set the file position to newpos, which must be the result of calling seekoff or seekpos on the same file. If which includes the ios_base::in bit, the input sequence is updated; if which includes the ios_base::out bit, the output sequence is updated, and any necessary unshift characters are written prior to setting the file position. If neither bit is set in which, an error results. The return value is -1 for an error or newpos for success.

virtual basic_streambuf<charT, traits>* **setbuf**(char_type* s, streamsize n)

> Sets the buffer. If you call setbuf(0, 0) before any I/O operations are performed on a file, the file is set to unbuffered. The behavior is implementation-defined for any other argument values. The return value is this.

virtual streamsize **showmanyc**( )
>   Returns an estimate of the number of characters immediately available for input. In other words, it does the same thing as the base class showmanyc function.

virtual int **sync**( )
>   Flushes output to the external file. The behavior for input is implementation-defined.

virtual int_type **uflow**( )
>   Fills the input buffer in the same manner as underflow.

virtual int_type **underflow**( )
>   Fills the input buffer. Multibyte characters are read from the external file and converted to charT characters by calling the equivalent of *a_codecvt*.in.

See Also

filebuf class, wfilebuf class, basic_streambuf in <streambuf>

---

basic_fstream class template

Class template for file input and output streams

```
template <class charT, class traits=char_traits<charT> >
class basic_fstream : public basic_iostream<charT,traits>
{
public:
  typedef charT char_type;
  typedef typename traits::int_type int_type;
  typedef typename traits::pos_type pos_type;
  typedef typename traits::off_type off_type;
  typedef traits traits_type;

  basic_fstream( );
  explicit basic_fstream(const char* filename,
                         ios_base::openmode mode = ios_base::in|ios_base::out);

  basic_filebuf<charT,traits>* rdbuf( ) const;
  bool is_open( );
  void open(const char* filename,
            ios_base::openmode mode = ios_base::in|ios_base::out);
  void close( );
};
```

The basic_fstream class template supports reading and writing to and from named files using a basic_filebuf<charT, traits> object. (See <istream> for a description of the base-class template, basic_iostream.) In the following member function descriptions, the file buffer object is assumed to be a private data member with the name *buf*.

basic_fstream( )
>   Constructor initializes the base class with basic_iostream(&*buf*) and initializes *buf* with its default constructor.

explicit **basic_fstream**(const char* filename,
  ios_base::openmode mode = ios_base::in | ios_base::out)
>   Initializes the base class and *buf*, then calls open(filename, mode). If open returns a null pointer, the constructor calls setstate(failbit).

basic_filebuf<charT, traits>* **rdbuf**( ) const
>   Returns &*buf*.

---

bool **is_open**( )
     Returns rdbuf( )->is_open( ).

void **open**(const char* filename,
  ios_base::openmode mode = ios_base::in | ios_base::out)
     Calls rdbuf( )->open(filename, mode). If that function returns a null pointer, open
     calls setstate(failbit).

void **close**( )
     Calls rdbuf( )->close( ). If that function fails, close calls setstate(failbit).

See Also

basic_filebuf class template, basic_ios in <ios>, basic_iostream in <istream>

---

basic_ifstream class template
Class template for file input streams

```
template <class charT, class traits = char_traits<charT> >
class basic_ifstream : public basic_istream<charT,traits>
{
public:
  typedef charT char_type;
  typedef typename traits::int_type int_type;
  typedef typename traits::pos_type pos_type;
  typedef typename traits::off_type off_type;
  typedef traits traits_type;
  basic_ifstream( );
  explicit basic_ifstream(const char* s, ios_base::openmode mode = ios_base::in);

  basic_filebuf<charT,traits>* rdbuf( ) const;
  bool is_open( );
  void open(const char* s, ios_base::openmode mode = ios_base::in);
  void open(const char* s, ios_base::open_mode mode);
  void close( );
};
```

The basic_ifstream class template supports reading from named files using a basic_
filebuf<charT, traits> object. (See <istream> for a description of the base-class
template, basic_istream.) In the following member function descriptions, the file
buffer object is assumed to be a private data member with the name *buf*:

basic_ifstream( )
     Initializes the base class with basic_istream(&*buf*) and initializes *buf* with its
     default constructor.

explicit **basic_ifstream**(const char* filename,
  ios_base::openmode mode = ios_base::in)
     Initializes the base class and *buf*, then calls open(filename, mode). If open returns a
     null pointer, the constructor calls setstate(failbit).

basic_filebuf<charT, traits>* **rdbuf**( ) const
     Returns &*buf*.

bool **is_open**( )
     Returns rdbuf( )->is_open( ).

```
void open(const char* filename, ios_base::openmode mode = ios_base::in)
void open(const char* filename,ios_base::open_mode mode)
```
> Calls rdbuf()->open(filename, mode). If that function returns a null pointer, open calls setstate(failbit). The second form is deprecated. It has the same functionality as the first form. See ios_base::openmode in <ios> for details.

```
void close()
```
> Calls rdbuf()->close(). If that function fails, close calls setstate(failbit).

See Also

basic_filebuf class template, basic_ios in <ios>, basic_istream in <istream>

---

basic_ofstream class template

Class template for file output streams

```
template <class charT, class traits = char_traits<charT> >
class basic_ofstream : public basic_ostream<charT,traits>
{
public:
  typedef charT char_type;
  typedef typename traits::int_type int_type;
  typedef typename traits::pos_type pos_type;
  typedef typename traits::off_type off_type;
  typedef traits traits_type;

  basic_ofstream();
  explicit basic_ofstream(const char* s, ios_base::openmode mode =
                          ios_base::out);
  basic_filebuf<charT,traits>* rdbuf() const;
  bool is_open();
  void open(const char* s, ios_base::openmode mode = ios_base::out);
  void open(const char* s, ios_base::open_mode mode);
  void close();
};
```

The basic_ofstream class template supports writing to named files using a basic_filebuf<charT, traits> object. (See <ostream> for a description of the base-class template, basic_ostream.) In the following member function descriptions, the file buffer object is assumed to be a private data member with the name *buf*:

```
basic_ofstream()
```
> Initializes the base class with basic_ostream(&*buf*) and initializes *buf* with its default constructor.

```
explicit basic_ofstream(const char* filename,
  ios_base::openmode mode = ios_base::out)
```
> Initializes the base class and *buf*, then calls open(filename, mode). If open returns a null pointer, the constructor calls setstate(failbit).

```
basic_filebuf<charT, traits>* rdbuf() const
```
> Returns &*buf*.

```
bool is_open()
```
> Returns rdbuf()->is_open().

void **open**(const char* filename, ios_base::openmode mode = ios_base::out)
void **open**(const char* filename,ios_base::open_mode mode)
> Calls rdbuf( )->open(filename, mode). If that function returns a null pointer, open calls setstate(failbit). The second form is deprecated. It has the same functionality as the first form. See ios_base::openmode in <ios> for details.

void **close**( )
> Calls rdbuf( )->close( ). If that function fails, close calls setstate(failbit).

See Also

basic_filebuf class template, basic_ios in <ios>, basic_ostream in <ostream>

filebuf class   File buffer

typedef basic_filebuf<char> **filebuf**;
The filebuf class is a specialization of the basic_filebuf template for char characters.

See Also

basic_filebuf class template, wfilebuf class

fstream class   Input and output file stream

typedef basic_fstream<char> **fstream**;
The fstream class is a specialization of the basic_fstream template for char characters.

See Also

basic_fstream class template, wfstream class, iostream in <istream>

ifstream class   Input file stream

typedef basic_ifstream<char> **ifstream**;
The ifstream class is a specialization of the basic_ifstream template for char characters. Example 13-9 shows a simple use of the ifstream and ofstream classes.

Example 13-9. Copying a file using ifstream and ofstream

```
#include <cstdlib>
#include <fstream>
#include <cstdio>    // For perror( )
#include <iostream>  // For cerr

int main(int argc, char** argv)
{
  if (argc != 3) {
    std::cerr << "usage: copy FROM TO\n";
    return EXIT_FAILURE;
  }

  // Open the input file.
  std::ifstream in(argv[1]);
```

Example 13-9. Copying a file using ifstream and ofstream (continued)

```
if (! in) {
  std::perror(argv[1]);
  return EXIT_FAILURE;
}

// Open the output file.
std::ofstream out(argv[2]);
if (! out) {
  std::perror(argv[2]);
  return EXIT_FAILURE;
}

// Copy the input to the output, one character at a time.
char c;
while (in.get(c))
  out.put(c);
out.close();
// Make sure the output was written.
if (! out) {
  std::perror(argv[2]);
  return EXIT_FAILURE;
}
}
```

See Also

basic_ifstream class template, wifstream class, istream in <istream>

---

ofstream class   Output file stream

typedef basic_ofstream<char> **ofstream**;

The ofstream class is a specialization of the basic_ofstream template for char characters.

See Also

basic_ofstream class template, wofstream class, ostream in <ostream>

---

wfilebuf class   Wide character file buffer

typedef basic_filebuf<wchar_t> **wfilebuf**;

The wfilebuf class is a specialization of the basic_filebuf template for wchar_t characters.

See Also

basic_filebuf class template, filebuf class

wfstream class
Wide character input and output stream

typedef basic_fstream<wchar_t> **wfstream**;

The wfstream class is a specialization of the basic_fstream template for wchar_t characters.

See Also

basic_fstream class template, fstream class, wiostream in <istream>

wifstream class
Wide character input stream

typedef basic_ifstream<wchar_t> **wifstream**;

The wifstream class is a specialization of the basic_ifstream template for wchar_t characters.

See Also

basic_ifstream class template, ifstream class, wistream in <istream>

wofstream class
Wide character output stream

typedef basic_ofstream<wchar_t> **wofstream**;

The wofstream class is a specialization of the basic_ofstream template for wchar_t characters.

See Also

basic_ofstream class template, ofstream class, wostream in <ostream>

Library
Reference

<functional>

The <functional> header defines several *functionals*, or *function objects*. A function object is an object that has an operator( ), so it can be called using the same syntax as a function. Function objects are most often used with the standard algorithms.

For example, to copy a sequence of integers, adding a fixed amount (42) to each value, you could use the following expression:

```
std::transform(src.begin( ), src.end( ), dst.begin( ),
            std::bind2nd(std::plus<int>( ), 42))
```

The result of combining bind2nd and plus<int> is a function object that adds the value 42 when it is applied to any integer. The transform algorithm copies all the elements from src to dst, applying the functional argument to each element. See the detailed description of bind2nd and plus in this section for details.

The standard function objects are defined for C++ operators; for binding function arguments; and for adapting functions, member functions, etc., as function objects.

Boost defines functionals that extend and improve on those in the standard library. See Appendix B for information about Boost.

binary_function class template   Base class for binary functionals

```
template <typename Arg1, typename Arg2, typename Result>
struct binary_function {
  typedef Arg1 first_argument_type;
  typedef Arg2 second_argument_type;
  typedef Result result_type;
};
```

The binary_function template is a base-class template for all the function classes that represent binary operations. It provides standard names for the argument and result types.

The base template has separate template parameters for each of the argument types and the return type. Many of the predefined function objects in this section use the same type for all three parameters, but you can use different types when defining your own function object, as shown in Example 13-10.

Example 13-10. Functional to round off a floating-point number

```
// Functional for a binary function that rounds off a floating-point number (of
// type FltT) to a certain number of decimal places (supplied as an unsigned)
template<typename FltT>
struct roundoff : std::binary_function<FltT,unsigned,FltT> {
  FltT operator()(FltT x, unsigned digits) const {
    FltT y = std::pow(10.0, static_cast<FltT>(digits));
    FltT z = x * y;
    return (z < 0 ? std::ceil(z - 0.5) : std::floor(z + 0.5)) / y;
  }
};
...
// Copy seq to seq2, rounding off to two decimal places.
std::transform(seq.begin(), seq.end(), seq2.begin(),
  std::bind2nd(roundoff<double>(), 2));
```

See Also

binary_negate class template, const_mem_fun1_ref_t class template, const_mem_fun1_t class template, mem_fun1_ref_t class template, mem_fun1_t class template, pointer_to_binary_function class template, unary_function class template

binary_negate class template   Logical negation of a binary predicate

```
template <typename P>
class binary_negate : public
  binary_function<typename P::first_argument_type,
            typename P::second_argument_type, bool>
{
public:
  explicit binary_negate(const P& predicate);
  bool operator()(const typename P::first_argument_type& x,
            const typename P::second_argument_type& y) const;
};
```

The `binary_negate` class template is a binary functional that returns the logical negation of another binary functional—that is, `operator( )` returns `!predicate(x, y)`. The simplest way to use `binary_negate` is to use the `not2` function template.

See Also

`unary_negate` class template, `not2` function template

bind1st function template
Creates a binder1st function object

```
template <typename Operation, typename T>
binder1st<Operation> bind1st(const Operation& op, const T& x);
```

The `bind1st` function is a convenient way to construct a `binder1st` object. Use `bind1st` when you have a binary function and always want to supply the same value as the first argument to the function.

Example

Suppose you have a container of data points, and you want to count the number of points that exceed a threshold—in other words, where the threshold is less than or equal to the data point. Here is one way to do this:

```
std::cout
  << std::count_if(data.begin( ), data.end( ),
      std::bind1st(std::less_equal<double>( ), threshold))
  << '\n';
```

See Also

`bind2nd` function template, `binder1st` class template

bind2nd function template
Creates a binder2nd function object

```
template <typename Operation, typename T>
binder2nd<Operation> bind2nd(const Operation& op, const T& x);
```

The `bind2nd` function is a convenient way to construct a `binder2nd` object. Use `bind2nd` when you have a binary function and always want to supply the same value as the first argument to the function.

Example

Suppose you have a container of data points, and you want to count the number of points that exceed a threshold. Here is one way to do this:

```
std::cout << std::count_if(data.begin( ), data.end( ),
            std::bind2nd(std::greater<double>( ), threshold)) << '\n';
```

See Also

`bind1st` function template, `binder2nd` class template

binder1st class template
Binds a value to the first argument of a binary function

```
template <typename Operation>
class binder1st : public unary_function<
  typename Operation::second_argument_type,
  typename Operation::result_type>
{
```

```
protected:
  Operation op;
  typename Operation::first_argument_type value;
public:
  binder1st(const Operation& x,
            const typename Operation::first_argument_type& y);
  typename Operation::result_type operator()
    (const typename Operation::second_argument_type& x)const;
};
```

The binder1st class template is a unary functional that binds a fixed value as the first argument to a binary function object. The constructor initializes the op and value data members with the x and y arguments. The operator() member function returns op(value, x).

See the bind1st function template for an easier way to construct and use the binder1st class template.

See Also

bind1st function template, binder2nd class template

---

binder2nd class template   Binds a value to the second argument of a binary function

```
template <typename Operation>
class binder2nd : public unary_function<
  typename Operation::first_argument_type,
  typename Operation::result_type>
{
protected:
  Operation op;
  typename Operation::second_argument_type value;
public:
  binder2nd(const Operation& x,
            const typename Operation::second_argument_type& y);
  typename Operation::result_type operator()
    (const typename Operation::first_argument_type& x) const;
};
```

The binder2nd class template is a unary functional that binds a fixed value as the second argument to a binary function object. The constructor initializes the op and value data members with the x and y arguments. The operator() member function returns op(x, value).

See the bind2nd function template for an easier way to construct and use the binder2nd class template.

See Also

bind2nd function template, binder1st class template

---

const_mem_fun_ref_t class template   Calls a member function of a constant reference object

```
template <typename Rtn, typename T>
class const_mem_fun_ref_t : public unary_function<T, Rtn>
{
```

```
public:
    explicit const_mem_fun_ref_t(Rtn (T::*p)() const);
    Rtn operator()(const T& p) const;
};
```

The const_mem_fun_ref_t class template is a unary functional that wraps a member function pointer. The Rtn template parameter is the member function's return type, and the T template parameter is the class that declares the member function. The argument to the constructor is a pointer to the member function, which takes no arguments. The member function is called from operator() using a reference to the const object.

See the mem_fun_ref function template for an easier way to construct and use the const_mem_fun_ref_t class template.

See Also

const_mem_fun_t class template, const_mem_fun1_ref_t class template, mem_fun_ref function template, mem_fun_ref_t class template

const_mem_fun_t class template   Calls a member function of a constant object

```
template <class Rtn, class T>
class const_mem_fun_t : public unary_function<T*, Rtn>
{
public:
    explicit const_mem_fun_t(Rtn (T::*p)() const);
    Rtn operator()(const T* p) const;
};
```

The const_mem_fun_t class template is a unary functional that wraps a member function pointer. The Rtn template parameter is the member function's return type, and the T template parameter is the class that declares the member function. The argument to the constructor is a pointer to the member function, which takes no arguments. The member function is called from operator() using a pointer to the const object.

See the mem_fun function template for an easier way to construct and use the const_mem_fun_t class template.

See Also

const_mem_fun_ref_t class template, const_mem_fun1_t class template, mem_fun function template, mem_fun_t class template

const_mem_fun1_ref_t class template   Calls a member function of a constant reference object with an argument

```
template <typename Rtn, typename T, typename Arg>
class const_mem_fun1_ref_t :
    public binary_function<T, Arg, Rtn>
{
public:
    explicit const_mem_fun1_ref_t(Rtn (T::*p)(Arg) const);
    Rtn operator()(const T& p, Arg x) const;
};
```

The const_mem_fun1_ref_t class template is a binary functional that wraps a member function pointer. The Rtn template parameter is the member function's return type, the T template parameter is the class that declares the member function, and the Arg template parameter is the type of the member function's sole argument.

The argument to the constructor is a pointer to the member function. The member function is called from operator( ) using a reference to the const object.

See the mem_fun_ref function template for an easier way to construct and use the const_mem_fun1_ref_t class template.

See Also

const_mem_fun_ref_t class template, const_mem_fun1_t class template, mem_fun_ref function template, mem_fun1_ref_t class template

const_mem_fun1_t class template

Calls a member function of a constant object with an argument

```
template <typename Rtn, typename T, typename Arg>
class const_mem_fun1_t: public binary_function<T*, Arg, Rtn>
{
public:
  explicit const_mem_fun1_t(Rtn (T::*p)(Arg) const);
  Rtn operator( )(const T* p, Arg x) const;
};
```

The const_mem_fun1_t class template is a binary functional that wraps a member function pointer. The Rtn template parameter is the member function's return type, the T template parameter is the class that declares the member function, and the Arg template parameter is the type of the member function's sole argument.

The argument to the constructor is a pointer to the member function. The member function is called from operator( ) using a pointer to the const object.

See the mem_fun function template for an easier way to construct and use the const_mem_fun1_t class template.

See Also

const_mem_fun_t class template, const_mem_fun1_ref_t class template, mem_fun function template, mem_fun1_t class template

divides class template

Binary functional to divide

```
template <typename T>
struct divides : binary_function<T, T, T> {
  T operator( )(const T& x, const T& y) const;
};
```

The divides class template is a binary functional in which operator( ) returns x / y.

See Also

binary_function class template, minus class template, modulus class template, multiplies class template, negate class template, plus class template

equal_to class template
Binary functional to compare for equality

```
template <typename T>
struct equal_to : binary_function<T, T, bool> {
  bool operator( )(const T& x, const T& y) const;
};
```

The equal_to class template is a binary functional in which operator( ) returns x == y.

See Also

binary_function class template, greater class template, greater_equal class template, less class template, less_equal class template, not_equal_to class template

greater class template
Binary functional to compare for greater-than

```
template <typename T>
struct greater : binary_function<T, T, bool> {
  bool operator( )(const T& x, const T& y) const;
};
```

The greater class template is a binary functional in which operator( ) returns x > y.

See Also

binary_function class template, equal_to class template, greater_equal class template, less class template, less_equal class template, not_equal_to class template

greater_equal class template
Binary functional to compare for greater-than-or-equal

```
template <typename T>
struct greater_equal : binary_function<T, T, bool> {
  bool operator( )(const T& x, const T& y) const;
};
```

The greater_equal class template is a binary functional in which operator( ) returns x >= y.

See Also

binary_function class template, equal_to class template, greater class template, less class template, less_equal class template, not_equal_to class template

less class template
Binary functional to compare for less-than

```
template <typename T>
struct less : binary_function<T, T, bool> {
  bool operator( )(const T& x, const T& y) const;
};
```

The less class template is a binary functional in which operator( ) returns x < y.

See Also

binary_function class template, equal_to class template, greater class template, greater_equal class template, less_equal class template, not_equal_to class template

less_equal class template   Binary functional to compare for less-than-or-equal

```
template <typename T>
struct less_equal : binary_function<T, T, bool> {
  bool operator()(const T& x, const T& y) const;
};
```
The less_equal class template is a binary functional in which operator( ) returns x <= y.

See Also

binary_function class template, equal_to class template, greater class template, greater_equal class template, less class template, not_equal_to class template

logical_and class template   Binary functional for logical conjunction

```
template <typename T>
struct logical_and : binary_function<T, T, bool> {
  bool operator()(const T& x, const T& y) const;
};
```
The logical_and class template is a binary functional in which operator( ) returns x && y. Note that no short-circuiting occurs because both arguments must be evaluated before operator( ) can be called.

See Also

logical_not class template, logical_or class template

logical_not class template   Binary functional for logical negation

```
template <typename T>
struct logical_not : unary_function<T, bool> {
  bool operator()(const T& x) const;
};
```
The logical_not class template is a unary functional in which operator( ) returns !x.

See Also

logical_and class template, logical_or class template, not1 function template, not2 function template

logical_or class template   Binary functional for logical disjunction

```
template <typename T>
struct logical_or : binary_function<T, T, bool> {
  bool operator()(const T& x, const T& y) const;
};
```
The logical_or class template is a binary functional in which operator( ) returns x || y. Note that no short-circuiting occurs because both arguments must be evaluated before operator( ) can be called.

See Also

logical_and class template, logical_not class template

mem_fun function template   Creates a function object to call a member function via a pointer

```
template<typename Rtn, typename T>
  const_mem_fun_t<Rtn,T> mem_fun(Rtn (T::*f)() const);
template<typename Rtn, typename T, typename Arg>
  const_mem_fun1_t<Rtn,T,Arg> mem_fun(Rtn (T::*f)(Arg) const);
template<typename Rtn, typename T>
  mem_fun_t<Rtn,T> mem_fun(Rtn (T::*f)());
template<typename Rtn, typename T, typename Arg>
  mem_fun1_t<Rtn,T,Arg> mem_fun(Rtn (T::*f)(Arg));
```

The mem_fun function template takes a pointer to a member function as an argument and returns a function object that can call the member function. The function object must be applied to a pointer to T (or a derived class). The Rtn template parameter is the return type of the member function, and the T template parameter is the object that has the member function. The optional Arg template parameter is the type of the argument to the member function.

The mem_fun function is usually the simplest way to create a function object that wraps a member function. In normal use, the compiler deduces the template parameters.

Suppose you have an Employee class and a container of Employee pointers. One of the member functions of Employee is gets_bonus, which returns a bool: true if the employee is lucky and gets a bonus this year, and false if the employee is unlucky. Example 13-11 shows how to remove all the unlucky employees from the container.

Example 13-11. Wrapping a member function called via a pointer as a function object

```
class Employee {
public:
  int        sales()      const { return sales_; }
  std::string name()      const { return name_; }
  bool       gets_bonus() const { return sales() > bonus; }
...
};

std::list<Employee*> empptrs;
// Fill empptrs with pointers to Employee objects.
...
// Remove the employees who will NOT receive bonuses.
std::list<Employee*>::iterator last =
  std::remove_if(empptrs.begin(), empptrs.end(),
              std::not1(std::mem_fun(&Employee::gets_bonus)));
```

See Also

const_mem_fun_t class template, const_mem_fun1_t class template, mem_fun_ref function template, mem_fun_t class template, mem_fun1_t class template, ptr_fun function template

mem_fun_ref function template

Creates a function object to call a member
function via a reference

```
template<typename Rtn, typename T>
  const_mem_fun_ref_t<Rtn,T>
    mem_fun_ref(Rtn (T::*f)() const);
template<typename Rtn, typename T, typename Arg>
  const_mem_fun1_ref_t<Rtn,T,Arg>
    mem_fun_ref(Rtn (T::*f)(Arg) const);
template<typename Rtn, typename T>
  mem_fun_ref_t<Rtn,T> mem_fun_ref(Rtn (T::*f)());
template<typename Rtn, typename T, typename Arg>
  mem_fun1_ref_t<Rtn,T,A> mem_fun_ref(Rtn (T::*f)(Arg));
```

The mem_fun_ref function template takes a pointer to a member function as an argument and returns a function object that can call the member function. The function object must be applied to an object of type T (or a derived class). The object is passed by reference to the functional. The Rtn template parameter is the return type of the member function; the T template parameter is the object that has the member function. The optional Arg template parameter is the type of the argument to the member function.

The mem_fun_ref function is usually the simplest way to create a function object that wraps a member function. In normal use, the compiler deduces the template parameters.

Suppose you have an Employee class and a container of Employee objects. As in Example 13-11, one of the member functions of Employee is gets_bonus, which returns a bool: true if the employee is lucky and gets a bonus this year, or false if the employee is unlucky. Example 13-12 shows how to remove all the unlucky employees from the container.

Example 13-12. Wrapping a member function called via a reference as a function object

```
class Employee {
public:
  int         sales()      const { return sales_; }
  std::string name()       const { return name_; }
  bool        gets_bonus() const { return sales() > bonus; }
...
};

std::list<Employee> emps;
// Fill emps with Employee objects.
...
// Erase the employees who will NOT receive bonuses. The call to remove_if
// rearranges emps; the call to erase removes the unlucky employees from the
// list.
emps.erase(
  std::remove_if(emps.begin(), emps.end(),
        std::not1(std::mem_fun_ref(&Employee::gets_bonus))),
  emps.end());
```

See Also

const_mem_fun_ref_t class template, const_mem_fun1_ref_t class template, mem_fun function template, mem_fun_ref_t class template, mem_fun1_ref_t class template, ptr_fun function template

mem_fun_ref_t class template   Calls a member function of a reference object

```
template <typename Rtn, typename T>
class mem_fun_ref_t : public unary_function<T, Rtn>
{
public:
  explicit mem_fun_ref_t(Rtn (T::*p)( ));
  Rtn operator( )(T& p) const;
};
```

The mem_fun_ref_t class template is a unary functional that wraps a member function pointer. The Rtn template parameter is the member function's return type, and the T template parameter is the class that declares the member function. The argument to the constructor is a pointer to the member function, which takes no arguments. The member function is called from operator( ) using a reference to the object.

See the mem_fun_ref function template for an easier way to construct and use the mem_fun_ref_t class template.

See Also

const_mem_fun_ref_t class template, mem_fun_ref function template, mem_fun_t class template, mem_fun1_ref_t class template

mem_fun_t class template   Calls a member function of a constant object

```
template <class Rtn, class T>
class mem_fun_t : public unary_function<T*, Rtn>
{
public:
  explicit mem_fun_t(Rtn (T::*p)( ) const);
  Rtn operator( )(const T* p) const;
};
```

The mem_fun_t class template is a unary functional that wraps a member function pointer. The Rtn template parameter is the member function's return type, and the T template parameter is the class that declares the member function. The argument to the constructor is a pointer to the member function, which takes no arguments. The member function is called from operator( ) using a pointer to the object.

See the mem_fun function template for an easier way to construct and use the mem_fun_t class template.

See Also

const_mem_fun_t class template, mem_fun function template, mem_fun_ref_t class template, mem_fun1_t class template

mem_fun1_ref_t class template

Calls a member function of a constant
reference object with an argument

```
template <typename Rtn, typename T, typename Arg>
class mem_fun1_ref_t :
  public binary_function<T, Arg, Rtn>
{
public:
  explicit mem_fun1_ref_t(Rtn (T::*p)(Arg) const);
  Rtn operator()(const T& p, Arg x) const;
};
```

The mem_fun1_ref_t class template is a binary functional that wraps a member function pointer. The Rtn template parameter is the member function's return type, the T template parameter is the class that declares the member function, and the Arg template parameter is the type of the member function's sole argument.

The argument to the constructor is a pointer to the member function. The member function is called from operator( ) using a const reference to the object.

See the mem_fun_ref function template for an easier way to construct and use the mem_fun1_ref_t class template.

See Also

const_mem_fun1_ref_t class template, mem_fun_ref function template, mem_fun_ref_t class template, mem_fun1_t class template

mem_fun1_t class template

Calls a member function of an object with an argument

```
template <typename Rtn, typename T, typename Arg>
class mem_fun1_t: public binary_function<T*, Arg, Rtn>
{
public:
  explicit mem_fun1_t(Rtn (T::*p)(Arg));
  Rtn operator()(T* p, Arg x) const;
};
```

The mem_fun1_t class template is a binary functional that wraps a member function pointer. The Rtn template parameter is the member function's return type, the T template parameter is the class that declares the member function, and the Arg template parameter is the type of the member function's sole argument.

The argument to the constructor is a pointer to the member function. The member function is called from operator( ) using a pointer to the object.

See the mem_fun function template for an easier way to construct and use the mem_fun1_t class template.

See Also

const_mem_fun1_t class template, mem_fun function template, mem_fun_t class template, mem_fun1_ref_t class template

minus class template

Binary functional for subtraction

```
template <typename T>
struct minus : binary_function<T, T, T> {
  T operator()(const T& x, const T& y) const;
};
```

The minus class template is a binary functional in which operator( ) returns x - y.

See Also

binary_function class template, divides class template, modulus class template, multiplies class template, negate class template, plus class template

modulus class template

Binary functional for modulus (remainder)

```
template <typename T>
struct modulus : binary_function<T, T, T> {
  T operator()(const T& x, const T& y) const;
};
```

The modulus class template is a binary functional in which operator( ) returns x % y.

See Also

binary_function class template, divides class template, minus class template, multiplies class template, negate class template, plus class template

multiplies class template

Binary functional for multiplication

```
template <typename T>
struct multiplies : binary_function<T, T, T> {
  T operator()(const T& x, const T& y) const;
};
```

The multiplies class template is a binary functional in which operator( ) returns x * y.

See Also

binary_function class template, divides class template, minus class template, modulus class template, negate class template, plus class template

negate class template

Unary functional for arithmetic negation

```
template <typename T>
struct negate : unary_function<T,T> {
  T operator()(const T& x) const;
};
```

The negate class template is a unary functional that performs arithmetic negation, that is, operator( ) returns -x.

See Also

divides class template, minus class template, modulus class template, multiplies class template, plus class template, unary_function class template

not1 function template

Returns a unary_negate object

```
template <typename Predicate>
unary_negate<Predicate> not1(const Predicate& pred);
```

The not1 function template is a convenient way to construct a unary_negate function object that performs the logical negation of pred. See Example 13-11 earlier in this section.

See Also

logical_not class template, not2 function template, unary_negate class template

not2 function template

Returns a binary_negate object

```
template <typename Predicate>
binary_negate<Predicate> not2(const Predicate& pred);
```

The not2 function template is a convenient way to construct a binary_negate function object that performs the logical negation of pred.

See Also

binary_negate class template, logical_not class template, not1 function template

not_equal_to class template

Binary functional for inequality

```
template <typename T>
struct not_equal_to : binary_function<T, T, bool>
{
  bool operator()(const T& x, const T& y) const;
};
```

The not_equal_to class template is a binary functional in which operator() returns x != y.

See Also

binary_function class template, equal_to class template, greater class template, greater_equal class template, less class template, less_equal class template

plus class template

Binary functional for addition

```
template <typename T>
struct plus : binary_function<T, T, T>
{
  T operator()(const T& x, const T& y) const;
};
```

The plus class template is a binary functional in which operator() returns x + y.

See Also

binary_function class template, divides class template, minus class template, modulus class template, multiplies class template, negate class template

pointer_to_binary_function class template Functional for a pointer to a binary function

```
template <class Arg1, class Arg2, class Rtn>
class pointer_to_binary_function :
  public binary_function<Arg1,Arg2,Rtn>
{
public:
  explicit pointer_to_binary_function(Rtn (*f)(Arg1, Arg2));
  Rtn operator( )(Arg1 x, Arg2 y) const;
};
```

The pointer_to_binary_function class template is a function object that wraps a pointer to a function, in which the function is an ordinary (nonmember) function that takes two arguments. The ptr_fun function template is the most convenient way to create a pointer_to_binary_function object.

See Also

pointer_to_unary_function class template, ptr_fun function template

pointer_to_unary_function class template Functional for a pointer to a unary function

```
template <typename Arg, typename Rtn>
class pointer_to_unary_function :
  public unary_function<Arg, Rtn>
{
public:
  explicit pointer_to_unary_function(Result (*f)(Arg));
  Rtn operator( )(Arg x) const;
};
```

The pointer_to_unary_function class template is a function object that wraps a pointer to a function, in which the function is an ordinary (nonmember) function that takes one argument. The ptr_fun function template is the most convenient way to create a pointer_to_unary_function object.

See Also

pointer_to_binary_function class template, ptr_fun function template

ptr_fun function template Creates a pointer to a function object

```
template <typename Arg1, typename Arg2, typename Rtn>
  pointer_to_binary_function<Arg1,Arg2,Rtn>
    ptr_fun(Rtn (*f)(Arg1, Arg2));
template <typename Arg, typename Rtn>
  pointer_to_unary_function<Arg, Rtn>
    ptr_fun(Rtn (*f)(Arg));
```

The ptr_fun function template creates a function object from a pointer to a function. The resulting function object has an operator( ) that calls the function. Functions of one and two arguments are supported.

For example, suppose you have two numeric vectors, a and b, and you want to raise each element of a to the power of the corresponding element in b, saving the result in a third vector, c. There is no predefined power function object, so you can use ptr_fun and your own power function instead, as shown in Example 13-13.

Example 13-13. Wrapping the pow function in a function object

```
std::vector<double> a, b, c;
double power(double x, double y)
{
  return std::pow(x, y);
}
...
std::transform(a.begin(), a.end(), b.begin(), c.begin(),
               std::ptr_fun(power));
```

See Also

mem_fun function template, mem_fun_ref function template, pointer_to_binary_ function class template, pointer_to_unary_function class template

---

unary_negate class template   Logical negation of a unary predicate

```
template <typename P>
class unary_negate :
  public unary_function<typename P::argument_type,bool>
{
public:
  explicit unary_negate(const P& predicate);
  bool operator()(const typename P::argument_type& x) const;
};
```

The unary_negate class template is a binary functional that returns the logical negation of another unary functional—that is, operator( ) returns !predicate(x). The simplest way to use unary_negate is to use the not1 function template.

See Also

binary_negate class template, not1 function template

---

unary_function class template   Base class for unary functionals

```
template <typename Arg, typename Result>
struct unary_function {
  typedef Arg argument_type;
  typedef Result result_type;
};
```

The unary_function template is a base class for all the function classes that represent unary operations. It provides standard names for the argument and result types.

See Also

binary_function class template, binder1st class template, binder2nd class template, const_mem_fun_ref_t class template, const_mem_fun_t class template, mem_fun_ref_t class template, mem_fun_t class template, negate class template, pointer_to_unary_function class template, unary_negate class template

---

<iomanip>

The <iomanip> header declares several I/O manipulators. An I/O manipulator is a function object that can be used in a sequence of input or output operators to manipulate the I/O stream. The manipulators are simple wrappers for functionality that is available as member functions of the ios_base class, but manipulators are simpler to use in some situations.

For example, to print formatted output, the following two code fragments are equivalent:

```
// Using manipulators
std::cout << std::setw(16) << std::setprecision(12) << x;

// Without manipulators
std::cout.width(16);
std::cout.precision(12);
std::cout << x;
```

At a basic level, manipulators are easy to use. If you want to understand exactly how they work, perhaps to write your own, see Chapter 9 for a thorough discussion of I/O, including manipulators.

 The return type of each manipulator is implementation-defined. For the following function descriptions, this type is shown as *manip_t*.

Use a manipulator by applying it to a stream—that is, *out* << *manip*, in which *out* is an instance of basic_ostream, or *in* >> *manip*, in which *in* is an instance of basic_istream. In the following function descriptions, *stream* refers to the input or output stream to which the manipulator is being applied.

---

resetiosflags function
Clears specified flags

manip_t **resetiosflags**(ios_base::fmtflags mask)

The resetiosflags function clears the flag bits in mask for a stream. In other words, it performs the equivalent of *stream*.setf(ios_base::fmtflags(0), mask).

See Also

setiosflags function, ios_base in <ios>

---

setbase function
Sets conversion radix

manip_t **setbase**(int base)

The setbase function sets the conversion radix for a stream. In other words, it performs the equivalent of *stream*.setf(*newbase,* ios_base::basefield), in which *newbase* depends on base, as shown in Table 13-11. Notice that any value of a base other than 8, 10, or 16 is treated the same as 0.

Table 13-11. Conversion radix

setbase argument	fmtflags equivalent
8	ios_base::oct
10	ios_base::dec
16	ios_base::hex
Anything else	0

Library Reference

See Also

ios_base in <ios>

---

setfill function template   Sets pad character

```
template <typename charT>
manip_t setfill(charT c)
```

The setfill function template sets the fill character for a stream to c. In other words, it performs the equivalent of *stream*.fill(c).

See Also

ios_base in <ios>

---

setiosflags function   Sets specified flags

```
manip_t setiosflags(ios_base::fmtflags mask)
```

The setiosflags function sets the flag bits in mask for a stream. In other words, it performs the equivalent of *stream*.setf(mask).

See Also

resetiosflags function, ios_base in <ios>

---

setprecision function   Sets precision

```
manip_t setprecision(int n)
```

The setprecision function template sets the output precision for a stream to n. In other words, it performs the equivalent of *stream*.precision(n).

See Also

ios_base in <ios>

---

setw function   Sets field width

```
manip_t setw(int n)
```

The setw function template sets the output field width for a stream to n. In other words, it performs the equivalent of *stream*.width(n).

See Also

ios_base in <ios>

<ios>

The <ios> header declares the classes, types, and manipulator functions that form the foundation of the C++ I/O library (which is often called *I/O streams*). The class ios_base is the base class for all I/O stream classes. The class template basic_ios derives from ios_base and declares the behavior that is common to all I/O streams (e.g., establishing a stream buffer and defining the I/O state).

Refer to Chapter 9 for more information about input and output, including the use of manipulators, formatting flags, streams, and stream buffers.

The <ios> header #includes <iosfwd>.

basic_ios class template

```
template <class charT, class traits = char_traits<charT> >
class basic_ios : public ios_base
{
public:
  typedef charT char_type;
  typedef typename traits::int_type int_type;
  typedef typename traits::pos_type pos_type;
  typedef typename traits::off_type off_type;
  typedef traits traits_type;
  // Status
  operator void*();
  const bool operator!();
  const iostate rdstate() const;
  void clear(iostate state = goodbit);
  void clear(io_state state);
  void setstate(iostate state);
  void setstate(io_state state);
  bool good() const;
  bool eof() const;
  bool fail() const;
  bool bad() const;
  iostate exceptions() const;
  void exceptions(iostate except);
  void exceptions(io_state except);
  explicit basic_ios(basic_streambuf<charT,traits>* sb);
  virtual ~basic_ios();
  basic_ostream<charT,traits>* tie() const;
  basic_ostream<charT,traits>* tie(basic_ostream<charT,traits>* tiestr);
  basic_streambuf<charT,traits>* rdbuf() const;
  basic_streambuf<charT,traits>* rdbuf(basic_streambuf<charT,traits>* sb);
  basic_ios& copyfmt(const basic_ios& rhs);
  char_type fill() const;
  char_type fill(char_type ch);
  locale imbue(const locale& loc);
  char narrow(char_type c, char deflt) const;
  char_type widen(char c) const;
protected:
  basic_ios();
  void init(basic_streambuf<charT,traits>* buf);
private:
  basic_ios(const basic_ios& );        // Not defined
  basic_ios& operator=(const basic_ios&); // Not defined
};
```

The basic_ios class template is the root of all I/O stream class templates. It provides a common functionality for all derived stream classes; in particular, it manages a stream buffer. In the following descriptions, the name *buf* refers to a private data member that points to the stream buffer. An implementation can use any name.

The following are the member functions of basic_ios:

basic_ios( )
>   The default constructor leaves the data members uninitialized. In a derived class, the default constructor must call init to initialize the members.

basic_ios(const basic_ios&)
>   The copy constructor is declared private and is not defined, which prevents the copying of any I/O stream objects.

explicit **basic_ios**(basic_streambuf<charT,traits>* sb)
>   Calls init(sb) to initialize the members.

operator void*( )
>   If fail( ) returns true, the void* operator returns a null pointer; otherwise, it returns a non-null pointer to indicate success. operator void* is most often used as an implicit conversion in a conditional (e.g., while (cin) cin >> data[i++]).

const bool **operator!**( )
>   Returns fail( ). operator ! is most often used in a conditional (e.g., if (!cout) cerr << "output error\n").

basic_ios& **operator=**(const basic_ios&)
>   The assignment operator, like the copy constructor, is private, so it cannot be used and is not defined. Assigning or copying an I/O stream would corrupt the stream buffer.

bool **bad**( ) const
>   Returns true if badbit is set in rdstate( ), or false otherwise.

void **clear**(iostate state = goodbit)
void **clear**(io_state state)
>   Sets the I/O state to state. If rdbuf( ) is a null pointer, badbit is also set (to state | ios_base::badbit). After setting the state, if any state bit is an exception bit ((rdstate( ) & exceptions( )) != 0), basic_ios::failure is thrown.
>
>   The second form is deprecated. See ios_base::iostate later in this section for details.

basic_ios& **copyfmt**(const basic_ios& rhs)
>   Copies formatting information from rhs. In particular, the format flags, fill character, locale, and the contents of the iword( ) and pword( ) arrays are copied. The I/O state and stream buffer are not copied. Before copying any callback functions, each one is called with erase_event. The callbacks are then replaced with those copied from rhs, and each one is called with copyfmt_event. (See ios_base for information about callbacks.) The exceptions( ) mask is copied last. The return value is *this.

bool **eof**( ) const
>   Returns true if eofbit is set in rdstate( ), or false otherwise.

iostate **exceptions**( ) const
void **exceptions**(iostate except)
void **exceptions**(io_state except)
>   Returns or sets the exception mask. (See the clear function for how and when an exception is thrown.) The third form is deprecated. See ios_base::iostate later in this section for details.

bool **fail**( ) const
> Returns true if badbit is set or if failbit is set in rdstate( ), or false if neither bit is set.

char_type **fill**( ) const
char_type **fill**(char_type ch)
> Returns or changes the fill character (also called the *pad character*). When setting the fill character, the old fill character is returned.

bool **good**( ) const
> Returns true if the I/O state is clean—that is, it returns rdstate( ) == 0.

locale **imbue**(const locale& loc)
> Calls ios_base::imbue(loc) and rdbuf( )->pubimbue(loc) (if rdbuf( ) is not null). The return value is the previous value of ios_base::imbue( ).

void **init**(basic_streambuf<charT,traits>* buf)
> Initializes the basic_ios object. Table 13-12 lists the observable effects of initialization. Also, the arrays for iword( ) and pword( ) are initially null pointers.

Table 13-12. *Effects of calling basic_ios::init*

Member function	Return value
exceptions( )	goodbit
fill( )	widen(' ')
flags( )	skipws | dec
getloc( )	Current global locale, that is, std::locale( )
precision( )	6
rdbuf( )	*buf*
rdstate( )	*buf* !=0 ? goodbit : badbit
tie( )	Null pointer
width( )	0

char **narrow**(char_type c, char deflt) const
> Narrows the character c by returning the following:
>
>   std::use_facet<ctype<char_type> >(getloc( )).narrow(c, deflt)

basic_streambuf<charT,traits>* **rdbuf**( ) const
basic_streambuf<charT,traits>*
rdbuf(basic_streambuf<charT,traits>* sb)
> Returns or changes the stream buffer, *buf*. After changing the stream buffer, the rdbuf function calls clear( ). The function returns the previous value of rdbuf( ).

const iostate **rdstate**( ) const
> Returns the current I/O state bitmask. See the bad, eof, fail, and good functions for convenient ways to test different bits in the state mask.

void **setstate**(iostate state)
void **setstate**(io_state state)
> Sets the specified bits in the I/O state bitmask—that is, it calls clear(rdstate( ) \| state). The second form is deprecated. See ios_base::iostate later in this section for details.

```
basic_ostream<charT,traits>* tie( ) const
basic_ostream<charT,traits>* tie(basic_ostream<charT,traits>* tiestr)
```
Ties a stream (typically an input stream) to an output stream, tiestr. Any input operation on this stream is prefaced by flushing tiestr. Tying streams can be used to ensure that prompts appear at the proper time. With no arguments, the tie function returns the currently tied stream, or 0 if no stream is tied.

```
char_type widen(char c) const
```
Widens the character c by returning the following:

```
        std::use_facet<ctype<char_type> >(getloc( )).widen(c)
```

See Also

ios_base class, ctype in <locale>, basic_streambuf in <streambuf>

boolalpha function
Manipulator for reading and writing bool as text

```
ios_base& boolalpha(ios_base& stream)
```

The boolalpha function is a manipulator that sets the boolalpha flag, which tells the stream to read or write a bool value as text, according to the stream's locale. Specifically, the function calls stream.setf(ios_base::boolalpha) and returns stream.

See Also

ios_base::fmtflags type, noboolalpha function, num_get in <locale>, num_put in <locale>

dec function
Manipulator for decimal integers

```
ios_base& dec(ios_base& stream)
```

The dec function is a manipulator that sets the conversion radix to base 10. The function calls stream.setf(ios_base::dec, ios_base::basefield) and returns stream.

See Also

hex function, ios_base::fmtflags type, noshowbase function, oct function, showbase function, num_get in <locale>, num_put in <locale>

fixed function
Manipulator for fixed-point output

```
ios_base& fixed(ios_base& stream)
```

The fixed function is a manipulator that sets the floating-point output style to fixed-point. The function calls stream.setf(ios_base::fixed, ios_base::floatfield) and returns stream.

See Also

ios_base::fmtflags type, noshowpoint function, scientific function, showpoint function, num_get in <locale>, num_put in <locale>

fpos class template
Represents a file position

```
template <typename stateT>
class fpos
{
```

```
public:
  stateT state( ) const;
  void state(stateT);

  // The following functionality is required, although not necessarily as member
  // functions.
  fpos(int i);
  fpos(streamoff offset);
  operator streamoff( ) const;
  bool operator==(const fpos& rhs) const;
  bool operator!=(const fpos& rhs) const;
  fpos operator+(streamoff offset) const;
  fpos operator-(streamoff offset) const;
  fpos& operator+=(streamoff offset);
  fpos& operator-=(streamoff offset);
  streamoff operator-(const fpos& rhs) const;
};
```

The fpos class template represents a position in a stream. The stateT template parameter is a multibyte shift state, such as mbstate_t. Objects of type fpos can be compared for equality or inequality, they can be subtracted to yield a stream offset, or a stream offset can be added to an fpos position to produce a new fpos. Also, stream offsets can be converted to and from fpos values. Although the declaration in this section shows these functions as member functions, they might be global functions or be provided in some other fashion.

The Shift State Problem

The C++ standard requires a library implementation to implement fpos<> and the streamoff types so that you can convert an object whose type is any fpos<> instance into a streamoff object and back again, recovering the original value.

Most library implementations do not work this way.

Instead, streamoff is usually implemented as an integral type, such as int or long. The problem is that fpos<> must store a stream position and a shift state, and the stream position is usually implemented with the same type as streamoff. In other words, converting from fpos<> to streamoff discards the shift state. The library cannot convert streamoff back to the original fpos<> because the original shift state is gone.

Note that char_traits has the same problem when specialized for char and wchar_t because its pos_type is defined to be streampos, which is defined in <iosfwd> to be fpos<mbstate_t>, and off_type is defined as streamoff.

The solution is not to convert a stream position to a stream offset. If you must do this, remember that you might be sacrificing the shift state. Save the shift state separately so you can restore it when converting a stream offset back to a stream position.

See Also
streamoff type, mbstate_t in <cwchar>

---

hex function   Manipulator for hexadecimal integers

ios_base& **hex**(ios_base& stream)

The hex function is a manipulator that sets the conversion radix to base 16. The function calls stream.setf(ios_base::hex, ios_base::basefield) and returns stream.

See Also
dec function, ios_base::fmtflags type, noshowbase function, oct function, showbase function, num_get in <locale>, num_put in <locale>

---

internal function   Manipulator to align output on an internal point

ios_base& **internal**(ios_base& stream)

The internal function is a manipulator that sets the stream's alignment to internal. The function calls stream.setf(ios_base::internal, ios_base::adjustfield) and returns stream. Internal padding works as follows:

- If the formatted number begins with a sign, insert the padding after the sign.
- If the formatted number begins with 0x or 0X, insert the padding after the x or X.
- Otherwise, insert the padding before the number (like ios_base::right).

See Also
ios_base::fmtflags type, left function, right function

---

ios_base class   Root class for I/O declarations

```
class ios_base
{
public:
  class failure;
  typedef ... fmtflags;
  typedef ... iostate;
  typedef ... io_state;
  typedef ... openmode;
  typedef ... open_mode;
  typedef ... seekdir;
  typedef ... seek_dir;
  typedef ... streamoff;
  typedef ... streampos;
  class Init;

  // Destructor
  virtual ~ios_base();
  // Formatting
  fmtflags flags() const;
  fmtflags flags(fmtflags fmtfl);
  fmtflags setf(fmtflags fmtfl);
  fmtflags setf(fmtflags fmtfl, fmtflags mask);
  void unsetf(fmtflags mask);
```

```
streamsize precision( ) const;
streamsize precision(streamsize prec);
streamsize width( ) const;
streamsize width(streamsize wide);
// Locales
locale imbue(const locale& loc);
locale getloc( ) const;
// Storage
static int xalloc( );
long& iword(int index);
void*& pword(int index);
// Callbacks
enum event { erase_event, imbue_event, copyfmt_event };
typedef void (*event_callback)(event, ios_base&, int index);
void register_callback(event_callback fn, int index);
static bool sync_with_stdio(bool sync = true);
protected:
ios_base( );
private:
ios_base(const ios_base&);
ios_base& operator=(const ios_base&);
};
```

The ios_base class is the root class for all the I/O stream classes. It declares fundamental types that are used throughout the I/O library. It also has members to keep track of formatting for input and output, storing arbitrary information for derived classes, and registering functions to be called when something interesting happens to the stream object.

The io_state, open_mode, seek_dir, streamoff, and streampos types are deprecated and might not be included in a future revision of the C++ standard. The first three are integer types that are equivalent to iostate, openmode, and seekdir. (See their respective subsections later in this section for details.) The streamoff and streampos types have equivalent types at namespace scope. See streamoff later in this section and streampos in <iosfwd> for details.

The following are the member functions of ios_base:

ios_base( )
> The default constructor is protected so you cannot accidentally declare an object of type ios_base. It does not initialize its members. That is left to the basic_ios::init function.

ios_base(const ios_base&)
> The copy constructor is private and not defined so you cannot copy objects of type ios_base or its derived classes.

virtual ~ios_base( )
> Calls every registered callback with the erase_event if the ios_base object has been properly initialized. See basic_ios::init.

ios_base& operator=(const ios_base&)
> The assignment operator is private and not defined to prevent the assignment of ios_base objects or its derivatives.

Library
Reference

fmtflags **flags**( ) const
fmtflags **flags**(fmtflags fmtfl)
> Returns the current format flags or sets the flags. When setting the flags, the previous flags are returned.

locale **getloc**( ) const
> Returns the stream's currently imbued locale.

locale **imbue**(const locale& loc)
> Saves loc as the new locale and calls all registered callbacks with imbue_event. The new locale is stored before calling any callbacks, so if a callback function calls getloc, it gets the new locale.

long& **iword**(int index)
> Returns a reference to a long integer that is stored in a private array, at index index. If iword has been called before with the same index, a reference to the array element is returned. Otherwise, the array is extended as needed so that index is a valid index, and the new entry is initialized to 0. A reference to the new element is returned.
>
> The structure of the internal array is implementation-defined, and it might be a sparse array. The internal array grows as needed, and all prior values stored in the array are preserved, although the references might become invalid in any of the following situations:
>
> - After a call to iword with a different index
> - After calling basic_ios::copyfmt for this object
> - When the object is destroyed
>
> If iword fails (perhaps because the internal array cannot grow), it returns a reference to a valid long& with a value that is initially 0. If the member function is called for an object whose class derives from basic_ios<>, badbit is set (which might throw ios_base::failure).
>
> See the xalloc member function to learn how to obtain a suitable index.

streamsize **precision**( ) const
streamsize **precision**(streamsize prec)
> Returns or sets the precision (places after the decimal point) used to format floating-point numbers for output. When setting a new precision, the previous precision is returned.

void*& **pword**(int index)
> Returns a reference to a void* that is stored in a private array, at index index. If pword has been called before with the same index, a reference to the array element is returned. Otherwise, the array is extended as needed so that index is a valid index, and the new entry is initialized to a null pointer. A reference to the new element is returned.
>
> The structure of the internal array is implementation-defined, and it might be a sparse array. The internal array grows as needed, and all prior values stored in the array are preserved, although the references might become invalid in any of the following situations:
>
> - After a call to pword with a different index
> - After calling basic_ios::copyfmt for this object
> - When the object is destroyed

If pword fails (perhaps because the internal array cannot grow), it returns a reference to a valid void*& with a value that is initially 0. If the object derives from basic_ios<>, badbit is set (which might throw ios_base::failure).

See the xalloc member function to learn how to obtain a suitable index.

void **register_callback**(event_callback fn, int index)
Registers a function fn to be called when one of three events occurs for the ios_base object:

- The object is destroyed (erase_event)
- copyfmt is called (erase_event followed by copyfmt_event)
- imbue is called (imbue_event)

Each callback function is registered with an integer index. The index is passed to the callback function. Functions are called in the opposite order of registration. The callback function must not throw exceptions.

For example, suppose a program stores some debugging information with each stream. It allocates a struct and stores a pointer to the struct in the stream's pword array. When copyfmt is called, the debugging information should also be copied. Example 13-14 shows how to use callbacks to make sure the memory is managed properly.

Example 13-14. Copying information associated with streams

```
void manage_info(std::ios_base::event event,
                 std::ios_base& stream, int index)
{
  infostruct* ip;

  switch(event) {
  case std::ios_base::erase_event:
    ip = static_cast<infostruct*>(stream.pword(index));
    stream.pword(index) = 0;
    delete ip;
    break;
  case std::ios_base::copyfmt_event:
    stream.pword(index) = new infostruct;
    break;
  default:
    break; // imbue_event does not affect storage.
  }
}

void openread(std::ifstream& f, const char* name)
{
  f.open(name);
  int index = f.xalloc();
  f.pword(index) = new infostruct;
  f.register_callback(manage_info, index);
}
```

fmtflags **setf**(fmtflags addflags)
> Sets the addflags bits of the formatting flags. It is equivalent to calling flags(flags( ) | addflags).

fmtflags **setf**(fmtflags newflags, fmtflags mask)
> Clears the mask bits from the formatting flags and then sets the newflags & mask bits. It is equivalent to calling flags((flags( ) & ~mask) | (newflags & mask)). The two-argument version of setf is most often used with multiple-choice flags (e.g., setf(ios_base::dec, ios_base::basefield)).

static bool **sync_with_stdio**(bool sync = true)
> Determines whether the standard C++ I/O objects are synchronized with the C I/O functions. Initially, they are synchronized.
>
> If you call sync_with_stdio(false) after any I/O has been performed, the behavior is implementation-defined.

void **unsetf**(fmtflags mask)
> Clears the mask bits from the formatting flags. It is equivalent to calling flags(flags( ) & ~mask).

streamsize **width**( ) const

streamsize **width**(streamsize wide)
> Returns or sets the minimum field width. When setting the width, the previous width is returned.

static int **xalloc**( )
> Returns a unique integer, suitable for use as an index to the iword or pword functions. You can think of ios_base as having a static integer data member, *xalloc_ index*, and xalloc is implemented so it returns *xalloc_index*++.

See Also

basic_ios class template

---

ios_base::event type   Callback event type

enum **event** { erase_event, imbue_event, copyfmt_event };

The ios_base::event type denotes an interesting event in the lifetime of an I/O stream object. See the register_callback function in the ios_base class, earlier in this section, to learn how to register a function that is called when one of these events occurs.

See Also

ios_base class, ios_base::event_callback type

---

ios_base::event_callback type   Callback function type

typedef void (***event_callback**)(event, ios_base&, int index);

The ios_base::event_callback type denotes a callback function. See the register_ callback function in the ios_base class, earlier in this section, to learn how to register a callback function, which a stream object calls when an interesting event occurs.

See Also

ios_base class, ios_base::event type

---

ios_base::failure class

```
class ios_base::failure : public exception
{
public:
  explicit failure(const string& msg);
  virtual ~failure();
  virtual const char* what() const throw();
};
```

The ios_base::failure class is the base class for I/O-related exceptions. Its use of the constructor's msg parameter and what() member function are consistent with the conventions of the exception class.

See Also

basic_ios::clear function, exception in <exception>

ios_base::fmtflags type

```
typedef ... fmtflags;
static const fmtflags boolalpha;
static const fmtflags dec;
static const fmtflags fixed;
static const fmtflags hex;
static const fmtflags internal;
static const fmtflags left;
static const fmtflags oct;
static const fmtflags right;
static const fmtflags scientific;
static const fmtflags showbase;
static const fmtflags showpoint;
static const fmtflags showpos;
static const fmtflags skipws;
static const fmtflags unitbuf;
static const fmtflags uppercase;
static const fmtflags adjustfield;
static const fmtflags basefield;
static const fmtflags floatfield;
```

The fmtflags type is an integer, enum, or bitmask type (the exact type is implementation-defined) that represents formatting flags for input and output. In the ios_base class, several static constants are also defined, which can be implemented as enumerated literals or as explicit constants. Table 13-13 lists the flag literals.

Table 13-13. fmtflags literals

Literal name	Description
boolalpha	Reads and writes bool values as text, according to the locale
dec	Reads and writes decimal integers
fixed	Writes floating-point values in fixed notation
hex	Reads and writes hexadecimal integers
internal	Aligns output to internal point (e.g., after sign or 0x)
left	Left-aligns output

Library
Reference

Table 13-13. fmtflags literals (continued)

Literal name	Description
oct	Reads and writes octal integers
right	Right-aligns output
scientific	Writes floating-point values in scientific notation
showbase	Writes a prefix for an integer radix (e.g., 0x for hexadecimal)
showpoint	Writes decimal point, even if not needed
showpos	Writes plus sign (+), even if not needed
skipws	Skips whitespace before input
unitbuf	Flushes output after each operation
uppercase	Uses uppercase in generated output (e.g., 0X prefix)

Some formatting items are Boolean: a flag is set or cleared. For example, the uppercase flag can be set to perform output in uppercase (that is, the 0X hexadecimal prefix or E in scientific notation), or the flag can be cleared for lowercase output. Other flags are set in *fields*. You can set a field to one of a number of values. Table 13-14 lists the field names, definitions, and the default behavior if the field value is 0. Each field name is used as a mask for the two-argument form of the ios_base::setf function.

Table 13-14. fmtflags constants

Constant name	Value	Default
adjustfield	left | internal | right	right
basefield	dec | hex | oct	Output: dec Input: leading 0x or 0x is hex, 0 is oct, anything else is dec
floatfield	fixed | scientific	scientific if exponent is < −4 or ≥ precision, else fixed; strip trailing zeros and unneeded decimal point

See Also
ios_base class, ctype in <locale>, num_get in <locale>, num_put in <locale>

---

ios_base::Init class   Initialization class

```
class ios_base::Init {
public:
  Init( );
  ~Init( );
};
```

The Init class is used to ensure that the construction of the standard I/O stream objects occurs. The first time an ios_base::Init object is constructed, it constructs and initializes cin, cout, cerr, clog, wcin, wcout, wcerr, and wclog. A static counter keeps track of the number of times ios_base::Init is constructed and destroyed. When the last instance is destroyed, flush( ) is called for cout, cerr, clog, wcout, wcerr, and wclog.

For example, suppose a program constructs a static object, and the constructor prints a warning to cerr if certain conditions hold. To ensure that cerr is properly initialized and ready to receive output, declare an ios_base::Init object before your static object, as shown in Example 13-15.

Example 13-15. Ensuring proper initialization of standard I/O streams

```
class myclass {
public:
  myclass( ) {
    if (! okay( ))
      std::cerr << "Oops: not okay!\n";
  }
};
static std::ios_base::Init init;
static myclass myobject;
```

See Also

<iostream>

ios_base::iostate type   I/O status

```
typedef ... iostate
typedef ... io_state
static const iostate badbit
static const iostate eofbit
static const iostate failbit
static const iostate goodbit = iostate(0);
```

The ios_base::iostate type is an integer, enum, or bitset type (the exact type is implementation-defined) that represents the status of an I/O stream. The io_state type is an integral type that represents the same information. Some functions that take an iostate parameter have an overloaded version that accepts an io_state parameter and has the same functionality as its iostate counterpart. The io_state type and related functions are deprecated, so you should use the iostate versions.

Table 13-15 lists the iostate literals and their meanings. The basic_ios class template has several member functions for setting, testing, and clearing iostate bits.

Table 13-15. iostate literals

Literal	Description
badbit	Irrecoverable error, such as a null streambuf pointer or a write failure
eofbit	End-of-file when reading
failbit	Failure to read or write expected characters (e.g., trying to read an integer from nonnumeric input)
goodbit	No problems; value is 0

See Also

basic_ios class template, <bitset>

ios_base::openmode type

```
typedef ... openmode
typedef ... open_mode
static const openmode app
static const openmode ate
static const openmode binary
static const openmode in
static const openmode out
static const openmode trunc
```

The ios_base::openmode type is an integer, enum, or bitset type (the exact type is implementation-defined) that defines the mode for opening a file. The open_mode type is an integral type that represents the same information. Some functions that take an openmode parameter have an overloaded version that accepts an open_mode parameter and has the same functionality as its openmode counterpart. The open_mode type and related functions are deprecated, so you should use the openmode versions.

Table 13-16 lists the openmode literals and their meanings. (Refer to the <fstream> section of this chapter for the most common use of ios_base::openmode and the permitted combinations of openmode literals.) The openmode type is also used for the basic_streambuf::pubseekoff and pubseekpos functions, and for related functions.

Table 13-16. openmode literals

Literal	Description
app	Seeks to end-of-file before each write
ate	Seeks to end-of-file immediately after opening
binary	Reads and writes in binary mode (default is text)
in	Opens for input (reading)
out	Opens for output (writing)
trunc	Truncates file to zero length

See Also

<bitset>, basic_filebuf in <fstream>, basic_streambuf in <streambuf>

ios_base::seekdir type

```
typedef ... seekdir
typedef ... seek_dir
static const seekdir beg
static const seekdir cur
static const seekdir end
```

The ios_base::seekdir type is an implementation-defined enumerated type that specifies the origin for seeking to a new file position. The seek_dir type is an integral type that represents the same information. Some functions that take a seekdir parameter have overloaded versions that accept a seek_dir parameter and have the same functionality as their seekdir counterparts. The seek_dir type and related functions are deprecated, so you should use the seekdir versions.

Table 13-17 lists the seekdir literals. Note that the order and integer values of the literals are implementation-defined.

Table 13-17. seekdir literals

Literal	Description
beg	Seeks from the beginning of the stream (e.g., offset is absolute position)
cur	Seeks from the current position; positive is toward end of stream, and negative offsets are toward the beginning of the stream
end	Seeks relative to the end of the stream; negative offsets are towards the beginning

See Also

basic_istream in <istream>, basic_ostream in <ostream>, basic_streambuf in <streambuf>

left function
Manipulator to left-align output

ios_base& **left**(ios_base& stream)

The left function is a manipulator that selects left-alignment for output to stream. The function calls stream.setf(ios_base::left, ios_base::adjustfield) and returns stream.

See Also

internal function, ios_base::fmtflags type, right function

noboolalpha function
Manipulator to disable reading and writing bool as text

ios_base& **noboolalpha**(ios_base& stream)

The noboolalpha function is a manipulator that clears the boolalpha flag, causing the stream to read or write bool values as integers. Specifically, the function calls stream.unsetf(ios_base::boolalpha) and returns stream.

See Also

boolalpha function, ios_base::fmtflags type, ctype in <locale>

noshowbase function
Manipulator to disable showing output radix

ios_base& **noshowbase**(ios_base& stream)

The noshowbase function is a manipulator that clears the showbase flag, which tells an output stream to write a prefix for integer output: 0x for hexadecimal or 0 for octal. Specifically, the function calls stream.unsetf(ios_base::showbase) and returns stream.

See Also

hex function, ios_base::fmtflags type, oct function, nouppercase function, showbase function, uppercase function, num_put in <locale>

noshowpoint function

```
ios_base& noshowpoint(ios_base& stream)
```

The noshowpoint function is a manipulator that clears the showpoint flag, causing an output stream to write a decimal point for floating-point output, even if the point is unnecessary (only zeros appear after the decimal point). Specifically, the function calls stream.unsetf(ios_base::showpoint) and returns stream.

See Also

fixed function, ios_base::fmtflags type, scientific function, showpoint function, num_put in <locale>

noshowpos function

```
ios_base& noshowpos(ios_base& stream)
```

The noshowpos function is a manipulator that clears the showpos flag, which causes an output stream to always write a plus sign (+) in front of a number even if the sign is unnecessary (the value is 0 or positive). Specifically, the function calls stream.unsetf(ios_base::showpos) and returns stream.

See Also

ios_base::fmtflags type, showpos function, num_put in <locale>

noskipws function

```
ios_base& noskipws(ios_base& stream)
```

The noskipws function is a manipulator that clears the skipws flag, which tells an input stream to skip whitespace before reading most fields. Specifically, the function calls stream.unsetf(ios_base::skipws) and returns stream.

See Also

ios_base::fmtflags type, skipws function, num_get in <locale>

nounitbuf function

```
ios_base& nounitbuf(ios_base& stream)
```

The nounitbuf function is a manipulator that clears the unitbuf flag, so the stream is not flushed after each output operation. Specifically, the function calls stream.unsetf(ios_base::unitbuf) and returns stream.

See Also

ios_base::fmtflags type, unitbuf function

nouppercase function

```
ios_base& nouppercase(ios_base& stream)
```

The nouppercase function is a manipulator that clears the uppercase flag, which tells an output stream to use uppercase letters for generated output (e.g., 0X for hexadecimal prefix or E for exponents). Specifically, the function calls stream.unsetf(ios_base::uppercase) and returns stream.

See Also

hex function, ios_base::fmtflags type, scientific function, uppercase function, num_put in <locale>

---

oct function
Manipulator for octal integers

ios_base& **oct**(ios_base& stream)

The oct function is a manipulator that sets the conversion radix to base 8. The function calls stream.setf(ios_base::oct, ios_base::basefield) and returns stream.

See Also

dec function, hex function, ios_base::fmtflags type, noshowbase function, showbase function, num_get in <locale>, num_put in <locale>

---

right function
Manipulator to right-align output

ios_base& **right**(ios_base& stream)

The right function is a manipulator that selects right-alignment for output to stream. The function calls stream.setf(ios_base::right, ios_base::adjustfield) and returns stream.

See Also

internal function, ios_base::fmtflags type, left function

---

scientific function
Manipulator to use scientific notation for output

ios_base& **scientific**(ios_base&)

The fixed function is a manipulator that sets the floating-point output style to scientific or exponential notation. The function calls stream.setf(ios_base::scientific, ios_base::floatfield) and returns stream.

See Also

fixed function, ios_base::fmtflags type, num_get in <locale>, num_put in <locale>

---

showbase function
Manipulator to show output radix

ios_base& **showbase**(ios_base& stream)

The showbase function is a manipulator that sets the showbase flag, which tells an output stream to write a prefix for integer output: 0x for hexadecimal or 0 for octal. Specifically, the function calls stream.setf(ios_base::showbase) and returns stream.

See Also

hex function, ios_base::fmtflags type, oct function, noshowbase function, nouppercase function, uppercase function, num_put in <locale>

---

showpoint function
Manipulator to show decimal point even when unnecessary

ios_base& **showpoint**(ios_base& stream)

The showpoint function is a manipulator that sets the showpoint flag, which tells an output stream to write a decimal point for floating-point output, even if the point is

Library Reference

unnecessary (only zeros appear after the decimal point). Specifically, the function calls stream.setf(ios_base::showpoint) and returns stream.

See Also

fixed function, ios_base::fmtflags type, noshowpoint function, scientific function, num_put in <locale>

---

showpos function
Manipulator to show plus sign for nonnegative numbers

ios_base& **showpos**(ios_base& stream)

The showpos function is a manipulator that sets the showpos flag, which tells an output stream to write a plus (+) sign, even if the sign is unnecessary (the value is 0 or positive). Specifically, the function calls stream.setf(ios_base::showpos) and returns stream.

See Also

ios_base::fmtflags type, noshowpos function, num_put in <locale>

---

skipws function
Manipulator to skip whitespace before reading

ios_base& **skipws**(ios_base& stream)

The skipws function is a manipulator that sets the skipws flag, which tells an input stream to skip whitespace before reading most fields. Specifically, the function calls stream.setf(ios_base::skipws) and returns stream.

See Also

ios_base::fmtflags type, noskipws function, num_get in <locale>

---

streamoff type
Stream offset type

typedef ... **streamoff**

 The streamoff type is an implementation-defined type that represents a signed offset in a stream. See the fpos type for more information about working with file positions and offsets.

See Also

fpos type, char_traits in <string>

---

streamsize type
Stream size type

typedef ... **streamsize**

 The streamsize type is an implementation-defined type that is used to represent the size of various stream entities, such as number of characters to read or write. It is a synonym for one of the signed integral types. You can convert a streamsize to a streamoff without loss of information. You can also convert a streamoff back to a streamsize. If the streamoff is the result of converting a streamsize, converting the streamoff back to streamsize yields the original streamsize.

See Also

fpos type, char_traits in <string>

---

unitbuf function
Manipulator to use unit buffering

ios_base& **unitbuf**(ios_base& stream)

The unitbuf function is a manipulator that sets the unitbuf flag, which causes the stream to be flushed after each output operation. Specifically, the function calls stream.setf(ios_base::unitbuf) and returns stream.

See Also

ios_base::fmtflags type, nounitbuf function

uppercase function
Manipulator to use uppercase for generated output

ios_base& **uppercase**(ios_base& stream)

The uppercase function is a manipulator that sets the uppercase flag, which tells an output stream to use uppercase letters for generated output (e.g., 0X for hexadecimal prefix or E for exponents). Specifically, the function calls stream.setf(ios_base::uppercase) and returns stream.

See Also

hex function, ios_base::fmtflags type, nouppercase function, scientific function, num_put in <locale>

<iosfwd>

The <iosfwd> header provides forward declarations of the various I/O-related classes and templates. The forward declarations are incomplete type declarations. (Read about complete and incomplete types in Chapter 6.) By using <iosfwd> you can sometimes avoid including the complete definitions of the I/O classes, and thereby save some compilation time.

It is always safe to include <iosfwd> and any of the other I/O headers, even if they both declare the same type.

Because <iosfwd> does not provide any complete type declarations, this section contains only Table 13-18, which lists each type name with a reference to the header (if any) that is required for the complete type.

Table 13-18. Forward type declarations in <iosfwd>

Type declaration	Header
template<typename T> class **allocator**	<memory>
template<typename charT, typename traits=char_traits<charT> > class **basic_filebuf**	<fstream>
template<typename charT, typename traits=char_traits<charT> > class **basic_fstream**	<fstream>
template<typename charT, typename traits=char_traits<charT> > class **basic_ifstream**	<fstream>
template<typename charT, typename traits=char_traits<charT> > class **basic_ios**	<ios>

Table 13-18. Forward type declarations in <iosfwd> (continued)

Type declaration	Header
template<typename charT, typename traits=char_traits<charT> > class **basic_iostream**	<istream>
template<typename charT, typename traits=char_traits<charT> > class **basic_istream**	<istream>
template<typename charT, typename traits=char_traits<charT>, typename Alloc = allocator<charT> > class **basic_istringstream**	<sstream>
template<typename charT, typename traits=char_traits<charT> > class **basic_ofstream**	<fstream>
template<typename charT, typename traits=char_traits<charT> > class **basic_ostream**	<ostream>
template<typename charT, typename traits=char_traits<charT>, typename Alloc = allocator<charT> > class **basic_ostringstream**	<sstream>
template<typename charT, typename traits=char_traits<charT> > class **basic_streambuf**	<streambuf>
template<typename charT, typename traits=char_traits<charT>, typename Alloc = allocator<charT> > class **basic_stringbuf**	<sstream>
template<typename charT, typename traits=char_traits<charT>, typename Alloc = allocator<charT> > class **basic_stringstream**	<sstream>
template<typename charT> class **char_traits**	<string>
template<> class **char_traits<char>**	<string>
template<> class **char_traits<wchar_t>**	<string>
typedef basic_filebuf<char> **filebuf**	<fstream>
template <typename state> class **fpos**	<ios>
typedef basic_fstream<char> **fstream**	<fstream>
typedef basic_ifstream<char> **ifstream**	<fstream>
typedef basic_ios<char> **ios**	<ios>
typedef basic_iostream<char> **iostream**	<istream>
typedef basic_istream<char> **istream**	<istream>
template<typename charT, typename traits=char_traits<charT> > class **istreambuf_iterator**	<iterator>
typedef basic_istringstream<char> **istringstream**	<sstream>
typedef basic_ofstream<char> **ofstream**	<fstream>
typedef basic_ostream<char> **ostream**	<ostream>
template<typename charT, typename traits=char_traits<charT> > class **ostreambuf_iterator**	<iterator>
typedef basic_ostringstream<char> **ostringstream**	<sstream>
typedef basic_streambuf<char> **streambuf**	<streambuf>
typedef fpos<char_traits<char>::state_type> **streampos**	N/A
typedef basic_stringbuf<char> **stringbuf**	<sstream>
typedef basic_stringstream<char> **stringstream**	<sstream>
typedef basic_filebuf<wchar_t> **wfilebuf**	<fstream>
typedef basic_fstream<wchar_t> **wfstream**	<fstream>
typedef basic_ifstream<wchar_t> **wifstream**	<fstream>
typedef basic_ios<wchar_t> **wios**	<ios>

Table 13-18. Forward type declarations in <iosfwd> (continued)

Type declaration	Header
typedef basic_iostream<wchar_t> **wiostream**	<istream>
typedef basic_istream<wchar_t> **wistream**	<istream>
typedef basic_istringstream<wchar_t> **wistringstream**	<sstream>
typedef basic_ofstream<wchar_t> **wofstream**	<fstream>
typedef basic_ostream<wchar_t> **wostream**	<ostream>
typedef basic_ostringstream<wchar_t> **wostringstream**	<sstream>
typedef basic_streambuf<wchar_t> **wstreambuf**	<streambuf>
typedef fpos<char_traits<wchar_t>::state_type> **wstreampos**	N/A
typedef basic_stringbuf<wchar_t> **wstringbuf**	<sstream>
typedef basic_stringstream<wchar_t> **wstringstream**	<sstream>

<iostream>

The <iostream> header declares the eight standard stream objects: cerr, cin, clog, cout, wcerr, wcin, wclog, and wcout. These objects are initialized when the first instance of ios_base::Init is constructed (or earlier), or before the main program starts. They are not destroyed during normal program execution, so any static object's destructor or other function can use the standard I/O objects.

Each of the standard I/O objects is associated with a standard C FILE pointer (see <cstdio>). (You can sever the connection by calling ios_base::sync_with_stdio(false), as described in <ios>.) You can use narrow or wide I/O objects, but once you have performed any I/O on an underlying C stream, you cannot switch from narrow to wide or wide to narrow. For example, after writing to cerr, you cannot write to wclog because both objects use the same C stream, stderr. See Chapter 9 for more information about I/O.

Many C++ programmers assume that <iostream> automatically #includes <istream> and <ostream>, but the standard does not guarantee that behavior. Always #include every header you need, for example:

```
#include <cstdlib>
#include <iostream>
#include <istream>
#include <ostream>

// Copy standard input to standard output.
int main( )
{
  std::cout << std::cin.rdbuf( );
  return std::cout ? EXIT_SUCCESS : EXIT_FAILURE;
}
```

cerr variable

`extern ostream cerr`

The cerr object is a standard output stream associated with the C stderr file. It is typically used for error messages. When the cerr object is initialized, it sets the unitbuf flag, causing cerr to flush the output buffer after every operation.

See Also

clog variable, wcerr variable, ostream in <ostream>

cin variable

`extern istream cin`

The cin object is a standard input stream associated with the C stdin file. It is used for normal program input. It is tied to cout (see the tie member function of basic_ios in <ios>).

See Also

wcin variable, basic_ios in <ios>, istream in <istream>

clog variable

`extern ostream clog`

The clog object is a standard output stream associated with the C stderr file. Unlike cerr, the clog object does not set the unitbuf flag. This makes it more suitable for writing less critical messages that are not considered normal program output, such as debugging or logging messages.

See Also

cerr variable, wclog variable, ostream in <ostream>

cout variable

`extern ostream cout`

The cout object is a standard input stream associated with the C stdout file. It is used for normal program output.

See Also

wcout variable, ostream in <ostream>

wcerr variable

`extern wostream wcerr`

The wcerr object is a wide character standard output stream associated with the C stderr file. It is typically used for error messages. When the wcerr object is initialized, it sets the unitbuf flag, causing wcerr to flush the output buffer after every operation.

See Also

cerr variable, wclog variable, wostream in <ostream>

wcin variable

```
extern wistream wcin
```

The wcin object is a wide character standard input stream associated with the C stdin file. It is used for wide program input. It is tied to wcout (see the tie( ) member function of basic_ios in <ios>).

See Also

cin variable, basic_ios in <ios>, wistream in <istream>

wclog variable

```
extern wostream wclog
```

The wclog object is a wide character standard output stream associated with the C stderr file. Unlike wcerr, the wclog object does not set the unitbuf flag. This makes it more suitable for writing less critical messages that are not considered normal program output, such as debugging or logging messages.

See Also

clog variable, wcerr variable, wostream in <ostream>

wcout variable

```
extern wostream wcout
```

The wcout object is a wide character standard input stream associated with the C stdout file. It is used for wide program output.

See Also

cout variable, wostream in <ostream>

<istream>

The <istream> header declares the input stream classes, templates, and an input manipulator.

istream is declared in <istream>, and ostream is declared in <ostream>, but iostream is declared in <istream>, not <iostream>.

See <fstream> for derived-class templates that read from files and <sstream> for derived-class templates that read from strings. See <ios> for the base-class declarations. Refer to Chapter 9 for general information about I/O.

basic_iostream class template   Base class for input and output stream

```
template <typename charT, typename traits = char_traits<charT> >
class basic_iostream : public basic_istream<charT,traits>,
                       public basic_ostream<charT,traits>
{
public:
  explicit basic_iostream(basic_streambuf<charT,traits>* sb);
  virtual ~basic_iostream( );
};
```

The basic_iostream class template represents a stream that can perform input and
output. (For details, see its base class templates, basic_istream in this section and
basic_ostream in <ostream>.) Note that the two base-class templates share a common
stream buffer, sb. Note also that basic_istream and basic_ostream inherit virtually
from basic_ios; basic_iostream inherits a single instance of the formatting flags,
iostate, and so on.

See Also

basic_istream class template, iostream class, wiostream class, basic_iostream in <ios>,
basic_ostream in <ostream>

basic_istream class template   Base class for input stream

```
template <typename chT, typename traits = char_traits<chT> >
class basic_istream : virtual public basic_ios<chT,traits>
{
public:
  // Types
  typedef chT char_type;
  typedef typename traits::int_type int_type;
  typedef typename traits::pos_type pos_type;
  typedef typename traits::off_type off_type;
  typedef traits traits_type;

  explicit basic_istream(basic_streambuf<chT,traits>* sb);
  virtual ~basic_istream( );
  class sentry;
  // Formatted input
  basic_istream<chT,traits>& operator>>(basic_istream<chT,traits>&
    (*pf)(basic_istream<chT,traits>&));
  basic_istream<chT,traits>& operator>> (basic_ios<chT,traits>& |
    (*pf)(basic_ios<chT,traits>&));
  basic_istream<chT,traits>& operator>>(ios_base& (*pf)(ios_base&));
  basic_istream<chT,traits>& operator>>(bool& n);
  basic_istream<chT,traits>& operator>>(short& n);
  basic_istream<chT,traits>& operator>>(unsigned short& n);
  basic_istream<chT,traits>& operator>>(int& n);
  basic_istream<chT,traits>& operator>>(unsigned int& n);
  basic_istream<chT,traits>& operator>>(long& n);
  basic_istream<chT,traits>& operator>>(unsigned long& n);
  basic_istream<chT,traits>& operator>>(float& f);
  basic_istream<chT,traits>& operator>>(double& f);
```

```
basic_istream<chT,traits>& operator>>(long double& f);
basic_istream<chT,traits>& operator>>(void*& p);
basic_istream<chT,traits>& operator>> (basic_streambuf<char_type,traits>* sb);
// Unformatted input
streamsize gcount( ) const;
int_type get( );
basic_istream<chT,traits>& get(char_type& c);
basic_istream<chT,traits>& get(char_type* s, streamsize n);
basic_istream<chT,traits>& get(char_type* s, streamsize n, char_type delim);
basic_istream<chT,traits>& get(basic_streambuf<char_type,traits>& sb);
basic_istream<chT,traits>& get(basic_streambuf<char_type,traits>& sb,
                               char_type delim);
basic_istream<chT,traits>& getline(char_type* s, streamsize n);
basic_istream<chT,traits>& getline(char_type* s, streamsize n,
                                   char_type delim);
basic_istream<chT,traits>& ignore (streamsize n = 1, int_type
                                   delim=traits::eof( ));
int_type peek( );
basic_istream<chT,traits>& read(char_type* s, streamsize n);
streamsize readsome(char_type* s, streamsize n);
basic_istream<chT,traits>& putback(char_type c);
basic_istream<chT,traits>& unget( );
int sync( );
pos_type tellg( );
basic_istream<chT,traits>& seekg(pos_type);
basic_istream<chT,traits>& seekg(off_type, ios_base::seekdir);
};
```

The basic_istream class template is the base for all input streams. It declares members for reading from streams and for managing streams. The act of reading from a stream is also known as *extracting* from the stream.

All reads go through a stream buffer, which provides the low-level access to the stream data. (See the sbumpc and sgetc functions for basic_streambuf in the <streambuf> header.) If the stream buffer returns traits::eof( ) for an input operation, the stream sets failbit | eofbit in the stream's I/O state. If the buffer object throws an exception, the stream sets badbit.

Before performing an input operation (e.g., operator>> or a get( ) function), the stream constructs a sentry object. If the sentry evaluates to true, the read operation continues. If the read throws an exception, badbit is set. The second (noskipws) argument to the sentry constructor is false for the formatted functions (operator>>) and true for all other input operations. The sentry object is destroyed before the input function returns. See basic_istream::sentry later in this section for more information.

When an input operation throws an exception, the stream sets badbit. If badbit is set in the exceptions( ) mask, the stream does not throw ios_base::failure, but instead rethrows the original exception. If any input operation sets eofbit or failbit, and that bit is set in the exceptions( ) mask, the usual ios_base::failure exception is thrown.

The following are the basic_istream member functions:

explicit **basic_istream**(basic_streambuf<chT,traits>* sb)
> Calls the basic_ios(sb) constructor and initializes gcount( ) to 0.

basic_istream<chT,traits>& **operator>>**
> (basic_istream<chT,traits>& (*manip)(basic_istream<chT,traits>&))
>> Returns manip(*this). See the ws function for an example of such a manipulator.

```
basic_istream<chT,traits>& operator>>(basic_ios<chT,traits>&
    (*manip)(basic_ios<chT,traits>&))
basic_istream<chT,traits>& operator>>
    (ios_base& (*manip)(ios_base&))
```
Calls manip(*this) and returns *this. See the dec function in <ios> for an example of such a manipulator.

```
basic_istream<chT,traits>& operator>>(bool& n)
basic_istream<chT,traits>& operator>>(short& n)
basic_istream<chT,traits>& operator>>(unsigned short& n)
basic_istream<chT,traits>& operator>>(int& n)
basic_istream<chT,traits>& operator>>(unsigned int& n)
basic_istream<chT,traits>& operator>>(long& n)
basic_istream<chT,traits>& operator>>(unsigned long& n)
basic_istream<chT,traits>& operator>>(float& f)
basic_istream<chT,traits>& operator>>(double& f)
basic_istream<chT,traits>& operator>>(long double& f)
basic_istream<chT,traits>& operator>>(void*& p)
```
Reads a formatted item from the stream. These formatted input functions use the num_get facet of the stream's imbued locale as shown in Example 13-16. See the <locale> header for information about num_get and locales.

Example 13-16. Using the num_get facet to format input

```
typedef
    std::num_get<char_type,
        std::istreambuf_iterator<char_type, traits_type> >
    numget;
std::ios_base::iostate err = 0;
std::use_facet<numget>(getloc()).(*this, 0, *this, err, val);
this->setstate(err);
```

```
basic_istream<chT,traits>& operator>>(basic_streambuf<char_type,traits>* sb)
```
Copies input to the stream buffer sb. If sb is a null pointer, the stream sets failbit and returns immediately. Otherwise, the function copies characters from the input stream to sb until it reaches the end of the input stream, writing to sb fails, or an exception is caught. If no characters are copied to sb, failbit is set. The return value is *this.

```
streamsize gcount() const
```
Returns the number of characters extracted by the most recent call to an unformatted member function (get, getline, ignore, peek, putback, read, readsome, and unget).

```
int_type get()
```
Reads a single character and returns it. If no character is available, the function sets failbit and returns traits::eof().

```
basic_istream<chT,traits>& get(char_type& c)
```
Reads a single character and stores it in c. If no character is available, the function sets failbit and does not modify c. The return value is *this.

```
basic_istream<chT,traits>& get(char_type* s, streamsize n)
```
  Returns get(s, n, widen('\n')).

```
basic_istream<chT,traits>& get(char_type* s, streamsize n, char_type delim)
```
  Reads up to n − 1 characters into the character array that s points to. Reading stops at the end-of-file (which sets eofbit) or when the next character would be delim (but the delimiter character is not read from the buffer). If no characters are stored in s, failbit is set.

  A null character is always appended to the end of s. The return value is *this.

```
basic_istream<chT,traits>& get(basic_streambuf<char_type,traits>& sb)
```
  Returns get(sb, widen('\n')).

```
basic_istream<chT,traits>& get(basic_streambuf<char_type,traits>& sb,
  char_type delim)
```
  Copies characters to the output buffer sb. Copying stops when an end-of-file is reached, when writing to sb fails, or when the next character to read would be delim (the delimiter is not read from the input buffer). If no characters are copied to sb, failbit is set.

```
basic_istream<chT,traits>& getline(char_type* s, streamsize n)
```
  Returns getline(s, n, widen('\n')).

```
basic_istream<chT,traits>& getline(char_type* s, streamsize n, char_type delim)
```
  Reads up to n − 1 characters into the character array that s points to. Reading stops at the end-of-file (which sets eofbit) or when delim is read (the delimiter character is read from the buffer but not stored in s).

  If no characters are read from the stream, failbit is set. If exactly n − 1 characters are read before reaching the end-of-file, eofbit is set; otherwise, if the limit of n − 1 characters is reached before reading a delimiter, failbit is set.

  A null character is always appended to the end of s. The return value is *this.

```
basic_istream<chT,traits>& ignore (streamsize n=1, int_type delim=traits::eof())
```
  Reads characters from the input buffer and discards them. The operation stops when one of the following occurs:

  - n characters have been read and discarded if n != numeric_limits<streamsize>::max().
  - End-of-file is reached, in which case eofbit is set.
  - delim is read if delim != traits::eof().

  The return value is *this.

```
int_type peek( )
```
  Looks ahead to the next character in the input stream. If good( ) returns true, rdbuf( )->sgetc( ) is returned; otherwise, traits::eof( ) is returned. No characters are extracted from the stream, so a subsequent call to gcount( ) returns 0.

```
basic_istream<chT,traits>& read(char_type* s, streamsize n)
```
  Reads up to n characters and stores them in the array that s points to. Before reading anything, if good( ) is false, failbit is set, and nothing is read. Otherwise, if end-of-file is reached before reading n characters, eofbit and failbit are set. A null character is not appended to s. The return value is *this.

```
streamsize readsome(char_type* s, streamsize n)
```
  Tries to read as many immediately available characters as possible into the array that s points to. If good( ) is false before reading, failbit is set, and readsome

returns immediately. Otherwise, readsome calls rdbuf()->in_avail() and does one of the following:

- in_avail() == -1: eofbit is set and no characters are read
- in_avail() == 0: no characters are read
- in_avail() > 0: min(in_avail(), n) characters are read into s

A null character is not appended to s. The return value is the number of characters stored in s.

basic_istream<chT,traits>& **putback**(char_type c)

Tries to push back the character c so it will be the next character read from the input stream. If good() is false, failbit is set and putback returns. Otherwise, if rdbuf() is not null, putback calls rdbuf()->sputbackc(c). If rdbuf() is null or sputbackc returns traits::eof(), badbit is set. The return value is *this. A subsequent call to gcount() returns 0.

basic_istream<chT,traits>& **seekg**(pos_type pos)
basic_istream<chT,traits>& **seekg**(off_type off, ios_base::seekdir dir)

Tries to seek to a new position in the stream. The first form specifies the position explicitly; the second form specifies the new position as an offset from a known position (beginning of file, current position, or end-of-file). If fail() is false, seekg calls rdbuf()->pubseekoff(pos) or rdbuf()->pubseekoff(off, dir). The return value is *this.

int **sync**()

Synchronizes the stream buffer. If rdbuf() is null, sync returns -1; otherwise, sync calls rdbuf()->pubsync(). If pubsync returns -1, badbit is set, and sync returns -1. Otherwise, sync returns 0.

pos_type **tellg**()

Returns the current position in the stream. If fail() is true, the return value is pos_type(-1); otherwise, the return value is rdbuf()->pubseekoff(0, ios_base::cur, ios_base::in).

basic_istream<chT,traits>& **unget**()

Tries to push back the last input character. If good() is false, failbit is set and unget returns. Otherwise, if rdbuf() is not null, putback calls rdbuf()->sungetc(). If rdbuf() is null or sungetc returns traits::eof(), badbit is set. The return value is *this. A subsequent call to gcount() returns 0.

See Also

istream class, wistream class

---

basic_istream::sentry class

Sentry class for input streams

```
template <typename chT, typename traits=char_traits<chT> >
class basic_istream<chT,traits>::sentry
{
  public: explicit sentry(basic_istream<chT,traits>& stream,
                          bool noskipws = false);
  ~sentry();
  operator bool() const;
```

```
private:
  sentry(const sentry&);            // Not defined
  sentry& operator=(const sentry&); // Not defined
};
```

A basic_istream object constructs a temporary sentry object prior to each input operation. The sentry object is destroyed when the input operation finishes and the function returns. The sentry manages tied streams and is responsible for skipping whitespace prior to a formatted read.

The stream passes itself and a flag to the sentry's constructor. Formatted reads (operator>>) use false for the second argument; unformatted reads (get, getline, etc.) use true.

If stream.good( ) is true, the sentry first flushes any tied stream. That is, if stream.tie( ) is not null, the sentry calls stream.tie( )->flush( ). This ensures that prompts and similar output appears before the input is requested. Then, if the noskipws argument is false, and if the skipws bit is not set in the stream's formatting flags ((ios_base::skipws & stream.fmtflags( )) == 0), the sentry's constructor reads and discards whitespace characters. The sentry uses code similar to that shown in Example 13-17.

Example 13-17. Skipping whitespace in an input sentry

```
const std::ctype<char_type>& ctype =
  std::use_facet<ctype<char_type> >(stream.getloc( ));
int_type c;
while ((c = stream.rdbuf( )->snextc( )) != traits::eof( ))
  if (ctype.is(ctype.space,c) == 0) {
    // Put back the non-space character.
    stream.rdbuf( )->sputbackc(c);
    break;
  }
```

If anything goes wrong, the sentry calls stream.setstate(failbit). The sentry's operator bool( ) returns true if stream.good( ) is true, and false otherwise.

See Also

basic_istream class template, basic_ostream::sentry in <ostream>

---

iostream class   Narrow input and output stream

typedef basic_iostream<char> **iostream**;

The iostream class specializes basic_iostream for the char type.

See Also

basic_iostream class template, istream class, wiostream class, ostream in <ostream>

---

istream class   Input stream

typedef basic_istream<char> **istream**;

The istream class specializes basic_istream for the char type.

See Also

basic_istream class template, iostream class, wistream class, ostream in <ostream>

---

operator>> function template
Input operator for single characters

```
template<typename charT, typename traits>
  basic_istream<charT,traits>& operator>>
  (basic_istream<charT,traits>& stream, charT& c);
```

```
template<typename traits> basic_istream<char,traits>&
  operator>>(basic_istream<char,traits>& stream, unsigned char& c);
template<typename traits> basic_istream<char,traits>&
  operator>>(basic_istream<char,traits>& stream, signed char& c);
```

The operator>> function reads a character from an input stream using the rules for a formatted read (that is, a sentry object is constructed and initial whitespace is skipped). The character is stored in c. If no character is available, failbit is set. The return value is stream.

Note that the first form of operator>> reads the stream's character type. If the stream's character type is char, the second and third forms read signed char and unsigned char.

See Also

basic_istream class template

---

operator>> function template
Input operator for character arrays

```
template<typename charT, typename traits>
  basic_istream<charT,traits>& operator>>
  (basic_istream<charT,traits>& stream, charT* str);
```

```
template<typename traits> basic_istream<char,traits>&
  operator>>(basic_istream<char,traits>& stream, unsigned char* str);
template<typename traits> basic_istream<char,traits>&
  operator>>(basic_istream<char,traits>& stream, signed char* str);
```

The operator>> function reads characters from stream into str. As with any formatted input, a sentry object is created and initial whitespace is skipped. Characters are then read from the stream into str until an end-of-file is reached or the next character read would be a whitespace character (the space is not read from the stream).

To limit the number of characters read (always a good idea), set the stream's width to n. At most, $n - 1$ characters will be read into s. The function resets the width to 0 after reading the stream. A null character is always appended to the end of the string.

If no characters are read from the stream, failbit is set.

Note that the first form of operator>> reads with the stream's character type. If the stream's character type is char, the second and third forms read signed char and unsigned char.

See Also

basic_istream class template

---

wiostream class
Wide input and output stream

```
typedef basic_iostream<wchar_t> wiostream;
```

The wiostream class specializes basic_iostream for the wchar_t type.

See Also

`basic_iostream` class template, `iostream` class, `wistream` class, `wostream` in `<ostream>`

---

wistream class

Wide input stream

`typedef basic_istream<wchar_t>` **`wistream`**`;`

The `wistream` class specializes `basic_istream` for the `wchar_t` type.

See Also

`basic_istream` class template, `istream` class, `wiostream` class, `wostream` in `<ostream>`

---

ws function

Skips whitespace manipulator

```
template <class charT, class traits>
  basic_istream<charT,traits>& ws(basic_istream<charT,traits>& stream);
```

The `ws` function is an input stream manipulator that skips whitespace characters in stream using the same technique as `basic_istream::sentry`. If the manipulator reaches the end-of-file, it sets `eofbit`, but not `failbit`.

Example

Suppose you want to read a line of text by calling `getline`, but you also want to skip whitespace at the beginning of the line. (Because `getline` is an unformatted input function, it does not automatically skip whitespace.) The following example shows one way to skip whitespace and read the line using `ws`:

```
char buffer[BUFSIZ];
...
in >> ws;
in.getline(buffer, sizeof(buffer));
```

See Also

`basic_istream` class template, `basic_istream::sentry` class template

<iterator>

The `<iterator>` header declares classes and templates for defining and using iterators. (See Chapter 10.) Iterators are especially important when using the standard algorithms in `<algorithm>`.

An iterator gives a program access to the contents of a container or other sequence, such as an I/O stream. You can think of an iterator as an abstraction of a pointer; the syntax for using iterators resembles that of pointers. Conceptually, an iterator points to a single element in a container or sequence and can be advanced to the next element with the ++ (increment) operator. The unary * (dereference) operator returns the element that the iterator points to. Iterators (except for output iterators) can be compared: two iterators are equal if they point to the same position in the same sequence, or if they both point to one position past the end of the same sequence.

There are five categories of iterators:

Input iterators

> Permit one pass to read a sequence. The increment operator advances to the next element, but there is no decrement operator. The dereference operator does not return an lvalue, so you can read elements but not modify them.

Output iterators

> Permit one pass to write a sequence. The increment operator advances to the next element, but there is no decrement operator. You can dereference an element only to assign a value to it. You cannot compare output iterators.

Forward iterators

> Are like a combination of an input and an output iterator. You can use a forward iterator anywhere an input iterator is required or where an output iterator is required. A forward iterator, as its name implies, permits unidirectional access to a sequence. You can refer to a single element and modify it multiple times before advancing the iterator.

Bidirectional iterators

> Are like forward iterators but also support the decrement operator (--) to move the iterator backward by one position.

Random access iterators

> Are like bidirectional iterators but also support the [] (subscript) operator to access any index in the sequence. Also, you can add or subtract an integer to move a random access iterator by more than one position at a time. Subtracting two random access iterators yields an integer distance between them. Thus, a random access iterator is most like a conventional pointer, and, in fact, a pointer can be used as a random access iterator.

An input, forward, bidirectional, or random access iterator can be a const_iterator. Dereferencing a const_iterator yields a constant (an rvalue or a const lvalue). Chapter 10 discusses const_iterators in more depth.

An iterator can point to any element in a sequence or to one position past the end. You cannot dereference an iterator that points to one past the end, but you can compare it with other iterators (provided it is not an output iterator) or, if it is a bidirectional or random access iterator, decrease its position so it points to a valid element of the sequence.

Iterators are often used in *ranges*. A range has two iterators: a starting point and an ending point. The end iterator typically points to one position past the last element in the range. Thus, a range is often written using the mathematical notation of [first, last), in which the square bracket means first is included in the range, and the parenthesis means last is excluded from the range.

Like ordinary pointers, iterators can be uninitialized or otherwise have invalid values, such as x.begin( ) - 1, in which x is any container. It is your responsibility to ensure that you dereference only valid iterators, that you don't let iterators run past their valid end-points, and so on.

To create your own iterator class, see the iterator class template.

---

advance function template   Moves iterator forward or backward

```
template <typename InputIterator, typename Distance>
    void advance(InputIterator& i, Distance n);
```

The advance function template advances an input iterator i by a distance n. If the iterator is bidirectional or random access, n can be negative. If the iterator is random

---

access, the advance function is specialized as i + n; other iterators apply the ++ operator n times (or -- for a bidirectional iterator when n is negative).

See Also

distance function template

---

back_insert_iterator class template

Output iterator to push items back onto a container

```
template <typename Container>
  class back_insert_iterator :
    public iterator<output_iterator_tag,void,void,void,void>
{
protected:
  Container* container;
public:
  typedef Container container_type;
  explicit back_insert_iterator(Container& x);
  back_insert_iterator<Container>&
    operator=(typename Container::const_reference value);
  back_insert_iterator<Container>& operator*();
  back_insert_iterator<Container>& operator++();
  back_insert_iterator<Container> operator++(int);
};
```

The back_insert_iterator class template implements an output iterator that stores elements in a container by calling the container's push_back function. The most convenient way to create a back_insert_iterator object is to use the back_inserter function template.

The way back_insert_iterator works seems slightly unconventional, although it is perfectly reasonable for an output iterator: the * operator returns the iterator, not an element of the container. Thus, the expression *iter = value assigns value to the iterator itself. The iterator's assignment operator appends value to the underlying container by calling the container's push_back function. Thus, the iterator does not maintain any notion of a position, and the increment operator is a no-op.

The following are the member functions of back_insert_iterator:

explicit **back_insert_iterator**(Container& x)
> Initializes the container member with &x.

back_insert_iterator<Container>& **operator=**(typename
Container::const_reference value)
> Calls container->push_back(value). The return value is *this.

back_insert_iterator<Container>& **operator***( )
> Returns *this.

back_insert_iterator<Container>& **operator++**( )
back_insert_iterator<Container> **operator++**(int)
> Returns *this with no side effects.

See Also

back_inserter function template, front_insert_iterator class template, insert_iterator class template

back_inserter function template

```
template <typename Container>
  back_insert_iterator<Container> back_inserter(Container& x);
```

The back_inserter function template constructs a back_insert_iterator object for the container x. Example 13-18 shows how to use back_inserter to read integers from a file into a vector.

Example 13-18. Using back_inserter to add numbers to a vector

```
std::ifstream in("experiment.dat");
std::vector<int> data;
std::copy(std::istream_iterator<int>(in),
          std::istream_iterator<int>( ),
          std::back_inserter(data));
```

See Also

back_insert_iterator class template, front_inserter function template, inserter function template

bidirectional_iterator_tag class

```
struct bidirectional_iterator_tag :
  public forward_iterator_tag {};
```

Use the bidirectional_iterator_tag class as the iterator category when declaring a new bidirectional iterator class. When writing a generic algorithm or similar function, you can use the iterator's category to write specialized implementations for different kinds of iterators. See Example 13-19 (under the distance function template).

See Also

bidirectional_iterator_tag class, forward_iterator_tag class, input_iterator_tag class, iterator class template, output_iterator_tag class, random_access_iterator_tag class

distance function template

```
template<typename InputIterator>
  typename iterator_traits<InputIterator>::difference_type
    distance(InputIterator first, InputIterator last);
```

The distance function returns the number of elements between first and last. The function is specialized for random access iterators to use the - operator; for other input iterators, the function applies the ++ operator to first until first == last. The behavior is undefined if first and last refer to different containers or if last points to an element earlier than first.

Example 13-19 shows a simple implementation of the distance function. The first specialized implementation works for any iterator (except output iterators, which do not support comparison with the != operator). The second one works only with random access iterators and uses the subtraction operator to compute the distance in constant time. The compiler picks the more specialized function when it can, so random access iterators can compute distances in constant time, compared to linear time for other iterators.

Example 13-19. A simple implementation of distance

```
namespace std {
  template<typename InputIter>
  typename iterator_traits<InputIter>::difference_type
  specialize_distance(InputIter first, InputIter last, ...)
  {
    typename iterator_traits<InputIter>::difference_type n;
    for (n = 0; first != last; ++first)
      ++n;
    return n;
  }

  template<typename InputIter>
  typename iterator_traits<InputIter>::difference_type
  specialize_distance(InputIter first, InputIter last,
                      random_access_iterator_tag)
  {
    return last - first;
  }

  template<typename InputIter>
  typename iterator_traits<InputIter>::difference_type
  distance(InputIter first, InputIter last)
  {
    return specialize_distance(first, last,
      iterator_traits<InputIter>::iterator_category());
  }
}
```

See Also

advance function template

forward_iterator_tag class
Tag for a forward iterator

```
struct forward_iterator_tag : public input_iterator_tag {};
```

Use the forward_iterator_tag class as the iterator category when declaring a new forward iterator class. When writing a generic algorithm or similar function, you can use the iterator's category to write specialized implementations for different kinds of iterators. See Example 13-19 (under the distance function template).

See Also

bidirectional_iterator_tag class, forward_iterator_tag class, input_iterator_tag class, iterator class template, output_iterator_tag class, random_access_iterator_tag class

front_insert_iterator class template
Iterator to insert elements at the front of a container

```
template <typename Container>
class front_insert_iterator :
  public iterator<output_iterator_tag,void,void,void,void>
{
```

```
protected:
  Container* container;
public:
  typedef Container container_type;
  explicit front_insert_iterator(Container& x);
  front_insert_iterator<Container>&
    operator=(typename Container::const_reference value);
  front_insert_iterator<Container>& operator*( );
  front_insert_iterator<Container>& operator++( );
  front_insert_iterator<Container> operator++(int);
};
```

The front_insert_iterator class template implements an output iterator that stores elements in a container by calling the container's push_front function. The most convenient way to create a front_insert_iterator object is to use the front_inserter function template.

The way front_insert_iterator works seems slightly unconventional, although it is perfectly reasonable for an output iterator: the * operator returns the iterator, not an element of the container. Thus, the expression *iter = value assigns value to the iterator itself. The iterator's assignment operator adds value to the underlying container by calling the container's push_front function. Thus, the iterator does not maintain any notion of a position, and the increment operator is a no-op.

The following are the member functions of front_insert_iterator:

explicit **front_insert_iterator**(Container& x)
> Initializes the container member with &x.

front_insert_iterator<Container>& **operator=**(typename
  Container::const_reference value)
> Calls container->push_front(value). The return value is *this.

front_insert_iterator<Container>& **operator***( )
> Returns *this.

front_insert_iterator<Container>& **operator++**( )
front_insert_iterator<Container> **operator++**(int)
> Returns *this with no side effects.

See Also

back_insert_iterator class template, front_inserter function template, insert_iterator class template

---

front_inserter function template

Creates a front_insert_iterator

```
template <typename Container>
  front_insert_iterator<Container>
    front_inserter(Container& x);
```

The front_inserter function template constructs a front_insert_iterator object for the container x. Example 13-20 shows how to use front_inserter to read integers from a file into a list in reverse order.

Example 13-20. Using a front_inserter to add numbers to a list

```
std::ifstream in("experiment.dat");
std::list<int> data;
std::copy(std::istream_iterator<int>(in),
          std::istream_iterator<int>( ),
          std::front_inserter(data));
```

See Also

back_inserter function template, front_insert_iterator class template, inserter function template

---

input_iterator_tag class
Tag for an input iterator

```
struct input_iterator_tag {};
```

Use the input_iterator_tag class as the iterator category when declaring a new input iterator class. When writing a generic algorithm or similar function, you can use the iterator's category to write specialized implementations for different kinds of iterators. See Example 13-19 (under the distance function template).

See Also

bidirectional_iterator_tag class, forward_iterator_tag class, iterator class template, output_iterator_tag class, random_access_iterator_tag class

---

insert_iterator class template
Iterator to insert elements in a container

```
class insert_iterator :
  public iterator<output_iterator_tag,void,void,void,void>
{
protected:
  Container* container;
  typename Container::iterator iter;
public:
  typedef Container container_type;
  insert_iterator(Container& cont, typename Container::iterator iter);
  insert_iterator<Container>&
    operator=(typename Container::const_reference value);
  insert_iterator<Container>& operator*( );
  insert_iterator<Container>& operator++( );
  insert_iterator<Container>& operator++(int);
};
```

The insert_iterator class template implements an output iterator that stores elements in a container by calling the container's insert function. The most convenient way to create a insert_iterator object is to use the inserter function template.

The way insert_iterator works seems slightly unconventional, although it is perfectly reasonable for an output iterator: the * operator returns the iterator, not an element of the container. Thus, the expression *iter = value assigns value to the iterator itself. The iterator's assignment operator adds value to the underlying container by calling the container's insert function. Thus, the iterator does not maintain any notion of a position, and the increment operator is a no-op.

The following are the member functions of insert_iterator:

insert_iterator(Container& x, typename Container::iterator i)
> Initializes the container member with &x and iter with i. Thus, the elements to be inserted in the container will be inserted at position i.

insert_iterator<Container>& **operator=**(typename
  Container::const_reference value)
> Assigns a value to an element in the iterator's container, performing the equivalent of the following:

```
iter = container->insert(iter, value);
++iter;
return *this;
```

insert_iterator<Container>& **operator***( )
> Returns *this.

insert_iterator<Container>& **operator++**( )
insert_iterator<Container>& **operator++**(int)
> Returns *this with no side effects.

See Also

back_insert_iterator class template, front_insert_iterator class template, inserter function template

---

inserter function template   Creates an insert_iterator

```
template <typename Container, typename Iterator>
  insert_iterator<Container>
    inserter(Container& x, Iterator i);
```

The inserter function template constructs an insert_iterator object for the container x to insert items starting at position i. Figure 13-22 illustrates a simple use of the inserter function.

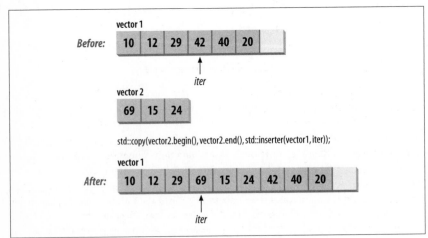

Figure 13-22. Using inserter to insert a vector in the middle of another vector

See Also

back_inserter function template, front_inserter function template, insert_iterator class template

istream_iterator class template

Input iterator to read items from an istream

```
template <typename T, typename charT = char,
          typename traits = char_traits<charT>, typename Distance = ptrdiff_t>
class istream_iterator :
  public iterator<input_iterator_tag,
    T, Distance, const T*, const T&>
{
public:
  typedef charT char_type;
  typedef traits traits_type;
  typedef basic_istream<charT,traits> istream_type;
  istream_iterator();
  istream_iterator(istream_type& stream);
  istream_iterator(const istream_iterator<T,charT,traits,Distance>& x);
  ~istream_iterator();
  const T& operator*() const;
  const T* operator->() const;
  istream_iterator<T,charT,traits,Distance>& operator++();
  istream_iterator<T,charT,traits,Distance> operator++(int);
};
```

The istream_iterator class template wraps an input iterator around an input stream (an instance of basic_istream), making the stream appear to be a sequence of items, each of type T.

Example 13-20 (under the front_inserter function template) shows how an istream_iterator can be used to read a series of integers from a file.

The following are the member functions of istream_iterator:

istream_iterator( )
> Constructs an istream_iterator that denotes the end of the stream. End-of-stream iterators are equal to each other and are not equal to any other istream_iterator.

istream_iterator(istream_type& stream)
> Constructs an istream_iterator to read from a stream. The constructor might read the first item from the stream. An istream_iterator that wraps a stream is equal to an end-of-stream iterator when stream.eof( ) is true.

istream_iterator(const istream_iterator<T,charT,traits,Distance>& iter)
> Constructs a copy of iter. Note that two istream_iterator objects are the same (operator== is true) if they point to the same stream object.

const T& **operator*( ) const**
> Returns the item that was read most recently from the stream.

const T* **operator->( ) const**
> Returns a pointer to the item that was read most recently from the stream.

istream_iterator<T,charT,traits,Distance>& **operator++( )**
> Reads the next item from the stream using operator>>. The return value is a copy of *this, made prior to reading from the stream.

See Also

istreambuf_iterator class template, ostream_iterator class template, basic_istream in <istream>

---

istreambuf_iterator class template   Input iterator to read characters from a streambuf

```
template<typename charT, typename traits=char_traits<charT> >
class istreambuf_iterator :
  public iterator<input_iterator_tag, charT, typename traits::off_type, charT*,
                  charT&>
{
public:
  typedef charT char_type;
  typedef traits traits_type;
  typedef typename traits::int_type int_type;
  typedef basic_streambuf<charT,traits> streambuf_type;
  typedef basic_istream<charT,traits> istream_type;
  class proxy; // Exposition only

  istreambuf_iterator() throw();
  istreambuf_iterator(istream_type& s) throw();
  istreambuf_iterator(streambuf_type* s) throw();
  istreambuf_iterator(const proxy& p) throw();
  charT operator*() const;
  istreambuf_iterator<charT,traits>& operator++();
  proxy operator++(int);
  bool equal(istreambuf_iterator& b) const;
};
```

The istreambuf_iterator class template wraps a stream buffer object (instance of basic_streambuf) as an input iterator to read characters from the stream buffer. Example 13-21 shows how to use streambuf_iterators to copy files.

Example 13-21. Copying files using streambuf iterators

```
void copyfile(const char* from, const char* to)
{
  std::ifstream in(from);
  std::ofstream out(to);

  std::copy(std::istreambuf_iterator<char>(in),
            std::istreambuf_iterator<char>(),
            std::ostreambuf_iterator<char>(out));
}
```

The post-increment operator (++) returns a *proxy object*, which is an object that stands in for the istreambuf_iterator object. Its use is largely transparent, and you rarely need to think about it. The definition and name of the proxy class are implementation-defined, but the class has at least the capability to return the input character and the underlying stream buffer. This section assumes that the class name is *proxy*. Example 13-22 shows a prototypical implementation of *proxy*.

Example 13-22. A trivial implementation of the proxy class

```
template<typename charT, typename traits=char_traits<charT> >
class istreambuf_iterator<charT, traits>::proxy
{
  friend template<typename charT, typename traits>
    class istreambuf_iterator<charT,traits>;
  charT keep;
  basic_streambuf<charT,traits>* sbuf;
  proxy(charT c, basic_streambuf<charT,traits>* sbuf);
    : keep(c), sbuf(sbuf) {}
public:
  charT operator*() { return keep; }
};
```

In the following descriptions of the member functions of istreambuf_iterator, the data member *sbuf* is a pointer to the iterator's stream buffer. The *sbuf* member serves only to keep the function descriptions clear and simple; the class is not required to have such a member, nor is the class required to have a member with that name.

istreambuf_iterator( ) throw( )
> Constructs the end-of-stream iterator.

istreambuf_iterator(istream_type& s) throw( )
istreambuf_iterator(streambuf_type* sb) throw( )
istreambuf_iterator(const *proxy*& p) throw( )
> Constructs an istreambuf_iterator and initializes *sbuf* to s.rdbuf( ), sb, or p.sbuf. If sb == 0, an end-of-stream iterator is constructed.

charT **operator***( ) const
> Returns *sbuf*->sgetc( ).

istreambuf_iterator<charT,traits>& **operator++**( )
> Calls *sbuf*->sbumpc( ) and returns *this.

proxy **operator++**(int)
> Returns *proxy*(*sbuf*->sbumpc( ), sbuf).

bool **equal**(istreambuf_iterator& b) const
> Returns true if both iterators are end-of-stream iterators or if neither iterator is an end-of-stream iterator. The iterators do not have to use the same stream buffer.

See Also

istream_iterator class template, ostreambuf_iterator class template, basic_streambuf in <streambuf>

---

iterator class template

Iterator base-class template

```
template<typename Category, typename T, typename Difference = ptrdiff_t,
         typename Pointer = T*, typename Reference = T&>
struct iterator
{
  typedef T value_type;
  typedef Difference difference_type;
  typedef Pointer pointer;
```

```
  typedef Reference reference;
  typedef Category iterator_category;
};
```

The iterator class template is a convenient base-class template to use when implementing your own iterator.

The following are the template parameters, which are all type parameters:

Category
> Must be one of the five iterator category tags: bidirectional_iterator_tag, forward_iterator_tag, input_iterator_tag, output_iterator_tag, or random_access_iterator_tag.

T   The element type. It can be void for an output iterator because you cannot dereference an output iterator.

Difference
> An integral type that represents the distance between two iterators. It can be void for an output iterator because you cannot measure the distance between two output iterators. This parameter is optional; the default is ptrdiff_t, which is suitable for typical pointer-like iterators.

Pointer
> The pointer-to-element type. This parameter is optional; the default is T*, which is correct for most iterators.

Reference
> The reference-to-element type. This parameter is optional; the default is T&, which is correct for most iterators.

See Also

iterator_traits class template, reverse_iterator class template

---

iterator_traits class template   Iterator traits

```
template<typename Iterator>
struct iterator_traits
{
  typedef typename Iterator::difference_type difference_type;
  typedef typename Iterator::value_type value_type;
  typedef typename Iterator::pointer pointer;
  typedef typename Iterator::reference reference;
  typedef typename Iterator::iterator_category iterator_category;
};
```

The iterator_traits class template declares traits for an iterator. If you use the iterator class template as the base for your custom iterator, you don't need to specialize iterator_traits. If you are writing a custom container or algorithm, you should always use iterator_traits to obtain the traits of an iterator. If you use a plain pointer as an iterator, the standard library specializes iterator_traits for you. See the next subsection.

If you write your own specialization, the iterator_category type must be one of the five iterator tag classes. (See the iterator class template.) For an output iterator, difference_type and value_type are void.

When writing a generic algorithm or other function that uses iterators, you can use iterator_traits to specialize the behavior for certain kinds of iterators. See

---

Example 13-19 (under distance), which shows how iterator traits can be used to improve the performance of a function.

See Also

iterator class template

iterator_traits<T*> template specialization
Iterator traits specialized for pointers

```
template<typename  T>
struct iterator_traits<T*>
{
  typedef ptrdiff_t difference_type;
  typedef T value_type;
  typedef T* pointer;
  typedef T& reference;
  typedef random_access_iterator_tag iterator_category;
};
```

The iterator_traits class template is specialized for pointers. This specialization lets you use a pointer as a random access iterator.

See Also

iterator_traits class template

iterator_traits<const T*> template specialization
Iterator traits specialized
for pointers to const

```
template<typename  T>
struct iterator_traits<const T*>
{
  typedef ptrdiff_t difference_type;
  typedef T value_type;
  typedef const T* pointer;
  typedef const T& reference;
  typedef random_access_iterator_tag iterator_category;
};
```

The iterator_traits class template is specialized for pointers to const. This specialization lets you use a pointer as a random access iterator.

See Also

iterator_traits class template

ostream_iterator class template
Output iterator to write items to an ostream

```
template <typename T, typename charT = char,
          typename traits = char_traits<charT> >
class ostream_iterator :
  public iterator<output_iterator_tag,void,void,void,void>
{
public:
  typedef charT char_type;
  typedef traits traits_type;
  typedef basic_ostream<charT,traits> ostream_type;
```

```
  ostream_iterator(ostream_type& s);
  ostream_iterator(ostream_type& s, const charT* delimiter);
  ostream_iterator(const ostream_iterator<T,charT,traits>& x);
  ~ostream_iterator( );
  ostream_iterator<T,charT,traits>& operator=(const T& value);
  ostream_iterator<T,charT,traits>& operator*( );
  ostream_iterator<T,charT,traits>& operator++( );
  ostream_iterator<T,charT,traits>& operator++(int);
};
```

The ostream_iterator class template wraps an output iterator around an output stream (instance of basic_ostream), making the stream appear to be a sequence of items, each of type T. For example, suppose you have a vector of data. You can print the data, one number per line, by using an ostream_iterator:

```
  std::vector<int> data;
  ... // Acquire data.
  std::copy(data.begin( ), data.end( ),
        std::ostream_iterator(std::cout, "\n"));
```

The following are the member functions of ostream_iterator:

ostream_iterator(ostream_type& stream)
ostream_iterator(ostream_type& stream, const charT* delimiter)
ostream_iterator(const ostream_iterator<T,charT,traits>& x)

Prepares to write items to stream. If delimiter is present, it will be written after each item. The copy constructor copies the reference to the stream and to the delimiter from x.

ostream_iterator<T,charT,traits>& **operator=**(const T& value)

Writes value to the stream using operator<<. If the ostream_iterator has a delimiter, it is written after value. The return value is *this.

ostream_iterator<T,charT,traits>& **operator*( )**

Returns *this.

ostream_iterator<T,charT,traits>& **operator++( )**
ostream_iterator<T,charT,traits>& **operator++**(int)

Returns *this with no side effects.

See Also

istream_iterator class template, ostreambuf_iterator class template, basic_ostream in <ostream>

---

ostreambuf_iterator class template   Output iterator to write characters to a streambuf

```
template<typename charT, typename traits=char_traits<charT> >
class ostreambuf_iterator :
  public iterator<output_iterator_tag,void,void,void,void>
{
public:
  typedef charT char_type;
  typedef traits traits_type;
  typedef basic_streambuf<charT,traits> streambuf_type;
  typedef basic_ostream<charT,traits> ostream_type;

  ostreambuf_iterator(ostream_type& s) throw( );
  ostreambuf_iterator(streambuf_type* s) throw( );
```

```
  ostreambuf_iterator& operator=(charT c);
  ostreambuf_iterator& operator*();
  ostreambuf_iterator& operator++();
  ostreambuf_iterator& operator++(int);
  bool failed() const throw();
};
```

The ostreambuf_iterator class template wraps a basic_streambuf object as an output iterator to write characters to the stream buffer. Example 13-21 (under istreambuf_iterator) shows how to use streambuf iterators to copy files.

In the following descriptions of the member functions of ostreambuf_iterator, the data member *sbuf* is a pointer to the iterator's stream buffer. The *sbuf* member serves only to keep the function descriptions clear and simple; the class is not required to have such a member, or a member with that name.

ostreambuf_iterator(ostream_type& s) throw( )
ostreambuf_iterator(streambuf_type* sb) throw( )
  Saves the stream buffer s.rdbuf( ) or sb in *sbuf*.

ostreambuf_iterator& **operator=**(charT c)
  Calls *sbuf*->sputc(c) (only if failed( ) returns false) and returns *this.

ostreambuf_iterator& **operator***( )
  Returns *this.

ostreambuf_iterator& **operator++**( )
ostreambuf_iterator& **operator++**(int)
  Returns *this.

bool **failed**( ) const throw( )
  Returns true if *sbuf*->sputc( ) ever returned traits::eof( ). Otherwise, it returns false.

See Also

istreambuf_iterator class template, ostream_iterator class template, basic_streambuf in <streambuf>

---

output_iterator_tag class   Tag for an output iterator

struct **output_iterator_tag** {};

Use the output_iterator_tag class as the iterator category when declaring a new output iterator class. When writing a generic algorithm or similar function, you can use the iterator's category to write specialized implementations for different kinds of iterators. See Example 13-19 (under the distance function template).

See Also

bidirectional_iterator_tag class, forward_iterator_tag class, input_iterator_tag class, iterator class template, random_access_iterator_tag class

---

random_access_iterator_tag class   Tag for a random access iterator

struct **random_access_iterator_tag** :
  public bidirectional_iterator_tag {};

Use the random_access_iterator_tag class as the iterator category when declaring a new random access iterator class. When writing a generic algorithm or similar function, you can use the iterator's category to write specialized implementations for different kinds of iterators. See Example 13-19 (under the distance function template).

See Also

bidirectional_iterator_tag class, forward_iterator_tag class, input_iterator_tag class, iterator class template, output_iterator_tag class

---

reverse_iterator class template   Iterator wrapper to reverse direction

```
template <typename Iterator>
class reverse_iterator : public iterator<
  typename iterator_traits<Iterator>::iterator_category,
  typename iterator_traits<Iterator>::value_type,
  typename iterator_traits<Iterator>::difference_type,
  typename iterator_traits<Iterator>::pointer,
  typename iterator_traits<Iterator>::reference>
{
protected:
  Iterator current;
public:
  typedef Iterator iterator_type;
  typedef typename iterator_traits<Iterator>::difference_type
    difference_type;
  typedef typename iterator_traits<Iterator>::reference reference;
  typedef typename iterator_traits<Iterator>::pointer pointer;
  reverse_iterator();
  explicit reverse_iterator(Iterator x);
  template <typename U>
  reverse_iterator(const reverse_iterator<U>& u);
  Iterator base() const;  // Explicit
  reference operator*() const;
  pointer operator->() const;
  reverse_iterator& operator++();
  reverse_iterator operator++(int);
  reverse_iterator& operator--();
  reverse_iterator operator--(int);
  reverse_iterator operator+(difference_type n) const;
  reverse_iterator& operator+=(difference_type n);
  reverse_iterator operator-(difference_type n) const;
  reverse_iterator& operator-=(difference_type n);
  reference operator[](difference_type n) const;
};
```

The reverse_iterator class template is an adapter for a bidirectional or random access iterator to iterate the sequence in the opposite direction of the adapted iterator. In other words, if the adapted iterator advances from the first to the last item in a container, a reverse iterator starts with the last items and "advances" to the first item. In addition to the reverse_iterator template, there are also several function templates for the comparison and arithmetic (+ and -) operators.

The standard containers return reverse_iterator objects from the rbegin() and rend() functions. The following example shows a simple implementation of these functions:

```
reverse_iterator rbegin() { return reverse_iterator(end()); }
reverse_iterator rend() { return reverse_iterator(begin()); }
```

Because an iterator can point to one past the last item in a container but cannot point to one item before the first, a reverse iterator conceptually points to one item *before* the position to which the adapted iterator points. In other words, given an iterator, iter, which points to 42 in Example 13-23, if you construct a reverse iterator that adapts iter, the reverse iterator appears to point to 29. When you increment the reverse iterator, it decrements the adapted iterator. Thus, the "next" element in the sequence of the reverse iterator is 12. (The adapted iterator points to 29.) The adapted iterator is also called the *base iterator*. See Chapter 10 for a discussion of some of the interesting ramifications of using reverse_iterator.

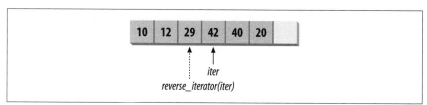

Figure 13-23. How a reverse iterator works

The following member functions of reverse_iterator refer to *adapted* as the data member that stores the base() iterator. The *adapted* member is actually named current, and is a protected data member of reverse_iterator:

reverse_iterator( )
 Initializes the *adapted* data member with its default constructor.

explicit **reverse_iterator**(Iterator iter)
 Initializes the *adapted* data member to iter.

template <typename U> **reverse_iterator**(const reverse_iterator<U>& ri)
 Initializes the *adapted* data member to ri.base( ).

Iterator **base( )** const
 Returns the adapted iterator, *adapted*. Note that the adapted iterator points to one position *after* the reverse iterator's logical position.

reference **operator***( ) const
 Returns a reference to the item that the reverse iterator logically points to, which is one item *before* the item to which base( ) points. Thus, you can think of the dereference function working as follows:

```
reference operator*( ) const {
  iterator_type tmp = base( );
  --tmp;
  return *tmp;
}
```

pointer **operator->**( ) const
 Returns a pointer to the item that the reverse iterator logically points to, that is, &(operator*( )).

reverse_iterator& **operator++**( )
 Decrements *adapted* and returns *this.

reverse_iterator **operator++**(int)
 Saves a copy of *this, decrements *adapted*, and returns the saved copy of *this.

reverse_iterator& **operator**--( )
>   Increments *adapted* and returns *this.

reverse_iterator **operator**--(int)
>   Saves a copy *this, increments *adapted*, and returns the saved copy of *this.

reverse_iterator **operator+**(difference_type n) const
>   Returns reverse_iterator(base( ) − n).

reverse_iterator& **operator+=**(difference_type n)
>   Subtracts n from *adapted* and returns *this.

reverse_iterator **operator-**(difference_type n) const
>   Returns reverse_iterator(base( ) + n).

reverse_iterator& **operator-=**(difference_type n)
>   Adds n to *adapted* and returns *this.

reference **operator[]**(difference_type n) const
>   Returns base( )[-n-1].

The following are several nonmember functions that compare reverse iterators and perform basic arithmetic such as finding the distance between two reverse iterators and advancing a reverse iterator by an integer:

template <typename Iterator>
bool **operator==**(const reverse_iterator<Iterator>& x, const
  reverse_iterator<Iterator>& y)
>   Returns true when the base iterators are equal, that is, x.base( ) == y.base( ).

template <typename Iterator>
bool **operator!=**(const reverse_iterator<Iterator>& x, const
  reverse_iterator<Iterator>& y)
>   Returns true when x and y have different base iterators, that is, x.base( ) != y.base( ).

template <typename Iterator>
bool **operator<**(const reverse_iterator<Iterator>& x, const
  reverse_iterator<Iterator>& y)
>   Returns true when x is closer than y to the beginning of the sequence. Because x and y are reverse iterators, the function returns y.base( ) < x.base( ).

template <typename Iterator>
bool **operator>**(const reverse_iterator<Iterator>& x, const
  reverse_iterator<Iterator>& y)
>   Returns true when x is farther than y from the beginning of the sequence. Because x and y are reverse iterators, the function returns y.base( ) > x.base( ).

template <typename Iterator>
bool **operator>=**(const reverse_iterator<Iterator>& x, const
  reverse_iterator<Iterator>& y)
>   Returns true when x is farther than y from the beginning of the sequence or x equals y. Because x and y are reverse iterators, the function returns y.base( ) >= x.base( ).

template <typename Iterator>
bool **operator<=**(const reverse_iterator<Iterator>& x, const
  reverse_iterator<Iterator>& y)
>   Returns true when x is closer than y to the beginning of the sequence or x equals y. Because x and y are reverse iterators, the function returns y.base( ) <= x.base( ).

```
template <typename Iterator>
typename reverse_iterator<Iterator>::difference_type
operator-(const reverse_iterator<Iterator>& x, const
   reverse_iterator<Iterator>& y)
```
Returns the distance between two reverse iterators, that is, y.base( ) - x.base( ).

```
template <typename Iter>
reverse_iterator<Iter>
operator+(typename reverse_iterator<Iter>::difference_type n, const
   reverse_iterator<Iter>& ri)
```
Advances a reverse iterator ri by n. This function is a counterpart to the operator+ member function, allowing you to write ri + n and n + ri, which yield the same result.

See Also

iterator class template, Chapter 10

<limits>

The <limits> header declares the numeric_limits class template and related types and specializations that define the limits and characteristics of the fundamental arithmetic types (such as the largest possible int). It is the C++ equivalent of the C headers <cfloat> and <climits> (and the wchar_t limits in <cwchar>).

The <limits> header has a number of advantages over the <cfloat> and <climits> declarations. In particular, by using a template, you can write your own template-based classes that depend on the characteristics of a template parameter; this is not possible with the macro-based C headers.

float_denorm_style type
Represents existence of denormalized, floating-point values

```
enum float_denorm_style {
  denorm_indeterminate = -1;
  denorm_absent = 0;
  denorm_present = 1;
};
```
The float_denorm_style type is an enumerated type that represents whether denormalized floating-point values are supported.

float_round_style type
Represents the floating-point rounding style

```
enum float_round_style {
  round_indeterminate = -1,
  round_toward_zero = 0,
  round_to_nearest = 1,
  round_toward_infinity = 2,
  round_toward_neg_infinity = 3
};
```

The float_round_style type is an enumerated type that represents how floating-point numbers are rounded.

---

numeric_limits class template

Represents the limits and characteristics of an arithmetic type

```
template<typename T>
class numeric_limits
{
public:
  static const bool is_specialized = false;
  static T min( ) throw( );
  static T max( ) throw( );
  static const int digits = 0;
  static const int digits10 = 0;
  static const bool is_signed = false;
  static const bool is_integer = false;
  static const bool is_exact = false;
  static const int radix = 0;
  static T epsilon( ) throw( );
  static T round_error( ) throw( );
  static const int min_exponent = 0;
  static const int min_exponent10 = 0;
  static const int max_exponent = 0;
  static const int max_exponent10 = 0;
  static const bool has_infinity = false;
  static const bool has_quiet_NaN = false;
  static const bool has_signaling_NaN = false;
  static const float_denorm_style has_denorm = denorm_absent;
  static const bool has_denorm_loss = false;
  static T infinity( ) throw( );
  static T quiet_NaN( ) throw( );
  static T signaling_NaN( ) throw( );
  static T denorm_min( ) throw( );
  static const bool is_iec559 = false;
  static const bool is_bounded = false;
  static const bool is_modulo = false;
  static const bool traps = false;
  static const bool tinyness_before = false;
  static const float_round_style round_style = round_toward_zero;
};
```

The numeric_limits class template represents the limits and characteristics of an arithmetic type. The data members that are shown as static const are constants that you can use in other integral constant expressions.

The default is for all members to be 0 or false. The header has specializations for all fundamental types, and only for the fundamental types. Every specialization in the standard library defines every member, even if the member does not pertain to the type (e.g., floating-point characteristics of an integral type). Meaningless members are defined as 0 or false.

You can specialize numeric_limits for your own types. For example, suppose you write a class, bigint, to represent integers of arbitrary size. You can define your specialization to show that the type is unbounded, signed, integral, etc. You should follow the convention of the standard library, namely, by defining all members, even if they do not apply to your type. Be sure to define is_specialized as true.

Use numeric_limits to query the properties or traits of a numeric type. For example, suppose you are writing a data analysis program. Among the data are points you want to ignore, but you need to keep their places in the data array. You decide to insert a special marker value. Ideally, the marker value (such as infinity) cannot possibly appear in the actual data stream. If the floating-point type that you are using does not support infinity, you can use the maximum finite value. Example 13-23 lists the no_data function, which returns the value used for the no-data marker.

Example 13-23. Using infinity or maximum finite value to mean "no data"

```
// Define a template that will differentiate types that have a specialized
// numeric_limits and an explicit value for infinity.
template<typename T, bool is_specialized, bool has_infinity>
struct max_or_infinity
{};

// Specialize the template to obtain the value of infinity.
template<typename T>
struct max_or_infinity<T, true, true>
{
  static T value()
    { return std::numeric_limits<T>::infinity(); }
};

// Specialize the template if infinity is not supported.
template<typename T>
struct max_or_infinity<T, true, false>
{
  static T value() { return std::numeric_limits<T>::max(); }
};

// Note that a type without a numeric_limits specialization does not have a
// max_or_infinity specialization, so the no_data function would result in
// compile-time errors when applied to such a type.
//
// The no_data function returns a value that can be used to mark points that do
// not have valid data.
template<typename T>
T no_data()
{
  return max_or_infinity<T,
    std::numeric_limits<T>::is_specialized,
    std::numeric_limits<T>::has_infinity>::value();
}
```

The C++ standard mandates that all integers are binary and use two's complement, ones' complement, or signed magnitude representation. The representation of floating-point numbers is not specified. The numeric_limits template assumes that a number is represented as a sign, a significand (sometimes called the *mantissa*), a base, and an exponent:

$$x = sign \times significand \times base^{\,exponent}$$

In everyday arithmetic, we are used to working with a *base* of 10. (The base is also called the *radix*.) The most common bases for computer arithmetic, however, are 16 and 2. Many modern workstations use the IEC 60559 (IEEE 754) standard for floating-point arithmetic, which uses a base of 2.

The *significand* is a string of digits in the given base. There is an implied radix point at the start of the significand, so the value of the significand is always less than one. (A *radix point* is the generalization of a decimal point for any radix.)

A finite floating-point value is *normalized* if the first digit of its significand is nonzero, or if the entire value is 0. The term *denormalized* means a finite value is not normalized.

The *precision* of a floating-point type is the maximum number of places in the significand. The *range* of a floating-point type depends primarily on the minimum and maximum values for the exponent.

The following are descriptions of the members of numeric_limits:

static T **denorm_min**( ) throw( )
> Returns the smallest positive, denormalized floating-point value. If has_denorm is false, it returns the smallest positive normalized value. For non-floating-point types, it returns 0.

static const int **digits**
> The number of radix digits that can be represented. For integer types, it is the number of non-sign bits; for floating-point types, it is the number of places in the significand.

static const int **digits10**
> The number of decimal digits that can be represented. If is_bounded is false, digits10 is 0.

static T **epsilon**( ) throw( )
> Returns the difference between 1.0 and the smallest representable value greater than 1.0. For integral types, epsilon returns 0.

static const float_denorm_style **has_denorm**
> Indicates the denormalized, floating-point style. It is denorm_indeterminate if the style cannot be determined at compile time. It is meaningful for all floating-point types.

static const bool **has_denorm_loss**
> Indicates whether the loss of accuracy in a floating-point computation is a denormalization loss rather than an inexact result.

static const bool **has_infinity**
> Indicates whether the floating-point type can represent positive infinity. In particular, has_infinity is true when is_iec559 is true.

static const bool **has_quiet_NaN**
> Indicates whether the floating-point type can represent a quiet (nonsignaling) NaN (not-a-number). In particular, this is true when is_iec559 is true.

static const bool **has_signaling_NaN**
> Indicates whether the floating point type can represent a signaling NaN. In particular, this is true when is_iec559 is true.

static T **infinity**( ) throw( )
> Returns the value of positive infinity if has_infinity is true.

static const bool **is_bounded**
> Indicates whether the type represents a finite set of values. This is `true` for all fundamental types.

static const bool **is_exact**
> Indicates whether the type represents values exactly. It is `true` for all integral types and `false` for the fundamental floating-point types.

static const bool **is_iec559**
> Indicates whether the type follows the IEC 60559 (IEEE 754) standard for floating-point arithmetic. It is meaningful only for floating-point types. Among the requirements of the IEC 60559 standard are support for positive and negative infinity, and for values that are NaN.

static const bool **is_integer**
> `true` for all integral types.

static const bool **is_modulo**
> Indicates whether the type uses modulo arithmetic. This is always `true` for unsigned integral types and often `true` for signed integral types. It is `false` for typical floating-point types.

static const bool **is_signed**
> Indicates whether the type is signed, that is, supports positive and negative values.

static const bool **is_specialized**
> Indicates whether numeric_limits is specialized for the type. It is `false` by default, so you can detect whether numeric_limits<> has been specialized for a particular type, and therefore determine whether a `false` or 0 value is meaningful.

static T **max**( ) throw( )
> Returns the maximum finite value when is_bounded is `true`.

static const int **max_exponent**
> The largest allowable exponent for a finite floating-point number.

static const int **max_exponent10**
> The largest allowable decimal exponent for a finite floating-point number.

static T **min**( ) throw( )
> Returns the minimum finite value. It is meaningful when is_bounded is `true` or when is_bounded and is_signed are both `false`.

static const int **min_exponent**
> The smallest allowable exponent for a floating-point number such that radix raised to min_exponent - 1 is representable as a normalized floating-point number.

static const int **min_exponent10**
> The smallest negative decimal exponent such that 10 raised to min_exponent10 is representable as a normalized floating-point number.

static T **quiet_NaN**( ) throw( )
> Returns a quiet NaN value if has_quiet_NaN is `true`.

static const int **radix**
> The base used in the representation of a numeric value. For floating-point numbers, it is the base of the exponent.

static T **round_error**( ) throw( )
> Returns the maximum rounding error.

static const float_round_style **round_style**
> Indicates the rounding style used by the floating-point type. (See the float_round_style type for a definition of the possible return values.) For integral types, the return value is always round_toward_zero.

static T **signaling_NaN**( ) throw( )
> Returns a signaling NaN value if has_signaling_NaN is true.

static const bool **tinyness_before**
> Indicates whether a floating-point type tests for denormalized values before rounding.

static const bool **traps**
> Indicates whether arithmetic errors *trap*, that is, result in signals or exceptions. It is false if errors are quietly ignored.

The numeric_limits template is specialized for all the fundamental numeric types and for no other types in the C++ standard. In each case, is_specialized is true, and other members are set as appropriate. The C++ standard (by way of the C standard) defines the minimum requirements for an implementation. The requirements for integral types are given in <climits>, and for floating-point types in <cfloat>.

The following are the standard specializations:

```
numeric_limits<bool>
numeric_limits<char>
numeric_limits<double>
numeric_limits<float>
numeric_limits<int>
numeric_limits<long>
numeric_limits<long double>
numeric_limits<short>
numeric_limits<signed char>
numeric_limits<unsigned char>
numeric_limits<unsigned int>
numeric_limits<unsigned long>
numeric_limits<unsigned short>
numeric_limits<wchar_t>
```

<list>

The <list> header is one of the standard container template headers. It declares the list class template and a few global function templates that operate on list objects.

A list is a sequence container that has constant performance when adding to or removing from any point in the container. It supports bidirectional iterators, but not random access. Although the standard does not mandate any particular implementation, the obvious choice is to use a doubly-linked list to implement the list class template.

See Chapter 10 for information about containers.

list class template

```
template <typename T, typename Alloc = allocator<T> >
class list
{
public:
  // Types
  typedef typename Alloc::reference reference;
  typedef typename Alloc::const_reference const_reference;
  typedef ... iterator;
  typedef ... const_iterator;
  typedef ... size_type;
  typedef ... difference_type;
  typedef T value_type;
  typedef Alloc allocator_type;
  typedef typename Alloc::pointer pointer;
  typedef typename Alloc::const_pointer const_pointer;
  typedef std::reverse_iterator<iterator> reverse_iterator;
  typedef std::reverse_iterator<const_iterator> const_reverse_iterator;

  // Construct/copy/destroy
  explicit list(const Alloc& = Alloc());
  explicit list(size_type n, const T& value = T(), const Alloc& = Alloc());
  template <class InputIterator>
  list(InputIterator first, InputIterator last, const Alloc& = Alloc());
  list(const list<T,Alloc>& x);
  ~list();
  list<T,Alloc>& operator=(const list<T,Alloc>& x);
  template <class InputIterator>
  void assign(InputIterator first, InputIterator last);
  void assign(size_type n, const T& t);
  allocator_type get_allocator() const;
  // Iterators
  iterator begin();
  const_iterator begin() const;
  iterator end();
  const_iterator end() const;
  reverse_iterator rbegin();
  const_reverse_iterator rbegin() const;
  reverse_iterator rend();
  const_reverse_iterator rend() const;
  // Capacity
  bool empty() const;
  size_type size() const;
  size_type max_size() const;
  void resize(size_type sz, T c = T());
  // Element access
  reference front();
  const_reference front() const;
  reference back();
  const_reference back() const;
  // Modifiers
  void push_front(const T& x);
```

```
    void pop_front( );
    void push_back(const T& x);
    void pop_back( );
    iterator insert(iterator position, const T& x);
    void insert(iterator position, size_type n, const T& x);
    template <class InputIterator>
    void insert(iterator position, InputIterator first, InputIterator last);
    iterator erase(iterator position);
    iterator erase(iterator position, iterator last);
    void swap(list<T,Alloc>&);
    void clear( );
    // List operations
    void splice(iterator position, list<T,Alloc>& x);
    void splice(iterator position, list<T,Alloc>& x, iterator i);
    void splice(iterator position, list<T,Alloc>& x, iterator first,
                iterator last);
    void remove(const T& value);
    template <class Predicate>
    void remove_if(Predicate pred);
    void unique( );
    template <class BinaryPredicate>
    void unique(BinaryPredicate binary_pred);
    void merge(list<T,Alloc>& x);
    template <class Compare>
    void merge(list<T,Alloc>& x, Compare comp);
    void sort( );
    template <class Compare> void sort(Compare comp);
    void reverse( );
};
```

The list class template is one of the standard container types, like deque and vector. A list stores a sequence of items such that inserting or erasing an item at any position requires constant time. The list template supports all the usual operations for a sequence container plus some functions that are unique to list.

When an item is erased from the list (by calling pop_back, erase, remove, etc.), all iterators that point to that item become invalid. All pointers and references to the item become invalid. No other iterators, pointers, or references are invalidated when inserting or erasing any items.

The size function can have constant or linear complexity. The standard encourages library vendors to implement the list class template so that size has constant complexity, but it permits worse performance (namely, linear in the size of the list). If size does not have constant complexity, you should expect all versions of splice to have constant complexity in all cases. (The last constraint is not mandated by the standard, but by common sense.)

The following are the member functions of list:

explicit **list**(const Alloc& = Alloc( ))
    Initializes an empty list that uses the given allocator.

explicit **list**(size_type n, const T& value = T( ), const Alloc& = Alloc( ))
    Initializes a list that contains n copies of value.

```
template < typename InputIterator>
list(InputIterator first, InputIterator last, const Alloc& = Alloc( ))
```
Initializes the list with a copy of the items in the range [first, last), unless InputIterator is an integral type, in which case the list is constructed as though the arguments were cast:

```
list(static_cast<size_type>(first), static_cast<value_type>(last),
    alloc);
```

```
list(const list<T,Alloc>& x)
```
Constructs a copy of the contents and allocator of the list x.

```
list<T,Alloc>& operator=(const list<T,Alloc>& x)
```
Replaces the list's contents with copies of the contents of x.

```
template <typename InputIterator>
void assign(InputIterator first, InputIterator last)
```
Replaces the list's contents with the items in the range [first, last), unless InputIterator is an integral type, in which case the arguments are interpreted as though they were cast:

```
assign(static_cast<size_type>(first), static_cast<value_type>(last));
```

```
void assign(size_type n, const T& value)
```
Replaces the list's contents with n copies of value.

```
reference back( )
const_reference back( ) const
```
Returns the last item in the list. The behavior is undefined if the list is empty.

```
iterator begin( )
const_iterator begin( ) const
```
Returns an iterator that points to the first item in the list.

```
void clear( )
```
Erases all the items in the list, invalidating all iterators that point to the list.

```
bool empty( ) const
```
Returns true if the list is empty. Note that empty( ) has constant complexity even if size( ) does not.

```
iterator end( )
const_iterator end( ) const
```
Returns an iterator that points one past the last item in the list.

```
iterator erase(iterator position)
iterator erase(iterator first, iterator last)
```
Erases the item at position or all the items in the range [first, last).

```
reference front( )
const_reference front( ) const
```
Returns the first item in the list. The behavior is undefined if the list is empty.

```
allocator_type get_allocator( ) const
```
Returns the list's allocator.

```
iterator insert(iterator position, const T& x)
void insert(iterator position, size_type n, const T& x)
template <typename InputIterator>
void insert(iterator position, InputIterator first, InputIterator last)
```
Inserts one or more items before position. The performance is linear in the number of items inserted, and the T copy constructor is invoked once for each

item inserted in the list. The first form inserts the item x; the second form inserts n copies of x; the third form copies the items in the range [first, last), unless InputIterator is an integral type, in which case the arguments are interpreted as though they were cast:

```
insert(position, static_cast<size_type>(first),
        static_cast<value_type>(last));
```

If an exception is thrown, such as bad_alloc when there is insufficient memory for a new element, the list is unchanged.

size_type **max_size**( ) const
> Returns the size of the largest possible list.

void **merge**(list<T,Alloc>& x)
template <class Compare>
void **merge**(list<T,Alloc>& x, Compare comp)
> Merges another sorted list, x, into the current list, which must also be sorted. Items are erased from x, so after merge returns, x is empty. Items are compared using the < operator or comp. The same function used to sort the items must be used to compare items. The merge is stable, so the relative order of items is unchanged; if the same item is already in the list and in x, the item from x is added after the item already in the list.
>
> The performance of the merge is linear: exactly size( ) + x.size( ) - 1 comparisons are performed.

void **pop_back**( )
> Erases the last item from the list. The behavior is undefined if the list is empty.

void **pop_front**( )
> Erases the first item from the list. The behavior is undefined if the list is empty.

void **push_back**(const T& x)
> Inserts x at the end of the list.

void **push_front**(const T& x)
> Inserts x at the beginning of the list.

reverse_iterator **rbegin**( )
const_reverse_iterator **rbegin**( ) const
> Returns a reverse iterator that points to the last item in the list.

void **remove**(const T& value)
> Erases all occurrences of value from the list. The performance is linear; exactly size( ) comparisons are performed.

template <typename Predicate>
void **remove_if**(Predicate pred)
> Erases all items for which pred(item) returns true. The performance is linear: pred is called exactly size( ) times.

reverse_iterator **rend**( )
const_reverse_iterator **rend**( ) const
> Returns a reverse iterator that points to one position before the first item in the list.

void **resize**(size_type sz, T c = T( ))
> Changes the size of the list to n. If n > size( ), one or more copies of c are added to the end of the list to reach the desired size. If the new size is smaller than the current size, elements are erased from the end to reach the new size.

void **reverse**( )
> Reverses the order of the entire list. The performance is linear.

 size_type **size**( ) const
> Returns the number of elements in the list. The complexity of size( ) can be constant or linear, depending on the implementation.

void **sort**( )
template <typename Compare>
void **sort**(Compare comp)
> Sorts the items in the list, comparing items with the < operator or by calling comp. The sort is stable, so the relative positions of the items do not change. The performance is $N \log N$, in which N is size( ).

> You must call the sort member function to sort a list. The generic sort algorithm requires a random access iterator, but list provides only a bidirectional iterator.

void **splice**(iterator position, list<T,Alloc>& x)
void **splice**(iterator position, list<T,Alloc>& x, iterator i)
void **splice**(iterator position, list<T,Alloc>& x, iterator first, iterator last)
> Moves one or more items from x, inserting the items just before position. The first form moves every item from x to the list. The second form moves the item at position i. The third form moves all items in the range [first, last); position must not be in that range. The third form requires no more than linear time when &x != this; all other cases work in constant time. If size( ) has linear complexity, you should expect splice( ) to have constant complexity in all cases.

void **swap**(list<T,Alloc>& x)
> Swaps all the items in this list with all the items in x. The performance should be constant.

void **unique**( )
template <typename BinaryPredicate>
void **unique**(BinaryPredicate pred)
> Erases adjacent duplicate items from the list. Items are compared with the == operator or by calling pred. When adjacent equal items are found in the list, the first one is retained, and the second and subsequent items are erased. The performance is linear: size( ) - 1 comparisons are performed (unless the list is empty).

See Also

deque in <deque>, vector in <vector>

---

operator== function template
Compares lists for equality

template <typename T, typename A>
bool **operator==**(const list<T,A>& x, const list<T,A>& y);

The == operator returns true if x and y have the same size and their elements are equal, that is, x.size( ) == y.size( ) && equals(x.begin( ), x.end( ), y.begin( )).

See Also

equals in <algorithm>

Library Reference

operator!= function template

Compares lists for inequality

```
template <typename T, typename A>
bool operator!=(const list<T,A>& x, const list<T,A>& y);
```

The != operator is equivalent to ! (x == y).

operator< function template

Compares lists for less-than

```
template <typename T, typename A>
bool operator<(const list<T,A>& x, const list<T,A>& y);
```

The < operator determines whether x is less than y using the same algorithm as lexicographical_compare(x.begin( ), x.end( ), y.begin( ), y.end( )).

See Also

lexicographical_compare in <algorithm>

operator<= function template

Compares lists for less-than-or-equal

```
template <typename T, typename A>
bool operator<=(const list<T,A>& x, const list<T,A>& y);
```

The <= operator is equivalent to ! (y < x).

operator> function template

Compares lists for greater-than

```
template <typename T, typename A>
bool operator>(const list<T,A>& x, const list<T,A>& y);
```

The > operator is equivalent to (y < x).

operator>= function template

Compares lists for greater-than-or-equal

```
template <typename T, typename A>
bool operator>=(const list<T,A>& x, const list<T,A>& y);
```

The >= operator is equivalent to ! (x < y).

swap function template

Swaps the contents of two lists

```
template<typename T, typename A>
void swap(list<T, A>& x, list<T, A>& y)
```

The swap function template specialization is equivalent to calling x.swap(y).

See Also

swap in <algorithm>

<locale>

The <locale> header declares class and function templates for internationalization and localization. It supports conversion between narrow and wide character sets, character classification and collation, formatting and parsing numbers, currency, dates and times, and retrieving messages. For example, every I/O stream has a locale, which it uses to parse formatted input or to format output.

A *locale* is an embodiment of a set of cultural conventions, including information about the native character set, how dates are formatted, which symbol to use for currency, and so on. Each set of related attributes is called a *facet*, which are grouped into categories.

The categories are fixed and defined by the standard (see Table 13-20, under locale::category, for a complete list), and each category has several predefined facets. For example, one of the facets in the time category is time_get<charT, InputIter>, which specifies rules for parsing a time string. You can define additional facets; see the description of the locale::facet class in this section for details.

Many of the facets come in two flavors: plain and named. The plain versions implement default behavior, and the named versions implement the behavior for a named locale. See the locale class later in this section for a discussion of locale names.

When a program starts, the global locale is initialized to the "C" locale, and the standard I/O streams use this locale for character conversions and formatting. A program can change the locale at any time; see the locale class in this section for details.

The C++ <locale> header provides more functionality than the C <clocale>, <cctype>, and <cwchar> headers, especially the ability to extend a locale with your own facets. On the other hand, facets and the locale class template are more complicated than the C functions. For simple character classification in a single locale, you are probably better off using the C functions. If a program must work with multiple locales simultaneously, use the C++ locale template.

codecvt class template

Facet for mapping one character set to another

```
template <typename internT,typename externT,typename stateT>
class codecvt : public locale::facet, public codecvt_base
{
public:
  typedef internT intern_type;
  typedef externT extern_type;
  typedef stateT state_type;
  explicit codecvt(size_t refs = 0);
  result out(stateT& state, const internT* from, const internT* from_end,
             const internT*& from_next, externT* to, externT* to_limit,
             externT*& to_next) const;
  result unshift(stateT& state, externT* to, externT* to_limit,
                 externT*& to_next) const;
  result in(stateT& state, const externT* from, const externT* from_end,
            const externT*& from_next, internT* to, internT* to_limit,
            internT*& to_next) const;
  int encoding() const throw();
  bool always_noconv() const throw();
  int length(stateT&, const externT* from, const externT* end, size_t max)
    const;
  int max_length() const throw();
  static locale::id id;
protected:
  virtual ~codecvt();
```

```
virtual result do_out(stateT& state, const internT* from,
                const internT* from_end, const internT*& from_next,
                externT* to, externT* to_limit, externT*& to_next)
    const;
virtual result do_in(stateT& state, const externT* from,
                const externT* from_end, const externT*& from_next,
                internT* to, internT* to_limit, internT*& to_next)
    const;
virtual result do_unshift(stateT& state, externT* to, externT* to_limit,
                externT*& to_next) const;
virtual int do_encoding( ) const throw( );
virtual bool do_always_noconv( ) const throw( );
virtual int do_length(stateT&, const externT* from, const externT* end,
                size_t max) const;
virtual int do_max_length( ) const throw( );
};
```

The codecvt template converts characters from one character encoding to another. It is most often used to convert multibyte characters to and from wide characters.

The following template specializations are required by the standard:

codecvt<wchar_t, char, mbstate_t>
: Converts multibyte narrow characters to wide characters (in) and wide to multibyte (out)

codecvt<char, char, mbstate_t>
: A no-op, "converting" characters to themselves

As with other facets, the public members of codecvt call virtual, protected members with the same name prefaced by do_. Thus, to use the facet, call the public functions, such as in and out, which in turn call do_in and do_out. The descriptions below are for the virtual functions because they do the real work. Imagine that for each virtual function description, there is a corresponding description for a public, nonvirtual function, such as:

bool always_noconv( ) const throw( )
: Returns do_always_noconv( )

The following are the virtual, protected members of codecvt:

virtual bool do_always_noconv( ) const throw( )
: Returns true if the codecvt object does not actually perform any conversions, that is, in and out are no-ops. For example, for the specialization codecvt<char,char,mbstate_t>, do_always_noconv always returns true.

virtual int do_encoding( ) const throw( )
: Returns the number of externT characters needed to represent a single internT character. If this number is not a fixed constant, the return value is 0. The return value is -1 if externT character sequences are not state-dependent.

virtual result do_in(stateT& state, const externT* from, const externT* from_end, const externT*& from_next, internT* to, internT* to_limit, internT*& to_next) const
: Converts externT characters to internT characters. The characters in the range [from, from_end) are converted and stored in the array starting at to. The number of characters converted is the minimum of from_end – from and to_limit – to.

  The from_next parameter is set to point to the value in [from, from_end) where the conversion stopped, and to_next points to the value in [to, to_limit) where the conversion stopped. If no conversion was performed, from_next is the same as from, and to_next is equal to to.

The return value is a result, as described in Table 13-19 (under the codecvt_base class).

virtual int **do_length**(stateT&, const externT* from, const externT* from_end, size_t max) const

Returns the number of externT characters in the range [from, from_end) that are used to convert to internT characters. At most, max internT characters are converted.

virtual int **do_max_length**( ) const throw( )

Returns the maximum number of externT characters needed to represent a single internT character, that is, the maximum value that do_length can return when max is 1.

virtual result **do_out**(stateT& state, const internT* from, const internT* from_end, const internT*& from_next, externT* to, externT* to_limit, externT*& to_next) const

Converts internT characters to externT characters. The characters in the range [from, from_end) are converted and stored in the array starting at to. The number of characters converted is the minimum of from_end – from and to_limit – to.

The from_next parameter is set to point to the value in [from, from_end) where the conversion stopped, and to_next points to the value in [to, to_limit) where the conversion stopped. If no conversion was performed, from_next is the same as from, and to_next is equal to to.

The return value is a result, as described in Table 13-19 (under codecvt_base class).

virtual result **do_unshift**(stateT& state, externT* to, externT* to_limit, externT*& to_next) const

Ends a shift state by storing characters in the array starting at to such that the characters undo the state shift given by state. Up to to_limit – to characters are written, and to_next is set to point to one past the last character written into to.

The return value is a result, as described in Table 13-19 (under codecvt_base class).

See Also

codecvt_base class, codecvt_byname class template, locale::facet class

---

codecvt_base class

Base class for the codecvt template

```
class codecvt_base {
public:
  enum result { ok, partial, error, noconv };
};
```

The codecvt_base class is the base class for the codecvt and codecvt_byname class templates. It declares the result type, which is the type returned by the do_in and do_out conversion functions. Table 13-19 lists the literals of the result enumerated type.

Table 13-19. codecvt_base::result literals

Literal	Description
error	Error in conversion (e.g., invalid state or multibyte character sequence)
noconv	No conversion (or unshift terminated) needed
ok	Conversion finished successfully
partial	Not all source characters converted, or unshift sequence is incomplete

See Also

codecvt class template, codecvt_byname class template

---

codecvt_byname class template
Facet for mapping one character set to another

```
template<typename internT, typename externT, typename stateT>
class codecvt_byname :
  public codecvt<internT, externT, stateT>
{
public:
  explicit codecvt_byname(const char*, size_t refs = 0);
protected:
  // ... Same virtual functions as in codecvt
};
```

The codecvt_byname class template converts characters from one character encoding to another using the rules of a named locale. The codecvt_byname<char,char,mbstate_t> and codecvt_byname<wchar_t,char,mbstate_t> instantiations are standard.

See Also

codecvt class template, locale::facet class

---

collate class template
Facet for comparing strings in collation order

```
template <typename charT>
class collate : public locale::facet
{
public:
  typedef charT char_type;
  typedef basic_string<charT> string_type;
  explicit collate(size_t refs = 0);
  int compare(const charT* low1, const charT* high1, const charT* low2,
              const charT* high2) const;
  string_type transform(const charT* low, const charT* high) const;
  long hash(const charT* low, const charT* high) const;
  static locale::id id;
protected:
  virtual ~collate( );
  virtual int do_compare(const charT* low1, const charT* high1,
                         const charT* low2, const charT* high2) const;
  virtual string_type do_transform (const charT* low, const charT* high) const;
  virtual long do_hash (const charT* low, const charT* high) const;
};
```

The collate class template is a facet used to compare strings. In some locales, the collation order of characters is not the same as the numerical order of their encodings, and some characters might be logically equivalent even if they have different encodings.

You can use a locale object as a comparator for algorithms that need a comparison function; the locale's operator() function uses the collate facet to perform the comparison.

The standard mandates the collate<char> and collate<wchar_t> instantiations, which perform lexicographical (element-wise, numerical) comparison. See lexicographical_compare in <algorithm> earlier in this chapter.

As with other facets, the public members call virtual, protected members with the same name prefaced by do_. Thus, to use the facet, call the public functions, such as compare, which calls do_compare. The descriptions below are for the virtual functions because they do the real work. Imagine that for each virtual function description, there is a corresponding description for a public, nonvirtual function, such as:

```
int compare(const charT* low1, const charT* high1, const charT* low2, const charT*
    high2) const
```
> Returns do_compare(low1, high1, low2, high2)

The following are the virtual, protected members of collate:

```
virtual int do_compare(const charT* low1, const charT* high1, const charT* low2,
    const charT* high2) const
```
> Compares the character sequences [low1, high1) with the character sequence [low2, high2). The return value is one of the following:
>
> - -1 if sequence 1 is less than sequence 2
> - 0 if the sequences are equal
> - 1 if sequence 1 is greater than sequence 2

```
virtual long do_hash (const charT* low, const charT* high) const
```
> Returns a hash value for the character sequence [low, high). If do_compare returns 0 for two character sequences, do_hash returns the same value for the two sequences. The reverse is not necessarily the case.

```
virtual string_type do_transform(const charT* low, const charT* high) const
```
> Transforms the character sequence [low, high) into a string that can be compared (as a simple lexicographical comparison) with another transformed string to obtain the same result as calling do_compare on the original character sequences. The do_transform function is useful if a program needs to compare the same character sequence many times.

See Also

collate_byname class template, locale class, locale::facet class

collate_byname class template
Facet for comparing strings in collation order

```
template <typename charT>
class collate_byname : public collate<charT>
{
public:
  typedef basic_string<charT> string_type;
```

```
  explicit collate_byname(const char*, size_t refs = 0);
protected:
  // ... Same virtual functions as in collate
};
```

Compares strings using a named locale's collation order. The collate_byname<char>
and collate_byname<wchar_t> instantiations are standard.

See Also

collate class template, locale::facet class

___

ctype class template   Facet for classifying characters

```
class ctype : public locale::facet, public ctype_base
{
public:
  typedef charT char_type;
  explicit ctype(size_t refs = 0);
  bool is(mask m, charT c) const;
  const charT* is(const charT* low, const charT* high, mask* vec) const;
  const charT* scan_is(mask m, const charT* low, const charT* high) const;
  const charT* scan_not(mask m, const charT* low, const charT* high) const;
  charT toupper(charT c) const;
  const charT* toupper(charT* low, const charT* high) const;
  charT tolower(charT c) const;
  const charT* tolower(charT* low, const charT* high) const;
  charT widen(char c) const;
  const char* widen(const char* low, const char* high, charT* to) const;
  char narrow(charT c, char dfault) const;
  const charT* narrow(const charT* low, const charT*, char dfault, char* to)
    const;
  static locale::id id;
protected:
  virtual ~ctype();
  virtual bool do_is(mask m, charT c) const;
  virtual const charT* do_is(const charT* low, const charT* high, mask* vec)
    const;
  virtual const charT* do_scan_is(mask m, const charT* low,
                                  const charT* high) const;
  virtual const charT* do_scan_not(mask m, const charT* low,
                                   const charT* high) const;
  virtual charT do_toupper(charT) const;
  virtual const charT* do_toupper(charT* low, const charT* high) const;
  virtual charT do_tolower(charT) const;
  virtual const charT* do_tolower(charT* low, const charT* high) const;
  virtual charT do_widen(char) const;
  virtual const char* do_widen(const char* low, const char* high, charT* dest)
    const;
  virtual char do_narrow(charT, char dfault) const;
  virtual const charT* do_narrow(const charT* low, const charT* high,
                                 char dfault, char* dest) const;
};
```

The ctype class template is a facet for classifying characters.

The ctype<char> specialization is described in its own section later in this chapter. The standard also mandates the ctype<wchar_t> instantiation. Both instantiations depend on the implementation's native character set.

As with other facets, the public members call virtual, protected members with the same name prefaced by do_. Thus, to use the facet, call the public functions, such as narrow, which calls do_narrow. The descriptions below are for the virtual functions because they do the real work. Imagine that for each virtual function description, there is a corresponding description for a public, nonvirtual function, such as:

bool **is**(mask m, charT c) const
    Returns do_is(m, c)

The following are the virtual, protected members of ctype:

virtual bool **do_is**(mask m, charT c) const
virtual const charT* **do_is**(const charT* low, const charT* high, mask* dest) const
    Classifies a single character c or a sequence of characters [low, high). The first form tests the classification mask, *M*, of c and returns (*M* & m) != 0. The second form determines the mask for each character in the range and stores the mask values in the dest array (which must be large enough to hold high − low masks), returning high. See Table 13-19 (under the ctype_base class) for a description of the mask type.

virtual char **do_narrow**(charT c, char dfault) const
virtual const charT* **do_narrow**(const charT* low, const charT* high, char dfault, char* dest) const
    Converts a character c or a sequence of characters [low, high) to narrow characters of type char. The first form returns the narrow character, and the second form stores the characters in the array dest (which must be large enough to hold high − low characters), returning high. If a charT source character cannot be converted to a narrow character, the first function returns dfault, and the second function stores dfault in dest as the narrow version of that character.

virtual const charT* **do_scan_is**(mask m, const charT* low, const charT* high) const
    Searches the sequence of characters [low, high) for the first character that matches m, that is, for which do_is(m, c) is true. The return value is a pointer to the first matching character, or high if no characters match m.

virtual const charT* **do_scan_not**(mask m, const charT* low, const charT* high) const
    Searches the sequence of characters [low, high) for the first character that does not match m, that is, for which do_is(m, c) is false. The return value is a pointer to the first matching character, or high if every character matches m.

virtual charT **do_tolower**(charT c) const
virtual const charT* **do_tolower**(charT* low, const charT* high) const
    Converts a character c or a sequence of characters [low, high) to lowercase. The first form returns the lowercase version of c, or it returns c if c does not have a lowercase counterpart.

    The second form modifies the character sequence: each character in [low, high) is replaced by its lowercase counterpart; if a character cannot be converted to lowercase, it is not touched. The function returns high.

virtual charT **do_toupper**(charT c) const
virtual const charT* **do_toupper**(charT* low, const charT* high) const

> Converts a character c or a sequence of characters [low, high) to uppercase. The first form returns the uppercase version of c, or it returns c if c does not have a uppercase counterpart.
>
> The second form modifies the character sequence: each character in [low, high) is replaced by its uppercase counterpart; if a character cannot be converted to uppercase, it is not touched. The function returns high.

virtual charT **do_widen**(char c) const
virtual const char* **do_widen**(const char* low, const char* high, charT* dest) const

> Converts a narrow character c or a sequence of narrow characters [low, high) to characters of type charT. The first form returns the new character, and the second form stores the characters in the array dest (which must be large enough to hold high − low characters), returning high.

See Also

ctype_base class, ctype_byname class template, locale::facet class

---

ctype<char> class

Facet for classifying narrow characters

```
template <>
class ctype<char> : public locale::facet, public ctype_base
{
    ...
public:
    explicit ctype(const mask* tab = 0, bool del = false, size_t refs = 0);
    static const size_t table_size = ...;
    inline bool is(mask m, char c) const;
    inline const char* is(const char* low, const char* high, mask* vec) const;
    inline const char* scan_is(mask m, const char* low, const char* high) const;
    inline const char* scan_not(mask m, const char* low, const char* high) const;
protected:
    virtual ~ctype();
    inline const mask* table() const throw();
    inline static const mask* classic_table() throw();
};
```

The ctype<> class template is specialized for type char (but not signed char or unsigned char) so the member functions can be implemented as inline functions. The standard requires the implementation to have the protected member functions table and classic_table. Each of these functions returns an array of mask values indexed by characters cast to unsigned char. The number of elements in a table must be at least table_size, which is an implementation-defined constant value.

The following are the key member functions:

explicit **ctype**(const mask* tab = 0, bool del = false, size_t refs = 0)

> Initializes the table() pointer with tab. If tab is a null pointer, table() is set to classic_table(). If tab is not null, and del is true, the ctype object owns the table, and when the ctype destructor is called, it will delete the table. The refs parameter is passed to the base class, as with any facet.

```
virtual ~ctype( )
```
If the constructor's del flag was true, and tab was not a null pointer, performs delete[ ] tab.

```
inline bool is(mask m, charT c) const
inline const charT* is(const charT* low, const charT* high, mask* dest) const
```
Tests character classifications. The first form returns:

```
(table( )[static_cast<unsigned char>(c)] & m) != 0
```

The second form stores the following in dest for each element c of the range [low, high):

```
table( )[static_cast<unsigned char>(c)]
```

Note that is does not call do_is, so is can be implemented as an inline function.

```
inline static const mask* classic_table( ) throw( )
```
Returns a table that corresponds to the "C" locale.

```
inline const char* scan_is(mask m, const char* low, const char* high) const
```
Searches the sequence of characters [low, high) for the first character that matches m, that is, for which is(m, c) is true. The return value is a pointer to the first matching character, or high if no characters match m.

```
inline const char* scan_not(mask m, const char* low, const char* high) const
```
Searches the sequence of characters [low, high) for the first character that does not match m, that is, for which is(m, c) is false. The return value is a pointer to the first matching character, or high if every character matches m.

```
inline const mask* table( ) throw( )
```
Returns the value that was passed to the constructor as the tab parameter, or, if tab was null, classic_table( ) is returned.

See Also

ctype class template, locale::facet class, <cctype>, <cwctype>

---

ctype_base class

Base class for ctype facet

```
class ctype_base
{
public:
  enum mask {
    space, print, cntrl, upper, lower, alpha, digit, punct, xdigit,
    alnum=alpha|digit, graph=alnum|punct
  };
};
```

The ctype_base class is the base class for the ctype and ctype_byname class templates. It declares the mask enumerated type, which is used for classifying characters. Table 13-20 describes the mask literals and their definitions for the classic "C" locale.

Table 13-20. mask literals for classifying characters

Literal	Description	"C" locale
alpha	Alphabetic (a letter)	lower or upper
alnum	Alphanumeric (letter or digit)	alpha or digit
cntrl	Control (nonprintable)	Not print

Table 13-20. mask literals for classifying characters (continued)

Literal	Description	"C" locale
digit	'0'-'9'	All locales
graph	Character that occupies graphical space	print but not space
lower	Lowercase letter	'a'-'z'
print	Printable character (alphanumeric, punctuation, space, etc.)	Depends on character set; in ASCII: '\x20'-'\x7e')
space	Whitespace	' ','\f','\n','\r','\t','\v'
upper	Uppercase letter	'A'-'Z'
xdigit	Hexadecimal digit ('0'-'9','a'-'f','A'-'F')	All locales

See Also

ctype class template, ctype_byname class template

---

ctype_byname class template

Facet for classifying characters

```
template <typename charT>
class ctype_byname : public ctype<charT>
{
public:
  typedef ctype<charT>::mask mask;
  explicit ctype_byname(const char*, size_t refs = 0);
protected:
  // ... Same virtual functions as in ctype
};
```

The ctype_byname class template is a facet for classifying characters; it uses a named locale. The ctype_byname<char> and ctype_byname<wchar_t> instantiations are standard.

See Also

ctype class template, ctype_byname<char> class

---

ctype_byname<char> class

Facet for classifying narrow characters

```
template <>
class ctype_byname<char> : public ctype<char>
{
public:
  explicit ctype_byname(const char*, size_t refs = 0);
protected:
  // ... Same virtual functions as in ctype<char>
};
```

The ctype_byname<char> class specializes the ctype_byname template for type char. (No specialization exists for signed char and unsigned char.) It derives from ctype<char>, so it inherits its table-driven implementation.

See Also

ctype<char> class, ctype_byname class template

has_facet function template

```
template <typename Facet>
bool has_facet(const locale& loc) throw( );
```

The has_facet function determines whether the locale loc supports the facet Facet. It returns true if the facet is supported or false if it is not. Call has_facet to determine whether a locale supports a user-defined facet. (Every locale must support the standard facets that are described in this section.) Example 13-24 shows how has_facet is used.

Example 13-24. Testing whether a locale supports a facet

```
// The units facet is defined under the locale::facet class (later in this
// section).

using std::locale;
if (std::has_facet<units>(locale( )) {
  // Get a reference to the units facet of the locale.
  const units& u = std::use_facet<units>(locale( ));
  // Construct a value of 42 cm.
  units::value_t len = u.make(42, units::cm);
  // Print the length (42 cm) in the locale's preferred units.
  u.length_put(std::cout, len);
}
```

See Also

locale class, use_facet function template

isalnum function template

```
template <typename charT>
bool isalnum(charT c, const locale& loc);
```

The isalnum function determines whether the character c is an alphanumeric character in the locale loc. It returns the following:

```
use_facet<ctype<charT> >(loc).is(ctype_base::alnum, c)
```

See Also

ctype_base class, ctype class template, isalpha function template, isdigit function template

isalpha function template

```
template <typename charT>
bool isalpha(charT c, const locale& loc);
```

The isalpha function determines whether the character c is a letter in the locale loc. It returns the following:

```
use_facet<ctype<charT> >(loc).is(ctype_base::alpha, c)
```

See Also

ctype_base class, ctype class template, isalnum function template, islower function template, isupper function template

iscntrl function template
Determines whether a character is a control character in a locale

```
template <typename charT>
bool iscntrl(charT c, const locale& loc);
```

The iscntrl function determines whether the character c is a control character in the locale loc. It returns the following:

```
use_facet<ctype<charT> >(loc).is(ctype_base::cntrl, c)
```

See Also
ctype_base class, ctype class template, isprint function template

isdigit function template
Determines whether a character is a digit in a locale

```
template <typename charT>
bool isdigit(charT c, const locale& loc);
```

The isdigit function determines whether the character c is a digit in the locale loc. It returns the following:

```
use_facet<ctype<charT> >(loc).is(ctype_base::digit, c)
```

See Also
ctype_base class, ctype class template, isalnum function template, isxdigit function template

isgraph function template
Determines whether a character is graphical in a locale

```
template <typename charT>
bool isgraph(charT c, const locale& loc);
```

The isgraph function determines whether the character c is graphical (alphanumeric or punctuation) in the locale loc. It returns the following:

```
use_facet<ctype<charT> >(loc).is(ctype_base::graph, c)
```

See Also
ctype_base class, ctype class template, isalnum function template, isprint function template, ispunct function template

islower function template
Determines whether a character is lowercase in a locale

```
template <typename charT>
bool islower(charT c, const locale& loc);
```

The islower function determines whether the character c is a lowercase letter in the locale loc. It returns the following:

```
use_facet<ctype<charT> >(loc).is(ctype_base::lower, c)
```

See Also
ctype_base class, ctype class template, isalpha function template, isupper function template

isprint function template

Determines whether a character is printable in a locale

```
template <typename charT>
bool isprint(charT c, const locale& loc);
```

The isprint function determines whether the character c is printable in the locale loc. It returns the following:

```
use_facet<ctype<charT> >(loc).is(ctype_base::print, c)
```

See Also

ctype_base class, ctype class template, iscntrl function template, isgraph function template, isspace function template

ispunct function template

Determines whether a character is punctuation in a locale

```
template <typename charT>
bool ispunct(charT c, const locale& loc);
```

The ispunct function determines whether the character c is punctuation in the locale loc. It returns the following:

```
use_facet<ctype<charT> >(loc).is(ctype_base::punct, c)
```

See Also

ctype_base class, ctype class template, isgraph function template

isspace function template

Determines whether a character is whitespace in a locale

```
template <typename charT>
bool isspace(charT c, const locale& loc);
```

The isspace function determines whether the character c is whitespace in the locale loc. It returns the following:

```
use_facet<ctype<charT> >(loc).is(ctype_base::space, c)
```

See Also

ctype_base class, ctype class template, isgraph function template, isprint function template

isupper function template

Determines whether a character is uppercase in a locale

```
template <typename charT>
bool isupper(charT c, const locale& loc);
```

The isupper function determines whether the character c is an uppercase letter in the locale loc. It returns the following:

```
use_facet<ctype<charT> >(loc).is(ctype_base::upper, c)
```

See Also

ctype_base class, ctype class template, isalpha function template, islower function template

isxdigit function template
Determines whether a character is a hexadecimal digit in a locale

```
template <typename charT>
bool isxdigit(charT c, const locale& loc);
```

The isxdigit function determines whether the character c is a hexadecimal digit in the locale loc. It returns the following:

```
    use_facet<ctype<charT> >(loc).is(ctype_base::xdigit, c)
```

See Also

ctype_base class, ctype class template, isdigit function template

locale class
Represents a locale as a set of facets

```
class locale
{
public:
  class facet;
  class id;
  typedef int category;
  static const category
    none, collate, ctype, monetary, numeric, time, messages,
    all = collate|ctype|monetary|numeric|time|messages;
  // Construct/copy/destroy
  locale() throw();
  locale(const locale& other) throw();
  explicit locale(const char* std_name);
  locale(const locale& other, const char* std_name,category);
  template <typename Facet>
  locale(const locale& other, Facet* f);
  locale(const locale& other, const locale& one, category);
  ~locale() throw();

  const locale& operator=(const locale& other) throw();
  template <typename Facet>
  locale combine(const locale& other) const;

  basic_string<char> name() const;
  bool operator==(const locale& other) const;
  bool operator!=(const locale& other) const;
  template <typename charT, typename Traits, typename Alloc>
  bool operator()(const basic_string<charT,Traits,Alloc>& s1,
                  const basic_string<charT,Traits,Alloc>& s2) const;

  static locale global(const locale&);
  static const locale& classic();
};
```

The locale class template represents the information for a locale. This information is stored as a set of facets. Several facets are defined by the C++ standard, and user-defined facets can be added to any locale. The has_facet function template tests whether a locale supports a particular facet. The use_facet function template retrieves a facet of a locale.

References to a facet are safe until all locale objects that use that facet have been destroyed. New locales can be created from existing locales, with modifications to a particular facet.

Some locales have names. A locale can be constructed for a standard name, or a named locale can be copied or combined with other named locales to produce a new named locale.

When interacting with the user, either through the standard I/O streams or through a graphical user interface, you should use the native locale, that is, locale(""). When performing I/O—especially to external files where the data must be portable to other programs, systems, or environments—always use the "C" locale (locale::classic( )).

Example 13-25 shows locales that control input and output formats.

Example 13-25. Using locales for input and output

```
// Open a file and read floating-point numbers from it, computing the mean.
// Return the mean or 0 if the file contains no data. The data is in the classic
// format, that is, the same format used by C++.
double mean(const char* filename)
{
  std::ifstream in(filename);
  // Force the datafile to be interpreted in the classic locale, so the same
  // datafile can be used everywhere.
  in.imbue(std::locale::classic( ));
  double sum = 0;
  unsigned long count = 0;
  std::istream_iterator<double> iter(in), end;
  for ( ; iter != end; ++iter) {
    ++count;
    sum += *iter;
  }
  return count == 0 ? 0.0 : sum / count;
}

int main( )
{
  // Print results in the user's native locale.
  std::cout.imbue(std::locale(""));
  std::cout << mean("data.txt") << '\n';
}
```

The following are the member functions of locale:

locale( ) throw( )
> Initializes the locale with a copy of the current global locale. The initial global locale is locale::classic( ).

locale(const locale& other) throw( )
> Copies the other locale.

explicit **locale**(const char* std_name)

> Initializes the locale using a standard name. The names "C" and "" (empty string) are always defined, in which "C" is the locale returned by the classic( ) function, and "" identifies the implementation-defined native locale.

> An implementation can define additional names. Many C++ implementations use ISO language codes and country codes to identify a locale. For example, the ISO 639 language code for English is "en", and the ISO 3166 country code for the United States is "US", so "en_US" could identify the locale for U.S. English.

locale(const locale& other, const char* std_name, category mask)

> Copies the locale from other, except for those categories identified by mask, which are copied from the standard locale identified by std_name. The new locale has a name only if other has a name.

template <typename Facet>
locale(const locale& other, Facet* f)

> Copies the locale from other except for the facet Facet, which is obtained from f if f is not null.

locale(const locale& other, const locale& one, category mask)

> Copies the locale from other except for those categories identified by mask, which are copied from one. The new locale has a name only if other and one have names.

template <typename Facet>
locale **combine**(const locale& other) const

> Returns a new locale that is a copy of *this, except for Facet, which is copied from other. If other does not support the facet—that is, has_facet<Facet>(other) is false—runtime_error is thrown. The new locale has no name.

basic_string<char> **name**( ) const

> Returns the locale's name or "*" if the locale has no name. The exact contents of the name string are implementation-defined, but you can use the string to construct a new locale that is equal to *this—that is, *this == locale(name( ).c_str( )).

const locale& **operator=**(const locale& other) throw( )

> Copies other and returns *this.

bool **operator==**(const locale& other) const

> Returns true if the two locales are the same object, one locale object is a copy of the other, or the two locales are named and have the same name. Otherwise, the function returns false.

bool **operator!=**(const locale& other) const

> Returns !(*this == other).

template <typename charT, typename Tr, typename A>
bool **operator()**(const basic_string<charT, Tr, A>& s1,
  const basic_string<charT,Tr,A>& s2) const

> Compares two strings using the collate<charT> facet and returns true if s1 < s2. You can use the locale object as a comparator predicate to compare strings. See <string> for more information.

static locale **global**(const locale& loc)

> Sets the global locale to loc and returns the previous global locale. If the new locale has a name, the C locale is set by calling setlocale(LC_ALL, loc.name( ).c_str( )); if the locale does not have a name, the effect on the C locale is implementation-defined.

static const locale& **classic**( )

> Returns a locale that implements the "C" locale.

See Also

has_facet function template, use_facet function template, setlocale in <clocale>, <string>

locale::category type

Bitmask of facet categories

typedef int **category**;
static const category
  none, collate, ctype, monetary, numeric, time, messages,
  all = collate|ctype|monetary|numeric|time|messages;

The category type is an int and represents a bitmask of category identifiers, as listed in Table 13-21. Each category represents a set of one or more related facets. When combining locales, you can copy all the facets in one or more categories. Category identifiers can be combined using bitwise operators.

Table 13-21. Standard categories and their facets

Literal	Facets
collate	collate<char> collate<wchar_t>
ctype	ctype<char> ctype<wchar_t> codecvt<char,char,mbstate_t> codecvt<wchar_t,char,mbstate_t>
messages	messages<char> messages<wchar_t>
monetary	money_get<char> money_get<wchar_t> money_put<char> money_put<wchar_t> moneypunct<char> moneypunct<wchar_t> moneypunct<char,true> moneypunct<wchar_t,true>
numeric	num_get<char> num_get<wchar_t> num_put<char> num_put<wchar_t> numpunct<char> numpunct<wchar_t>
time	time_get<char> time_get<wchar_t> time_put<char> time_put<wchar_t>

See Also

locale class

locale::facet class

Base class for locale facets

```
class locale::facet
{
protected:
  explicit facet(size_t refs = 0);
```

```
  virtual ~facet( );
private:
  facet(const facet&);        // Not defined
  void operator=(const facet&); // Not defined
};
```

The facet class is the base class for all facets. A derived class must also declare a public, static data member of type locale::id whose name is id. Even a derived class must declare its own id member because it must have an identifier that is distinct from that of the base-class facet. Any other members for a custom facet are entirely up to the programmer; the derived class does not need to provide a copy or default constructor or an assignment operator.

The locale class assigns a value to id when the facet object is added to a locale. You never need to examine or alter the id member; it is managed entirely by locale.

The explicit constructor for facet takes a single argument, ref. If ref == 0, the facet object is not deleted until the last locale that uses the facet is destroyed. If ref == 1, the facet object is never destroyed. The standard facet classes (ctype, etc.) also take a ref parameter and pass it directly to the inherited facet constructor. Custom facets can do whatever the programmer wants, such as relying on the default value of 0 to manage the facet's lifetime automatically.

For example, suppose you want to define a facet that captures the locale-specific preferences for units of measure, such as length and weight. A program can store and manipulate values in a common base unit and convert to the preferred unit for output. Example 13-26 shows a units facet that allows you to do these things.

Example 13-26. A simple facet for working with units of measure

```
class units : public std::locale::facet
{
public:
  enum length_units {
     length_base=1,
     mm=10, cm=10*mm, m=10*cm, km=1000*m,
     in=254, ft=12*in, yd=3*ft, mi=5280*ft };

  typedef double value_t;

  // All facets must have a static ID member.
  static std::locale::id id;

  // Constructor initializes length_units_ according to local preferences.
  units( );

  // Read a length and its units, and return the length in base units.
  value_t length_get(std::istream& stream) const;

  // Convert value to the preferred units, and print the converted value followed
  // by the unit name.
  void length_put(std::ostream& stream, value_t value) const;

  // Make a base unit value from a value in src_units.
  value_t make(value_t src_value, length_units src_units)
    const;
```

Example 13-26. A simple facet for working with units of measure (continued)

```
  // Convert base units to dst_unit.
  value_t convert(value_t src_value, length_units dst_units)
    const;
  // Return the name of a unit.
  const char* unit_name(length_units units) const;
  // Return the preferred unit for length.
  length_units get_length_unit( ) const;
private:
  length_units length_units_;
};

int main( )
{
  // Add the units facet to the global locale:
  // 1. Construct a new locale that is a copy of the global locale, with the new
  //    units facet added to it.
  // 2. Set the new locale as the global locale.
  std::locale loc(std::locale(std::locale( ), new units));
  std::locale::global(loc);

  // Now anyone can get the units facet from the global locale.
  const units& u = std::use_facet<units>(std::locale( ));
  units::value_t size = u.make(42, units::cm);
  u.length_put(std::cout, size);
}
```

See Also

locale class, locale::id class

---

locale::id class   Facet identification

```
class locale::id
{
public:
  id( );
private:
  void operator=(const id&); // Not defined
  id(const id&);              // Not defined
};
```

The id class identifies a facet. It is used only to declare a public, static member of type
locale::id in every facet class. See locale::facet for more information.

See Also

locale::facet class

---

messages class template   Facet for retrieving strings from a message catalog

```
template <typename charT>
class messages : public locale::facet, public messages_base
{
public:
  typedef charT char_type;
```

```
    typedef basic_string<charT> string_type;
    explicit messages(size_t refs = 0);
    catalog open(const basic_string<char>& fn, const locale&) const;
    string_type get(catalog c, int set, int msgid, const string_type& dfault)
      const;
    void close(catalog c) const;
    static locale::id id;
protected:
    virtual ~messages();
    virtual catalog do_open(const basic_string<char>&, const locale&) const;
    virtual string_type do_get(catalog, int set, int msgid,
                               const string_type& dfault) const;
    virtual void do_close(catalog) const;
};
```

The messages class template is a facet for a message catalog. A message catalog is a database of textual messages that can be translated into different languages. The messages<char> and messages<wchar_t> instantiations are standard.

How a message catalog is found is implementation-defined. For example, a catalog name could be the name of an external file, or it could be the name of a special resource section in the program's executable file. The mapping of message identifiers to a particular message is also implementation-defined.

As with other facets, the public members call virtual, protected members with the same name prefaced by do_. Thus, to use the facet, call the public functions, such as get, which calls do_get. The descriptions below are for the virtual functions because they do the real work. Imagine that for each virtual-function description, there is a corresponding description for a public, nonvirtual function, such as:

void close(catalog cat) const
    Calls do_close(cat).

The following are the virtual, protected members of messages:

virtual void do_close(catalog cat) const
    Closes the message catalog cat.

virtual string_type do_get(catalog cat, int set, int msgid, const string_type& dfault) const
    Gets a message that is identified by set, msgid, and dfault from catalog cat. If the message cannot be found, dfault is returned.

virtual catalog do_open(const basic_string<char>& name, const locale& loc) const
    Opens a message catalog name. If the catalog cannot be opened, a negative value is returned. Otherwise, the catalog value can be passed to get to retrieve messages. Call close to close the catalog.

See Also

messages_base class, messages_byname class template

---

messages_base class   Base class for message facets

```
class messages_base {
public:
    typedef int catalog;
};
```

The message_base class is the base class for messages and message_byname. It declares the catalog type, which stores a handle for an open message catalog.

See Also

messages class template, message_byname class template

messages_byname class template

```
template <typename charT>
class messages_byname : public messages<charT>
{
public:
  typedef messages_base::catalog catalog;
  typedef basic_string<charT> string_type;
  explicit messages_byname(const char*, size_t refs = 0);
protected:
  // ... Same virtual functions as in messages
};
```

The messages_byname class template is a facet for a message catalog; it uses a named locale. The messages_byname<char> and messages_byname<wchar_t> instantiations are standard.

See Also

messages class template, messages_base class

money_base class

```
class money_base {
public:
  enum part { none, space, symbol, sign, value };
  struct pattern { char field[4]; };
};
```

The money_base class is a base class for the moneypunct and moneypunct_byname class templates. It declares the part and pattern types. A pattern actually stores four part values, but they are stored as four char values for space efficiency. See moneypunct for an explanation of how part and pattern are used.

See Also

moneypunct class template, moneypunct_byname class template

money_get class template

```
template <typename charT,
          typename InputIterator = istreambuf_iterator<charT> >
class money_get : public locale::facet
{
public:
  typedef charT char_type;
  typedef InputIterator iter_type;
  typedef basic_string<charT> string_type;
  explicit money_get(size_t refs = 0);
```

```
  iter_type get(iter_type s, iter_type end, bool intl, ios_base& f,
                ios_base::iostate& err, long double& units) const;
  iter_type get(iter_type s, iter_type end, bool intl, ios_base& f,
                ios_base::iostate& err, string_type& digits) const;
  static locale::id id;
protected:
  virtual ~money_get( );
  virtual iter_type do_get(iter_type begin, iter_type end, bool intl,
                           ios_base& strean, ios_base::iostate& err,
                           long double& units) const;|  virtual iter_type
                 do_get(iter_type begin, iter_type end, bool intl,
                        ios_base& stream, ios_base::iostate& err,
                        string_type& digits) const;
};
```

The money_get class template is a facet for parsing monetary values from an input stream. The money_get<char> and money_get<wchar_t> instantiations are standard. Example 13-27 shows a simple use of money_get and money_put.

Example 13-27. Reading and writing monetary values

```
#include <iostream>
#include <locale>
#include <ostream>

int main( )
{
  std::ios_base::iostate err = std::ios_base::goodbit;
  long double value;
  std::cout << "What is your hourly wage? ";
  std::use_facet<std::money_get<char> >(std::locale( )).get(
    std::cin, std::istreambuf_iterator<char>( ),
    false, std::cin, err, value);
  if (err)
    std::cerr << "Invalid input\n";
  else {
    std::cout << value << '\n';
    std::cout << "You make ";
    std::use_facet<std::money_put<char> >(std::locale( )).put(
      std::cout, false, std::cout, std::cout.fill( ),
      value * 40);
    std::cout << " in a 40-hour work week.\n";
  }
}
```

As with other facets, the public members call virtual, protected members with the same name prefaced by do_. Thus, to use the facet, call the public function get, which calls do_get. The description below is for the virtual functions because they do the real work. Imagine that for each virtual-function description, there is a corresponding description for a public, nonvirtual function, such as:

```
iter_type get(iter_type begin, iter_type end, bool intl, ios_base& stream,
  ios_base::iostate& err, long double& units) const
    Calls do_get(begin, end, intl, stream, err, units)
```

The following are the virtual, protected members of money_get:

virtual iter_type **do_get**(iter_type begin, iter_type end, bool intl, ios_base&
   stream, ios_base::iostate& err, long double& units) const
virtual iter_type **do_get**(iter_type begin, iter_type end, bool intl, ios_base&
   stream, ios_base::iostate& err, string_type& digits) const

> Reads characters in the range [begin, end) and interprets them as a monetary value.
> If intl is true, the value is parsed using international format; otherwise, local
> format is used. That is, the intl value is used as the Intl template parameter to
> moneypunct<char_type, Intl>. If a valid monetary value is read from the input
> stream, the integral value is stored in units or is formatted as a string in digits. (For
> example, the input "$1,234.56" yields the units 123456 or the digits "123456".) The
> digit string starts with an optional minus sign ('-') followed by digits ('0'–'9'), in
> which each character c is produced by calling ctype<char_type>.widen(c).
>
> If a valid sequence is not found, err is modified to include stream.failbit. If the
> end of the input is reached without forming a valid monetary value, stream.eofbit
> is also set.
>
> If the showbase flag is set (stream.flags( ) & stream.showbase is not 0), the currency
> symbol is required; otherwise, it is optional. Thousands grouping, if the local
> format supports it, is optional.
>
> The sign of the result is dictated by positive_sign( ) and negative_sign( ) from
> the moneypunct facet.
>
> The return value is an iterator that points to one past the last character of the
> monetary value.

See Also

money_put class template, moneypunct class template, num_get class template

---

money_put class template
Facet for output of monetary values

```
template <typename charT,
  typename OutputIterator = ostreambuf_iterator<charT> >
class money_put : public locale::facet
{
public:
  typedef charT char_type;
  typedef OutputIterator iter_type;
  typedef basic_string<charT> string_type;
  explicit money_put(size_t refs = 0);
  iter_type put(iter_type s, bool intl, ios_base& f, char_type fill,
                long double units) const;
  iter_type put(iter_type s, bool intl, ios_base& f, char_type fill,
                const string_type& digits) const;
  static locale::id id;
protected:
  virtual ~money_put();
  virtual iter_type do_put(iter_type, bool, ios_base&, char_type fill,
                           long double units) const;
  virtual iter_type do_put(iter_type, bool, ios_base&, char_type fill,
                           const string_type& digits) const;
};
```

The money_put class template is a facet for formatting and printing monetary values. See Example 13-27 (under money_get), which shows how to use the money_put facet. The money_put<char> and money_put<wchar_t> instantiations are standard.

As with other facets, the public members call virtual, protected members with the same name prefaced by do_. Thus, to use the facet, call the public functions, such as put, which calls do_put. The descriptions below are for the virtual functions because they do the real work. Imagine that for each virtual function description, there is a corresponding description for a public, nonvirtual function, such as:

iter_type **put**(iter_type iter, bool intl, ios_base& stream, char_type fill, long double units) const
    Returns do_put(iter, intl, stream, fill, units)

The following are the virtual, protected members of money_put:

virtual iter_type **do_put**(iter_type iter, bool intl, ios_base& stream, char_type fill, long double units) const

virtual iter_type **do_put**(iter_type iter, bool intl, ios_base& stream, char_type fill, const string_type& digits) const

    Formats a monetary value and writes the formatted characters to iter. The value to format is either an integer, units, or a string of digit characters in digits. If the first character of digits is widen('-'), the remaining digits are interpreted as a negative number.

    The formatting pattern and punctuation characters are obtained from the moneypunct facet. For positive values, pos_format( ) is used; for negative values, neg_format( ) is used. The pattern dictates the output format. (See moneypunct later in this section for information on patterns.) The currency symbol is printed only if the showbase flag is set (that is, stream.flags( ) & stream.showbase is nonzero). Thousands separators and a decimal point are inserted at the appropriate places in the formatted output.

    If necessary, fill characters are inserted until the formatted width is stream.width( ). The stream's adjustfield flag dictates how fill characters are inserted. That is, stream.flags( ) & stream.adjustfield is tested, and if it is equal to:

ios_base::internal
    Fill characters are inserted where the pattern is none or space.

ios_base::left
    Fill characters are appended to the end of the formatted field.

None of the above
    Fill characters are inserted at the start of the formatted field.

    Finally, stream.width(0) is called to reset the field width to 0. The return value is an iterator that points to one past the last output character.

See Also

money_get class template, moneypunct class template, num_put class template

---

moneypunct class template   Facet for punctuation of monetary values

```
template <typename charT, bool International = false>
class moneypunct : public locale::facet, public money_base
{
public:
  typedef charT char_type;
```

```
  typedef basic_string<charT> string_type;
  explicit moneypunct(size_t refs = 0);
  charT decimal_point() const;
  charT thousands_sep() const;
  string grouping() const;
  string_type curr_symbol() const;
  string_type positive_sign() const;
  string_type negative_sign() const;
  int frac_digits() const;
  pattern pos_format() const;
  pattern neg_format() const;
  static locale::id id;
  static const bool intl = International;
protected:
  virtual ~moneypunct();
  virtual charT do_decimal_point() const;
  virtual charT do_thousands_sep() const;
  virtual string do_grouping() const;
  virtual string_type do_curr_symbol() const;
  virtual string_type do_positive_sign() const;
  virtual string_type do_negative_sign() const;
  virtual int do_frac_digits() const;
  virtual pattern do_pos_format() const;
  virtual pattern do_neg_format() const;
};
```

The moneypunct class template is a facet that describes the punctuation characters used to format a monetary value.

The moneypunct<char,false>, moneypunct<wchar_t,false>, moneypunct<char,true>, and moneypunct<wchar_t,true> instantiations are standard.

Specify true for the International template parameter to obtain an international format, or false to obtain a local format. In an international format, the currency symbol is always four characters, usually three characters followed by a space.

The money_get and money_put facets use a pattern to parse or format a monetary value. The pattern specifies the order in which parts of a monetary value must appear. Each pattern has four fields, in which each field has type part (cast to char). The symbol, sign, and value parts must appear exactly once, and the remaining field must be space or none. The value none cannot be first (field[0]); space cannot be first or last (field[3]).

Where sign appears in the pattern, the first character of the sign string (positive_sign() or negative_sign()) is output, and the remaining characters of the sign string appear at the end of the formatted output. Thus, if negative_sign() returns "()", the value -12.34 might be formatted as "(12.34)".

As with other facets, the public members call virtual, protected members with the same name prefaced by do_. Thus, to use the facet, call the public functions, such as grouping, which calls do_grouping. The descriptions below are for the virtual functions because they do the real work. Imagine that for each virtual-function description, there is a corresponding description for a public, nonvirtual function, such as:

string_type curr_symbol() const
    Returns do_curr_symbol()

The following are the virtual, protected members of moneypunct:

virtual string_type **do_curr_symbol**( ) const
> Returns the currency symbol, such as "$" (which is used by some U.S. locales) or "USD " (which is the international currency symbol for U.S. dollars). In the "C" locale, the currency symbol is "" or L"".

virtual charT **do_decimal_point**( ) const
> Returns the character used before the fractional part when do_frac_digits is greater than 0. For example, in the U.S., this is typically '.', and in Europe, it is typically ','. In the "C" locale, the decimal point is '.' or L'.'.

virtual int **do_frac_digits**( ) const
> Returns the number of digits to print after the decimal point. This value can be 0. In the "C" locale, the number of digits is std::numeric_limits<char>.max( ).

virtual string **do_grouping**( ) const
> Returns a string that specifies the positions of thousands separators. The string is interpreted as a vector of integers, in which each value is a number of digits, starting from the right. Thus, the string "\3" means every three digits form a group. In the "C" locale, the grouping is "" or L"".

virtual pattern **do_neg_format**( ) const
> Returns the pattern used to format negative values. In the "C" locale, the negative format is { symbol, sign, none, value }.

virtual string_type **do_negative_sign**( ) const
> Returns the string (which may be empty) used to identify negative values. The position of the sign is dictated by the do_neg_format pattern. In the "C" locale, the negative sign is "-" or L"-".

virtual pattern **do_pos_format**( ) const
> Returns the pattern used to format positive values. In the "C" locale, the positive format is { symbol, sign, none, value }.

virtual string_type **do_positive_sign**( ) const
> Returns the string (which may be empty) used to identify positive values. The position of the sign is dictated by the do_pos_format pattern. In the "C" locale, the positive sign is "" or L"".

virtual charT **do_thousands_sep**( ) const
> Returns the character used to separate groups of digits, in which the groups are specified by do_grouping. In the U.S., the separator is typically ',', and in Europe, it is often '.'. In the "C" locale, the thousands separator is '\0' or L'\0'.

See Also

money_base class, money_get class template, money_put class template, moneypunct_byname class template, numpunct class template

---

moneypunct_byname class template
Facet for punctuation of monetary values

```
template <typename charT, bool Intl = false>
class moneypunct_byname : public moneypunct<charT, Intl>
{
public:
  typedef money_base::pattern pattern;
  typedef basic_string<charT> string_type;
  explicit moneypunct_byname(const char*, size_t refs = 0);
```

```
protected:
  // ... Same virtual functions as in moneypunct
};
```

The moneypunct_byname class template provides formatting characters and information for monetary values using the rules of a named locale. The moneypunct_byname<char,International> and moneypunct_byname<wchar_t,International> instantiations are standard.

See Also

moneypunct class template

num_get class template

```
template <typename charT,
          typename InputIterator = istreambuf_iterator<charT> >
class num_get : public locale::facet
{
public:
  typedef charT char_type;
  typedef InputIterator iter_type;
  explicit num_get(size_t refs = 0);
  iter_type get(iter_type in, iter_type end, ios_base&,
                ios_base::iostate& err, bool& v) const;
  iter_type get(iter_type in, iter_type end, ios_base&,
                ios_base::iostate& err, long& v) const;
  iter_type get(iter_type in, iter_type end, ios_base&,
                ios_base::iostate& err, unsigned short& v) const;
  iter_type get(iter_type in, iter_type end, ios_base&,
                ios_base::iostate& err, unsigned int& v) const;
  iter_type get(iter_type in, iter_type end, ios_base&,
                ios_base::iostate& err, unsigned long& v) const;
  iter_type get(iter_type in, iter_type end, ios_base&,
                ios_base::iostate& err, float& v) const;
  iter_type get(iter_type in, iter_type end, ios_base&,
                ios_base::iostate& err, double& v) const;
  iter_type get(iter_type in, iter_type end, ios_base&,
                ios_base::iostate& err, long double& v) const;
  iter_type get(iter_type in, iter_type end, ios_base&,
                ios_base::iostate& err, void*& v) const;
  static locale::id id;
protected:
  virtual ~num_get();
  virtual iter_type do_get(iter_type, iter_type, ios_base&,
                           ios_base::iostate& err, bool& v) const;
  virtual iter_type do_get(iter_type, iter_type, ios_base&,
                           ios_base::iostate& err, long& v) const;
  virtual iter_type do_get(iter_type, iter_type, ios_base&,
                           ios_base::iostate& err, unsigned short& v) const;
  virtual iter_type do_get(iter_type, iter_type, ios_base&,
                           ios_base::iostate& err, unsigned int& v) const;
  virtual iter_type do_get(iter_type, iter_type, ios_base&,
                           ios_base::iostate& err, unsigned long& v) const;
```

```
    virtual iter_type do_get(iter_type, iter_type, ios_base&,
                             ios_base::iostate& err, float& v) const;
    virtual iter_type do_get(iter_type, iter_type, ios_base&,
                             ios_base::iostate& err, double& v) const;
    virtual iter_type do_get(iter_type, iter_type, ios_base&,
                             ios_base::iostate& err, long double& v) const;
    virtual iter_type do_get(iter_type, iter_type, ios_base&,
                             ios_base::iostate& err, void*& v) const;
};
```

The num_get class template is a facet for parsing and reading numeric values from an input stream. The istream extraction operators (>>) use num_get. The num_get<char> and num_get<wchar_t> instantiations are standard.

As with other facets, the public members call virtual, protected members with the same name prefaced by do_. Thus, to use the facet, call the public functions, such as get, which calls do_get. The descriptions below are for the virtual functions because they do the real work. Imagine that for each virtual function description, there is a corresponding description for a public, nonvirtual function, such as:

iter_type **get**(iter_type begin, iter_type end, ios_base& stream,
  ios_base::iostate& err, bool& v) const
    Returns do_get(begin, end, stream, err, v)

The following are the virtual, protected members of num_get:

virtual iter_type **do_get**(iter_type begin, iter_type end, ios_base& stream,
  ios_base::iostate& err, bool& v) const
    Reads a bool value, which can be represented as a number or as a character string. The function first tests the boolalpha flag, that is, stream.flags( ) & stream.boolalpha. If the flag is 0, a numeric value is read; if the flag is 1, a string is read from [begin, end).

    If boolalpha is false, the input is interpreted as a long int. If the numeric value is 1, v is assigned true; if the value is 0, v is assigned false; otherwise, failbit is set in err, and v is not modified.

    If boolalpha is true, characters are read from begin until one of the following happens:

- The input matches truename( ) from the numpunct facet:

      use_facet<numpunct<char_type> >(stream.getloc( )).truename( )

  v is assigned true, and err is assigned goodbit. A match is determined by the shortest input sequence that uniquely matches truename( ) or falsename( ).

- The input matches falsename( ): v is assigned false, and err is assigned goodbit.

- begin == end, in which case eofbit is set in err.

- The input does not match truename( ) or falsename( ); failbit is set in err.

virtual iter_type **do_get**(iter_type begin, iter_type end, ios_base& stream,
  ios_base::iostate& err, *type*& v) const
    Reads a single value. The do_get function is overloaded for most of the fundamental types. The behavior of each function is essentially the same (except for the bool version described earlier) and depends on stream.flags( ), the ctype facet, and the numpunct facet. Both facets are obtained for the locale stream.getloc( ).

First, input characters are collected from the range [begin, end) or until the input character is not part of a valid number according to the flags and numpunct facet. A locale-dependent decimal point is replaced with the character '.'. Thousands separators are read but not checked for valid positions until after the entire number has been read. The set of valid characters depends on the type of v and the flags, in particular the basefield flags. If stream.flags() & basefield is hex, hexadecimal characters are read; if it is oct, only octal characters are read ('0'–'7'). If the basefield is 0, the prefix determines the radix: 0x or 0X for hexa-decimal, 0 for octal, and anything else for decimal. Floating-point numbers can use fixed or exponential notation, regardless of the flags.

If v is of type void*, the format is implementation-defined in the same manner as the %p format for scanf (in <cstdio>).

After all the valid characters have been read, they are interpreted as a numeric value. If the string is invalid, or if the thousands groupings are incorrect, failbit is set in err and v is not changed. If the string is valid, its numeric value is stored in v and err is set to goodbit. If the entire input stream is read (up to end), eofbit is set in err.

See Also

money_get class template, num_put class template, numpunct class template, basic_istream in <istream>

num_put class template
Facet for output of numbers

```
template <typename charT,
          typename OutputIterator = ostreambuf_iterator<charT> >
class num_put : public locale::facet
{
public:
  typedef charT char_type;
  typedef OutputIterator iter_type;
  explicit num_put(size_t refs = 0);
  iter_type put(iter_type s, ios_base& f, char_type fill, bool v) const;
  iter_type put(iter_type s, ios_base& f, char_type fill, long v) const;
  iter_type put(iter_type s, ios_base& f, char_type fill, unsigned long v) const;
  iter_type put(iter_type s, ios_base& f, char_type fill, double v) const;
  iter_type put(iter_type s, ios_base& f, char_type fill, long double v) const;
  iter_type put(iter_type s, ios_base& f, char_type fill, const void* v) const;
  static locale::id id;
protected:
  virtual ~num_put();
  virtual iter_type do_put(iter_type, ios_base&, char_type fill, bool v) const;
  virtual iter_type do_put(iter_type, ios_base&, char_type fill, long v) const;
  virtual iter_type do_put(iter_type, ios_base&, char_type fill, unsigned long)
    const;
  virtual iter_type do_put(iter_type, ios_base&, char_type fill, double v) const;
  virtual iter_type do_put(iter_type, ios_base&, char_type fill, long double v)
    const;
  virtual iter_type do_put(iter_type, ios_base&, char_type fill, const void* v)
    const;
};
```

The num_put class template is a facet for formatting and outputing a numeric value. The ostream output operators (>>) use num_put. The num_put<char> and num_put<wchar_t> instantiations are standard.

As with other facets, the public members call virtual, protected members with the same name prefaced by do_. Thus, to use the facet, call the public functions, such as put, which calls do_put. The descriptions below are for the virtual functions because they do the real work. Imagine that for each virtual function description, there is a corresponding description for a public, nonvirtual function, such as:

iter_type **put**(iter_type out, ios_base& stream, char_type fill, bool v) const
    Returns do_put(out, stream, fill, v)

The following are the virtual, protected members of num_put:

virtual iter_type **do_put**(iter_type out, ios_base& stream, char_type fill, bool v) const
    Writes a bool value to out. If the boolalpha flag is clear, that is, stream.flags() & stream.boolalpha is 0, the integer value of v is written as a number. If boolalpha is set, v is written as a word: if v is true, truename() is written; if v is false, falsename() is written using the numpunct facet. For example:

```
const numpunct<charT>& n = use_facet<numpunct<charT> >;
string_type s = v ? n.truename() : n.falsename();
// Write characters of s to out.
```

virtual iter_type **do_put**(iter_type out, ios_base& stream, char_type fill, *type* v) const
    Formats v as a string and writes the string contents to out using the flags of stream to control the formatting and the imbued locale of stream to obtain the ctype and numpunct facets for punctuation rules and characters. The format also depends on *type*:

Integral types (long, unsigned long)
    The format depends on the basefield flags (stream.flags() & basefield). If oct, the number is formatted as octal; if hex, the number is formatted as hexadecimal (using 'a'–'f' for the digits 10–16, or 'A'–'F' if the uppercase flag is set); or else the number is decimal. If the showbase flag is set, a prefix is used: 0 for octal, or 0x or 0X for hexadecimal (depending on the uppercase flag).

Floating-point types (double, long double)
    The format depends on the floatfield flags (stream.flags() & floatfield). If fixed, the format is fixed-point: an integer part, a decimal point, and a fractional part. If scientific, the format is exponential.

    If the floatfield flags do not indicate fixed or scientific, the general format is used: exponential if the exponent is -4 or less or greater than the precision (number of places after the decimal point), or fixed otherwise. Trailing zeros are dropped, as is the decimal point if would be the last character in the string.

    If the uppercase flag is set, the exponent is introduced by 'E', or else by 'e'. If the showpoint flag is set, the decimal point is always present.

Pointer (void*)
    The output format for a pointer is implementation-defined.

If the number is negative, it is prefaced with a minus sign ('-'). If the number is positive, no sign is output unless the showpos flag is set, in which case a positive sign ('+') appears at the start of the string.

If a decimal point character is needed, it is obtained from the numpunct facet's decimal_point( ) function. Integers have thousands separators inserted according to the grouping( ) function. See numpunct later in this section for more information.

If necessary, fill characters are inserted until the formatted width is stream.width( ). The stream's adjustfield flag dictates how fill characters are inserted. That is, stream.flags( ) & stream.adjustfield is tested, and if it is equal to:

ios_base::internal
> Fill characters are inserted after a sign (if present) or, if there is no sign, after a leading 0x or 0X, or else at the start of the field.

ios_base::left
> Fill characters are appended to the end of the formatted field.

Any other value
> Fill characters are inserted at the start of the formatted field.

Finally, stream.width(0) is called to reset the field width to 0. The return value is an iterator that points to one past the last output character.

See Also

money_put class template, num_get class template, numpunct class template, basic_ostream in <ostream>

---

numpunct class template   Facet for punctuation of numbers

```
template <typename charT>
class numpunct : public locale::facet
{
public:
  typedef charT char_type;
  typedef basic_string<charT> string_type;
  explicit numpunct(size_t refs = 0);
  char_type decimal_point( ) const;
  char_type thousands_sep( ) const;
  string grouping( ) const;
  string_type truename( ) const;
  string_type falsename( ) const;
  static locale::id id;
protected:
  virtual ~numpunct( );
  virtual char_type do_decimal_point( ) const;
  virtual char_type do_thousands_sep( ) const;
  virtual string do_grouping( ) const;
  virtual string_type do_truename( ) const;
  virtual string_type do_falsename( ) const;
};
```

The numpunct class template is a facet for numeric formatting and punctuation. The num_get and num_put facets use numpunct. The numpunct<char> and numpunct<wchar_t> instantiations are standard.

As with other facets, the public members call virtual, protected members with the same name prefaced by do_. Thus, to use the facet, call the public functions, such as grouping, which calls do_grouping. The descriptions below are for the virtual functions because they do the real work. Imagine that for each virtual-function description, there is a corresponding description for a public, nonvirtual function, such as:

char_type **decimal_point**( ) const
    Returns do_decimal_point( )

The following are the virtual, protected members of numpunct:

virtual char_type **do_decimal_point**( ) const
    Returns the decimal point character, which is typically '.' in U.S. locales and ','
    in European locales. In the "C" locale, the decimal point is '.' or L'.'.

virtual string_type **do_falsename**( ) const
    Returns the textual representation for the value false. In the standard instantia-
    tions (numpunct<char> and numpunct<wchar_t>), the value is "false" or L"false".

virtual string **do_grouping**( ) const
    Returns a string that specifies the positions of thousands separators. The string is
    interpreted as a vector of integers, in which each value is a number of digits,
    starting from the right. Thus, the string "\3" means every three digits form a
    group. In the "C" locale, the grouping is "" or L"".

virtual char_type **do_thousands_sep**( ) const
    Returns the character used to separate digit groups. (See do_grouping earlier in
    this section.) In U.S. locales, this is typically ',', and in European locales, it is
    typically '.'. In the "C" locale, the thousands separator is '\0' or L'\0'.

virtual string_type **do_truename**( ) const
    Returns the textual representation for the value true. In the standard instantia-
    tions (numpunct<char> and numpunct<wchar_t>), the value is "true" or L"true".

See Also

moneypunct class template, num_get class template, num_put class template

---

numpunct_byname class template   Facet for punctuation of numbers

```
template <typename charT>
class numpunct_byname : public numpunct<charT>
{
// This class is specialized for char and wchar_t.
public:
  typedef charT char_type;
  typedef basic_string<charT> string_type;
  explicit numpunct_byname(const char*, size_t refs = 0);
protected:
  // ... Same virtual functions as in numpunct
};
```

The numpunct_byname class template is a facet for numeric formatting and punctuation; it uses the rules of a named locale. The numpunct_byname<char> and numpunct_byname<wchar_t> instantiations are standard.

See Also

numpunct class template

---

time_base class

```
class time_base {
public:
  enum dateorder { no_order, dmy, mdy, ymd, ydm };
};
```

The time_base class is a base class for the time_get class template. It declares the dateorder type. See time_get for more information.

See Also

time_get class template

time_get class template

```
template <typename charT, typename InputIterator = istreambuf_iterator<charT> >
class time_get : public locale::facet, public time_base
{
public:
  typedef charT char_type;
  typedef InputIterator iter_type;
  explicit time_get(size_t refs = 0);
  dateorder date_order() const;
  iter_type get_time(iter_type s, iter_type end, ios_base& f,
                     ios_base::iostate& err, tm* t) const;
  iter_type get_date(iter_type s, iter_type end, ios_base& f,
                     ios_base::iostate& err, tm* t) const;
  iter_type get_weekday(iter_type s, iter_type end,
                        ios_base& f, ios_base::iostate& err, tm* t) const;
  iter_type get_monthname(iter_type s, iter_type end,
                          ios_base& f, ios_base::iostate& err, tm* t) const;
  iter_type get_year(iter_type s, iter_type end, ios_base& f,
                     ios_base::iostate& err, tm* t) const;
  static locale::id id;
protected:
  virtual ~time_get();
  virtual dateorder do_date_order() const;
  virtual iter_type do_get_time(iter_type s, iter_type end, ios_base&,
                                ios_base::iostate& err, tm* t) const;
  virtual iter_type do_get_date(iter_type s, iter_type end, ios_base&,
                                ios_base::iostate& err, tm* t) const;
  virtual iter_type do_get_weekday(iter_type s, iter_type end, ios_base&,
                                   ios_base::iostate& err, tm* t) const;
  virtual iter_type do_get_monthname(iter_type s, iter_type end, ios_base&,
                                     ios_base::iostate& err, tm* t) const;
  virtual iter_type do_get_year(iter_type s, iter_type end, ios_base&,
                                ios_base::iostate& err, tm* t) const;
};
```

The time_get class template is a facet for parsing and reading dates and times from an input stream. The components of the date and time value are stored in a tm structure. (See <ctime> for more information about tm.) The time_get<char> and time_get<wchar_t> instantiations are standard.

Most of the time_get functions take an err parameter in much the same way other facets and their functions do. Unlike other facets, however, the time_get functions do not set err to goodbit upon success. Instead, they only set failbit for an error. They do not set eofbit if the end of the input sequence is reached.

Most of the time_get functions take a t parameter, which is a pointer to a tm object, which is filled in with the relevant parts of the date and time. If a function fails, the state of the tm object is undefined.

As with other facets, the public members call virtual, protected members with the same name prefaced by do_. Thus, to use the facet, call the public functions, such as get_date, which calls do_get_date. The descriptions below are for the virtual functions because they do the real work. Imagine that for each virtual-function description, there is a corresponding description for a public, nonvirtual function, such as:

dateorder **date_order**( ) const
> Returns do_date_order( )

The following are the virtual, protected members of time_get:

virtual dateorder **do_date_order**( ) const
> Returns the order in which the day, month, and year appear in a locale-specific date. If the formatted date includes additional elements, the return value is no_order. See the time_base class for the declaration of the dateorder type.

virtual iter_type **do_get_time**(iter_type begin, iter_type end, ios_base& stream, ios_base::iostate& err, tm* t) const
> Reads characters from [begin, end) and interprets them as a time, according to the format of time_put<>::put, using the 'X' format. The time elements are stored in *t. If the input is invalid, the state of t's members is undefined, and err is set to failbit. The return value is an iterator that points to one past where the input stopped.

virtual iter_type **do_get_date**(iter_type begin, iter_type end, ios_base& stream, ios_base::iostate& err, tm* t) const
> Reads characters from [begin, end) and interprets them as a date, according to the format of time_put<>::put, using the 'x' format. The date elements are stored in *t. If the input is invalid, the state of t's members is undefined, and err is set to failbit. The return value is an iterator that points to one past where the input stopped.

virtual iter_type **do_get_weekday**(iter_type begin, iter_type end, ios_base& stream, ios_base::iostate& err, tm* t) const
> Reads characters from [begin, end) until it reads the name of a day of the week, either abbreviated or spelled out. The appropriate date elements are stored in *t. If the input is invalid, the state of t's members is undefined, and err is set to failbit. The return value is an iterator that points to one past where the input stopped.

virtual iter_type **do_get_monthname**(iter_type begin, iter_type end, ios_base& stream, ios_base::iostate& err, tm* t) const
> Reads characters from [begin, end) until it reads the name of a month, either abbreviated or spelled out. The appropriate date elements are stored in *t. If the input is invalid, the state of t's members is undefined, and err is set to failbit. The return value is an iterator that points to one past where the input stopped.

virtual iter_type **do_get_year**(iter_type begin, iter_type end, ios_base& stream, ios_base::iostate& err, tm* t) const

> Reads characters from [begin, end) until it reads a year. It is up to the implementation to determine whether two-digit years are accepted, and if so, which century to apply to the abbreviated year. The t->tm_year member is set appropriately. If the input is invalid, the state of t's members is undefined, and err is set to failbit. The return value is an iterator that points to one past where the input stopped.

See Also

time_base class, time_get_byname class template, time_put class template, tm in <ctime>

---

time_get_byname class template
Facet for input of dates and times

```
template <typename charT, typename InputIterator = istreambuf_iterator<charT> >
class time_get_byname : public time_get<charT, InputIterator>
{
public:
  typedef time_base::dateorder dateorder;
  typedef InputIterator iter_type;
  explicit time_get_byname(const char*, size_t refs = 0);
protected:
  // ... Same virtual functions as in time_get
};
```

The time_get_byname class template is a facet for reading dates and times from an input stream using a named locale. The time_get_byname<char> and time_get_byname<wchar_t> instantiations are standard.

See Also

time_get class template

---

time_put class template
Facet for output of dates and times

```
template <typename charT, typename OutputIterator = ostreambuf_iterator<charT> >
class time_put : public locale::facet
{
public:
  typedef charT char_type;
  typedef OutputIterator iter_type;
  explicit time_put(size_t refs = 0);
  iter_type put(iter_type s, ios_base& f, char_type fill, const tm* tmb,
                const charT* pattern, const charT* pat_end) const;
  iter_type put(iter_type s, ios_base& f, char_type fill, const tm* tmb,
                char format, char modifier = 0) const;
  static locale::id id;
protected:
  virtual ~time_put();
  virtual iter_type do_put(iter_type s, ios_base&, char_type, const tm* t,
                           char format, char modifier) const;
};
```

The time_put class template is a facet for formatting and writing dates and times. The time_put<char> and time_put<wchar_t> instantiations are standard.

Note that time_put is unlike other facets. The public put function does not always directly call do_put. Here are the complete descriptions of put and do_put:

iter_type **put**(iter_type out, ios_base& stream, char_type fill, const tm* t, const charT* pattern, const charT* pat_end) const

> Reads the pattern in [pattern, pat_end) and writes formatted date and time information to out. The pattern contains ordinary characters (which are written directly to out) interspersed with format specifiers. A format specifier starts with '%' and is followed by an optional modifier character, which is followed in turn by a format specifier character. The put function checks format characters by first calling narrow from the ctype<charT> facet, then checking the narrowed character.
>
> For each format specifier, put calls do_put(out, stream, fill, t, format, modifier), in which format is the format specifier and modifier is the modifier character or 0 if no modifier is present.
>
> The use of modifier characters is implementation-defined. The standard does not define any modifiers. See the do_put member function for more information.

iter_type **put**(iter_type out, ios_base& stream, char_type fill, const tm* t, char format, char modifier = 0) const

> Returns do_put(out, stream, fill, t, format, modifier).

virtual iter_type **do_put**(iter_type out, ios_base& stream, char_type fill, const tm* t, char format, char modifier) const

> Formats a single date or time element and writes the formatted characters to out. The format character specifies what to output (as shown in Table 13-22). The date and time information is obtained from t.
>
> The do_put function, unlike some of the other output facets, does not use stream's flags or field width. The fill parameter is used by implementation-defined formatting.

Table 13-22. Format specifiers for do_put

Specifier	Description
a	Abbreviated weekday name
A	Full weekday name
b	Abbreviated month name
B	Full month name
C	Complete date and time
D	Day of the month (01–31)
H	Hour (00–23); 24-hour clock
I	Hour (01–12); 12-hour clock
j	Day of the year (001–366)
m	Month (01–12)
M	Minutes (00–59)
P	A.M./P.M. designation for use with a 12-hour clock
S	Second (00–61); up to two leap seconds
U	Week number (00–53); week 1 starts with the first Sunday
w	Weekday (0–6); Sunday is day 0
W	Week number (00–53); week 1 starts with first Monday

Table 13-22. *Format specifiers for do_put (continued)*

Specifier	Description
x	Date
X	Time
y	Year in century (00–99)
Y	Year
Z	Time zone name or abbreviation, or empty string if time zone is unknown
%	Literal %

The use of modifier is implementation-defined. The C++ standard recommends the use of POSIX modifiers, which are 'E' and 'O'. These modifiers request the use of an alternative format if the locale has one. The 'E' modifier applies to certain format specifiers to request an alternative representation for dates and times. The 'O' modifier applies to certain format specifiers to request the use of alternative numeric symbols. If a locale cannot honor the modified request, it uses the unmodified format specifier.

See Also

time_get class template, time_put_byname class template, <ctime>

time_put_byname class template
Facet for output of dates and times

```
template <typename charT, typename OutputIterator = ostreambuf_iterator<charT> >
class time_put_byname : public time_put<charT,OutputIterator>
{
public:
  typedef charT char_type;
  typedef OutputIterator iter_type;
  explicit time_put_byname(const char*, size_t refs = 0);
protected:
  // ... Same virtual functions as in time_put
};
```

The time_put class template is a facet for formatting and writing dates and times using a named locale. The time_put_byname<char> and time_put_byname<wchar_t> instantiations are standard.

See Also

time_put class template

tolower function template
Converts a character to lowercase in a locale

```
template <typename charT>
charT tolower(charT c, const locale& loc);
```

The tolower function converts the character c to lowercase using the locale loc:

```
use_facet<ctype<charT> >(loc).tolower(c)
```

See Also

ctype class template, `islower` function template, `toupper` function template

toupper function template
Converts a character to uppercase in a locale

```
template <typename charT>
charT toupper(charT c, const locale& loc);
```

The toupper function converts the character c to uppercase using the locale loc:

```
use_facet<ctype<charT> >(loc).toupper(c)
```

See Also

ctype class template, `isupper` function template, `tolower` function template

use_facet function template
Retrieves a facet for a locale

```
template <typename Facet>
const Facet& use_facet(const locale& loc)
```

The use_facet function template obtains a facet from locale loc. See Examples 13-24 and 13-27, earlier in this section.

See Also

has_facet function template, `locale::facet` class

<map>

The <map> header is one of the standard container template headers. It declares the map and multimap class templates and a few global function templates that operate on map and multimap objects.

A *map* is a container that stores pairs of keys and values. Looking up keys, inserting keys, and deleting keys can all be performed in logarithmic or better time. Maps support bidirectional iterators (no random access). In other languages and libraries, maps are also called dictionaries and associative arrays.

See Chapter 10 for information about containers. See the <utility> section later in this chapter for information about the pair class template.

map class template
Associative map container with unique keys

```
template <typename Key, typename T, typename Compare = less<Key>,
          typename Alloc = allocator<pair<const Key, T> > >
class map {
public:
  typedef Key key_type;
  typedef T mapped_type;
  typedef pair<const Key, T> value_type;
  typedef Compare key_compare;
  typedef Alloc allocator_type;
  typedef typename Alloc::reference reference;
```

```
typedef typename Alloc::const_reference const_reference;
typedef ... iterator;
typedef ... const_iterator;
typedef ... size_type;
typedef ... difference_type;
typedef typename Alloc::pointer pointer;
typedef typename Alloc::const_pointer const_pointer;
typedef std::reverse_iterator<iterator> reverse_iterator;
typedef std::reverse_iterator<const_iterator> const_reverse_iterator;
class value_compare :
    public binary_function<value_type,value_type,bool>
{
   friend class map;
protected:
  Compare comp;
  value_compare(Compare c) : comp(c) {}
public:
  bool operator()(const value_type& x, const value_type& y) const
      { return comp(x.first, y.first); }
};
explicit map(const Compare& comp = Compare(), const Alloc& = Alloc());
template <class InputIterator>
map(InputIterator first, InputIterator last,
    const Compare& comp = Compare(), const Alloc& = Alloc());
map(const map<Key,T,Compare,Alloc>& x);
~map();
map<Key,T,Compare,Alloc>& operator=(const map<Key,T,Compare,Alloc>& x);

allocator_type get_allocator() const;
// Iterators
iterator begin();
const_iterator begin() const;
iterator end();
const_iterator end() const;
reverse_iterator rbegin();
const_reverse_iterator rbegin() const;
reverse_iterator rend();
const_reverse_iterator rend() const;
// Capacity
bool empty() const;
size_type size() const;
size_type max_size() const;
// Element access
T& operator[](const key_type& x);
// Modifiers
pair<iterator, bool> insert(const value_type& x);
iterator insert(iterator hintpos, const value_type& x);
template <class InputIterator>
  void insert(InputIterator first, InputIterator last);
void erase(iterator position);
size_type erase(const key_type& x);
void erase(iterator first, iterator last);
void swap(map<Key,T,Compare,Alloc>&);
void clear();
```

Library
Reference

```
// Observers
key_compare key_comp( ) const;
value_compare value_comp( ) const;
// Map operations
iterator find(const key_type& x);
const_iterator find(const key_type& x) const;
size_type count(const key_type& x) const;
iterator lower_bound(const key_type& x);
const_iterator lower_bound(const key_type& x) const;
iterator upper_bound(const key_type& x);
const_iterator upper_bound(const key_type& x) const;
pair<iterator,iterator> equal_range(const key_type& x);
pair<const_iterator,const_iterator>
  equal_range(const key_type& x) const;
};
```

The map class template represents a map container. A map stores pairs of unique keys and associated objects, in which the key type is specified by the Key template parameter, and the associated type is the T template parameter. The values stored in the map are of type pair<const Key, T> (which has the convenience typedef value_type).

A map's iterators are bidirectional. They return value_type references; use the first member to access the key or second to access the associated object.

Note that keys are const in the map. You must not change the key while it is stored in a map. More precisely, you must not change the key in a way that alters its relative order with the other keys in the map. If you need to modify a key, you can erase the key from the map, modify the key, and insert the new key with its original associated value, as shown in Example 13-28.

Example 13-28. One way to modify a key in a map

```
template <typename Key, typename T, typename C, typename A>
void change_key(std::map<Key, T, C, A>& m,
  const Key& oldkey, const Key& newkey)
{
  using std::map;
  typedef typename map<Key, T, C, A>::iterator map_iterator;
  map_iterator i = m.find(oldkey);
  if (i != m.end( )) {
    // Save a copy of i->second because erase invalidates i.
    T tmp = i->second;
    m.erase(i);
    m[newkey] = tmp;
  }
  // Exercise: What if newkey is already in m?
}
```

Within a map, keys are ordered in ascending order, according to the Compare template parameter (which can be a function pointer or functor that compares two objects of type Key and returns true if the first argument should come before the second). Keys must be unique, but note that uniqueness is determined only by calling Compare, not by using the == operator. That is, two objects, a and b, are different (and therefore can both be present in a single map object) if Compare(a, b) is true or Compare(b, a) is true. See multimap later in this section for a map container that can store non-unique keys.

Inserting into a map does not invalidate any iterators for that map or references to pairs in the map. Erasing an element invalidates only iterators and references that refer to that element.

Inserting into a map and searching for an element in a map usually take logarithmic time. Erasing a single element, given an iterator, takes amortized constant time.

The subscript operator ([ ]) lets you use a map as an associative array, for which the array indices are keys. If a key is not already present in the map, it is added. Using operator[ ] allows for compact, easy-to-read code, as you can see in Example 13-29, which shows how to use map to count word frequencies in the standard input.

Example 13-29. Using a map to count word frequencies

```cpp
#include <cstddef>
#include <iostream>
#include <istream>
#include <map>
#include <ostream>
#include <string>

typedef std::map<std::string, std::size_t> freqmap;

// Print a single word and its count.
void print(const freqmap::value_type info)
{
  std::cout << info.first << '\t' << info.second << '\n';
}

int main( )
{
  freqmap fm;
  std::string word;
  // Count words. If a word is not in the map, add it. When a new word is added,
  // its count is initially 0. Each time, including the first, increment the
  // count.
  while (std::cin >> word)
    ++fm[word];
  // Print the frequencies of each word, in order.
  std::for_each(fm.begin( ), fm.end( ), print);
}
```

The following are the member functions of map:

explicit **map**(const Compare& comp = Compare( ), const Alloc& = Alloc( ))
> Creates an empty map.

template <class InputIterator>
map(InputIterator first, InputIterator last, const Compare& comp = Compare( ),
const Alloc& = Alloc( ))
> Creates an empty map and then copies all pairs in the range [first, last) into the new map.

map(const map<Key,T,Compare,Alloc>& x)
> Creates a new map and copies the allocator and all the pairs from x to the new map.

Library
Reference

```
iterator begin( )
const_iterator begin( ) const
```
Returns an iterator that points to the first item in the map.

```
void clear( )
```
Erases every item in the map.

```
size_type count(const key_type& x) const
```
Returns the number of pairs whose keys are equivalent to x. This value is always 0 or 1.

```
bool empty( ) const
```
Returns size( ) == 0.

```
iterator end( )
const_iterator end( ) const
```
Returns an iterator that points to one past the last item in the map.

```
pair<iterator,iterator> equal_range(const key_type& x)
pair<const_iterator,const_iterator> equal_range(const key_type& x) const
```
Returns the lower bound and upper bound as a pair:

```
      std::make_pair(lower_bound(x), upper_bound(x))
```

```
void erase(iterator position)
size_type erase(const key_type& x)
void erase(iterator first, iterator last)
```
Erases one or more pairs from the map. The first version erases the pair at position in constant time (amortized over many calls). The second version erases the pair equivalent to x, if it is present, returning a count of the number of pairs erased, that is, 0 or 1. It runs in logarithmic time. The third version erases all elements in the range [first, last) in a time proportional to log size( ) + (last − first).

```
iterator find(const key_type& x)
const_iterator find(const key_type& x) const
```
Searches for a pair whose key is equivalent to x and returns an iterator that points to that pair or end( ) if it is not found. It runs in logarithmic time.

```
allocator_type get_allocator( ) const
```
Returns the map's allocator.

```
pair<iterator, bool> insert(const value_type& x)
iterator insert(iterator hintpos, const value_type& x)
template <class InputIterator>  void insert(InputIterator first, InputIterator last)
```
Inserts one or more pairs into the map, but only if an equivalent key is not already present in the map. If the key is already present, the insert attempt is ignored. The first version attempts to insert the pair x in logarithmic time.

The second version inserts the pair x using hintpos as a position hint. If x is inserted immediately after hintpos, the performance is constant (amortized over many insertions); at any other position, the performance is logarithmic. Use this form when inserting many items that are already in the desired order.

The third version copies all the pairs in the range [first, last), which must be pointing to a different map object. If the items are already in the desired order, the performance is linear; otherwise, it is N log (size( ) + N), in which N is last − first.

key_compare **key_comp**( ) const
> Returns the comparator function pointer or object, which compares keys. The key_compare type is the same as the Compare template parameter. See also the value_comp member.

iterator **lower_bound**(const key_type& x)
const_iterator **lower_bound**(const key_type& x) const
> Returns an iterator that points to the first pair in the map that does not come before x. That is, if x is in the map, the iterator points to its position; otherwise, the iterator points to the first position where x should be inserted. Performance is logarithmic.

size_type **max_size**( ) const
> Returns the largest number of pairs that can be in the map.

reverse_iterator **rbegin**( )
const_reverse_iterator **rbegin**( ) const
> Returns a reverse iterator that points to the last element of the map.

reverse_iterator **rend**( )
const_reverse_iterator **rend**( ) const
> Returns a reverse iterator that points to one position before the first element of the map.

size_type **size**( ) const
> Returns the number of pairs in the map.

void **swap**(map<Key,T,Compare,Alloc>&)
> Swaps the contents of the map with the contents of x.

iterator **upper_bound**(const key_type& x)
const_iterator **upper_bound**(const key_type& x) const
> Returns an iterator that points to the first pair in the map that comes after x. Performance is logarithmic.

value_compare **value_comp**( ) const
> Returns a value_compare object, which can be used to compare pairs. The value_compare object takes two value_type arguments and compares their keys, returning true if the first should come before the second in the map.

map<Key,T,Compare,Alloc>& **operator=**(const map<Key,T,Compare,Alloc>& x)
> Erases all the elements of the map and replaces them with copies of the elements of x.

T& **operator[ ]**(const key_type& x)
> Returns a reference to the object associated with the key x. If x is not in the map, it is added with a default associated object, and a reference to that new object is returned. That is, operator[ ] returns:
>
>   (*((insert(std::make_pair(x, T()))).first)).second
>
> Note that there is no const version of this operator.

See Also

multimap class template, set in <set>

multimap class template

Associative map container with duplicate keys

```
template <class Key, class T, class Compare = less<Key>,
          class Alloc = allocator<pair<const Key, T> > >
class multimap {
public:
  typedef Key key_type;
  typedef T mapped_type;
  typedef pair<const Key,T> value_type;
  typedef Compare key_compare;
  typedef Alloc allocator_type;
  typedef typename Alloc::reference reference;
  typedef typename Alloc::const_reference const_reference;
  typedef ... iterator;
  typedef ... const_iterator;
  typedef ... size_type;
  typedef ... difference_type;
  typedef typename Alloc::pointer pointer;
  typedef typename Alloc::const_pointer const_pointer;
  typedef std::reverse_iterator<iterator> reverse_iterator;
  typedef std::reverse_iterator<const_iterator> const_reverse_iterator;
  class value_compare :
    public binary_function<value_type,value_type,bool>
  {
    friend class multimap;
  protected:
    Compare comp;
    value_compare(Compare c) : comp(c) {}
  public:
    bool operator()(const value_type& x, const value_type& y)
      const { return comp(x.first, y.first); }
  };

  explicit multimap(const Compare& comp = Compare(),
    const Alloc& = Alloc());
  template <class InputIterator>
  multimap(InputIterator first, InputIterator last,
    const Compare& comp = Compare(), const Alloc& = Alloc());
  multimap(const multimap<Key,T,Compare,Alloc>& x);
  ~multimap();
  multimap<Key,T,Compare,Alloc>&
    operator=(const multimap<Key,T,Compare,Alloc>& x);
  allocator_type get_allocator() const;
  // Iterators
  iterator begin();
  const_iterator begin() const;
  iterator end();
  const_iterator end() const;
  reverse_iterator rbegin();
  const_reverse_iterator rbegin() const;
  reverse_iterator rend();
  const_reverse_iterator rend() const;
```

```
    // Capacity
    bool empty( ) const;
    size_type size( ) const;
    size_type max_size( ) const;
    // Modifiers
    iterator insert(const value_type& x);
    iterator insert(iterator hintpos, const value_type& x);
    template <class InputIterator>
    void insert(InputIterator first, InputIterator last);
    void erase(iterator position);
    size_type erase(const key_type& x);
    void erase(iterator first, iterator last);
    void swap(multimap<Key,T,Compare,Alloc>&);
    void clear( );
    // Observers
    key_compare key_comp( ) const;
    value_compare value_comp( ) const;
    // Map operations
    iterator find(const key_type& x);
    const_iterator find(const key_type& x) const;
    size_type count(const key_type& x) const;
    iterator lower_bound(const key_type& x);
    const_iterator lower_bound(const key_type& x) const;
    iterator upper_bound(const key_type& x);
    const_iterator upper_bound(const key_type& x) const;
    pair<iterator,iterator> equal_range(const key_type& x);
    pair<const_iterator,const_iterator>
    equal_range(const key_type& x) const;
};
```

The multimap class template represents a map container that can store duplicate keys. A map stores pairs of keys and associated objects, in which the key type is specified by the Key template parameter, and the associated type is the T template parameter. The values stored in the map are of type pair<const Key, T> (which has the convenience typedef value_type).

A map's iterators are bidirectional. They return value_type references; use the first member to access the key or second to access the associated object.

Note that keys are const in the map. You must not change the key while it is stored in a map. More precisely, you must not change the key in a way that alters its relative order with the other keys in the map. See Example 13-28 (earlier in this section), which shows how to change a key by erasing and reinserting an object.

Within a map, keys are ordered in ascending order, according to the Compare template parameter (which can be a function pointer or functor that compares two objects of type Key and returns true if the first argument should come before the second).

Inserting into a map does not invalidate any iterators for that map. Erasing an element invalidates only iterators that refer to that element.

Inserting a single item into a map and searching for an element in a map usually take logarithmic time. Erasing a single element, given an iterator, takes amortized constant time.

The following are the member functions of multimap. Note that multimap does not have a subscript operator.

Library
Reference

explicit **multimap**(const Compare& comp = Compare( ), const Alloc& = Alloc( ))
> Creates an empty map.

template <class InputIterator>
multimap(InputIterator first, InputIterator last,
  const Compare& comp = Compare( ), const Alloc& = Alloc( ))
> Creates an empty map and then copies all pairs in the range [first, last) into the new map.

multimap(const multimap<Key,T,Compare,Alloc>& x)
> Creates a new map and copies all the pairs from x to the new map.

iterator **begin**( )
const_iterator **begin**( ) const
> Returns an iterator that points to the first item in the map.

void **clear**( )
> Erases every item in the map in linear time.

size_type **count**(const key_type& x) const
> Returns the number of pairs whose keys are equivalent to x. Complexity is proportional to log(size( )) + the return value.

bool **empty**( ) const
> Returns size( ) == 0.

iterator **end**( )
const_iterator **end**( ) const
> Returns an iterator that points to one past the last item in the map.

pair<iterator,iterator> **equal_range**(const key_type& x)
pair<const_iterator,const_iterator> **equal_range**(const key_type& x) const
> Returns the lower bound and upper bound as a pair:
>
> > std::make_pair(lower_bound(x), upper_bound(x))

void **erase**(iterator position)
size_type **erase**(const key_type& x)
void **erase**(iterator first, iterator last)
> Erases one or more pairs from the map. The first version erases the pair at position in constant time (amortized over many calls). The second version erases all the pairs equivalent to x if any are present, returning a count of the number of pairs erased. The third version erases all elements in the range [first, last). The last two forms take time proportional to log(size( )) + the number of elements erased.

iterator **find**(const key_type& x)
const_iterator **find**(const key_type& x) const
> Searches for a pair whose key is equivalent to x and returns an iterator that points to that pair or end( ) if it is not found. If x occurs more than once, the iterator might point to any of the equivalent pairs.

allocator_type **get_allocator**( ) const
> Returns the map's allocator.

pair<iterator, bool> **insert**(const value_type& x)
iterator **insert**(iterator hintpos, const value_type& x)
template <class InputIterator> void **insert**(InputIterator first, InputIterator last)
> Inserts one or more pairs into the map. The first version inserts the pair x in logarithmic time.

The second version inserts the pair x using hintpos as a position hint. If x is inserted immediately after hintpos, the performance is constant (amortized over many insertions); at any other position, the performance is logarithmic. Use this form when inserting many items that are already in the desired order.

The third version copies all the pairs in the range [first, last), which must be pointing to a different multimap object. If the items are already in the desired order, the performance is linear; otherwise, it is N log (size( ) + N), in which N is last − first.

key_compare **key_comp**( ) const

> Returns the comparator function pointer or object, which compares keys. The key_compare type is the same as the Compare template parameter. See also the value_comp member.

iterator **lower_bound**(const key_type& x)
const_iterator **lower_bound**(const key_type& x) const

> Returns an iterator that points to the first pair in the map that does not come before x. That is, if x is in the map, the iterator points to the position of its first occurrence; otherwise, the iterator points to the first position where x should be inserted. Performance is logarithmic.

size_type **max_size**( ) const

> Returns the largest number of pairs that can be in the map.

reverse_iterator **rbegin**( )
const_reverse_iterator **rbegin**( ) const

> Returns a reverse iterator that points to the last element of the map.

reverse_iterator **rend**( )
const_reverse_iterator **rend**( ) const

> Returns a reverse iterator that points to one position before the first element of the map.

size_type **size**( ) const

> Returns the number of pairs in the map.

void **swap**(multimap<Key,T,Compare,Alloc>&)

> Swaps the contents of the map with the contents of x.

iterator **upper_bound**(const key_type& x)
const_iterator **upper_bound**(const key_type& x) const

> Returns an iterator that points to the first pair in the map that comes after all occurrences of x. Performance is logarithmic.

value_compare **value_comp**( ) const

> Returns a value_compare object, which can be used to compare pairs. The value_compare object takes two value_type arguments and compares their keys, returning true if the first should come before the second in the map.

multimap<Key,T,Compare,Alloc>& **operator=**(const multimap<Key,T,Compare,Alloc>& x)

> Erases all the elements of the map and replaces them with copies of the elements of x.

See Also

map class template, multiset in <set>

operator== function template
Compares maps for equality

```
template <class Key, class T, class Comp, class Alloc>
bool operator==(const map<Key,T,Comp,Alloc>& x,
                const map<Key,T,Comp,Alloc>& y);
template <class Key, class T, class Comp, class Alloc>
bool operator==(const multimap<Key,T,Comp,Alloc>& x,
                const multimap<Key,T,Comp,Alloc>& y);
```

The == operator returns true if x and y have the same size and their elements are equal, that is, x.size( ) == y.size( ) && equals(x.begin( ), x.end( ), y.begin( )).

See Also
equals in <algorithm>

operator!= function template
Compares maps for inequality

```
template <class Key, class T, class Comp, class Alloc>
bool operator!=(const map<Key,T,Comp,Alloc>& x,
                const map<Key,T,Comp,Alloc>& y);
template <class Key, class T, class Comp, class Alloc>
bool operator!=(const multimap<Key,T,Comp,Alloc>& x,
                const multimap<Key,T,Comp,Alloc>& y);
```

The != operator is equivalent to ! (x == y).

operator< function template
Compares maps for less-than

```
template <class Key, class T, class Comp, class Alloc>
bool operator<(const map<Key,T,Comp,Alloc>& x,
               const map<Key,T,Comp,Alloc>& y);
template <class Key, class T, class Comp, class Alloc>
bool operator<(const multimap<Key,T,Comp,Alloc>& x,
               const multimap<Key,T,Comp,Alloc>& y);
```

The < operator determines whether x is less than y, using the same algorithm as lexicographical_compare(x.begin( ), x.end( ), y.begin( ), y.end( )).

See Also
lexicographical_compare in <algorithm>

operator<= function template
Compares maps for less-than-or-equal

```
template <class Key, class T, class Comp, class Alloc>
bool operator<=(const map<Key,T,Comp,Alloc>& x,
                const map<Key,T,Comp,Alloc>& y);
template <class Key, class T, class Comp, class Alloc>
bool operator<=(const multimap<Key,T,Comp,Alloc>& x,
                const multimap<Key,T,Comp,Alloc>& y);
```

The <= operator is equivalent to ! (y < x).

operator> function template

```
template <class Key, class T, class Comp, class Alloc>
bool operator>(const map<Key,T,Comp,Alloc>& x,
               const map<Key,T,Comp,Alloc>& y);
template <class Key, class T, class Comp, class Alloc>
bool operator>(const multimap<Key,T,Comp,Alloc>& x,
               const multimap<Key,T,Comp,Alloc>& y);
```

The > operator is equivalent to (y < x).

operator>= function template

```
template <class Key, class T, class Comp, class Alloc>
bool operator>=(const map<Key,T,Comp,Alloc>& x,
                const map<Key,T,Comp,Alloc>& y);
template <class Key, class T, class Comp, class Alloc>
bool operator>=(const multimap<Key,T,Comp,Alloc>& x,
                const multimap<Key,T,Comp,Alloc>& y);
```

The >= operator is equivalent to ! (x < y).

swap function template

```
template <class Key, class T, class Comp, class Alloc>
  void swap(map<Key,T,Comp,Alloc>& x, map<Key,T,Comp,Alloc>& y);
template <class Key, class T, class Comp, class Alloc>
  void swap(multimap<Key,T,Comp,Alloc>& x, multimap<Key,T,Comp,Alloc>& y);
```

The swap function template specialization is equivalent to calling x.swap(y).

See Also

swap in <algorithm>

<memory>

The <memory> header declares function and class templates for allocating and using memory, such as the auto_ptr<> smart pointer, algorithms for working with uninitialized memory, and a standard allocator for use with the standard containers.

The auto_ptr class template provides a simple ownership model for working with pointers. It can be extremely useful for writing exception-safe code. On the other hand, copying an auto_ptr<> object does not produce an exact copy (ownership of the pointer is transferred), so auto_ptr<> objects cannot be stored in standard containers.

Several functions work with uninitialized memory, which can be helpful when implementing a container. For example, an implementation of vector must allocate an uninitialized array of objects and initialize elements of the array as they are needed. The uninitialized_... functions can come in handy for that purpose.

The allocator class template manages memory allocation and deallocation and the construction and destruction of objects in the memory it manages. It is the default allocator for all the standard containers.

allocator class template

```
template <class T>
class allocator {
public:
  typedef size_t size_type;
  typedef ptrdiff_t difference_type;
  typedef T* pointer;
  typedef const T* const_pointer;
  typedef T& reference;
  typedef const T& const_reference;
  typedef T value_type;
  template <class U> struct rebind {
    typedef allocator<U> other;
  };
  allocator() throw();
  allocator(const allocator&) throw();
  template <class U> allocator(const allocator<U>&) throw();
  ~allocator() throw();
  pointer address(reference x) const;
  const_pointer address(const_reference x) const;
  pointer allocate(size_type, allocator<void>::const_pointer hint = 0);
  void deallocate(pointer p, size_type n);
  size_type max_size() const throw();
  void construct(pointer p, const T& val);
  void destroy(pointer p);
};
```

The allocator class template encapsulates basic allocation and deallocation functions. The standard containers rely on allocators for memory management and use allocator as the default allocator.

Most programmers do not need to use allocator, which offers few advantages over plain new and delete. However, if you want to write your own container, or provide a custom allocator for the standard containers, you should take the time to understand allocator.

Perhaps the easiest way to understand allocator is to take a look at a trivial implementation in Example 13-30. Note that a library might have a more complicated implementation to handle multithreading, improve performance, etc. Some libraries offer allocators for special purposes, such as allocating memory that can be shared among multiple processes. This particular implementation is just a sample.

Example 13-30. Sample allocator implementation

```
template<typename T>
class myallocator {
public:
  typedef std::size_t size_type;
  typedef std::ptrdiff_t difference_type;
  typedef T* pointer;
  typedef const T* const_pointer;
  typedef T& reference;
  typedef const T& const_reference;
  typedef T value_type;
```

Example 13-30. Sample allocator implementation (continued)

```
  template <class U> struct rebind {
    typedef myallocator<U> other;
  };
  myallocator( ) throw( )                         {}
  myallocator(const myallocator&) throw( )        {}
  template <class U>
  myallocator(const myallocator<U>&) throw( )     {}
  ~myallocator( ) throw( )                        {}
  pointer address(reference x) const              {return &x;}
  const_pointer address(const_reference x) const  {return &x;}
  pointer allocate(size_type n, void* hint = 0) {
    return static_cast<T*>(::operator new (n * sizeof(T)) );
  }
  void deallocate(pointer p, size_type n) {
    ::operator delete(static_cast<void*>(p));
  }
  size_type max_size( ) const throw( ) {
    return std::numeric_limits<size_type>::max( ) / sizeof(T);
  }
  void construct(pointer p, const T& val) {
    new(static_cast<void*>(p)) T(val);
  }
  void destroy(pointer p) {
    p->~T( );
  }
};

template<typename T>
bool operator==(const myallocator<T>&, const myallocator<T>&)
{
  return true;
}

template<typename T>
bool operator!=(const myallocator<T>&, const myallocator<T>&)
{
   return false;
}

template<>
class myallocator<void> {
public:
  typedef void* pointer;
  typedef const void* const_pointer;
  typedef void value_type;
  template <class U> struct rebind {
    typedef myallocator<U> other;
  };
};
```

The following are the members of allocator:

allocator( ) throw( )
allocator(const allocator&) throw( )
template<class U> **allocator**(const allocator<U>&) throw( )

> Constructs a new allocator object, possibly copying an existing allocator. Remember that all instances must be equivalent, so an allocator typically does not have any data members to initialize.

pointer **address**(reference x) const
const_pointer **address**(const_reference x) const

> Returns the address of x, that is, &x.

pointer **allocate**(size_type n, allocator<void>::const_pointer hint = 0)

> Calls the global new operator to allocate enough memory to hold n objects of type T. The hint argument must be 0 or a pointer obtained from a prior call to allocate that has not been passed to deallocate. The return value is a pointer to the newly allocated memory. If the memory cannot be allocated, bad_alloc is thrown.
>
> An implementation might use hint to improve performance.

typedef const T* **const_pointer**

> A type for a pointer to const. In a custom allocator, the type should be equivalent to const T*.

typedef const T& **const_reference**

> A type for a const lvalue. In a custom allocator, the type should be equivalent to const T&.

void **construct**(pointer p, const T& val)

> Calls the global new operator to construct an instance of T with value val using the memory that p points to. That is, it calls new(static_cast<void*>(p)) T(val).

void **deallocate**(pointer p, size_type n)

> Calls the global delete operator to free the memory that p points to. The n argument is the number of items of type T—the same value passed to allocate.

void **destroy**(pointer p)

> Calls the destructor for the object at address p. That is, it calls reinterpret_cast<T*>(p)->~T( ).

typedef ptrdiff_t **difference_type**

> A type that represents the difference of any two pointers that the allocator returns from allocate( ).

size_type **max_size**( ) const throw( )

> Returns the maximum size that can be passed to allocate.

typedef T* **pointer**

> A pointer type. In a custom allocator, the type should be equivalent to T*.

template <class U> struct **rebind**

> Binds the allocator object to a different value type. The rebind class has a single typedef, other, which is an instance of the same allocator template, but with U as the template parameter. The rebind template is necessary for standard containers that allocate helper objects, such as link nodes, rather than allocating values directly. If you are not implementing a standard container, you probably don't need to understand rebind.

typedef T& **reference**

> An lvalue type. In a custom allocator, the type should be equivalent to T&.

---

typedef size_t **size_type**
>   A type that can represent the size of the largest allocation request.

typedef T **value_type**
>   The type of allocated values, which is typically T.

See Also

allocator<void> class, <new>, new operator, delete operator

---

allocator<void> class
Specializes allocator for void pointers

```
template <> class allocator<void> {
public:
  typedef void* pointer;
  typedef const void* const_pointer;
  typedef void value_type;
  template <class U> struct rebind {
    typedef allocator<U> other;
  };
};
```

The allocator<void> specialization is necessary to represent pointers to void without permitting the allocation of objects of type void.

See Also

allocator class template

---

auto_ptr class template
Smart pointer to manage ownership of pointers

```
template <class T> struct auto_ptr_ref {};
template<class T>
class auto_ptr {
public:
  typedef T element_type;
  explicit auto_ptr(T* p = 0) throw();
  auto_ptr(auto_ptr&) throw();
  template<class U> auto_ptr(auto_ptr<U>&) throw();
  auto_ptr(auto_ptr_ref<T>) throw();
  ~auto_ptr() throw();
  auto_ptr& operator=(auto_ptr&) throw();
  template<class U>
  auto_ptr& operator=(auto_ptr<U>&) throw();
  auto_ptr& operator=(auto_ptr_ref<T> r) throw();

  T& operator*() const throw();
  T* operator->() const throw();
  T* get() const throw();
  T* release() throw();
  void reset(T* p = 0) throw();

  template<class U> operator auto_ptr_ref<U>() throw();
  template<class U> operator auto_ptr<U>() throw();
};
```

The auto_ptr class template implements a smart pointer to manage ownership of pointers. Proper use of auto_ptr ensures that a pointer has exactly one owner (which prevents accidental double deletes), and the owner automatically frees the memory when the owner goes out of scope (which prevents memory leaks). Assignment of auto_ptr values transfers ownership from the source to the target of the assignment.

The auto_ptr_ref type holds a reference to an auto_ptr. Implicit conversions between auto_ptr and auto_ptr_ref facilitate the return of auto_ptr objects from functions. Usually, you can ignore the auto_ptr_ref type and let the implicit conversions handle the details for you. All you need to do is use auto_ptr as a return type. The details of auto_ptr_ref are implementation-defined.

Some of the typical uses for auto_ptr are:

Data members

> Data members of pointer type that point to dynamically allocated objects are prime candidates for auto_ptr, which ensures that the memory is properly freed when the owning object is destroyed. Be sure to implement a copy constructor and assignment operator for any class that uses auto_ptr<> for its data members.

Local variables

> If a function must dynamically allocate a temporary object, store the pointer in an auto_ptr variable. When the function returns (normally or as the result of an exception), the object is destroyed automatically. This can drastically reduce the need for try-catch statements.

Transferring ownership

> In a complex program, objects are frequently allocated in one part of the program and freed in another. It can be difficult to keep track of when it is safe or proper to free an object. Using auto_ptr, you can safely ensure that each object has exactly one owner, and ownership is properly passed via assignment and function calls. When the object is no longer needed, it is freed automatically.

Because you cannot simply copy or assign an auto_ptr, you cannot use auto_ptr objects in a standard container. Another limitation is that auto_ptr cannot hold a pointer to an array. Allocating and freeing a single object (e.g., new int) is different from allocating and freeing an array of objects, (e.g., new int[42]), and auto_ptr is designed to work only with single objects.

 A useful guideline is that a program should avoid bare pointers (e.g., int* x). Bare pointers are error-prone: they are subject to memory leaks, double-freeing, and dangling references. Instead, use some form of ownership, such as auto_ptr<>, or one of the Boost smart pointers.

The Boost project has additional smart-pointer class templates that permit copying, arrays, and shared ownership. See Appendix B for more information about Boost.

Example 13-31 shows some uses of auto_ptr.

Example 13-31. Sample uses of auto_ptr

```
class brush { ... };
class pen { ... };

// A function can return an auto_ptr<> object.
std::auto_ptr<brush> default_brush( )
```

Example 13-31. Sample uses of auto_ptr (continued)

```
{
  return std::auto_ptr<brush>(new brush);
}

class DisplayContext {
  // Display or graphics context for drawing on a window.
public:
  DisplayContext()
  : brush_(default_brush()), pen_(new pen) {...}
  ...
private:
  // Make sure caller never tries to copy or assign
  // DisplayContext, but uses only objects that are
  // managed by auto_ptr<>.
  DisplayContext(const DisplayContext& dc);
  DisplayContext& operator=(const DisplayContext& dc);
  // Automatically manage lifetime of the pen and brush.
  // When the DisplayContext is freed, so are the pen
  // and brush instances.
  std::auto_ptr<brush> brush_;
  std::auto_ptr<pen>   pen_;
};

void repaint()
{
  // Allocate a new display context. Use auto_ptr to ensure
  // that it will be freed automatically.
  std::auto_ptr<DisplayContext> dc(new DisplayContext());
  // Draw stuff on the display context.
  dc->draw(...);
  // No need to call release; the display context is
  // automatically released when repaint() returns.
}

int main()
{
  std::auto_ptr<DisplayContext> dc1(new DisplayContext);
  std::auto_ptr<DisplayContext> dc2(dc1);

  dc1 = dc2;
  repaint();
}
```

The following are the members of auto_ptr:

explicit **auto_ptr**(T* p = 0) throw()
> Initializes the auto_ptr object to own the pointer p.

auto_ptr(auto_ptr& x) throw()
template<class U> **auto_ptr**(auto_ptr<U>& x) throw()
> Initializes the auto_ptr object with the pointer returned from x.release(). In the second version, the type U* must be implicitly convertible to T*. Note that x is not

const. It is not possible to copy a const auto_ptr because to do so would break the ownership rules.

auto_ptr(auto_ptr_ref<T> r) throw( )
>   Initializes the auto_ptr object with the pointer obtained from calling release on r's auto_ptr.

~auto_ptr( ) throw( )
>   Deletes the owned pointer (e.g., delete get( )).

T* **get**( ) const throw( )
>   Returns the owned pointer.

T* **release**( ) throw( )
>   Returns get( ) and resets the owned pointer to 0.

void **reset**(T* p = 0) throw( )
>   Deletes the owned pointer (if it is not equal to p) and saves p as the new owned pointer.

template<class U> **operator auto_ptr_ref<U>**( ) throw( )
>   Returns a temporary auto_ptr_ref object that owns the pointer. The pointer must be convertible to U*. Ownership is released and transferred to the new auto_ptr_ref object.

template<class U> **operator auto_ptr<U>**( ) throw( )
>   Returns a new auto_ptr object. The owned pointer is converted to type U*, and ownership is transferred to the new auto_ptr object.

auto_ptr& **operator=**(auto_ptr& x) throw( )
template<class U>
auto_ptr& **operator=**(auto_ptr<U>& x) throw( )
auto_ptr& **operator=**(auto_ptr_ref<T> r) throw( )
>   Transfers ownership of the pointer that is owned by x or by the auto_ptr object held by r to *this. That is, it calls reset(x.release( )).

T& **operator***( ) const throw( )
>   Returns *get( ). If the owned pointer is a null pointer, the behavior is undefined.

T* **operator**->( ) const throw( )
>   Returns get( ).

See Also

new operator

---

get_temporary_buffer function template   Allocates temporary memory buffer

```
template <class T>
pair<T*, ptrdiff_t> get_temporary_buffer(ptrdiff_t n);
```

The get_temporary_buffer function template allocates memory for temporary use. The request is for up to n adjacent objects of type T. The return value is a pair of the pointer to the newly allocated memory and the actual size of the memory allocated (in units of sizeof(T)). If the memory cannot be allocated, the return value is a pair of 0s. The allocated memory must be freed by calling return_temporary_buffer. The temporary buffer is uninitialized.

This function has limited usefulness. You must test the return value to see how much memory was allocated and ensure that the memory is properly freed if an exception is thrown. It is usually simpler to call new and save the pointer in an auto_ptr<>.

See Also

auto_ptr class template, return_temporary_buffer function template, pair in <utility>

---

operator== function template

```
template <class T1, class T2>
bool operator==(const allocator<T1>&, const allocator<T2>&)
  throw( );
```

The operator== function template always returns true. In other words, any object of type allocator is considered to be the same as every other allocator.

See Also

allocator class template

---

operator!= function template

```
template <class T1, class T2>
bool operator!=(const allocator<T1>&, const allocator<T2>&)
  throw( );
```

The operator!= function template always returns false. In other words, any object of type allocator is considered to be the same as every other allocator.

See Also

allocator class template

---

raw_storage_iterator class template

```
template <class OutputIterator, class T>
class raw_storage_iterator :
  public iterator<output_iterator_tag,void,void,void,void> {
public:
  explicit raw_storage_iterator(OutputIterator x);
  raw_storage_iterator<OutputIterator,T>& operator*( );
  raw_storage_iterator<OutputIterator,T>&
    operator=(const T& element);
  raw_storage_iterator<OutputIterator,T>& operator++( );
  raw_storage_iterator<OutputIterator,T> operator++(int);
};
```

The raw_storage_iterator class template implements an output iterator that writes to uninitialized memory. It adapts another output iterator that must have operator& return a pointer to T. The adapted iterator is typically used as a pointer to uninitialized memory.

Use the raw_storage_iterator as you would any other output iterator.

See Also

uninitialized_copy function template, uninitialized_fill function template, uninitialized_fill_n function template, <iterator>

return_temporary_buffer function template   Frees temporary memory buffer

```
template <class T>
void return_temporary_buffer(T* p);
```

The return_temporary_buffer function reclaims the memory that was previously allocated by get_temporary_buffer.

See Also

get_temporary_buffer function template

---

uninitialized_copy function template   Copies into uninitialized memory

```
template <class InputIter, class FwdIter>
FwdIter uninitialized_copy(InputIter first, InputIter last, FwdIter result);
```

The uninitialized_copy function template is like the copy algorithm, except the result iterator is assumed to point to uninitialized memory. The range [first, last) is copied to result using placement new.

See Also

raw_storage_iterator class template, uninitialized_fill function template, copy in <algorithm>, new operator

---

uninitialized_fill function template   Fills uninitialized memory

```
template <class FwdIter, class T>
void uninitialized_fill(FwdIter first, FwdIter last, const T& x);
```

The uninitialized_fill function template is like the fill algorithm, except that it fills uninitialized memory. Every item in the range [first, last) is constructed as a copy of x using placement new.

See Also

raw_storage_iterator class template, uninitialized_copy function template, uninitialized_fill_n function template, fill in <algorithm>, new keyword

---

uninitialized_fill_n function template   Fills uninitialized memory

```
template <class FwdIter, class Size, class T>
void uninitialized_fill_n(FwdIter first, Size n, const T& x);
```

The uninitialized_fill_n function template is like the fill_n algorithm, except it fills uninitialized memory. Starting with first, n copies of x are constructed using placement new.

See Also

raw_storage_iterator class template, uninitialized_fill function template, fill_n in <algorithm>, new keyword

---

<new>

The <new> header declares types and functions related to dynamic memory management. (See Chapter 3 for more information about the new and delete expressions, including placement new and delete, and the operator new and operator delete functions.) Most programs do not need to use <new>. The header is typically used by libraries and programs that implement their own operator new and operator delete functions or otherwise provide custom management of dynamic memory.

If a source file uses the standard new and delete expressions, it does not need to #include <new>. You can also use the pointer placement new without including this header. In order to use the nothrow placement new, or catch bad_alloc, you must include this header.

Most programs do not call the operators directly, but instead use new and delete expressions, and the compiler generates calls using the appropriate operators. Library implementors sometimes make direct calls to the operators, especially to allocate uninitialized memory. See <memory> earlier in this chapter for examples.

Some specialized applications might implement the global operator new and operator delete functions or provide additional overloaded operators for specialized circumstances, such as allocating memory that is shared across process boundaries. If you write your own operator new, you should obey the following guidelines:

- Implement operator new and operator new[ ].

- Implement operator delete and operator delete[ ]. Even if your operator new is a placement new function, you should have a corresponding placement delete function (which is called if a new expression throws an exception).

- Return a pointer that meets the strictest alignment requirements of any type. (Note that malloc in <cstdlib> and the standard operator new function return aligned pointers.)

- Handle out-of-memory situations by throwing bad_alloc (or a class that derives from bad_alloc) or returning a null pointer. If you return a null pointer, your operator new function must have an empty exception specification.

- If operator new and operator delete are member functions, include the static keyword as a reminder to the human reader. The compiler always treats these functions as static, even if you omit the keyword.

Example 13-32 shows a trivial implementation of the global operator new and operator delete functions.

Example 13-32. Implementing operator new and operator delete with malloc and free

```
#include <cstdlib>
#include <new>

void* operator new(std::size_t size) throw(std::bad_alloc)
{
  void* ptr = std::malloc(size);
  if (ptr == 0)
    throw std::bad_alloc( );
  return ptr;
}
```

Example 13-32. Implementing operator new and operator delete with malloc and free (continued)

```
void* operator new(std::size_t size, const std::nothrow_t&)
throw( )
{
  return std::malloc(size);
}

void* operator new[](std::size_t size) throw(std::bad_alloc)
{
  return operator new(size);
}

void* operator new[](std::size_t size, const std::nothrow_t&)
throw( )
{
  return operator new(size, std::nothrow);
}

void operator delete(void* ptr) throw( )
{
  std::free(ptr);
}

void operator delete(void* ptr, const std::nothrow_t&)
throw( )
{
  std::free(ptr);
}

void operator delete[](void* ptr) throw( )
{
  operator delete(ptr);
}

void operator delete[](void* ptr, const std::nothrow_t&)
throw( )
{
  operator delete(ptr);
}
```

bad_alloc class

Exception class for failed memory allocation

```
class bad_alloc : public exception {
public:
  bad_alloc( ) throw( );
  bad_alloc(const bad_alloc&) throw( );
  bad_alloc& operator=(const bad_alloc&) throw( );
  virtual ~bad_alloc( ) throw( );
  virtual const char* what( ) const throw( );
};
```

The bad_alloc class is an exception class that is thrown when operator new is unable to fulfill a request to allocate memory. As with any of the standard exception classes, what( ) returns an implementation-defined character string.

See Also

operator new, set_new_handler, exception in <exception>

---

nothrow object
Requests null pointer return when out of memory

```
struct nothrow_t {};
extern const nothrow_t nothrow;
```

The nothrow object is used in placement new expressions to request that the new operator return a null pointer instead of throwing bad_alloc if the memory allocation request cannot be fulfilled.

The nothrow_t type does not do anything; it is used only in overloaded placement new and delete operators.

Note that nothrow is also accepted by overloaded operator delete for symmetry with new. The nothrow version of operator delete behaves just like the ordinary operator delete. Like any placement delete function, it is called only if the placement new expression throws an exception.

See Also

operator delete, operator new

---

operator delete
Global operator delete

```
void operator delete(void* ptr) throw( );
void operator delete[](void* ptr) throw( );
void operator delete(void* ptr, const std::nothrow_t&) throw( );
void operator delete[](void* ptr, const std::nothrow_t&) throw( );
void operator delete(void* ptr, void*) throw( );
void operator delete[](void* ptr, void*) throw( );
```

The global operator delete function is called from a delete expression to free memory. The memory, which ptr points to, must have been returned by a corresponding call to operator new or be a null pointer. You must not call operator delete more than once for the same pointer. If ptr is null, operator delete returns without doing anything.

The first two versions of operator delete free the memory that ptr points to, which must have been allocated by calling the plain form of operator new. These forms of operator delete are called from a delete expression. The first is called for a scalar delete, and the second is called for an array delete[].

The remaining forms are called only when the corresponding placement new expression throws an exception during construction. The nothrow functions free the memory that ptr points to. The last two forms do nothing. See the new expression in Chapter 3 to learn how and when placement operator delete is called.

Unlike other identifiers in the standard library, operator delete is global and is not in the std namespace. Also, unlike with other functions in the standard library, you can provide your own implementation of operator delete, which replaces the standard implementation. You cannot, however, replace the last two versions of delete with your own implementation.

Library Reference

See Also

operator new

---

operator new   Global operator new

```
void* operator new(std::size_t size) throw(std::bad_alloc);
void* operator new(std::size_t size, const std::nothrow_t&) throw( );
void* operator new[](std::size_t size) throw(std::bad_alloc);
void* operator new[](std::size_t size, const std::nothrow_t&) throw( );
void* operator new(std::size_t size, void* ptr) throw( );
void* operator new[](std::size_t size, void* ptr) throw( );
```

The global operator new function allocates memory and returns a pointer to the newly allocated memory. The memory must later be released by a corresponding delete expression or an explicit call to operator delete.

The first version of new allocates at least size bytes of memory, suitably aligned to store any type, and returns a pointer to the memory. If the request cannot be fulfilled, it throws bad_alloc.

The second version is like the first, but it returns a null pointer instead of throwing bad_alloc if sufficient memory cannot be allocated.

The third version is like the first, but it allocates memory for storing an array of objects. It might allocate more than size bytes to permit the library to store additional bookkeeping information. You must use the array form of delete[] to free this memory.

The fourth version is like the third, but it returns a null pointer instead of throwing bad_alloc if sufficient memory cannot be allocated.

To allocate memory, the operator new functions first try to allocate size bytes. If they cannot, they call the handler function set by the most recent call to set_new_handler. Then they try again to allocate size bytes. This loop repeats until the request is fulfilled or the handler function fails to return. The nothrow versions of the function return 0 if the most recent call to set_new_handler was a null pointer or if the new handler function throws bad_alloc.

The final two versions do nothing except return ptr. These forms permit placement new expressions to specify a memory location where an object will be constructed.

Unlike other identifiers in the standard library, operator new is global and is not in the std namespace. Also, unlike with other functions in the standard library, you can provide your own implementation of operator new, which replaces the standard implementation. You cannot, however, replace the last two versions of new with your own implementation.

See Also

nothrow object, operator delete, set_new_handler function

---

set_new_handler function   Sets handler for obtaining memory

```
typedef void (*new_handler)( );
new_handler set_new_handler(new_handler new_p) throw( );
```

The set_new_handler function stores a function pointer for a function that obtains additional memory from the operating system for use by the new operator. When the default operator new is unable to fulfill a request to allocate memory, it calls the

---

handler that was set by the most recent call to set_new_handler. This handler must do one of the following:

- Obtain more memory from the host environment
- Throw bad_alloc (or a type that derives from bad_alloc)
- Call abort( ) or exit( ) to halt the program

The return value is the pointer to the previous handler, or 0 for the first call to set_new_handler.

<numeric>

The <numeric> header declares several function templates for numerical algorithms. See <algorithm> earlier in this chapter for most of the standard algorithms. See <cmath> for math functions that operate on scalar quantities. The <functional> section contains the standard functors, which might be useful when calling the numeric algorithms.

Refer to Chapter 10 for general information about algorithms and iterators. See Appendix B for information about other libraries that provide additional numeric functions.

accumulate function template   Computes a value from all items in a range

```
template <typename InputIter, typename T>
T accumulate(InputIter first, InputIter last, T init);
template < typename InputIter, typename T, typename BinaryOp>
T accumulate(InputIter first, InputIter last, T init, BinaryOp binary_op);
```

The accumulate function template sums all the values in the range [first, last) added with init and returns the result. The result and intermediate sum have the same type as init. The second version calls binary_op instead of using the addition (+) operator.

Technical Notes

The result is computed as follows: for each i in the range [*first*, *last*), *tmp* = binary_op(*tmp*, **i*), in which *tmp* is initialized to *init*. The final value of *tmp* is returned.

The binary_op function or functor must not have any side effects.

Complexity is linear: binary_op is called exactly *last* − *first* times.

adjacent_difference function template   Computes differences of adjacent elements in a range

```
template <typename InIter, typename OutIter>
OutIter adjacent_difference(InIter first, InIter last, OutIter result);
template <typename InIter, typename OutIter, typename BinOp>
OutIter adjacent_difference(InIter first, InIter last, OutIter result,
                            BinOp binary_op);
```

The adjacent_difference function computes the differences of adjacent elements in the range [first, last) and assigns those differences to the output range starting at result. The second version calls binary_op instead of using the subtraction (-) operator.

Technical Notes

For each i in [$first + 1$, $last$) and j in [$result$, $result + (last - first)$), assign $*j = *i - tmp$, in which tmp is initially $*first$; it becomes $*i$ after each assignment to $*j$.

The return value is the result iterator pointing to one past the last element written.

The binary_op function or functor must not have any side effects. The result iterator can be the same as first.

Complexity is linear: binary_op is called exactly $last - first - 1$ times.

---

inner_product function template
Computes inner product of two ranges

```
template <typename InIter1, typename InIter2, typename T>
T inner_product(InIter1 first1, InIter1 last1, InIter2 first2, T init);
template <typename InIter1, typename InIter2, typename T,
         typename BinaryOp1, typename BinaryOp2>
T inner_product(InIter1 first1, InIter1 last1, InIter2 first2, T init,
                BinaryOp1 binary_op1, BinaryOp2 binary_op2);
```

The inner_product function template computes an inner product of two ranges. It accumulates the products of corresponding items in [first1, last1) and [first2, last2), in which last2 = first2 + (last1 − first1). The second version calls binary_op1 as the accumulator operator (instead of addition) and binary_op2 as the multiplication operator.

Technical Notes

The result is computed as follows: for each i in the range [$first1$, $last1$), and for each j in [$first2$, $last2$), in which $last2 = first2 + (last1 - first1)$, assign tmp = binary_op1(tmp, binary_op2($*i$, $*j$)), in which tmp is initialized to $init$. The final value of tmp is returned.

The binary_op1 and binary_op2 functions or functors must not have side effects.

Complexity is linear: binary_op1 and binary_op2 are called exactly $last - first$ times.

See Also

accumulate function template

---

partial_sum function template
Compute sums of subranges in a range

```
template <typename InIter, typename OutIter>
OutIter partial_sum(InIter first, InIter last, OutIter result);
template <typename InIter, typename OutIter, typename BinOp>
OutIter partial_sum(InIter first, InIter last, OutIter result, BinOp binary_op);
```

The partial_sum function template assigns partial sums to the range that starts at result. The partial sums are computed by accumulating successively larger subranges of [first, last). Thus, the first result item is *first, the second is *first + *(first + 1), and so on. The second version calls binary_op instead of using the addition operator (+).

Technical Notes

For each i in [$first$, $last$), assign $*(result + k) = sum(first, i)$, in which $k = i - first$, and $sum(a, b)$ computes the sum in the manner of accumulate($a + 1$, b, $*a$, binary_op).

The return value is the result iterator, pointing to one past the last item written.

The `binary_op` function or functor must not have any side effects. The `result` iterator can be the same as `first`.

Complexity is linear: binary_op is called exactly $(last - first) - 1$ times.

<ostream>

The <ostream> header declares the output stream class template, specializations, and manipulators.

See <fstream> for derived classes that write to files and <sstream> for derived classes that write to strings. See <ios> for the base-class declarations. See <string> for information about the char_traits template. Refer to Chapter 9 for general information about I/O.

basic_ostream class template

```
template <class charT, class traits = char_traits<charT> >
class basic_ostream : virtual public basic_ios<charT,traits>
{
public:
  // Types (inherited from basic_ios)
  typedef charT char_type;
  typedef typename traits::int_type int_type;
  typedef typename traits::pos_type pos_type;
  typedef typename traits::off_type off_type;
  typedef traits traits_type;

  explicit basic_ostream(basic_streambuf<charT,traits>* sb);
  virtual ~basic_ostream( );

  class sentry;

  // Formatted output
  basic_ostream<charT,traits>& operator<<(basic_ostream<charT,traits>&
    (*pf)(basic_ostream<charT,traits>&));
  basic_ostream<charT,traits>& operator<<(basic_ios<charT,traits>&
    (*pf)(basic_ios<charT,traits>&));
  basic_ostream<charT,traits>& operator<<(ios_base&(*pf)(ios_base&));
  basic_ostream<charT,traits>& operator<<(bool n);
  basic_ostream<charT,traits>& operator<<(short n);
  basic_ostream<charT,traits>& operator<<(unsigned short n);
  basic_ostream<charT,traits>& operator<<(int n);
  basic_ostream<charT,traits>& operator<<(unsigned int n);
  basic_ostream<charT,traits>& operator<<(long n);
  basic_ostream<charT,traits>& operator<<(unsigned long n);
  basic_ostream<charT,traits>& operator<<(float f);
  basic_ostream<charT,traits>& operator<<(double f);
  basic_ostream<charT,traits>& operator<<(long double f);
  basic_ostream<charT,traits>& operator<<(const void* p);
```

```
basic_ostream<charT,traits>& operator<<
  (basic_streambuf<char_type,traits>* sb);
// Unformatted output
basic_ostream<charT,traits>& put(char_type c);
basic_ostream<charT,traits>& write(const char_type* s, streamsize n);
basic_ostream<charT,traits>& flush( );

pos_type tellp( );
basic_ostream<charT,traits>& seekp(pos_type);
basic_ostream<charT,traits>& seekp(off_type, ios_base::seekdir);
};
```

The basic_ostream class template is the base for all output streams. It declares members for writing to streams and for managing streams. The act of writing to a stream is also known as *inserting* to the stream.

All writes go through a stream buffer, which provides low-level access to the stream data. (See the sputc function for basic_streambuf in the <streambuf> header.) If the stream buffer object throws an exception, the stream sets badbit.

Before performing an output operation (e.g., operator<<, put, or write), a stream constructs a sentry object. If the sentry evaluates to true, the write operation continues. If the write throws an exception, badbit is set. The sentry object is destroyed before the output function returns. See basic_ostream::sentry later in this section for more information.

When an output operation throws an exception, the stream sets badbit. If badbit is set in the exceptions( ) mask, the stream does not throw ios_base::failure, but instead rethrows the original exception.

The following are the basic_ostream member functions:

explicit **basic_ostream**(basic_streambuf<char_type,traits>* sb)
> Constructs a basic_ostream object and then initializes it by calling init(sb).

virtual **~basic_ostream**( )
> Destroys the basic_ostream object without calling any functions of the stream buffer. Derived classes that might have buffered, unflushed data must take appropriate action to ensure that the buffer is flushed before the stream object is destroyed.

basic_ostream<charT,traits>& **flush**( )
> Flushes the output buffer. If rdbuf( ) is not null, flush calls rdbuf( )->pubsync( ). If pubsync returns -1, flush sets badbit. The return value is *this.

basic_ostream<charT,traits>& **put**(char_type c)
> Writes a single character c. If the write fails, put sets badbit. The return value is *this.

basic_ostream<charT,traits>& **seekp**(pos_type pos)
basic_ostream<charT,traits>& **seekp**(off_type off, ios_base::seekdir dir)
> Tries to seek to a new position in the stream. The first form specifies the position explicitly; the second form specifies the new position as an offset from a known position (start-of-file, current position, or end-of-file). If fail( ) is false, seekp calls rdbuf( )->pubseekoff(pos) or rdbuf( )->pubseekoff(off, dir). If fail( ) is true, seekp does nothing. The return value is *this.

pos_type **tellp**( )

> Returns the current position in the stream. If fail( ) is true, the return value is
> pos_type(-1); otherwise, the return value is rdbuf( )->pubseekoff(0,ios_
> base::cur,ios_base::out).

basic_ostream<charT,traits>& **write**(const char_type* s, streamsize n)

> Writes n characters from s. If the output fails after any character, write sets badbit
> and stops writing. The return value is *this.

basic_ostream<charT,traits>& **operator<<**
  (basic_ostream<charT,traits>& (*pf)(basic_ostream<charT,traits>&))

> Calls pf(*this) and returns *this. See endl later in this section for an example of
> a manipulator that uses this operator.

basic_ostream<charT,traits>& **operator<<**
  (basic_ios<charT,traits>& (*pf)(basic_ios<charT,traits>&))
basic_ostream<charT,traits>& **operator<<**(ios_base& (*pf)(ios_base&))

> Calls pf(*this) and returns *this. See the dec function in <ios> for an example of
> a manipulator that uses this operator.

basic_ostream<charT,traits>& **operator<<**(bool n)
basic_ostream<charT,traits>& **operator<<**(short n)
basic_ostream<charT,traits>& **operator<<** (unsigned short n)
basic_ostream<charT,traits>& **operator<<**(int n)
basic_ostream<charT,traits>& **operator<<** (unsigned int n)
basic_ostream<charT,traits>& **operator<<**(long n)
basic_ostream<charT,traits>& **operator<<** (unsigned long n)
basic_ostream<charT,traits>& **operator<<**(float f)
basic_ostream<charT,traits>& **operator<<**(double f)
basic_ostream<charT,traits>& **operator<<**(long double f)
basic_ostream<charT,traits>& **operator<<**(const void* p)

> Formats a value and writes the formatted characters to the output stream. These
> functions start by creating a sentry object; they then use the num_put facet of the
> stream's imbued locale as shown in Example 13-33. If the formatting fails,
> failbit is set. If an exception is thrown, badbit is set. See the <locale> header for
> information about num_put and locales.

> *Example 13-33. Using the num_put facet to format output*

```
typedef
    std::num_put<char_type,
    std::ostreambuf_iterator<char_type, traits_type> >
  numput;
std::ostreambuf_iterator<char_type, traits_type> iter =
  std::use_facet<numput>(getloc( )).(*this,*this,fill( ),val);
if (iter.failed( ))
  setstate(ios_base::badbit);
```

basic_ostream<charT,traits>& **operator<<**(basic_streambuf<char_type,traits>* sb)

> Writes characters from the stream buffer sb. If sb is null, badbit is set. Otherwise,
> characters are read from sb and written to *this until one of the following
> happens:

> - The end-of-file is reached on sb
> - Writing fails (badbit is set)
> - An exception is thrown when reading from sb (failbit is set)

If no characters are written, failbit is set.

See Also

ostream class, wostream class, iostream in <istream>

---

basic_ostream::sentry class
Sentry class for output streams

```
template <class charT,class traits = char_traits<charT> >
class basic_ostream<charT,traits>::sentry {
public:
  explicit sentry(basic_ostream<charT,traits>& os);
  ~sentry();
  operator bool() const;
private:
  sentry(const sentry&);              // Not defined
  sentry& operator=(const sentry&);   // Not defined
};
```

A basic_ostream object constructs a temporary sentry object prior to each output operation. The sentry object is destroyed when the output operation finishes and the function returns. The sentry manages tied streams and unit buffering.

The stream passes itself to the sentry's constructor. If stream.good() is true, the sentry first flushes any tied stream. That is, if stream.tie() is not null, the sentry calls stream.tie()->flush().

If sentry preparation fails, badbit is set.

The sentry destructor flushes the buffer if the unitbuf flag is on and the output function did not throw an exception:

```
if ((os.flags() & ios_base::unitbuf) && !uncaught_exception())
  os.flush();
```

See Also

basic_ostream class template, basic_ios in <ios>

---

endl function template
Manipulator to write an end-of-line character

```
template <class charT, class traits>
basic_ostream<charT,traits>& endl(basic_ostream<charT,traits>& os);
```

The endl function template is a manipulator that writes a newline to os and then calls os.flush():

```
std::cout << "Hello, world." << std::endl;
```

If you do not need to flush the output stream, do not use endl; write a plain '\n' character instead. If you feel you need to flush the output stream after finishing a line of output, consider using unit buffering for the stream, or if you need to flush the output prior to reading an input stream, you can tie the streams instead of using endl. See the basic_ios class template (in <ios>) for information about tied streams and the ios_base class (also in <ios>) for information about unit buffering.

See Also

basic_ios in <ios>, ios_base::fmtflags in <ios>

ends function template
Manipulator to write an end-of-string character

```
template <class charT, class traits>
basic_ostream<charT,traits>& ends(basic_ostream<charT,traits>& os);
```

The ends function template is a manipulator that writes a null character (defined by charT( )) to os to mark the end of a string. Typically, ends is used only when writing to a character array stream, that is, ostrstream:

```
std::ostrstream out1;
out1 << "Hi" << std::ends; // out1.str( ) has length 2.
```

See Also

<strstream>

flush function template
Manipulator to flush output buffer

```
template <class charT, class traits>
basic_ostream<charT,traits>& flush(basic_ostream<charT,traits>& os);
```

The flush function template is a manipulator that calls os.flush:

```
std::cout << "This is important!" << std::flush;
```

See Also

basic_ostream class template

operator<< function template
Character output operator

```
template<class charT, class traits>
basic_ostream<charT,traits>&
  operator<<(basic_ostream<charT,traits>& out, charT c);
template<class charT, class traits>
basic_ostream<charT,traits>&
  operator<<(basic_ostream<charT,traits>& out, char c);
template<class traits>
basic_ostream<char,traits>&
  operator<<(basic_ostream<char,traits>& out, char c);
template<class traits>
basic_ostream<char,traits>&
  operator<<(basic_ostream<char,traits>& out, signed char c);
template<class traits>
basic_ostream<char,traits>& operator<<(basic_ostream<char,traits>& out,
                                       unsigned char c);
template<class charT, class traits>
basic_ostream<charT,traits>& operator<<(basic_ostream<charT,traits>& out,
                                        const charT* s);
template<class charT, class traits>
basic_ostream<charT,traits>& operator<<(basic_ostream<charT,traits>& out,
                                        const char* s);
template<class traits>
basic_ostream<char,traits>&
  operator<<(basic_ostream<char,traits>& out, const char* s);
template<class traits>
basic_ostream<char,traits>& operator<<(basic_ostream<char,traits>& out,
                                       const signed char* s);
```

Library Reference

```
template<class traits>
basic_ostream<char,traits>& operator<<(basic_ostream<char,traits>& out,
                                       const unsigned char* s);
```

The << operator writes a single character c, or a character string s, to the output stream out. As with other formatted output functions, a sentry object is created, and the character or string is written with appropriate padding. Each character is converted to the stream's character type by calling widen. Finally, width(0) is called.

See Also

basic_ostream class template, basic_ostream::sentry class

---

ostream class   Output stream

```
typedef basic_ostream<char> ostream;
```

The ostream class specializes basic_ostream for the char type.

See Also

basic_ostream class template, wostream class, iostream in <istream>

---

wostream class   Wide output stream

```
typedef basic_ostream<wchar_t> wostream;
```

The wostream class specializes basic_ostream for the wchar_t type.

See Also

basic_ostream class template, ostream class, wiostream in <istream>

<queue>

The <queue> header declares the queue and priority_queue container adapters. These class templates are not containers in their own rights, but they adapt containers to present the behavior of a queue or priority queue.

A *queue* is a sequence of items that supports insertion at one end and removal from the other end. Because the first item inserted into a queue is the first item removed, a queue is sometimes called a FIFO (first-in, first-out) container.

Instead of preserving FIFO order, a *priority queue* maintains heap order, which ensures that the largest item is always first. In strict C++ terms, the first item in a priority queue is not less than any other item in the queue. This is called the "largest" item, but you can also think of it as the most important item or the one with the highest priority.

See Chapter 10 for information about containers.

---

operator== function template   Compares queues for equalilty

```
template <typename T, typename Container>
bool operator==(const queue<T, Container>& x, const queue<T, Container>& y);
```

The == operator compares two queues for equality by comparing the adapted containers (e.g., the return value is x.c == y.c).

---

operator!= function template

```
template <typename T, typename Container>
bool operator!=(const queue<T, Container>& x, const queue<T, Container>& y);
```

The != operator compares two queues for inequality by comparing the adapted containers (e.g., the return value is x.c != y.c).

operator< function template

```
template <typename T, typename Container>
bool operator<(const queue<T, Container>& x, const queue<T, Container>& y);
```

The < operator compares two queues by comparing the adapted containers (e.g., the return value is x.c < y.c).

operator<= function template

```
template <typename T, typename Container>
bool operator<=(const queue<T, Container>& x, const queue<T, Container>& y);
```

The <= operator compares two queues by comparing the adapted containers (e.g., the return value is x.c <= y.c).

operator> function template

```
template <typename T, typename Container>
bool operator>(const queue<T, Container>& x, const queue<T, Container>& y);
```

The > operator compares two queues by comparing the adapted containers (e.g., the return value is x.c >= y.c).

operator>= function template

```
template <typename T, typename Container>
bool operator>=(const queue<T, Container>& x, const queue<T, Container>& y);
```

The >= operator compares two queues by comparing the adapted containers (e.g., the return value is x.c >= y.c).

priority_queue class template

```
template <typename T, typename Container = vector<T>,
          typename Compare = less<typename Container::value_type> >
class priority_queue {
public:
  typedef typename Container::value_type value_type;
  typedef typename Container::size_type size_type;
  typedef Container container_type;

  explicit priority_queue(const Compare& x = Compare(),
                          const Container& = Container());
  template <class InputIterator>
  priority_queue(InputIterator first, InputIterator last,
                 const Compare& x = Compare(),
                 const Container& = Container());
```

```
    bool empty( ) const { return c.empty( ); }
    size_type size( ) const { return c.size( ); }
    const value_type& top( ) const { return c.front( ); }
    void push(const value_type& x);
    void pop( );
protected:
    Container c;
    Compare comp;
};
```

The priority_queue class template is an adapter for any sequence container that supports random access, such as deque and vector. (The default is vector.) The priority queue keeps its elements in heap order, so it requires a comparator (the Compare template parameter).

Because priority_queue is not itself a standard container, it cannot be used with the standard algorithms. (In particular, note the lack of begin and end member functions.) Thus, the priority_queue adapter is useful only for simple needs.

Unlike queue, priority_queue has no comparison operators.

Most of the members of priority_queue are straightforward mappings from a simple queue protocol to the underlying container protocol. The members are:

explicit **priority_queue**(const Compare& cmp = Compare( ), const Container&
  cont = Container( ))
    Copies cont to the data member c, copies cmp to comp, and then calls make_heap(c.
    begin( ), c.end( ), comp) to initialize the priority queue.

template <class InputIter>
priority_queue(InputIter first, InputIter last, const Compare& cmp =
  Compare( ), const Container& cont = Container( ))
    Copies cont to the data member c, copies cmp to comp, and then adds the elements
    [first, last) to the container by calling c.insert(c.end( ), first, last). Finally,
    this method initializes the priority queue by calling make_heap(c.begin( ), c.end( ),
    comp).

bool **empty**( ) const
    Returns true if the priority queue is empty.

void **pop**( )
    Erases the largest (last) item from the priority queue by calling pop_heap and then
    erasing the last element in the container.

void **push**(const value_type& x)
    Inserts x in the container and then calls push_heap to restore priority queue order.

size_type **size**( ) const
    Returns the number of items in the priority queue.

const value_type& **top**( ) const
    Returns the largest (last) item in the priority queue.

See Also

make_heap, pop_heap, and push_heap in <algorithm>, list in <list>, vector in <vector>

---

queue class template   Queue container adapter

```
template <class T, class Container = deque<T> >
class queue {
```

```
public:
    typedef typename Container::value_type value_type;
    typedef typename Container::size_type size_type;
    typedef Container container_type;

    explicit queue(const Container& = Container());
    bool empty() const { return c.empty(); }
    size_type size() const { return c.size(); }
    value_type& front() { return c.front(); }
    const value_type& front() const { return c.front(); }
    value_type& back() { return c.back(); }
    const value_type& back() const { return c.back(); }
    void push(const value_type& x) { c.push_back(x); }
    void pop() { c.pop_front(); }
protected:
    Container c;
};
```

The queue class template is an adapter for any sequence container that supports the front(), back(), push_back(), and pop_front() members. See the list and deque class templates for the standard containers that are suitable. (The default is deque.)

Because queue is not itself a standard container, it cannot be used with the standard algorithms. (In particular, note the lack of begin and end member functions.) Thus, the queue adapter is useful only for simple needs.

Most of the members of queue are straightforward mappings from a simple queue protocol to the underlying container protocol. The members are:

explicit queue(const Container& cont = Container())

> Takes an existing container cont and copies its contents into the queue. With no argument, the constructor creates a new, empty container for the queue.

value_type& back()
const value_type& back() const

> Returns the last item in the queue, that is, the item that was added most recently to the queue.

bool empty() const

> Returns true if the queue is empty.

value_type& front()
const value_type& front() const

> Returns the first item in the queue.

void pop()

> Erases the first item from the queue.

void push(const value_type& x)

> Inserts x at the end of the queue.

size_type size() const

> Returns the number of items in the queue.

See Also

deque in <deque>, list in <list>, stack in <stack>

\<set\>

The \<set\> header is one of the standard container template headers. It declares the set and multiset class templates and a few global function templates that operate on set and multiset objects.

A set is a container that stores keys. Looking up keys, inserting keys, and deleting keys can all be performed in logarithmic or better time. Sets support bidirectional iterators (not random access).

See Chapter 10 for information about containers.

---

multiset class template

Set container with duplicate keys

```
template <typename Key, typename Compare = less<Key>,
          typename Alloc = allocator<Key> >
class multiset {
public:
  typedef Key key_type;
  typedef Key value_type;
  typedef Compare key_compare;
  typedef Compare value_compare;
  typedef Alloc allocator_type;
  typedef typename Alloc::reference reference;
  typedef typename Alloc::const_reference const_reference;
  typedef ... iterator;
  typedef ... const_iterator;
  typedef ... size_type;
  typedef ... difference_type;
  typedef typename Alloc::pointer pointer;
  typedef typename Alloc::const_pointer const_pointer;
  typedef std::reverse_iterator<iterator> reverse_iterator;
  typedef std::reverse_iterator<const_iterator> const_reverse_iterator;

  explicit multiset(const Compare& comp = Compare(), const Alloc& = Alloc());
  template <class InputIterator>
  multiset(InputIterator first, InputIterator last,
           const Compare& comp = Compare(), const Alloc& = Alloc());
  multiset(const multiset<Key,Compare,Alloc>& x);
  ~multiset();
  multiset<Key,Compare,Alloc>& operator=(const multiset<Key,Compare,Alloc>& x);
  allocator_type get_allocator() const;
  // Iterators
  iterator begin();
  const_iterator begin() const;
  iterator end();
  const_iterator end() const;
  reverse_iterator rbegin();
  const_reverse_iterator rbegin() const;
  reverse_iterator rend();
  const_reverse_iterator rend() const;

  bool empty() const;
  size_type size() const;
  size_type max_size() const;
```

```
iterator insert(const value_type& x);
iterator insert(iterator hintpos, const value_type& x);
template <class InputIterator>
void insert(InputIterator first, InputIterator last);
void erase(iterator position);
size_type erase(const key_type& x);
void erase(iterator first, iterator last);
void swap(multiset<Key,Compare,Alloc>&);
void clear();

key_compare key_comp() const;
value_compare value_comp() const;

iterator find(const key_type& x) const;
size_type count(const key_type& x) const;
iterator lower_bound(const key_type& x) const;
iterator upper_bound(const key_type& x) const;
pair<iterator,iterator> equal_range(const key_type& x) const;
};
```

The multiset class template is a standard container that contains an ordered set of keys of type T. The keys can be duplicated, that is, the multiset can contain more than one instance of a particular key.

A multiset's iterators are bidirectional. Note that keys are const in the set. You must not change the key while it is stored in a set. More precisely, you must not change the key in a way that alters its relative order with the other keys in the set. If you need to modify a key, erase the key from the set, modify the key, and insert the new key, as shown in Example 13-34 (in the set class template).

Within a multiset, keys are ordered in ascending order, according to the Compare template parameter (which can be a function pointer or functor that compares two objects of type Key and returns true if the first argument should come before the second). Keys do not need to be unique. When searching for keys, they are compared using the function or functor specified by the Compare template parameter. Two objects, a and b, are different if Compare(a, b) is true or Compare(b, a) is true. See set later in this section for a set container that stores unique keys.

Inserting into a multiset does not invalidate any iterators for that set or references to items in the set. Erasing an element invalidates only iterators and references that refer to that element.

Inserting into a set and searching for an element in a set usually take logarithmic time. Erasing a single element, given an iterator, takes constant time, amortized over many erasures.

The following are the member functions of multiset:

explicit **multiset**(const Compare& comp = Compare(), const Alloc& = Alloc())
    Constructs an empty multiset.

template <class InputIterator>
multiset(InputIterator first, InputIterator last, const Compare& comp = Compare(), const Alloc& = Alloc())
    Constructs an empty multiset and then copies all items in the range [first, last) into the new set. The complexity is linear if the keys in [first, last) are already sorted. If they are not sorted, the complexity is $N \log N$, in which N is last − first.

multiset(const multiset<Key,Compare,Alloc>& x)
> Constructs a new multiset and copies the allocator and all the items from x to the new set.

iterator **begin**( )
const_iterator **begin**( ) const
> Returns an iterator that points to the first element of the set.

void **clear**( )
> Erases every item in the set.

size_type **count**(const key_type& x) const
> Returns the number of keys that are equivalent to x. The complexity is log(size( )) + r, in which r is the return value.

bool **empty**( ) const
> Returns size( ) == 0.

iterator **end**( )
const_iterator **end**( ) const
> Returns an iterator that points to one past the last element of the set.

pair<iterator,iterator> **equal_range**(const key_type& x) const
> Returns the lower bound and upper bound as a pair:
>
>   std::make_pair(lower_bound(x), upper_bound(x))
>
> The complexity is log(size( )).

void **erase**(iterator position)
size_type **erase**(const key_type& x)
void **erase**(iterator first, iterator last)
> Erases one or more elements from the set. The first version erases the item at position in constant time (amortized over many calls). The second version erases the items equivalent to x, if any are present, returning a count of the number of items erased. The third version erases all elements in the range [first, last). The last two forms run in time proportional to log(size( )) + r, in which r is the number of items erased.

iterator **find**(const key_type& x) const
> Searches for a key that is equivalent to x and returns an iterator that points to that key or end( ) if it is not found. If x occurs more than once, the iterator might point to any of its occurrences in the multiset. The complexity is log(size( )).

allocator_type **get_allocator**( ) const
> Returns the set's allocator.

pair<iterator,bool> **insert**(const value_type& x)
iterator **insert**(iterator hintpos, const value_type& x)
template <class InputIterator>
void **insert**(InputIterator first, InputIterator last)
> Inserts one or more items into the set. The first version inserts x in logarithmic time.
>
> The second version inserts x using hintpos as a position hint. If x is inserted immediately after hintpos, the performance is constant (amortized over many insertions); at any other position, the performance is logarithmic.
>
> The third version copies all the items in the range [first, last), which must be pointing to a different multiset object. If the items are already in the desired

order, the performance is linear; otherwise, it is N log (size( ) + N), in which N is last − first.

key_compare **key_comp**( ) const
> Returns the comparator function pointer or object. The key_compare type is the same as the Compare template parameter.

iterator **lower_bound**(const key_type& x) const
> Returns an iterator that points to the first item in the set that does not come before x. That is, if x is in the set, the iterator points to the position of its first occurrence; otherwise, the iterator points to the first position where x should be inserted. The complexity is log(size( )).

size_type **max_size**( ) const
> Returns the largest number of items that can be in the set.

reverse_iterator **rbegin**( )
const_reverse_iterator **rbegin**( ) const
> Returns a reverse iterator that points to the last element of the set.

reverse_iterator **rend**( )
const_reverse_iterator **rend**( ) const
> Returns a reverse iterator that points to one position before the first element of the set.

size_type **size**( ) const
> Returns the number of items in the set.

void **swap**(multiset<Key,Compare,Alloc>&)
> Swaps the contents of the set with the contents of x.

iterator **upper_bound**(const key_type& x) const
> Returns an iterator that points to the first item in the set that comes after all occurrences of x. The complexity is log(size( )).

value_compare **value_comp**( ) const
> Returns the comparator function pointer or functor object. The value_compare type is the same as the Compare template parameter.

multiset<Key,Compare,Alloc>& **operator=**(const multiset<Key,Compare,Alloc>& x)
> Erases all the elements of the set and replaces them with copies of the elements of x.

See Also

set class template, multimap in <map>

---

operator== function template

```
template <typename Key, typename T, typename C, typename A>
bool operator==(const set<Key,T,C,A>& x, const set<Key,T,C,A>& y);
template <typename Key, typename T, typename C, typename A>
bool operator==(const multiset<Key,T,C,A>& x, const multiset<Key,T,C,A>& y);
```

The == operator returns true if x and y have the same size and their elements are equal, that is, x.size( ) == y.size( ) && equals(x.begin( ), x.end( ), y.begin( )).

See Also

equals in <algorithm>

---

operator!= function template
Compares sets for inequality

```
template <typename Key, typename T, typename C, typename A>
bool operator!=(const set<Key,T,C,A>& x, const set<Key,T,C,A>& y);
template <typename Key, typename T, typename C, typename A>
bool operator!=(const multiset<Key,T,C,A>& x, const multiset<Key,T,C,A>& y);
```

The != operator returns ! (x == y).

operator< function template
Compares sets for less-than

```
template <typename Key, typename T, typename C, typename A>
bool operator<(const set<Key,T,C,A>& x, const set<Key,T,C,A>& y);
template <typename Key, typename T, typename C, typename A>
bool operator<(const multiset<Key,T,C,A>& x, const multiset<Key,T,C,A>& y);
```

The < operator determines whether x is less than y using the same algorithm as
lexicographical_compare(x.begin( ), x.end( ), y.begin( ), y.end( )).

See Also

lexicographical_compare in <algorithm>

operator<= function template
Compares sets for less-than-or-equal

```
template <typename Key, typename T, typename C, typename A>
bool operator<=(const set<Key,T,C,A>& x, const set<Key,T,C,A>& y);
template <typename Key, typename T, typename C, typename A>
bool operator<=(const multiset<Key,T,C,A>& x, const multiset<Key,T,C,A>& y);
```

The <= operator returns ! (y < x).

operator> function template
Compares sets for greater-than

```
template <typename Key, typename T, typename C, typename A>
bool operator>(const set<Key,T,C,A>& x, const set<Key,T,C,A>& y);
template <typename Key, typename T, typename C, typename A>
bool operator>(const multiset<Key,T,C,A>& x, const multiset<Key,T,C,A>& y);
```

The > operator returns (y < x).

operator>= function template
Compares sets for greater-than-or-equal

```
template <typename Key, typename T, typename C, typename A>
bool operator>=(const set<Key,T,C,A>& x, const set<Key,T,C,A>& y);
template <typename Key, typename T, typename C, typename A>
bool operator>=(const multiset<Key,T,C,A>& x, const multiset<Key,T,C,A>& y);
```

The >= operator returns ! (x < y).

set class template
Set container with unique keys

```
template <typename Key, typename Compare = less<Key>,
          typename Alloc = allocator<Key> >
class set {
public:
  typedef Key key_type;
```

```
typedef Key value_type;
typedef Compare key_compare;
typedef Compare value_compare;
typedef Alloc allocator_type;
typedef typename Alloc::reference reference;
typedef typename Alloc::const_reference const_reference;
typedef ... iterator;
typedef ... const_iterator;
typedef ... size_type;
typedef ... difference_type;
typedef typename Alloc::pointer pointer;
typedef typename Alloc::const_pointer const_pointer;
typedef std::reverse_iterator<iterator> reverse_iterator;
typedef std::reverse_iterator<const_iterator> const_reverse_iterator;

explicit set(const Compare& comp = Compare(),
             const Alloc& = Alloc());
template <class InputIterator>
set(InputIterator first, InputIterator last,
    const Compare& comp = Compare(), const Alloc& = Alloc());
set(const set<Key,Compare,Alloc>& x);
~set();
set<Key,Compare,Alloc>& operator=(const set<Key,Compare,Alloc>& x);

allocator_type get_allocator() const;

iterator begin();
const_iterator begin() const;
iterator end();
const_iterator end() const;
reverse_iterator rbegin();
const_reverse_iterator rbegin() const;
reverse_iterator rend();
const_reverse_iterator rend() const;

bool empty() const;
size_type size() const;
size_type max_size() const;

pair<iterator,bool> insert(const value_type& x);
iterator insert(iterator hintpos, const value_type& x);
template <class InputIterator>
void insert(InputIterator first, InputIterator last);
void erase(iterator position);
size_type erase(const key_type& x);
void erase(iterator first, iterator last);
void swap(set<Key,Compare,Alloc>&);
void clear();
// Observers
key_compare key_comp() const;
value_compare value_comp() const;
// Set operations
iterator find(const key_type& x) const;
size_type count(const key_type& x) const;
```

```
    iterator lower_bound(const key_type& x) const;
    iterator upper_bound(const key_type& x) const;
    pair<iterator,iterator> equal_range(const key_type& x) const;
};
```

The set class template is a standard container that contains an ordered set of unique keys of type T.

A set's iterators are bidirectional. Note that keys are const in the set. You must not change the key while it is stored in a set. More precisely, you must not change the key in a way that alters its relative order with the other keys in the set. If you need to modify a key, erase the key from the set, modify the key, and insert the new key, as shown in Example 13-34.

Example 13-34. One way to modify a key in a set

```
template <typename T, typename C, typename A>
void change_key(std::set<T, C, A>& s,
  const T& oldkey, const T& newkey)
{
  using std::set;
  typedef typename set<T, C, A>::iterator set_iterator;
  set_iterator i = s.find(oldkey);
  if (i != s.end()) {
    m.erase(i);
    m.insert(newkey);
  }
  // Exercise: What if newkey is already in s?
}
```

Within a set, keys are ordered in ascending order, according to the Compare template parameter (which can be a function pointer or functor that compares two objects of type Key and returns true if the first argument should come before the second). Keys must be unique, but note that uniqueness is determined only by calling Compare, not by using the == operator. That is, two objects, a and b, are different (and therefore can both be present in a single set object) if Compare(a, b) is true or Compare(b, a) is true. See multiset earlier in this section for a set container that can store non-unique keys.

Inserting into a set does not invalidate any iterators for that set or any references to items in the set. Erasing an element invalidates only iterators or references that refer to that element.

Inserting into a set and searching for an element in a set usually take logarithmic time. Erasing a single element, given an iterator, takes constant time, amortized over many erasures.

The following are the member functions of set:

explicit **set**(const Compare& comp = Compare( ), const Alloc& = Alloc( ))
    Constructs an empty set.

template <class InputIterator>
set(InputIterator first, InputIterator last, const Compare& comp = Compare( ),
    const Alloc& = Alloc( ))
    Constructs an empty set and then copies all items in the range [first, last) into the new set. The complexity is linear if the keys in [first, last) are already sorted. If they are not sorted, the complexity is $N \log N$, in which N is last − first.

set(const set<Key,Compare,Alloc>& x)
>   Constructs a new set and copies the allocator and all the items from x to the new set.

iterator **begin**( )
const_iterator **begin**( ) const
>   Returns an iterator that points to the first element of the set.

void **clear**( )
>   Erases every item in the set.

size_type **count**(const key_type& x) const
>   Returns the number of keys that are equivalent to x. This value is always 0 or 1. The complexity is log(size( )).

bool **empty**( ) const
>   Returns size( ) == 0.

iterator **end**( )
const_iterator **end**( ) const
>   Returns an iterator that points to one past the last element of the set.

pair<iterator,iterator> **equal_range**(const key_type& x) const
>   Returns the lower bound and upper bound as a pair:
>
>   >   std::make_pair(lower_bound(x), upper_bound(x))
>
>   The complexity is log(size( )).

void **erase**(iterator position)
size_type **erase**(const key_type& x)
void **erase**(iterator first, iterator last)
>   Erases one or more elements from the set. The first version erases the item at position in constant time (amortized over many calls). The second version erases the item equivalent to x, if it is present, returning a count of the number of items erased, that is, 0 or 1. It runs in logarithmic time. The third version erases all elements in the range [first, last) in a time proportional to log(size( )) + r, in which r is last − first.

iterator **find**(const key_type& x) const
>   Searches for a key that is equivalent to x and returns an iterator that points to that key or end( ) if it is not found. The complexity is log(size( )).

allocator_type **get_allocator**( ) const
>   Returns the set's allocator.

pair<iterator,bool> **insert**(const value_type& x)
iterator **insert**(iterator hintpos, const value_type& x)
template <class InputIterator>
void **insert**(InputIterator first, InputIterator last)
>   Inserts one or more items into the set, but only if an equivalent key is not already present in the set. If the key is already present, the insert attempt is ignored. The first version attempts to insert x in logarithmic time.
>
>   The second version inserts x using hintpos as a position hint. If x is inserted immediately after hintpos, the performance is constant (amortized over many insertions); at any other position, the performance is logarithmic.
>
>   The third version copies all the items in the range [first, last), which must be pointing to a different set object. If the items are already in the desired order, the performance is linear; otherwise, it is N log(size( ) + N), in which N is last − first.

key_compare **key_comp**( ) const
> Returns the comparator function pointer or object. The key_compare type is the same as the Compare template parameter.

iterator **lower_bound**(const key_type& x) const
> Returns an iterator that points to the first item in the set that does not come before x. That is, if x is in the set, the iterator points to its position; otherwise, the iterator points to the first position where x should be inserted. The complexity is log(size( )).

size_type **max_size**( ) const
> Returns the largest number of items that can be in the set.

reverse_iterator **rbegin**( )
const_reverse_iterator **rbegin**( ) const
> Returns a reverse iterator that points to the last element of the set.

reverse_iterator **rend**( )
const_reverse_iterator **rend**( ) const
> Returns a reverse iterator that points to one position before the first element of the set.

size_type **size**( ) const
> Returns the number of items in the set.

void **swap**(set<Key,Compare,Alloc>&)
> Swaps the contents of the set with the contents of x.

iterator **upper_bound**(const key_type& x) const
> Returns an iterator that points to the first item in the set that comes after x. The complexity is log(size( )).

value_compare **value_comp**( ) const
> Returns the comparator function pointer or functor object. The value_compare type is the same as the Compare template parameter.

set<Key,Compare,Alloc>& **operator=**(const set<Key,Compare,Alloc>& x)
> Erases all the elements of the set and replaces them with copies of the elements of x.

See Also

multiset class template, multimap in <map>

---

swap function template

Swaps the contents of two sets

```
template <typename Key, typename T, typename C, typename A>
 void swap(set<Key,T,C,A>& x,
           set<Key,T,C,A>& y);

template <typename Key, typename T, typename C, typename A>
 void swap(multiset<Key,T,C,A>& x,
           multiset<Key,T,C,A>& y);
```

The swap function template specialization is equivalent to calling x.swap(y).

See Also

swap in <algorithm>

<sstream>

The <sstream> header declares classes, templates, and other types for reading from and writing to strings in the same manner as reading from and writing to files.

See Chapter 9 for a general discussion of I/O, Chapter 1 for more information about character sets, and the <iostream> section in this chapter for information about the base-class templates required by the stringstream class templates. Refer to Chapter 8 for information about traits in general and to the <string> section in this chapter for detailed information about the char_traits template. Refer to the <streambuf> section in this chapter for information about the basic_streambuf template. See also <strstream> for classes that are similar to the string streams, except they work with arrays of narrow characters.

To read from a string, use istringstream; for writing, use ostringstream; for reading and writing, use stringstream. For wide character I/O, use wistringstream, wostringstream, or wstringstream. Example 13-35 shows tostring, a simple use of ostringstream to convert a value to a string. (Think of tostring as the inverse of strtol and friends.)

Example 13-35. Converting a value to a string

```
template<typename T>
std::string tostring(const T& x)
{
  std::ostringstream out;
  out << x;
  return out.str( );
}
```

Example 13-36 shows a use of istringstream to interpret HTML colors. In HTML, a color can be a name, such as white, or a hexadecimal digit string that begins with #. The digit string is interpreted as a triplet of red, green, and blue color elements, each expressed as two hexadecimal digits. For the sake of simplicity, the example omits error handling and assumes that the order of the color elements matches the order needed by the program. The known color names are stored in a map.

Example 13-36. Interpreting an HTML color string

```
typedef std::map<std::string, unsigned long> colormap;
colormap colors;

unsigned long get_color(const std::string& text)
{
  unsigned long rgb;
  colormap::iterator i = colors.find(text);
  if (i != colors.end( ))
    return i->second;
  else if (text.length( ) == 0)
    return 0;
  else {
    std::istringstream in(text);
    if (in.peek( ) == '#')
      in.ignore( );
    in >> std::noskipws >> std::hex >> rgb;
```

Library Reference

Example 13-36. Interpreting an HTML color string (continued)

```
      if (in)
        return rgb;
      else
        return 0;
    }
}

void initcolors(colormap& colors)
{
  ...
  colors["black"] = 0x000000;
  colors["blue"]  = 0x0000FF;
  colors["green"] = 0x00FF00;
  colors["red"]   = 0xFF0000;
  colors["white"] = 0xFFFFFF;
}
```

basic_istringstream class template

Base class for input string streams

```
template <class charT, class traits = char_traits<charT>,
          class Alloc = allocator<charT> >
class basic_istringstream: public basic_istream<charT,traits>
{
public:
  typedef charT char_type;
  typedef typename traits::int_type int_type;
  typedef typename traits::pos_type pos_type;
  typedef typename traits::off_type off_type;
  typedef traits traits_type;

  explicit basic_istringstream(ios_base::openmode which = ios_base::in);
  explicit basic_istringstream(const basic_string<charT,traits,Alloc>& str,
                               ios_base::openmode which = ios_base::in);

  basic_stringbuf<charT,traits,Alloc>* rdbuf() const;
  basic_string<charT,traits,Alloc> str() const;
  void str(const basic_string<charT,traits,Alloc>& s);
};
```

The basic_istringstream class template is the base class for input string streams. Typically, you would construct an istringstream with a string argument and then read from the string stream just as you would from any other input stream.

The following are the methods of basic_istringstream:

explicit **basic_istringstream**(ios_base::openmode which = ios_base::in)
> Initializes an empty input string stream by constructing an internal basic_stringbuf object, passing which | ios_base::in to that object's constructor, and passing the address of the string buffer to the base-class constructor for basic_istream.

explicit **basic_istringstream**(const basic_string<charT,traits,Alloc>& str, ios_base::openmode which = ios_base::in)
> Initializes a string stream with str as the initial string contents by constructing an internal basic_stringbuf object, passing str and which | ios_base::in to that

object's constructor, and passing the address of the string buffer to the base-class constructor for basic_istream.

basic_stringbuf<charT,traits,Alloc>* **rdbuf**( ) const
  Returns a pointer to the internal basic_stringbuf object.

basic_string<charT,traits,Alloc> **str**( ) const
  Returns the buffer contents as a string, that is, rdbuf( )->str( ).

void **str**(const basic_string<charT,traits,Alloc>& s)
  Calls rdbuf( )->str(s) to set the buffer contents.

See Also

basic_stringstream class template, istringstream class, wistringstream class, basic_ifstream in <fstream>, basic_istream in <istream>

---

basic_ostringstream class template
Base class for output string streams

```
template <class charT, class traits = char_traits<charT>,
          class Alloc = allocator<charT> >
class basic_ostringstream: public basic_ostream<charT,traits>
{
public:
  typedef charT char_type;
  typedef typename traits::int_type int_type;
  typedef typename traits::pos_type pos_type;
  typedef typename traits::off_type off_type;
  typedef traits traits_type;

  explicit basic_ostringstream(ios_base::openmode which = ios_base::out);
  explicit basic_ostringstream(const basic_string<charT,traits,Alloc>& str,
                               ios_base::openmode which = ios_base::out);

  basic_stringbuf<charT,traits,Alloc>* rdbuf() const;
  basic_string<charT,traits,Alloc> str() const;
  void str(const basic_string<charT,traits,Alloc>& s);
};
```

The basic_ostringstream class template is the base class for output string streams. Typically, you would construct an ostringstream with no string and let the string stream allocate the string as you write to the stream. You would then call the str member function to read the resulting string.

The following are the methods of basic_ostringstream:

explicit **basic_ostringstream**(ios_base::openmode which = ios_base::out)
  Initializes an empty output string stream by constructing an internal basic_stringbuf object, passing which | ios_base::out to that object's constructor, and passing the address of the string buffer to the base-class constructor for basic_ostream.

explicit **basic_ostringstream**(const basic_string<charT,traits,Alloc>& str, ios_base::openmode which = ios_base::out)
  Initializes a string stream with str as the initial string contents by constructing an internal basic_stringbuf object, passing str and which | ios_base::out to that object's constructor, and passing the address of the string buffer to the base-class constructor for basic_ostream.

```
basic_stringbuf<charT,traits,Alloc>* rdbuf() const
```
    Returns a pointer to the internal basic_stringbuf object.

```
basic_string<charT,traits,Alloc> str() const
```
    Returns the buffer contents as a string, that is, rdbuf()->str().

```
void str(const basic_string<charT,traits,Alloc>& s)
```
    Calls rdbuf()->str(s) to set the buffer contents.

See Also

basic_stringstream class template, ostringstream class, wostringstream class, basic_ofstream in <fstream>, basic_ostream in <ostream>

---

basic_stringbuf class template   Base class for string buffers

```
template <class charT, class traits = char_traits<charT>,
          class Alloc = allocator<charT> >
class basic_stringbuf : public basic_streambuf<charT,traits>
{
public:
  typedef charT char_type;
  typedef typename traits::int_type int_type;
  typedef typename traits::pos_type pos_type;
  typedef typename traits::off_type off_type;
  typedef traits traits_type;
  explicit basic_stringbuf(ios_base::openmode mode = ios_base::in |
                           ios_base::out);
  explicit basic_stringbuf(const basic_string<charT,traits,Alloc>& str,
                           ios_base::openmode mode = ios_base::in |
                           ios_base::out);
  basic_string<charT,traits,Alloc> str() const;
  void str(const basic_string<charT,traits,Alloc>& s);
protected:
  virtual int_type underflow();
  virtual int_type pbackfail(int_type c = traits::eof());
  virtual int_type overflow (int_type c = traits::eof());
  virtual basic_streambuf<charT,traits>* setbuf(charT*, streamsize);
  virtual pos_type seekoff(off_type off, ios_base::seekdir way,
                           ios_base::openmode which = ios_base::in |
                           ios_base::out);
  virtual pos_type seekpos(pos_type sp,
                           ios_base::openmode which = ios_base::in |
                           ios_base::out);
};
```

The basic_stringbuf class template implements a stream buffer for string-based streams. A string buffer maintains a single character buffer with separate positions for reading and writing. That is, the buffer has *begin*, *next*, and *end* pointers for reading and separate *begin*, *next*, and *end* pointers for writing. The *begin* pointer points to the start of a buffer, and the *end* pointer points to one past the end of the buffer. The *next* pointer points to the position where the next character will be read or written. Refer to basic_streambuf in <streambuf> for details about buffer positions.

In the following descriptions of the member functions of basic_stringbuf, *mode* refers to a private copy of the mode parameter that is passed to the constructors. The

---

implementation is not required to have such a data member, but the descriptions below are clearer with the assumption that it exists.

explicit **basic_stringbuf**(ios_base::openmode mode = ios_base::in |
  ios_base::out)

    Initializes the buffer with an empty string and remembers the mode.

explicit **basic_stringbuf**(const basic_string<charT,traits,Alloc>& str,
  ios_base::openmode mode = ios_base::in | ios_base::out)

    Initializes the buffer with a copy of str and remembers the mode. If mode & ios_base::in is nonzero, the input position is initialized to read from the start of the buffer. If mode & ios_base::out is nonzero, the output position is initialized to overwrite the buffer.

virtual int_type **overflow** (int_type c = traits::eof( ))

    Attempts to append c to the end of the buffer as follows:

- If c is an end-of-file character (c is traits::eof( )), nothing happens, and a non-end-of-file character is returned to indicate success.
- If c is not end-of-file, and a write position is available, c is appended to the buffer by calling sputc(c).
- If a write position is not available, and the *mode* allows writing (*mode* & ios_base::out is nonzero), the buffer is extended by one character and c is appended. If the *mode* allows reading (*mode* & ios_base::in is nonzero), the read end pointer egptr( ) is set to point to one position past the end of the buffer.

    The return value is traits::not_eof(c) for success or traits::eof( ) for failure.

virtual int_type **pbackfail**(int_type c = traits::eof( ))

    Attempts to push c back onto the buffer for reading as follows:

- If c is an end-of-file character (c is traits::eof( )), and a putback position is available, gptr( ) is set to gptr( ) − 1.
- If c is not an end-of-file character, and a putback position is available, and gptr( )[-1] is equal to c, gptr( ) is set to gptr( ) − 1.
- If c is not an end-of-file character, and a putback position is available, and the *mode* allows writing (*mode* & ios_base::out is nonzero), gptr( ) is set to gptr( ) − 1, and *gptr( ) is assigned c.

    The return value is traits::not_eof(c) for success or traits::eof( ) for failure.

virtual pos_type **seekoff**(off_type off, ios_base::seekdir way,
  ios_base::openmode which = ios_base::in|ios_base::out)

    Sets the stream position. The input position, output position, or both can be set, depending on (which & (ios_base::in | ios_base::out)). The following are the possible results of this expression:

    ios_base::in
        Sets the input position

    ios_base::out
        Sets the output position

    ios_base::in | ios_base::out, *and* way *is either* ios_base::beg *or*
      ios_base::end
        Sets input and output positions

    Otherwise
        The function fails and returns pos_type(-1)

The new position is determined as an offset off, which is added to the position at the start of the stream, the current position, or at the end of the stream, depending on way (ios_base::beg, ios_base::cur, or ios_base::end). If the desired position is negative or past the end of the buffer, the function fails and returns pos_type(-1). If the function succeeds, it returns the new position.

virtual pos_type **seekpos**(pos_type sp, ios_base::openmode which = ios_base::in|ios_base::out)

Sets the stream position to sp. The input position is set if which & ios_base::in is nonzero. The output position is set if which & ios_base::out is nonzero. If sp is not a valid position, or if neither the input nor the output position is set, seekpos fails and pos_type(-1) is returned. The return value is sp for success. If sp was not returned from a prior call to a positioning function (that is, seekoff, seekpos, tellg, or tellp), the results are undefined.

virtual basic_streambuf<charT,traits>* **setbuf**(charT*, streamsize)

Calling setbuf(0, 0) has no effect other than to return this. The result of any other call to setbuf is implementation-defined.

basic_string<charT,traits,Alloc> **str**( ) const

Returns the contents of the buffer as a string. If the mode allows output (mode & ios_base::out is nonzero), the buffer contents are taken from the output positions; otherwise, the buffer contents are copied from the input positions.

void **str**(const basic_string<charT,traits,Alloc>& s)

Deallocates the current buffer if one exists and replaces it with a copy of s. If *mode* & ios_base::in is nonzero, the input positions are set to read from the start of the buffer. If *mode* & ios_base::out is nonzero, the output positions are set to overwrite the buffer.

virtual int_type **underflow**( )

Returns *gptr( ) if more input is available, that is, if there is a read position. Otherwise, the function returns traits::eof( ).

See Also

stringbuf class, wstringbuf class, basic_filebuf in <fstream>, basic_streambuf in <streambuf>

---

basic_stringstream class template
Base class for input and output string streams

```
template <class charT, class traits = char_traits<charT>,
          class Alloc = allocator<charT> >
class basic_stringstream: public basic_iostream<charT,traits>
{
public:
  typedef charT char_type;
  typedef typename traits::int_type int_type;
  typedef typename traits::pos_type pos_type;
  typedef typename traits::off_type off_type;
  typedef traits traits_type;

  explicit basic_stringstream(ios_base::openmode which =
                              ios_base::out|ios_base::in);
  explicit basic_stringstream(const basic_string<charT,traits,Alloc>& str,
                              ios_base::openmode which =
                              ios_base::out|ios_base::in);
```

```
basic_stringbuf<charT,traits,Alloc>* rdbuf() const;
basic_string<charT,traits,Alloc> str() const;
void str(const basic_string<charT,traits,Alloc>& str);
};
```

The basic_stringstream class template is the base class for string streams that permit input and output. You can start with an empty string and write to the stream, or start with a string and read from the stream. If you initialize the stream with a string and start writing, the output overwrites the string. You can switch between reading and writing at any time and set the read and write positions independently.

The following are the methods of basic_stringstream:

explicit **basic_stringstream**(ios_base::openmode which = ios_base::in | ios_base::out)

> Initializes an empty string stream by constructing an internal basic_stringbuf object, passing which | ios_base::in | ios_base::out to that object's constructor and the address of the string buffer to the base-class constructor for basic_iostream.

explicit **basic_stringstream**(const basic_string<charT,traits,Alloc>& str, ios_base::openmode which = ios_base::in|ios_base::out)

> Initializes a string stream with str as the initial string contents by constructing an internal basic_stringbuf object, passing str and which | ios_base::in | ios_base::out to that object's constructor and the address of the string buffer to the base-class constructor for basic_iostream.

basic_stringbuf<charT,traits,Alloc>* **rdbuf**() const

> Returns a pointer to the internal basic_stringbuf object.

basic_string<charT,traits,Alloc> **str**() const

> Returns the buffer contents as a string, that is, rdbuf()->str().

void **str**(const basic_string<charT,traits,Alloc>& s)

> Calls rdbuf()->str(s) to set the buffer contents.

See Also

basic_istringstream class template, basic_ostringstream class template, stringstream class, wstringstream class, basic_fstream in <fstream>, basic_iostream in <istream>

---

istringstream class   Input string stream

typedef basic_istringstream<char> **istringstream**;

The istringstream class is a specialization of the basic_istringstream template for char characters.

See Also

basic_istringstream class template, wistringstream class, ifstream in <fstream>, istream in <istream>

---

ostringstream class   Output string stream

typedef basic_ostringstream<char> **ostringstream**;

The ostringstream class is a specialization of the basic_ostringstream template for char characters.

See Also

basic_ostringstream class template, wostringstream class, ofstream in <fstream>, ostream in <ostream>

---

stringbuf class   Narrow character string buffer

typedef basic_stringbuf<char> **stringbuf**;

The stringbuf class is a specialization of the basic_stringbuf template for char characters.

See Also

basic_stringbuf class template, wstringbuf class, filebuf in <fstream>, streambuf in <streambuf>

---

stringstream class   Input and output string stream

typedef basic_stringstream<char> **stringstream**;

The stringstream class is a specialization of the basic_stringstream template for char characters.

See Also

basic_stringstream class template, wstringstream class, fstream in <fstream>, iostream in <istream>

---

wistringstream class   Wide input string stream

typedef basic_istringstream<wchar_t> **wistringstream**;

The wistringstream class is a specialization of the basic_istringstream template for wchar_t characters.

See Also

basic_istringstream class template, istringstream class, wifstream in <fstream>, wistream in <istream>

---

wostringstream class   Wide output string stream

typedef basic_ostringstream<wchar_t> **wostringstream**;

The wostringstream class is a specialization of the basic_ostringstream template for wchar_t characters.

See Also

basic_ostringstream class template, ostringstream class, wofstream in <fstream>, wostream in <ostream>

---

wstringbuf class   Wide character string buffer

typedef basic_stringbuf<wchar_t> **wstringbuf**;

The wstringbuf class is a specialization of the basic_stringbuf template for wchar_t characters.

See Also

basic_stringbuf class template, stringbuf class, wfilebuf in <fstream>, wstreambuf in <streambuf>

wstringstream class
Wide input and output string stream

typedef basic_stringstream<wchar_t> **wstringstream**;

The wstringstream class is a specialization of the basic_stringstream template for wchar_t characters.

See Also

basic_stringstream class template, stringstream class, wfstream in <fstream>, wiostream in <istream>

<stack>

The <stack> header declares the stack container adapter. This class template is not a container in its own right, but adapts other containers to present the behavior of a stack.

A stack is a sequence of items that supports insertion and removal at one end. Because the last item inserted into a stack is the first item removed, a stack is sometimes called a LIFO (last-in, first-out) container.

See Chapter 10 for information about containers.

operator== function template
Compares stacks for equality

```
template <typename T, typename Container>
bool operator==(const stack<T, Container>& x, const stack<T, Container>& y);
```

The == operator compares two stacks for equality by comparing the adapted containers (e.g., the return value is x.c == y.c).

operator!= function template
Compares stacks for inequality

```
template <typename T, typename Container>
bool operator!=(const stack<T, Container>& x, const stack<T, Container>& y);
```

The != operator compares two stacks for inequality by comparing the adapted containers (e.g., the return value is x.c != y.c).

operator< function template
Compares stacks for less-than

```
template <typename T, typename Container>
bool operator<(const stack<T, Container>& x, const stack<T, Container>& y);
```

The < operator compares two stacks by comparing the adapted containers (e.g., the return value is x.c < y.c).

operator<= function template   Compares stacks for less-than-or-equal

```
template <typename T, typename Container>
bool operator<=(const stack<T, Container>& x, const stack<T, Container>& y);
```

The <= operator compares two stacks by comparing the adapted containers (e.g., the return value is x.c <= y.c).

operator> function template   Compares stacks for greater-than

```
template <typename T, typename Container>
bool operator>(const stack<T, Container>& x, const stack<T, Container>& y);
```

The > operator compares two stacks by comparing the adapted containers (e.g., the return value is x.c >= y.c).

operator>= function template   Compares stacks for greater-than-or-equal

```
template <typename T, typename Container>
bool operator>=(const stack<T, Container>& x, const stack<T, Container>& y);
```

The >= operator compares two stacks by comparing the adapted containers (e.g., the return value is x.c >= y.c).

stack class template   Stack container adapter

```
template <class T, class Container = deque<T> >
class stack {
public:
  typedef typename Container::value_type value_type;
  typedef typename Container::size_type size_type;
  typedef Container container_type;
protected:
  Container c;
public:
  explicit stack(const Container& = Container());
  bool empty() const { return c.empty(); }
  size_type size() const { return c.size(); }
  value_type& top() { return c.back(); }
  const value_type& top() const { return c.back(); }
  void push(const value_type& x) { c.push_back(x); }
  void pop() { c.pop_back(); }
};
```

The stack class template is an adapter for any sequence container—such as deque, list, and vector—that supports the back, push_back, and pop_back members. (The default is deque.)

Because stack is not itself a standard container, it cannot be used with the standard algorithms. (In particular, note the lack of begin and end member functions.) Thus, the stack adapter is useful only for simple needs.

Most of the members of stack are straightforward mappings from a simple stack protocol to the underlying container protocol. The members are:

explicit **stack**(const Container& cont = Container())
    Copies the elements from cont to the c data member

bool **empty**( ) const
> Returns true if the stack is empty

void **pop**( )
> Erases the item at the top of the stack

void **push**(const value_type& x)
> Adds x at the top of the stack

size_type **size**( ) const
> Returns the number of items in the stack

value_type& **top**( )
const value_type& **top**( ) const
> Returns the item at the top of the stack

See Also

<deque>, <list>, <queue>, <vector>

<stdexcept>

The <stdexcept> header defines several standard exception classes. (Refer to <exception> for the base exception class.) Figure 13-24 shows all the exception classes in the standard library, including a few that are declared in other headers. Note that the standard library has very few places that throw exceptions. The exceptions in <stdexcept> are available primarily for your use.

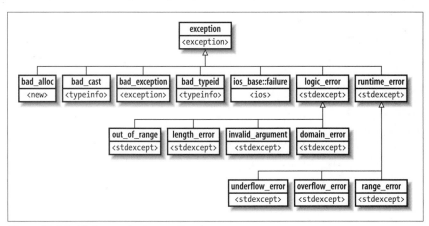

Figure 13-24. All the standard exception classes

See Chapter 3 for more information about throw expressions and Chapter 4 for information about handling exceptions with try statements.

domain_error class

```
class domain_error : public logic_error {
public:
  explicit domain_error(const string& what_arg);
};
```

The domain_error class is used to report domain errors, that is, arguments to functions that are outside the valid domain for input to the functions. For example, a function that converts a color from the Hue, Saturation, Lightness colorspace to the Red, Green, Blue colorspace might require a Saturation in the range [0.0, 1.0] and throw domain_error for any other value.

See Also

logic_error class

invalid_argument class

```
class invalid_argument : public logic_error {
public:
  explicit invalid_argument(const string& what_arg);
};
```

The invalid_argument class is thrown to report invalid arguments to functions. Specific kinds of invalid arguments are covered by the other logic errors; use invalid_argument for any other situations. For example, constructing a bitset from a string throws invalid_argument if any character is other than '0' or '1'.

See Also

logic_error class

length_error class

```
class length_error : public logic_error {
public:
  explicit length_error(const string& what_arg);
};
```

The length_error class is used to attempt to set or change the size of an object that exceeds the maximum size. For example, the string class throws length_error if you attempt to create a string longer than max_size( ) characters.

See Also

logic_error class

logic_error class

```
class logic_error : public exception {
public:
  explicit logic_error(const string& what_arg);
};
```

The logic_error class is a base class for logic-error exceptions. A *logic error* is a violation of the preconditions or other requirements for a function.

See Also

domain_error class, invalid_argument class, length_error class, out_of_range class, runtime_error class

---

out_of_range class

Argument out of range

```
class out_of_range : public logic_error {
public:
  explicit out_of_range(const string& what_arg);
};
```

The out_of_range class is used when an index or similar value is out of its expected or allowed range. For example, the at member (of deque, string, and vector) throws out_of_range if the index is invalid.

See Also

logic_error class

---

overflow_error class

Arithmetic overflow

```
class overflow_error : public runtime_error {
public:
  explicit overflow_error(const string& what_arg);
};
```

The overflow_error class can be used for arithmetic overflow. For example, bitset::to_ulong throws overflow_error if the arithmetic value of the bitset exceeds the maximum value of an unsigned long.

 Note that overflow in most arithmetic expressions has undefined behavior; an implementation might throw overflow_error, but there is no guarantee that it will throw this or any other exception.

See Also

runtime_error class

---

range_error class

Arithmetic range error

```
class range_error : public runtime_error {
public:
  explicit range_error(const string& what_arg);
};
```

The range_error class can be used when a function's results would fall outside its valid range. Note that the <cmath> functions do not throw any exceptions, but a third-party math library might throw range_error for, say, computing a power that exceeds the limits of its return type.

See Also

runtime_error class

runtime_error class   Base class for runtime errors

```
class runtime_error : public exception {
public:
  explicit runtime_error(const string& what_arg);
};
```

The runtime_error class is the base class for runtime errors, which are errors that cannot reasonably be detected by a static analysis of the code but can be revealed only at runtime.

See Also

overflow_error class, range_error class, underflow_error class

---

underflow_error class   Arithmetic underflow

```
class underflow_error : public runtime_error {
public:
  explicit underflow_error(const string& what_arg);
};
```

The underflow_error class can be used for arithmetic underflow. Note that underflow in most arithmetic expressions has undefined behavior; an implementation might throw underflow_error, but there is no guarantee that it will throw this or any other exception.

See Also

runtime_error class

<streambuf>

The <streambuf> header declares the basic_streambuf class template and its two specializations: streambuf and wstreambuf. A stream buffer object manages low-level access to a sequence of characters. The characters might be stored in an external file or reside entirely in memory. See the <fstream>, <sstream>, and <strstream> headers for examples of different kinds of stream buffers that are derived from basic_streambuf.

Most programs do not use stream buffers directly, but use stream classes instead because they provide a higher-level interface. Each stream object has an associated stream buffer object.

See Chapter 9 for general information on input and output using the stream classes.

basic_streambuf class template   Stream buffer

```
template <class charT, class traits = char_traits<charT> >
class basic_streambuf
{
public:
  typedef charT char_type;
  typedef typename traits::int_type int_type;
```

```
  typedef typename traits::pos_type pos_type;
  typedef typename traits::off_type off_type;
  typedef traits traits_type;
  virtual ~basic_streambuf();

  locale pubimbue(const locale &loc);
  locale getloc() const;
  basic_streambuf<char_type,traits>* pubsetbuf(char_type* s, streamsize n);
  pos_type pubseekoff(off_type off, ios_base::seekdir way,
                      ios_base::openmode which = ios_base::in | ios_base::out);
  pos_type pubseekoff(off_type off, ios_base::seekdir way,
                      ios_base::open_mode which=ios_base::in | ios_base::out);
  pos_type pubseekpos(pos_type sp, ios_base::openmode which = ios_base::in |
                      ios_base::out);
  pos_type pubseekpos(pos_type sp,ios_base::open_mode which);
  int pubsync();
  // Input
  streamsize in_avail();
  int_type snextc();
  int_type sbumpc();
  int_type stossc();
  int_type sgetc();
  streamsize sgetn(char_type* s, streamsize n);
  // Putback
  int_type sputbackc(char_type c);
  int_type sungetc();
  // Output
  int_type sputc(char_type c);
  streamsize sputn(const char_type* s, streamsize n);
protected:
  basic_streambuf();
  // Input
  char_type* eback() const;
  char_type* gptr() const;
  char_type* egptr() const;
  void gbump(int n);
  void setg(char_type* gbeg, char_type* gnext, char_type* gend);
  // Output
  char_type* pbase() const;
  char_type* pptr() const;
  char_type* epptr() const;
  void pbump(int n);
  void setp(char_type* pbeg, char_type* pend);
  // Locales
  virtual void imbue(const locale &loc);
  // Buffer management and positioning
  virtual basic_streambuf<char_type,traits>*
    setbuf(char_type* s, streamsize n);
  virtual pos_type seekoff(off_type off, ios_base::seekdir way,
                      ios_base::openmode which = ios_base::in |
                      ios_base::out);
  virtual pos_type seekpos(pos_type sp, ios_base::openmode which = ios_base::in |
                      ios_base::out);
  virtual streamsize showmanyc();
```

```
   virtual int sync( );
   virtual int_type underflow( );
   virtual int_type uflow( );
   virtual streamsize xsgetn(char_type* s, streamsize n);
   // Putback
   virtual int_type pbackfail(int_type c = traits::eof( ));
   // Output
   virtual int_type overflow(int_type c = traits::eof( ));
   virtual streamsize xsputn(const char_type* s, streamsize n);
};
```

The basic_streambuf class template manages an input buffer and an output buffer, in which each buffer is an array of characters. The base character type is a template parameter, charT. A buffer has the following three pointers to the array (the names below are not part of the standard but are used for informational purposes only):

begin
> Points to the beginning of the array

next
> Points to the next element in the array, that is, the next character to read or the position at which to write the next character

end
> Points to one past the end of the array

The pointers in this list can all be null pointers, which makes the stream "buffer" unbuffered. If the pointers are not null, the following rules apply:

* If *next* < *end* for an output array, the stream buffer is said to have a *write position*. The next output character is written to **next*.

* If *begin* < *next* for an input array, the stream buffer is said to have a *push back position*. When a character is pushed back, it is stored in *next*[-1].

* If *next* < *end* for an input array, the stream buffer is said to have a *read position*. The next character to read from the buffer is **next*.

Figure 13-25 depicts an input buffer, in which the characters "Hello, world." have been fetched from the input source. So far, the first six characters have been read from the input buffer, and the next character to read is the space between "Hello," and "world."

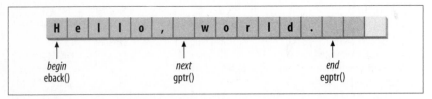

Figure 13-25. Input stream buffer

Figure 13-26 depicts an output buffer, which has room for 12 characters. So far, the buffer contains the five characters "Hello".

Several functions come in pairs: a public function that is the public interface and a protected, virtual function to do the actual work. For example, pubsync is a public function that simply calls sync, which is protected and virtual. The name of the public function is pub followed by the name of the protected function. The two exceptions are

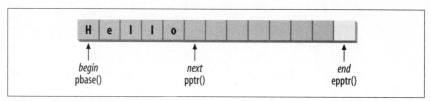

Figure 13-26. Output stream buffer

sgetn and sputn, which are public, with xsgetn and xsputn as their protected counterparts.

The basic_streambuf class template implements minimal functionality for managing the buffer pointers. Derived-class templates must override the virtual functions to provide concrete behavior. See basic_filebuf in <fstream>, basic_stringbuf in <sstream>, and strstreambuf in <strstream> for examples of derived classes and templates.

The following descriptions start with the expected public behavior. If you are writing a stream class that uses a stream buffer, you can rely on that behavior from the stream buffer object. If you are writing your own derived-class template, that is the behavior you must implement. Each description ends with the actual implementation in basic_streambuf.

When comparing characters, converting characters to integers or integers to characters, and obtaining the end-of-file marker, basic_streambuf uses the character traits specified by the traits template parameter. See <string> for information about the default character traits, char_traits.

The following are the public member functions of basic_streambuf:

locale **getloc**( ) const
> Returns the current locale, which can be set by calling pubimbue.

streamsize **in_avail**( )
> Returns the number of characters available for input. The return value is egptr( ) − gptr( ) if the stream buffer has a read position, or the result of calling showmanyc( ) if the stream buffer does not have a read position.

locale **pubimbue**(const locale &loc)
> Saves a copy of the locale, loc. Subsequent calls to getloc return a copy of the imbued locale. The basic_streambuf class does not use the locale, but a derived class can use the locale to interpret multibyte characters and for other purposes. When a stream buffer is created, it is initially imbued with the global locale.

pos_type **pubseekoff**(off_type off, ios_base::seekdir way, ios_base::openmode which=ios_base::in|ios_base::out)
pos_type **pubseekoff**(off_type off, ios_base::seekdir way, ios_base::open_mode which=ios_base::in|ios_base::out)
> Returns seekoff(off, way, which), which changes the stream position. The second form is deprecated. See ios_base::openmode in <ios> for details.

pos_type **pubseekpos**(pos_type sp, ios_base::openmode which=ios_base::in|ios_base::out)
pos_type **pubseekpos**(pos_type sp, ios_base::open_mode which)
> Returns seekpos(off, way, which), which changes the stream position. The second form is deprecated. See ios_base::openmode in <ios> for details.

Library
Reference

basic_streambuf<char_type,traits>* **pubsetbuf**(char_type* s, streamsize n)
> Returns setbuf(s, n), which typically sets the *begin*, *next*, and *end* array pointers.

int **pubsync**( )
> Returns sync( ), which synchronizes the internal arrays with the external I/O source, if any. The pubsync function returns -1 for a failure and any other value for success.

int_type **snextc**( )
> Returns the next input character and advances the input pointers. Specifically, snextc calls sbumpc( ), and if sbumpc returns traits::eof( ), snextc returns traits::eof( ); otherwise, it returns sgetc( ).

int_type **sbumpc**( )
int_type **stossc**( )
> Returns the next input character (if one is available) and increments the input array's *next* pointer. If there is no read position, sbumpc returns uflow( ); otherwise, it returns *gptr( ).

> The stossc function is deprecated. If it is implemented, it calls sbumpc( ).

int_type **sgetc**( )
> Returns the next available input character without advancing the input pointer. If no read position is available, sgetc returns underflow( ); otherwise, it returns *gptr( ).

streamsize **sgetn**(char_type* s, streamsize n)
> Returns xsgetn(s, n).

virtual streamsize **showmanyc**( )
> Returns an estimate of the number of characters immediately available for input. If showmanyc returns a positive value, at least that many characters can be read before underflow returns traits::eof( ). If showmanyc returns -1, calls to underflow or uflow will fail. If the return value is 0, input might be available, but there is no guarantee. Read the function name as s-how-many-c.

int_type **sputbackc**(char_type c)
> Tries to push back the character c so the next read will return c. If a push-back position is available (gptr( ) > ebase( )), and the most recently read character (gptr( )[-1]) is c, the input *next* pointer is decremented, and *gptr( ) is returned. Otherwise, pbackfail(c) is returned.

int_type **sputc**(char_type c)
> Writes the character c to the output array and returns c if an output position is available. Otherwise, sputc returns overflow(c).

streamsize **sputn**(const char_type* s, streamsize n);
> Calls xsputn(s, n) to write a string s of length n.

int_type **sungetc**( )
> Pushes back the character that was read most recently from the input stream. If a push-back position is available, the function decrements the input *next* pointer and returns *gptr( ); otherwise, it returns pbackfail( ).

The following are the protected member functions of basic_streambuf. Those marked as virtual should probably be overridden in a derived class template.

basic_streambuf( )
> Initializes all pointers to null pointers. The locale (as returned from getloc( )) is initialized to the current global locale.

---

char_type* **eback**( ) const
Returns the *begin* pointer for the input array.

char_type* **egptr**( ) const
Returns the *end* pointer for the input array.

char_type* **epptr**( ) const
Returns the *end* pointer for the output array.

void **gbump**(int n)
Advances the *next* pointer for the input array by n characters.

char_type* **gptr**( ) const
Returns the *next* pointer for the input array.

virtual void **imbue**(const locale &loc)
A derived class overrides the imbue function to take whatever action is needed when the stream buffer's locale is changed. For example, the stream buffer might cache facets or other information from the new locale.

The pubimbue function calls imbue *before* storing a new locale; thus, within the call to imbue, the getloc function returns the old locale, and the loc parameter is the new locale.

The default behavior for imbue is to do nothing.

virtual int_type **overflow** (int_type c = traits::eof( ))
The stream buffer calls overflow to flush the output buffer when it is full. The overflow function handles the sequence of characters stored in the buffer array, or an empty string if the *begin* and other pointers are null. If c is not traits::eof( ), c is appended to the output sequence. For example, a file stream buffer might write the array to the file. If an output error occurs, an exception is thrown or traits::eof( ) is returned. For success, any value other than traits::eof( ) is returned.

The default behavior is to do nothing and return traits::eof( ).

virtual int_type **pbackfail**(int_type c = traits::eof( ))
Handles a push-back failure. When the sungetc or sputbackc functions try to push back a character, they first attempt to adjust the current input *next* pointer. This can fail for one of three reasons:

- Input is unbuffered (gptr( ) == 0).
- The input buffer is empty (gptr( ) == eback( )).
- The push-back character, c, is not the same character that was most recently read (that is, c != gptr( )[-1]).

If the push-back attempt fails, pbackfail mediates with the external input source, if any, to try to complete the push-back operation. For example, a file stream buffer might adjust the external file position so the next character read from the input array will retrieve the pushed-back character.

If c is traits::eof( ), the input sequence is moved back one position to reread the character at that position. If c is not traits::eof( ), pbackfail tries to ensure that the next character read will be c; the derived class is free to modify the input source, change the stream position, or take another action to push back c.

The return value is traits::eof( ) for failure or any other value for success.

The default behavior is to do nothing and return traits::eof( ).

char_type* **pbase**( ) const
>   Returns the output buffer's *begin* pointer.

void **pbump**(int n)
>   Increments the output buffer's *next* pointer by n characters.

char_type* **pptr**( ) const
>   Returns the output buffer's *next* pointer.

Virtual pos_type **seekoff**(off_type off, ios_base::seekdir way,
> ios_base::openmode which=ios_base::in|ios_base::out)
>   Changes the stream position. The default behavior is to do nothing except return
>   pos_type(-1).

virtual pos_type **seekpos**(pos_type sp,
> ios_base::openmode which=ios_base::in|ios_base::out)
>   Changes the stream position. The default behavior is to do nothing except return
>   pos_type(-1).

virtual basic_streambuf<char_type,traits>* **setbuf**(char_type* s,
> streamsize n)
>   Typically sets the internal array pointers. The default behavior is to do nothing
>   and return this.

void **setg**(char_type* gbegin, char_type* gnext, char_type* gend)
>   Sets the input array pointers: *begin* = gbegin, *next* = gnext, and *end* = gend.

void **setp**(char_type* pbegin, char_type* pend)
>   Sets the output array pointers: *begin* = *next* = pbegin and *end* = pend.

virtual int **sync**( )
>   Synchronizes the stream buffer with its external source, if any. Any characters in
>   the output array are written, and all pointers are adjusted as needed. The return
>   value is -1 for failure and anything else for success.
>
>   The default behavior is to do nothing and return 0.

virtual int_type **uflow**( )
>   Fills the input array and fetches the first character from the array. It is called from
>   sbumpc if the input is not buffered (gptr( ) == 0) or if the input buffer is empty
>   (gptr( ) >= egptr( )). Input is obtained from the external source, and the input
>   pointers are reset.
>
>   The key difference between uflow and underflow is that uflow advances the input
>   *next* pointer after returning the first character in the buffer, but underflow does
>   not.
>
>   The return value from uflow is *gptr( ) if there is a read position or traits::eof( )
>   if there is no more input or some other failure occurs.
>
>   The default behavior is to do nothing and return traits::eof( ).

virtual int_type **underflow**( )
>   Fills the input array and returns the first character in the array. The sgetc( ) func-
>   tion calls underflow when the input is not buffered (gptr( ) == 0) or when the
>   input buffer is empty (gptr( ) >= egptr( )). Input is obtained from the external
>   source, and the input pointers are reset.
>
>   The key difference between uflow and underflow is that uflow advances the input
>   *next* pointer after returning the first character in the buffer, but underflow does
>   not.

The return value is *gptr( ) if there is a read position or traits::eof( ) if there is no more input or some other failure occurs.

The default behavior is to do nothing and return traits::eof( ).

virtual streamsize **xsgetn**(char_type* s, streamsize n)

Reads up to n characters from the input stream into the character array that s points to. No null character is appended to s. It is equivalent to calling sbumpc up to n times or until it returns traits::eof( ). The number of characters actually read and stored in s is returned. Derived classes can override this function to provide a more efficient implementation.

virtual streamsize **xsputn**(const char_type* s, streamsize n)

Writes up to n characters from s to the output stream. It is equivalent to calling sputc up to n times or until it returns traits::eof( ). The number of characters actually written is returned. Derived classes can override this function to provide a more efficient implementation.

See Also

basic_filebuf in <fstream>, basic_stringbuf in <sstream>

---

streambuf class
Stream buffer specialization

typedef basic_streambuf<char> streambuf;

The streambuf class specializes basic_streambuf for the char type.

See Also

char_traits<char> in <string>

---

wstreambuf class
Stream buffer, wide character specialization

typedef basic_streambuf<wchar_t> wstreambuf;

The wstreambuf class specializes basic_streambuf for the wchar_t type.

See Also

char_traits<wchar_t> in <string>

<string>

The <string> header declares the class templates and functions that support the string and wstring types, which are specializations of the basic_string class template. The string types are easier to use and safer than C-style character arrays. Another important class template is char_traits, which describes a character type and is used throughout the standard library.

The complete declarations of the overloaded operators can be daunting to read. To help you, each function template declaration is followed by a comment that shows the equivalent declaration that uses the common typedefs for narrow characters (e.g., string instead of basic_string<charT, traits, Allocator>).

Example 13-37 shows a function that classifies a string as an identifier, integer, floating point, or other. The example demonstrates the use of the string class and several of its member functions.

Example 13-37. Classifying a string

```cpp
#include <iostream>
#include <string>

enum kind { empty, ident, integer, floatingpt, error };

kind classify(const std::string& s)
{
  using std::string;
  const string lower("abcdefghijklmnopqrstuvwxyz");
  const string upper("ABCDEFGHIJKLMNOPQRSTUVWXYZ");
  const string letters = lower + upper + '_';
  const string digits("0123456789");
  const string identchars = letters + digits;

  if (s.empty())
    return empty;

  else if (letters.find_first_of(s[0]) != string::npos) {
    // Check for valid identifier.
    if (s.find_first_not_of(identchars, 1) == string::npos)
      return ident;
    else
      return error;
  }

  // Skip a leading sign, if present.
  string::size_type pos;
  if (s[0] == '+' or s[0] == '-')
    pos = 1;
  else
    pos = 0;

  // The number must start with a digit.
  if (pos == s.length())
    return error;
  if (not digits.find_first_of(s[pos]))
    return error;
  // Find where the digit string ends.
  pos = s.find_first_not_of(digits, pos);
  if (pos == string::npos)
    // Only digits => integer
    return integer;

  else if (s[pos] == '.') {
    // There is a decimal point.
    pos = s.find_first_not_of(digits, pos+1);
    if (pos == string::npos)
```

Example 13-37. Classifying a string (continued)

```
      // Integer part "." fractional part
      return floatingpt;
  }

  // Look for optional exponent.
  if (s[pos] == 'e' or s[pos] == 'E') {
    if (pos == s.length() - 1)
      return error; // 'e' or 'E' is last char
    else if (s[pos+1] == '+' or s[pos+1] == '-')
      ++pos;          // skip over sign;
    if (pos == s.length() - 1)
      return error; // Sign is last char.
    pos = s.find_first_not_of(digits, pos+1);
    if (pos == string::npos)
      return floatingpt;
  }

  return error;
}
```

---

basic_string class template

Base class for string types

```
template<class charT, class traits = char_traits<charT>,
         class Alloc = allocator<charT> >
class basic_string {
public:
  typedef traits traits_type;
  typedef typename traits::char_type value_type;
  typedef Alloc allocator_type;
  typedef typename Alloc::size_type size_type;
  typedef typename Alloc::difference_type difference_type;
  typedef typename Alloc::reference reference;
  typedef typename Alloc::const_reference const_reference;
  typedef typename Alloc::pointer pointer;
  typedef typename Alloc::const_pointer const_pointer;
  typedef ... iterator;
  typedef ... const_iterator;
  typedef std::reverse_iterator<iterator> reverse_iterator;
  typedef std::reverse_iterator<const_iterator> const_reverse_iterator;
  static const size_type npos = -1;

  explicit basic_string(const Alloc& a = Alloc());
  basic_string(const basic_string& str);
  basic_string(const basic_string& str, size_type pos, size_type n = npos,
               const Alloc& a = Alloc());
  basic_string(const charT* s, size_type n, const Alloc& a = Alloc());
  basic_string(const charT* s, const Alloc& a = Alloc());
  basic_string(size_type n, charT c, const Alloc& a=Alloc());
  template<class InputIterator>
  basic_string(InputIterator begin, InputIterator end,
               const Alloc& a = Alloc());
  ~basic_string();
```

```
basic_string& operator=(const basic_string& str);
basic_string& operator=(const charT* s);
basic_string& operator=(charT c);

iterator begin( );
const_iterator begin( ) const;
iterator end( );
const_iterator end( ) const;
reverse_iterator rbegin( );
const_reverse_iterator rbegin( ) const;
reverse_iterator rend( );
const_reverse_iterator rend( ) const;
// Size and capacity
size_type size( ) const;
size_type length( ) const;
size_type max_size( ) const;
void resize(size_type n, charT c);
void resize(size_type n);
size_type capacity( ) const;
void reserve(size_type res_arg = 0);
void clear( );
bool empty( ) const;
// Element access
const_reference operator[](size_type pos) const;
reference operator[](size_type pos);
const_reference at(size_type n) const;
reference at(size_type n);
basic_string substr(size_type pos = 0, size_type n = npos) const;
// Modifiers
basic_string& operator+=(const basic_string& str);
basic_string& operator+=(const charT* s);
basic_string& operator+=(charT c);
basic_string& append(const basic_string& str);
basic_string& append(const basic_string& str, size_type pos, size_type n);
basic_string& append(const charT* s, size_type n);
basic_string& append(const charT* s);
basic_string& append(size_type n, charT c);
template<class InputIter>
basic_string& append(InputIter first, InputIter last);
void push_back(charT c);
basic_string& assign(const basic_string& str);
basic_string& assign(const basic_string& str, size_type pos, size_type n);
basic_string& assign(const charT* s, size_type n);
basic_string& assign(const charT* s);
basic_string& assign(size_type n, charT c);
template<class InputIter>
basic_string& assign(InputIter first, InputIter last);
basic_string& insert(size_type pos1, const basic_string& str);
basic_string& insert(size_type pos1, const basic_string& str, size_type pos2,
                     size_type n);
basic_string& insert(size_type pos, const charT* s, size_type n);
basic_string& insert(size_type pos, const charT* s);
basic_string& insert(size_type pos, size_type n, charT c);
iterator insert(iterator p, charT c);
```

```
void insert(iterator p, size_type n, charT c);
template<class InputIter>
void insert(iterator p, InputIter first, InputIter last);
basic_string& erase(size_type pos = 0, size_type n = npos);
iterator erase(iterator position);
iterator erase(iterator first, iterator last);
basic_string& replace(size_type pos1, size_type n1, const basic_string& str);
basic_string& replace(size_type pos1, size_type n1, const basic_string& str,
                      size_type pos2,  size_type n2);
basic_string& replace(size_type pos, size_type n1, const charT* s,
                      size_type n2);
basic_string& replace(size_type pos, size_type n1, const charT* s);
basic_string& replace(size_type pos, size_type n1, size_type n2, charT c);
basic_string& replace(iterator i1, iterator i2, const basic_string& str);
basic_string& replace(iterator i1, iterator i2, const charT* s, size_type n);
basic_string& replace(iterator i1, iterator i2, const charT* s);
basic_string& replace(iterator i1, iterator i2, size_type n, charT c);
template<class InputIterator>
basic_string& replace(iterator i1, iterator i2, InputIterator j1,
                      InputIterator j2);
size_type copy(charT* s, size_type n, size_type pos = 0) const;
void swap(basic_string& str);
// String operations
const charT* c_str( ) const;
const charT* data( ) const;
allocator_type get_allocator( ) const;
// Searching
size_type find(const basic_string& str, size_type pos = 0) const;
size_type find(const charT* s, size_type pos, size_type n) const;
size_type find(const charT* s, size_type pos = 0) const;
size_type find(charT c, size_type pos = 0) const;
size_type rfind(const basic_string& str, size_type pos = npos) const;
size_type rfind(const charT* s, size_type pos, size_type n) const;
size_type rfind(const charT* s, size_type pos=npos) const;
size_type rfind(charT c, size_type pos = npos) const;
size_type find_first_of(const basic_string& str, size_type pos = 0) const;
size_type find_first_of(const charT* s, size_type pos, size_type n) const;
size_type find_first_of(const charT* s, size_type pos = 0) const;
size_type find_first_of(charT c, size_type pos = 0) const;
size_type find_last_of(const basic_string& str, size_type pos = npos) const;
size_type find_last_of(const charT* s, size_type pos, size_type n) const;
size_type find_last_of(const charT* s, size_type pos = npos) const;
size_type find_last_of(charT c, size_type pos=npos) const;
size_type find_first_not_of(const basic_string& str, size_type pos = 0) const;
size_type find_first_not_of(const charT* s, size_type pos, size_type n) const;
size_type find_first_not_of(const charT* s, size_type pos = 0) const;
size_type find_first_not_of(charT c, size_type pos = 0) const;
size_type find_last_not_of(const basic_string& str, size_type pos = npos)
                          const;
size_type find_last_not_of(const charT* s, size_type pos, size_type n) const;
size_type find_last_not_of(const charT* s, size_type pos = npos) const;
size_type find_last_not_of(charT c, size_type pos = npos) const;
// Comparisons
int compare(const basic_string& str) const;
```

```
   int compare(size_type pos1, size_type n1, const basic_string& str) const;
   int compare(size_type pos1, size_type n1, const basic_string& str,
               size_type pos2, size_type n2) const;
   int compare(const charT* s) const;
   int compare(size_type pos1, size_type n1, const charT* s) const;
   int compare(size_type pos1, size_type n1, const charT* s, size_type n2)
     const;
};
```

The basic_string class template is the base for the string and wstring types. A string object holds a sequence, or string, of characters and provides a number of useful member functions for searching and modifying the string. You can also work with C-style, null-terminated character strings as arguments to basic_string members, including constructors. A basic_string object keeps track of an explicit length instead of using the C convention of null-terminated character arrays. The string and wstring types are therefore much easier to use and offer greater safety (see the at member function), while still offering ease-of-use with many functions that take C-style strings as arguments.

If you need a sequence of characters that you don't need to treat as a character string, you can use vector<char> or vector<wchar_t>, but in most cases you will probably find string or wstring to be more convenient. You can usually use a string or wstring as a container that supports random access iterators, so you can use strings with the standard algorithms.

Many of the member functions can throw exceptions. Specifying an index out of range often throws out_of_range. An attempt to construct a string or modify a string so its length exceeds max_size( ) throws length_error. The basic_string class uses an allocator object for memory allocation, which can throw an exception (such as bad_alloc) almost any time the string is modified.

Iterators, pointers, and references to elements of a string become invalid in the following situations:

- The string is the target of the swap member function or an argument to the swap function template.

- The string is an argument to operator>> or getline.

- You call the data or c_str member function.

- You call any non-const member function except operator[], at, begin, end, rbegin, or rend.

- You call the non-const version of operator[], at, begin, end, rbegin, or rend after any of the above situations, except after calling a form of insert or erase that returns an iterator (so the returned iterator remains valid).

The following are the members of basic_string. Several small examples appear throughout this section, illustrating the use of some of the more complex member functions. Some of the functions are described in terms of temporary string objects or calls to other member functions. The actual implementation might be different, provided the behavior is the same.

explicit **basic_string**(const Alloc& a = Alloc( ))
    Constructs an empty string.

basic_string(const basic_string& str)
    Constructs a string that is a copy of str, with Alloc( ) as the allocator.

basic_string(const basic_string& str, size_type pos, size_type n = npos, const Alloc& a = Alloc( ))
> Copies a substring of str, starting at pos. If pos is out of range (that is, pos > str.size( )), out_of_range is thrown. The number of characters copied is n or the number of characters left in the string (str.size( ) - pos), whichever is smaller.

basic_string(const charT* s, size_type n, const Alloc& a = Alloc( ))
> Copies the first n characters from s.

basic_string(const charT* s, const Alloc& a = Alloc( ))
> Copies a null-terminated character array, s. More precisely, this constructor copies traits::length(s) characters from s.

basic_string(size_type n, charT c, const Alloc& a = Alloc( ))
> Initializes the string with n copies of the character c.

template<class InputIterator>
basic_string(InputIterator begin, InputIterator end, const Alloc& a = Alloc( ))
> The constructor depends on the type of InputIterator:
>
> * For any input iterator, the string is initialized by copying the contents of the range [begin, end).
>
> * If InputIterator is an integral type, the string is initialized with static_cast<size_type>(begin) copies of the character static_cast<value_type>(end).

basic_string& **append**(const basic_string& str, size_type pos, size_type n)
> Appends characters to the end of the string. If pos > str.size( ), out_of_range is thrown. Otherwise, up to n characters are copied from str, starting at position pos. The return value is *this. See also operator+= later in this section.

basic_string& **append**(const basic_string& str)
> Returns append(str, 0, npos).

basic_string& **append**(const charT* s, size_type n)
basic_string& **append**(const charT* s)
basic_string& **append**(size_type n, charT c)
template<class InputIter>
basic_string& **append**(InputIter first, InputIter last)
> Constructs a temporary string *str*, passing the arguments to the constructor, and returns append(*str*).

basic_string& **assign**(const basic_string& str, size_type pos, size_type n)
> Erases the current contents of the string and replaces them with the substring of str that starts at pos and extends for up to n characters. The return value is *this. See also operator= later in this section.

basic_string& **assign**(const basic_string& str)
> Returns assign(str, 0, npos).

basic_string& **assign**(const charT* s, size_type n)
basic_string& **assign**(const charT* s)
basic_string& **assign**(size_type n, charT c)
template<class InputIter>
basic_string& **assign**(InputIter first, InputIter last)
> Constructs a temporary string *str*, passing the arguments to the constructor, and returns assign(*str*).

const_reference **at**(size_type n) const
reference **at**(size_type n)
> Returns the character at position n. If n >= size( ), out_of_range is thrown. See also operator[] later in this section.

iterator **begin**( )
const_iterator **begin**( ) const
> Returns an iterator that points to the first character of the string.

const charT* **c_str**( ) const
> Returns a pointer to a null-terminated (C-style) character array that contains the same characters as the string followed by a terminating null character. The pointer becomes invalid after calling any non-const member function of the string. The typical use of c_str is to interface with C functions that require a null-terminated character string:
>
>   std::printf(fmtstr.c_str( ), value);
>
> See also the data member function.

size_type **capacity**( ) const
> Returns the number of characters allocated for use by the string. The string grows as needed; capacity tells you how much you can put in the string before it must grow again.

void **clear**( )
> Erases all the characters in the string.

int **compare**(const basic_string& str) const
> Returns traits::compare(data( ), str.data( ), *len*), in which *len* is the smaller of size( ) and str.size( ).

int **compare**(size_type pos1, size_type n1, const basic_string& str) const
> Constructs a temporary string *tmp*(*this, pos1, n1), and returns *tmp*.compare(str).

int **compare**(const charT* s) const
> Constructs a temporary string *tmp*(s), and returns this->compare(*tmp*).

int **compare**(size_type pos1, size_type n1, const basic_string& str, size_type pos2, size_type n2) const
int **compare**(size_type pos1, size_type n1, const charT* s) const
int **compare**(size_type pos1, size_type n1, const charT* s, size_type n2) const
> Constructs two temporary strings *tmp1*(*this, pos1, n1) and *tmp2*: *tmp2*(str, pos2, n2), *tmp2*(s), or *tmp2*(s, n2). The function returns *tmp1*.compare(*tmp2*).

size_type **copy**(charT* dst, size_type n, size_type pos = 0) const
> Copies up to n characters from the string, starting at position pos, to the character array dst. If pos > size( ), out_of_range is thrown. The number of characters copied, *len*, is the smaller of n and size( ) - pos. The return value is *len*.

const charT* **data**( ) const
> Returns a pointer to a character array that has the same character contents as the string. Note that the character array is not null-terminated. If size( ) == 0, data returns a valid, non-null pointer. Do not modify the contents of the data string. The pointer becomes invalid after calling any non-const member function of the string. See also the c_str member function.

bool **empty**( ) const
> Returns true if the string is empty (size( ) == 0).

iterator **end**( )
const_iterator **end**( ) const
> Returns an iterator that points to one position past the end of the string.

basic_string& **erase**(size_type pos = 0, size_type n = npos)
> Erases characters from the string, starting at position pos and erasing n or size( ) - pos characters, whichever is smaller. If pos > size( ), out_of_range is thrown. The return value is *this. For example:

```
std::string s("hello, world");
s.erase(9, 1) == "hello, wold"
s.erase(5)    == "hello"
```

iterator **erase**(iterator position)
> Erases the character at position and returns an iterator that points to the next character (if there is one) or end( ).

iterator **erase**(iterator first, iterator last)
> Erases characters in the range [first, last) and returns an iterator that points to the character that last pointed to (prior to the erasure) or end( ).

size_type **find**(const basic_string& str, size_type pos = 0) const
size_type **find**(const charT* s, size_type pos, size_type n) const
size_type **find**(const charT* s, size_type pos = 0) const
size_type **find**(charT c, size_type pos = 0) const
> Returns the smallest index of a string or character, or npos if the search fails. The search starts at position pos. The string to search for is str or a temporary string *tmp* constructed as *tmp*(s, n), *tmp*(s), or *tmp*(1, c). In other words, find returns the smallest i such that $i >= pos$, $i + str.size( ) <= size( )$, and $at(i+j) == str.at(j)$ for all j in $[0, str.size( ))$. For example:

```
string("hello").find('l')     == 2
string("hello").find("lo", 2) == 3
string("hello").find("low")   == string::npos
```

> See also rfind later in this section.

size_type **find_first_not_of**(const basic_string& str, size_type pos = 0) const
> Finds the first character at or after position pos that does not appear in str, or npos if every character appears in str. For example:

```
string("hello").find_first_not_of("aeiou")    == 0
string("hello").find_first_not_of("aeiou", 1) == 2
string("hello").find_first_not_of("aeiou", 6) == string::npos
```

size_type **find_first_not_of**(charT c, size_type pos = 0) const
size_type **find_first_not_of**(const charT* s, size_type pos = 0) const
size_type **find_first_not_of**(const charT* s, size_type pos, size_type n) const
> Constructs a temporary string *tmp* and returns find_first_not_of(*tmp*, pos), in which *tmp* is constructed as *tmp*(1, c), *tmp*(s), or *tmp*(s, n).

size_type **find_first_of**(const basic_string& str, size_type pos = 0) const
> Finds the first character at or after position pos that appears in str, or npos if no character appears in str. For example:

```
string("hello").find_first_of("aeiou")    = 1
string("hello").find_first_of("aeiou", 2) = 4
string("hello").find_first_of("aeiou", 6) = string::npos
```

```
size_type find_first_of(charT c, size_type pos = 0) const
size_type find_first_of(const charT* s, size_type pos = 0) const
size_type find_first_of(const charT* s, size_type pos, size_type n) const
```
> Constructs a temporary string *tmp* and returns find_first_of(*tmp*, pos), in which *tmp* is constructed as *tmp*(1, c), *tmp*(s), or *tmp*(s, n).

```
size_type find_last_not_of(const basic_string& str, size_type pos = npos) const
```
> Finds the last character at or before position pos that does not appear in str, or npos if every character appears in str. For example:
> ```
> string("hello").find_last_not_of("aeiou")    == 3
> string("hello").find_last_not_of("aeiou", 1) == 0
> string("hello").find_last_not_of("aeiou", 0) == 0
> ```

```
size_type find_last_not_of(charT c, size_type pos = npos) const
size_type find_last_not_of(const charT* s, size_type pos = npos) const
size_type find_last_not_of(const charT* s, size_type pos, size_type n) const
```
> Constructs a temporary string *tmp* and returns find_last_not_of(*tmp*, pos), in which *tmp* is constructed as *tmp*(1, c), *tmp*(s), or *tmp*(s, n).

```
size_type find_last_of(const basic_string& str, size_type pos = npos) const
```
> Finds the last character at or before position pos that appears in str, or npos if no character appears in str. For example:
> ```
> string("hello").find_last_of("aeiou")    == 4
> string("hello").find_last_of("aeiou", 3) == 1
> string("hello").find_last_of("aeiou", 0) == string::npos
> ```

```
size_type find_last_of(charT c, size_type pos = npos) const
size_type find_last_of(const charT* s, size_type pos = npos) const
size_type find_last_of(const charT* s, size_type pos, size_type n) const
```
> Constructs a temporary string *tmp* and returns find_last_of(*tmp*, pos), in which *tmp* is constructed as *tmp*(1, c), *tmp*(s), or *tmp*(s, n).

```
allocator_type get_allocator() const
```
> Returns the string's allocator object.

```
basic_string& insert(size_type pos1, const basic_string& str, size_type pos2, size_type n)
```
> Inserts a substring of str into the string starting at position pos1. The substring to insert starts at pos2 and extends for up to n characters. If pos1 > size() or pos2 > str.size(), out_of_range is thrown. The number of characters inserted is the smaller of n and str.size() - pos2. The return value is *this. For example:
> ```
> string s("hello");
> s.insert(5, ", world")          // s == "hello, world"
> s.insert(5, "out there", 3, 42) // s == "hello there, world"
> ```

```
basic_string& insert(size_type pos, const basic_string& str)
basic_string& insert(size_type pos, const charT* s, size_type n)
basic_string& insert(size_type pos, const charT* s)
basic_string& insert(size_type pos, size_type n, charT c)
```
> Returns insert(pos, str, 0, npos), in which the last three versions construct a temporary string *tmp* as *tmp*(s, n), *tmp*(s), or *tmp*(n, c), and then returns insert(pos, *tmp*, 0, npos).

```
iterator insert(iterator p, charT c)
void insert(iterator p, size_type n, charT c)
template<class InputIter>
void insert(iterator p, InputIter first, InputIter last)
```
Inserts text before the character that p points to. The first version inserts the character c and returns an iterator that points to c, the second version inserts n copies of the character c, and the third version inserts the temporary string constructed from the arguments (first, last). If InputIter is an integral type, the temporary string contains static_cast<size_type>(first) copies of the character static_cast<value_type>(last).

```
size_type length( ) const
```
Returns size( ).

```
size_type max_size( ) const
```
Returns the size of the largest possible string.

```
const_reference operator[](size_type pos) const
reference operator[](size_type pos)
```
Returns the character at position pos. If pos == size( ), the return value is charT( ), that is, a null character. The behavior is undefined if pos > size( ).

```
basic_string& operator=(const basic_string& str)
```
If *this and str are the same object, the assignment operator does nothing and returns *this. If they are different objects, the operator replaces the current string contents with the contents of str and returns *this.

```
basic_string& operator=(const charT* s)
basic_string& operator=(charT c)
```
Constructs a temporary string, *tmp*(s) or *tmp*(1, c), and assigns *this = *tmp*. The return value is *this.

```
basic_string& operator+=(const basic_string& str)
basic_string& operator+=(const charT* s)
basic_string& operator+=(charT c)
```
Calls append with the same arguments and returns *this.

```
void push_back(charT c)
```
Appends c to the end of the string. Its existence lets you use basic_string with a back_insert_iterator.

```
reverse_iterator rbegin( )
const_reverse_iterator rbegin( ) const
```
Returns a reverse iterator that points to the last character of the string.

```
reverse_iterator rend( )
const_reverse_iterator rend( ) const
```
Returns a reverse iterator that points to one position before the first character of the string.

```
basic_string& replace(size_type pos1, size_type n1, const basic_string& str,
  size_type pos2, size_type n2)
```
Erases a substring and inserts another string in its place. The string to erase starts at pos1 and extends for up to n1 characters (the smaller of n1 and size( ) - pos1). The string to insert is a substring of str, starting at pos2 and extending for up to n2 characters (the smaller of n2 and str.size( ) - pos2). The replacement string is

inserted at pos1. If pos1 > size( ) or pos2 > str.size( ), out_of_range is thrown. The return value is *this.

```
basic_string& replace(size_type pos, size_type n1, const basic_string& str)
basic_string& replace(size_type pos, size_type n1, const charT* str)
basic_string& replace(size_type pos, size_type n1, const charT* s, size_type n2)
basic_string& replace(size_type pos, size_type n1, size_type n2, charT c)
```
Returns replace(pos, n1, *tmp*, 0, npos), in which *tmp* is a temporary string constructed as *tmp*(str), *tmp*(s, n2), or *tmp*(n2, c). For example:

```
std::string s("hello");
s.replace(1, 4, "appy")              s=="happy"
s.replace(5, 0, "your birthday !", 4, 10) s=="happy birthday"
s.replace(1, 1, 1, 'i')              s=="hippy birthday"
```

```
basic_string& replace(iterator first, iterator last, const basic_string& str)
```
Erases the text in the range [first, last) and inserts str at the position first pointed to. The return value is *this.

```
basic_string& replace(iterator first, iterator last, const charT* s, size_type n)
basic_string& replace(iterator first, iterator last, const charT* s)
basic_string& replace(iterator first, iterator last, size_type n, charT c)
template<class InputIterator>
basic_string& replace(iterator first, iterator last, InputIterator i1,
    InputIterator i2)
```
Returns replace(first, last, *tmp*), in which *tmp* is a temporary string constructed as *tmp*(s, n), *tmp*(s), *tmp*(n, c), or *tmp*(i1, i2).

```
void reserve(size_type res_arg = 0)
```
Ensures that the capacity( ) is at least as large as res_arg. Call reserve to avoid the need to reallocate the string data repeatedly when you know the string will grow by small increments to a large size. Note that size( ) does not change.

```
void resize(size_type n, charT c)
void resize(size_type n)
```
Changes the size of the string to n characters. If n <= size( ), the new string has the first n characters of the original string. If n > size( ), the new string has n − size( ) copies of c appended to the end. The second version returns resize(n, charT( )).

```
size_type rfind(const basic_string& str, size_type pos = npos) const
size_type rfind(const charT* s, size_type pos, size_type n) const
size_type rfind(const charT* s, size_type pos = npos) const
size_type rfind(charT c, size_type pos = npos) const
```
Returns the largest index at or before pos of a string or character or npos if the search fails. The string to search for is str or a temporary string *tmp* constructed as *tmp*(s, n), *tmp*(s), or *tmp*(1, c). In other words, rfind returns the largest i such that $i <=$ pos, $i +$ str.size( ) $<=$ size( ), and at($i+j$) == str.at(j) for all j in [0, str.size( )). (See also find, earlier in this section.) For example:

```
string("hello").rfind('l')     == 3
string("hello").rfind("lo", 2) == string::npos
string("hello").rfind("low")   == string::npos
```

```
size_type size( ) const
```
Returns the number of characters (not bytes) in the string.

basic_string **substr**(size_type pos = 0, size_type n = npos) const
> Returns a substring that starts at position pos and extends for up to n characters (the smaller of n and size( ) - pos). If pos > size( ), out_of_range is thrown.

void **swap**(basic_string& str)
> Exchanges string contents with str in constant time.

See Also

char_traits class template, <sstream>, <vector>

---

char_traits class template

Base class for character traits

template<typename charT> struct **char_traits**;

The char_traits template describes a character type and provides basic functions for comparing, converting, and copying character values and arrays. (See the char_traits<char> and char_traits<wchar_t> specializations later in this section for details.) If you create a custom character type, you should specialize char_traits<> or define your own traits class, which you can provide to basic_string and other templates as the traits template parameter. Your traits class should define the same members that char_traits<char> defines. See Chapter 8 for an example.

See Also

char_traits<char> class, char_traits<wchar_t> class

---

char_traits<char> class

Character traits of char type

```
template<> struct char_traits<char> {
  typedef char char_type;
  typedef int int_type;
  typedef streamoff off_type;
  typedef streampos pos_type;
  typedef mbstate_t state_type;

  static void assign(char_type& dst, const char_type& src);
  static char_type* assign(char_type* dst, size_t n, const char_type& c);
  static bool eq(const char_type& c1, const char_type& c2);
  static bool lt(const char_type& c1, const char_type& c2);
  static size_t length(const char_type* str);
  static int compare(const char_type* s1, const char_type* s2, size_t n);
  static const char_type* find(const char_type* str, size_t n,
                               const char_type& c);
  static char_type* copy(char_type* dst, char_type* src, size_t n);
  static char_type* move(char_type* dst, char_type* src, size_t n);
  static bool eq_int_type(const int_type& i1, const int_type& i2);
  static int_type eof( );
  static int_type not_eof(const int_type& i);
  static char_type to_char_type(const int_type& i);
  static int_type to_int_type(const char_type& c);
};
```

The char_traits<char> class specializes char_traits for narrow characters. The streamoff type is implementation-defined. The streampos type is defined as fpos<mbstate_t> in <iosfwd>. The character traits are defined for the type char and

---

have the same meaning in all locales. The other types are self-explanatory. The following are the member functions:

static void **assign**(char_type& dst, const char_type& src)
> Assigns dst = src.

static char_type* **assign**(char_type* dst, size_t n, const char_type& c)
> Fills dst with n copies of c, that is, dst[0] through dst[n-1] = c.

static int **compare**(const char_type* s1, const char_type* s2, size_t n)
> Compares the first n characters of the arrays s1 and s2, returning an integer result:
>
> - 0 if eq(s1[i], s2[i]) is true for all i in [0, n)
> - Negative if eq(s1[i], s2[i]) is true for all i in [0, k), and lt(s1[k], s2[k]) is true for some k in [0, n)
> - Positive otherwise

static char_type* **copy**(char_type* dst, char_type* src, size_t n)
> Copies n characters from src to dst. The arrays src and dst must not overlap.

static int_type **eof**( )
> Returns the end-of-file marker, EOF (in <cstdio>). The end-of-file marker is different from all characters, that is, for all character values c, eq_int_type(eof( ), to_int_type(c)) is false.

static bool **eq**(const char_type& c1, const char_type& c2)
> Returns c1 == c2.

static bool **eq_int_type**(const int_type& i1, const int_type& i2)
> Returns true if i1 is the same as i2. Specifically, for all character values c1 and c2, eq(c1, c2) has the same value as eq_int_type(to_int_type(c1), to_int_type(c2)). Also, eof( ) is always equal to eof( ) and not equal to to_int_type(c) for any character c. The value is unspecified for any other integer values.

static const char_type* **find**(const char_type* str, size_t n,
  const char_type& c)
> Returns a pointer p to the first character in str such that eq(*p, c) is true. It returns a null pointer if there is no such character in the first n characters of str.

static size_t **length**(const char_type* str)
> Returns the length of the null-terminated character string str, that is, it returns the smallest i such that eq(str[i], charT( )) is true.

static bool **lt**(const char_type& c1, const char_type& c2)
> Returns c1 < c2.

static char_type* **move**(char_type* dst, char_type* src, size_t n)
> Copies n characters from src to dst. The arrays src and dst are allowed to overlap.

static int_type **not_eof**(const int_type& i)
> Returns a value that is guaranteed to be different from eof( ). If i is not eof( ), i is returned. Otherwise, some other value is returned.

static char_type **to_char_type**(const int_type& i)
> Converts i to its equivalent character value (for which eq_int_type(i, to_int_type(to_char_type(i))) is true). If i is not equivalent to any character, the behavior is unspecified.

static int_type **to_int_type**(const char_type& c)
> Converts c to its equivalent integer representation.

See Also

char_traits<wchar_t> class, mbstate_t in <cwchar>, fpos in <ios>, <iosfwd>

---

char_traits<wchar_t> class
Character traits of wchar_t type

```
template<> struct char_traits<wchar_t> {
  typedef wchar_t char_type;
  typedef wint_t int_type;
  typedef streamoff off_type;
  typedef wstreampos pos_type;
  typedef mbstate_t state_type;

  static void assign(char_type& dst, const char_type& src);
  static char_type* assign(char_type* dst, size_t n, const char_type& c);
  static bool eq(const char_type& c1, const char_type& c2);
  static bool lt(const char_type& c1, const char_type& c2);
  static size_t length(const char_type* str);
  static int compare(const char_type* s1, const char_type* s2, size_t n);
  static const char_type* find(const char_type* str, size_t n,
                               const char_type& c);
  static char_type* copy(char_type* dst, char_type* src, size_t n);
  static char_type* move(char_type* dst, char_type* src, size_t n);
  static bool eq_int_type(const int_type& i1, const int_type& i2);
  static int_type eof();
  static int_type not_eof(const int_type& i);
  static char_type to_char_type(const int_type& i);
  static int_type to_int_type(const char_type& c);
};
```

The char_traits<wchar_t> class specializes char_traits for wide characters. The wstreamoff type is implementation-defined. The wstreampos type is defined as fpos<mbstate_t> in <iosfwd>. The other types are self-explanatory. The character traits are defined for the type wchar_t and have the same meaning in all locales.

See char_traits<char> earlier in this section for a description of the member functions. The eof() function returns WEOF (in <cwchar>).

See Also

char_traits<char> class, mbstate_t in <cwchar>, fpos in <ios>, <iosfwd>

---

getline function template
Reads a line into a string

```
template<class charT, class traits, class Allocator>
  basic_istream<charT,traits>& getline(basic_istream<charT,traits>& in,
                                        basic_string<charT,traits,Allocator>& str,
                                        charT delim);
// istream& getline(istream& in, string& str, char delim);
template<class charT, class traits, class Allocator>
  basic_istream<charT,traits>& getline(basic_istream<charT,traits>& in,
                                        basic_string<charT,traits,Allocator>&
                                        str);
// istream& getline(istream& in, string& str);
```

The getline function template reads a line of text from an input stream into the string str. It starts by creating a basic_istream::sentry(in, true) object. If the sentry object evaluates to true, getline erases str then reads characters from in and appends them to str until end-of-file is reached or delim is read. (The delim character is read from the stream but not appended to the string.) Reading also stops if max_size( ) characters have been stored in the string, in which case ios_base::failbit is set. If no characters are read from the stream, ios_base::failbit is set. The return value is in.

The second form of getline uses a newline as the delimiter, that is, it returns getline(in, str, in.widen('\n')).

See Also

operator>> function template, basic_istream in <istream>, basic_istream::sentry in <istream>

---

operator+ function template   Concatenates two strings

```
template<class charT, class traits, class Allocator>
  basic_string<charT,traits,Allocator> operator+(
    const basic_string<charT,traits,Allocator>& a,
    const basic_string<charT,traits,Allocator>& b);
// string& operator+(const string& a, const string& b);
template<class charT, class traits, class Allocator>
  basic_string<charT,traits,Allocator> operator+(const charT* a,
    const basic_string<charT,traits,Allocator>& b);
// string& operator+(const char* a, const string& b);
template<class charT, class traits, class Allocator>
  basic_string<charT,traits,Allocator> operator+(
    const basic_string<charT,traits,Allocator>& a, const charT* b);
// string& operator+(const string& a, const char* b);
template<class charT, class traits, class Allocator>
  basic_string<charT,traits,Allocator> operator+(
    const basic_string<charT,traits,Allocator>& a, charT b);
// string& operator+(const string& a, char b);
```

The + operator concatenates two strings and returns the result. It constructs a new string as a copy of a, then calls a.append(b) and returns the copy.

See Also

basic_string class template

---

operator== function template   Compares strings for equality

```
template<class charT, class traits, class Allocator>
  bool operator==(
    const basic_string<charT,traits,Allocator>& a,
    const basic_string<charT,traits,Allocator>& b);
// bool operator==(const string& a, const string& b);
template<class charT, class traits, class Allocator>
  bool operator==(const charT* a, const basic_string<charT,traits,Allocator>& b);
// bool operator==(const char* a, const string& b);
template<class charT, class traits, class Allocator>
  bool operator==(const basic_string<charT,traits,Allocator>& a, const charT* b);
// bool operator==(const string& a, conat char* b);
```

The == operator compares two strings for equality or compares a string and a null-terminated character array. It returns a.compare(b) == 0, converting a or b from a character array to a string, as needed.

See Also

basic_string class template

---

operator!= function template

```
template<class charT, class traits, class Allocator>
  bool operator!=(
    const basic_string<charT,traits,Allocator>& a,
    const basic_string<charT,traits,Allocator>& b);
// bool operator!=(const string& a, const string& b);
template<class charT, class traits, class Allocator>
  bool operator!=(const charT* a, const basic_string<charT,traits,Allocator>& b);
// bool operator!=(const char* a, const string& b);
template<class charT, class traits, class Allocator>
  bool operator!=(const basic_string<charT,traits,Allocator>& a, const charT* b);
// bool operator!=(const string& a, conat char* b);
```

The != operator compares two strings for inequality or compares a string and a null-terminated character array. It returns !(a == b).

See Also

basic_string class template

---

operator< function template

```
template<class charT, class traits, class Allocator>
  bool operator<(
    const basic_string<charT,traits,Allocator>& a,
    const basic_string<charT,traits,Allocator>& b);
// bool operator<(const string& a, const string& b);
template<class charT, class traits, class Allocator>
  bool operator<(const charT* a, const basic_string<charT,traits,Allocator>& b);
// bool operator<(const char* a, const string& b);
template<class charT, class traits, class Allocator>
  bool operator<(const basic_string<charT,traits,Allocator>& a, const charT* b);
// bool operator<(const string& a, conat char* b);
```

The < operator compares two strings or compares a string and a null-terminated character array. It returns a.compare(b) < 0, converting a or b from a character array to a string, as needed.

See Also

basic_string class template

---

operator<= function template

```
template<class charT, class traits, class Allocator>
  bool operator<=(
    const basic_string<charT,traits,Allocator>& a,
    const basic_string<charT,traits,Allocator>& b);
```

```
// bool operator<=(const string& a, const string& b);
template<class charT, class traits, class Allocator>
  bool operator<=(const charT* a, const basic_string<charT,traits,Allocator>& b);
// bool operator<=(const char* a, const string& b);
template<class charT, class traits, class Allocator>
  bool operator<=(const basic_string<charT,traits,Allocator>& a, const charT* b);
// bool operator<=(const string& a, conat char* b);
```

The <= operator compares two strings or compares a string and a null-terminated character array. It returns a.compare(b) <= 0, converting a or b from a character array to a string, as needed.

See Also

basic_string class template,

---

operator> function template
Compares strings for greater-than

```
template<class charT, class traits, class Allocator>
  bool operator>(
    const basic_string<charT,traits,Allocator>& a,
    const basic_string<charT,traits,Allocator>& b);
// bool operator>(const string& a, const string& b);
template<class charT, class traits, class Allocator>
  bool operator>(const charT* a, const basic_string<charT,traits,Allocator>& b);
// bool operator>(const char* a, const string& b);
template<class charT, class traits, class Allocator>
  bool operator>(const basic_string<charT,traits,Allocator>& a, const charT* b);
// bool operator>(const string& a, conat char* b);
```

The > operator compares two strings or compares a string and a null-terminated character array. It returns a.compare(b) > 0, converting a or b from a character array to a string, as needed.

See Also

basic_string class template

---

operator>= function template
Compares strings for greater-than-or-equal

```
template<class charT, class traits, class Allocator>
  bool operator>=(
    const basic_string<charT,traits,Allocator>& a,
    const basic_string<charT,traits,Allocator>& b);
// bool operator>=(const string& a, const string& b);
template<class charT, class traits, class Allocator>
  bool operator>=(const charT* a, const basic_string<charT,traits,Allocator>& b);
// bool operator>=(const char* a, const string& b);
template<class charT, class traits, class Allocator>
  bool operator>=(const basic_string<charT,traits,Allocator>& a, const charT* b);
// bool operator>=(const string& a, conat char* b);
```

The >= operator compares two strings or compares a string and a null-terminated character array. It returns a.compare(b) >= 0, converting a or b from a character array to a string, as needed.

See Also

basic_string class template

---

operator<< function template

```
template<class charT, class traits, class Allocator>
  basic_ostream<charT, traits>& operator<<(
    basic_ostream<charT, traits>& out,
    const basic_string<charT,traits,Allocator>& str);
// ostream& operator<<(ostream& out, const string& str);
```

The << operator writes the string str to out. Like any formatted output function, it first creates a sentry object, and if the sentry evaluates to true, it writes the string contents by calling out.rdbuf( )->sputn. If str.size( ) < out.width( ), fill characters are added to achieve the desired width. If sputn fails, ios_base::failbit is set.

See Also

ios_base in <ios>, basic_ostream in <ostream>, basic_ostream::sentry in <ostream>

---

operator>> function template

```
template<class charT, class traits, class Allocator>
  basic_istream<charT,traits>& operator>>(
    basic_istream<charT,traits>& in,
    basic_string<charT,traits,Allocator>& str);
// istream& operator>>(istream& in,  string& str);
```

The >> operator reads a string from in and stores the string in str. Like any other formatted input operator, it first creates a sentry object basic_istream::sentry(in), and if the sentry evaluates to true, it erases str and then reads characters from in and appends the characters to str. If in.width( ) is greater than 0, no more than in.width( ) characters are read from in; otherwise, up to max_size( ) characters are read. Reading also stops at end-of-file or when reading a whitespace character (isspace is true for locale in.getloc( )). The whitespace character is left in the input stream. The return value is in.

See Also

getline function template, basic_istream in <istream>, basic_istream::sentry in <istream>

---

string class

```
typedef basic_string<char> string;
```

The string class specializes basic_string for type char.

See Also

basic_string class template, wstring class

swap function template

Swaps two strings

```
template<class charT, class traits, class Allocator>
  void swap(basic_string<charT,traits,Allocator>& a,
          basic_string<charT,traits,Allocator>& b);
// void swap(string& a, string& b);
```

The swap function template specialization is equivalent to calling a.swap(b).

See Also

swap in <algorithm>

wstring class

Wide character string class

```
typedef basic_string<wchar_t> wstring;
```

The wstring class specializes basic_string for type wchar_t.

See Also

basic_string class template, string class

<strstream>

The <strstream> header declares several classes for reading from character arrays and writing to character arrays in the same manner as reading from and writing to files.

This header and its classes are deprecated in the standard, meaning they might disappear from a future version of the standard. Instead, you are encouraged to use the <sstream> header and its class templates. Nonetheless, the <strstream> classes have their uses; when you are dealing exclusively with narrow characters, and are using character arrays instead of string objects, these classes sometimes offer better performance than their <sstream> counterparts.

See Chapter 10 for a general discussion of I/O, and the <istream> and <ostream> sections in this chapter for information about the base classes from which the strstream classes derive. Refer to the <streambuf> section in this chapter for information about the streambuf class.

istrstream class

Input character array streams

```
class istrstream: public istream
{
public:
  explicit istrstream(const char* str);
  explicit istrstream(char* str);
  istrstream(const char* str, streamsize n);
  istrstream(char* str, streamsize n);

  strstreanbuf* rdbuf() const;
  char* str();
};
```

The istrstream class represents an input string stream. To construct an istrstream, pass a character array (with an optional size). You can then read from the string stream just as you would from any other input stream.

The following are the methods of istrstream:

explicit **istrstream**(const char* str)
explicit **istrstream**(char* str)

> Initializes an input string stream by constructing an internal stream buffer as strstreambuf(str, 0) and passing the address of the stream buffer to the base-class constructor for istream.

explicit **istrstream**(const char* str, streamsize n)
explicit **istrstream**(char* str, streamsize n)

> Initializes an input string stream by constructing an internal stream buffer as strstreambuf(str, n) and passing the address of the stream buffer to the base-class constructor for istream.

strstreambuf* **rdbuf**( ) const

> Returns a pointer to the internal strstreambuf object.

char* **str**( )

> Returns the internal string, rdbuf( )->str( ).

See Also

ostrstream class, strstream class, strstreambuf class, istream in <istream>, istringstream in <sstream>

---

ostrstream class
Output character array streams

```
class ostrstream: public ostream
{
public:
  ostrstream( );
  ostrstream(char* str, int n, ios_base::openmode mode = ios_base::out);

  strstreambuf* rdbuf( ) const;
  void freeze(bool flag = true);
  char* str( );
  int pcount( ) const;
};
```

The ostrstream class represents an output string stream. You can provide a character array, and the stream contents are written to that array. Another typical usage is to construct an ostrstream with no argument and let the string stream allocate the string as you write to the stream. Then call str( ) to obtain the resulting character array. Once you call str( ), the stream is *frozen* and cannot be modified. The pointer returned from str( ) remains valid until the ostrstream object is destroyed or until you *thaw* the stream to allow writing again.

The following are the methods of ostrstream:

ostrstream( )

> Initializes an empty output string stream by constructing an internal strstreambuf object and passing the address of the string buffer to the base-class constructor for ostream.

ostrstream(char* str, int n, ios_base::openmode mode = ios_base::out)
 Initializes a string stream with str as the initial string contents by constructing an
 internal strstreambuf object and passing the address of the buffer to the base-
 class constructor for ostream. If the ios_base::app bit is set in mode, the buffer is
 constructed like this:

   strstreambuf(str, n, str + std::strlen(str));

 If the ios_base::app bit is clear in mode, the buffer is constructed like this:

   strstreambuf(str, n, str);

void **freeze**(bool flag = true)
 Freezes or thaws the buffer by calling rdbuf( )->freeze(flag).

strstreambuf* **rdbuf**( ) const
 Returns a pointer to the internal strstreambuf object.

char* **str**( )
 Returns a pointer to the buffer's character array, that is, rdbuf( )->str( ).

int **pcount**( ) const
 Returns the number of bytes in the output buffer by calling rdbuf( )->pcount( ).

See Also

istrstream class, strstream class, strstreambuf class, ostream in <ostream>,
ostringstream in <sstream>

---

strstream class   Input and output character array streams

```
class strstream: public iostream
{
public:
  typedef char char_type;
  typedef typename char_traits<char>::int_type int_type;
  typedef typename char_traits<char>::pos_type pos_type;
  typedef typename char_traits<char>::off_type off_type;

  strstream( );
  strstream(char* s, int n,
            ios_base::openmode mode = ios_base::in|ios_base::out);
  virtual ~strstream( );

  strstreambuf* rdbuf( ) const;
  void freeze(bool freezefl = true);
  int pcount( ) const;
  char* str( );
};
```

The strstream class is a stream class that performs input and output to a character
array. You can start with an empty string and write to the stream, or start with a string
and read from the stream. You can switch between reading and writing at any time. If
you use the default constructor and write to the stream, the stream buffer grows as
needed. Then you can call str( ) to obtain the resulting character array. Once you call
str( ), the stream is frozen and cannot be modified. The pointer returned from str( )
remains valid until the ostrstream object is destroyed or until you thaw the stream to
allow writing again.

The following are the methods of strstream:

strstream( )
>Initializes an empty string stream by constructing an internal strstreambuf object and passing the address of the string buffer to the base-class constructor for iostream.

basic_strstream(char* str, int n, ios_base::openmode mode =
  ios_base::in|ios_base::out)
>Initializes a string stream with str as the initial string contents by constructing an internal strstreambuf object and passing the address of the buffer to the base-class constructor for iostream. If the ios_base::app bit is set in mode, the buffer is constructed like this:

>>strstreambuf(str, n, str + std::strlen(str));

>If the ios_base::app bit is clear in mode, the buffer is constructed like this:

>>strstreambuf(str, n, str);

void **freeze**(bool flag = true)
>Freezes or thaws the buffer by calling rdbuf( )->freeze(flag).

strstreambuf* **rdbuf**( ) const
>Returns a pointer to the internal strstreambuf object.

char* **str**( )
>Returns a pointer to the buffer's character array, that is, rdbuf( )->str( ).

int **pcount**( ) const
>Returns the number of bytes in the output buffer by calling rdbuf( )->pcount( ).

See Also

istrstream class, ostrstream class, strstreambuf class, basic_iostream in <istream>, stringstream in <sstream>

---

strstreambuf class
I/O buffer for character array streams

```
class strstreambuf : public basic_streambuf<char> {
public:
  explicit strstreambuf(streamsize alsize_arg = 0);
  strstreambuf(void* (*palloc_arg)(size_t), void (*pfree_arg)(void*));
  strstreambuf(char* gnext_arg, streamsize n, char* pbeg_arg = 0);
  strstreambuf(const char* gnext_arg, streamsize n);
  strstreambuf(signed char* gnext_arg, streamsize n,
               signed char* pbeg_arg = 0);
  strstreambuf(const signed char* gnext_arg, streamsize n);
  strstreambuf(unsigned char* gnext_arg, streamsize n,
               unsigned char* pbeg_arg = 0);
  strstreambuf(const unsigned char* gnext_arg, streamsize n);
  virtual ~strstreambuf( );

  void freeze(bool freezefl = true);
  char* str( );
  int pcount( );

protected:
  virtual int_type overflow (int_type c = EOF);
  virtual int_type pbackfail(int_type c = EOF);
```

```
   virtual int_type underflow( );
   virtual pos_type seekoff(off_type off, ios_base::seekdir way,
                            ios_base::openmode which = ios_base::in |
                            ios_base::out);
   virtual pos_type seekpos(pos_type sp,
                            ios_base::openmode which = ios_base::in |
                            ios_base::out);
};
```

The strstreambuf class implements a stream buffer for character array streams. An internal buffer maintains a single character array with separate positions for reading and writing. That is, the buffer has *begin*, *next*, and *end* pointers for reading and separate *begin*, *next*, and *end* pointers for writing. The *begin* pointer points to the start of a buffer, and the *end* pointer points to one past the end of the buffer. The *next* pointer points to the position where the next character is to be read or written. Refer to basic_streambuf in <streambuf> for details about buffer positions.

A strstreambuf object maintains a set of flags, an allocated buffer size, and two function pointers for an allocation and deallocation function. If the allocation function pointer is null, the new[] operator is used for allocating the character array; if the deallocation function pointer is null, the delete[] operator is used.

The flags are:

allocated
> Indicates that the character array has been allocated, so the destructor should delete it

constant
> Indicates that the character array is const, so it cannot be used for output

dynamic
> Indicates that the character array has been dynamically allocated and can grow as needed to accommodate output

frozen
> Indicates that the character array can no longer be modified, extended, or freed

The following are the public member functions of strstreambuf:

explicit **strstreambuf**(streamsize alloc_size = 0)
> Saves alloc_size as the suggested size of the character array, and sets the *dynamic* flag. The allocation and deallocation functions are set to null pointers.

strstreambuf(void* (*palloc)(size_t), void (*pfree)(void*))
> Sets the *dynamic* flag and saves palloc and pfree as the allocation and deallocation functions.

strstreambuf(char* gnext_arg, streamsize n, char* pbeg_arg = 0)
strstreambuf(signed char* gnext_arg, streamsize n, signed char* pbeg_arg = 0)
strstreambuf(unsigned char* gnext_arg, streamsize n, unsigned char*
  pbeg_arg = 0)
> Clears all flags and sets the allocation and deallocation functions to null pointers. If pbeg_arg is null, the output pointers are null and the input buffer is set to n bytes starting at gnext_arg by calling setg(gnext_arg, gnext_arg, gnext_arg + N). If pbeg_arg is not null, the input pointers are set by calling

setg(gnext_arg, gnext_arg, pbeg_arg), and the output pointers are set by calling setp(pbeg_arg, pbeg_arg + N). N is determined as follows:

n > 0
> N is n.

n == 0
> N is strlen(gnext_arg).

n < 0
> N is INT_MAX.

strstreambuf(const char* gnext_arg, streamsize n)
strstreambuf(const signed char* gnext_arg, streamsize n)
strstreambuf(const unsigned char* gnext_arg, streamsize n)
> Initializes the buffer pointers in the same manner as constructing strstreambuf(const_cast<char*>(gnext_arg), n). The only difference is that the *constant* flag is set.

virtual **~strstreambuf**( )
> The destructor frees the character array if the *allocated* flag is set and the *frozen* flag is clear.

void **freeze**(bool freezefl = true)
> Freezes or thaws the character buffer. If the *dynamic* flag is set, the freeze function sets or clears the *frozen* flag to match the freezefl parameter. If the *dynamic* flag is clear, freeze( ) does nothing.

char* **str**( )
> Returns the internal character buffer by calling freeze( ) and returning gbase( ).

int **pcount**( )
> Returns the number of output bytes in the buffer. If pptr( ) is null, 0 is returned; otherwise, pptr( ) - pbase( ) is returned.

The overridden virtual functions are:

virtual int_type **overflow** (int_type c = EOF)
> Attempts to append c to the end of the character array as follows:
>
> - If c == EOF, nothing happens and a non-end-of-file character is returned to indicate success.
> - If c != EOF, and a write position is available, c is appended to the character array by calling sputc(c).
> - If a write position is not available, the *dynamic* flag is set, and the *frozen* flag is clear, then the character array is extended and c is appended to the array. The array is extended by allocating a new, larger character array; copying the old contents (if any); updating the read and write pointers. If the array is successfully extended, the *allocated* flag is set.
> - Otherwise, the array cannot be extended, so the function fails.
>
> The return value is c for success or EOF for failure. If c is EOF, a value other than EOF is returned for success.

virtual int_type **pbackfail**(int_type c = traits::eof( ))
> Attempts to push back c onto the input array for reading as follows:
>
> - If c == EOF, and a putback position is available, gptr( ) is set to gptr( ) − 1.
> - If c != EOF, a putback position is available, and gptr( )[-1] is equal to c, gptr( ) is set to gptr( ) − 1.

- If c != EOF, the *constant* flag is clear, and a putback position is available, gptr( ) is set to gptr( ) − 1, and *gptr( ) is assigned c.
- Otherwise, the character cannot be put back, so the function fails.

The return value is c for success or EOF for failure. If c is EOF, a value other than EOF is returned for success.

virtual pos_type **seekoff**(off_type off, ios_base::seekdir way,
 ios_base::openmode which = ios_base::in|ios_base::out)

Sets the stream position. The input position, output position, or both can be set, depending on (which & (ios_base::in | ios_base::out)). The following are the possible results of this expression:

os_base::in
 Sets the input position

os_base::out
 Sets the output position

ios_base::in | ios_base::out, *and* way *is either* ios_base::beg *or* ios_base::end
 Sets input and output positions

Otherwise
 The function fails and returns pos_type(-1)

The new position is determined by adding the offset off to a base position given by way, which must be one of the following:

ios_base::beg
 The base position is the at start of the stream—that is, off is an absolute position.

ios_base::cur
 The base position is the current stream position.

ios_base::end
 The base position is at the end of the stream.

In all cases, a positive offset is toward the end of the stream, and a negative offset is toward the start of the stream. If the desired position is negative or past the end of the string, the function fails and returns pos_type(-1). If the function succeeds, it returns the new position.

virtual pos_type **seekpos**(pos_type sp, ios_base::openmode which =
 ios_base::in|ios_base::out)

Sets the stream position to sp. The input position is set if which & ios_base::in is nonzero. The output position is set if which & ios_base::out is nonzero. If sp is not a valid position, or if neither the input nor the output position is set, seekpos fails and pos_type(-1) is returned. The return value is sp for success. If sp was not returned from a prior call to a positioning function (that is, seekoff, seekpos, tellg, or tellp), the results are undefined.

virtual basic_streambuf<charT,traits>* **setbuf**(charT*, streamsize)

Calling setbuf(0, 0) has no effect. The result of any other call to setbuf is implementation-defined.

virtual int_type **underflow**( )

Gets another character from the input range without moving the input pointer. If the stream has a read position, the function returns *gptr( ). If there is no read position, but there is a non-null write pointer past the end of the input range—that is, pptr( ) > gend( )—then the read end pointer (gend( )) is advanced at least one position but still less than or equal to pptr( ). The return value is EOF for failure or *gnext( ) for success.

See Also

stringbuf in <sstream>, basic_streambuf in <streambuf>

<typeinfo>

The <typeinfo> header declares the type_info class (for the typeid operator) and two exception classes related to type information and casting.

bad_cast class   Exception for dynamic_cast<>

```
class bad_cast : public exception {
public:
  bad_cast( ) throw( );
  bad_cast(const bad_cast&) throw( );
  bad_cast& operator=(const bad_cast&) throw( );
  virtual ~bad_cast( ) throw( );
  virtual const char* what( ) const throw( );
};
```

The dynamic_cast<> operator throws bad_cast when the cast of a reference fails. See dynamic_cast in Chapter 3 for more information.

See Also

dynamic_cast operator

bad_typeid class   Exception for null pointer in typeid expressions

```
class bad_typeid : public exception {
public:
  bad_typeid( ) throw( );
  bad_typeid(const bad_typeid&) throw( );
  bad_typeid& operator=(const bad_typeid&) throw( );
  virtual ~bad_typeid( ) throw( );
  virtual const char* what( ) const throw( );
};
```

The typeid operator throws bad_typeid when it is applied to an expression of the form *p, in which p is a null pointer. See typeid in Chapter 3 for more information.

See Also

typeid operator

type_info class   Type information

```
class type_info {
public:
  virtual ~type_info( );
```

```
  bool operator==(const type_info& rhs) const;
  bool operator!=(const type_info& rhs) const;
  bool before(const type_info& rhs) const;
  const char* name( ) const;
private:
  type_info(const type_info& rhs);
  type_info& operator=(const type_info& rhs);
};
```

The typeid operator (described in Chapter 3) returns a static type_info object. The type information includes the type's name and a collation order, both of which are implementation-defined. An implementation might derive classes from type_info to provide additional information.

Note that the copy constructor and assignment operators are inaccessible, so you must store pointers if you want to use a standard container. Example 13-38 shows how to store type_info pointers in a set, where the order is determined by the before member function.

Example 13-38. Storing type information

```
#include <algorithm>
#include <functional>
#include <iostream>
#include <ostream>
#include <set>
#include <typeinfo>

typedef bool (*type_info_compare) (const std::type_info*, const std::type_info*);

typedef std::set<const std::type_info*, type_info_compare>
  typeset;

// Return true if *a comes before *b (comparison function to store type_info
// pointers in an associative container).
bool type_info_less(const std::type_info* a, const std::type_info* b)
{
  return a->before(*b);
}

// Print a type_info name on a line.
void print(const std::type_info* x)
{
  std::cout << x->name( ) << '\n';
}

void demo( )
{
  // Construct and initialize the set.
  typeset types(&type_info_less);

  types.insert(&typeid(int));
  types.insert(&typeid(char));
  types.insert(&typeid(std::type_info));
  types.insert(&typeid(std::bad_alloc));
```

Example 13-38. Storing type information (continued)

```
  types.insert(&typeid(std::exception));
  ...
  // Print the types in the set.
  std::for_each(types.begin( ), types.end( ), print);
}
```

The members of type_info are:

bool **before**(const type_info& rhs) const
> Returns true if this type_info object comes before rhs in the implementation-defined order. The relative order of types can vary between programs, even for the same types.

const char* **name**( ) const
> Returns the type's name as a null-terminated string, which might be a multibyte string. The contents of the name string are implementation-defined.

bool **operator==**(const type_info& rhs) const
bool **operator!=**(const type_info& rhs) const
> Compares type_info objects, which are equal when the types they describe are the same.

See Also

typeid operator

<utility>

The <utility> header declares the pair<> class template, which has many uses, especially by maps in the <map> header. It also defines the rel_ops namespace, which defines relational operators in terms of == and <.

make_pair function template   Constructs a pair object

```
template <typename T1, typename T2>
pair<T1,T2> make_pair(T1 a, T2 b);
```

Constructs a pair<T1,T2> object and initializes it with the values a and b. The advantage of using make_pair over a simple pair<> constructor is that the compiler can deduce the types T1 and T2 from the values a and b. Example 13-39 shows a typical use of make_pair.

Example 13-39. Making pairs of objects

```
std::map<std::string, int> wordcounts;
wordcounts.insert(std::make_pair("hello", 1));

// Functor, suitable for passing to for_each to find minimum and maximum values
// in a range
template<typename T>
class minmax
{
```

Example 13-39. Making pairs of objects (continued)

```
public:
  minmax( ) : min_(std::numeric_limits<T>::max( )),
              max_(std::numeric_limits<T>::min( ))
              {}
  void operator( )(const T& x) {
    if (x < min_) min_ = x;
    if (max_ < x) max_ = x;
  }
  operator std::pair<T,T>( ) const {
    return std::make_pair(min_, max_);
  }
private:
  T min_;
  T max_;
};

int main( )
{
  std::vector<int> v;
  // Fill v with data.
  std::pair<int,int> mm =
    std::for_each(v.begin( ), v.end( ), minmax<int>( ));
  // Do something with mm.
}
```

See Also

pair class template

---

operator== function template
Compares for equality

```
template <typename T1, typename T2>
bool operator==(const pair<T1,T2>& a, const pair<T1,T2>& b);
```

Returns true if a and b are equal, that is, a.first == b.first && a.second == b.second.

---

operator!= function template
Compares for inequality

```
namespace rel_ops {
  template<typename T>
  bool operator!=(const T& a, const T& b);
}
template <typename T1, typename T2>
bool operator!=(const pair<T1,T2>& a, const pair<T1,T2>& b);
```

Returns true if a and b are not equal, that is, ! (a == b).

---

operator< function template
Compares for less-than

```
template <typename T1, typename T2>
bool operator<(const pair<T1,T2>& a, const pair<T1,T2>& b);
```

Returns true if a is less than b, assuming that the first member is more significant than second. That is, the return value is a.first < b.first || (!(b.first < a.first) && a.second < b.second).

---

operator<= function template

```
namespace rel_ops {
  template<typename T>
  bool operator<=(const T& a, const T& b);
}
template <typename T1, typename T2>
bool operator<=(const pair<T1,T2>& a, const pair<T1,T2>& b);
```

Returns true if a is less than or equal to b, that is, ! (b < a).

operator> function template

```
namespace rel_ops {
  template<typename T>
  bool operator>(const T& a, const T& b);
}
template <typename T1, typename T2>
bool operator>(const pair<T1,T2>& a, const pair<T1,T2>& b);
```

Returns true if a is greater than b, that is, b < a.

operator>= function template

```
namespace rel_ops {
  template<typename T>
  bool operator>=(const T& a, const T& b);
}
template <typename T1, typename T2>
bool operator>=(const pair<T1,T2>& a, const pair<T1,T2>& b);
```

Returns true if a is greater than or equal to b, that is, ! (a < b).

pair class template

```
template <typename T1, typename T2>
struct pair {
  typedef T1 first_type;
  typedef T2 second_type;
  T1 first;
  T2 second;
  pair( );
  pair(const T1& x, const T2& y);
  template<typename U, typename V> pair(const pair<U, V> &p);
};
```

The pair class template represents a pair of related objects, in which the relationship is defined by the programmer. The most common use of pairs is by the map class template, which stores pairs of keys and associated objects.

The Boost project has a generalization of pair, called tuple. See Appendix B for information about Boost.

The pair constructors are straightforward:

pair( )

> Initializes first as T1( ) and second as T2( )

pair(const T1& x, const T2& y)
> Initializes first with x and second with y

template<typename U, typename V>
pair(const pair<U, V> &p)
> Initializes first with p.first and second with p.second, performing implicit conversions as needed

See Also

make_pair function template

---

rel_ops namespace   Relational operators

```
namespace std {
 namespace rel_ops {
  template<typename T> bool operator!=(const T&, const T&);
  template<typename T> bool operator> (const T&, const T&);
  template<typename T> bool operator<=(const T&, const T&);
  template<typename T> bool operator>=(const T&, const T&);
 }
}
```

The std::rel_ops namespace declares four comparison operators. The four operators are implemented in terms of the == and < operators. The rel_ops namespace has limited utility. If you are using an unusual class, which has only operator== and operator<, you can add a using namespace std::rel_ops directive to a function that makes heavy use of comparison operators and this unusual class. Even better, though, is fixing the class declaration to provide all necessary comparison operators. If you are writing a class that represents an ordered value, you should provide all six operators and not force your users to rely on rel_ops. The Boost project has templates that you can derive from to fill in all the relational operators, based on equality and less-than. See Appendix B for information about Boost.

See Also

operator!= function template, operator> function template, operator<= function template, operator >= function template

---

<valarray>

The <valarray> header declares types and functions for operating on arrays of numerical values. The intention is to provide types that could be optimized on certain hardware platforms for computationally-intensive programs. The consensus in the C++ user community seems to be that the standard failed to live up to the intentions. Several other numerical libraries, such as Blitz++ and MTL, provide high-performance matrix solutions. (See Appendix B for more information about Blitz++.) Most programs do not need <valarray>.

A valarray is a class template that represents a one-dimensional array of numerical values. The array can grow at runtime. All the arithmetic operators and mathematical functions are overloaded to work with two valarray arguments or with a valarray and

---

a scalar. You can also work with parts of an array: slices, generalized slices, masks, and indirect arrays.

A *slice* is a set of elements of a valarray, with a starting index, a count, and a stride (an index interval). A *generalized slice* (gslice) lets the stride count and length vary, which can be used to implement multidimensional arrays. A *mask* is a valarray of flags, in which the flags indicate whether the corresponding item is part of the masked array. An *indirect array* is an array of indices. Each of these concepts is explained in this section.

The most important distinguishing feature of valarrays is that they do not allow aliasing, that is, an object cannot be an element of more than one valarray. This enables additional optimizations that are not possible on ordinary arrays.

Because valarray is optimized for performance, no error-checking is performed. Referring to an index out of range or operating on arrays of different size result in undefined behavior—the same as with ordinary arrays. Unlike ordinary arrays, a convenient size( ) member function helps to ensure that you do not make mistakes.

See the <cmath> header for scalar mathematical functions and <numeric> for a few numeric algorithms. See <complex> for complex numbers.

Throughout this section, examples show valarray objects and subsets printed using operator<<, which is shown in Example 13-40.

Example 13-40. Printing a valarray or subset array

```
// Print a valarray on one line, enclosed by curly braces. For example:
// "{ 1 2 3 }".
template<typename T>
void print_valarray(std::ostream& out, const std::valarray<T>& a)
{
  out << '{';
  for (size_t i = 0; i < a.size(); ++i)
    out << ' ' << a[i];
  out << " }";
}

// Print a slice_array, gslice_array, etc. by converting to a valarray.
// Converting a valarray to a valarray is wasteful, but harmless for these simple
// examples.
template<template<typename T> class U, typename T>
std::ostream& operator<<(std::ostream& out, const U<T>& x)
{
  print_valarray(out, static_cast<std::valarray<T> >(x));
  return out;
}
```

abs function template   Computes absolute value

```
template<typename T> valarray<T> abs(const valarray<T>& a);
```
The abs function computes the absolute value of each element of a.

See Also

abs in <cmath>, abs in <cstdlib>

acos function template
Computes inverse cosine

```
template<typename T> valarray<T> acos(const valarray<T>& a);
```
The acos function computes the inverse cosine of each element of a.

See Also

acos in <cmath>

asin function template
Computes inverse sine

```
template<typename T> valarray<T> asin(const valarray<T>& a);
```
The asin function computes the inverse sine of each element of a.

See Also

asin in <cmath>

atan function template
Computes inverse tangent

```
template<typename T> valarray<T> atan(const valarray<T>& a);
```
The atan function computes the inverse tangent of each element of a.

See Also

atan2 function template, atan in <cmath>

atan2 function template
Computes inverse tangent of two arguments

```
template<typename T>
valarray<T> atan2(const valarray<T>& b, const valarray<T>& a);
template<typename T> valarray<T> atan2(const valarray<T>& b, const T& x);
template<typename T> valarray<T> atan2(const T& y, const valarray<T>& a);
```
The atan2 function computes the inverse tangent of y/x, in which y is a scalar or an element of b, and x is a scalar or an element of a.

See Also

atan function template, atan2 in <cmath>

cos function template
Computes cosine

```
template<typename T> valarray<T> cos(const valarray<T>& a);
```
The cos function computes the cosine of each element of a.

See Also

cos in <cmath>

cosh function template
Computes hyperbolic cosine

```
template<typename T> valarray<T> cosh(const valarray<T>& a);
```
The cosh function computes the hyperbolic cosine of each element of a.

See Also

cosh in <cmath>

---

exp function template

```
template<typename T> valarray<T> exp(const valarray<T>& a);
```

The exp function computes the exponential e^x for each element x of a.

See Also

exp in <cmath>

---

gslice class

```
class gslice {
public:
  gslice( );
  gslice(size_t start, const valarray<size_t>& size,
         const valarray<size_t>& stride);
  size_t start( ) const;
  valarray<size_t> size( ) const;
  valarray<size_t> stride( ) const;
};
```

The gslice class describes a generalized slice of a valarray. A generalized slice is a subset of the elements of a valarray, characterized by a starting index and a set of sizes and strides. The size and stride arrays must have the same size. Each size/stride pair denotes a set of elements at periodic indices. The number of elements in the generalized slice is equal to the product of the values in the size array. The elements are taken from a valarray at each index i:

$$i = \text{start} + \Sigma\, k_j \times \text{stride}_j$$

in which k_j takes all the values in the range [0, size[j]), and j is in the range [0, stride.size( )). The highest value of j varies fastest. With a single element in stride and size, gslice is the same as plain slice. Example 13-41 demonstrates gslice more clearly. Pay particular attention to the final gslice, where you can see how the indices advance, first with a stride of 3 (k_1 ranges from 0 to 2), then with a stride of 2 (k_0 ranges from 0 to 3)

Example 13-41. Generalized slicing of a valarray

```
// Construct valarray objects from a few integers.
std::valarray<std::size_t> va(std::size_t a0)
{
  std::valarray<std::size_t> result(1);
  result[0] = a0;
  return result;
}

std::valarray<std::size_t> va(std::size_t a0, std::size_t a1)
{
  std::valarray<std::size_t> result(2);
  result[0] = a0;
  result[1] = a1;
```

Example 13-41. Generalized slicing of a valarray (continued)

```
  return result;
}

int main( )
{
  using namespace std;
  valarray<int> a(24);
  for (size_t i = 0; i < a.size( ); ++i)
    a[i] = i;
  cout << a << '\n';
// Prints { 0 1 2 3 4 5 6 7 8 9 10 11 ... 20 21 22 23 }

  cout << a[slice(1, 4, 3)] << '\n';
// Prints { 1 4 7 10 }
  cout << a[gslice(1, va(4), va(3))] << '\n';
// Prints { 1 4 7 10 }

  const valarray<int> const_a(a);
  cout << const_a[gslice(2, va(4, 3), va(2, 3))] << '\n';
// Prints { 2 5 8 4 7 10 6 9 12 8 11 14 }
}
```

Notice also that the final gslice requires a const valarray. This is because it contains degenerate slices, in which an element (e.g., 8) appears more than once in the result. The aliasing rules of a valarray prohibit multiple references to the same element, so if a const valarray were not used, the results would be undefined. By using a const valarray, the result is a copy of the sliced elements, so the two occurrences of element 8 are separate objects, not aliases for the same object, and disaster is averted.

A generalized slice is most often used to represent a multidimensional array. For example, you can treat a valarray of 24 elements as a 2 × 3 × 4 matrix. To extract a plane of the matrix, you can use a gslice. Figure 13-27 depicts the matrix and the plane. Example 13-42 shows the code.

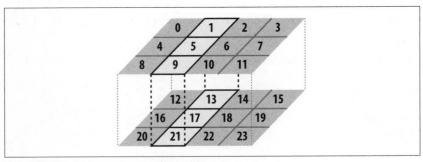

Figure 13-27. A 3-D matrix stored in a valarray

Example 13-42. Using gslice for multidimensional arrays

```
// See Example 13-41 for the va function.
int main( )
{
```

Example 13-42. Using gslice for multidimensional arrays (continued)

```
  using namespace std;
  valarray<int> a(24);
  for (size_t i = 0; i < a.size( ); ++i)
    a[i] = i;
  cout << a[gslice(1, va(2, 3), va(12, 4))] << '\n';
// Prints: { 1 5 9 13 17 21 }
}
```

To create an *n*-dimensional submatrix of an *m*-dimensional matrix, the size and stride arrays must both have length *n*. The size array determines the dimensions of the result.

Use the subscript operator to take a generalized slice of a valarray. You can assign a valarray to a generalized slice, in which the righthand side of the assignment must have the same size as the size of the slice. You can also convert the slice to a valarray, which copies only those elements of the slice to the new valarray.

When you take a generalized slice of a valarray, the result is a gslice_array object, but the gslice_array type is mostly transparent to the programmer. See gslice_array later in this section for details.

See Also

gslice_array class template, slice class

---

gslice_array class template

Helper class for generalized slices

```
template <typename T>
class gslice_array {
public:
  typedef T value_type;
  void operator=(const valarray<T>&) const;
  void operator*=(const valarray<T>&) const;
  void operator/=(const valarray<T>&) const;
  void operator%=(const valarray<T>&) const;
  void operator+=(const valarray<T>&) const;
  void operator-=(const valarray<T>&) const;
  void operator^=(const valarray<T>&) const;
  void operator&=(const valarray<T>&) const;
  void operator|=(const valarray<T>&) const;
  void operator<<=(const valarray<T>&) const;
  void operator>>=(const valarray<T>&) const;
  void operator=(const T&);
  ~gslice_array( );
private:
  gslice_array( );
  gslice_array(const gslice_array&);
  gslice_array& operator=(const gslice_array&);
};
```

The gslice_array class template represents a subset of the elements of a valarray, called a generalized slice. To create a generalized slice, use valarray's operator[ ] with an argument of type gslice.

For some operations, the gslice_array object is transparent. In particular, you can assign a valarray to a gslice_array object (provided they have the same size), or you can construct a new valarray from a gslice_array.

If you want to perform other operations, such as non-assignment arithmetic, you must explicitly convert the gslice_array to valarray, as demonstrated in Example 13-43.

Example 13-43. Using gslice_array

```
// See Example 13-41 for the va function.
int main( )
{
  using namespace std;
  const int data[] = { 1, 2, 3, 4, 5, 6, 7, 8 };
  valarray<int> a(data, sizeof(data)/sizeof(data[0]));
  cout << a << '\n';
// Prints { 1 2 3 4 5 6 7 8 }

  cout << a[gslice(1, va(2, 2), va(4, 2))] << '\n'
       << a[gslice(0, va(2, 2), va(4, 2))] << '\n';
// prints:
//  { 2 4 6 8 }
//  { 1 3 5 7 }

  // operator+ is not defined for gslice_array, so cast to valarray to perform
  // addition.
  cout <<
    static_cast<valarray<int> >(a[gslice(1, va(2,2), va(4,2))]) +
    static_cast<valarray<int> >(a[gslice(0, va(2,2), va(4,2))])
       << '\n';
// Prints: { 3 7 11 15 }

  // Simple assignment does not require casting.
  a[gslice(0, va(2, 2), va(4, 2))] = 0;
  cout << a << '\n';
// Prints: { 0 2 0 4 0 6 0 8 }

  // Computational assignment does not require casting.
  valarray<int> ten(10, 4);
  a[gslice(1, va(2, 2), va(4, 2))] *= ten;
  cout << a << '\n';
// Prints: { 0 20 0 40 0 60 0 80 }
}
```

The members of gslice_array are straightforward. When using any of the assignment operators, the valarray on the righthand side must be the same size as the gslice_array on the lefthand side. You can also assign a scalar to every element of the array. Note that the default constructor, copy constructor, and copy assignment operator are all private. The purpose of this is to restrict the use of gslice_array so it can be used only as a return value from valarray's operator[].

See Also

gslice class, indirect_array class template, mask_array class template, slice_array class template, valarray class template

indirect_array class template

```
template <typename T>
class indirect_array {
public:
  typedef T value_type;
  void operator=(const valarray<T>&) const;
  void operator*=(const valarray<T>&) const;
  void operator/=(const valarray<T>&) const;
  void operator%=(const valarray<T>&) const;
  void operator+=(const valarray<T>&) const;
  void operator-=(const valarray<T>&) const;
  void operator^=(const valarray<T>&) const;
  void operator&=(const valarray<T>&) const;
  void operator|=(const valarray<T>&) const;
  void operator<<=(const valarray<T>&) const;
  void operator>>=(const valarray<T>&) const;
  void operator=(const T&);
  ~indirect_array( );
private:
  indirect_array( );
  indirect_array(const indirect_array&);
  indirect_array& operator=(const indirect_array&);
};
```

The indirect_array class template represents a subset of the elements of a valarray. To create an indirect subset, use valarray's operator[] with an argument of type valarray<size_t>. The elements of the argument are the desired indices in the subset.

For some operations, the indirect_array object is transparent. In particular, you can assign a valarray to an indirect_array object (provided they have the same size), or you can construct a new valarray from an indirect_array.

If you want to perform other operations, such as non-assignment arithmetic, you must explicitly convert the indirect_array to valarray, as demonstrated in Example 13-44.

Example 13-44. Using indirect_array

```
int main( )
{
  using namespace std;
  const int data[] = { 1, 2, 3, 4, 5, 6, 7, 8 };
  valarray<int> a(data, sizeof(data)/sizeof(data[0]));
  cout << a << '\n';
// Prints: { 1 2 3 4 5 6 7 8 }

  // Specify the indices into a.
  const size_t p[] = { 2, 3, 5, 7 };
  valarray<size_t> indices(p, sizeof(p)/sizeof(p[0]));
  cout << a[indices] << '\n';
// Prints: { 3 4 6 8 }

  // Add 10 to the elements at the desired indices.
  valarray<int> ten(10, 4);
  a[indices] += ten;
```

Example 13-44. Using indirect_array (continued)

```
  cout << a << '\n';
// Prints: { 1 2 13 14 5 16 7 18 }

  // Must cast to perform ordinary arithmetic.
  cout << static_cast<valarray<int> >(a[indices])
         * ten << '\n';
// Prints: { 130 140 160 180 }
}
```

The members of indirect_array are straightforward. When using any of the assignment operators, the valarray on the righthand side must be the same size as the indirect_array on the lefthand side. You can also assign a scalar to every element of the array. Note that the default constructor, copy constructor, and copy assignment operator are all private. The purpose of this is to restrict the use of indirect_array so it can be used only as a return value from valarray's operator[].

See Also

gslice_array class template, mask_array class template, slice_array class template, valarray class template

---

log function template   Computes natural logarithm

```
template<typename T> valarray<T> log(const valarray<T>& a);
```

The log function computes the natural (base *e*) logarithm of each element of a.

See Also

log in <cmath>

---

log10 function template   Computes common logarithm

```
template<typename T> valarray<T> log10(const valarray<T>& a);
```

The log10 function computes the common (base 10) logarithm of each element of a.

See Also

log10 in <cmath>

---

mask_array class template   Helper class for mask arrays

```
template <typename T>
class mask_array {
public:
  typedef T value_type;
  void operator=(const valarray<T>&) const;
  void operator*=(const valarray<T>&) const;
  void operator/=(const valarray<T>&) const;
  void operator%=(const valarray<T>&) const;
  void operator+=(const valarray<T>&) const;
  void operator-=(const valarray<T>&) const;
  void operator^=(const valarray<T>&) const;
  void operator&=(const valarray<T>&) const;
```

```
  void operator|=(const valarray<T>&) const;
  void operator<<=(const valarray<T>&) const;
  void operator>>=(const valarray<T>&) const;
  void operator=(const T&);
  ~mask_array( );
private:
  mask_array( );
  mask_array(const mask_array&);
  mask_array& operator=(const mask_array&);
};
```

The mask_array class template represents a subset of the elements of a valarray. To create a mask subset, use valarray's operator[] with an argument of type valarray<bool>. An element is included in the result set if the corresponding element in the argument is true.

For some operations, the mask_array object is transparent. In particular, you can assign a valarray to a mask_array object (provided they have the same size), or you can construct a new valarray from a mask_array.

If you want to perform other operations, such as non-assignment arithmetic, you must explicitly convert the mask_array to valarray, as demonstrated in Example 13-45.

Example 13-45. Using mask_array

```
// Simple average
template<typename T>
T avg(const std::valarray<T>& a)
{
  return a.sum( ) / a.size( );
}

int main( )
{
  using namespace std;
  const int data[] = { 1, -3, 10, 42, -12, 13, -7, 69 };
  valarray<int> a(data, sizeof(data)/sizeof(data[0]));
  cout << a << '\n';
// Prints: { 1 -3 10 42 -12 13 -7 69 }

  // Print the values that are above average.
  cout << "avg=" << avg(a) << '\n';
  cout << a[a > avg(a)] << '\n';
// Prints: { 42 69 }

  // Force all negative values to be 0. Notice how no cast is needed for the
  // simple assignment.
  a[a < 0] = 0;
  cout << a << '\n';
// Prints: { 1 0 10 42 0 13 0 69 }

  // Other operations, such as multiplication by a scalar, are defined only for
  // valarray, so a cast is needed.
  cout << static_cast<valarray<int> >(a[a > 0]) * -1 << '\n';
// Prints: { -1 -10 -42 -13 -69 }
}
```

The members of mask_array are straightforward. When using any of the assignment operators, the valarray on the righthand side must be the same size as the mask_array on the lefthand side. You can also assign a scalar to every element of the array. Note that the default constructor, copy constructor, and copy assignment operator are all private. The purpose of this is to restrict the use of mask_array so it can be used only as a return value from valarray's operator[].

See Also

gslice_array class template, indirect_array class template, slice_array class template, valarray class template

---

operator* function template   Performs multiplication

```
template<typename T>
valarray<T> operator*(const valarray<T>& a, const valarray<T>& b);
template<typename T>
valarray<T> operator*(const valarray<T>& a, const T& y);
template<typename T>
valarray<T> operator*(const T& x, const valarray<T>& b);
```

The * operator performs elementwise multiplication. It multiplies each x * y, in which x is a scalar or an element of a, and y is a scalar or an element of b. When multiplying two arrays, they must have the same size. The resulting array has the same size as the argument array(s).

---

operator/ function template   Performs division

```
template<typename T>
valarray<T> operator/(const valarray<T>& a, const valarray<T>& b);
template<typename T>
valarray<T> operator/(const valarray<T>& a, const T& y);
template<typename T>
valarray<T> operator/(const T& x, const valarray<T>& b);
```

The / operator performs elementwise division. It divides each x / y, in which x is a scalar or an element of a, and y is a scalar or an element of b. When dividing two arrays, they must have the same size. The resulting array has the same size as the argument array(s).

---

operator+ function template   Performs addition

```
template<typename T>
valarray<T> operator+(const valarray<T>& a, const valarray<T>& b);
template<typename T>
valarray<T> operator+(const valarray<T>& a, const T& y);
template<typename T>
valarray<T> operator+(const T& x, const valarray<T>& b);
```

The + operator performs elementwise addition. It adds each x + y, in which x is a scalar or an element of a, and y is a scalar or an element of b. When adding two arrays, they must have the same size. The resulting array has the same size as the argument array(s).

---

operator- function template
Performs subtraction

```
template<typename T>
valarray<T> operator-(const valarray<T>& a, const valarray<T>& b);
template<typename T>
valarray<T> operator-(const valarray<T>& a, const T& y);
template<typename T>
valarray<T> operator-(const T& x, const valarray<T>& b);
```

The - operator performs elementwise subtraction. It subtracts each x - y, in which x is a scalar or an element of a, and y is a scalar or an element of b. When subtracting two arrays, they must have the same size. The resulting array has the same size as the argument array(s).

operator& function template
Performs bitwise and

```
template<typename T>
valarray<T> operator&(const valarray<T>& a, const valarray<T>& b);
template<typename T>
valarray<T> operator&(const valarray<T>& a, const T& y);
template<typename T>
valarray<T> operator&(const T& x, const valarray<T>& b);
```

The & operator performs *bitwise and* on each x & y, in which x is a scalar or an element of a, and y is a scalar or an element of b. When operating on two arrays, they must have the same size. The resulting array has the same size as the argument array(s). The type T must be one for which operator & is defined.

operator| function template
Performs bitwise or

```
template<typename T>
valarray<T> operator|(const valarray<T>& a, const valarray<T>& b);
template<typename T>
valarray<T> operator|(const valarray<T>& a, const T& y);
template<typename T>
valarray<T> operator|(const T& x, const valarray<T>& b);
```

The | operator performs *bitwise inclusive or* on each x | y, in which x is a scalar or an element of a, and y is a scalar or an element of b. When operating on two arrays, they must have the same size. The resulting array has the same size as the argument array(s). The type T must be one for which operator | is defined.

operator^ function template
Performs bitwise exclusive or

```
template<typename T>
valarray<T> operator^(const valarray<T>& a, const valarray<T>& b);
template<typename T>
valarray<T> operator^(const valarray<T>& a, const T& y);
template<typename T>
valarray<T> operator^(const T& x, const valarray<T>& b);
```

The ^ operator performs *bitwise exclusive or* on each x ^ y, in which x is a scalar or an element of a, and y is a scalar or an element of b. When operating on two arrays, they must have the same size. The resulting array has the same size as the argument array(s). The type T must be one for which operator ^ is defined.

operator>> function template
Performs right shift

```
template<typename T>
valarray<T> operator>>(const valarray<T>& a, const valarray<T>& b);
template<typename T>
valarray<T> operator>>(const valarray<T>& a, const T& y);
template<typename T>
valarray<T> operator>>(const T& x, const valarray<T>& b);
```

The >> operator performs right shift on each x >> y, in which x is a scalar or an element of a, and y is a scalar or an element of b. When operating on two arrays, they must have the same size. The resulting array has the same size as the argument array(s). The type T must be one for which operator >> is defined.

operator<< function template
Performs left shift

```
template<typename T>
valarray<T> operator<<(const valarray<T>& a, const valarray<T>& b);
template<typename T>
valarray<T> operator<<(const valarray<T>& a, const T& y);
template<typename T>
valarray<T> operator<<(const T& x, const valarray<T>& b);
```

The << operator performs left shift on each x << y, in which x is a scalar or an element of a, and y is a scalar or an element of b. When operating on two arrays, they must have the same size. The resulting array has the same size as the argument array(s). The type T must be one for which operator << is defined.

operator&& function template
Performs logical and

```
template<typename T>
valarray<bool> operator&&(const valarray<T>& a, const valarray<T>& b);
template<typename T>
valarray<bool> operator&&(const valarray<T>& a, const T& y);
template<typename T>
valarray<bool> operator&&(const T& x, const valarray<T>& b);
```

The && operator performs *logical and* on each x && y, in which x is a scalar or an element of a, and y is a scalar or an element of b. When operating on two arrays, they must have the same size. The resulting array has the same size as the argument array(s). The type T must be one for which operator && is defined. As with any other overloaded operator &&, short-cut evaluation is not supported.

operator|| function template
Performs logical or

```
template<typename T>
valarray<bool> operator||(const valarray<T>& a, const valarray<T>& b);
template<typename T>
valarray<bool> operator||(const valarray<T>& a, const T& y);
template<typename T>
valarray<bool> operator||(const T& x, const valarray<T>& b);
```

The || operator performs *logical or* on each x || y, in which x is a scalar or an element of a, and y is a scalar or an element of b. When operating on two arrays, they must have the same size. The resulting array has the same size as the argument array(s). The type T must be one for which operator || is defined and yields a bool result or a result that can be converted to bool. As with any other overloaded operator ||, short-cut evaluation is not supported.

operator== function template

```
template<typename T>
valarray<bool> operator==(const valarray<T>& a, const valarray<T>& b);
template<typename T>
valarray<bool> operator==(const valarray<T>& a, const T& y);
template<typename T>
valarray<bool> operator==(const T& x, const valarray<T>& b);
```

The == operator compares each x == y, in which x is a scalar or an element of a, and y is a scalar or an element of b. When operating on two arrays, they must have the same size. The resulting array has the same size as the argument array(s). The type T must be one for which operator == is defined and yields a bool result or a result that can be converted to bool.

operator!= function template

```
template<typename T>
valarray<bool> operator!=(const valarray<T>& a, const valarray<T>& b);
template<typename T>
valarray<bool> operator!=(const valarray<T>& a, const T& y);
template<typename T>
valarray<bool> operator!=(const T& x, const valarray<T>& b);
```

The != operator compares each x != y, in which x is a scalar or an element of a, and y is a scalar or an element of b. When operating on two arrays, they must have the same size. The resulting array has the same size as the argument array(s). The type T must be one for which operator != is defined and yields a bool result or a result that can be converted to bool.

operator< function template

```
template<typename T>
valarray<bool> operator<(const valarray<T>& a, const valarray<T>& b);
template<typename T>
valarray<bool> operator<(const valarray<T>& a, const T& y);
template<typename T>
valarray<bool> operator<(const T& x, const valarray<T>& b);
```

The < operator compares each x < y, in which x is a scalar or an element of a, and y is a scalar or an element of b. When operating on two arrays, they must have the same size. The resulting array has the same size as the argument array(s). The type T must be one for which operator < is defined and yields a bool result or a result that can be converted to bool.

operator<= function template

```
template<typename T>
valarray<bool> operator<=(const valarray<T>& a, const valarray<T>& b);
template<typename T>
```

```
valarray<bool> operator<=(const valarray<T>& a, const T& y);
template<typename T>
valarray<bool> operator<=(const T& x, const valarray<T>& b);
```

The <= operator compares each x <= y, in which x is a scalar or an element of a, and y is a scalar or an element of b. When operating on two arrays, they must have the same size. The resulting array has the same size as the argument array(s). The type T must be one for which operator <= is defined and yields a bool result or a result that can be converted to bool.

operator> function template   Compares for greater-than

```
template<typename T>
valarray<bool> operator>(const valarray<T>& a, const valarray<T>& b);
template<typename T>
valarray<bool> operator>(const valarray<T>& a, const T& y);
template<typename T>
valarray<bool> operator>(const T& x, const valarray<T>& b);
```

The > operator compares each x > y, in which x is a scalar or an element of a, and y is a scalar or an element of b. When operating on two arrays, they must have the same size. The resulting array has the same size as the argument array(s). The type T must be one for which operator > is defined and yields a bool result or a result that can be converted to bool.

operator>= function template   Compares for greater-than-or-equal

```
template<typename T>
valarray<bool> operator>=(const valarray<T>& a, const valarray<T>& b);
template<typename T>
valarray<bool> operator>=(const valarray<T>& a, const T& y);
template<typename T>
valarray<bool> operator>=(const T& x, const valarray<T>& b);
```

The >= operator compares each x >= y, in which x is a scalar or an element of a, and y is a scalar or an element of b. When operating on two arrays, they must have the same size. The resulting array has the same size as the argument array(s). The type T must be one for which operator >= is defined and yields a bool result or a result that can be converted to bool.

pow function template   Computes power

```
template<typename T>
valarray<T> pow(const valarray<T>& a, const valarray<T>& b);
template<typename T>
valarray<T> pow(const valarray<T>& a, const T& y);
template<typename T>
valarray<T> pow(const T& x, const valarray<T>& b);
```

The pow function computes the power x^y, in which x is a scalar or an element of a, and y is a scalar or an element of b.

See Also

pow in <cmath>

sin function template
Computes sine

```
template<typename T> valarray<T> sin(const valarray<T>& a);
```

The sin function computes the sine of the elements of a.

See Also

sin in <cmath>

sinh function template
Computes hyperbolic sine

```
template<typename T> valarray<T> sinh(const valarray<T>& a);
```

The sinh function computes the hyperbolic sine of the elements of a.

See Also

sinh in <cmath>

slice class
Slice of an array

```
class slice {
public:
  slice( );
  slice(size_t, size_t, size_t);
  size_t start( ) const;
  size_t size( ) const;
  size_t stride( ) const;
};
```

The slice class describes a slice of a valarray. A slice is a subset of the elements of a valarray at periodic indices. The slice has a starting index, a size, and a stride, in which the stride is the index interval. Figure 13-28 depicts slice(1,3,4) of a valarray.

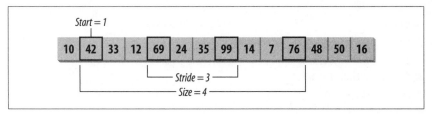

Figure 13-28. Slicing a valarray

Use the subscript operator to take a slice of a valarray. You can assign a valarray to a slice, in which the righthand side of the assignment must have the same size as the size of the slice. You can also convert the slice to a valarray, which copies only those elements of the slice to the new valarray.

When you take a slice of a valarray, the result is a slice_array object, but the slice_array type is mostly transparent to the programmer. See slice_array later in this section for details.

You can use a slice to treat a valarray as a two-dimensional matrix. A slice can specify a row or column of the matrix. For an $n \times m$ matrix, row r is slice(r*m, m, 1), and column c is slice(c, n, m), as you can see in Example 13-46.

Example 13-46. A simple 2-D matrix class

```
template<typename T>
class matrix2D {
public:
  matrix2D(std::size_t rows, std::size_t columns) :
    rows_(rows), cols_(columns), data_(rows * columns) {}
  std::size_t rows() const { return rows_; }
  std::size_t cols() const { return cols_; }
  std::valarray<T> row(std::size_t r) const
    { return data_[std::slice(r*cols(),cols(), 1)]; }
  std::valarray<T> col(std::size_t c) const
    { return data_[std::slice(c, rows(), cols())]; }
  std::slice_array<T> row(std::size_t r)
    { return data_[std::slice(r*cols(),cols(), 1)]; }
  std::slice_array<T> col(std::size_t c)
    { return data_[std::slice(c, rows(), cols())]; }
  T& operator()(std::size_t r, std::size_t c)
    { return data_[r*cols()+c]; }
  T operator()(std::size_t r, std::size_t c) const
    { return row(r)[c]; }
  matrix2D<T> transpose() {
    matrix2D<T> result(cols(), rows());
    for (std::size_t i = 0; i < rows(); ++i)
      result.col(i) = static_cast<std::valarray<T> >(row(i));
    return result;
  }
private:
  std::size_t rows_;
  std::size_t cols_;
  std::valarray<T> data_;
};
```

See Also

gslice class, slice_array class template

---

slice_array class template   Helper class for slice

```
template <typename T>
class slice_array {
public:
  typedef T value_type;
  void operator=(const valarray<T>&) const;
  void operator*=(const valarray<T>&) const;
  void operator/=(const valarray<T>&) const;
  void operator%=(const valarray<T>&) const;
  void operator+=(const valarray<T>&) const;
  void operator-=(const valarray<T>&) const;
  void operator^=(const valarray<T>&) const;
  void operator&=(const valarray<T>&) const;
  void operator|=(const valarray<T>&) const;
  void operator<<=(const valarray<T>&) const;
  void operator>>=(const valarray<T>&) const;
  void operator=(const T&);
```

```
  ~slice_array( );
private:
  slice_array( );
  slice_array(const slice_array&);
  slice_array& operator=(const slice_array&);
};
```

The slice_array class template represents a subset of the elements of a valarray, taken at periodic indices, called a slice. To create a slice, use valarray's operator[] with an argument of type slice.

For some operations, the slice_array object is transparent. In particular, you can assign a valarray to a slice_array object (provided they have the same size), or you can construct a new valarray from a slice_array.

If you want to perform other operations, such as non-assignment arithmetic, you must explicitly convert the slice_array to valarray, as demonstrated in Example 13-47.

Example 13-47. Slicing a valarray

```
int main( )
{
  using namespace std;
  const int data[] = { 1,2,3,4,5,6,7,8,9,10,11,12,13 };
  valarray<int> v(data, sizeof(data)/sizeof(data[0]));
  const int newdata[] = { 30, 70, 110 };
  valarray<int> rpl(newdata, 3);
  v[slice(2, 3, 4)] = rpl;
  cout << v << '\n';
// Prints: { 1 2 30 4 5 6 70 8 9 10 110 12 13}
  v[slice(3, 4, 2)] = -1;
  cout << v << '\n';
// Prints: { 1 2 30 -1 5 -1 70 -1 9 -1 110 12 13}
  valarray<int> mult(3, 2);
  v[slice(8, 2, 3)] *= mult;
  cout << v << '\n';
// Prints: { 1 2 30 -1 5 -1 70 -1 27 -1 110 36 13}
  cout << static_cast<valarray<int> >(v[slice(1, 5, 2)])
       << '\n';
// Prints: { 2 -1 -1 -1 -1}
  cout << static_cast<valarray<int> >(v[slice(4, 3, 2)]) +
          static_cast<valarray<int> >(v[slice(2, 3, 2)])
       << '\n';
// Prints: { 35 75 97}
}
```

The members of slice_array are straightforward. When using any of the assignment operators, the valarray on the righthand side must be the same size as the slice_array on the lefthand side. You can also assign a scalar to every element of the array. Note that the default constructor, copy constructor, and copy assignment operator are all private. The purpose of this is to restrict the use of slice_array so it can be used only as a return value from valarray's operator[].

See Also

gslice_array class template, indirect_array class template, mask_array class template, slice class, valarray class template

sqrt function template   Computes square root

```
template<typename T> valarray<T> sqrt(const valarray<T>& a);
```
The sqrt function computes the square root of the elements of a.

See Also
sqrt in <cmath>

tan function template   Computes tangent

```
template<typename T> valarray<T> tan(const valarray<T>& a);
```
The tan function computes the tangent of the elements of a.

See Also
tan in <cmath>

tanh function template   Computes hyperbolic tangent

```
template<typename T> valarray<T> tanh(const valarray<T>& a);
```
The tanh function computes the hyperbolic tangent of the elements of a.

See Also
tanh in <cmath>

valarray class template   Array of values

```
template<typename T>
class valarray {
public:
  typedef T value_type;

  valarray( );
  explicit valarray(size_t);
  valarray(const T&, size_t);
  valarray(const T*, size_t);
  valarray(const valarray&);
  valarray(const slice_array<T>&);
  valarray(const gslice_array<T>&);
  valarray(const mask_array<T>&);
  valarray(const indirect_array<T>&);
  ~valarray( );

  valarray<T>& operator=(const valarray<T>&);
  valarray<T>& operator=(const T&);
  valarray<T>& operator=(const slice_array<T>&);
  valarray<T>& operator=(const gslice_array<T>&);
  valarray<T>& operator=(const mask_array<T>&);
  valarray<T>& operator=(const indirect_array<T>&);

  T operator[](size_t) const;
  T& operator[](size_t);
```

```
valarray<T> operator[](slice) const;
slice_array<T> operator[](slice);
valarray<T> operator[](const gslice&) const;
gslice_array<T> operator[](const gslice&);
valarray<T> operator[](const valarray<bool>&) const;
mask_array<T> operator[](const valarray<bool>&);
valarray<T> operator[](const valarray<size_t>&) const;
indirect_array<T> operator[](const valarray<size_t>&);

valarray<T> operator+() const;
valarray<T> operator-() const;
valarray<T> operator~() const;
valarray<bool> operator!() const;

valarray<T>& operator*= (const T&);
valarray<T>& operator/= (const T&);
valarray<T>& operator%= (const T&);
valarray<T>& operator+= (const T&);
valarray<T>& operator-= (const T&);
valarray<T>& operator^= (const T&);
valarray<T>& operator&= (const T&);
valarray<T>& operator|= (const T&);
valarray<T>& operator<<=(const T&);
valarray<T>& operator>>=(const T&);
valarray<T>& operator*= (const valarray<T>&);
valarray<T>& operator/= (const valarray<T>&);
valarray<T>& operator%= (const valarray<T>&);
valarray<T>& operator+= (const valarray<T>&);
valarray<T>& operator-= (const valarray<T>&);
valarray<T>& operator^= (const valarray<T>&);
valarray<T>& operator|= (const valarray<T>&);
valarray<T>& operator&= (const valarray<T>&);
valarray<T>& operator<<=(const valarray<T>&);
valarray<T>& operator>>=(const valarray<T>&);

size_t size() const;
T sum() const;
T min() const;
T max() const;
valarray<T> shift (int) const;
valarray<T> cshift(int) const;
valarray<T> apply(T func(T)) const;
valarray<T> apply(T func(const T&)) const;
void resize(size_t sz, T c = T());
};
```

The valarray class template represents an array of numeric values, with restrictions that permit an implementation to optimize performance. In particular, an object cannot be an element of more than one array. A subset, such as a generalized slice or indirect array, cannot specify a single element more than once, or else the behavior is undefined.

You can instantiate valarray with any numerical type as its template parameter if you limit yourself to using only operations that are defined for that type. For example, you cannot use operator<< on valarray<double> because you cannot use operator<< on scalars of type double.

Examples of using valarray can be found throughout this section.

The following are the members of valarray:

valarray( )
> Constructs an empty valarray.

explicit **valarray**(size_t n)
> Constructs a valarray of length n, in which all elements are initialized to T( ).

valarray(const T& x, size_t n)
> Construct a valarray that contains n copies of x.

valarray(const T* x, size_t n)
> Constructs a valarray by copying n elements from the array x.

valarray(const valarray& a)
> Constructs a valarray by copying a.

valarray(const slice_array<T>& a)
valarray(const gslice_array<T>& a)
valarray(const mask_array<T>& a)
valarray(const indirect_array<T>& a)
> Constructs a valarray by copying the elements referenced by a.

valarray<T> **apply**(T func(T)) const
valarray<T> **apply**(T func(const T&)) const
> Returns a new array whose contents are the result of calling func for each element of the original array.

valarray<T> **cshift**(int n) const
> Performs a circular shift (rotation) by n places. The return value is a new array that has the same size as the original, but the element at new index i comes from $(i + n)$ % size( ) in the original.

T **max**( ) const
> Returns the largest element of the array or an undefined value if the array is empty. Elements are compared using operator<.

T **min**( ) const
> Returns the smallest element of the array or an undefined value if the array is empty. Elements are compared using operator<.

valarray<T>& **operator=**(const valarray<T>& a)
> Each element of this array is assigned the corresponding elements of a. If size( ) != a.size( ), the behavior is undefined.

valarray<T>& **operator=**(const T& x)
> Each element of this array is assigned the scalar value x.

valarray<T>& **operator=**(const slice_array<T>& a)
valarray<T>& **operator=**(const gslice_array<T>& a)
valarray<T>& **operator=**(const mask_array<T>& a)
valarray<T>& **operator=**(const indirect_array<T>& a)
> Each element of this array is assigned the corresponding element from the subset array a. The value being assigned to an element must not depend on any other value in this array, that is, a cannot be a subset of *this, or, if it is, the element assigned to index i must depend only on index i and not on values at any other index.

```
T operator[](size_t i) const
T& operator[](size_t i)
```
Returns the element at index i. The behavior is undefined for i >= size( ). The anti-aliasing rule means that for any two distinct valarray objects a and b, and for all valid indices *i* and *j*, you can safely assume that the following is true: &a[*i*] != &b[*j*]. All values in a single valarray object are stored contiguously, just as in an ordinary array. References become invalid after a call to resize.

```
valarray<T> operator[](slice) const
slice_array<T> operator[](slice)
valarray<T> operator[](const gslice&) const
gslice_array<T> operator[](const gslice&)
valarray<T> operator[](const valarray<bool>&) const
mask_array<T> operator[](const valarray<bool>&)
valarray<T> operator[](const valarray<size_t>&) const
indirect_array<T> operator[](const valarray<size_t>&)
```
Returns a subset of this valarray. A subset of a const valarray is a new valarray. A subset of a non-const valarray is a helper object that maintains a reference to the original valarray. (See the descriptions of the helper classes earlier in this section for details.) Briefly, the four kinds of subsets are:

- A slice object specifies a simple slice, suitable for extracting a row or column of a 2-D array.

- A gslice is a generalized slice, which permits multidimensional matrices.

- A mask_array is created by specifying an array of bool as the argument. If an element is true, that element is part of the resulting subset.

- An indirect_array is created by specifying an array of size_t indices as the argument. Each element specifies an index, and the element at that index is added to the resulting array.

```
valarray<T> operator+( ) const
valarray<T> operator-( ) const
valarray<T> operator~( ) const
valarray<bool> operator!( ) const
```
Returns a new valarray in which each new element is the result of applying the unary operator to the corresponding element in the original array.

```
valarray<T>& operator*= (const T& x)
valarray<T>& operator/= (const T& x)
valarray<T>& operator%= (const T& x)
valarray<T>& operator+= (const T& x)
valarray<T>& operator-= (const T& x)
valarray<T>& operator^= (const T& x)
valarray<T>& operator&= (const T& x)
valarray<T>& operator|= (const T& x)
valarray<T>& operator<<=(const T& x)
valarray<T>& operator>>=(const T& x)
```
Modifies this valarray by applying the assignment operator to each element of the array. The return value is *this.

```
valarray<T>& operator*= (const valarray<T>& a)
valarray<T>& operator/= (const valarray<T>& a)
valarray<T>& operator%= (const valarray<T>& a)
valarray<T>& operator+= (const valarray<T>& a)
valarray<T>& operator-= (const valarray<T>& a)
valarray<T>& operator^= (const valarray<T>& a)
valarray<T>& operator|= (const valarray<T>& a)
valarray<T>& operator&= (const valarray<T>& a)
valarray<T>& operator<<=(const valarray<T>& a)
valarray<T>& operator>>=(const valarray<T>& a)
```
> Modifies this valarray by applying the assignment operator to each element of the array and to the corresponding element of a. The behavior is undefined if size( ) != a.size( ). The return value is *this.

`void resize(size_t sz, T x = T())`
> Changes the size of the array to sz and reinitializes every element of the array to x.

`valarray<T> shift (int n) const`
> Performs a shift by n places. The return value is a new array with the same size as the original array, but the element at index i in the new array comes from index i + n in the original array. If i + n < 0 or $\geq$ size( ), the new element is set to T( ).

`size_t size( ) const`
> Returns the number of elements in the array.

`T sum( ) const`
> Returns the sum of all the elements in the array using operator+=. If the array is empty, the value is undefined.

See Also

gslice class, gslice_array class template, indirect_array class template, mask_array class template, slice class, slice_array class template

---

<vector>

The <vector> header is one of the standard container template headers. It declares the vector class template and a few global function templates that operate on vector objects.

A vector is a sequence container that yields linear performance for inserting and erasing at any point in the container, except the end, for which performance is constant. A vector supports random access iterators. A vector is best thought of as a generalization of arrays.

See Chapter 10 for information about containers in.

---

operator== function template   Compares for equality

```
template <typename T, typename A>
bool operator==(const vector<T,A>& x, const vector<T,A>& y);
template <typename Alloc>
bool operator==(const vector<bool,Alloc>& x, const vector<bool,Alloc>& y);
```

The == operator returns true if x and y have the same size and their elements are equal, that is, x.size() == y.size() && equals(x.begin(), x.end(), y.begin()).

See Also

equals in <algorithm>

---

operator!= function template

Compares for inequality

```
template <typename T, typename A>
bool operator!=(const vector<T,A>& x, const vector<T,A>& y);
template <typename Alloc>
bool operator!=(const vector<bool,Alloc>& x, const vector<bool,Alloc>& y);
```

The != operator returns ! (x == y).

---

operator< function template

Compares for less-than

```
template <typename T, typename A>
bool operator<(const vector<T,A>& x, const vector<T,A>& y);
template <typename Alloc>
bool operator<(const vector<bool,Alloc>& x, const vector<bool,Alloc>& y);
```

The < operator determines whether x is less than y using the same algorithm as lexicographical_compare(x.begin(), x.end(), y.begin(), y.end()).

See Also

lexicographical_compare in <algorithm>

---

operator<= function template

Compares for less-than-or-equal

```
template <typename T, typename A>
bool operator<=(const vector<T,A>& x, const vector<T,A>& y);
template <typename Alloc>
bool operator<=(const vector<bool,Alloc>& x, const vector<bool,Alloc>& y);
```

The <= operator returns ! (y < x).

---

operator> function template

Compares for greater-than

```
template <typename T, typename A>
bool operator>(const vector<T,A>& x, const vector<T,A>& y);
template <typename Alloc>
bool operator>(const vector<bool,Alloc>& x, const vector<bool,Alloc>& y);
```

The > operator returns (y < x).

---

operator>= function template

Compares for greater-than-or-equal

```
template <typename T, typename A>
bool operator>=(const vector<T,A>& x, const vector<T,A>& y);
template <typename Alloc>
bool operator>=(const vector<bool,Alloc>& x, const vector<bool,Alloc>& y);
```

The >= operator returns ! (x < y).

swap function template

Swaps contents of two vectors

```
template <typename T, typename Alloc>
void swap(vector<T,Alloc>& x, vector<T,Alloc>& y);
template <typename Alloc>
void swap(vector<bool,Alloc>& x, vector<bool,Alloc>& y);
```

The swap function template specialization is equivalent to calling x.swap(y).

See Also

swap in <algorithm>

vector class template

Array-like container

```
template <typename T, typename Alloc = allocator<T> >
class vector {
public:
  typedef typename Alloc::reference reference;
  typedef typename Alloc::const_reference const_reference;
  typedef ... iterator;
  typedef ... const_iterator;
  typedef ... size_type;
  typedef ... difference_type;
  typedef T value_type;
  typedef Alloc allocator_type;
  typedef typename Alloc::pointer pointer;
  typedef typename Alloc::const_pointer const_pointer;
  typedef std::reverse_iterator<iterator> reverse_iterator;
  typedef std::reverse_iterator<const_iterator> const_reverse_iterator;

  explicit vector(const Alloc& = Alloc());
  explicit vector(size_type n, const T& value = T(), const Alloc& = Alloc());
  template <class InpIt>
  vector(InpIt first, InpIt last, const Alloc& = Alloc());
  vector(const vector<T,Alloc>& x);
  ~vector();
  vector<T,Alloc>& operator=(const vector<T,Alloc>& x);
  template <class InputIterator>
  void assign(InputIterator first, InputIterator last);
  void assign(size_type n, const T& u);
  allocator_type get_allocator() const;

  iterator begin();
  const_iterator begin() const;
  iterator end();
  const_iterator end() const;
  reverse_iterator rbegin();
  const_reverse_iterator rbegin() const;
  reverse_iterator rend();
  const_reverse_iterator rend() const;
```

```
  size_type size( ) const;
  size_type max_size( ) const;
  void resize(size_type sz, T c = T( ));
  size_type capacity( ) const;
  bool empty( ) const;
  void reserve(size_type n);
  // Element access
  reference operator[](size_type n);
  const_reference operator[](size_type n) const;
  const_reference at(size_type n) const;
  reference at(size_type n);
  reference front( );
  const_reference front( ) const;
  reference back( );
  const_reference back( ) const;
  // Modifiers
  void push_back(const T& x);
  void pop_back( );
  iterator insert(iterator position, const T& x);
  void insert(iterator position, size_type n, const T& x);
  template <class InpIt>
  void insert(iterator position, InpIt first, InpIt last);
  iterator erase(iterator position);
  iterator erase(iterator first, iterator last);
  void swap(vector<T,Alloc>&);
  void clear( );
};
```

Library
Reference

The vector class template is a standard sequence container that is like an array: adding or removing from the end of the vector takes constant time (amortized over many such operations), adding or removing from anywhere else takes linear time, and random access happens in constant time.

Elements of a vector are stored contiguously, just like an ordinary array. For most cases in which you need an array, you should use a vector instead because a vector offers greater safety (no need for dynamic memory and raw pointers, the at member function checks array bounds, etc.)

All iterators and references to a vector's elements become invalid when the vector's internal array is resized, which can happen for an insertion when the size matches the capacity, or when you explicitly change the size (e.g., by calling resize). You can ensure that an insertion does not force a resize by calling reserve to set the capacity prior to inserting one or more items. Iterators and references also become invalid when they are past (at a higher index) the point where an item is inserted or erased.

If you need a vector of Boolean values, consider using deque<bool> instead of vector<bool>. See vector<bool> for an explanation.

The following are the members of vector:

explicit **vector**(const Alloc& = Alloc( ))
    Constructs an empty vector.

explicit **vector**(size_type n, const T& value = T( ), const Alloc& = Alloc( ))
    Constructs a vector of size n, in which each element is initialized to value.

```
template <class InpIt>
```
vector(InpIt first, InpIt last, const Alloc& = Alloc( ))
> Constructs an empty vector and copies [first, last) into the new vector unless InputIterator is an integral type, in which case the vector is constructed as though the arguments were cast as follows:
>
> > vector(static_cast<size_type>(first), static_cast<value_type>(last), alloc);

vector(const vector<T,Alloc>& v)
> Constructs a copy of v.

vector<T,Alloc>& **operator=**(const vector<T,Alloc>& v)
> Erases all the elements of the vector, then copies the elements from v into the vector.

```
template <class InputIterator>
```
void **assign**(InputIterator first, InputIterator last)
> Erases all the elements of the vector, then copies the elements from [first, last) into the vector, unless InputIterator is an integral type, in which case the arguments are interpreted as though they were cast as follows:
>
> > assign(static_cast<size_type>(first), static_cast<value_type>(last));

void **assign**(size_type n, const T& value)
> Erases all the elements of the vector, then inserts n copies of value.

const_reference **at**(size_type n) constreference **at**(size_type n)
> Returns the element at index n. If n >= size( ), throws out_of_range.

reference **back**( )
const_reference **back**( ) const
> Returns the last element of the vector. Behavior is undefined if the vector is empty.

iterator **begin**( )
const_iterator **begin**( ) const
> Returns an iterator that points to the first element of the vector.

size_type **capacity**( ) const
> Returns the number of elements the vector can store before it resizes itself.

void **clear**( )
> Erases all elements of the vector.

iterator **end**( )
const_iterator **end**( ) const
> Returns an iterator that points to one past the last element of the vector.

bool **empty**( ) const
> Returns size( ) == 0.

iterator **erase**(iterator position)
> Erases the element at position.

iterator **erase**(iterator first, iterator last)
> Erases all the elements in the range [first, last).

reference **front**( )
const_reference **front**( ) const
> Returns the first element of the vector. Behavior is undefined if the vector is empty.

locator_type **get_allocator**( ) const
>   Returns the allocator object.

iterator **insert**(iterator position, const T& x)
>   Inserts x before position.

void **insert**(iterator pos, size_type n, const T& x)
>   Inserts n copies of x at pos.

template <class InpIt>
void **insert**(iterator pos, InpIt first, InpIt last)
>   Inserts the elements in the range [first, last) starting at position pos, unless InputIterator is an integral type, in which case the arguments are interpreted as though they were cast as follows:

>   > insert(pos, static_cast<size_type>(first),
>   >   static_cast<value_type>(last));

>   If an exception is thrown, such as bad_alloc when there is insufficient memory for a new element, the vector is unchanged, and all iterators and references remain valid. If the exception is thrown from an element's copy constructor or assignment operator, however, the behavior is unspecified.

size_type **max_size**( ) const
>   Returns the size of the largest possible vector.

reference **operator[ ]**(size_type n)
const_reference **operator[ ]**(size_type n) const
>   Returns the element at index n. If n >= size( ), the behavior is undefined.

void **pop_back**( )
>   Erases the last element of the vector. The behavior is undefined if the vector is empty.

void **push_back**(const T& x)
>   Inserts x as the new last element of the vector.

reverse_iterator **rbegin**( )
const_reverse_iterator **rbegin**( ) const
>   Returns a reverse iterator that points to the last element of the vector.

reverse_iterator **rend**( )
const_reverse_iterator **rend**( ) const
>   Returns a reverse iterator that points to one position before the first element of the vector.

void **reserve**(size_type n)
>   Ensures that capacity( ) is at least n. Call reserve to avoid the need to reallocate the vector repeatedly when you know the vector will grow by small increments to a large size, or when you want to ensure that iterators do not become invalid after inserting one or more items. Note that size( ) does not change.

void **resize**(size_type sz, T c = T( ))
>   Changes the size of this vector to n. If n > size( ), one or more copies of c are added to the end of the vector to reach the desired size. If the new size is smaller than the current size, elements are erased from the end to reach the new size.

size_type **size**( ) const
>   Returns the number of elements in the vector.

void **swap**(vector<T,Alloc>& that)
>   Exchanges all the elements in this vector with all the elements in that.

Library
Reference

See Also
vector<bool> class, deque in <deque>, list in <list>

---

vector<bool> class   Specialized vector of bool

```
template <typename Alloc>
class vector<bool, Alloc> {
public:
  typedef bool const_reference;
  typedef ... iterator;
  typedef ... const_iterator;
  typedef ... size_type;
  typedef ... difference_type;
  typedef bool value_type;
  typedef Alloc allocator_type;
  typedef ... pointer;
  typedef ... const_pointer
  typedef std::reverse_iterator<iterator> reverse_iterator;
  typedef std::reverse_iterator<const_iterator> const_reverse_iterator;

  class reference;
  static void swap(reference x, reference y);
  void flip();
  ... // Same as vector<> ...
};
```

The vector<bool> specialization is an interesting beast. It is an attempt to demonstrate how to define a container that uses a *proxy* to represent the elements of the container. The bool elements are packed into integers, and the vector<bool>::reference type is a proxy that represents a single bool element by keeping track of the bit number within the integer and the integer's index in the vector.

However, by using a proxy, vector<bool> violates the constraints of a container, so it cannot be used in many situations that call for a standard container. In particular, the pointer type cannot point to an element of the container because C++ does not have a type that can point to a single bit. Many algorithms require the pointer type, and so they cannot work with a vector<bool> object.

If you need to use a compact, fixed-size set of bits, use the bitset class template. If you need a standard container that contains bool elements, use deque<bool>.

In addition to the members of the vector<> template, vector<bool> also defines the following functions:

static void swap(reference x, reference y)
    Swaps two bit values

void flip()
    Flips all the bits in the vector

See Also
vector class template, vector<bool>::reference class, bitset in <bitset>, deque in <deque>

---

vector<bool>::reference class

```
class reference {
  friend class vector;
  reference();
public:
  ~reference();
  operator bool() const;
  reference& operator=(const bool x);
  reference& operator=(const reference& x);
  void flip();
};
```

The reference class represents a single bit in a vector<bool>. The constructor is private, so only vector<bool> can create reference objects. The reference keeps track of the position of an individual bit in a vector<bool>, so you can get, set, or flip the bit. The following are the members of reference:

void **flip**( )
> Flips or toggles the bit, that is, performs the equivalent of *this = ! *this

operator **bool**( ) const
> Returns the bit value as a bool

reference& **operator**=(const bool x)
reference& **operator**=(const reference& x)
> Assigns x to *this

See Also

vector<bool> class

A

Compiler Extensions

When writing portable code, you should stick to the standard, but sometimes you have to use compiler-specific extensions of the standard. This appendix lists some of the more interesting extensions in a few compilers. It is not a reference of compiler extensions, but more an illustration of the kinds of extensions that compiler writers choose to implement.

Borland C++ Builder and Kylix

Borland has several extensions to C++ to support its Rapid Application Development products: C++ Builder (for Microsoft Windows) and Kylix (for Linux). This section presents highlights of the RAD extensions.

__closure

> In C++ Builder, a closure is like a pointer to a member function that has been bound to a specific object. Given a closure, you can call it the way you would call an ordinary function. To declare a closure type or object, use __closure as a modifier for the name of a function pointer:

```
typedef int (* __closure MemFunc)(int);
MemFunc func;
struct demo {
  int sqr(int x) { return x * x; }
};
demo d;
func = d.sqr;
int n = func(10); // n = 100
```

__declspec

> The __declspec keyword takes an attribute in parentheses and serves as a declaration specifier. Depending on the attribute, it can be used to modify a function, object, or class. For example, __declspec(noreturn) is a function specifier that tells the compiler that the function does not return, which

permits additional optimization and error-checking (for example, eliminating statements that follow a call to the noreturn function):

```
void __declspec(noreturn) abort( );
```

Other attributes include:

thread
> A storage-class specifier that declares an object to be local to a thread; that is, each runtime thread has a separate copy of the object.

dllexport
> A function specifier that tells the linker to export the function name from a dynamic-link library (DLL).

uuid(*string-literal*)
> Modifies a class declaration. It associates a universally unique identifier (UUID) with the class, which is required for implementing COM objects in Windows. A class's UUID can be retrieved with the __uuidof operator.

__int64
> The __int64 type is a 64-bit integer type. In current releases of C++ Builder and Kylix, long is 32 bits. A 64-bit integer literal is written with a suffix of i64 (e.g., 10000000000000i64).

__property
> A property is a class member that is used like a data member, but it can have the semantics of a member function. Properties are the foundation for the RAD features of C++ Builder and Kylix. A property is associated with a reader and writer, which can be data member names or member function names:

```
class TControl {
private:
  int height_;
  void set_height(int h);
  ...
__published:
  __property int height { read=height_, write=set_height };
};
TControl * ctl = new TControl;
ctl->height = 10;    // Calls ctl->set_height(10)
int h = ctl->height; // Gets ctl->height_
```

__published
> The __published access specifier label yields the same accessibility as the public keyword, but it also directs the compiler to store additional runtime type information (RTTI) for the published declarations. The RAD features use the RTTI when the user designs an application

__thread
> The __thread keyword is a synonym for __declspec(thread).

__uuidof
> The __uuidof operator takes an expression as an operand and returns the UUID of the expression's class. The class declares its UUID with

`__declspec(uuid(...))`. A class can implement the standard COM member function, `QueryInterface`, with `__uuidof`:

```
class demo {
  virtual HRESULT QueryInterface(const UUID& iid, void** obj)
  {
    if (iid == __uuidof(IUnknown)) {
      *obj = reinterpret_cast<IUnknown*>(this);
      static_cast<IUnknown*>(*obj)->AddRef( );
      return S_OK;
    }
    return E_NOINTERFACE;
  }
};
```

GNU Compiler Collection

The GNU C++ compiler has many extensions to the standard. The most wide-spread version, 2.95, is mature, stable, but very much outdated with regard to the C++ standard. The new 3.*x* version hews much closer to the standard, while retaining the familiar GNU extensions. This section presents highlights of only a few of the extensions.

`__attribute__`
> A function can be modified with attributes to tell the compiler about the function. For example, `__attribute__((noreturn))` tells the compiler that the function does not return, which enables the compiler to remove unneeded code, such as statements that follow calls to the function. Some attributes can apply to objects, labels, and types. Several different attributes are supported, such as:

`always_inline`
> Always expand this function inline, even if optimizations are disabled.

`const`
> The function has no side effects and does not depend on any global variables; therefore, the compiler can replace repeated calls to the function with a single call, saving the result.

`deprecated`
> The function, object, or type is deprecated. Using a deprecated entity results in a compiler warning.

`dllexport`
> On Windows, marks the function as exported from a DLL.

`pure`
> Slightly less strong than `const`, a pure function has no side effects but can depend on global variables. The compiler can optimize away repeated calls when it knows intervening code does not modify any global variables.

case *range*

In a switch statement, a single case label can specify a range of values:

```
switch(c) {
case 'a' ... 'z': case 'A' ... 'Z':
  do_english_letter(c);
  break;
  // ... Other cases, etc.
}
```

long long

The long long type is an integral type that has at least 64 bits. A long long literal is written with a suffix of LL (e.g., 10000000000000LL).

Minimum and maximum operators

The operators <? and >? return the minimum and maximum of their two operands. You can overload these operators the way you would any other operator:

```
template<typename T>
T max3(const T& a, const T& b, const T& c)
{
  return a >? b >? c;
}
```

typeof

The typeof keyword takes an expression as an operand and yields the type of the expression. You can use typeof wherever you can use a type identifier. Templates create a need for typeof because when writing the template, you have no way of knowing the return type of an operator or function. For example:

```
template<typename T, typename U>
typeof(T+U) incr(const T& t, const U& u)
{
  return t + u;
}
```

Microsoft Visual C++

Microsoft's latest C++ compiler has a split personality. It can generate a conventional program following the standard (more or less), or it can produce .NET output using a modified language called Managed C++, which restricts some features and adds others. The following are some highlights of the Managed C++ extensions:

__box

The __box operator takes a value object as an argument and returns a managed (__gc) object that wraps the value in a managed "box." You can also declare a pointer to a value type with the __box specifier so the pointer can store boxed values. The compiler treats boxed values specially and lets you access the members of the value transparently, as though the box were not present. Nonetheless, the box manages the lifetime of the value it contains.

__declspec

The __declspec keyword takes a list of attributes in parentheses and serves as a declaration specifier. Depending on the attributes, it can be used to modify a function, object, or class. See "Borland C++ Builder and Kylix" for more information.

__gc

The key feature of Managed C++ is that objects are garbage-collected. This means the lifetime and memory are managed automatically by the runtime environment. As long as the object is in use, it remains alive. When the object is no longer used anywhere in the program, it is up for reclamation.

Declare a class using the __gc specifier to mark the class as managed. A managed class has numerous restrictions, such as:

- No more than one base class (which must also be managed)
- No unmanaged data members (except POD types)
- No friends
- No operator new or operator delete members
- No user-defined copy constructors
- No const or volatile qualified member functions

Managed objects are created with the global new operator. They are freed automatically when they are no longer needed. If the class has a destructor, you can invoke the delete operator, which calls the destructor but does not free the memory.

__int64

The __int64 type is a 64-bit integer type. In the current releases of Visual C++, long is 32 bits. A 64-bit integer literal is written with a suffix of i64 (e.g., 1000000000000i64).

__pin

Sometimes, a managed application must call an unmanaged library or system call. The __pin keyword locks a managed object at its address in memory and prevents the garbage collector from moving the object. The address of the object can safely be passed to the unmanaged function. When the __pin pointer goes out of scope, the managed object is no longer pinned and can be moved or reclaimed.

__property

A property is a pseudo-member that is used like a data member, but it can have the semantics of a member function. Properties are the foundation of the Visual Studio RAD features. A property is associated with a getter and setter, which have the forms get_*name*( ) and set_*name*( ) for the property named *name*:

```
__gc class Control {
private:
  int height_;
public:
  __property int get_height() const { return height_; }
  __property void set_height(int h);
};
```

```
Control * ctl = new Control;
ctl->height = 10;     // Calls ctl->set_height(10)
int h = ctl->height; // Calls ctl->get_height( )
```

__value

A __value class is intended for small objects with short lifetimes, which are allocated on the runtime stack, not the managed heap (the way __gc objects are managed). A managed class can have __value data members, but not the other way around.

#using

The #using directive is similar to #include, except the included object is not a header or file but a .NET assembly, which contains all the information the compiler needs to use the classes, types, and functions that are defined in the assembly.

B

Projects

This appendix lists three interesting C++ projects. Of course, many, many more projects exist. These were chosen because they best reflect the capabilities or future directions of C++. This book's web site (*http://www.tempest-sw.com/cpp/*) has links to these and other projects.

Blitz++

The Blitz++ project brings high-performance numerical computing to C++. In some respects, it is what `valarray<>` should have been. Blitz++ has powerful array and matrix classes, operators, and functions, with strides, subarrays, and so on. The package is written to minimize the number of unnecessary temporary objects and take advantage of compile-time computation (via template metaprogramming) whenever possible.

One of the key optimizations is that arithmetic operators and mathematical functions involving Blitz++ arrays do not compute values immediately. Instead, they return expression objects. When an expression object is assigned to an array, the expression is computed, storing the results directly in the target of the assignment, without the need for large temporary arrays.

Example B-1 shows a program that demonstrates a few of the features of Blitz++.

Example B-1. Working with matrices

```
#include <iostream>
#include <ostream>
#include "blitz/array.h"

// Blitz formats output in a manner that is best suited for subsequent input by a
// program, not for reading by a human. The print( ) function uses a format that
// is slightly better for human readers. (Further improvement is left as an
// exercise.)
```

Example B-1. Working with matrices (continued)

```
template<typename T>
void print(const blitz::Array<T, 3>& a)
{
  std::cout << a.extent(0) << " x " << a.extent(1) <<
              " x " << a.extent(2) << ":\n[";
  for (size_t i = a.lbound(0); i <= a.ubound(0); ++i)
  {
    // Blitz can print a 2-D array well enough, so extract each 2-D plane and
    // print it. Note that plane shares storage with a, so even if a is large,
    // memory is not wasted by needlessly copying data.
    blitz::Array<T, 2>
      plane(a(i, blitz::Range::all( ), blitz::Range::all( )));
    std::cout << plane;
  }
  std::cout << "]\n";
}

int main( )
{
  // Math with TinyVector and TinyMatrix uses template metaprogramming to produce
  // fast code, even for complicated operations, such as matrix multiplication.
  blitz::TinyMatrix<double,2,4> a;
  blitz::TinyMatrix<double,4,3> b;
  blitz::TinyMatrix<double,2,3> c;
  a = 1, 2, 3,  4,          // Set elements of a.
      0, 1, -2, -1;
  b = 3.14159;              // Set all elements of b.
  c = blitz::product(a, b); // Matrix multiplication
  std::cout << a << b << c;

  // Arrays can have more than two dimensions and offer more computing power.
  blitz::Array<double,3> d(2,3,4), e(2,3,4), f(2,3,4);
  // Set elements of d to values that depend on the indices.
  d = blitz::firstIndex( ) + blitz::secondIndex( ) +
      blitz::thirdIndex( );
  // Set a subarray of d to 42.
  d(blitz::Range::all( ),blitz::Range(1,2),blitz::Range(2,3))
    = 42;
  print(d);

  // Call sin for each element of d.
  e = sin(d);
  print(e);

  // If an element of e is negative, set corresponding element of f to 1; set
  // other elements to -1.
  f = blitz::where(e < 0, 1.0, -1.0);
  print(f);

  // Elementwise multiplication
  e *= f;
  print(e);
```

Example B-1. Working with matrices (continued)

```
  // Add all elements of f.
  std::cout << blitz::sum(f) << '\n';
}
```

Boost

The Boost project was started by members of the C++ Standard Committee as a way to explore future directions for the C++ library and to provide a high-quality library that extends what is available in the standard C++ library. Boost has grown to encompass many areas, such as dates and times, regular expressions, lambda expressions, mathematical functions, graphs (the mathematical kind, not the pictorial kind), type traits, multithreaded programming, and more.

Some of the Boost packages have already been proposed as extensions to the standard library. By the time you read this, the Standard Committee might already have accepted a formal Technical Specification for an extension to the standard library. See my web site at *http://www.tempest-sw.com/cpp/* for current information.

This section presents two of the packages in Boost that are part of the proposed library extension: tuples and smart pointers. A *tuple* is a generalization of the standard pair class template. Instead of being limited to 2 elements, a tuple can contain up to 10 elements (and the maximum can be extended if necessary). Example B-2 shows one way to use boost::tuple.

Example B-2. Using a tuple

```
#include <numeric>
#include <iostream>
#include <ostream>
#include <vector>
#include "boost/tuple/tuple.hpp"

// Store count, sum, and sum of squares.
typedef boost::tuple<std::size_t, double, double> Stats;

// Accumulate statistics.
Stats stats(Stats s, double x)
{
  ++s.get<0>();
  s.get<1>() += x;
  s.get<2>() += x * x;
  return s;
}

int main()
{
  std::vector<double> v;
  ... fill v with data ...

  Stats s = std::accumulate(v.begin(), v.end(),
                 boost::make_tuple(0U, 0.0, 0.0), stats);
```

Example B-2. Using a tuple (continued)

```
  std::cout << "count = " << s.get<0>() << '\n';
  std::cout << "mean  = " << s.get<1>() / s.get<0>() << '\n';
}
```

Boost has several smart pointer class templates. They solve a number of problems that the standard auto_ptr<> class template does not. For example, you cannot store an auto_ptr<> object in a standard container, but you can store a boost::shared_ptr<> object. Boost has several other smart pointer templates; for the sake of brevity, Example B-3 shows only shared_ptr<>.

Example B-3. Using shared pointers

```
#include <algorithm>
#include <iostream>
#include <iterator>
#include <ostream>
#include <string>
#include <vector>
#include "boost/smart_ptr.hpp"

// A company has employees. Each employee can be Exempt or NonExempt. Certain
// Exempt employees are Managers, which are distinguished by having a group of
// Employees. All the memory for said employees is managed automatically by Boost
// shared_ptr<> templates.

class Employee {
public:
  Employee(const std::string& name) : name_(name) {}
  virtual ~Employee() {}
  const std::string name() const { return name_; }
  virtual void print(std::ostream&);
private:
  const std::string name_;
};
typedef boost::shared_ptr<Employee> employee;

void Employee::print(std::ostream& out)
{
  out << name() << '\n';
}

class Exempt : public Employee {
public:
  Exempt(const std::string& name) : Employee(name) {}
};

class NonExempt : public Employee {
public:
  NonExempt(const std::string& name) : Employee(name) {}
};
```

Example B-3. Using shared pointers (continued)

```cpp
class Manager : public Exempt {
public:
  Manager(const std::string& name) : Exempt(name) {}
  void add(Employee* e) { group_.push_back(employee(e)); }
  void add(employee e) { group_.push_back(e); }
  virtual void print(std::ostream&);
private:
  std::vector<employee> group_;
};
typedef boost::shared_ptr<Manager> manager;

void Manager::print(std::ostream& out)
{
  out << name() << " { ";
  std::copy(group_.begin(), group_.end(),
    std::ostream_iterator<employee>(out, ""));
  out << "}\n";
}

// Make it easier to print any kind of employee.
template<typename charT, typename traits>
std::basic_ostream<charT,traits>& operator<<(std::basic_ostream<charT,traits>&
  out, employee e)
{
  e->print(out);
  return out;
}

int main()
{
  manager ceo(new Manager("I. M. Portant"));
  manager muddle(new Manager("Muddled manager"));
  ceo->add(muddle);
  muddle->add(new Exempt("J. Doe"));
  muddle->add(new NonExempt("J. Dough"));
  ceo->print(std::cout);
}
```

STLport

The STLport project is a free, open source implementation of the C++ standard library. Although every modern compiler comes with a more-or-less complete standard library, there remain differences, omissions, and errors in most vendor-supplied libraries. If portability across compilers and platforms is a major concern, you might want to use the same library implementation on all platforms.

You might also want to use STLport for its additional features, such as debug mode, which helps detect programming errors. You can also use the library safely in a multithreaded program; for example, reading from a standard container is thread-safe. Of course, writing to any shared data must be properly synchronized. See the Boost project for help with threads and synchronization.

Also included are extensions to the standard library: hashed containers, singly-linked lists, and *ropes* (strings that scale well for very large sizes).

See my web page at *http://www.tempest-sw.com/cpp/* for links and more information.

Glossary

This brief glossary defines words and phrases that are used often in this book. Also included are terms that the C++ community often uses, even though this book does not use them. Frequent and judicious use of the terms in this glossary will convince all your friends and coworkers of your remarkable C++ skills.

Algorithm

A generic function, usually one that operates on a sequence specified by a pair of iterators. See Chapter 10.

Argument

An expression that is used in a function call to initialize a function parameter (Chapter 3). Can also be a template argument (Chapter 7).

***cv*-qualifier**

A const or volatile qualifier, or both (in any order). See Chapter 2.

Deprecated

Obsolete. A language or library feature that is deprecated might be removed from the next version of the standard. You should avoid using deprecated features if you can.

Explicit specialization

The C++ standard term for a template definition that defines a special case of an earlier template, supplying one or more template arguments that apply only to the

explicit specialization. In this book, plain *specialization* means the same thing. See Chapter 7.

Ill-formed

A source file or program that does not follow the rules of the C++ standard. This book uses informal terms, such as "illegal" or "invalid," to refer to programs that are ill-formed or that invoke undefined behavior. See also *Well-formed*.

Implementation-defined behavior

Behavior that is well-defined but varies from one implementation to another. The vendor is required to document the precise behavior. For example, the size of an int is implementation-defined. It might be 16 bits, 32 bits, 48 bits, or some other size. The C++ standard can mandate limits on the implementation-defined behavior—for example, the minimum size for an int is 16 bits.

Instance or instantiation

Can be a template instance or class instance. A template instance applies a set of template arguments to a template name, creating a specific function or class. Each template argument is matched with a template parameter; arguments can be explicit, or can be deduced for a function template or supplied by default arguments for a class template. See Chapter 7.

A class instance is an object of class type. See *Object*, Chapter 6.

Iterator

An abstraction of a pointer that can point to an element of a container or other sequence. Most algorithms work with iterators. See Chapter 10.

Lvalue

An object reference. You can take the address of an lvalue, but you cannot take the address of an rvalue. The lefthand operand of the built-in assignment operator must be a non-const lvalue (hence the l in lvalue). See also *Rvalue*, Chapter 3.

NRVO

Named Return Value Optimization. A compiler is free to optimize away the call to a copy constructor when an object is returned from a function. Some compilers perform this optimization only when the return expression is the name of an object. See also *RVO*.

Object

A region of storage with a type. Unlike some object-oriented languages, the term "object" is not restricted to instances of class type. An object of class type can be an lvalue or an rvalue. An object of fundamental or enumerated type is an lvalue. See Chapter 2.

ODR

One Definition Rule. A program can have any number of declarations of an entity, such as a function, template, or global variable. It must have at most one definition of these entities. See Chapter 2 for details and exceptions to this rule.

Opaque type

A type whose implementation is hidden. A pimpl is one way to implement an opaque type. See also *Pimpl idiom*.

Parameter

Function parameter or template parameter. A function parameter is an object that is local to the function and is initialized with the value of a function argument in a function call. See Chapter 5.

A template parameter can be a value, a type, or a template; it gets its "value" from a template argument in a template instantiation. See Chapter 7.

Parametric polymorphism

Generic programming, such that a function can have a single definition that applies regardless of the type of its parameters. See Chapter 7.

Pimpl idiom

A way of implementing an opaque type that uses a wrapper class that holds a pointer to a hidden implementation class. The name can mean pointer-to-implementation. See *Opaque type*, Chapter 6.

POD

Plain Old Data. A C-style type: a fundamental type, enumerated type, a pointer to a POD type, or an array of POD types. A class, structure, or union can be a POD type if its nonstatic data members all have POD types. See Chapter 6.

Polymorphism

Greek for "having many shapes." Usually means *type polymorphism*. See also *Parametric polymorphism*.

RAII

Resource Allocation Is Initialization applies to a style of programming that ensures that resources are correctly allocated and deallocated. The auto_ptr<> template is an example of RAII.

Rvalue

A value that does not necessarily have any storage or address. An rvalue of fundamental type can appear only on the right side of an assignment (hence the R in Rvalue). An lvalue can be implicitly converted to an rvalue, but not the other way around. See Chapter 3.

RVO

Return Value Optimization. A compiler is free to optimize away the call to a copy constructor when an object is returned from a function. See also *NRVO*.

SFINAE

Substitution Failure Is Not An Error. When the compiler looks for candidate functions for overload resolution, all function templates with the desired name are initially considered. If the compiler cannot generate a template instance to match the function call's arguments, that function template is not considered. That is, failure to substitute the arguments is not an error.

Specialization

Defining a template for a specific set of template arguments. A specialization can be *total* (specifying all template arguments) or *partial* (specifying only some of the template arguments). Only class templates can have partial specializations. See Chapter 7.

Type polymorphism

An object can have a pointer or reference to a base class as its type. At runtime, it can take a pointer or reference to a derived class as its value. At runtime, calls to virtual functions bind to the functions in the derived class. The derived-class type is known as the object's *dynamic type*; the declared type of the object is the *static type*. See Chapter 6.

Undefined behavior

Anything can happen. Maybe an exception will be thrown; maybe a signal will be raised; maybe the application will crash and burn. A particular implementation might have well-defined behavior, but different implementations are free to choose different behaviors. For example, dereferencing a null pointer produces undefined behavior. A desktop application might raise a segmentation fault signal. An embedded control for a toy robot might reset itself. An operating system kernel might panic and shut down, possibly corrupting filesystems and databases. Anything can happen.

Well-formed

A program that obeys the syntactic rules, the diagnosable semantic rules, and the one-definition rule of the C++ standard. Note that the compiler is not required to diagnose all errors, so you can have a program that is well-formed but still incorrect. See also *Ill-formed*.

Index

Symbols

& (ampersand)
  example, 70
  returning address of lvalue or
     qualified-name, 69
&& (logical and), 59, 80
\ (backslash) (see backslash (\))
! (bang) (see operator!)
, (comma), 82
... (ellipsis) (see ellipsis (...))
=0 (pure specifier), 161
== (equality operator) (see operator==)
^ (exclusive or), 79
(expression), defined, 61
:: identifier, defined, 62
:: scope operator, 17
:: operator symbol, defined, 62
| (inclusive or), 79
|| (logical or), 59, 80
- (minus sign) (see operator-)
operator, 277
  example, 277
operator and directive, 276
  example, 277
. operator, calling member
        functions, 112
++ operator (see operator++)
-> operator (see operator->)
+ (plus sign)(see operator+)

* pointer, dereferencing pointer, 69
< (relational operator) (see operator<)
<= (relational operator) (see
        operator<=)
> (relational operator) (see operator>)
>= (relational operator) (see operator>
        =)
<< (shift operator) (see operator<<)
>> (shift operator) (see operator>>)
~ (tilde), 70
  destructor names, 151

A

abort function (<cstdlib> header), 429
abs function
  (<cmath> header), 391
  (<cstdlib> header), 430
abs function template
  (<complex> header), 397
  (<valarray> header), 699
abstract classes, 162
abstract functions, 161
access specifiers, 167–170
  labels, 135
accumulate function template
        (<numeric> header), 627
acos function (<cmath> header), 392
acos function template (<valarray>
        header), 700

We'd like to hear your suggestions for improving our indexes. Send email to *index@oreilly.com*.

fwide function (<cwchar> header), 451
fwprintf function (<cwchar> header), 452
fwrite function (<cstdio> header), 422
fwscanf function (<cwchar> header), 452

G

gbump function (basic_streambuf class template), 665
_ _gc specifier (Managed C++ extension), 733
gcount function (basic_istream class template), 530
generate function template (<algorithm> header), 272, 338
generate_n function template (<algorithm> header), 272, 339
get function, 237
  (auto_ptr class template), 620
  (basic_istream class template), 530
  (message class), 584
  (num_get class template), 592
get_allocator function
  (basic_string class template), 676
  (deque class template), 472
  (list class template), 561
  (map class template), 606
  (multimap class template), 610
  (multiset class template), 640
  (set class template), 645
  (valarray class template), 725
getc macro (<cstdio> header), 423
getchar macro (<cstdio> header), 423
get_date function (time_get class template), 598
getenv function (<cstdlib> header), 433
getline function (basic_istream class template), 531
getline function template (<string> header), 681
getloc function
  (basic_streambuf class template), 663
  (ios_base class), 512
get_monthname function (time_get class template), 598
gets function (<cstdio> header), 423
get_temporary_buffer function template (<memory> header), 620

get_time function (time_get class template), 598
getwc macro (<cwchar> header), 452
getwchar macro (<cwchar> header), 452
get_weekday function (time_get class template), 598
get_year function (time_get class template), 599
global function (locale class template), 580
global namespace, 45
global objects, 57
global scope operator, using, 17
global static declarations, 45
glossary, 741–743
gmtime function (<ctime> header), 447
GNU C++ compiler, 731
good function (basic_ios class template), 507
goodbit literal (ios_base class), 244, 517
goto statement, 306
  example, 306
  loops and, 93
gptr function (basic_streambuf class template), 665
greater class template (<functional> header), 493
greater_equal class template (<functional> header), 493
grouping function
  (lconv member), 388
  (moneypunct class template), 590
gslice class (<valarray> header), 701
gslice_array class template (<valarray> header), 703

H

has_denorm member (numeric_limits class template), 556
has_denorm_loss member (numeric_limits class template), 556
has_facet function template (<locale> header), 575
hash function (collate class template), 569
has_infinity member (numeric_limits class template), 556
has_quiet_NaN member (numeric_limits class template), 556

push_front function
    (deque class template), 474
    (list class template), 562
    (optional container function), 252
push_heap function template
    (<algorithm> header), 274,
    352
put function, 237
    (basic_ostream class template), 630
    (money_put class template), 588
    (num_put class template), 594
    (time_put class template), 600
putback function (basic_istream class
    template), 532
putc macro (<cstdio> header), 424
putchar macro (<cstdio> header), 424
puts function (<cstdio> header), 424
putwc macro (<cwchar> header), 455
putwchar function (<cwchar>
    header), 455
pword function (ios_base class), 512

Q

qsort function (<cstdlib> header), 435
qualified member function call, 112
qualified name, defined, 62
qualified name lookup, 17
queue class template (<queue>
    header), 248, 636
<queue> header, 214, 634–637
    operator!= function template, 635
    operator< function template, 635
    operator<= function template, 635
    operator== function template, 634
    operator> function template, 635
    operator>= function template, 635
    priority_queue class template, 635
    queue class template, 636
quiet_NaN function (numeric_limits
    class template), 557

R

RAD extensions, 729–731
radix member (numeric_limits class
    template), 557
RAII (Resource Allocation Is
    Initialization) (glossary
    definition), 742
raise function (<csignal> header), 407
rand function (<cstdlib> header), 436

RAND_MAX macro (<cstdlib>
    header), 436
random access iterators, 536
random-access iterators, 261
random_access_iterator_tag class
    (<iterator> header), 549
random_shuffle function template
    (<algorithm> header), 272,
    353
range_error class (<stdexcept>
    header), 659
Rapid Application Development
    products, 729–731
rational class, I/O for, 231
rational class template for rational
    numbers, 225–228
rational objects in a valarray, 225
raw_storage_iterator class template
    (<memory> header), 621
rbegin function
    (basic_string class template), 677
    (deque class template), 474
    (list class template), 562
    (map class template), 607
    (multimap class template), 611
    (multiset class template), 641
    (set class template), 646
    (valarray class template), 725
rdbuf function
    (basic_fstream class template), 482
    (basic_ifstream class template), 483
    (basic_ios class template), 507
    (basic_istringstream class
    template), 649
    (basic_ofstream class template), 484
    (basic_ostringstream class
    template), 650
    (istrstream class), 687
    (ostrstream class), 688
    (strstream class), 689
rdstate function (basic_ios class
    template), 507
read function (basic_istream class
    template), 237, 531
readsome function (basic_istream class
    template), 531
real function (complex class
    template), 398
real function template (<complex>
    header), 405
realloc function (<cstdlib> header), 436

About the Author

Ray Lischner began his career as a software developer but dropped out of the corporate rat race to become an author. He started using C++ in the late 1980s, working at a company that was rewriting its entire product line in C++. Over the years, he has witnessed the evolution of C++ from *cfront* to native compilers to integrated development environments to visual, component-based tools. Ray has taught C++ at Oregon State University. He is the author of *Delphi in a Nutshell* (O'Reilly) and other books.

Colophon

Our look is the result of reader comments, our own experimentation, and feedback from distribution channels. Distinctive covers complement our distinctive approach to technical topics, breathing personality and life into potentially dry subjects.

The animal on the cover of *C++ in a Nutshell* is an Eastern chipmunk, a striped ground squirrel found mostly in eastern North America. Eastern chipmunks have five dark and two light stripes on their backs, extending from head to rump, and two stripes on their long, bushy tails. They are distinguished from other ground squirrels by the white stripes above and below their eyes. The coloration of chipmunks throughout North America varies but is quite uniform within regions.

Chipmunks often make their homes in sparse forests or farms, where they can build the entrances to their lodges in stone walls, broken trees, or thick underbrush. A lodge consists of a maze of tunnels leading to a large, leaf-lined nest. Chipmunks spend most of the daylight hours outdoors but head for their lodges before nightfall. Although they are excellent climbers, chipmunks live primarily on the ground.

Chipmunks eat nuts, seeds, insects, and occasionally birds' eggs. Like all ground squirrels, they have large cheek pouches, sometimes extending as far back as their shoulders, in which they can store food. They collect and store nuts and seeds through the summer and fall. When the weather starts to get cool, all the chipmunks in a region suddenly disappear into their lodges, where they begin hibernation. On warm winter days one can often see chipmunk pawprints in the snow, as they will sometimes wake up and leave their lodges for brief periods when the temperature rises.

Mating season for Eastern chipmunks is mid-March to early April. The gestation period is 31 days, after which a litter of three to six is born. Baby chipmunks leave the lodge after one month and are mature by July.

The chipmunk most likely got its name from the noise it makes, which sounds like a loud "cheep." You can occasionally see a chipmunk hanging upside down from a tree branch "cheeping" its call.

Matt Hutchinson was the production editor and copyeditor for *C++ in a Nutshell*. Sarah Sherman and Claire Cloutier provided quality control. Julie Hawks wrote the index. Derek Di Matteo and Mary Brady provided production assistance

Ellie Volckhausen designed the cover of this book, based on a series design by Edie Freedman. The cover image is a 19th-century engraving from the Dover Pictorial Archive. Emma Colby produced the cover layout with QuarkXPress 4.1 using Adobe's ITC Garamond font.

David Futato designed the interior layout. This book was converted by Joe Wizda and Andrew Savikas to FrameMaker 5.5.6 with a format conversion tool created by Erik Ray, Jason McIntosh, Neil Walls, and Mike Sierra that uses Perl and XML technologies. The text font is Linotype Birka; the heading font is Adobe Myriad Condensed; and the code font is LucasFont's TheSans Mono Condensed. The illustrations that appear in the book were produced by Robert Romano and Jessamyn Read using Macromedia FreeHand 9 and Adobe Photoshop 6. The tip and warning icons were drawn by Christopher Bing. This colophon was written by Clairemarie Fisher O'Leary.

Related Titles Available from O'Reilly

C and C++ Programming

C Pocket Reference

C++ Pocket Reference

C++: The Core Language

Mastering Algorithms with C

Objective-C Pocket Reference

Practical C Programming, *3rd Edition*

Practical C++ Programming, *2nd Edition*

Programming Embedded Systems in C and C++

Secure Programming Cookbook for C and C++

STL Pocket Reference

O'REILLY®

Our books are available at most retail and online bookstores.
To order direct: 1-800-998-9938 • *order@oreilly.com* • *www.oreilly.com*
Online editions of most O'Reilly titles are available by subscription at *safari.oreilly.com*

Keep in touch with O'Reilly

1. Download examples from our books

To find example files for a book, go to:

www.oreilly.com/catalog

select the book, and follow the "Examples" link.

2. Register your O'Reilly books

Register your book at *register.oreilly.com*

Why register your books? Once you've registered your O'Reilly books you can:

- Win O'Reilly books, T-shirts or discount coupons in our monthly drawing.
- Get special offers available only to registered O'Reilly customers.
- Get catalogs announcing new books (US and UK only).
- Get email notification of new editions of the O'Reilly books you own.

3. Join our email lists

Sign up to get topic-specific email announcements of new books and conferences, special offers, and O'Reilly Network technology newsletters at:

elists.oreilly.com

It's easy to customize your free elists subscription so you'll get exactly the O'Reilly news you want.

4. Get the latest news, tips, and tools

http://www.oreilly.com

- "Top 100 Sites on the Web"—PC Magazine
- CIO Magazine's Web Business 50 Awards

Our web site contains a library of comprehensive product information (including book excerpts and tables of contents), downloadable software, background articles, interviews with technology leaders, links to relevant sites, book cover art, and more.

5. Work for O'Reilly

Check out our web site for current employment opportunities:

jobs.oreilly.com

6. Contact us

O'Reilly & Associates, Inc.
1005 Gravenstein Hwy North
Sebastopol, CA 95472 USA

TEL: 707-827-7000 or 800-998-9938
       (6am to 5pm PST)

FAX: 707-829-0104

order@oreilly.com
For answers to problems regarding your order or our products.
To place a book order online, visit:

www.oreilly.com/order_new

catalog@oreilly.com
To request a copy of our latest catalog.

booktech@oreilly.com
For book content technical questions or corrections.

corporate@oreilly.com
For educational, library, government, and corporate sales.

proposals@oreilly.com
To submit new book proposals to our editors and product managers.

international@oreilly.com
For information about our international distributors or translation queries. For a list of our distributors outside of North America check out:

international.oreilly.com/distributors.html

adoption@oreilly.com
For information about academic use of O'Reilly books, visit:

academic.oreilly.com

O'REILLY®

Our books are available at most retail and online bookstores.
To order direct: 1-800-998-9938 • *order@oreilly.com* • *www.oreilly.com*
Online editions of most O'Reilly titles are available by subscription at *safari.oreilly.com*